Marketing Management

RUSSELL S. WINER

University of California, Berkeley

Prentice Hall

Prentice Hall
Upper Saddle River, New Jersey

Acquisitions Editor: Leah Johnson
Managing Editor (Editorial): Bruce Kaplan
Editor-in-Chief: Natalie E. Anderson
Marketing Manager: Shannon Moore
Permissions Coordinator: Monica Stipanov
Associate Managing Editor: John Roberts
Manufacturing Supervisor: Arnold Vila
Manufacturing Manager: Vincent Scelta
Design Manager: Patricia Smythe
Interior Design: Electronic Publishing Services, Inc., NYC
Cover Design: Kevin Kall
Composition: Electronic Publishing Services, Inc., NYC

Library of Congress Cataloging-in-Publication Data

Winer, Russell S.
   Marketing management / Russell S. Winer
      p.   cm.
   Includes bibliographical references and index.
   ISBN 0-321-01421-9.
   1. Marketing—Management.   I. Title.
 HF5415.13.W5476   1999
   658.8—dc21   99-28523
                                                                        CIP

Prentice-Hall International (UK) Limited, London
Prentice-Hall of Australia Pty. Limited, Sydney
Prentice-Hall Canada, Inc., Toronto
Prentice-Hall Hispanoamericana, S.A., Mexico
Prentice-Hall of India Private Limited, New Delhi
Prentice-Hall of Japan, Inc., Tokyo
Pearson Education Asia Pte. Ltd., Singapore
Editora Prentice-Hall do Brasil, Ltda., Rio de Janeiro

Printed in the United States of America

10 9 8 7 6 5 4

Dedication

With much love to Toby, Jessica, and Andrew

Brief Contents

Contents

Part 2: The Development of a Marketing Strategy

9 CHANNELS OF DISTRIBUTION   233

Part 4: Special Topics in Marketing Management

13   CUSTOMER RELATIONSHIP MANAGEMENT   357

Preface

In the 1970s and early 1980s, American visitors to the Soviet Union and eastern Europe could almost be guaranteed that they would be accosted by young people wondering whether they had any extra pairs of Levi's jeans they were willing to sell. Such was the strength of Levi's as a worldwide brand. In the 1990s, something changed. Where 31 percent of the jeans sold in the U.S. market in 1990 were Levi's, this had shrunk to 16.9 percent by 1998, a drop of nearly 50 percent. Young people can now be heard saying that they do not want to be seen in the same jeans as their parents. What happened in so short a time? How could a world-renowned brand from a world-renowned company have stumbled so badly?

To understand this fully, a marketing management textbook must go beyond a careful explication of basic concepts—it must bring in a strategic perspective. *Marketing Management* was written because after teaching the core marketing management course for more than 20 years, I thought this strategic perspective was missing from other textbooks. Readers of this book will find a strategic framework set up in chapter 3 and then used through most of the rest of the book (chapters 4–12). In this way, strategy becomes a chief distinguishing feature of this book.

Marketing Management's strategic framework facilitates understanding of the second distinguishing feature of this text: its emphasis on the rapid changes that are being thrust upon marketing managers by information technology, especially the Internet. No existing marketing management text presents the basics of marketing management in a way that reflects the impact of the Internet. I did not achieve this by simply adding a separate chapter on the Internet; rather, I have woven the impact of information technology and the Internet throughout the book. In every chapter, company names appear in blue to simulate Web "hot links." Where these hot links appear, students will also find a Web icon in the margin. This icon is a signal to students that they can find, and link to, the Web site for the company cited by accessing the main Web site for this text at www.prenhall.com/winer.

While looking at the transformations that information technology has brought, *Marketing Management* also takes a unique look at high technology. Chapter 15 covers marketing management in high-technology markets. It is not only my geographical location near Silicon Valley, and the interests of Berkeley MBAs, that have led me to include material on this topic. In discussions with business students at a variety of schools, I have found that many are interested in careers in computer software, biotechnology, semiconductors, and other technology-based industries. While the basics of marketing are the same across all industries, there are some features of high-technology markets (e.g., short product life cycles) that make being a marketing manager for one of these companies a somewhat different experience than being a brand manager for, say, Proctor & Gamble's Crest toothpaste.

The technology orientation is reinforced by a running case study on the personal computer industry that is introduced in chapter 2. The background information provided in this case serves as the basis for end-of-chapter assignments in the chapters that follow. This is another unique feature of the book, as marketing management texts normally include only end-of-chapter questions rather than in-depth analyses of a particular industry. The personal computer industry was chosen both because it has a technology dimension and because it spans both consumer and business-to-business markets. It has also been heavily influenced by the Internet; witness the explosive growth of Dell Computers, which has been driven by sales at its Web site.

I would like to note here that this book is not biased toward any particular industry. All students, whether they are interested in consumer packaged goods, high-tech marketing, services, or industrial marketing (business-to-business), will find something in this book for them.

I have also attempted to include many examples from global contexts. Although there is a separate chapter on global marketing (chapter 16), as is the case with technology, I have tried to weave non-U.S. examples throughout the text to convey to the reader that thinking about global markets is a natural part of the job for many marketing managers. It is no longer a separate activity.

Another feature of the book is the chapter on customer relationship management (chapter 13). Few topics have received as much attention in recent years as the question of how to maintain and enhance long-term relationships with customers. Considerable research has shown that it is less expensive and more profitable to retain customers than it is to try to get customers to switch from competitors. A good example of this recent emphasis on customer retention is the proliferation of loyalty programs. I discuss these programs in chapter 13 and also provide several examples.

With all of the above features, it is necessary to point out one more key feature of *Marketing Management:* The book you hold in your hand is much shorter than the standard marketing management text, yet it covers all the critical topics, helping students understand why marketing can be so difficult. Both instructors and students are encouraged to add supplementary cases and articles to customize marketing to their own interests. After all, we are in the era of "mass customization." In addition, students can use the fundamental knowledge about marketing provided in the book as a springboard to other marketing courses.

This manageable length and the flexibility provided both to instructors and to students makes *Marketing Management* an ideal text to use in better undergraduate, MBA, and EMBA classes.

ORGANIZATION OF THE BOOK

This book is divided into four parts, the contents of which follow this sequence: (1) introduction to marketing and the marketing concept, (2) overview of marketing strategy, (3) marketing-mix decision making, and (4) special topics such as services marketing that cut across all of the preceding material.

The key benefit of this approach is that it shows very clearly that strategic decisions must be made before tactical decisions. I have taken this approach because I do not believe that a discussion about pricing, for example, can take place before students are given a sense of how price must fit into the product's positioning and value proposition as well as be suitable for the particular market segment being pursued. In other words, marketing managers cannot make pricing decisions without clear direction from the strategy. This is an important feature of the book and distinguishes it clearly from competing texts. In addition, chapters 4–12 repeat the figure describing the overall strategic structure with indications of "where we are" in the structure. This has the benefit of continually reinforcing the strategic perspective I advocate.

Part 1: Customer Focus and Marketing Management. These two chapters provide a general overview of marketing and how difficult the job is.

Chapter 1, "The Concept of Marketing," covers the basics of marketing: what it is, why it is important, the importance of a customer/competitor orientation, and the controversy over being customer led versus leading the customer. *Key benefits:* introduces students to the importance of being customer-oriented and having an external rather than internal focus.

Chapter 2, "The Marketing Manager's Job," covers topics such as marketing organizations, the marketing plan, changes in the marketing manager's job, and how technology is changing marketing management. This chapter introduces the introduction to the personal computer case that runs throughout the book. *Key benefits:* gives students a better understanding of the organizational environment within which marketing decisions are made.

Part 2: The Development of a Marketing Strategy. This set of chapters covers the "behind the scenes" work that marketing managers do in framing the specific decisions that are ultimately made such as what price to charge. This is a unique aspect of the book since, as noted earlier, I cover this material earlier than other textbooks.

Chapter 3, "A Strategic Framework," introduces a basic strategic framework that ties together the rest of the book. Topics include the development of a complete marketing strategy, differentiation, product positioning, developing a value proposition, the product life cycle, and product line management. I have put much of the traditional material on one of the "four Ps"—product—in this chapter to show that my emphasis on the book is how product decisions must fit within an overall strategic framework. *Key benefits:* provides readers with the backbone of the book, a practical guide to the development of marketing strategy that is a key takeaway.

Chapter 4, "Marketing Research," shows how market research is fundamental to the development of a marketing strategy. This chapter covers primary and secondary data collection, electronic sources of information, forecasting, and methods of estimating market potential. *Key benefit:* introduces students both to the general point that research is critical to the marketing management function and to some specific pointers about what to do.

Chapter 5, "Consumer Behavior and Analysis," covers the basics of understanding how and why consumers (individuals) make purchasing decisions. Market segmentation is discussed, and special attention is given to secondary sources of information that are useful for segmentation. *Key benefit:* An understanding of consumer behavior is crucial to the development of a marketing strategy.

Chapter 6, "Organizational Buying Behavior," highlights the differences between consumer and organizational (business-to-business) buying behavior. *Key benefit:* Many readers may be unfamiliar with industrial buying behavior, and this chapter provides the background for developing marketing strategies targeting business customers.

Chapter 7, "Market Structure and Competitor Analysis," covers competitor definition (against whom are you competing?), analysis, and where information can be obtained for these two activities. A game-theoretic approach to competitive strategy is introduced. *Key benefit:* Students will obtain a "hands on" approach and concrete methods for determining competitors and analyzing their strengths/weaknesses. The simple game-theoretic illustrations are generally not included in other texts.

Part 3: Marketing Mix Decision-Making. These chapters cover the actual decisions marketing managers have to make that customers see. This is the section instructors would consider to be the four Ps, although, as noted earlier, "product" is integrated into the strategy discussion in chapter 3.

Chapter 8, "Communications and Advertising Strategy," covers the basic communications model and emphasizes how it is changing due to the Internet and the Web. After reviewing the elements of the communications mix, the bulk of the remainder of the chapter covers advertising decision making, including new approaches to advertising on the Internet. *Key benefits:* Students will have a better understanding of integrated marketing communications (IMC) and advertising's role in the communications mix.

Chapter 9, "Channels of Distribution," covers channel structure and management. In addition, using the Internet as a channel, multilevel marketing, direct marketing, and current issues in supermarket retailing are also discussed. *Key benefit:* Students will better appreciate the wide variety of channel options that exist today as well as some of the management problems involved with channels.

Chapter 10, "The Personal Sales Channel," introduces personal selling as a mixture of communications and distribution and thus logically follows chapters 8 and 9. Selling is portrayed as a channel—that is, a way for customers to gain access to the company's products and services. The basics of sales management (e.g., setting sales quotas) is discussed, with an emphasis on the impact of information technology on the salesperson's job. *Key benefit:* understanding how personal selling fits into the marketing mix.

Chapter 11, "Pricing," focuses on the importance of understanding the concept of customer value, or how much customers are willing to pay for a product or service. Thus, the chapter focuses on how to measure and use that concept to make pricing decisions. Specific pricing issues such as EDLP (everyday low pricing) and private label competition are covered. *Key benefit:* Students should understand that pricing decisions can be made systematically versus the ad hoc approaches that are often taken.

Chapter 12, "Sales Promotion," covers the essentials of sales promotion (different types, objectives, trade vs. retailer promotions) as well as budgeting and Internet applications. *Key benefit:* Students will better appreciate how sales promotion complements other elements of the communications mix.

Part 4: Special Topics in Marketing Management. These topics are particularly relevant for marketing in the twenty-first century.

Chapter 13, "Customer Relationship Management," is a unique part of the book. A considerable literature has developed around the concept of lifetime customer value and the economics of brand loyalty. Various topics in customer retention are covered in this chapter, including loyalty programs, mass customization, and using information technology to create customer databases. *Key benefit:* The management of customer relationships is an absolutely critical area of marketing; this is a unique feature of the book.

Chapter 14, "Strategies for Service Markets," discusses the unique aspects of service markets and what makes services marketing different. Topics covered include the service quality model, strategic and tactical issues, and the impact of technology on service markets paying special attention to financial services. *Key benefit:* Given that about 80 percent of the U.S. economy is service based, students must understand how marketing services is different from marketing physical goods.

Chapter 15, "Strategies for Technology-Based Markets," is another unique chapter that covers the difficulties of marketing in turbulent, high-tech markets. Topics include customer behavior, new approaches to high-tech marketing strategy, and particular tactical issues such as marketing through OEMs (original equipment manufacturers) and VARs (value-added resellers). *Key benefit:* Another unique aspect of the book, this chapter is particularly important for students interested in careers in technology-based industries.

Chapter 16, "Global Marketing Strategies," covers the essential elements of global marketing strategy, including the debate over global marketing, and focuses in particular on marketing mix implications such as channels (e.g., joint ventures), advertising, and pricing (e.g., exchange rate risk). *Key benefit:* Given that the world economy is becoming increasingly global, marketing students cannot consider themselves to be knowledgeable without understanding the important aspects of global marketing.

Chapter 17, "New Product Development," discusses various approaches to new product development; for example, the classical linear process vs. the "rugby," interfunctional approach vs. target costing. New product forecasting and new issues such as how to decrease time to market are given special attention. *Key benefit:* New products are the lifeline of any business; students will better appreciate the complexities of developing and introducing new products.

KEY PEDAGOGICAL FEATURES

A variety of pedagogical features have been integrated throughout this text to enhance the learning experience for students.

Chapter Briefs. Each chapter in this text begins with a brief roadmap to the chapter, titled "Chapter Brief." This feature briefly outlines what material will be covered.

Chapter-Opening Case. Following this outline, a chapter-opening case provides the reader with (1) an interesting, contemporary, real-world company situation, and (2) a context within which the reader can easily see how the chapter material can be applied in the marketing decision-making process.

Extended Illustrations. Each chapter includes at least one Illustration feature, set off by the word *Illustration* without interrupting the flow of text. Each Illustration is an extended example that provides a more in-depth look at a particular company, in order to illustrate its practice of a particular marketing concept.

Examples of Real Companies and Real Strategies. In all of the chapters, real company examples are used liberally. Also, throughout each chapter, strategy examples that highlight how an actual company has applied a specific marketing strategy are indicated by an icon in the margin.

Figures, Photos, and Hot-Linked Company Names. Figures and photos are used liberally to reinforce the concepts raised. To reinforce the relationship of the material to information technology and to help students follow up when interested, company names are "hot-linked" in blue and the text's Web site address is provided in the margin. By accessing this site, students are led to the Web addresses of the hot-linked companies.

Executive Summaries. At the end of each chapter, the "Executive Summary" summarizes the main points covered.

End-of-Chapter Questions. Following the "Executive Summary," a series of chapter questions is given to permit students to review and apply the material they have learned in the chapter.

Case Exercises. At the end of every chapter, a section titled "Application Exercises" provides assignment questions related to the personal computer case introduced in chapter 2. These hands-on exercises reinforce the material in each chapter by offering an opportunity for students to apply what they have learned.

Further Reading. A section of "Further Reading" contains references for additional reading on the material covered in the chapter. Readings are drawn from both academic and professional sources.

SUPPLEMENTS

A strong package has been compiled to help you teach your course as effectively as possible.

Instructor's Manual. This helpful teaching resource contains chapter objectives, extensive lecture outlines, chapter summaries, and answers to all end of chapter questions.

Test Item File. The Test Item File contains more than 1,500 items, including multiple-choice, true/false, and essay questions. They are graded for difficulty and page-referenced to the text. The questions are also available electronically through the Prentice Hall Test Manager program (Windows version).

Electronic Transparencies. The PowerPoint set contains slides that cover key concepts of the text and includes text figures and tables.

Companion Web Site. Available for students is the Prentice Hall Companion Web Site. Students can go online and answer multiple-choice, true/false, and essay questions covering the concepts of each chapter. Each question contains hints and page references to the text. Students also have the option to submit their answers via the Web to their professor or to professors at other schools.

ACKNOWLEDGMENTS

While I am the sole author of this book, no project like this one can be completed without help from a large number of people. For their influence on my thinking about marketing management, I am indebted to many of the colleagues at my current and previous institutions. These include Don Lehmann, Mac Hulbert, and Bill Brandt at Columbia; Al Shocker at Vanderbilt; and Dave Aaker, Rashi Glazer, and Debu Purohit at Berkeley. Former students at Columbia, Vanderbilt, and Berkeley and in various executive and MBA programs around the world have forced me to think and rethink how to present material and have provided valuable insights from their work and life experiences.

I also acknowledge the professionals at Addison Wesley Longman who encouraged and assisted in the development of this book. Substantial credit should go to Anne Smith, my original editor, who in a low-key way pestered and finally convinced me to write it in the first place. A similar acknowledgment should go to my friend and former colleague Joel Steckel (NYU), Addison Wesley's consulting editor for marketing. Credit is also due to my former editor, Mike Roche, for some of the format and production ideas that have made this a unique book. Developmental editor Ann Sass has spent about as much time as I have on the book; she has devoted many hours to reading and critiquing the chapters as well as going through the reviews and distilling the widely varied comments down to a manageable set of very useful suggestions.

My editor at Prentice Hall, Leah Johnson, helped me complete the project as did her PH colleagues Natalie Anderson, Shannon Moore, Bruce Kaplan, John Larkin, John Roberts, and Pat Smythe. David M. Andrus (Kansas State University), Kevin Gwinner (Kansas State University), and Andrew P. Yap (Florida International University) prepared the supplementary material for which I am grateful.

As any author knows, reviewers have the thankless task of reading rough manuscripts and giving valuable advice. The long list of reviewers involved with this project follows:

Tom Gillpartick, *Portland State University*
Raj Sisodia, *George Mason University*
Danny Bellenger, *Georgia State University*
Ronald C. Goodstein, *Indiana University*
Kristiaan Helsen, *Hong Kong University of Science and Technology*
Murphy Sewall, *University of Connecticut*
Charles B. Weinberg, *University of British Columbia*
Percy J. Vaughn, *Alabama State University*
Ray Andrus, *Brigham Young University*
Charles Noble, *Boston College*
Michael d'Amico, *University of Akron*
Douglas Lincoln, *Boise State University*

Michael Hutt, *Arizona State University*
Peter Boatwright, *Carnegie Mellon University*
Joseph A. Cote, *Washington State University*
Joel Huber, *Duke University*
William Dillon, *Southern Methodist University*
Joel Steckel, *New York University*
Jim Lattin, *Stanford University*
Carol Bruenau, *University of Montana*
S. Ram, *Thunderbird*
Sandy Jap, *Massachusetts Institute of Technology*
Jerman Rose, *Washington State University*
Carol Harvey, *Assumption College*
Brett Boyle, *DePaul University*

Finally, I would be remiss if I did not acknowledge the love and support given to me by my family: Toby, Jessica, and Andrew. This book's for you.

Russell S. Winer
University of California at Berkeley
Winer@haas.berkeley.edu

The Concept of Marketing

1

CHAPTER BRIEF

The purpose of this chapter is to introduce what marketing is and how marketing managers and the marketing environment are being buffeted by major changes in the business environment. Key areas of learning are

The marketing concept
Different organizational philosophies about marketing
The importance of being customer focused
How marketing is changing
The focus of this book

THE FIRST PUBLIC BROADCAST of black-and-white television took place at the New York World's Fair in 1939.[1] Nine commercial TV stations were on the air in the United States in 1945, and by 1950, 145 companies were manufacturing TV sets. By 1953, the Federal Communications Commission adopted a color transmission standard, and in 1956 sets that could receive the color signals were being sold. Today, nearly 100% of U.S. households own at least one color TV set.

In the early 1970s, the Electronics Industries Association (EIA), a global trade association of manufacturers of electronic products, became interested in improving the quality of color TV transmissions. Picture quality is measured by the number of horizontal and vertical lines scanned on the screen, with greater picture quality delivered by more lines scanned. The standard in North America for many years has been the National Television Systems Committee (NTSC) standard, which has 525 scanning lines, an aspect ratio (ratio of picture width to height) of 4:3, and 300,000 pixels (picture elements, a measure of picture resolution). In much of the rest of the world, the Phase Alternating Line (PAL) or Sequential Color with Memory (SECAM) standard is used, which offers better picture resolution, but the difference is not dramatic. The EIA became interested in high-definition TV (HDTV), which would scan many more lines and have twice the horizontal and vertical resolution. The picture quality of HDTV sets would rival the quality of a 35-millimeter photograph.

In 1970, NHK, the state-owned TV broadcasting company in Japan, proposed a new standard for HDTV. Setting a standard in an industry such as television is important because it determines how many different types of TVs would have to be manufactured around the world. For example, having PAL, NTSC, and SECAM standards means that a TV set purchased in Hong Kong cannot be used in the United States.[2] However, standard-setting often involves complex global politics as different countries jockey for preeminent positions for

1

their own companies to manufacture and supply customers around the world. This occurred in the HDTV standard-setting situation; more than 25 years have passed since the initial NHK attempt to set standards before products were developed.

Fast-forward to the late 1990s: HDTVs, now called digital TVs (DTVs), were on the U.S. market in the fall 1998 (Matsushita's Panasonic brand was the first), following the first digital transmissions from TV stations on November 1. Today's DTVs are large, with 60-inch screens, and cost about $10,000. The picture quality is outstanding: 1,080 lines per frame (vs. NTSC's 525), 2 million pixels (vs. 300,000), and an aspect ratio of 16:9 (vs. 4:3). Major manufacturers entering the market are Hitachi, Thomson, Samsung, Sony, and Zenith.

A schedule of the rollout of DTV programming in the United States is shown in Table 1–1. The technology is here, but are the customers? Without many digital programs, customers will receive the normal-quality signal on a better TV, an improvement but not worth $10,000. Customers will purchase the TVs only if the supply of digital programming makes the purchase worth the expense. The TV stations must purchase new equipment to transmit the digital signal (satellite broadcasters already transmit digitally). However, the rate at which they invest in such equipment will depend on the penetration rate of DTVs. To complicate the situation further, TV manufacturers are designing set-top boxes that will attach to existing TVs and act as receivers for digital programs. As a marketing manager for one of the companies manufacturing DTVs, how do you gain customers for your product? Is it possible that the technology is great but that customers will not be willing to pay the necessary price? How will sales of digital DTVs affect the sales of traditional analog TVs until the latter are phased out?[3]

In an attempt to answer these questions and many others, this book was written to help marketing managers in organizations, in both the commercial and the nonprofit sectors, develop better marketing strategies, make better decisions, and ultimately create more successful products and services in the markets in which they compete.

Marketing is very difficult to define. Many organizations, such as the American Marketing Association, and many authors struggle to pin down what marketing is and what marketers do. A particularly dangerous concept is the ubiquitous marketing department in many organizations. In some of these organizations, managers think that marketing is what the

---

Table 1–1 Rollout of DTV Programming in the United States

May 1999: Network stations in top 10 markets must simulcast at least half of their analog programming on DTV.

November 1999: Network stations in the next 20 markets must broadcast DTV.

May 2002: All commercial stations must start DTV.

April/May 2003: Noncommercial stations must begin DTV broadcasts, with 50% simulcasting of analog programming.

April 2004: All stations must broadcast at least 75% of their analog programming on DTV.

April 2005: All stations must broadcast all programs in both analog and DTV.

December 31, 2006: Target date for all stations to cease analog broadcasting and relinquish their analog channels. However, this is subject to further review and appears unlikely to be met.

Source: *The Digital Television Transition Guide* (1998), published by *Twice* Magazine, p. 6.

people in the marketing department do—creating brochures, developing advertisements, organizing promotional events, and similar activities. This concept is dangerous because it gives people who are not in marketing the sense that those who work in the traditional marketing department are the only people charged with performing marketing activities.

Let me give you an example. The customer newsletter for a small community bank in California contained an article about a teller at a branch in a small town outside of San Francisco. This article described how a customer was very frustrated at being unable to balance her checkbook—not an unusual situation. This customer called the branch several times seeking assistance until the teller took it upon herself to drive to the customer's home (about 30 minutes from her own home) and help her balance the checkbook. Naturally, the customer was delighted with this level of personal service and probably will be a long-term customer of the bank.

From an organizational perspective, the teller was not in the marketing department. However, she had a significant impact on the short- and long-term likelihood that the customer would maintain her accounts at the bank. In addition, the teller was not performing what might normally be considered marketing activities. She did not talk about price, she did not communicate any of the benefits of banking with her employer, and she was not trying to persuade the customer to do anything.

The point is that what marketing is and who is involved with marketing is very difficult to determine. I would argue that *any* employee of an organization who either has or could have contact with customers is actually in a marketing job, whether it is in his or her title or not. Any person who can potentially win or lose customers is in marketing. Of course, this creates a very broad set of marketers in organizations, from the receptionist who greets customers, to the actual marketing managers making strategic decisions about the products, to the people on the manufacturing line attempting to ensure that the product is made at the level of quality consistent with the marketing strategy.

And what about the definition of marketing? It is not really worth struggling over a definition of what it is; rather, it is more useful to describe when one would use the marketing tools and techniques described in this book. **Marketing** is involved and necessary *whenever an individual or organization has a choice to make.* This is obviously a very broad definition, but it is intended to be. It includes what are normally thought to be marketing situations (e.g., "What brand of toothpaste should I buy?") and personal situations (e.g., "Should I take a vacation in Europe or visit my family in Los Angeles?"). Marketing is involved in both kinds of situations because there is a choice to be made *and* some individual, organization, or institution has or is attempting to have influence on the decision. The set of activities attempting to influence choice is marketing.[4]

The reason marketing is such an exciting field is that choices are made in a wide variety of contexts and the influences and influencers can be very different from context to context and from each other in the same situation. The archetypal marketing situation is the brand manager at Coca-Cola trying to persuade you to buy Diet Coke rather than Diet Pepsi. Similarly, Gateway 2000 spends a considerable amount of money trying to persuade personal computer customers to purchase their brand rather than Dell, Compaq, Hewlett-Packard, or some other competing brand. In Japan, the marketing manager at Kao is interested in consumers buying their brands of disposable diapers rather than Proctor & Gamble's. Visa wants you to use its card rather than MasterCard and American Express. And, continuing our DTV example, Zenith needs to convince customers both to buy a DTV *and* to buy one that has the Zenith brand name on it.

However, these situations are only a subset of the applications of marketing concepts. Consider the U.S. government's attempts to reduce the incidence of smoking. Similarly, the leaders of China have succeeded in reducing their country's population by marketing the

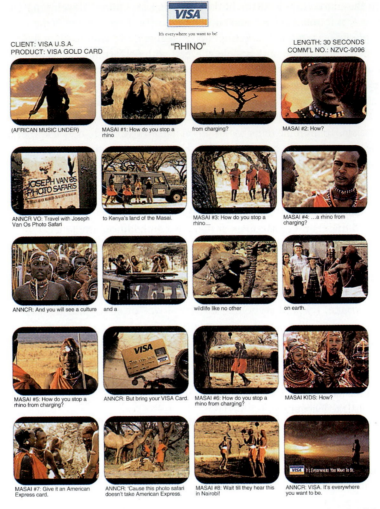

This advertisement for the Visa Gold card exemplifies the marketing strategies used for brands that are close competitors. Visa's ad campaign emphasizes the card's more universal acceptance, in contrast to the more exclusive American Express card. Whereas American Express's ad campaign presents this exclusivity as desirable, Visa casts it in a more negative light, as limiting the card user's options. (Courtesy of Visa)

importance of having only one child. What about the local art museum's attempts to draw people away from staying at home or a baseball game? Students graduating from business schools must convince corporate recruiters to pick them from a large number of qualified candidates. Churches, synagogues, and other religious groups must increase their congregations and keep their current members. Even the local utility that has a monopoly is often interested in convincing customers to cut back on their consumption of electricity to reduce the need to add expensive new capacity.

Thus most kinds of organizations need to understand marketing and use marketing techniques to increase the number of "customers" that choose their options instead of others. That is why marketing is pervasive in most developed economies: There are simply too many choices that customers can make, including doing nothing, so organizations that want to be sustainable successes and achieve their organizational objectives cannot ignore marketing and what it can do for them.

At the same time, marketing is also very difficult. The correct decision rarely (if ever) pops out of a formula such as a net present value calculation, as it might in accounting or finance. An infinite number of combinations of market segments, positioning statements, advertising budgets, prices, and other factors could make up a marketing strategy for a product. Although most of these combinations can be eliminated because of financial constraints, the product or service characteristics, what the competition is doing, or other reasons, the marketing manager still must consider a large set of options. Usually there is no obvious answer.

That marketing is difficult is clear when one views the vast graveyard of marketing mistakes and products that have gone from greatness to sadness: New Coke, Sony Betamax VCRs, Lotus 1-2-3, the Newton personal digital assistant, videodiscs, Pan American Airlines, and many others. Although some of these products still exist and have a loyal base of customers, they all either disappeared or have significantly lower sales than they once had. Product failures and depressed sales do not always result from decisions made by poor marketers. John Sculley, the CEO of Apple who is widely blamed for its decline, had a reputation as one of the world's best marketers when he was at PepsiCo.[5] Besides organizational failures such as not spending any money on marketing research, some of the reasons that marketing is difficult are as follows:

- Unlike successful corporate financial, accounting, or production personnel, a marketing manager cannot be successful without spending a considerable amount of time talking to customers.
- At the same time, customers are not always able to tell you what products they want with 100% accuracy.
- Competitors' actions are difficult to predict, particularly those of new competitors from other countries.
- Changes in customer tastes and general societal trends occur frequently.
- Implementing strategies precisely as they are written in the marketing plan is difficult.

In other words, the environment in which marketing and marketers operate is dynamic and usually outside the control of marketing management. The fact that the environment is so dynamic is perhaps the greatest threat to successful implementation of marketing strategies and tools.

Although marketing is difficult, some organizations consistently produce winning products and services, including McDonald's (fast food), Johnson & Johnson (baby and medical supplies), Nestlé (food products), Proctor & Gamble (household products), General Electric (diversified consumer and industrial products and financial services), and Hewlett-Packard (computers, printers, medical equipment, and measurement devices). Although some of their success resulted from nonmarketing factors, these companies are all lauded for their marketing capabilities.

Table 1–2 shows some very interesting data on brand leadership from 1923 and 1983 for a variety of consumer products. Of the 25 leaders in 1923, 19 were still first in 1983! This is strong evidence that although marketing is very much a creative activity, some things clearly can be taught and passed down through the fabric of an organization. Much like a sports team with great natural talent, a marketing team still needs strong training in the fundamentals to be a winner. One of the goals of this book is to provide the fundamentals that will lend a marketing structure to the reader's natural creative abilities.

Table 1–2 Market Share Rank of Brands: 1923 and 1983

Brand	1923 Rank	1983 Rank
Swift's Premium bacon	1	1
Kellogg's corn flakes	1	3
Eastman Kodak cameras	1	1
Del Monte canned fruit	1	1
Hershey's chocolates	1	2
Crisco shortening	1	2
Carnation canned milk	1	1
Wrigley chewing gum	1	1
Nabisco biscuits	1	1
Eveready flashlight batteries	1	1
Gold Medal flour	1	1
Life Savers mint candies	1	1
Sherwin-Williams paint	1	1
Hammermill paper	1	1
Prince Albert pipe tobacco	1	1
Gillette razors	1	1
Singer sewing machines	1	1
Manhattan shirts	1	top 5
Coca-Cola soft drinks	1	1
Campbell's soup	1	1
Ivory soap	1	1
Lipton tea	1	1
Goodyear tires	1	1
Palmolive toilet soap	1	2
Colgate toothpaste	1	2

Source: *Advertising Age* (1983), "Study: majority of 25 leaders in 1923 still on top," September 19, p. 32.

THE MARKETING CONCEPT

One of the most pervasive concepts in marketing is what is known as **the marketing concept.** In its simplest terms, the marketing concept emphasizes a customer focus, or organizing the resources of the firm toward understanding customers' needs and wants and offering products and services that meet those needs.

Although many definitions of the marketing concept exist and a number of people are credited with originating the concept,[6] perhaps the best way to put the importance of a customer focus has been stated by famous management guru Peter Drucker:[7]

> There is only one valid definition of business purpose: *to create a customer.*

According to Drucker, the focus of a business is not profits but customers: One generates profits by serving customers better than competitors do.

This was elegantly restated by well-known marketing theorist Theodore Levitt:[8]

> The purpose of a business is to create and keep a customer. To do that you have to produce and deliver goods and services that people want and value at prices and under conditions that are reasonably attractive relative to those offered by others to a proportion of customers large enough to make those prices and conditions possible.

Therefore, the marketing concept not only embraces the notion of being customer focused, but, as is less often perceived, is also consistent with being competitor focused and making a profit.

This latter point is particularly important because sometimes the marketing concept is interpreted as "serving all customer needs at all costs" and "the customer is always right" (i.e., there is no such thing as a bad customer). This is simply not true. The marketing concept is entirely consistent with serving only segments of the customer population and is also consistent with turning away customers and customer segments that are unprofitable to serve.[9] Some customers cost more in time, money, and morale than they add in terms of profit to the company. For example, companies such as AT&T and Citibank attempt to drive away customers who cost more to serve than the revenues they generate by offering them fewer services than those who are profitable to serve.

◆ Illustration: AT&T

Continuing the AT&T example, if you call the company with a question about your long-distance service, you will be routed to one of many different call centers. The company's computers use their caller-ID service to identify your phone number and match it against your monthly bill. If you spend a lot of money on long-distance calls each month, you get what AT&T calls "hot-towel service," which translates to speaking with a person. If you spend less than some predetermined amount (currently $3 per month), you get routed to more automated choices.

The company does not care if this routing to more computer-generated voices turns you off and causes you to switch to another carrier. AT&T loses $500 million each year on the 15 to 20 million customers who do not make many long-distance calls but cost a significant amount to acquire, bill, and service. As noted earlier, this is not inconsistent with the marketing concept.[10] ◆

The marketing concept and customer focus are core concepts not only in marketing but in general business practice today. Marketing does not have proprietary claim to customer orientation. Organizations have found that it is simply not enough to produce excellent products and services; to be successful and ultimately achieve their goals, they have to figure out what customers want and offer it in a better way than the competitors. As noted earlier, this is not easy to do. However, from preachers of the total quality management (TQM) trend in the 1980s[11] to today's business writers exhorting companies to concentrate on the long-term value of customer relationships,[12] the customer has been and should be the focus of attention.

Different Organizational Philosophies

Although it may seem obvious that it is important to focus on the customer in order to be successful, a casual inspection of marketing practices shows that this is not always done. Figure 1–1 shows four different strategic approaches to the marketplace, three of which are not consistent with the customer-focused marketing concept.

Strategic Approaches to the Marketplace

Sales Driven | Technology Driven | Marketing Driven

Customer Driven

Figure 1–1

Strategic Approaches to the Marketplace

One kind of organization is what might be called sales driven. In this kind of organization, the philosophy is "what we make, we sell." This is usually a very aggressive, push-the-catalogue approach to marketing. In these organizations, the sales function is the leader and marketing usually acts in a supporting role through the production of collateral material (e.g., sales literature) and coordination of promotional events. Usually little effort is expended in listening to what the customer is saying or even attempting to understand what the customer wants. The main focus is on selling and meeting sales targets, not marketing. The sales organization is interested in volume, not profits, sells to all comers, and uses flexible price, credit, and service policies in order to close the deal (i.e., give the customer everything she wants even if it is not in her long-term best interests).

Every reader of this book has undoubtedly been exposed to an organization like this. When your dinner is interrupted by a telemarketer selling stocks or some other opportunity that you simply cannot pass up, you clearly understand this approach to the marketplace. Retail salespeople who obviously are participating in sales contests or trying to cash in on manufacturers' promotions give the impression that they are not looking out for the customer's welfare. Sometimes this impression reflects a lack of investment in training. However, it is a clear signal of the company's attitudes toward customers.

A second common approach to the marketplace is the technology-driven organization. Here, the focus is on the research and development group as well as sales. In these companies, R&D develops products and "throws them over the wall" for marketing and sales to sell. The next technology (i.e., a newer and better mousetrap) will be even better. The problem with this kind of focus is not that the technology is bad; the problem is that the technology may not solve anyone's problem.

A good example of a product category developed under this kind of philosophy is personal digital assistants (PDAs). The term was introduced by Apple in 1992 when they introduced the Newton, a hand-held computer that had a pen-based interface and could send faxes, take notes, and organize your life. Many other large companies, such as Motorola, AT&T, Sony, and Casio, saw tremendous potential in this market and invested large amounts of money in product development. However, the Newton was a flop. Why? Most customers are not interested in technology for technology's sake.[13] There was a basic problem with the Newton: Although it was cute, it did not provide enough benefits to customers to make them want to pay more than $500 for it. The Newton is not the only flop in this market. In fact, the market for PDAs has been much smaller than anticipated. The reason can be summarized by one of the pioneers in the PDA market, Jerry Kaplan, who founded GO (which became EO when AT&T invested in them), a company that predated the development of the Newton:[14]

> In looking back over the entire GO–EO experience, it is tempting to blame the failure on management errors, aggressive actions by competitors, and indifference on the part of large corporate partners. While all these played important roles, the project might have withstood them if we had succeeded in building a useful product at a reasonable price that met a clear market need.

It is clear that having a great technology does not guarantee that a company will have customers. This is the risk that the DTV manufacturers will face.

One of the best-known cases of a technologically excellent product that did not meet customer needs was the Sony Betamax.[15] Although the home video market emerged in 1971, the current standard playing format, VHS, was not introduced until 1976. Other technologies promoted besides VHS and Betamax were Ampex's InstaVideo and Sony's U-matic formats. Betamax followed U-matic and was introduced in 1975, a full year before VHS. Not only was it introduced earlier, but Betamax was considered to be a superior technology. How could it fail?

THE MARKETING CONCEPT

When Sony introduced the Betamax format following the U-matic failure, it was the first compact, lightweight, and inexpensive VCR taping format (InstaVideo and U-matic tapes were bulky and expensive). A strength of the Betamax format was a broader carrier signal bandwidth than VHS; videophiles considered Betamax to have superior picture quality. Also contributing the better picture quality was Beta's higher signal-to-noise ratio. Although some commentators questioned whether consumers could tell the difference in picture quality, it was generally conceded that Beta was the higher-quality format.

However, a key difference between the two was playing time: Beta tapes had recording capacities of only 1 hour, whereas VHS tapes could record up to 6 hours of material. Sony's product development process focused on the technical aspect of the product and ignored customer preferences.[16] RCA, considering an alliance with Sony, conducted its own research and discovered that consumers required a minimum tape capacity of 2 hours. As a result, RCA did not enter into an agreement with Sony and instead waited to find a partner that could produce a tape format with greater capacity.

However, Sony launched the format in 1975. Although RCA and other companies such as Matsushita had a 1-year disadvantage, Beta's market share slumped from 100% in 1975 to only 28% in 1981. Extending the Beta format to longer playing times did not revive it because VHS had already become the de facto standard. Few Betamax machines survive today, although it is still the preferred format for videophiles.

The Betamax experience was traumatic for Sony. The failed attempt to set a product standard that did not meet customer needs was so crushing that the company reportedly gave serious consideration to abandoning consumer products altogether. This is another illustration of the fact that the best mousetrap does not always lead to market success. ◆

The third type of strategic approach to the marketplace is what might be called market*ing* driven. This kind of organization embraces marketing, but to excess. Much money is spent on marketing research and test marketing until the product is finely honed. These companies are great customers for the marketing research industry because they have large budgets and use every new and old technique that exists. They rely on customers to tell them what they want rather than take risks and anticipate customer needs. They typically have brand managers, associate brand managers, assistant brand managers, and multiple layers of decision making. This overmarketing approach is usually associated with the large consumer packaged goods companies, such as Proctor & Gamble and Kraft General Foods. Those companies have been much more successful introducing line extensions (i.e., new flavors of Jell-O) than establishing new product categories.

The main problem with this kind of organization is its speed of response to changes in the marketplace: It is dreadfully slow. The Coca-Cola company had been around for about 100 years before it attempted to introduce a new product with the Coke name, the very successful Diet Coke. However, the diet cola category had been around for many years before Diet Coke entered. Because of corporate downsizing, the introduction of multidisciplinary new product teams, and a general slimming down of marketing organizations within companies, the market*ing*-driven of organization is more difficult to find today.

What Is Customer Orientation?

We described three organizational attitudes toward the marketplace in the previous section. But how would we describe an organization that is customer oriented? It is important to start with a statement about what customers do not want:

Customers do *not* inherently want to buy products. Products cost money and reduce profits. Customers buy products for the *benefits* that the product features provide.

This is a critical distinction in understanding how you and your organization can become customer oriented. Companies sell automobiles; customers buy transportation, prestige, economy, and fun. Companies sell local area networks; customers buy the ability for their employees to easily share documents and send e-mail. Companies sell laundry detergent; customers buy clean clothes that smell nice. Banks sell mortgages; customers buy homes.

Customer-oriented organizations understand that there are differences between the physical products that engineers often describe and the products customers buy. Companies sell product attributes such as microprocessor speed, interest rates, the ability to detect the phone number of the person who is calling you, and antilock brakes. Customers buy the ability to get work done more quickly, the ability to finance a new car, security, and safety. The job of marketing is to understand what benefits customers are seeking, translate them into products, and then retranslate the physical products or services back into benefit terms the customers can understand.

We can also describe the customer orientation of an organization in terms of whether it views customer relationships as long or short term. Marketing is often criticized for making customers buy things they do not really want. We have all purchased something under those conditions. However, the keys are whether we repurchased the product or brand and what we said about it to other people. As noted earlier, the marketing concept involves creating *and* recreating customers. It is the rare product that can be successful creating unhappy customers. Companies, particularly those whose shares are traded on stock exchanges, have also often been criticized for being short-term oriented in order to post attractive quarterly earnings reports. That kind of activity is not consistent with a customer orientation. Marketers should be and are often in conflict with financially oriented managers.

A good example of the conflict between finance and marketing is the leveraged buyout of R.J. Reynolds by Kohlberg, Kravis, and Roberts (KKR) in 1987. In the 1980s and even through the 1990s, companies have been bought and sold and their brands and product lines considered assets in a financial sense. The problem from a marketing perspective is that concern for customers rarely plays a role in takeovers. In the case of R.J. Reynolds, the tobacco company suffered tremendously under KKR's management. If a company is taken private through a leveraged buyout, generating cash flow to pay down debt becomes of primary importance; spending money investing in brands in terms of understanding changing customer needs and benefits sought becomes much less important. Through 1995, their leading brands (Winston, Camel, and Salem) all suffered disastrous market share losses against Philip Morris's Marlboro, Brown & Williamson's Kool, and the new price brands. It is difficult to be customer oriented and market driven when the main objective is to sustain profit margins and generate cash. Another indicator of whether the company is customer oriented and maintains a long-term focus on its customers is how it reacts to a crisis.

 Johnson & Johnson is a classic example of a customer-oriented company because of its reaction to two Tylenol poisonings in 1982 and 1986. In 1982, seven people died after they consumed Tylenol Extra Strength pain reliever capsules filled with cyanide. McNeil Laboratories, the division of Johnson & Johnson that makes Tylenol, immediately pulled the product off store shelves and soon reintroduced the product in new tamper-resistant packaging. In 1986, another woman was poisoned by a tainted capsule. McNeil again immediately pulled the product from store shelves and subsequently decided to abandon capsules. In both cases, Tylenol's market share rebounded because of the immediate actions taken by the company and the resulting perception that McNeil and Johnson & Johnson put their customers and their long-term relationships with them ahead of short-term profits. ◆

German automobile company Audi (a subsidiary of Volkswagen) did not respond in such textbook fashion. In 1986, the company was accused by several U.S. government agencies of not disclosing a suspected problem with its 5000 model: "sudden acceleration" occurring when automatic transmission 5000s were shifted from park to reverse or drive. The problem was exacerbated when the sudden acceleration problem was highlighted on the popular TV show *60 Minutes* and, later, when Audi management denied that there was such a systematic problem with its cars and that its own customers were to blame for the problem. Because of the negative publicity surrounding Audi's lack of decisive action protecting its customers, sales dropped from around 74,000 in 1985 to 23,000 in 1988.[17]

Finally, it is useful to examine an organization's attitudes toward marketing expenditures. Is advertising considered a way of investing in the brand name and providing value to customers, or is it simply an expense? What about investments in customer service? Federal Express has invested hundreds of millions of dollars in its customer service operation, from its initial telephone-based system to the current PowerShip terminals, FedEx Ship software, and World Wide Web site that permit customers to track their own packages. Most observers credit the company's success in differentiating itself from its competitors (UPS, DHL, Emery, U.S. Postal Service) to its higher level of customer service.

To summarize,

- Customer-oriented organizations understand that customers buy benefits, not products. The job of marketing is to translate these benefits into products and services that satisfy enough customers better than competitors to make a profit.
- Customer-oriented organizations make their key investments in their customers and their customers' long-term satisfaction.

How does an organization achieve this kind of customer orientation? One writer suggests the following:[18]

- Information on all important buying influences should be distributed to every corporate function. Marketing research information should not be restricted to marketers and the sales force, but should be disseminated to production, R&D, application engineers, and everyone else in the organization with customer contact.
- Make strategic and tactical decisions interfunctionally and interdivisionally. Often, marketing managers in a division are competing for company-wide resources. It is important to be able to get key conflicts out on the table in order for each to be maximally successful. In addition, it is important for a variety of corporate functions to be involved with key processes such as new product development. Today, it is common for marketing, R&D, and customer service employees to work together on developing new products.
- Divisions and functions should make coordinated decisions and execute them with a sense of commitment. For example, the decision to serve customer needs better with a sophisticated information system based on the Internet is not just a one-product decision but one that could be adopted throughout the organization.

A checklist to see whether your organization is customer oriented is provided in Table 1–3.

An Alternative Perspective

Given the Sony Betamax example earlier in this chapter, readers will not be surprised by the following quote from Akio Morita, the late CEO and visionary leader of Sony:[19]

> Our plan is to lead the public with new products rather than ask them what kind of products they want. The public does not know what is possible, but we do. So instead of doing a lot of market research, we refine our thinking on a product and its use and try to create a market for it by educating and communicating with the public.

Table 1–3 Customer Orientation Checklist

1. Are we easy to do business with?
   Easy to contact?
   Fast to provide information?
   Easy to order from?
   Make reasonable promises?

2. Do we keep our promises?
   On product performance?
   Delivery?
   Installation?
   Training?
   Service?

3. Do we meet the standards we set?
   Specifics?
   General tone?
   Do we even know the standards?

4. Are we responsive?
   Do we listen?
   Do we follow up?
   Do we ask "why not," not "why"?
   Do we treat customers as individual companies and individual people?

5. Do we work together?
   Share blame?
   Share information?
   Make joint decisions?
   Provide satisfaction?

Source: Benson P. Shapiro (1988), "What the hell is 'market oriented'?" *Harvard Business Review*, 88 (November–December), pp. 119–125.

A best-selling book by Gary Hamel and C. K. Prahalad notes that consumers have never asked for cellular telephones, fax machines, copiers at home, compact disc players, automated teller machines, and other recent successful products.[20] Their position is that for a company to dominate its industry in the future, it must lead the customer rather than being customer led. To help conceptualize their ideas, they use the four-quadrant model shown in Fig. 1–2, where the two dimensions are customer needs (articulated, unarticulated) and customer types (served, unserved). As they note, most of today's business comes from customers who are currently being served with products that are being developed based on needs that they can clearly articulate in focus groups and surveys. Their point is that most of the good opportunities for a company to develop significant new growth are

Figure 1–2

The Dangers of Being Customer Led

Source: Gary Hamel and C. K. Prahalad (1994), *Competing for the Future* (Boston: Harvard Business School Press).

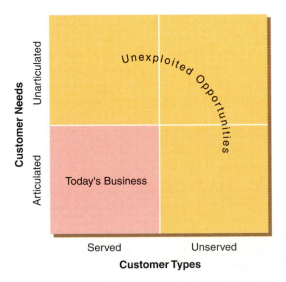

in the other three quadrants, with two-thirds of them in areas that customers cannot conceptualize very well and that are open to competitors with more foresight.

A 1995 magazine article with the provocative title "Ignore Your Customer" reiterated this point.[21] Some successful products developed without marketing research are the Chrysler minivan, the Compaq Systempro (the first PC network server), and Urban Outfitters (a retailer of cutting-edge clothing and furniture for urban youth). Some products that were unsuccessful despite considerable marketing research were New Coke, McDonald's McLean low-fat hamburger, and Pizza Hut's low-calorie pizza.

The laws of probability dictate that some products will be successful and more will fail, despite any amount of money spent on research. However, the point being made is more important: The marketing concept and a strong customer orientation will not produce true innovations. If the concept is useful only for marginal product improvements (i.e., line extensions), then how useful is it? How do we reconcile these seemingly opposing points of view?

One way to address this question is to consider the two components of R&D: the basic research component and development, which is the part of the process that takes the concept and develops actual products. Basic scientific advancements such as the microprocessor developed at Bell Labs, a better understanding of DNA patterns, flat panel display technology, and DTV will be researched whether customers can see benefits from them or not. However, a customer orientation is critical to development, and someone within the organization must have the foresight to see that there are commercial prospects for what has been developed. At that point, a company should say, "OK, we have the ability to develop high-resolution TV pictures that look like photographs; now, how do we make the products that customers will buy?" Customer input is absolutely essential in moving from research to development.

 As an illustration, Iomega had moderate success with its Bernoulli box, a $500 mass storage device for personal computers that featured removable 5-inch cartridges starting at 44 megabytes of storage. However, demand was low because the price was high and Iomega was unsuccessful in winning the original equipment manufacturer (OEM) market; that is, they could not get PC manufacturers to include the Bernoulli boxes in their computers, as they do with the traditional 31/2-inch 1.44-megabyte floppy disk drives that come standard with every PC. Without any customer research, they (along with other companies) developed the technology to store as much data as Bernoulli disks held but on standard 31/2-inch disks. Before developing a new drive, they conducted 1,000 personal interviews and 100 focus groups. They then built the Zip drive, which has removable 100-megabyte disks, sells for $150 and has sold over 1 million units since introduction in March 1995. With the success of the Zip drive in hand, Iomega developed the Jaz drive, which holds 1 gigabyte of information. ◆

In other words, the marketing concept is not limited to *current, expressed* needs.[22] The research must be translated into developed concepts. If a marketing manager sees a new product concept that has the potential to meet customer needs and is willing to develop this product while attempting to satisfy the customer, then the marketing concept is being applied.

Finally, you will be disappointed if you expect customers to be able to express what they want to see in products, particularly for newer technologies. As Morita said, you cannot ask consumers what kind of products they want because they do not always know what is possible to make. However, customers can always express their feelings in terms of needs or benefits. As Hamel and Prahalad noted, customers never did ask for cellular phones or fax machines. However, if you asked people whether they would like to be able to call their children at home from their cars when stuck in traffic, they would probably say "Yes." If you asked people whether they would like to be able to transmit nonconfidential documents instantly from one place to another, again, they would say "Yes." New Coke failed not because people lied about how much they liked it, but because Coke's marketing research did not place people in the context of having only the New Coke, with the original Coke pulled from the market. What is critical is not only what question is asked but *how the question is asked*.

An interesting (but probably apocryphal) story revolves around the development of the electric knife by General Electric in 1948. Their new product evaluation committee liked the concept because it was electric and fit with GE's other electrical appliances, it would only cost $10 retail, it cut almost as well as a real knife, and it was easy to use. They did their marketing research and asked people whether they liked the idea of an electric knife. Most said "No" and the project was shelved. In 1954, a new small appliance general manager looked at some past product ideas that did not make it to market. He immediately loved the concept of an electric knife because he saw it as the ideal gift for weddings and in-laws. Why? The price was right, it was unobtrusive, and would hardly ever be used. Research strongly supported the concept and the knife has had a long life cycle.

In sum, a customer orientation and being market driven are not inconsistent with revolutionary new products. It is the marketing manager's responsibility to put the concepts in terms that customers can understand: benefits. Customers will not always be able to tell you what products they want and need, but they will always be able to tell you what problems they are having with current products and the benefits they would like to obtain from new ones.

THE CHANGING NATURE OF MARKETING

Several major changes in the business environment have significantly affected the practice of marketing and the development of marketing strategies and programs. Some of these changes are related primarily to a particular aspect of strategy or program development. For example, there has been a dramatic increase in the use of direct mail to reach customers, both consumers and businesses. We discuss this issue in Chapter 9. In addition, significant changes in basic technologies continue to spur development of new products and improved business processes in many industries, including biotechnology, communication, and robotics.

However, four issues represent such fundamental change that they have created ripple effects across many aspects of marketing. As a result, the implications of the following issues permeate this textbook:

- The dramatic increase in the adoption of and investment in information technology by companies and members of distribution channels.
- The rapid commercialization of the Internet, particularly the World Wide Web.
- The continued trend toward globalization of business.
- The importance of customer relationship-building and maintaining customer databases.

The Increased Adoption of Information Technology

In 1995, companies in the United States spent a staggering sum—over $200 billion—on investments in information technology hardware, much of it focused on customers.[23] In addition, as of 1996 about 97% of the sales moving through grocery stores in the United States were being recorded by electronic scanners. Such scanning technology is rapidly diffusing throughout Europe as large retailers such as Sainsbury and Tesco seek to provide better information to themselves and manufacturers about the sales performance of brands and product categories. This technology is also being adopted by discount, drug, and convenience stores.

Clearly, more information is being collected at a more rapid pace.[24] This is largely because of improvements in telecommunication and computer technology, but is also a result

Now a common sight in grocery stores as well as many discount, drug, and convenience stores, electronic scanners capture useful information for marketing managers, retailers, and manufacturers. For the marketing manager, such information technology provides valuable data about the sales performance of brands and product categories. (Bob Rowan/Corbis)

of the increasingly competitive marketplace. Grocery stores need to be more efficient to compete against chains such as Wal-Mart and its subsidiary, Sam's Club. They cannot afford to devote their scarce resource—shelf space—to items that do not turn over rapidly. At the same time, manufacturers need to be able to show that their brands are selling better than competitors' and work with the retailers to help them be more profitable.[25]

As a result, a considerable amount of money is being poured into transaction-based information systems (TBISs) and electronic data interchange (EDI), the more general term for the electronic exchange of information. One estimate is that investments in EDI are increasing at the rate of 20–25% worldwide.[26] These systems take all the information available in a transaction through point-of-sale (POS) terminals (substitutes for the old cash registers) and make it available to all the entities in the distribution channel for better decision-making. In addition to Wal-Mart, companies such as Safeway, Nintendo of America, General Electric, and American Greetings use these systems to manage their inventory, test new product ideas, and learn more about their customers' behavior in order to serve them better. So much information is being collected and put to use that some writers are describing decision-making in the late twentieth century as being done in real time because of the ready availability of information and the need to act on it quickly.[27]

Some of this technology is also being applied in global settings:[28]

- In Italy, São Paolo Bank allows customers to purchase groceries and other products through its ATMs, with the costs being deducted from their accounts.

- British Airways permits customers to order duty-free merchandise from their seats with a system of handheld computers that can scan credit cards. The data are transmitted via satellite and the goods are delivered to the customers' hotels.
- A joint venture between South African and British firms, SuperTag, allows customers to scan their own purchases through an electromagnetic tag placed on every product.

However, this diffusion of information technology is in no way limited to this context. Companies are investing large sums for better customer service operations, improved database marketing to target narrowly defined segments, systems that help salespeople make presentations to potential customers with up-to-the-minute information about competitors, and many other ways. Marketing managers will continue to be affected by the amount of information available, the speed with which it can be processed, and the way it can be packaged to enable them to use it to make better decisions.

Fueling the growing use of information technology is the dramatic ascent of the personal computer (PC). About 90 million personal computers were sold worldwide in 1997, compared to 100 million TVs; many forecasters expect PCs to eventually overtake TVs in sales.[29] Two of the main corporate beneficiaries have been the leading PC manufacturers (Compaq, Dell, IBM) and the chief supplier of PC operating systems, Microsoft.[30] However, what is really driving the growth of PCs is the incredible increase in power delivered by the "brain" of the PCs, the microprocessor.

The combination of staggering computing power and small size has not only increased PC sales by virtually destroying the minicomputer and rendering mainframe computers obsolete for many applications, but has also spawned the multimedia industry, which is actually composed of a number of different uses of the microprocessor:

- Computing devices: PCs, servers (for computer networks), portable PCs, and handheld devices
- Communication devices: cellular phones, pagers, and smart phones
- Peripheral equipment: printers, scanners, digital cameras, liquid crystal display (LCD) projectors, fax machines, copiers, and videoconferencing equipment
- Consumer/home electronics: video cameras, CD players, and satellite dishes

The PC is the basis of the information technology revolution that has had a profound impact on marketing, business, and society in general.

The Rapid Commercialization of the Internet

Although the Internet has been around since the 1960s, only since the development of the World Wide Web (WWW, or the Web) has its potential for electronic commerce become apparent. The WWW is essentially a network of home pages on which companies (and other organizations and individuals) can place information about themselves, communicate with customers, receive information from customers, make transactions, and deliver customized messages, products, and services to customers. Through the use of layers of information called hypertext, hot links that permit easy flow from one WWW site to another, Web search engines that permit a user to search for information by simply typing in a keyword or phrase, and various methods of payment including credit cards and e-cash, the WWW has become a hot area of marketing.[31]

How hot? It has been estimated that $5–6 billion worth of goods were sold on the Web in 1998. This is expected to quintuple within 3 years.[32] Dell Computer Corporation sells approximately $10 million worth of PCs each day in the United States and $2 million in Europe via the Web. Although these are not large numbers in the overall global market, as more users are linked to the Web every day from each country in the world, the potential is enormous. The number of users of the Web has increased from 10 million in 1995 to a projected figure of 160 million in 2000,[33] and the number of Web sites by the end of 1998 had reached 4 billion.[34]

In addition to the Web, other PC-based technologies have changed sellers' relationships with buyers. With increased penetration of computers, particularly multimedia computers equipped with CD-ROM drives and modems, subscription-based services such as America Online (AOL) that allow consumers to check airline flight schedules and make reservations, purchase a wide variety of products, and discuss product performance with other consumers are becoming very popular. Households in Chicago and San Francisco and other U.S. cities can purchase groceries from home using computer software marketed by Peapod, Inc. This service allows consumers to search within a product category using attributes such as price, calories, sugar content, and package size. Car manufacturers such as BMW regularly mail out CD-ROMs with video shots of the cars and data about BMW's cars and their competitors' cars. Virtual shopping experiences enable marketing researchers to simulate a buyer's actual experience in a supermarket with remarkable accuracy.

These computer-based technologies are examples of what we call computer-mediated environments (CMEs).[35] In general, we define a CME as a link between a sponsor (e.g., a seller) and users (e.g., a customer) involving

- Information technology
- Feedback (i.e., interactivity)
- Customization.

A CME may or may not allow open access and communications among the users. For example, AOL is a subscription-based service, whereas in most cases the WWW permits open access. The WWW and AOL both allow for communication among users, whereas Peapod does not.

The WWW offers organizations a large variety of uses for marketers, but the main applications are the following:

- A communication vehicle. Many companies pay money to other Web site sponsors to advertise on their sites. Much of this is fairly conventional advertising, like print advertising. However, a user can normally click on an ad with a mouse and be transported to the sponsor's Web site, where further information about the sponsor can be found.
- A distribution channel. There are many estimates of the size of the Internet-based transactions market. Many companies have been successful selling products to customers from around the world via the Web. Examples are catalog retailer Land's End, Southwest Airlines, on-line computer auction site eBay, and Virtual Vineyards, a wine club.
- A means for disseminating information about the product or service. Almost every corporate Web site includes information about the company's product lines and who can be contacted for further information. Often, new product announcements and other kinds of useful information are also provided. Examples are Hewlett-Packard and Gateway 2000, the PC direct seller.
- A source for answering technical questions about product use. For example, customers can often e-mail questions to technical support staff via a company's Web site.

Many companies are turning to the Web as a distribution channel. Catalog retailer Land's End is among the more successful. This Web site serves as an additional distribution channel for the company's products and offers information about the company and links to useful sites for Land's End customers, such as a guide to national parks. (Courtesy of Lands' End)

Figure 1–3 shows part of the Web home page for Intuit, the software company best known for its Quicken program used for home finances. As you can see, Intuit's site features most of the four general categories of Web applications.

Two Internet-related technologies are **intranets** and **extranets.** Intranets are Web-based systems within a specific organization that cannot be accessed from the outside without special codes (the barriers between the outside world and the intranet are called firewalls). The beauty of an intranet is that people do not have to be geographically proximate to do joint work such as sharing information about a new advertising campaign. The actual advertising copy (including animation) can be shipped via an intranet for group discussion. Compare this to the poor quality of a fax. Extranets are pipelines from an organization to other specific organizations such as channel members. Again, a firewall protects the extranet from unauthorized use. Extranets can be established to share information with advertising agencies, to get customer feedback, and to supply channel members with up-to-date product information.

Marketing managers not equipped with knowledge of the applications of the Internet and its related technologies are truly behind the technology curve.

The Continued Globalization of Business

It is virtually impossible today to market a product and not be concerned about markets outside the manager's home market. Even in the United States, which has the largest economy in the world, marketing managers are thinking about how to launch their products in some foreign countries or are concerned about foreign competitors entering their markets. Often, the way to be successful is through joint ventures. An excellent example of such a partnership is the more than 30-year relationship between Xerox and Fuji Photo Film Company; the latter distributes the former's copiers in Japan.

The availability of better information through improved communications and increased exposure to marketing tools such as advertising has caused the worldwide consumer population to rise, thus increasing demand for goods and services. Therefore, when a home market matures and little growth potential is left, market opportunities abroad must be exploited. Although there are debates about how marketing should approach global populations with different cultures and histories, there is little question that marketing management is a global topic.

The need to be concerned about global marketing issues comes at a time when nearly every sector of the world is undergoing a dramatic political or economic shift, creating new opportunities for global companies who are attuned to these shifts and willing to take advantage of them:

- Europe is moving toward a common monetary unit with the introduction of the Euro in January 1, 1999. This will eventually facilitate the flow of goods and services across borders, and the improved economies in some of the former Eastern Bloc countries, such as Hungary and Poland. Taken together with an already large and sophisticated industrial base in traditional economies led by Germany, Britain, and France, this is the second largest market in the world and demands attention.
- The breakup of the Soviet Union and increased democratization of Russia are creating new market opportunities. Many entrepreneurs are establishing businesses and a financial infrastructure that will help the country modernize its distribution and communication systems if there is no social and political upheaval.

Figure 1–3

Intuit Web Site

Intuit, Inc.

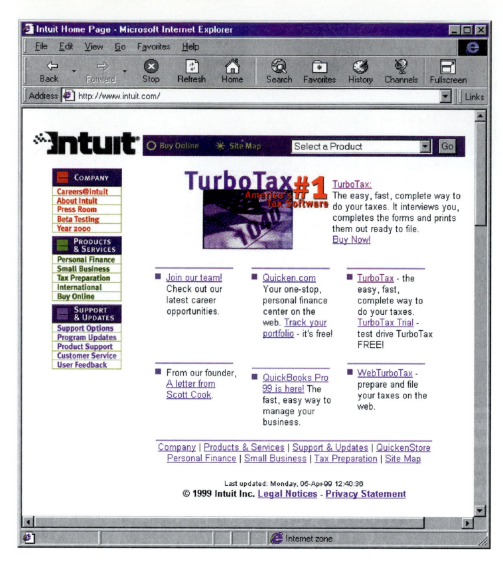

- Despite the economic turmoil of 1998 and 1999, Asia is creating many new markets through its developing economies. New markets in India, Vietnam, and Thailand are becoming fertile ground for Western and east Asian (Japanese and Korean) investment. These join emerging powers (Singapore, Malaysia, and Indonesia) and the more traditional powers (Hong Kong, Japan, Taiwan, and Korea). Potentially swamping all of these markets is China. Many companies such as Proctor & Gamble are struggling to create a consumer market in that country, which has the world's largest population but very poor infrastructure.
- Latin America is an emerging market. Although the Mexican economy has had its ups and downs, its large population and industrial base make it an attractive market and a competitor in many international markets. Strong economies in Chile, Brazil, and Argentina also create attractive opportunities as long as there is political stability.

This is only a brief overview of the global economy. Global marketers face many opportunities and problems, which are covered throughout this book.

The Value of the Customer Base

Many studies have shown that it costs more to get a new customer than to keep an existing one. That should be fairly obvious: Current customers are familiar with your products, are satisfied with their performance (ideally), and know your brand name. To convince a customer to leave a competitor and buy your product or service, it takes either a financial inducement (lower price through a price promotion) or a particularly convincing communication program targeted at that group, both of which are expensive to launch.

What is new, then? Marketers are discovering not only that pursuing their current customers is more efficient, but that over the long term, it pays to do this more proactively than has been done before. Much has been written about a concept called **lifetime customer value,** that is, the present value of a stream of revenue that can be produced by a customer. Many marketers have traditionally focused on the *transaction* as the consummation of their marketing efforts. Going into the next century, marketing managers will have to focus on the *relationship* between the organization and the customer as the end result of a successful marketing strategy.[36] Marketers that can retain more customers by satisfying them better than competitors will have profitable products in the long run, not just in the short run.

In other words, one way to quantify the value of a product or service is the lifetime value of the customer base. Two products with identical 1999 sales levels can have quite different lifetime values: One brand with customers who switch often between brands (low brand loyalty) has a much lower lifetime value of its customer base than a competitor with high brand loyalty.

The era of relationship marketing involves a number of different activities; each one helps to improve customers' lifetime values. These include the following:

- Database marketing. If a company is not actively creating a customer database and extensively using it to target products to customers and offer overall better service, it is definitely behind the competition. Databases are created through transactions, surveys, warranty cards, and a number of other ways. The purpose is mainly to take products that are traditionally mass marketed and make them appear to be targeted to you—hence the term **mass customization.**[37] For example, Levi Strauss has mass customized its women's jeans by allowing women to have them custom fit and ordered. Andersen Windows does this for their customers by permitting them to design their own windows at their retailers through computer-aided design; the design is automatically routed to the plant where the windows are produced. The growth in database marketing is highly related to the information technology revolution that is reshaping marketing.
- Customer satisfaction. A major area of emphasis of many organizations is continuing to satisfy customers, even when the physical product or service is identical to competitors' offerings. Some of this is done through extraordinary customer service; we cover this in Chapter 14. Achieving high levels of customer satisfaction also occurs through product and service quality. The TQM movement alluded to earlier in this chapter has been successful in increasing the average level of product quality in many product categories, such as automobiles. This has led to increased rates of customer satisfaction.

As a result, a key goal of a marketing manager today is to leverage the existing customer base by creating high degrees of brand loyalty and, therefore, high rates of repeat purchasing into the future.

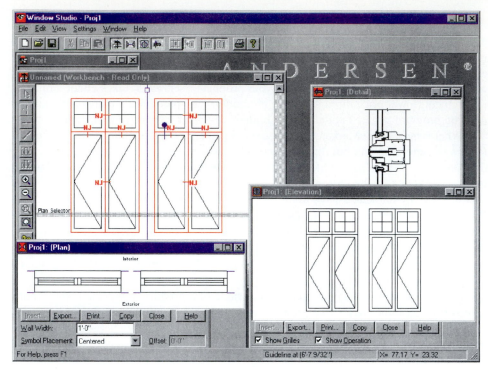

Many of today's companies are embracing the concept of mass customization, whereby products that traditionally have been mass marketed are customized to meet each customer's needs. At Andersen Windows, for example, customers are no longer limited to choosing from among a standard lineup of ready-made windows. Instead, they can actively participate in the design process, using computer-aided design to fashion unique windows that meet their specific needs. (Courtesy of Andersen Windows)

THE FOCUS OF THIS BOOK

Readers of this book should expect to be able to answer the following questions:

- What is the marketing manager's job? How is the marketing function organized? (Chapter 2)
- What are the components of a marketing strategy? How can I develop a strategy that differentiates my product or service from competition to improve my position in the marketplace? (Chapter 3)
- What information do I need to collect to make marketing decisions? How and where do I collect information about customers, competitors, and the external environment? (Chapters 4, 5, 6, and 7).
- How do I make the key marketing decisions of communications (Chapter 8), channels of distribution (Chapter 9), sales force (Chapter 10), price (Chapter 11), and sales promotion (Chapter 12)?
- What are the considerations for building strong, long-term customer relationships? (Chapter 13)
- What are the unique considerations for marketing services? (Chapter 14)
- What are the strategic implications of marketing high-technology products? (Chapter 15)

- How is global marketing different from domestic marketing? (Chapter 16)
- What are the different approaches to developing new products? (Chapter 17)

This book has a very strong technology flavor. As we discussed earlier in this chapter, no marketing manager can enter the twenty-first century without a solid understanding of how information and computer technology affect his or her job. The risk of this emphasis is that some of the examples and specific references are dated by the time you read them because of the speed with which technology is changing. Given the pervasiveness of technology in everyday life and business today, I am willing to take that risk. However, some of this risk is reduced by the treatment of Web site Universal Resource Locators (URLs, the address of the Web site) in this book. In the margins of the text, icons direct the reader to the book's Web site, where the specific URLs can be found. As these change (or disappear), the updates will be made on the Web site, a much more dynamic medium than a book.

EXECUTIVE SUMMARY

Key learning points in this chapter include the following:

- Marketing is pervasive; it is involved whenever a customer has a choice to make between alternatives, including a decision not to buy (or act, depending on the context).
- Marketing is a difficult area of decision-making because of the dynamics of the external market: Customers, competitors, and general societal and technological conditions change constantly.
- The purpose of marketing is to create and recreate a customer.
- The marketing concept involves being customer and competitor focused and making a profit as a result.
- Customer-oriented organizations understand that customers buy benefits, not products, and make their key investments in their customers and their customers' long-term satisfaction.
- Being customer oriented is not inconsistent with being technologically innovative.
- Key changes in the marketing environment affecting every marketing manager's job are the rapid diffusion of information technology, the growth of the Internet, the continued globalization of business, and the increased value of the organization's customer base.

CHAPTER QUESTIONS

1. Compare the situation facing DTV manufacturers with the problem of selling videocassette recorders in the late 1970s. From the consumer perspective, what are the similarities and differences?
2. Think of another product or service that suffered a significant decline in sales after being very popular. What were the reasons for the product's decline?
3. Give an example of a company or service provider that has treated you very well (i.e., one that appears to be customer focused). What particular steps has it taken to achieve this success? How do you feel about the company? Do you recommend it to friends and relatives? Do you pay a higher price for its products than you would for a competitor's?

4. Give examples of the four different kinds of organizations shown in Fig. 1–1.

5. Find a company or product that has recently suffered a disaster such as those suffered by Tylenol and Audi discussed in the chapter. How did the company handle the situation? Would you say that it was a customer-focused approach?

6. Marketing has often been criticized for forcing people to buy things they don't really want or need, or can't afford. Discuss.

FURTHER READING

A number of papers and books have appeared becoming more market oriented, measuring a firm's degree of market focus, and the relationship between market focus and profitability. These include the following:

Day, George S. (1994), "The capabilities of market-driven organizations," *Journal of Marketing,* 58 (October), pp. 37–52.

Han, Jin K., Namwoon Kim, and Rajendra K. Srivastava (1998), "Market orientation and organizational performance: is innovation a missing link?" *Journal of Marketing,* 62 (October), pp. 30–45.

Kohli, Ajay K., Bernard J. Jaworski, and Ajith Kumar (1993), "MARKOR: a measure of market orientation," *Journal of Marketing Research,* 30 (November), pp. 467–477.

Narver, John C., and Stanley F. Slater (1990), "The effect of a market orientation on business profitability," *Journal of Marketing,* 54 (October), pp. 20–35.

The Marketing Manager's Job

2

CHAPTER BRIEF

The purpose of this chapter is to give the reader an overview of the marketing manager's job. Key learning points include the following:

Examples of different kinds of marketing organizations
The structure of a marketing plan
The difficulty of the marketing manager's job
How to be a successful marketing manager
Introduction to the personal computer industry, the basis for the integrated case running throughout the book

The Becton Dickinson Division (BDD) of Becton Dickinson Company sells a wide variety of medical products to hospitals, medical research institutions, laboratories, the government, and a variety of alternative health-care providers.[1] The division has four major product lines: hypodermic needles and syringes (accounting for more than half of BDD's sales), medical gloves, technique needles (special needles used in anesthesia, biopsy, and radiology procedures), and thermometry (glass and digital thermometers).

In early 1992, these products were marketed by a large sales force organized by regions of the United States. Each region was headed by a regional sales manager who managed a district manager and 7–12 sales representatives, most of whom sold the full BDD product line. In the large and important hospital market, the salespeople typically negotiated with the director of purchasing or material management. After the hospital's representative had negotiated terms (price, product specifications, delivery) with the BDD sales representative, the hospital chose a medical product distributor for the actual delivery of the products. Virtually all sales were fulfilled through these distributors.

Four major trends affected BDD in the 1990s. The most important was a change in how the U.S. government reimbursed hospitals for Medicare patients, who account for 40% of all hospital patient days. Before 1983, hospitals were reimbursed for the full cost of serving these patients. However, in 1983 legislation mandated payment on the basis of national and regional average costs for diagnosis-related groups (DRGs), not on an individual hospital's cost structure. In addition, as hospitals lowered their costs to offset lower revenues, these average costs were updated and resulted in even lower reimbursements. Hospital admissions, the average length of a patient's stay, and profit margins all decreased. In addition, many companies adopted health plans that encouraged employees to reduce their hospital stays in favor of outpatient treatment.

This change in reimbursement policies affected BDD and similar companies significantly. First, hospitals reduced their inventories of medical products and pressured companies to cut their prices. Second, because of the hospitals' need for cost containment, the purchasing department's power in the decision-making process increased, at the expense of health-care professionals such as nurses. In fact, in the late 1990s the power of the purchasing department was reduced by the emergence of group purchasing organizations (GPOs), which buy in bulk from companies such as Becton Dickinson and then resell to hospitals. Third, because of hospital mergers and the growth of GPOs, increased purchasing power from these more centralized operations put even more pressure on prices. A somewhat counteracting trend, particularly for the sales of hypodermic needles and medical gloves, was the growing incidence of AIDS and the increased awareness of the health risks from formerly routine treatments.

A second factor was that BDD had two major competitors: Sherwood Medical, a division of American Home Products, and Terumo Corporation. Both companies focused on keeping costs low and passing these savings on to customers in the form of low prices.

A third major factor was the emerging nonhospital health-care market segment. Because of the increased demand for nontraditional facilities with lower cost structures, a variety of small, short-term health facilities proliferated. Additionally, hospitals were diversifying into outpatient surgical centers, rehabilitation centers, home health services, and other nonhospital facilities. Physicians were forming groups and competing with hospitals in some medical treatment areas.

A fourth factor was the rapid change in technology affecting BDD's product line. New ways of delivering drugs besides hypodermics and intravenous (IV) systems, such as new needleless systems and skin patches, were being developed. These products could obviously become significant competitors to BDD's hypodermic business.[2]

Finally, an important development occurred in the area of medical waste disposal. As much as 10% of the waste generated by a hospital was considered infectious by the Environmental Protection Agency. Between 1988 and 1990, the cost of disposing of medical waste doubled or tripled. As a result, hospitals put pressure on companies to develop products with more efficient packaging and other attributes to lower disposal costs. In addition, hospitals sought guidance from their vendors about more effective ways of reducing disposal costs. In a related matter, concerns were raised about Becton Dickinson's and other competitors' relaxed attitudes toward the safety of health professionals using products such as hypodermic needles, resulting in the slow development of newer, safer devices.

At BDD, the person charged with overseeing the marketing of the product line had the title *director of marketing*. Some of the important issues facing the director of marketing were the following:

- How should he adapt the product line and its marketing to the four key trends just identified?
- What is the appropriate organizational form for the people involved with marketing efforts?
- What marketing strategies should be used for the BDD product line?
- What are the necessary activities for developing and implementing the marketing strategies?
- As can be seen from the BDD organizational chart shown in Fig. 2–1, the director of marketing does not control the sales function. How should he interact with sales to implement the marketing strategies?
- Given public relations problems facing the industry over the delayed introduction of safer products, how should he interact with other company departments, senior managers, and external agencies to handle the problems?

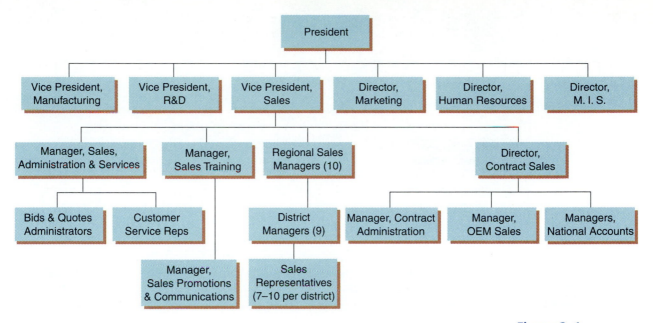

Figure 2–1

Becton Dickinson
Division
Organizational Chart

Source: Adapted from Frank
V. Cespedes (1992), "Becton
Dickinson Division:
marketing organization,"
Harvard Business School
case #9-593-070, p. 18.

This is only a small subset of the total number of duties a director of marketing or, more generically, any marketing manager has. However, it is clear that the marketing manager's job is difficult and challenging. The purpose of this chapter is to highlight some of these challenges by discussing the various jobs a marketing manager has and how she or he systematically goes about developing and implementing marketing strategies.

THE JOB OF THE MARKETING MANAGER

The title *marketing manager* is purposefully vague because usually a large number of people in an organization are managers involved with marketing. It is difficult to characterize the main job of the marketing manager because it depends on how the organization is structured, what industry is represented, and on what level in the organization we are focusing.

Perhaps the best way to show how varied the marketing manager's job can be is to describe the most common marketing organization: the product-focused organization. This is sometimes called the classic brand or product management system, pioneered by Proctor & Gamble in the 1930s.[3] Figure 2–2 illustrates a typical brand management system from the former General Foods Corporation's (now part of Kraft General Foods) Desserts Division in 1984.

In this organization, four different kinds of managers are involved with marketing. At the lowest level of the chart (not necessarily the lowest level of the organization), product managers (PMs) have responsibility for the success of individual brands such as Jell-O and Cool Whip. They develop marketing strategies for their brands and coordinate marketing activities such as advertising and sales promotion.[4] Above them, group product managers (or product group managers [PGMs]) are responsible for closely related clusters of brands (e.g., packaged desserts and dessert enhancers). They look at the marketing strategies and programs of the PMs and make sure that they will attain the objectives of the cluster or group. Above the group product managers are what General Foods called marketing managers, who are essentially super–group product managers because they manage larger clusters of brands

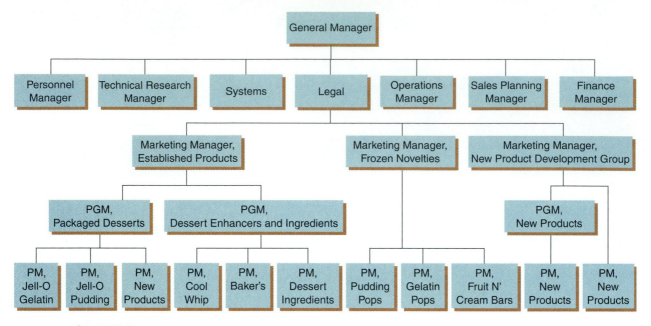

Figure 2–2

Desserts Division
Organizational
Chart, General Foods
Corporation

Source: Adapted from John
A. Quelch and Paul W. Farris
(1985), "General Foods
Corporation: the product
management system,"
Harvard Business School
case #9-586-057, p. 27.

such as established products, frozen novelties, and new products. Finally, at the top of the organization, the general manager of the division has the ultimate responsibility for dessert marketing. Thus, four levels of managers and four different job titles have marketing responsibility in this organization.

An internationally focused organizational structure for Grasse Fragrances SA, one of the world's largest producers of fragrances, is shown in Fig. 2–3. Like General Foods, this company has product managers for its four major product lines: fine fragrances, toiletries and cosmetics, soaps and detergents, and household and industrial applications. These managers report to a marketing director, who acts like the group and marketing managers in General Foods to coordinate the marketing strategies of the product managers to achieve the organization's objectives. However, these activities are limited to France. At the same level as the marketing director, reporting to the company's managing director, are country managers, who are responsible for all company activities in each country. These country managers have diverse responsibilities that include marketing.

An alternative to the product-focused organizational structure is a market-based structure. In some industries, particularly industrial or business-to-business products (the customer is an organization rather than a consumer or family), it would be awkward to have several people, selling different products or services, calling on the same customer. In addition, a market-based organization puts more emphasis on understanding particular customers or market segments than the product management organization does.

Figure 2–4 shows the marketing organization of one of the regional Bell Telephone operating companies (RBOCs). This organizational chart divides marketing into three large groups: consumer, business, and interindustry (business with other carriers, such as MCI). Each business market includes different operational functions and product management. For example, the consumer sector includes product managers for custom-calling features such as call waiting and special phone directory listings. The business sector includes product managers for pay telephones, central office phone services, local area network planning services, and many other services. Unlike the purely product-focused marketing organization, this type of organization does not give managers full profit/loss responsibility for their prod-

Figure 2–3

Partial
Organizational
Chart, Grasse
Fragrances SA

Source: Adapted from
Michael Hayes (1989),
"Grasse Fragrances SA,"
IMD International case
#M-369, p. 13.

ucts. Product managers are more like coordinators who implement marketing programs
developed by the staffs of the three marketing managers.

The marketing organization is dynamic and must adapt to internal (company) and external (competition, environment) changes. Let us return to the Becton Dickinson Division
(BDD) illustration. In the early 1980s, the marketing department was organized according
to the traditional product management model. Each product manager had profit/loss responsibility for his or her product line in all market segments, and each product manager reported

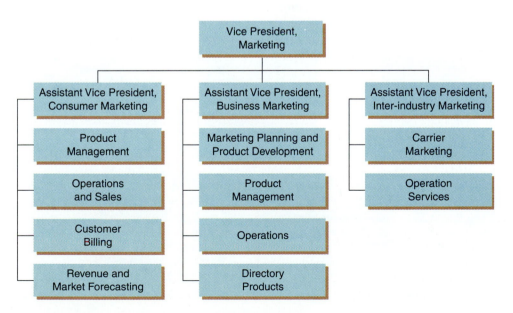

Figure 2–4

Regional Bell
Operating Company
Marketing
Organization

to one of three group product managers (hypodermics, technique products, gloves) who reported to the director of marketing. In 1985, hypodermics was made a separate business unit with three product managers (for needles/syringes, sharps collectors [containers for used needles and blades], and pharmacy products), each with profit/loss responsibility.

In 1987, the BDD marketing department was reorganized into a market management structure. This was done because of the growth in the number of nonhospital customers and the recognition that their needs were different from the hospital segment they knew so well. As a result, special programs had to be developed for that new, emerging segment. Four market manager positions were created (for hospital, alternate care, pharmacy, and safety/OEM/dental[5]), with specific product lines assigned to each market and some overlap between markets.

In 1987, the organization was changed to the one shown in Fig. 2–5. Each product manager has specific program responsibilities. Thus the senior product manager for hypodermic programs has worldwide marketing responsibilities for hypodermics but also syringe marketing in the allergist market, end-user advertising, and marketing intelligence. Most of the other positions in this organization have hybrid responsibilities of products, markets, and specific programs. The rationale was that this hybrid organization could be altered easily when competitors, customers, or the external environment changes.

Although it is difficult to generalize about the precise duties of marketing managers, *the main job of anyone in marketing is to create or implement a marketing strategy for the product or service that meets the needs of the targeted customers better than the competitors' offerings and achieves the objectives set by the organization.* That is, anyone with a marketing or marketing-related title (or, as argued in Chapter 1, possibly anyone in a company) is either setting and monitoring the strategic direction of the product or performing some activity such as serving customers, implementing a promotion, working with the advertising agency, or selling to a large customer account.

More specifically, based on the organizational charts shown earlier and this strategic orientation, the marketing manager's job can be described by a large number of interactions

Figure 2–5

Becton Dickinson Division Marketing Organization, *ca.* 1989

Source: Adapted from Frank V. Cespedes (1992), "Becton Dickinson Division: marketing organization," Harvard Business School case #9-593-070, p. 21.

Director of Marketing

Senior Product Manager, Hypodermic Programs
- End-User Advertising
- Marketing Intelligence
- Wordwide Hypodermic
- Allergist Syringe

Senior Product Manager, Distributor Programs
- BD Advantage Program
- Easy Draw Syringe
- Nursing Home Syringe
- Alternate Care Syringe

Product Manager, Safety Systems
- Sharps Collectors
- Safety Lok Syringe
- Solo Shot Syringe
- Syringe Disposal

Manager, Advertising
- Agency Interface
- Media Planning
- Ad Budget Approval

Senior Product Manager, Hospital Market
- Hospital Conversion Programs
- Forecasting
- Product Development
- Packaging

Senior Product Manager, National Accounts Service
- National Accounts Marketing
- Hospital Advantage Program
- Multidivisional program
- Pharmacy Products

Manager, Marketing Research
- Primary Research
- Market Share Reporting
- Customer/Market Analysis
- Competitor Analysis

both within and outside of the organization. Figure 2–6 shows many of these interactions. Within the box, the interactions may or may not occur, depending on the level of the position, the type of product, and the particular company. *External* interactions include working with the company's or brand's advertising agency, dealing with suppliers (e.g., raw materials, consultants), improving relationships with members of the channel of distribution system, talking about the firm's prospects with members of the media (e.g., business press, trade journals), and interacting with government agencies for export/import licenses. *Internal* interactions are with the parts of the firm that help the marketing manager to develop the marketing strategy and be successful within the company. These people include marketing researchers, the sales force management organization, public relations, purchasing (raw materials), manufacturing and distribution logistics, and research and development (new products). Many marketing managers also interact with the legal department, financial management, senior management, and board of trust.

These internal and external interactions are somewhat within the control of the marketing manager. The manager can make his or her own decisions about how much time to spend in the field with the channel members or with the advertising agency. The manager can also determine how much time he or she should spend with marketing researchers, sales, purchasing, and other personnel.

However, the three areas outside the box affect the marketing manager's job greatly and are beyond the manager's control. In addition, they are dynamic and can determine whether the product or service and, therefore, the manager are successful. *Customers'* needs are constantly changing, as are many other aspects of their buying behavior, such as the underlying process. *Competitors* are also changing, not only in who they are but in what strategies they use in the marketplace. The five key factors in the external environment must be

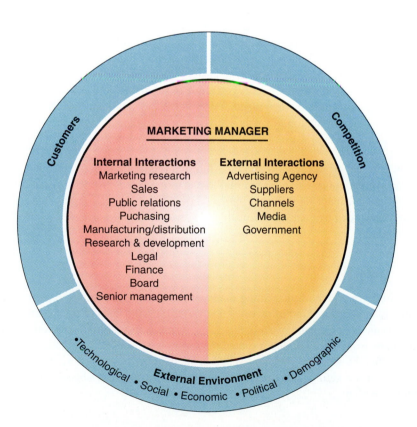

Figure 2–6

The Marketing Manager's Interactions

monitored closely. As noted in Chapter 1, *technology* is having a profound impact on marketing as we approach the twenty-first century. *Social* factors such as income distributions and birth rates in different countries affect marketing strategies. *Economic* factors such as the volatile exchange rates of the late 1990s have significant effects on raw materials and labor prices. Similarly, shifts in *political* situations affect global and domestic markets. Finally, *demographic* changes such as aging populations create new market segments and opportunities for growth.

◆ Illustration: Motorola

An example of how the interactions between marketing management and external and internal forces must be managed is provided by the electronic company Motorola.[6] In the early 1990s, Motorola was the trendsetter and clear leader in the global market for cellular phones. From 1992 through 1998, the number of U.S. users of the original analog technology (calls are broadcast like radio signals) grew from around 11 million to nearly 66 million. Motorola consistently developed new phones ahead of competitors. For example, its small StarTAC phone was a winner.

However, in the late 1990s and continuing into the early 2000s, the dominant technology is expected to be digital, which transmits calls in the binary language of computers. Digital communication brings better sound, more security, and more advanced features. What is the fastest-growing digital phone company? Unfortunately for Motorola, it is the Finnish company Nokia. In 1996, 53% of the portable phones sold in the United States were cellular (analog); by 1998, it was 41%. In 1998, Motorola's share of phone sales slid from 41% to 34%. At the same time, Nokia's share rose from 18% to 24%.

Motorola's problems relate directly to the interactions shown in Fig. 2–6. One problem was that the growth rate in general market for cellular phones declined because of market saturation. This is a customer–manager interaction. A second problem was that the company missed the shift in technology from analog to digital. This is actually two interactions, one with technological forces and one with customers, whose tastes are changing from analog to digital along with the technology. A third problem was that some competitors use semiconductor chips already developed and produced by companies such as Qualcomm. Motorola's slower production of chips delayed response time. This is an internal interaction with manufacturing.   ◆

What emerges from Fig. 2–6 and the Motorola illustration is a picture of the marketing manager interacting with both internal and external forces; some of these can be controlled and many cannot. In this environment, how does the marketing manager create the strategies for which he or she is responsible? The mechanism for accomplishing this is the marketing plan.

The Marketing Plan

One activity with which all marketing managers become (or should become) involved is marketing planning. The kind of involvement varies with the level of the manager: Product managers typically write and execute the plans, whereas more senior marketing managers take the plans from the individual product managers, give feedback and suggest revisions, and ensure that the specific objectives stated in the plans achieve the desired goals. In addition, the senior marketing personnel evaluate the product managers based on their abilities to execute the plan.

The definition of a marketing plan is as follows:[7]

A **marketing plan** is a written document containing the guidelines for the product's marketing programs and allocations over the planning period.

Thus, a key feature of the marketing plan is that it is written. This may seem obvious, but many plans exist only in the manager's head. A written plan is easy to communicate throughout the organization, provides a concrete history of the product's strategies over a period of time, which helps to educate new managers, and pinpoints responsibility for achieving particular results by a specified date.

The major benefit of the written marketing plan is that because it forces the marketing manager to analyze the external environment as well as internal factors, the customer and competitor orientations mentioned earlier in this chapter are automatically enforced. This disciplined thinking helps to ensure that before any marketing strategies or programs are developed, the manager first analyzes customer and competitor behavior and the general climate in the product category or industry. Market-focused decisions are more likely to emerge under this scenario than with a more random approach to decision making.

Because planning can occur at various levels of an organization, it is important to pinpoint where marketing planning most often takes place. Figure 2–7 shows a hierarchy of planning. More general strategic planning occurs at the corporate and group levels. These kinds of plans typically have broad objectives (e.g., return on investment) and focus on decisions such as which products or businesses to emphasize and what acquisitions should occur. Marketing plans are constructed at the strategic business unit (SBU) and, of course, on the product levels (the focus of the annual marketing plan). An SBU might be desserts or personal computers for the home and the product or brands would be Jell-O and the Hewlett-Packard Pavilion line of home PCs. Returning to the Becton Dickinson illustration, separate marketing plans are developed for the worldwide hypodermic products and allergist syringes. These plans would be evaluated by the senior product manager of hypodermic programs.

A typical marketing planning sequence followed by product or other marketing managers is shown in Fig. 2–8. In this process, the marketing manager first updates some of the facts (e.g., market shares) contained in the old plan. Because planning is always forward-looking, a plan to be implemented in 2000 would be developed in 1999. Thus the most recent facts might be from 1998 or, depending on the industry and the quality of data available, even earlier. The next major activity is to collect and analyze information about the current situation (1999) pertaining to customers, competitors, and the category environment. Based on this analysis, the manager develops objectives, strategies, and programs for the product,

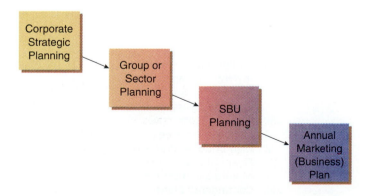

Figure 2–7

Hierarchy of Planning

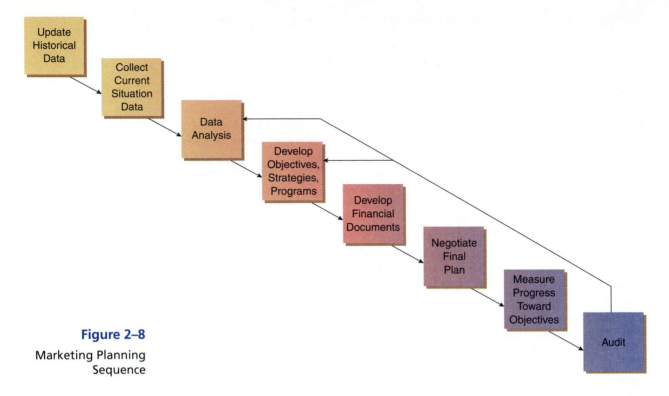

Figure 2–8

Marketing Planning Sequence

product line, or closely related group of products. The objectives and the expenditure budgets, along with data on labor, raw material, and other assigned costs, are put together to create a pro forma financial statement or projection. This projection is used in negotiations with senior management. They may want a more aggressive profit result, for example, or lower advertising expenditures. When the plan is finally implemented, progress toward achieving the goals must be measured. After the planning period is over, an audit of the plan reveals why something went wrong and what can be improved the next time.

A basic outline of a typical plan appears in Table 2–1. There are three major parts to the plan. First, the marketing manager conducts a background assessment, the "homework" part of the plan. In this part, the historical data are collected and updated; they are often stored in a product fact book. In addition, the manager analyzes the current competitive, customer, and category situation and determines how the firm's capabilities match these three external

Table 2–1 Marketing Plan Summary

    I. Executive summary
   II. Background assessment
      A. Historical appraisal
      B. Situation analysis
      C. Planning assumptions
  III. Marketing objectives
  IV. Marketing strategy
   V. Marketing programs
  VI. Financial documents
 VII. Monitors and controls
VIII. Contingency plans

Conducting a background assessment—gathering and analyzing current competitive information—is the first major step in creating a business plan. This marketing manager is recording updated information in a product fact book. (Robert Brenner/Photo Edit)

elements (i.e., he or she performs the situation analysis). Finally, forecasts, estimates of market potential, and other assumptions that must be made about the market environment are collected and put into a section called the planning assumptions. The second major part is the strategy section, which actually is composed of the product's or service's objectives (increase market share by x share points, for example), the marketing strategy itself, and the implementation of the strategy (i.e., the marketing mix of price, advertising, and personal selling effort). Finally, the plan includes the financial implications, the monitors and controls used to assess the progress being made toward the plan's objectives, and contingency plans.

Therefore, the overall purpose of the marketing plan is to enable the marketing manager to stay in touch with the three key parts of the business environment crucial to his or her success: customers, competitors, and factors outside the control of both customers and competitors. By doing this, the manager should be able to adapt the marketing strategies to changes in customer tastes, competitor strategies, and external factors such as exchange rates or global politics. That is the theory, at least. In practice, however, the problems facing a marketing manager and a particular product or brand cannot be solved so easily.

Before moving on, let's take a moment to examine the case of Cadillac and see how marketing has been at least partially responsible for the demise of this luxury car line, in large part because of management's inability to stay attuned to the business environment.[8]

 Illustration: Cadillac

The Tradition

"When I die, I don't want to go to heaven, I want to go to Cadillac."

"An American Standard for the World."

"This was the car that took a certain look all the way over the top. Big tailfins. Lots of chrome. Longer and wider than a city bus. These were the cars you needed to own if you wanted people to notice you. The Cadillac said you'd made it and you were, by God, going to enjoy it."

The Cadillac Automobile Company was organized on August 22, 1902. For over 70 years from its inception, the Cadillac brand name stood for quality. One of its founders, Henry Martyn Leland, insisted on precision manufacturing and the standardization and inter-changeability of parts. Cadillac produced several firsts in automobile history: the first elec-tric starter (1912), the first V-8 engine (1915), tilt-beam safety headlights (1915), and its trademark tailfins (1948). For nearly 80 years, the Cadillac models Fleetwood, DeVille, Eldorado, and LaSalle were the gold standard for luxury automobiles.

This reputation for quality and luxury produced large sales for General Motors, and, at gross margins estimated at $10,000 per car in 1994, a disproportionate amount of its prof-its. From sales of nearly 8,000 in 1909 (the first year Cadillac's sales were consolidated into General Motors' figures), sales of the Cadillac models peaked at nearly 351,000 in 1978 and nearly 33% of the luxury car segment. The marketing people at Cadillac and General Motors felt they had one of the strongest brand names in business and could hardly imag-ine that one day Caddys would not be the most sought-after car in their class.

The Problems

Fast-forward to the 1990s:

"Cadillac dealers often joke that instead of a first-time-buyer program, we need a last-time-buyer program."
"You don't want to drive your parents' car."
"Baby boomers have plenty of money, but they view Cadillacs and Lincolns as Grand-dad's car."

The following table is a graphic description of the problems facing Cadillac's market-ing managers in 1997:

	Age	Women	College Graduates
Cadillac's current customer profile	65	28%	45%
Average new luxury customer	44	53%	73%

Ask any group of prospective car buyers under 60 years old for their image of a Cadil-lac owner and you will invariably get phrases like "old," "men," "retired," and "the white-shoes set." The major demographic group of luxury car buyers, successful men and women in their 30s, 40s, and 50s, is not buying Cadillacs but is instead buying Mercedes-Benzes, BMWs, Lexuses, Acuras, and upscale four-wheel-drive sport utility vehicles, the hottest car segment in the United States. The worst part for Cadillac is that many of the younger buyers in this group would not even consider setting foot in a Cadillac dealer-ship or ever see themselves owning one. This is a complete turnabout from the earlier era when, even if you could not afford one, you still saw owning a Cadillac as the ultimate goal and symbol of success.

The ultimate result was a dramatic drop in Cadillac sales, from the peak of 351,000 in 1978 to 182,151 in 1998. The simple calculation of $10,000 in gross profit per car multi-plied by the 170,000-unit decline in sales gives you some idea of the total cost to General Motors between 1978 and 1998.

What went wrong? How could a brand name such as Cadillac become so devalued by customers to result in such dramatic declines in sales and attitudes?

The explanation begins in the early to mid-1970s and the first oil crisis. Cadillac's cars were big and consumed large quantities of gasoline. Consumer tastes began to shift to smaller, more energy-efficient cars to combat the rocketing prices at the gas pump. Because the design-and-build cycle for automobile manufacturers at this time was at least 5 years, there was not much Cadillac could do about the problem in the short term. In addition, traditional Cadillac owners liked the large size of their cars and were generally price insensitive because they came from the upper income groups. As a result, sales did not suffer; indeed, as noted earlier, they peaked in 1978. However, this was the beginning of the age cohort problem: Traditional Cadillac owners were not interested in downsizing, but the newer, younger buyers with the appropriate income levels were more conscious of energy efficiency because they had different values about the conservation of natural resources.

That the traditional Cadillac buyers were not interested in smaller cars was dramatically emphasized by the tepid reception given the Cimarron, "A New Kind of Cadillac for a New Kind of Cadillac Owner," in 1981. This was not entirely Cadillac's fault. General Motors decided to standardize some of its models on what it called its J-body. As a result, except for the price, customers had difficulty telling the difference between the Cadillac Cimarron and the Chevrolet Cavalier. Of course, not only was a smaller car not what the traditional buyers wanted, but the Cimarron did not draw in new, younger, upscale buyers to purchase a car that was essentially a low-end Chevy. Slimmed-down versions of the Seville and Eldorado introduced in 1985 also did not fare well.

The second problem facing Cadillac was increasing foreign competition in the luxury car segment: Mercedes and BMW in the 1980s and Lexus (Toyota), Acura (Honda), and Infiniti (Nissan) in the 1990s. The first wave of the competitors, the German cars, provided a combination of styling, handling, size, prestige, and fuel efficiency that Cadillac could not match through the mid-1980s. Although these cars were often more expensive than Cadillacs, customers valued the differential benefits provided by Mercedes and BMW and were willing to pay a higher price. Indeed, a large segment of Cadillac owners, physicians, moved to Mercedes. The later Japanese entrants appealed to luxury car buyers who were more interested in fit, finish, reliability, and good value for money at the high end of the market.

Cadillac did not sit idly by. In 1987, the division launched the Allanté, a $54,700 coupe that was intended to give the whole Cadillac line an aura of sexier European styling and simultaneously attempt to appeal to a younger buyer base. Unfortunately, the car was underpowered, not distinctively styled, and poorly made. The roof leaked and there was considerable road noise. Cadillac pulled the plug on the model in 1993. The Seville was introduced in 1975 and has been a moderate hit.

Observers commented that the new model introduced in 1997, the German-produced Catera, is Cadillac's last and best opportunity to create a success with younger buyers. The car is intended to compete head-to-head with the lower-end BMWs and Mercedes by being priced at $30,000. In addition, Cadillac is expected to benefit from the new brand management structure introduced by General Motors in 1995. Under this system (see the discussion later in this chapter), one person is fully in charge of the marketing for the Catera, including product development, the marketing strategy, and the implementation of the strategy, including advertising and pricing. The Catera brand manager took a very bold step by redesigning Cadillac's traditional "wreath and crest" emblem to create a cartoon mascot, distancing the image of the car from the other brands in the Cadillac product lineup. In a telling move, the marketing of the car emphasizes the car itself rather than the Cadillac brand name.

It is too early to tell whether the Catera will help to save the Cadillac brand, although the Catera did sell 25,331 units in 1998 (about the same as in 1997), helping the division to increase its total sales by 13,250 units over the period 1996–1998 (note that sales of the traditional cars continue to decline). The car has the appropriate physical characteristics that should appeal to the intended target customers. In addition, early results show that half the buyers are women, a considerable improvement over the data shown earlier. The advertising campaign featuring the tag line "The Caddy That Zigs" has been well received by industry critics. However, the median age of Catera buyers is 56, only slightly lower than the overall median of 65; in addition, the model ranked near the bottom of the influential 1997 J.D. Power quality rankings. It still has the Cadillac brand name and is sold by the same dealers as the larger models. In a 1996 U.S.-based survey of brand quality, Cadillac ranked 67th, behind Mercedes (5), Lexus (12), BMW (28), Jeep Grand Cherokee (55), and the GMC Suburban (63).[9]

The Lessons

One of the motivations for the Cadillac illustration is to demonstrate that marketing is a very difficult job. Although Cadillac (and General Motors) personnel must shoulder the blame for the introduction of the Cimarron, not responding quickly enough to the foreign car onslaught, and the inability to develop new models that appeal to younger customers, it is easy to say this only in hindsight. Although U.S. automobile manufacturers are often criticized for promoting only from within, their managers have considerable marketing and automobile expertise.

We can relate the insights learned from the Cadillac case to the points raised earlier about the difficulty of the marketing manager's job and all the interactions the manager has with the external environment (Fig. 2–6):

- Successful marketing managers talk to their customers. Not until 1979 did Cadillac establish its first formal product-planning group with formal marketing research. Before then, the division felt it had an excellent intuitive feel for its traditional buyer. As evidenced by the brand's historical success, Cadillac managers did and do have a good grasp on what its traditional buyer wants; the new buyers are the problem. In addition, although customers can usually express their basic needs and wants with respect to a product category, they are much less useful in telling you what features they are looking for. This makes it very difficult to design new products, particularly automobiles that have long production lead times. In addition, these preferences are unstable. The automobile industry has been whipsawed by consumers wanting change for a long time. When the industry makes small cars, customers want large cars, and vice versa.[10] This is not intended to discourage the reader from spending money on marketing research. Indeed, as was argued in Chapter 1, it is critical to do so. What it does mean is that the research should be conducted with the understanding that it is not perfect and should not be used to make decisions but rather as an aid to decision-making, along with judgment and other inputs. The success of the German and Japanese manufacturers in the luxury car segment shows that it is very possible to develop products that appeal to younger affluent buyers.
- It is critical to understand competitors' strategies and future intentions. Non-U.S. manufacturers have done a better job than Cadillac in developing products and marketing strategies in the luxury car segment. Toyota, Nissan, and Honda are particularly noteworthy because, unlike Mercedes's and BMW's, their product lines were not attractive to this segment. The Japanese firms not only developed good products but developed separate brand names and distribution structures (i.e., entirely new auto dealer networks) to reach these buyers. Thus prospective Lexus buyers who are thinking of spending up to $50,000 for a car do not even see Toyota Tercels costing much less. In addition, the customer service offered by the competitors was at a level not heretofore seen by U.S. auto makers (or customers). Cadillac recognizes this problem for the Catera and is shipping the new cars only to dealers who meet higher standards for customer satisfaction and service.

These two photos illustrate separate distribution structures. The used car lot features products that appeal to a distinct market segment: buyers interested in small to mid-sized used vehicles. In contrast, the cars featured in the showroom appeal to a different class of buyers: those interested in upscale, luxury cars. These separate distribution systems allow the marketing manager to better attract—and not distract— the right buyer. (Left: D. Young Wolff/Photo Edit; Right: John Neubauer/Photo Edit)

- The environment must be monitored constantly for changes in social trends and attitudes. In the luxury automobile market, customer standards for production quality are extraordinarily high. Part of this demand for quality resulted from not only the higher prices for cars in this segment, but also from the greater visibility of the quality movement in the United States in the 1980s. Greater attention by the general press to J.D. Power quality surveys and winners of the Malcolm Baldrige award, given by the Commerce Department for product quality, resulted in greater public awareness of quality issues. Cadillac did improve its quality and won the Baldrige award in 1990. However, because this award represented Cadillac's emphasis on manufacturing quality, it came far too late.

- Brand names and the images they evoke must be evaluated constantly against changes in customer perceptions. The implementation of marketing strategies for Cadillac has been handicapped by the brand name and what it connotes to potential buyers. The division has been extraordinarily successful over its history and has spent billions giving consumers an image of its products. Unfortunately, Cadillac has become a virtual prisoner of its success; if younger customers will not even visit Cadillac dealerships because of the dowdy image, of what value are new products? This is a good example of how brand names do not remain valuable in perpetuity but need constant invigorating. It is also an example of how becoming very well known for something can be a handicap if that something is not relevant to a market segment critical to your product's future.

In sum, the stories of Cadillac and Motorola tell us much about the difficulty of marketing and how important it is for the marketing manager to remain in touch with the external environment. The first three problems just mentioned are in precisely the areas outside the box in Fig. 2–6. Much of Motorola's difficulty has been in dealing with customer and technology changes, which are also external. Integrating information about changes in those areas into the marketing strategies is the rationale for the marketing plan.

Introduction to the Integrated Case

Part of a student's learning experience is pulling together the concepts learned throughout a textbook to develop a coherent and comprehensive knowledge of the subject matter. In this chapter, we have tried to provide the reader with some ideas about what the marketing manager's job is like. However, it is not until you implement those ideas that marketing concepts and strategies come alive.

To achieve that goal, at the end of each chapter, beginning with Chapter 3, we include a series of assignments related to what is called the Integrated Case, based on the personal computer (PC) industry. This industry was chosen because it is consistent with the technology theme of this textbook, material about it is widely available, and it is increasingly affecting our lives both at home and at work. A brief overview of the industry and some of its companies is given here. Completion of some or all of the chapter assignments will fill in many of the blanks purposely left out of the overview.

History of the PC Market

Until 1974, the computer industry was dominated by two kinds of machines: mainframe computers with large-scale computing capabilities, for which IBM was the dominant supplier, and minicomputers popularized by Digital Equipment Corporation (DEC). The choice between the two forms was based largely on the amount of computing power necessary and whether customers wanted large, centralized computer operations or smaller, distributed facilities.

In 1974, a rivalry between two electronics magazines, *Radio-Electronics* and *Popular Electronics,* began the PC (or microcomputer) industry.[11] The former magazine promoted the Mark 8 machine, which was a printed circuit board with a book of simulations selling for about $1,000. *Popular Electronics* promoted its better-known MITS Altair, which sold for $395 as a kit or $621 preassembled.

In 1977, four changes in technology created the PC industry as we know it today. First, Intel, Zilog, and Commodore launched 8-bit microprocessors that offered significant price and performance improvements over the processors in the early computers. Second, an operating system, CP/M-80, became standard, making it more profitable for software developers to create programs for PCs. Early leaders were Lotus's spreadsheet package 1-2-3 and the word processing program Wordstar. Third, Shugart Corporation developed a $5\frac{1}{4}$-inch disc drive for data storage, which was a vast improvement over the previously used external tape cassette drives. Finally, memory prices fell, further reducing prices.

Two companies were the leaders in expanding the PC market from the 100,000 units sold in 1977. First, Apple Computer offered a unique operating system and a very easy-to-use graphical user interface (GUI), which enabled users to run applications with a point and click of a mouse rather than typing in instructions. Apple attracted many first-time users and became an instant hit in the educational market. Second, in 1981 IBM entered the market with its IBM PC, now the generic term for the product. IBM took a completely different approach from Apple's. First, IBM focused on the business segment rather than the home. Second, it chose to outsource supply of hardware and software components. Third, in a critical contrast to Apple, IBM took an open architecture approach whereby it licensed its operating system, PC-DOS (developed in collaboration with Microsoft), to other manufacturers and software developers. By 1983, IBM held 42% of the PC market, with Apple having 20%.

IBM's strategy of focusing on the business market and having an open architecture was so successful that it created a huge demand among business customers that the company could not fill. As a result, many other companies, called clone manufacturers, started manufacturing PCs or were formed to meet the unmet demand. Improvements in technology, increased marketing expenditures, and better software caused the U.S. market to grow from 3,520,000 units sold in 1982 to about 20 million in 1996, and total revenues increased from $10.5 billion to nearly $60 billion annually. The global market for PCs also exploded.

The Situation in the Late 1990s

Table 2–2 shows the worldwide sales and market shares for the leading PC manufacturers in 1997 and 1998. The five leading suppliers of PCs in the world are Compaq, IBM, Dell, Hewlett-Packard, and Gateway 2000. These companies are briefly described here.[12]

DELL

Dell Computer was founded by Michael Dell, who started by selling PCs over the telephone in 1983 while he was a student at the University of Texas.[13] From the very beginning, Dell has focused on the direct model, that is, selling via direct mail and other methods directly from the company to the customer, with no retailers or other distributors in between. This permitted Dell to charge lower prices because there were no intermediate markups. The company also focused more on higher-profit-margin customers in businesses and government. Dell grew from $0 in 1983 to $3.5 billion in 1994.

In 1995, the company perfected its build-to-order system, which is now widely emulated. In this system, PCs are manufactured only when an order is received. As a result, the company's inventory holding costs are much lower than any competitor's. In the late 1990s, Dell's success continued to be built on its strategy of low-cost distribution, build-to-order manufacturing, and products and services targeted to distinct customer segments. As noted in Chapter 1, the company sells approximately $10 million worth of computers through its Web site every day and this amount is growing. The Dell model of build-to-order and direct selling to customers was widely considered the route to success in the desktop PC industry in the late 1990s as prices kept dropping, putting more pressure on lowering manufacturing and distribution costs.[14]

COMPAQ

Compaq was founded in 1982 to manufacture IBM clones.[15] Its first product was the Compaq Portable, which at the time was really a "luggable." Over time, Compaq added to its portable line a series of clone desktops based on whichever Intel microprocessor was the latest technology at the time. In addition, the company introduced its SystemPro file server for networked PCs in 1989. By 1990, Compaq had sales of $3.6 billion and was 136th in the Fortune 500 and 377th in the Global 500 rankings.

In 1991, the company began to falter with the rise of lower-priced brands such as Dell. This was part of a general trend in the industry, which began to see a polarization in the market between high-priced, feature-laden models for technical applications and enthusiasts

---

Table 2–2 Global Sales Shares of Leading PC Firms, 1997–1998

| Company | 1998 | | 1997 | | |
	Shipments (thousands)	Market Share	Shipments (thousands)	Market Share	Change
Compaq	12,789	13.8%	10,596	13.1%	+20.7%
IBM	7,617	8.2	6,958	8.6	+ 9.5
Dell	7,361	7.9	4,464	5.5	+64.9
Hewlett-Packard	5,391	5.8	4,297	5.3	+25.5
Packard Bell NEC	3,950	4.3	4,116	5.1	− 4.0
Others	55,816	60.1	51,150	63.5	+ 9.1
Total Market	92,925	100.0	80,608	100.0	+15.3

Note: Figures don't include server PCs.
Source: DataQuest

and budget computers for basic business applications and the home market. Up to this time, Compaq had used a premium price strategy. After changing CEOs, Compaq shifted strategies and began to focus more on lowering its costs to participate in the low-price part of the market. In addition, the company bet heavily on the file server product line.

This strategy has been wildly successful, culminating with Compaq being the number-one PC manufacturer in the world in the late 1990s. It is the leading supplier of Windows NT–based servers as the market for networked PCs has exploded. The company purchased Tandem Computers (a company making fail-safe machines) in 1997 and the once formidable DEC in 1998. Also in 1998, it won the right to be the exclusive supplier of Tandy Corporation's 6,800-store Radio Shack chain, replacing IBM. A cloud on the horizon is that its large bet on servers began to hurt the company as that segment of the market started to become price-competitive, like the desktop market. In addition, because Compaq uses dealers rather than selling directly to customers, its costs are still higher than Dell's, putting pressure on the company to move more fully to the Dell model, which it is attempting to do (see Fig. 2–9 for Compaq's home page).

IBM

Although IBM has been very successful with its ThinkPad line of portable computers, its once-dominant market position in desktop PCs has dropped markedly since the early 1980s.[16] Although it is the number-two supplier in the world, behind Compaq, it is far behind and Dell is nipping at its heels. The main reason for this is the company's steadfast policy of not selling computers at a low price to compete with the low-price vendors. In 1995, the company felt that it had turned the home PC situation around with its widely acclaimed Aptiva model. In addition, with a new CEO (Louis Gerstner) with a consumer packaged goods background, IBM established a consumer division to focus exclusively on PCs, hired a marketing expert from American Express, and put a considerable amount of money behind PC marketing. However, the move in 1997 and 1998 by the price-oriented companies to computers costing less than $1,000 caught IBM by surprise and without a competing model. Never the low-cost leader, as shown in Table 2–2, IBM is growing but at a rate much slower than those of its major competitors. In 1998, IBM began to hurt Compaq financially by dropping prices on its servers. In addition, the company moved significantly toward a build-to-order system by using some of its distributors to assemble the desktops when ordered.[17]

HEWLETT-PACKARD

Hewlett-Packard (HP) is a well-known company making a large variety of technical products, including measurement devices, medical equipment, laser printers, and electronic components. With annual revenues of about $40 billion, the company invests about $2 billion each year on research and development and has a worldwide reputation for excellent products and outstanding relationships with its customers. The company has made PCs since 1980 and its portable computers have been successful, but through 1992 its desktop PCs, though innovative, were considered to be overpriced and poorly marketed.

In 1993, the company introduced its Vectra line to the corporate market. In 1994, HP decided to enter the home computer market and created its Home Products Division. In 1995, it introduced the Pavilion line of PCs and sold them through major retail chains such as Circuit City. Prices were above the low end (Packard Bell) but below Compaq's. Together, the two lines have made HP the world's number-three supplier of PCs, behind Compaq and IBM.[18] The company is very motivated to overtake the top two companies and set a goal to be number one by the year 2001.[19]

GATEWAY 2000

Gateway 2000, founded in 1987, focused on selling low-cost computers to home users using direct marketing (telephone, mail). Their direct-selling model actually predates Dell's. The

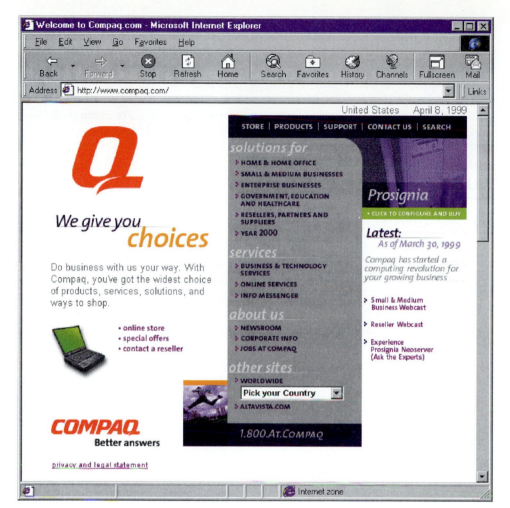

Figure 2–9

Compaq Computer
Web Site

Courtesy of Compaq
Computer Corporation.

company started in Iowa and is now located in South Dakota. From the beginning, Gateway has emphasized its rural roots by having a holstein cow as its symbol, black cowhide-patterned boxes and advertising motifs, and a folksy image (their first ads asked "Computers from Iowa?"). Obviously, given their 4% share of worldwide shipments and over $5 billion in annual revenue, Gateway is a well-managed company.

The company has never rested on its laurels and has always been willing to try new strategies. In 1997, Gateway decided to end its reliance on the home market and to make a big push into corporate sales. The company has been a leader in integrating new PC technology into its computers; it was the first to adopt Intel's Pentium processor, use color monitors, and include CD-ROM drives as standard equipment. In 1998, the company developed its innovative "Your :) Ware" program, which permits customers to finance their purchases with Gateway and to trade in their old PCs for a new one. The company is also boosting its direct selling with an expanded Internet site and 90 Gateway Country stores, located around the United States, where customers can try out, configure, and order Gateway computers for later delivery (the stores do not carry inventory).[20]

OTHERS

There are many other PC brands. Packard Bell–NEC, once the number-five brand in the world because of its low price, has slumped because of customer service and quality problems. A number of minor brands such as AST and Taiwan's Acer are attempting to gain footholds in the market. In addition, the computer retailer CompUSA began a limited version of Dell's build-to-order model, thus competing with the manufacturers. However, the PC business is very difficult because of its emphasis on low costs and because consumers have trouble seeing the differences between brands. In 1998, the giant Japanese company Toshiba decided to withdraw from the U.S. consumer desktop market and concentrate on its portable and corporate business. In addition, global competitors can vary by country. For example, the leading PC manufacturer in China is Legend Group, ahead of HP, IBM, and Compaq.

EXECUTIVE SUMMARY

Key learning points in this chapter include the following:

- The marketing manager's job is difficult and challenging.
- A major type of marketing organization is a product-focused organization, in which product managers have profit/loss responsibility for individual products or product lines.
- A second major type of marketing organization is a market-focused organization. In this structure, marketing managers are responsible for marketing the company's products to a market segment.
- The marketing organization must adapt to changes in the environment.
- The main job of the marketing manager is to be involved with the creation and implementation of marketing strategy.
- The marketing plan enables the manager to remain in touch with changes in the external environment and to incorporate those changes into the marketing strategy.

CHAPTER QUESTIONS

1. What are the pros and cons of the various marketing organizations shown in this chapter?
2. Are some organizations more appropriate for certain kinds of products than others? If so, why?
3. What are the benefits to the marketing manager of developing marketing plans? Are there any drawbacks?
4. Consider a well-known brand name or product (other than Cadillac and Motorola) that has had a serious decline in sales over the years. In your opinion, what caused the decline and how do these factors fit into the marketing manager interactions shown in Fig. 2–6?
5. Given the kinds of interactions shown in Fig. 2–6, what kind of educational background is appropriate for a marketing manager? What skills are needed?

FURTHER READING

For additional reading and examples on marketing organizations and the marketing manager's interactions with the environment, see Frank V. Cespedes (1991), *Organizing and Implementing the Marketing Effort: Text and Cases* (Reading, MA: Addison-Wesley). An interesting book that shows the difficulty of marketing through the mistakes companies have made is Steven P. Schnaars (1989), *Megamistakes* (New York: Free Press).

A Strategic Marketing Framework

3

CHAPTER BRIEF

The purpose of this chapter is to provide a framework for Chapters 4 through 12. That framework is the key part of the marketing manager's job: the development of a marketing strategy. Key learning points include the following:

The elements of a complete marketing strategy
Developing competitive advantage
Positioning products and services
The importance and development of a value proposition
The product life cycle and how it affects marketing strategies
Product line management

One of the most tumultuous industries in the world is the airline industry. It faces high operating costs (fuel, labor, reservation systems, landing rights at airports, etc.), significant competition, and myriad international and local regulations. For these reasons, many airlines have entered and exited the industry over the last 20 years.

In 1994, Western Pacific Airlines was born.[1] The fastest-growing part of the United States at that time was the Rocky Mountain region. A major airline, United Airlines, had Denver as a major hub, with many connections to other parts of the country. Denver had just completed construction of the controversial Denver International Airport (DIA), which promised much better landing and passenger facilities than its predecessor, Stapleton Airport. However, just 70 miles south of Denver was an airport in Colorado Springs that shared many of the advantages of Denver but without the high costs of DIA (the individual passenger facility charges range from $16 to $21 versus less than $3 at Colorado Springs) and no significant competition. This lack of competition allowed the incumbent carriers to charge premium prices in and out of Colorado Springs. Most significantly, many Denver residents, particularly those who lived in the fast-growing southern suburbs, preferred the Colorado Springs airport because it was much more accessible than DIA.

Although it operated 70 miles south of DIA, Western Pacific was not beyond United's influence. Because United has 70% of the gates at DIA, it was very important to the region. In addition, United could achieve tremendous economies of scale in customer service activities such as reservations, connections to international flights, and brand awareness. Thus, like its well-established counterpart, Southwest Airlines, Western Pacific had to become a low-cost, low-price airline that could compete with United for the region's passengers despite its lack of brand name awareness. Its routes would be between 30 and 1,000 miles.

Thus, the marketing managers at Western Pacific faced the following problems:

- To which customers should Western Pacific market its services? Should it market them to current United customers or customers of the airlines already serving Colorado Springs, or should it try to develop new customers?
- How should Western Pacific differentiate its products from competitors' offerings and what image should the company project to make these differences clear?
- What product features are customers demanding and which should be incorporated into Western Pacific's service?
- Over time, how should the company adapt its marketing to changes in competition, customer awareness and usage of the airline, and other changes in the environment?

In Chapter 2 we stated that the central job of the marketing manager or anyone involved with marketing is to develop or implement a marketing strategy for a product or service, based on the marketing plan. The key task facing Western Pacific marketing managers in 1994 was to develop a marketing strategy for their new airline and adapt that strategy over time to changes in the market environment. This chapter describes the basics of developing a marketing strategy for a product or service (sections III, IV, and V of the marketing plan outline shown in Table 2–1).

COMPLETE MARKETING STRATEGY

The marketing strategy framework used in this book is shown in Fig. 3–1. The components of a strategy are as follows:

- The objective to be achieved. This is the criterion by which the success or failure of the strategy is measured.
- The strategic alternatives to be considered. These are potential groups of customers that the marketing manager could pursue.
- The customer targets. This is a more specific statement of which customers (e.g., income over $40,000, small businesses with revenues under $10,000,000) the marketing manager wants to entice to buy the product or service.
- For each customer target, competitor targets must be identified. These are the brands or companies that offer the most likely competition for that customer.
- Given the customer and competitor targets, the marketing manager needs to choose which product or service features to offer.
- The marketing manager must target the customer group with the **core strategy.** This strategy has three parts: the differential advantage, or how the product or service is better than the competition; the product position, or how the customer is intended to perceive the product; and the value proposition, which summarizes the customer target, the differential advantage, and the product position in a statement that communicates the reason to buy.
- The marketing mix is the set of decisions about price, channels of distribution, and so on. This aspect of the marketing strategy is covered in later chapters.

This marketing strategy framework follows the flow of decision-making. The marketing manager first decides what the goal is and then how to get there. The key decision is which customer groups to target. As shown in Fig. 3–2, other decisions flow from that crucial decision. The customers' needs, an analysis of the competitors, and an understanding

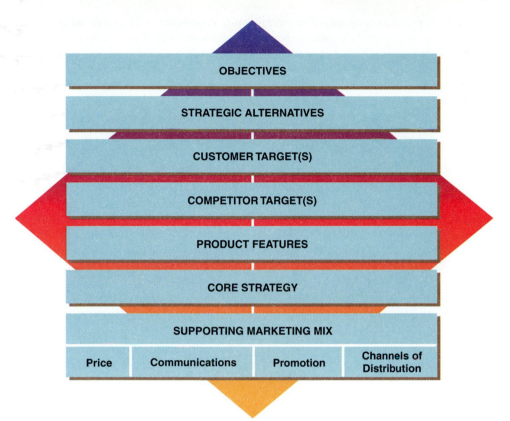

Figure 3–1

Elements of a
Complete Marketing
Strategy

of the industry environment lead to a core strategy that is tailored to each customer target. Finally, the marketing mix or implementation of the strategy is customized for each target, with an additional understanding of the key reasons to buy. Of course, this is a simplified model. In practice, the marketing manager often moves back and forth between steps of the strategy as new information about customers, changes in competitors' actions, and other changes emerge.

Often, steps 3 (choosing the customer targets), 5 (choosing the product features), and 6 (setting the core strategy) are called the marketing strategy. However, the "complete" marketing strategy shown in Fig. 3–1 reflects the importance of making decisions about all three major components—the objective, the strategy, and the marketing mix or tactics—in concert

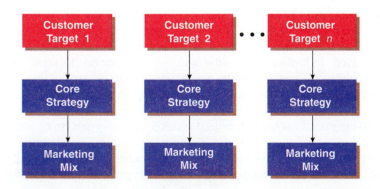

Figure 3–2

Ensuring a
Segment-Focused
Strategy

and in the appropriate sequence. For example, it is impossible to determine what price to charge unless you know how price sensitive your customer target is or whether your core strategy is to position the product as one with a premium image. Similarly, you cannot make advertising copy decisions without knowing the target market's media habits and what reason to buy must be communicated. Therefore, both the components of the strategy and the order in which they are completed are critical.

Objectives

Many different kinds of objectives are set in an organization. A company's **mission statement** usually describes in general terms its major business thrusts, customer orientation, or business philosophy. The corporate objective is an overall goal to be achieved, usually stated in financial (return on sales, margins, etc.) or stock price terms. Business units or divisions also have objectives, which might be stated in terms of sales growth or profitability. Brands or products have specific objectives, usually stated in either growth in volume-related measures (sales, market share) or profits. Finally, specific programs such as advertising can have objectives in terms that are relevant to the particular activity (e.g., awareness).

There is often tension between objectives such as increasing market share and increasing profits. Obviously, some of the activities required to increase share (e.g., lowering price, increasing the sales force) lower profit margins and increase costs, thus working against increasing profits simultaneously. Similarly, increasing profitability involves lowering costs or maintaining or increasing price, which make it more difficult to gain market share. Although managers can sometimes avoid this tradeoff by lowering costs in areas where customers are not likely to notice (e.g., the thickness of the metal of a can), one objective is normally given priority over the others.

For example, in 1991 Colgate-Palmolive reported that the profitability of its detergent product line had increased but that the line suffered a 40% decrease in market share.[2] The tradeoff between market share and profitability was also recognized by Japanese automakers, who held about 23% of the U.S. market in 1996. Because the market was not growing, the companies decided to set profit goals rather than market share goals.[3]

Returning to the Western Pacific airline illustration, the key to any service business is sales volume because the fixed costs are high and variable costs low.[4] In addition, generating cash to continue operations was of primary consideration for the first year. Thus, Western Pacific's main objective was to fill seats on as many flights as possible—a volume goal. More passengers means more revenues to cover fixed costs and more opportunity for satisfied customers to spread favorable word-of-mouth.

It is not sufficient to state an objective in terms such as "Increase market share" or "Increase profits." Characteristics of good objective statements include the following:

- Objectives should have a quantified standard of performance. In other words, an improved statement would be "Increase market share by 5 points."
- Objectives should have a clear time frame, that is, a period within which it should be achieved. To further improve the objective, it would be "Increase market share by 5 points by the end of calendar year 1999."
- Objectives should be stated in measurable terms. Although there is some variation between industries and companies, market share, profitability, and sales volume are easy to measure. Less tangible objectives such as quality need to be put into verifiable terms.
- Objectives should be ambitious enough to be challenging. One of the purposes of an objective is to push management to improve its performance. Objectives that are

not challenging do not test the management team and are therefore poor measures of the quality of the personnel. At the same time, the objectives should be realistic, taking external and internal constraints into consideration.

Strategic Alternatives, Customer Targets, and Competitor Targets

Once the objective for the brand or product line has been established, the next major decision is on which customer groups to focus. Although the motivation and methods for making this focus or **market segmentation** decision are elaborated upon in Chapters 5 and 6, the primary reason to think about the market in terms of groups or segments is market heterogeneity. Simply put, customers have different personal values, are looking for different benefits from products and services, and respond differently to the marketing mix variables. As a result, even if the manager decides to pursue all potential customers in the market, it is still important to consider the market as being composed of segments for which alternative marketing strategies must be developed.

Because there are many ways to segment a market, a useful first step is to consider the strategic alternatives shown in Fig. 3–3. The strategic alternatives divide the total potential market into two general strategies:

- A **market penetration strategy** targets current customers of the product or service. These are customers who are buying your product or a competitor's (often both).
- A **market development strategy** targets customers who have not purchased the product yet. These could be customers who have been targeted but simply have not been persuaded or they could be customers in segments that have not been pursued by any company in the industry or product category.

The market penetration strategy targeting current customers should always be a high priority for the marketing manager. Clearly, customers who have purchased your product or service are familiar with its benefits. Assuming that a high percentage of the customers enjoyed the consumption experience, there is often potential left in the market from the current customers who could be persuaded to buy more. For example,

- In an organizational buying or industrial marketing setting, where products or services are marketed to companies rather than households, it is often possible to get the organization to adopt the product more widely throughout the organization. This can be done at a particular location or, if the company has multiple locations throughout the country or the world, at other sites. Computer software programs used for

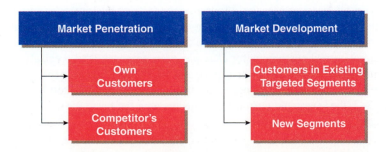

Figure 3–3
Strategic Alternatives

applications such as inventory control can be applied in a plant in Europe and then, if found to be useful, applied to the U.S. plants.

- Per capita consumption of consumer products can be increased by using larger package sizes or showing how the product can be used on other occasions or in other ways. American Express has attempted to get consumers to use the card even for small purchases. Kodak wants you to take everyday photos of family or guests. Pepsi-Cola would like you to drink it at breakfast or in the morning as a substitute for coffee.[5]

A more difficult strategy that also focuses on customers who have purchased the product is to target competitors' customers. This strategy is riskier and more expensive because it involves persuading customers who may be satisfied with their current supplier or brand to switch. This is often done in markets in which the growth rate is slowing, usually called a mature market; because new customers are unlikely to enter the market, competitors try to convince customers to switch brands. Often, this is done through price or price-related promotions. Customers often use reduced-price coupons delivered in magazines or direct mail for frequently purchased grocery items. A point-of-purchase machine developed by Catalina Marketing Corporation can be programmed to print coupons for a particular brand when a competitor's brand is scanned at the checkout. Long-distance telephone services have been a brand-switching battleground for several years as AT&T and MCI furiously attempt to get you to change carriers, mainly by advertising price comparisons. Computer software companies often offer reduced prices if a user of a competitor's product sends in a proof-of-purchase. Because Western Pacific Airlines is new, one of its key strategic alternatives is to take customers from United (from DIA) and other small airlines flying out of Colorado Springs.

A market development strategy expands the marketing effort beyond the current segments into new ones. This can be done with or without product modifications. The seed company Burpee developed small seed packages that were sold with plastic watering cans and tools aimed at penetrating the children's market. Kodak and Fuji have also focused on children by developing programs to link their products with school photography classes and featuring movie tie-ins on special packaging for their cameras. Private banking companies such as U.S. Trust have reduced the net worth threshold to obtain special services that are usually offered only to people with net worth of at least $1 million. By offering low fares and service to towns and cities not previously served by the other airlines, Western Pacific could expand the total market by attracting new customers.

Market development can also involve working harder to attract customers in segments that are already being targeted. In this case, the marketing manager has to assess whether it is profitable to do so. For example, a customer who fits the description of a targeted group may be located in a region of the country that makes the cost of attempting to gain the sale too high. Alternatively, the strategy may address some systematic reason (e.g., insufficient production or retail sites) that potential customers are not buying.

The marketing manager uses these four groups (existing customers, competitors' customers, nonbuying customers in currently targeted segments, and segments that have not been previously targeted) to give more focus to the market segment decision. Once you have decided to target current customers, for example, your next task is to precisely define who these customers are ("women between ages 20 and 40," "midsized companies," etc.). These specific, actionable definitions are necessary in implementing a marketing strategy. Following Fig. 3–2, these targeted customer groups become the basis for the rest of the marketing strategy.

The strategic alternatives chosen also help determine the competitor targets. For example, if a penetration strategy of stealing competitors' customers is chosen, the exact competitors must be specified. Even a decision to continue to pursue current customers should result in a set of competitors who may be trying to steal them from you.

The Grey Poupon brand of dijon mustard, now owned by a subsidiary of RJR Nabisco, Nabisco Holdings, featured one of the most memorable advertising campaigns ever developed: the "Pardon Me" campaign.[6] In this campaign, the marketing managers for the brand sought to give an element of prestige to a brand that cost more and brought an element of distinction to any dish in which it was used. The advertising developed a very high level of awareness and was parodied in different media, from the *Tonight Show* to the movie *Wayne's World*.

However, at some point every advertising campaign gets tired and must be replaced. In addition, the "special occasions" theme limits the perception of when it can be used and thereby reduces the purchase volume. Therefore, in 1998 the brand's managers decided to focus on getting current customers to buy more (penetration strategy) by encouraging them to use Grey Poupon not just on special occasions but for everyday use. A suggested advertising theme was "Pamper your family, not just your guests." The managers were also trying to attract new users, mainly by getting new customers in the targeted segments (development strategy). This was attempted through coupons with price discounts, recipes, and premiums such as measuring spoons that were obtained with purchases of the brand.

There is a risk in attempting to broaden the occasions when Grey Poupon can be used. By extending into everyday uses, the brand may lose its prestigious image and start to look more like lower-priced brands such as Guldens. As a result, it could be priced higher than the normal brands of mustards and less prestigious than the upper-end brands (i.e., stuck in the middle, which is discussed further later in this chapter). Therefore, it is risky to expand into other strategic alternatives because increasing the segments you are trying to attract may be inconsistent with the brand's image. ◆

Product Features

At this point in the process, you have formulated the objective and, after considering the various strategic alternatives, you have determined the customer and competitor targets. Given what you know about the customers' tastes and the competitors' products, you must make a decision about the specific features to be included in your product. These include the intrinsic product features (size, ingredients, color, etc.) as well as packaging and design, the latter of which have received a great deal of attention in the last few years.[7]

The notion of developing different product features for different segments is particularly appealing for services and information goods (e.g., computer software, entertainment, newspapers). For manufactured products, it is very expensive to tailor products to segments because of the implications for the manufacturing process. The Jeep division of Chrysler can offer two basic versions of the Cherokee sport utility vehicle (basic and Grand) to appeal to different customer interests for luxury. However, the number of versions is very limited. Services and information goods can be very tailored. For example, if you join a health club, there are usually several different membership options: family or single, 1-month, 6-month, 1-year, basic or basic plus swimming, and so on. It does not cost the health club any more to offer these options to customers because the options do not force the club to change its amenities for each segment.

In information goods, offering different product options for different segment needs is called versioning.[8] Consider the product line for Kurzweil, a producer of voice recognition software:

Product	Price	Description
VoicePad Pro	$ 79	Vocabulary of 20,000 words
Personal	295	Vocabulary of 30,000 words
Professional	595	Vocabulary of 50,000 words
Office Talk	795	General office staff
Law Talk	1,195	Legal vocabulary
Voice Med	6,000	Medical offices
Voice Ortho	8,000	Special-purpose medical vocabulary

In each case, the company has recognized that there are different segments with different needs, and that the greater the need, the higher the price the customers in the segment are willing to pay. The segments are differentiated by the size and the customization of the vocabulary that the software can recognize.   ◆

The Core Strategy: Competitive Advantage

One of the most important strategic decisions you make is the basis on which customers will choose your product over the competitors'. This is called developing a **competitive or differential advantage.** When customers cannot discriminate between products, they consider the products to be commodities and the main determinant of which product is purchased is price. Such competition is not necessarily bad if you are the low-cost producer or supplier; in fact, as we discuss later in this chapter, you might choose to compete on that basis. However, if you are not the low-cost producer and you are unable to differentiate your product on any basis other than price, you are unlikely to succeed.

There are many possible ways to develop competitive advantage. A successful basis for developing such an advantage should have three characteristics:[9]

- It should generate customer value. In other words, it should improve some characteristic or be relevant to some aspect of the product or service that is valued by the customer. For example, you could paint your mainframe computers red to differentiate them from the competition, but the color of the computer probably does not matter to the key decision-makers. Low price, speedy delivery, and Internet access are product dimensions that generate value to some set of customers. Thus, a point of difference is a competitive advantage only if, from the customer's perspective, your product delivers better value than the competition.
- The increased value must be perceived by the customer. In other words, even if your product is better than the competition, if the customer cannot discern this point of difference, it is not a competitive advantage. For example, Intel felt that its x86 line of microprocessor chips delivered superior value to customers. However, microprocessors are invisible to the user. By branding the Intel name with the "Intel Inside" advertising campaign, the company attempted to make the value visible and more tangible to personal computer buyers.
- The advantage should be difficult to copy. Clearly, a successful competitive advantage adopted by one product is going to be emulated by others, if possible. Although American Airlines was the first airline to offer a frequent-flier program,

Manufacturers of high-tech products confront a particular problem in communicating tangible points of difference to their customers. For example, faced with an array of similar products, the average PC buyer cannot easily distinguish among them. In response, Intel launched its highly successful "Intel Inside" campaign, making the value of its x86 line of chips more tangible to PC buyers. This ad for Gateway's E-Series workstations includes the "Intel Inside" logo, communicating the product's superior value. (Copyright 1999 Gateway 2000, Inc. Reprinted with permission.)

few people remember this because of the flood of imitators. A competitive advantage is more likely to be sustainable if it is difficult to copy because of unique organizational assets and skills that can be brought into play. For example, Federal Express has developed a sustainable competitive advantage over UPS, Emery, and other package delivery companies in the area of customer service. This is because of its pioneering use of information technology and the company's continued investments in such technology that the other companies have been unable or unwilling to match.

There are three general approaches to developing competitive advantage:

- Cost- or price-based advantage
- Quality-based or differentiation advantage
- Perceived quality or brand-based advantage

Cost- or Price-Based Competitive Advantage

Achieving the low-cost position among competitors does not necessarily imply lowering prices for competitive advantage. However, as in the market share–profitability tradeoff discussed earlier in this chapter, it is difficult to have both a low-cost competitive advantage and a quality advantage such as superior customer service because service costs money. However, being in the low-cost position enables the manager to choose whether to compete on price, depending on competitive conditions.

One of the most difficult approaches to competitive advantage is the cost-based approach. It is difficult for the following reasons: You need to know the competitors' costs to be sure that you can compete on this basis by matching price cuts, if necessary; because of improvements in technology, it is possible to be leapfrogged in terms of low costs; and only one supplier or producer can be the low-cost competitor in a market. As a result, it is not surprising that most marketing managers choose to compete on the other two bases (actual and perceived quality) while exercising as much cost control as possible.

It has been argued that there are two ways to attain the low-cost position in an industry or product category. One of these is by simply being the largest producer and taking advantages of **economies of scale** (sometimes called economies of size).[10] The rationale behind economies of scale is that larger sales mean that fixed costs of operations can be spread over more units, which lowers average unit costs. Originally developed for manufacturing plant construction, the economies of scale concept also applies to marketing, distribution, and other expenditures. For example, scale is critical to fast-food profitability. A fast-food chain has to spend the same amount on regional advertising whether it has 1 or 50 stores in the area. With more stores against which the advertising can be leveraged, revenues go up while advertising costs remain constant, thus increasing profits.

Further evidence of the benefits of size comes from the PIMS (Profit Impact of Market Strategies) project sponsored by the Strategic Planning Institute.[11] PIMS researchers have analyzed many relationships between company strategies and the resulting performance. One of the key findings of the PIMS study is that there is a positive relationship between market share and profitability. This result is shown in Fig. 3–4. On average, market leaders have rates of return that are three times greater than those of businesses with a market share rank of 5 or lower. Although not all market leaders achieved that position by using a low-price advantage, it is often the case that sales volume and market share are built through low-price strategies.

Figure 3–4

Relationship between Market Share and Return on Investment

Source: Robert D. Buzzell and Bradley T. Gale (1987), *The PIMS Principles* (New York: Free Press), p. 72.

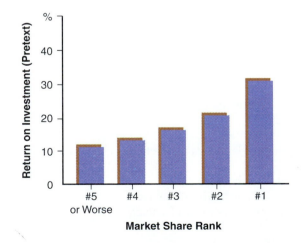

One of the major ways to achieve the low-cost position is by taking advantage of a phenomenon called the **experience curve.**[12] Simply put, costs fall with cumulative production or delivery of a service and, after some observations based on the first few years of a product's life, the continued decline in costs is predictable. The experience curve phenomenon has been observed in a wide variety of industries, from semiconductors to airline transportation to life insurance administration. As a product is produced over time, companies learn how to make it better and more efficiently through changes in the production process, work specialization, product standardization, and redesign. According to the proponents of the experience curve, a product that has more cumulative production (i.e., greater sales aggregated over time) is in the best cost position in the industry or product category and has the most flexibility for using price as a differential advantage.

Figure 3–5 shows learning curves for the computer software and semiconductor industries. The vertical axis is cost per unit, adjusted for inflation; the horizontal axis is time.[13] The costs for semiconductors are given in cost per transistor, whereas for software, they are given in terms of cost per software function point, a measure of the number of inputs, outputs, and internal and external files manipulated by the program. As can be seen, the experience curve is much steeper for semiconductors than for software. The figure implies that costs per transistor have declined 48% per year while costs per function point have declined only 4.5% per year.

Although using these two effects (scale and experience) to develop marketing strategies has been popular, it is possible to be the low-cost producer and use a low-price competitive advantage even if you are not the industry leader or have the greatest cumulative experience. In today's manufacturing environment, flexible manufacturing systems make it possible to have short production runs of different models of products tailored to segments and simultaneously have low costs. What is perhaps most important in attaining a low-cost–low-price advantage is to focus all the company's controls on costs. In other words, it is possible to compete on price without being the largest.

 For example, Southwest Airlines and other, smaller regional airlines in different parts of the world always compete on price and are not nearly as large as their international competitors, nor do they have as much experience. They succeed by having a maniacal approach to cost control. No meals (just peanuts and soft drinks), not much baggage handling, no fancy computerized reservation systems (mainly ticketless, no

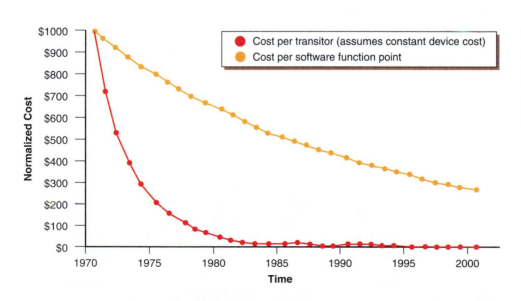

Figure 3–5

Learning Curves for Software and Hardware

Source: *Upside* (1996), March, p. 68.

reserved seats, no agents to whom they have to pay commissions, and greater use of the Web), standardized planes for easier maintenance (Boeing 737s), one class of seating, and flexible work rules keep their costs way down. Many small airlines also lease their planes and subcontract out maintenance to further reduce costs.   ◆

Some other examples of successful low-price competitive advantages are the following:

- Ikea, the Swedish furniture retailer with stores around the world, keeps its prices down by emphasizing self-service, low-cost modular designs, and customer pickup and delivery.
- Jiffy Lube International focuses on one area of automobile maintenance—lubricants—and does not do any other work.
- Agco, formed in 1990, is one of the leading farm equipment manufacturers. They have been successful by undercutting market leader Deere's prices by 10% through low-cost production processes and spending little on R&D.
- Mutual fund marketer the Vanguard Group has fund managers who keep trading levels low to keep costs down, as well as a low-cost approach to managing distribution, customer service, and marketing.
- Wal-Mart became the low-price leader in retailing by having the best information technology in the industry. They are supplied directly by manufacturers rather than going through distributors, using satellite-based links to track inventory. The suppliers provide Wal-Mart with inventory that is ready to be put directly on the shelves.

There are many other examples; most product categories have at least one product attempting to obtain a price-based advantage. The key to successful price competition is having the lowest costs.

Quality-Based Differentiation

A second approach to creating a competitive advantage is to develop an observable difference that is valued by the target customers. This approach is distinctly different from the low-cost–low-price competitive advantage because it usually implies higher costs but a concomitant higher price and often higher margins. You can think of this approach as a search for some point of difference that customers value and for which they are willing to pay a price premium. Thus, this approach is often called **differentiation.**[14]

Studies have shown that high perceived quality pays off. Figure 3–6 shows some results produced by the Strategic Planning Institute demonstrating the strong positive relationship between perceived quality and return on sales and return on investment.

Figure 3–6

Relationship between Quality and Profitability

Source: Robert D. Buzzell and Bradley T. Gale (1987), *The PIMS Principles* (New York: Free Press), p. 107.

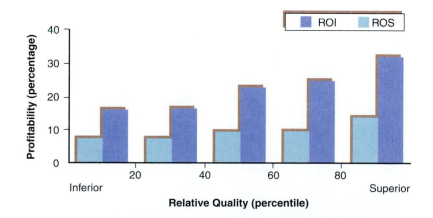

Some readers may argue that for some products, it is impossible to differentiate based on quality. This is the commodity mentality referred to earlier in this chapter. The problem is that if you are not the low-cost producer and you cannot differentiate on the basis of quality, real or perceived, then your product will be unsuccessful, "stuck in the middle,"[15] because other products in your category or industry are (or can be) priced lower and have better perceived or actual quality (recall the Grey Poupon illustration earlier in the chapter). Think of the most commodity-like products (e.g., gasoline, long-distance service, bulk chemicals). The challenge to the marketing manager is to find the dimensions of the product or service that differentiate it from the competition.

One way to differentiate is through what might be called a real difference, that is, one not built solely on the basis of perceptions. For example, Caterpillar markets the most reliable farm and construction equipment in the industry. This is an actual difference that can be supported with data on intervals between equipment breakdowns. For industrial and highly technical products and services, this kind of differentiation is common. However, for consumer products it is often more difficult to differentiate on the basis of an actual quality difference, presenting a greater challenge to the marketing manager.

One approach to conceptualizing ways to differentiate was developed by Porter and is called the value chain.[16] The value chain concept emphasizes that differentiation can be obtained through efforts of the whole corporation, not just marketing. The major parts of the value chain are shown in Fig. 3–7. One way to differentiate is through inbound logistics, that is, through the selection of the highest-quality raw materials and other inputs, including technology. Bottled waters, for example, often use their natural water sources as a point of difference. For years, supercomputer company Cray had a significant technological edge on other companies. A second way to gain competitive advantages is through operational advantages. One of the ways McDonald's has remained the fast-food market leader throughout the world is by significant investments in training programs that maintain consistency in service and product quality. Outbound logistics provides a third basis for differentiation. This can be through speedy and on-time delivery such as the Federal Express promise of being there "absolutely and positively overnight." A company called Premier Industrial Corporation distributes nuts and bolts, seemingly a commodity, but differentiates itself from competition (and has higher margins) by agreeing to ship in any quantity desired by the customer. Marketing and sales also differentiate. The IBM sales force has historically been a major asset to the company, enabling IBM to satisfy customer needs better than competitors. Finally, as is discussed further in Chapter 14, service can be an important differentiator, as the retailer

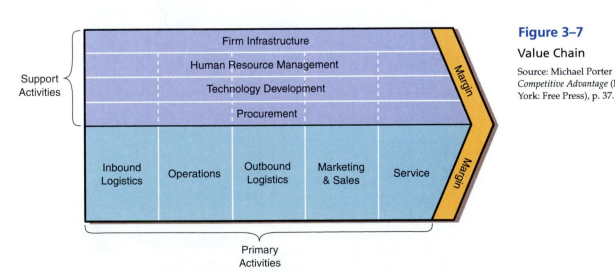

Figure 3–7

Value Chain

Source: Michael Porter (1980), *Competitive Advantage* (New York: Free Press), p. 37.

Nordstrom has found. Therefore, one way you can attempt to differentiate is by seeking advantage in one or more of the five dimensions of the value chain.

 Chevron is using two of the elements of the value chain to differentiate itself from other major brands such as Shell and Exxon as well as from low-price brands such as Arco and local brands. One way is through a proprietary additive, Techron (inbound logistics). This is an advantage if Chevron can convince customers that Techron actually enhances performance as claimed. Chevron is also developing a joint venture with McDonald's that will differentiate it from the other leading brands (marketing and sales), who often have mini-marts selling food and sundry items.

Other examples are the following:

- Kensington, a leading marketer of replacement mice for PCs, has developed a new eye-catching retail display with more user information than other brands provide (marketing and sales).
- Anheuser-Busch puts a "Born On" date on its beer labels to indicate when the product was brewed (operations).
- Marks & Spencer, the British retailer known for its own brands of clothing and food, maintains tight quality control standards that produce some of the highest-quality private label products in the world (inbound logistics).

Budweiser's "Born On" ad campaign uses product quality to create a competitive advantage. Building the case that "freshness is the key ingredient to great beer taste," this ad for Budweiser beer highlights the fact that many other breweries do not provide consumers with information about product freshness and establishes freshness as a point of difference between Budweiser and competing brands. (Anheuser Busch Advertisement)

WHEN WAS YOUR BEER BORN?

Freshness is the key ingredient to great beer taste. It's a fact that Fresh Beer Tastes Better.™ *How can you tell how fresh your beer is?*

INTRODUCING OUR NEW BORN ON DATE

- The "Born On" Date is easy-to-read and tells you the exact day our beers are packaged.
- Our beers are freshest within 110 days of the "Born On" Date.
- You know exactly how fresh your beer is and when it's at its peak of flavor.

MANY OTHER BREWERS USE A PULL DATE

- A Pull date is a "sell-by" date set by the brewer. It's the date the beer should be pulled from the shelf.
- Pull dates are often coded and cannot be easily read.
- Bottom line – a Pull date does not tell you how fresh the beer is, only when it should no longer be sold.

FRESH BEER TASTES BETTER.™

- Perkin Elmer Applied Biosystems Division has developed a new polymerase chain reaction thermal cycler (used in DNA analysis) that has a smaller footprint (takes up less space on the researcher's table), a better user interface, and higher reliability than currently exists in the industry (inbound logistics/operations).
- Fidelity Investments has invested more than $100 million in a new office park in Kentucky that brings state-of-the-art printing and mailing technology to its mutual funds business (operations).
- Although it is heavier and offers lower-quality picture resolution than competitors' products, Sony's Mavica digital camera is the market leader because it is the only one that stores the pictures on a conventional 3.5" disk, which permits the user to download the pictures easily and conveniently onto a PC.
- Amazon.com has developed a better interactive strategy than main competitors such as Barnesandnoble.com; it does a better job of providing tailored book offerings and building customer relationships.
- University National Bank & Trust in Palo Alto, California, offers superior service including free shoe shines and vans that travel to business customers' offices to pick up their deposits (service).

Perceived Quality or Brand-Based Differentiation

It is often said that in both marketing and politics, "The perception *is* the reality." Many products and services differentiate themselves from competitors by doing a better job of giving customers the perception that they are of higher overall quality or better on a particular product characteristic (part of the marketing and sales portion of the value chain shown in Fig. 3–7). Good examples are "taste," "freshness," or just "quality." Marketing managers might also attempt to differentiate their products in terms of image ("cool," "young," "sumptuous"). Perceptual differential advantages are often used when actual product differences are small, hard to achieve, or difficult to sustain. Although you might think that this would characterize only consumer products and services, many industrial and high-tech marketing managers attempt to develop perceptual differences in addition to the actual differences that their customers usually demand. For example, some high-tech companies try to differentiate by being on the leading edge of the technology they use.

Perceptual differential advantages can be conveyed using all elements of the marketing mix. High price can communicate high quality for product categories in which consumers perceive a price–quality correlation. Electronic and print advertising is an excellent vehicle for delivering images and feelings. Exclusive distribution channels can be used to provide the potential customer with the feeling that the product is rare and expensive.

The dimensions of a perceptual differential advantage are the same as for an actual one; that is, you can use the value chain shown in Fig. 3–7 to develop alternative ideas for how to deliver unique perceptions to customers. For example, you might want to deliver the image that your customer service is the best in the industry. Alternatively, you can tell customers that you use the best ingredients. Although you would clearly want to do this if you have a real or actual advantage in terms of that characteristic, the difference between this approach to competitive advantage and that based on real differences is that in this case, the claims are more difficult for customers to verify. Thus, categories that rely heavily on this approach to differentiation are beer, cosmetics, and many services such as airlines and banks.

An important tool in understanding how your brand or product is perceived is marketing research that measures customers' perceptions of your product on a variety of attributes. Although it is covered in more detail in Chapter 5, one way to conceptualize the output of this kind of research is a **perceptual map.** A perceptual map based on retail banks is shown

Figure 3–8

Perceptual Map:
Retail Banking

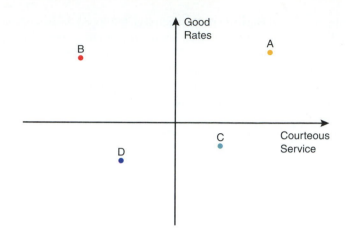

in Fig. 3–8. This perceptual map provides the marketing manager with information about how the bank is perceived on attributes or dimensions that customers consider important in choosing between competitors. The two key attributes in this example are courteous service and good interest rates offered (higher for deposits, lower for credit). The dimensions cannot be interpreted as actual scales; differences, whether horizontal or vertical, cannot be translated into actual rate differences. In addition, the location of the axes is arbitrary; what counts are the relative distances between the banks. However, the map gives you information about perceptions of your brand relative to competitors, or the **brand positions.** Customers are asked to provide ratings of how similar the banks are overall as well as supplemental information about how important different characteristics are in their bank selection process. The map indicates the following:

- Bank A is perceived to have the best rates and the most courteous service.
- Banks D and C are roughly comparable in terms of rates but C is perceived to offer better service.
- Bank B is well perceived on the rate dimension but is the poorest on the service dimension.

Note that this is very valuable diagnostic information, particularly to banks B, C, and D, who may have had little idea of the customers' perceptions about them. In addition, what is most interesting is that the perceptions could be at variance with reality; perhaps Bank C spends as much money as Bank A on teller and manager training, has the same hours, and so on. However, Bank C's position is inferior to A's on the service dimension. What you can do with this information is discussed in the next section.

One of the key ways to define a perceptual differential advantage is through the brand name. The value of a brand name in communicating quality or other aspects of the product is called **brand equity.**[17] Brand names by themselves are very powerful communicators of product quality that form an important part of the product's differential advantage. For example, the top 10 brand names as measured by consulting firm Interbrand are the following:[18]

1. McDonald's
2. Coca-Cola
3. Disney
4. Kodak
5. Sony
6. Gillette
7. Mercedes-Benz
8. Levi's
9. Microsoft
10. Marlboro

Independent of the individual products involved, each of these brand names adds considerable intangible value to the customer's perceptions.

Brand equity can be defined as follows:[19]

Brand equity is a set of assets (and liabilities) linked to a brand's name and symbol that adds to (or subtracts from) the value provided by a product or service to a firm or that firm's customers.

The assets and liabilities underlying brand value fall into five categories, as shown in Fig. 3–9:

- Brand loyalty. The strongest measure of a brand's value is the loyalty (repeat buying, word of mouth) it engenders in customers.

Figure 3–9

Brand Equity

Source: David A. Aaker (1996), *Building Strong Brands* (New York: Free Press), p. 9.

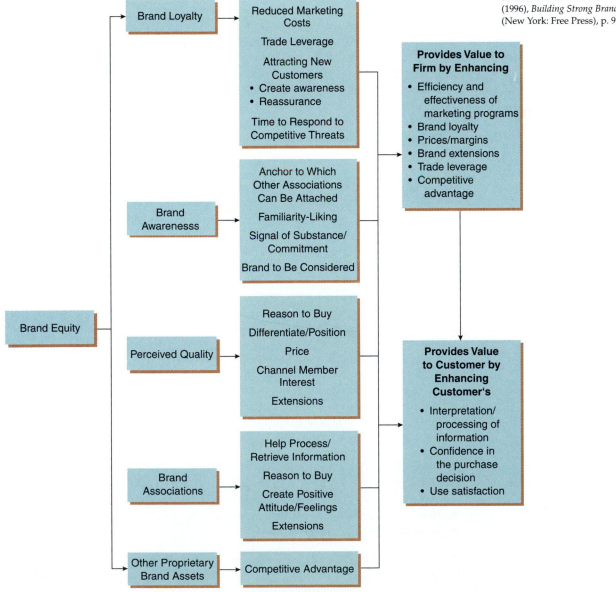

- Brand awareness. The simplest form of brand equity is familiarity. A familiar brand gives the customer a feeling of confidence, so he or she is more likely to consider and choose it.
- Perceived quality. A known brand often conveys an aura of quality (either good or bad). A quality association can be of the general halo type, such as Levi's outstanding reputation for both its products and as a place to work. It could also be a category-specific association, such as Gillette's reputation in razors and blades.
- Brand associations. Although quality associations are very important, more subjective and emotional associations are also important parts of brand value. These could include personal, emotional, and many other kinds of associations. Taken together, these associations form a brand personality that suggests situations for which a brand is (and is not) suitable.
- Other brand assets. Other assets, such as patents and trademarks, are also very valuable to products and services.

Thus, marketing managers must be aware that the brand name is a product characteristic like any other from which customer perceptions can be drawn. These can be positive or strong, such as those from the preceding list. They can also be negative or weak. For example, until recently, the giant retailer Sears had a negative image among wealthier customers, who would not think of buying clothes in the same store as you could buy power tools. The "mad cow" scare in England in 1996 tainted the image of all British beef and even some from other parts of Europe. The airline ValuJet is now part of joke routines. A brand name is part of the potential differential advantage linked heavily to customer perceptions.

PRODUCT POSITIONING

At this point in the development of the marketing strategy, you have established

- The product's objective
- The customer targets
- The competitor targets for each customer target
- The specific product features
- The possible ways to differentiate your product, based on either real or perceived (or both) advantages, in your target groups

The next task is to consider the alternative differentiation possibilities and determine what differential advantages are to be emphasized and communicated to the target customers.[20] This is called **product positioning.** Positioning takes the competitive advantage and plants it in the mind of the customer so that it is clear what the product stands for and how it is different from the other offerings in the product category.

In order to make a good positioning decision, we need to know the following:[21]

- What dimensions do consumers use to evaluate product offerings in the industry or category?
- How important is each of these dimensions in the decision process?
- How do you and the competition compare on the dimensions?
- What decision process do the customers use?

The marketing manager then determines the key points of differentiation that will make the most impact on the target market and communicates them to the customer. **Repositioning** occurs when the manager is dissatisfied with the current positioning and seeks a new perceived advantage.

It is important to note that positioning involves both actual and perceived differential advantages. For example, British Airways is the largest airline in the world, as measured by the total number of passengers carried annually. Recent advertising campaigns have emphasized that fact: British Airways is positioned as a global airline that is the world's largest. How potential customers interpret "largest" is ambiguous; it could mean a variety of things to them (financially secure, safe, etc.). The advertisement in Fig. 3–10 for Olympus Optical's SYS.230 Personal Storage System removable storage device for personal computers shows clearly that it is positioned as a low-cost alternative to the main competitors, including Iomega's Zip and Jaz drives, although the latter are not mentioned explicitly in the ad. The product is also positioned as being technologically different from Iomega's products, which rely on more traditional magnetic technology rather than the optical technology used in the SYS.230.

A point to keep in mind is that too many different product positionings aimed at different target markets are difficult to implement. Because target markets often overlap (e.g., 35- to 45-year-old adults and young families) and media such as television cannot exclude people not in the target group (can you tell people not to watch a particular program because

they are not in the show's target?), advertisements are often seen by unintended audiences. Returning to an earlier illustration, the managers of Grey Poupon will find it difficult to develop advertising and find media that are read or watched only by current users when developing the penetration strategy aimed at getting current users to buy more. Nonusers of the brand might watch the commercial and say "Hey, that's not me" and become confused about exactly what the Grey Poupon brand stands for.

◆ Illustration: Metaxa

Metaxa, a Greek brandy created in 1888 and owned by IDV/Grand Metropolitan Group, had been dormant since the 1980s.[22] By 1995, worldwide sales volume had dropped to less than 1 million cases per year, below the volume necessary to be considered a major spirits brand. The product had a poor image because it was associated with classical Greece, perceived to be long dead, and the Athens airport, generally considered to be one of the world's worst.

The manager of the brand went directly to the major market segment, Germany, where 40% of Metaxa's sales occur. Using basic marketing research methods, the manager found that the positive associations of the brand with Greece focused on the Greek attitude toward life, an easy-going informality with a Mediterranean feel. The brand was subsequently repositioned, focusing on the lifestyle differential advantage it had as the only Greek brandy, promoted with a carefree, optimistic Mediterranean feeling using the theme "Sunshine in a Bottle."[23] In addition, other target markets are Greece, Russia, the Ukraine, Eastern Europe, and the United States and the target age group is 25. The repositioning is being tested in Germany alone and it has been successful in pretesting. In Greece, where the brand was positioned as a cheap drink, Metaxa's management raised the price, developed a new package, and repositioned the brand using a cartoon image of the Greek god Dionysus. Sales volume has declined by 40% but profits are higher than before the price increase.   ◆

The Value Proposition

A convenient way to summarize the differentiation strategy and product positioning to each target customer group is the **value proposition.** In one paragraph, state the customer's reason to buy your product or service rather than the competitor's. The advantage of developing a succinct summary of the relative value of your product to the customer is that it forms the basis on which the programs (marketing mix) can be developed because the key point of differentiation is clear.

A model for a value proposition is the following:[24]

For (target customer) who (statement of the need), the (product/brand name) is a (product category) that (statement of the key benefit/compelling reason to buy). Unlike (primary competitive alternatives), (product/brand name) (statement of primary differentiation).

For example, Amazon.com is an Internet business that sells books through its Web site. Although the company faces strong competition from Barnes and Noble's site, it is one of the most successful Web-based businesses because it has a very sound value proposition:

For World Wide Web users who enjoy books, Amazon.com is a retail bookseller that provides instant access to over 1.1 million books. Unlike traditional book retailers, Amazon.com provides a combination of extraordinary convenience, low prices, and comprehensive selection.

A second example comes from the computer database software industry.[25] Databases store and retrieve records such as customer accounts and inventories and manage transactions such as hotel and airline reservation systems. Relational databases are the most common; these match different variables in a customer file, such as name and recent purchases. The dominant supplier of relational databases is Oracle, with over 40% of the worldwide market. Informix is another supplier and has about 15% of the market. However, because of the growing need to store images and sound for use on the Internet, databases must combine complex multimedia data with the text and numbers normally found in relational databases. Informix has developed such software; its value proposition is the following:

> For companies who need relational databases with advanced multimedia capabilities, Informix's Universal Server software is the first database product to successfully integrate text, graphics, and sound capabilities. Unlike Oracle's product under development, the Informix Universal Server is available for on-time delivery.

MARKETING STRATEGIES OVER THE PRODUCT LIFE CYCLE

One of the most important concepts in marketing is the **product life cycle (PLC).** The PLC is defined for a product category[26] and sketches the sales history of the category over time. The importance of the PLC is as a strategic tool: The strategic options available to the marketing manager vary over the life cycle, as does the importance of various marketing mix elements. Although the PLC should not be followed religiously because category characteristics can vary widely, it is useful as a conceptual tool.

Figure 3–11 shows a theoretical PLC. As can be seen, the curve is normally *S*-shaped and breaks down product sales over time into four discrete segments: introduction, growth, maturity, and decline. In the **introductory phase,** the growth rate and the size of the market are low. At this stage of the PLC, there is normally one company, the pioneer of the category. For example, MTV was the pioneer in the music television category, Cray in the supercomputer category. If the pioneer is successful in building demand or the category appears attractive to other companies, the sales in the category will increase, thus creating the growth stage. During this stage, the market grows rapidly at first and then begins to slow down. When the market growth becomes flat, the maturity phase has been reached. This is usually when competition is most intense; some of the earlier entrants

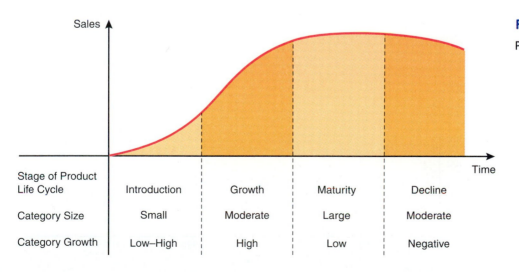

Figure 3–11

Product Life Cycle

Stage of Product Life Cycle	Introduction	Growth	Maturity	Decline
Category Size	Small	Moderate	Large	Moderate
Category Growth	Low–High	High	Low	Negative

have dropped out, and the ones that are left normally have substantial resources and are attempting to steal market share from each other (e.g., Coke vs. Pepsi). At some point, the market begins to decline. Firms must decide whether to continue investing in the category or to withdraw.

The PLC is a theoretical model because categories do not follow Fig. 3–11 perfectly (or even closely, in some cases). First, the curve is not smooth but bumpy. For example, Fig. 3–12 shows the PLC for videocassette recorders through 1996. Although it has the general shape characteristic of the theoretical PLC, sales dipped between 1987 and 1989 rather than being perfectly flat for some time, which is characteristic of the maturity stage. Second, there is no standard time interval for each stage. Some product categories, particularly for frequently purchased products such as beer and cigarettes, have maturity phases that can last for 20 or 30 years or more. In some cases, maturity and then decline are reached quickly. Witness the fast cycles for different classes of microprocessors such as the 286 (3 years to being technologically leapfrogged by the next-generation product), 386 (4 years), and 486 (4 years). Third, PLCs can decline and then be revived by new product introductions or marketing innovation. Witness the decline in the video game market after the previous market leader, Atari, died in the 1970s with an overproduction of cheap games. The market was resurrected by Nintendo, which continues to lead the market, along with Sega. This can also be seen in Fig. 3–12. Note the increase in VCR sales from 1992 to 1996, after what looked like a decline phase. This was probably caused by the substantial decrease in the price of VCRs, which permitted households to purchase several for different rooms of the house. Finally, it is not always easy to define the product. For example, should the PLC be defined by the sales of all personal computers or should there be separate life cycles depending on the microprocessor inside?

Strategies for the Introductory Phase

In this phase, because the product is new, sales volume increases slowly because of lack of marketing effort (only one or a very small number of firms) and the reluctance of customers to buy it. Selling and advertising focus on the *generic* product, that is, the basic concept; customers must be convinced that the benefits from this new product provide an improvement over the product or service that is being replaced. Distributors usually have power in the relationship with manufacturers or service suppliers because the product is still unproven with customers. Prices can be high or low depending on the entry strategy of the firms mar-

Figure 3–12

Product Life Cycle: Videocassette Recorders

Source: Electronic Industries Association (1998), *Electronic Market Data Book* (Washington, DC: Electronic Industries Association).

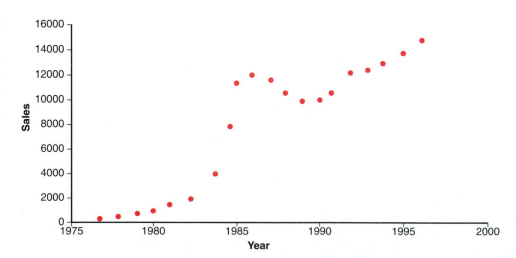

keting the product.[27] This is a very risky stage; however, as the data in Fig. 1–1 show, market pioneers often retain their leadership positions for decades.

There are strategic advantages to being first in the market and establishing a strong position, a situation consistent with a penetration strategy. Empirical research shows that the first mover in a category has an advantage (called the first-mover advantage) in that it tends to maintain its lead through the PLC. The advantage results from early access to distribution channels; also, the first mover establishes awareness of its product as the prototype against which later entrants must be compared.[28] However, some evidence indicates that this first-mover advantage is not as strong as was once believed.[29]

Growth Strategies

The **growth phase** of the PLC actually encompasses two different kinds of market behavior: early growth (the phase just following the introductory phase) and late growth (the phase in which the rapid increase in sales begins to flatten out). In general, however, the growth phase has several features beyond the obvious fact that product category sales are still growing. First, the number of competitors is increasing. This puts pressure on marketing managers to keep distribution channels and changes the focus of sales and communications to emphasize competitive advantage. As customers become more knowledgeable about the product and the available options, they put more pressure on price. Finally, with the increased competition, market segmentation begins to be a key issue.

The general strategic options relate to the product's position in the market, whether it is a leader (the brand with the leading market share) or a follower (the second or later entrant in the market). The leader can choose to fight, keeping the leadership position, or to flee, ceding market leadership to another product. If the leader chooses to fight, the manager can attempt to simply maintain the current position or to keep enhancing the product or service. Why would the leader choose to flee? It is possible that the new entrants in the market are just too strong and raise the stakes for competing to a level the incumbent cannot sustain. For example, Minnetonka established the liquid soap category. When Unilever and Proctor & Gamble entered with their own versions, Minnetonka sold out. Thus, exit is always an option. The other option implies an attempt to reposition the product so that it can be a strong number-two or number-three brand.

In many cases, the market leader is a small company that develops a new technology and a small market and faces the prospect of larger companies taking over. Storm Primax, Inc. makes hardware and software that lets users drop photos into computer documents. Their chief product is a mousepad-sized scanner named the EasyPhoto Reader. The user feeds in a snapshot and pushes a button, and the photo appears on the screen. You can then touch up the image, put the photo in a document, or send it over the Internet. That is the good news; the bad news is that large software producer Adobe and Hewlett-Packard, in conjunction with Microsoft, are looking at the market and will introduce products. It is difficult for a small company to fight in such circumstances.

However, a clear success story for a leader is the home finance software product Quicken. The manufacturer, Intuit, chose to enhance its product rather than flee. Although other large software companies, including Microsoft, have attempted to gain a large presence in this category, Intuit has done an excellent job enhancing its product and developing an outstanding customer service operation to maintain its leadership position.

The follower has a number of options depending on the strength of the leader, its own strength, and market conditions. One option is to simply exit quickly and invest in some product that has better long-term potential. A second option is to imitate the leader by developing a "me-too" product at perhaps a lower price. The follower can also be content to be a strong number two or three by fortifying its position. Finally, the riskiest move is to try to leapfrog the competition. Some companies do this with pure marketing muscle and an imitative product. For example, in over-the-counter yeast infection drugs, Schering-Plough established the market and Johnson & Johnson followed with its Monistat 7 brand, which quickly obtained more than half of the market. America Online leapfrogged Prodigy in the at-home electronic services market through more creative marketing and product features that appealed to consumers.

Strategies for Maturity

The maturity stage of the PLC is characteristic of most products, particularly consumer products and services. Product categories exhibiting fierce battles for market share, access to distribution channels, large amounts of money spent on trade and consumer promotion, and competitive pricing policies are probably in this stage of the PLC.

In the **maturity phase,** the sales curve has flattened out and few new buyers are in the market. Market potential usually remains, but it is either difficult or expensive to reach nonbuyers. Customers are sophisticated and well versed in product features and benefits. Where differential advantage can be obtained, it is through intangible or perceived product quality or from other innovations such as packaging, distribution, or customer service. Market segments are also well defined, and finding new ones that are untapped is difficult.

The general strategies in mature markets are similar to those in growth markets; they depend on the relative market position of the product in question. In this case, however, leaders sometimes look at the time horizon for cashing out the product. If the manager is committed to the product for an extended time period, the objective is usually to invest just enough money to maintain share. An alternative short-term objective is to "harvest" the product, that is, set an objective of gradual share decline with minimal investment to maximize short-run profits. The followers have some interesting alternatives that depend on the leader's strategy. If the leader is harvesting the product, the number-one position may be left open for an aggressive number-two brand. If the leader is intent on maintaining that position for a long time, the follower may choose to be a profitable number two or exit the category.

Keep in mind that the PLC is a conceptual model of how product or service strategies can shift with changes in the market. However, the life cycle model should not be followed mindlessly. As was noted earlier, life cycles can be rejuvenated by marketing or product innovation (the Nintendo example). Thus, just because a market appears to be maturing does not mean it is time to abandon ship; it can also mean that other managers will treat the market as a mature market, which creates a competitive opportunity. And there is always opportunity for a creative manager.

How can you develop this creative perspective? One way is to exploit the PLC by always looking ahead to the next stage and planning the product's evolutionary change. This helps to keep the product profitably alive and avoid profit margin squeezes at the maturity phase. This is called stretching out the life cycle.

How can you do this? You can consider using the strategic alternatives shown in Fig. 3–3 as a guide.

- Promote more frequent use of the product by current users (market penetration).
- Promote more varied use of the product (market penetration).
- Create new users by expanding the market (market development).
- Find new uses (market penetration).

Or, as Campbell Soup CEO David Johnson says, "There are no mature markets, only tired marketers."[30]

For example, DuPont's Nylon was originally developed for military uses (parachutes, thread, rope). They stretched the PLC to hosiery (new use), tinted hosiery (varied usage), and rugs, tires, and other products (new uses). 3M's Scotch tape was extended through the use of new dispensers (more usage), colored and waterproof varieties (varied usage), commercial applications (new users), and reflective and double-sided tape (new uses).

Strategies for Decline

You need not accept the fact that a market is in decline. Most strategies for reviving mature markets also can be used to revive declining markets. In addition, serendipity may come to your rescue. Witness the recent surge in demand for cigars in the United States. This was not caused by anything the manufacturers did; there was simply a revival in cigar smoking among certain higher-income segments of the population. Such changes in customer tastes not stimulated by marketers cannot always be explained but can profitably be exploited.

If the market is truly dying, it can be very profitable to be the "last iceman." By being last, a product gains monopoly rights to the remaining customers, which results in the ability to charge high prices. For example, Lansdale Semiconductor is the last firm making the 8080 computer chip introduced by Intel in 1974. Although most applications of computer chips are well beyond the 8080, it is still used in military systems that are typically built to last 20–25 years, such as the Hellfire and Pershing 2 missiles and the Aegis radar system for battleships. Where does the Department of Defense go when it needs 8080s? Lansdale.

PRODUCT LINE STRATEGY

The examples used in this chapter have been drawn primarily from single products or services. It is often the case that a manager has to develop a **product line strategy** for a group of closely related products. The product variants may be developed to appeal to different segments of the market. Alternatively, a line may be developed to compete more directly with major competition. Products lines are also developed in order to gain additional shelf space with distributors.

In some cases, the line may share a brand name. For example, Perkin Elmer's Applied Biosystems Division markets a line of thermal cyclers that perform polymerase chain reaction, used in DNA analysis. The line consists of the GeneAmp PCR System 2400, the GeneAmp PCR System 9600, and the GeneAmp PCR System 9700.

The products are differentiated largely by their production capacity, that is, how many tests can be run simultaneously, because research labs and pharmaceutical companies differ in their testing needs. When the same brand name is used, it is called **umbrella branding.** In this case, a divisional vice president is in charge of the line.

Alternatively, the brands may have totally unrelated brand names. An example would be Crest and Gleem toothpaste, both marketed by Proctor & Gamble. The Robert Mondavi Company markets a line of premium wines under the labels Robert Mondavi Reserves, Opus One, Napa Valley, Byron, Vichon "Napa," Coastal, Vichon "California," and Woodbridge. Again, each brand has its own positioning and image. Each label also represents a line broken down by variety of grape and vintage. Company president Michael Mondavi is in charge of the corporate marketing.

Product lines may also include complementary products, which are intended to be used together but also could be marketed separately. In the Perkin Elmer example, the company also markets reagents and enzymes to be used with the DNA samples as well as disposables such as slides and plastic tubes.

In developing a product line strategy, the marketing manager must address a number of important issues:[31]

- How many products should be in the line?
- How should the products in the line be targeted and differentiated?
- How should resources be allocated across the line to maximize profits or market share?

The answer to the first question looks simple from an economic perspective: Add variants to the line as long as the incremental sales exceed the incremental costs. Often, the direct costs of making the product or delivering the service when added to a line are low because there are cost interdependencies; that is, the new product uses machinery or other assets already in place. However, there are also hidden costs with product line additions. One such cost is that additional line elements take up additional shelf space or salesperson time. Unsuccessful additions to the line create loss of goodwill from both the retailer and the salesperson, which can have negative long-term consequences for the entire product line. A second such cost is called **cannibalization,** in which the sales for a new element of the line are not entirely incremental—some may come from an existing element of the line. Additional line elements also dissipate the advertising budget and management attention. Thus, the product line manager must fully account for all costs of line additions.

Therefore, the number of products and their targeting and differentiation should be determined *before* variants are added to a product line. If the addition to the line does not cover the hidden costs and it is difficult to position relative to existing products in the line, then it is questionable whether such a product should be added unless the other reasons (e.g., combating competition) are particularly compelling.

Resource allocation decisions depend on the nature of the product line. If the variations in the line are minor, the marketing strategy normally would not single out the individual elements for special advertising or promotion programs. For example, the Jell-O gelatin line varies only by flavor. In such a case, the whole product line is promoted together, except perhaps for particular seasonal or recipe purposes. Sony does not develop different strategies for its different sizes of televisions (within a range).

When the elements of the line appeal to different segments of the market with different characteristics such as growth rates and competition, another approach can be used. The product line can be considered a portfolio of products, with some aspects of one product (e.g., high cash flow) helping with another (e.g., a new product that needs investment). The most popular framework for this kind of analysis of a product line (or even larger groups of products such as a division or corporation) is the portfolio approach introduced by the Boston Consulting Group (BCG) in the 1970s.

The BCG portfolio, also called the growth share matrix, is shown in Fig. 3–13. The two dimensions, market share and market growth, incorporate the following definitions:

- The market is defined as the served market or market segment. Thus, if we are considering a line of wine, such as the Mondavi line, the served market would be defined at least on the basis of red versus white but more likely on a varietal (Chardonnay, rosé, burgundy, etc.) basis.
- Market share is defined as relative share: the ratio of the share of your product in the market segment to the next largest competitor. As can be seen in Fig. 3–13, high relative market share is greater than 1.0 and low is below 1.0.
- Market growth is the sales growth rate in the served market. The dividing line between high and low can be based on gross national product or gross domestic product growth rates, inflation, or more subjective criteria.

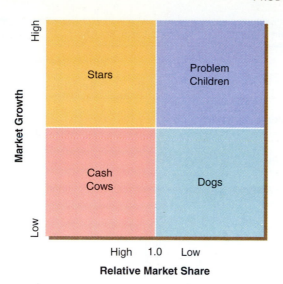

Figure 3–13
Growth Share Matrix

The rationale for using growth and share as the criteria for resource allocation decisions is the following. Market growth rate is a proxy for the PLC. In addition, it is easier to gain share when the market is in its early stages (i.e., in the growth stage) than in the maturity stage, when growth rates are stable. As we have seen in this chapter, market share is related to higher rates of profitability, lower costs, and other strengths such as brand awareness and strong channel relationships.

Products in the different quadrants have varying characteristics. The products in the lower right quadrant have low relative share in low-growth markets (usually called dogs). Typically, they are eliminated or they can resegment their markets to gain a better relative market position. The products in the upper right quadrant have low share in high-growth markets (called problem children or question marks). These products are net users of cash because they need money to make product improvements to compete in the lucrative, high-growth segment. The upper left quadrant are the stars, products in the dominant position in a high-growth market. These products also need cash to maintain their market leadership position but they are also generating some because of the high margins they can maintain. Cash cows reside in the lower left quadrant. These generate cash because they lead their markets, which are usually large by the maturity phase of the PLC. The cash generated by these products is used to feed R&D and marketing for the problem children and the stars.

Thus, the product portfolio's major use is as a device for managing cash over a diversified product line. One of the implied objectives of this kind of analysis is that the manager should strive to have a balanced portfolio. Too many of any kind of product is not good for the long-run health of the line or division. For example, too many cash cows means considerable revenue generation but no future (unless the PLCs are very long). Too many products in the upper quadrants implies significant cash flow requirements that are not being met.

Table 3–1 shows the portfolio for the wholesale (business-to-business) division of a large southern bank during the mid-1980s. As can be seen, the portfolio is very unbalanced, with only one cash cow, one star, five problem children, and three dogs. The obvious problem is that insufficient resources are being generated or allocated to the products on the right side of the matrix, as indicated by their poor market positions.[32]

Table 3–1 Example of a Product Portfolio: Large Southern U.S. Bank, ca. 1986

Product	Wholesale Product Line		
	Growth	**Relative Share**	**Status**
Pension management assets:			
Large	High	About 0	Problem child
Small	High	0.13	Problem child
Automation services	Low	0.20	Dog
Indentured trustee	Low	About 0	Dog
Municipal paying agent services	Low	2.0	Cash cow
International services:			
Pacific	High	2.5	Star
Europe	Low	0.50	Problem child
Foreign exchange	High	0.44	Problem child
Brokerage	High	0.20	Problem child
Bond sales	Low	0.33	Dog

EXECUTIVE SUMMARY

Key concepts from this chapter are the following:

- A complete marketing strategy features a statement of the product's objectives, strategic alternatives, customer targets, competitor targets, product features, a core strategy, and the marketing mix used to implement the strategy.
- Differential advantages can be obtained in three ways: low cost with concomitant low price, objective quality differences, and perceived quality differences, including strong brand equity.
- Product positioning involves developing an image in the mind of the customer about how you want him or her to perceive your product.
- The value proposition concisely summarizes the customer target and positioning, that is, the segment's reason to buy.
- The product life cycle consists of four stages determined by the market's growth rate: introduction, growth, maturity, and decline. The strategic options available to the marketing manager vary over the life cycle.
- For a product line, a group of related products, the marketing manager must consider three questions: How many items should be in the line? How should each be positioned? How should resources be allocated over the products?

CHAPTER QUESTIONS

1. Suppose that a marketing manager first develops an advertising campaign before the marketing strategy. How will this create problems for the product?
2. Choose a consumer product or service. How can you get current customers of the product or service to buy more? Do the same for a business-to-business product or service.
3. Pick a basic commodity such as steel or wheat. If you were the marketing manager for one of these products, how could you differentiate your product from the competitors' commodities?

4. Select several magazine advertisements. How are the companies positioning their products?
5. What would be a possible value proposition for your school?
6. Pick a product that is in the early stage of the product life cycle and pick one that you believe is a mature product. How is the marketing for the two products different?
7. Visit a consumer electronics store and analyze a company's product line. How are the products differentiated? Are there too many products in the line? How well does the salesperson know the differences between the products in the line?

Integrated Case

Application Exercises: Developing Marketing Strategy in the Personal Computer Industry

1. Select one of the PC brands. Using the outline of a complete marketing strategy described in this chapter and in Fig. 3–1, what is the current marketing strategy for that brand?
2. Diagnose that strategy; that is, determine whether you think the strategy is a good one. Be as detailed as possible about why you think it is good or bad.
3. Given current market conditions for PCs, develop a new strategy for the PC brand given your answer to assignment 2.
4. Collect sales data for the PC market in a country of your choosing since they were introduced in that country. Using those data, perform a PLC analysis by determining what stage you believe the PC market is in.
5. For a brand of PC, collect information about the company's product line (desktops, laptops, or servers). Evaluate the product line in terms of size, distinctiveness of the models, and any other characteristic you believe is important.

FURTHER READING

Although it is already referenced in the Notes, an excellent book on developing marketing strategy in the information age is Shapiro and Varian's *Information Rules*. Some research has examined the role of marketing in increasing shareholder value, usually thought of as the domain of financial managers. See Rajendra K. Srivastava, Tasadduq A. Shervani, and Liam Fahey (1998), "Market-based assets and shareholder value: a framework for analysis," *Journal of Marketing,* 62 (January), pp. 2–18.

Marketing Research 4

CHAPTER BRIEF

The purpose of this chapter is to provide insights into marketing research. After reading the chapter, the reader should be familiar with the following:

The scope of marketing research activities
Where to find secondary sources of information
Primary sources of marketing research information
Developing estimates of market potential
Developing sales forecasts
The impact of the Internet on marketing research

Dannon Yogurt, produced by France's Groupe Danone, is one of the world's leading brands of yogurt.[1] In 1993, although Dannon was the leading brand of yogurt, the number of competitors was increasing steadily (the major threat was from General Mills's Yoplait) and the company was concerned about maintaining its leadership position. The company had done an excellent job in the 1980s of repositioning yogurt from a narrowly defined health food to a more mainstream food through packaging, educational campaigns, and new products such as frozen yogurt. By 1990, consumer perception was that yogurt is a healthful and convenient snack or light meal and Dannon was primarily responsible for the category's significant growth. However, the Dannon marketing managers needed to better understand how consumers perceived Dannon in order to continue to differentiate the brand and maintain its market position.

Dannon turned to its Consumer Awareness, Attitude and Usage tracking study, developed in partnership with a market research company. Since 1992, Dannon had developed this study as an ongoing monitor of the yogurt market. The market research company interviewed 300 yogurt users each quarter, assessing consumers' category, brand, and advertising awareness, brand usage, and attitudes toward Dannon and competing brands. In 1993, they found that consumers valued Dannon's commitment to purity of ingredients and its packaging. The research also uncovered an emotional attachment to Dannon based on the care customers felt Dannon took in making the yogurt.

As a result of the research, a new advertising campaign was developed, stressing Dannon's superior taste and attributing it to the care Dannon takes in selecting its ingredients. The advertising agency developed two different executions of this theme and tested them on consumers. The campaign, "Taste Why It's Dannon," was launched in July 1994, and in

The success of Dannon's "Taste Why It's Dannon" advertising campaign can be traced to the company's investment in market research in the mid-1990s. Based on customer attitudes identified in this research, Dannon's ad campaign stresses the product's superior taste, a theme that the company has carried over to new lines such as its new chunky fruit yogurt. (Reprinted with permission of the Dannon Company, Inc. © 1997 the Dannon Company, Inc.)

the 9-week period following its introduction, Dannon's sales increased faster than those of other yogurt brands.

Although Dannon has had a good experience and has some success from its investments in marketing research, a number of general questions remain:

- Should the company make consistent investments in research or spend the money only when a revision in marketing strategy is called for?
- If the company decides continued investment is necessary, what kind of information should be collected?
- Dannon has done an excellent job of collecting diagnostic information that has captured changes in consumer attitudes. How much should it invest in forecasting future changes in consumer attitudes?

Chapters 1–3 emphasized the need for constant contact with the business environment. Indeed, such contact is essential to the situation analysis and planning assumption steps in the marketing plan (Table 2–1). Developing a marketing strategy that targets the right customers and competitors (see the marketing strategy diagram) also requires data collection from the environment and analysis. The mechanism for maintaining this contact is **marketing research.** The American Marketing Association defines marketing research as follows:

Marketing research is the function which links the consumer, customer, and public to the marketer through information—information used to identify and define marketing oppor-

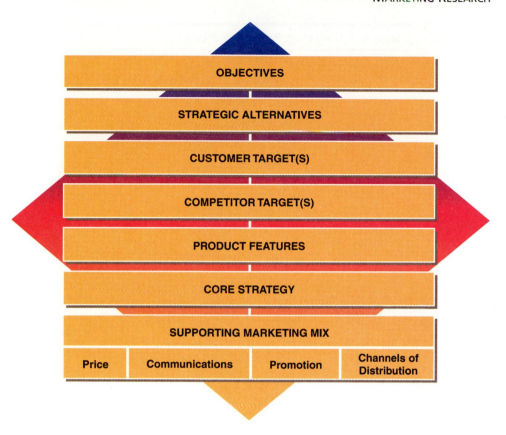

tunities and problems; generate, refine, and evaluate marketing actions; monitor marketing performance; and improve understanding of marketing as a process.

Also consider the mission statements of the market research departments at Thomas J. Lipton, Marriott Corporation, and Coca-Cola:

> The mission of the Market Research Department is to gather, analyze, and interpret marketing and other relevant information needed for decision making at all levels of management. These activities are to be carried out in a cost-effective manner consistent with high professional standards.[2]

Note that in this latter statement, the companies emphasize that marketing research information is not just for marketing managers, but for all managers in the organization.

Table 4–1 shows the three major functions of marketing research:

- Scanning for opportunities and threats. A good research[3] operation collects and analyzes information about customers, competitors, technology, global economic conditions, and other factors. It provides input to marketing managers that they can use to find new markets for existing products, uncover new market segments (see the marketing strategy diagram), and anticipate competitors' moves. These data are used in the situation analysis of the marketing plan and the development of a marketing strategy.

Table 4–1 Marketing Research Functions

Major Functions	Targets
Scanning (for opportunities and threats)	Markets Competitors Technology Environment Economic • Regulatory • Political • Social • Cultural
Risk assessment (of future programs)	Own customers Competitors' customers Non-users
Monitoring (of current programs)	Tracking performance evaluation among all intended segments, including: • Own customers • Competitors' customers • Non-users

Source: Eli Seggev (1995), "A role in flux," *Marketing Management*, 4 (Winter), p. 37.

- Risk assessment of future programs. When considering alternative marketing strategies, the marketing manager should test them against different scenarios. For example, if the manager is considering entering an international expansion into Hong Kong, the political and economic implications of Hong Kong becoming a part of China, such as new import/export laws, must be considered.
- Monitoring of current programs. As noted in Chapter 2, marketing research plays a key role in monitoring the progress of the plan toward its objectives. For example, to raise awareness of your brand from 60% to 70% in the target market, you need to develop a plan to measure customer awareness.

More specifically, marketing research is most commonly used to

- Forecast the sales of existing and new products
- Refine new product concepts
- Develop a new strategy for an existing product
- Understand competitors
- Identify marketing segmentation opportunities
- Understand how customers in different market segments make buying decisions
- Evaluate how customers in the target audience react to various advertising messages and executions
- Determine what price to charge
- Understand how customers perceive the product and the company

This is only a subset of the many valuable ways marketing research helps the manager develop a better marketing plan and ultimately a better, more competitive marketing strategy. Marketing research is so valuable that companies annually spend over $6 billion worldwide on it.

THE RESEARCH PROCESS

The standard approach to marketing research is shown in Fig. 4–1. The research process can be condensed into six steps:

1. Problem definition. A key to any kind of research is to establish the problem to be addressed. "Evaluation of advertising" is too vague to be operational. "Measuring current awareness levels of our current advertising theme" is better.
2. Information needs. The marketing researcher needs to establish what kinds of information are most appropriate for solving the problem.
3. Type of study or research. Many kinds of studies can be performed, ranging from exploratory ("We do not know much at this time so we are just trying to establish some basic facts") to descriptive ("We think that the major users of personal digital assistants are businesspeople on the road and we need to collect some information establishing that relationship") to causal ("We need to establish that our recent price reduction caused the increase in sales we observed"). Many different kinds of research data can be collected; we describe these later in this chapter.

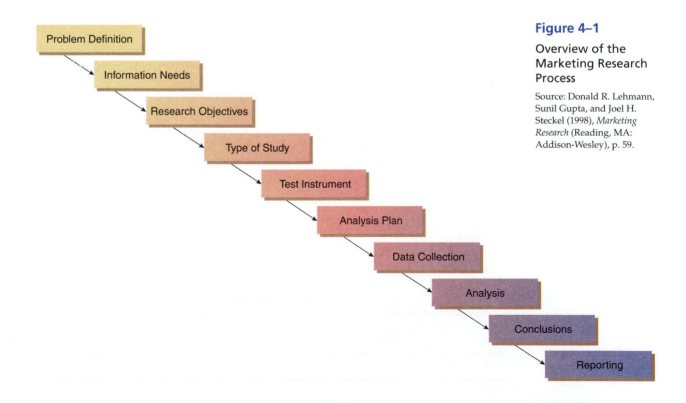

Figure 4–1

Overview of the Marketing Research Process

Source: Donald R. Lehmann, Sunil Gupta, and Joel H. Steckel (1998), *Marketing Research* (Reading, MA: Addison-Wesley), p. 59.

4. Data collection. At this stage, depending on the kind of information needed, the researcher must establish the specific data sources, including the sample of people or organizations studied, if appropriate.
5. Data analysis and conclusions. Some person, either internal to the organization or external (e.g., a marketing research firm), must analyze the data and draw conclusions that address the stated problem.
6. Reporting. If appropriate to the research problem, a report is usually written to communicate the findings to the marketing organization and other relevant groups (e.g., manufacturing, customer service).

Particularly relevant to this book are the different kinds of research information available to the marketing manager. Table 4–2 shows the different types. It is important to distinguish between secondary and primary sources of information. **Secondary information sources** are those that already exist and were not developed for the particular problem at hand. For example, U.S. government sources such as the census are secondary sources of information. **Primary information sources** are those that are generated for the particular problem being studied. The Dannon survey is an example of primary data collection.

Although we will go into further detail about these sources of information in this chapter, one useful generalization is that marketing managers almost always consult secondary sources before embarking on primary data collection. Because secondary sources are usually less expensive (particularly with advances in information technology), marketing managers are well advised to consult existing data before doing special-purpose surveys. These secondary sources can be either internal to the organization (e.g., past marketing plans) or external (e.g., computer databases).

As can be seen in Table 4–2, there are many ways of obtaining primary data. The advantage of primary data collection is that the study is tailored to the manager's needs. Other than cost, the disadvantages of primary data collection are the time it takes to collect the information needed and the fact that expertise for this kind of marketing research often lies outside the organization. Unless the manager has a list of trusted research suppliers based on past experience and performance, he or she must go through a vendor selection process.[4]

Table 4–2 Marketing Research Data Sources

Secondary	Observations	Experiments
Internal	Surveys	Laboratory
External	Personal	Field
Public domain	Phone	Models/simulations
Private	Mail	
Primary	Internet	
Informal	Panels	
Qualitative	Continuous reporting	
Introspection	Special purpose	
Depth interviews	Scanner	
Focus groups		

Source: Donald R. Lehmann, Sunil Gupta, and Joel H. Steckel (1988), *Marketing Research* (Reading, MA: Addison-Wesley), pp. 79, 88.

In this chapter, we focus on primary and secondary marketing research. In addition, two applications of secondary and primary research—market potential estimation and forecasting—are also discussed. The marketing manager must understand basic marketing research methods to better understand customers (Chapters 5 and 6) and competitors and the external environment (Chapter 7).

SECONDARY DATA SOURCES

As noted in Table 4–2, there are two kinds of secondary data sources: internal and external.

Internal

A good place to start collecting information is within your own organization. There is much more information here than you might expect. For example,

- In the marketing organization, past marketing plans are invaluable sources of statistical information (e.g., market shares) as well as strategic information (e.g., past marketing strategies). As noted in Chapter 2, analyzing the marketplace is a significant part of the marketing plan, so if your organization has a history of developing plans that roughly adhere to the outline presented, you are in luck.
- The sales organization should have information based on call reports submitted by the salespeople. These reports not only indicate what happened during the call but often contain valuable information about competitor activities (e.g., a special promotion or price cut) and changes in attitudes and behavior by the channels of distribution. Salespeople also have direct customer contact and are thus an invaluable (although sometimes biased) source of information about customer attitudes toward your products and services.
- The accounting department collects a considerable amount of detailed information on transactions. If you market a line of products with a large number of stock keeping units (SKUs, each representing a particular combination of size, color, flavor, and other attributes), the accounting department can tell you which sizes, for example, are selling better than others. Catalogue marketers, retailers, and distributors, which carry large numbers of SKUs, are particularly interested in this kind of sales analysis.
- Research and development departments not only focus on bringing your company's product ideas to market, but may also analyze competitors' products or services. This kind of analysis, called reverse engineering for manufactured products (taking the products apart to better understand their costs, technology, etc.) or benchmarking in service businesses,[5] provides excellent information about the competitors' costs, technology, and quality.

These are only some of the sources available within the organization that can help marketing managers to get a better picture of the environment. Often, larger companies have their own libraries with information specialists who are particularly focused on the industry in which the firm competes. In addition, many companies use intranets to make internal data available on-line to managers around the world. For example, many salespeople now file their call reports electronically via a notebook computer and modem. The information in these reports is instantaneously available to marketing managers.

To better understand the marketing environment and key competitors' products, manufacturing firms often turn to reverse engineering. This secondary data source is especially valuable for high-technology firms. (Sieplinga.HMS Images, Harry/The Image Bank)

The major problem marketing managers face with internal sources of information is getting it in a useful format. The accounting department's information system may be incompatible with the marketing system, for example. Similarly, a database established for direct mail purposes might not be appropriate for storing the broad range of information about customers provided by the sales force, marketing research studies, and other sources. Marketing management should be involved in the design and implementation of information systems to ensure that they provide the maximum value.

External

With the growth of the Internet as an information source and the concomitant ability of the marketing manager to access a large amount of information, it is sometimes difficult to distinguish between external and internal sources. However, there is a clear distinction between sources that the company has collected for the manager's use and those that are collected by external organizations for public use.

There are so many secondary sources of information that a good place to start would be with publications that produce lists of information sources. Figure 4–2 provides four general flowcharts for finding information about companies, individuals, industries, and products. Several of the better references for secondary sources of information are listed in Table 4–3.

The general categories of external secondary information are the following:[6]

- Trade associations. These industry organizations often collect information about their member companies, particularly on sales and profits.
- General business publications. Magazines such as *Business Week, Fortune,* and *Forbes* often include useful information about company product introductions and strategies. Newspapers such as the *Wall Street Journal* and its various global editions (Europe and Asia) are similarly valuable.
- Trade publications. Even better than general business publications for specific data about product categories are publications such as *Advertising Age, Twice* (consumer electronics), *Upside* (computers), and *Progressive Grocer* that target managers in particular industries. These media often provide detailed sales and share informa-

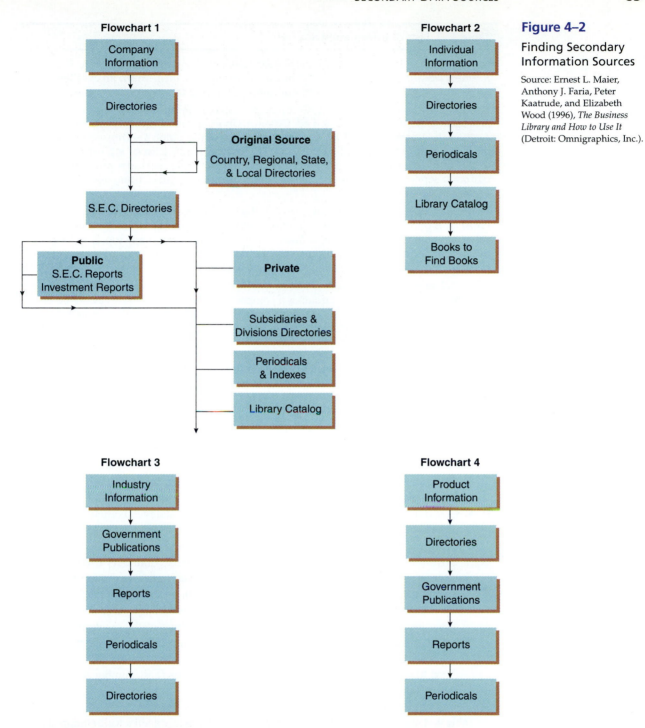

Figure 4–2

Finding Secondary Information Sources

Source: Ernest L. Maier, Anthony J. Faria, Peter Kaatrude, and Elizabeth Wood (1996), *The Business Library and How to Use It* (Detroit: Omnigraphics, Inc.).

tion along with personnel changes, new product announcements and strategies, promotional plans, and other useful data.

- Academic publications. Although these journals tend to target academic audiences, the *Harvard Business Review,* the *California Management Review,* the *Sloan Management Review,* and the *Journal of Marketing* do a good job of translating academic

---

Table 4–3 Lists of Information Sources

Maier, Ernest L., Anthony J. Faria, Peter Kaatrude, and Elizabeth Wood (1996), *The Business Library and How to Use It* (Detroit: Omnigraphics, Inc.). This is an excellent guide not only to specific sources of information but also to research strategies.

Barksdale, Hiram C., Jr., and Jac L. Goldstucker (1995), *Marketing Information: A Professional Reference Guide*, 3rd ed. (Atlanta: Georgia State University Business Press). As the title suggests, the information sources listed in this guide are those that are more relevant to the marketing manager. The book contains a list of marketing organizations and associations and sources of information in particular areas such as customer service/satisfaction, global marketing, franchising, advertising, and channels of distribution.

Peete, Gary R. (1995), *Business Resources on the Internet* (Berkeley, CA: Library Solutions Press). This book is an introduction to how to search the Internet for information. Topics covered include listservs, electronic discussion groups that cover many topics in different business areas including marketing, and how to use the variety of ways of accessing the Internet, including e-mail, gophers, FTP, Telnet, and the Web.*

Zakalik, Joanna ed. (1995), *Gale Guide to Internet Databases* (New York: Gale Research Inc.). As the title suggests, this guide is a comprehensive list of databases available on the Internet. Some are free, but some are subscription based. It should be noted that with the explosive growth of the Web, guides of this type are inevitably incomplete at the time of publication.

---

*The reader may be unfamiliar with some of these terms. Books such as the one cited are useful not only to show how information can be obtained via the Internet but also as a basic introduction for how to use the Internet most productively.

---

material for practitioners. They enable managers to keep abreast of new concepts being developed in universities. More academic journals such as the *Journal of Marketing Research* are methodologically oriented and better for marketing research professionals or managers who are academically inclined.

- Corporate reports. These include annual reports, 10K statements (detailed financial reports of publicly held companies), and other releases that are mandated by the Securities and Exchange Commission for publicly held firms.
- Government publications. These are some of the most commonly used sources of information. Almost every government in the world collects information about commerce in its own country. The Department of Commerce/Bureau of the Census publishes the *Statistical Abstract of the United States,* containing a large amount of data about the economy and various business sectors. Much of the government data is collected by Standard Industrial Classification (SIC) codes rather than product categories.[7] These codes range from broad two-digit codes (e.g., number 34 is Fabricated Metal Products) to more detailed four-digit codes (e.g., number 3442 is Metal Doors, Sash Frames, Molding, and Trim).

Table 4–4 shows the marketing data sources typically available in a well-equipped business library. Information on many topics, from demographics to specific product and industry data, can be obtained from the sources listed in Tables 4–3 and 4–4. Managers and students should not hesitate to ask the professional staff in these libraries to help locate the appropriate sources.

Much of this information is available on the Internet, including all U.S. Census statistics. General searches for business information can be conducted using the various search engines available on the Web. The most popular search engine is Yahoo!. Figure 4–3 shows

Table 4–4 Overview of Marketing Data Sources

Demographic data
  1990 Census of Population and
    Housing
  County and City Data Book
  The Ernst & Young Almanac and Guide
    to U.S. Business Cities: 65 Leading
    Places To Do Business
  Geographic Reference Report
  National Economic Projections Series
  Rand McNally Commercial Atlas and
    Marketing Guide
  Survey of Buying Power Data Service
  Upclose 1990 Economic Sourcebook
  Upclose 1990 Census Sourcebook

**Consumer surveys/market information
(domestic and foreign)**
  Almanac of Consumer Markets
  Consumer Europe
  Consumer Power: How Americans
    Spend Their Money
  Dentsu Japan Marketing/Advertising
    Yearbook
  Editor and Publisher Market Guide
  European Marketing Data and
    Statistics
  Hispanic Americans: A Statistical
    Sourcebook
  International Marketing Data and
    Statistics
  Lifestyle Market Analyst: A Reference
    Guide for Consumer Market Analysis
  Lifestyle Zip Code Analyst
  Market Research Europe
  Markets of the U.S. for Business
    Planners
  The Official Guide to the American
    Market-Place
  Panorama of European Union Industry
  Simmons Study of Media and Markets

Product/industry data
  Ad $ Summary
  Business Index on CD/ROM
  Economic Censuses
  F&S Index Plus Text/F&S Index Plus Text
    International
  Manufacturing USA: Industry Analyses,
    Statistics and Leading Companies

Service Industries USA: Industry
    Analyses, Statistics and Leading
    Organizations
  Standard & Poor's Industry Surveys
  U.S. Industrial Outlook

Market share
  Investext on CD-ROM
  Market Share Reporter
  Ward's Business Directory
  World Market Share Reporter

Marketing surveys/research reports
  Bradford's Directory of Marketing
    Research and Management
    Consultants
  Findex: The Directory of Market
    Research Reports, Studies, and
    Surveys

**Factbooks and statistical annuals
(examples)**
  Aerospace Facts and Figures
  Automotive News
  Beverage Industry Annual Manual
  Computer Industry Forecasts
  Electronic Market Data Book
  Liquor Handbook
  Sales of the Soft Drink Industry
  Sporting Goods Market
  Wine Marketing Handbook

**Trade periodicals and indexes
(databases)**
  ABI: indexes over 1,000 business,
    trade, and economic publications
  Business Index on CD-ROM: covers
    over 800 business periodical titles,
    including regional business
    publications
  Comp on Melvyl: indexes over 200
    computer-related journals and
    magazines
  F&S Index Plus Text/International:
    indexes industry and trade
    publications in the United States
    and around the world
  Nexis: full text of newspapers,
    magazines, and trade journals

the Web page for Yahoo! that points to sources on the Web for business and economics topics. The user simply types in a keyword on the search line or uses the mouse to click on the categories listed to do a more focused search. Additionally, most companies have their own Web sites from which information can be obtained (and purchases made). Figure 4–4 shows the home page for Texas Instruments (TI), best known for its calculators and semiconductors.

Figure 4–3

Yahoo! Web Site

Courtesy of Yahoo!

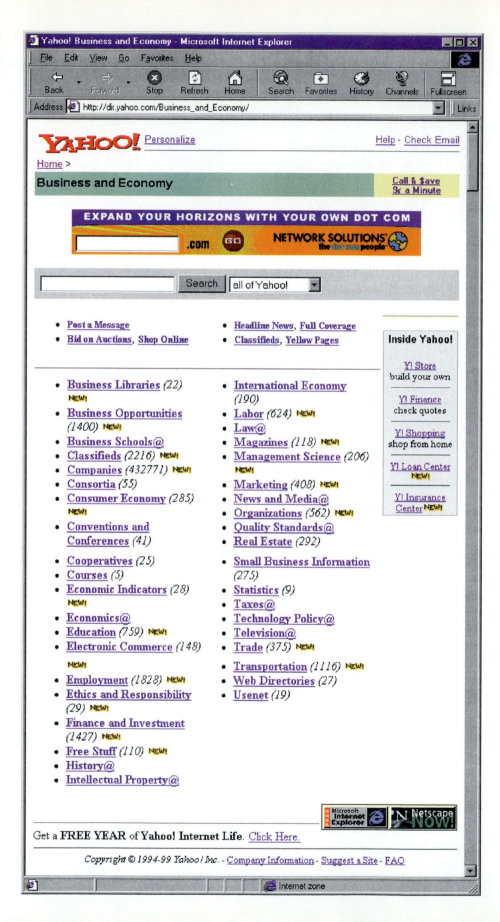

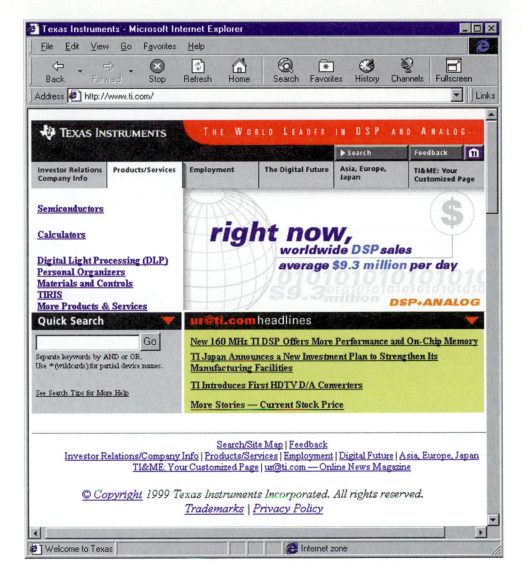

Figure 4–4

Texas Instruments Web Site

© Copyright 1999 Texas Instruments Incorporated.

You can quickly and easily find financial information, TI's product line, communication themes ("The World Leader in Digital Signal Processing Solutions"), and other useful information.

PRIMARY DATA SOURCES

As shown in Table 4–2, many different types of marketing information can be collected with the marketing manager's specific purpose in mind.

Informal

It is often useful to collect information from friends, relatives, customers, and informal observation. Although these sources may not be representative samples, such information can help you form hypotheses about the quality of a competitor's product, your own marketing strategy, and so forth. For example, a marketing manager for a product that is sold through a retailer would find it very useful to simply browse the store, looking at the point-of-purchase displays, talking with customers at the displays, and speaking with the store or department managers. Useful insights about channels of distribution relationships can be obtained. Manufacturers of farm equipment should talk to farmers who actually use the equipment. You can do this as a "mystery shopper" (i.e., posing as a real customer) or with full disclosure of your identity.

Qualitative Research

A large portion of marketing research budgets is spent on what is generally called **qualitative research.** Qualitative research is often defined in terms of what it is not: "not good enough, not large enough, not comprehensive enough to serve as a benchmark or a basis for statistical projection."[8] This definition may seem overly negative, but qualitative research usually involves small samples of customers and produces information that does not lead directly to decisions but is valuable as an input for further research.

Table 4–5 illustrates the difference between qualitative research and **quantitative research.** Quantitative research typically involves statistical analysis of data (not necessarily just primary) in order to provide descriptive results such as the relationship between variables such as age, income, country, and purchasing behavior, or to explicitly test a hypothesis, such as "Our product's advertising has a significant impact on its sales." Qualitative research may be of three types:[9]

- Phenomenological. Often, the marketing manager is interested in understanding how customers use products in everyday life. For example, a marketing manager for Toshiba might be interested in all the ways a businessperson uses a laptop computer (report writing, communicating with the home office, etc.). Phenomenological research elicits this kind of information.
- Exploratory. This kind of qualitative research generates hypotheses for further research, often quantitative. For example, a marketing manager would use qualitative research to test advertising campaigns at a very early stage of their develop-

Table 4–5 Qualitative Versus Quantitative Research

Subtypes	Knowledge	Examples
Quantitative Research		
Descriptive	General	Nielsen, Starch, Burke
Scientific	Causal	Quantitative techniques that test hypotheses
Qualitative Research		
Phenomenological	General	Focus groups
Exploratory	Precausal	Open-ended interviews
Clinical	Causal	Depth interviews

Source: Adapted from Bobby J. Calder (1977), "Focus groups and the nature of qualitative marketing research," *Journal of Marketing Research*, 14 (August), pp. 353–364.

ment. The manager would then develop hypotheses about which campaign does the best job achieving the stated objectives and then test these hypotheses using further research.

- Clinical. In this kind of qualitative research, the manager explores the reasoning behind customer purchasing behavior. The methods used are often psychoanalytic, including in-depth interviews and other techniques such as metaphors to understand customer motivations.

There are many kinds of qualitative research methods, but the best known and most widely used is the **focus group.** Focus groups are small groups of people typically chosen for their membership in various target groups of interest. The people could be consumers, influencers of buying decisions in organizations, former customers, or noncustomers, or they may be chosen for their personal characteristics (e.g., teenagers). These people are usually brought together in a room and have a discussion about a topic chosen by the marketing manager and led by a professional moderator. The focus group is often observed by members of the marketing group (through a one-way mirror), and a videotape and transcript of the proceedings are made. The moderator usually develops a report on his or her conclusions.

The different kinds of focus groups are compared in Table 4–6.[10] Probably the most popular use of focus groups is for phenomenological research, a basic understanding of how customers use the product or service in question. As noted in the table, these kinds of groups must not be used to develop generalizations and should be followed up with further research, usually quantitative. Because clinical focus groups are used to explore the psychological underpinnings of the customers through in-depth questioning, the results cannot be generalized so follow-up research is unnecessary. Likewise, the purpose of exploratory focus groups is to generate research hypotheses for further study; they are not intended to produce generalizable, actionable results.

The focus group is probably the most misused of all marketing research methods. This is because most marketing managers do not understand the various kinds of groups (exploratory, clinical, phenomenological), the purposes of each, and how to structure the

Table 4–6 Characteristics of Focus Groups

Key Questions	Exploratory	Clinical	Phenomenological
Should results be generalized with further study?	No	No	Yes
When should each type be used?	Support prior research; before quantitative research	When you need an indirect approach	When management needs to better understand customers
How many groups?		As many as deemed needed	
Interaction within the group?	Unnecessary	Considerable, but moderator is detached	Considerable, but moderator is involved
Homogeneity of the group?	Heterogeneous	Either	Homogeneous
Moderator expertise is important?	Yes, scientific	Yes, psychological	Yes, personal
Management observation?	Unnecessary	Unnecessary	Essential

Source: Adapted from Bobby J. Calder (1977), "Focus groups and the nature of qualitative marketing research," *Journal of Marketing Research,* 14 (August), pp. 353–364.

A small group of factory workers participates in a focus group session. Although this is an inexpensive way to gather valuable qualitative research, misuse of the information can lead to inaccurate conclusions. Marketing managers must use focus group research cautiously and avoid the temptation to generalize the results. (PhotoDisc)

group to achieve different kinds of results. The marketing manager must develop an objective for the focus group research, match it with the kind of group needed, and then structure the process accordingly. The most common misuse of focus groups is attempting to use them to draw general conclusions. This may be an inexpensive way to do research, but because the groups are small and not all behaviors are generalizable, the results can be misleading. Focus groups are a valuable source of information for keeping in touch with customers, but they have their limits.

Improvements in technology have changed focus group research. Videoconferencing is being used as a way to reduce costs and to make it more convenient for customers to participate. Videoconferencing also enables managers at different locations to observe sessions. The use of telephone focus groups is also expanding. Respondents are recruited from various geographic locations and asked to call a toll-free number at a prearranged time to participate in the group. Greater use is being made of the telephone as a way to conduct in-depth qualitative research as well.[11]

Many companies are looking for qualitative methods to help develop brand strategies that go beyond what focus groups and quantitative research can deliver. A San Francisco–based company named Tattoo has employees hang out on sidewalks with video cameras and ask people on the street for their impressions of a brand. In a project for a clothing retailer, researchers looked through people's closets and asked them to tell on-camera stories about their wardrobes, such as how they feel when they wear certain outfits.[12]

 Universal Studios Online, a subsidiary of Seagram, was interested in redesigning the Web site for Captain Morgan Original Spiced Rum.[13] To help accomplish this task, the company engaged Greenfield Online, a company specializing in focus group research developed in real time with on-line participants. Although it is not possible to view the interactions of the focus group members using such technology, the benefits include no geographic barriers, much lower costs, and faster turnaround time; also, participants are more open without having a moderator in their presence.

To put together the focus group, Greenfield sent out 6,000 e-mails to their database of 500,000 homes wired to the Internet. Two groups of eight panelists were formed after candidates were screened for age and certain drinking preferences.

During the focus group held in a private chat room at Greenfield's Web site, a moderator fields questions and answers on one side of a split screen, while the participants make suggestions on the left side of the screen. All the information is processed almost instantaneously and the client, Universal, has a report within days.   ◆

Observations

Not all observational research is informal. A common observational technique is to set up a one-way mirror in a supermarket or other retail outlet. In this way, the marketing manager or researcher can observe the behavior patterns of shoppers in different demographic groups. The observer might count the different items examined, calculate how much time is spent considering a purchase in a product category, or evaluate the interactions with a salesperson (if appropriate). Another observational approach is to go through a household's pantry to see what brands are being purchased and measure their consumption rates. Other observational methods are more intrusive and involve measuring the dilation of a person's pupil to measure attention to an advertisement or measuring the electric impulses transmitted through the skin to determine the subject's excitement level.

A new technology incorporating computer graphics and three-dimensional modeling allows marketing managers to observe how consumers choose between different brands in a virtual reality–like setting.[14] In **virtual shopping,** the consumer can use the simulation to view (on a screen) shelves stocked with any kind of product. The shopper can choose a package on the virtual shelf by touching its image on the screen. The product can be rotated and examined on all sides. The consumer can also "purchase" the product by touching the image of a shopping cart. Unlike the artificial environment in a focus group, the shopper can choose simulated brands in a realistic setting. New product concepts can be tested easily and quickly.

Surveys

A major portion of many research budgets is devoted to survey research, performed by administering questionnaires to people. This is a form of quantitative research and, as Table 4–5 shows, the major purposes of survey research are either descriptive, such as attempting to understand various market segmentation approaches, or scientific, such as testing a marketing manager's hypothesis that women consume more of a product than men. The two primary issues for the manager to consider are the sample from which the responses are taken and the various survey approaches that can be used.

Survey development and analysis are complex, and a full description is beyond the scope of this book. For example, the construction of useful survey questions is much more difficult than you might expect. The wording of a question may be biased, leading the respondent to a particular answer. In addition, the possible responses can be open-ended (e.g., "How many times did you go to the movies last month?") or fixed (e.g., "Check off from the following list how many times you went to the movies last month"). Each of these styles has different implications for analysis and opportunities for inaccurate responses. In addition, many questions on opinions and attitudes use scales (e.g., "On a 1–7 scale where 1 is very bad and 7 is excellent, please rate the quality of service you received at the hotel during your recent stay"); the number of points on the scale and whether it should be an even or odd number must be considered carefully.

Sampling Considerations

An important concept in marketing research is the population or universe from which the sample should be drawn. In this context, *universe* means the entire population of the target group. Suppose you are marketing a computer software product used in local area networks. One target audience is the population or universe of network managers in a country. Few companies can afford to administer a survey to every member of a population.[15] As a result, we would draw a sample from the network managers and assume that the results could be extrapolated to the population. Using statistical analysis, you can determine the range of results within which the "true" or population results would fall.[16]

The results of any survey are only as good as the sample taken. If the sample is biased, then the results cannot be considered representative of the population and any analysis of the survey results would be misleading without some adjustment.[17] It is usually assumed that samples are taken randomly, that is, every member of the population has a nonzero probability of being chosen for the sample. Note that this does not imply that every member of the population has an equal chance of being selected. Some random sampling approaches give more weight to subgroups or segments within the population. Samples in which some members of the population have a zero probability of being chosen are nonrandom and are sometimes called convenience samples because they are used for expediency rather than scientific reasons. Thus, one important characteristic of a survey is how the sample is taken; the marketing manager should always ask about the characteristics of the sample before using the results of the survey.

Note that any sampling process in which the customers can self-select to return a survey is not random. For example, it is common for hotels, restaurants, and other service organizations to give short surveys for customers to complete about the service quality. Obviously, many customers do not return these surveys. Those that are returned are not a random sample of customers; they are likely to represent the views of customers who are highly satisfied or highly dissatisfied.

Samples are usually pulled from lists of customers obtained from company records, industry associations, or companies that specialize in developing lists. In some cases, such lists are unnecessary because the universe is readily observable. For example, a researcher who wants to study the dishwashing habits of German households could use government records to randomly sample cities and blocks within cities, and then randomly choose houses within the blocks.

However, there is often a large difference between the original random sample and the final group of surveys obtained. Those who respond, even if randomly chosen, may not ultimately represent a random sample of the target population. This is called nonresponse bias: The people who did not respond may feel differently about the issue being surveyed than those who did. It is important for the marketing manager to make sure the sample has been inspected for nonresponse bias by examining the answers to some of the other questions on the survey (e.g., income, age) or the geographic distribution of the responses.

Survey Types

The three main approaches to collecting survey data are personal interviews, telephone interviews, and mail, although the Internet is becoming more popular as a survey tool as the number of users grows. The tradeoffs between these four approaches are highlighted in Table 4–7.

The main criteria for evaluating the survey alternatives are the following:

- Cost. Most marketing managers have a fixed budget for research, so cost considerations are important. Personal interviews are the most expensive choice.
- Control. This refers to how much control the data collector has in the data collection process. For example, because mail surveys are completed at a location distant from the organization collecting the data, there is no opportunity to answer clarification questions. In addition, there is no opportunity to prod the respondent to fill out the survey.
- Response rate. This is the percentage of surveys completed.

Table 4–7 Tradeoffs with Different Kinds of Surveys

Criteria for Evaluation	Personal Interview	Phone	Mail	Internet
Cost	High	Medium	Low	Low
Control	High	Medium	Low	Low
Response rate	High	Medium	Low	Low
Potential for interviewer bias	High	Medium	Low	Low
Time to obtain data	Long	Short	Long	Short
Flexibility	High	Medium	Low	Medium
Nonresponse bias	Low	Low	High	High

- Potential for interviewer bias. The inability of the data collector to interact with the respondent is not necessarily a bad thing. Personal interactions with survey respondents could lead to answers that would not be given otherwise.
- Time to obtain data. The marketing manager may need the data within 2 weeks or 2 months.
- Flexibility. This characteristic describes how many different kinds of survey formats and question types can be used. For example, with personal interviews, flexibility is high because a large variety of question-and-answer formats can be used, including video, and the surveys can be long.
- Nonresponse bias. A serious problem with survey research is that the people who choose to respond to the survey may be significantly different from those who do not. The different survey methods offer the marketing researcher varying ability to control and correct for this bias.

The tradeoffs noted in Table 4–7 are not surprising. If the manager needs a quick response, telephone surveys are the way to go, although the Internet is also fairly quick. If budget limitations are critical, mail surveys are the least expensive. In survey research, you get what you pay for.

Technology is also affecting survey research. Besides the Internet, fax and e-mail approaches have been used. A study on the use of fax surveys showed that the response time was about 40% faster than for mail surveys, but response rates and quality of information were the same.[18] The small number of fax machines in the home limits this approach, however. A similar study compared e-mail surveys to mail surveys; this study found a greater response rate and a much faster return rate for e-mail than for mail.[19] Of course, the problem with this approach is that only about one-third of U.S. households (and fewer in other countries) own PCs.

Some companies take surveys at fixed time intervals (e.g., every 3 months) in order to monitor advertising awareness, product usage, or strategy-related measures such as product positioning over time. These are called tracking studies. An example is Dannon's Consumer Awareness, Attitude and Usage study referred to at the beginning of the chapter.

Panels

A **panel** is a set of customers who are enlisted to give responses to questions or to provide data repeatedly over a period of time.[20] The main benefit of a panel is the ability to observe changes in behavior caused by changes in marketing variables or other factors in the marketplace. Conventional surveys and focus groups are called cross-sectional data because they provide a slice of life at one point in time. Panels provide both cross-sectional data and time-series data. When correlated with other factors, panel data can provide useful longitudinal results that cross-sectional data cannot match.

There are several problems with panels, however. The most important is panel dropout (also called mortality). It is difficult for a marketing researcher to keep panel members sufficiently interested to remain on panels. Because panels often involve a fair amount of work answering a detailed survey multiple times, a second problem is that people who agree to be on panels are not always representative of the underlying population. Finally, the researcher must ensure that being on a panel does not change the member's behavior, a problem sometimes called panel conditioning.

There are many types of panels:

- Continuous reporting panels. Some panels require the members to report all their purchases in certain product categories or to report other kinds of behavior as it occurs. An example is the Nielsen TV panel, which provides the ratings for the network and local shows. NFO Research has established an interactive media research panel with 50,000 U.S. households that use on-line services or the Internet.
- A special kind of continuous panel in a grocery purchasing context is a scanner panel. Consumers are enlisted to allow A.C. Nielsen and Information Resources Inc. (IRI) to track their supermarket purchases through the electronic checkout scanners. The consumer scans in his or her bar-coded ID card, and all of the purchases following are put into a data file. When combined with in-store data such as the existence of point-of-purchase displays, coupon usage, price paid, and, for some panels, TV advertising exposure, Nielsen and IRI can track consumer reaction to promotions, price changes, and new product introductions. Scanner panels eliminate several of the problems typical of panels; in particular, conditioning and the nonrepresentativeness of the panels are mitigated because of the unobtrusive nature of the data collection process.
- Special-purpose panels. A company may want to set up a panel for a particular reason. For example, software companies often engage potential customers to be beta testers for new versions in late stages of development. A panel of users can be established only for this development period and then disbanded. The panel provides feedback to the company on bugs in the program, the clarity and accuracy of the operating manuals, and other product characteristics.

Experiments

In science, an experiment is the only true way to determine cause and effect. Marketing managers can track the sales response to a new advertising campaign, but without controlling for other factors that could have also caused a sales change, it is impossible to determine how much of the change resulted from the advertising. The purpose of an experiment is to allow the marketing manager to conclusively show that a change in x produced y.

A marketing experiment has several important features:

- A **manipulation.** This is the marketing variable that is of central interest. It is called a manipulation because different levels or values of the variable are controlled by the researcher. For example, a company interested in finding out whether increasing its advertising budget by 25% would be profitable would choose some geographic areas in which to increase spending (the manipulation) and others in which to maintain the current level.

- A **control group.** A control group is a set of respondents or experimental units (e.g., cities) that receive the "normal" level of the manipulation; in other words, they are not subject to the experiment. The control group is used as a base against which the experimental group can be compared. Continuing the advertising example, the geographic areas receiving the current level of spending would be the control.
- **External validity.** A key issue in evaluating experimental results is validity. One kind of validity, external validity, is the degree to which the results can be generalized to the real world or, more generally, to the target population. For example, if a marketing researcher tests different advertising copy targeted to a broad audience on undergraduate students only, the experiment may not be externally valid.
- **Internal validity.** A second kind of validity, internal validity, is the degree to which the results found are actually caused by the experimental manipulation. For example, suppose a company increases its advertising in one city (the manipulation) and maintains the same level in another (the control). Let us assume that the cities are perfectly matched in terms of buying habits, demographics, and other relevant characteristics and that the results would be externally valid. If the company also launches a promotional campaign in the test city but not in the control city, then the results of the advertising experiment are not internally valid because the increased sales could result from the advertising or the promotional campaign.

Experiments can be conducted in a laboratory or in the field. A **laboratory experiment** is run in an artificial environment such as a classroom or movie theater. The advantage of lab experiments is that they generally have high internal validity because the experimenter can control the environment easily. However, they usually have low external validity because the controlled environment does not replicate the real world. **Field experiments** take place in realistic environments such as an actual city. The advantage of field experiments is that they generally have high external validity, but they suffer from potential internal validity problems because the experimenter cannot control events in the real-world business environment.

An excellent example of a field experiment is a study examining the profit impact of Everyday Low Pricing (EDLP), a pricing strategy that offers low prices and no promotions.[21] EDLP has been adopted by several firms such as Proctor & Gamble and some retailers (Sears, unsuccessfully) as an alternative to having higher prices with frequent price promotions (often called hi–lo pricing). Nineteen product categories in all 86 stores in a Chicago-area supermarket chain were chosen for the study. Stores were randomly assigned to three pricing conditions. In the control stores, all nonpromotional prices were maintained at current levels. In EDLP stores, prices of each brand in a product category were reduced by a constant factor ranging from 6% to 24%. In hi–lo stores, prices of each brand in a category were increased by 10% on average. In all stores, normal promotional activity occurred, with the promotional prices being the same across all stores. This resulted in a larger percentage discount in hi–lo stores than in EDLP stores. The main outcome was that although volume was higher in EDLP stores than in the control stores, the increased volume was not sufficient to offset the drop in profits; across all 19 categories, volume increased by 3% on average while profits dropped 18%. In hi–lo stores, volume dropped 3% but profits increased 15%. This study was the first comprehensive examination of EDLP pricing policies. Because of the controlled nature of the experiment and the concomitant cause-and-effect conclusions that could be drawn, it raised serious questions about the wisdom of EDLP pricing policies. ◆

Models and Simulations

Very different from focus groups are mathematical models developed to simulate a particular marketing problem. These are normally abstractions of the actual complexity of what is being modeled. For example, a researcher might develop a model assuming a mathematical relationship between two controllable marketing variables (such as price and advertising) and brand sales. The researcher knows that although these may be the main two variables affecting sales, several other factors (e.g., the weather, the salesperson's attitude toward the brand) also affect sales; because these factors are not controllable, they are omitted from the model. Normally, a statistical method such as regression analysis (discussed later in this chapter) is to estimate the assumed relationships.

MARKET POTENTIAL AND SALES FORECASTING

Two important applications of marketing research information are the calculations of **market potential** and the development of **sales forecasts.** These quantities aid the marketing manager in setting quotas for the sales force, setting product objectives, and performing a number of other tasks. These calculations depend on both primary and secondary research information and are themselves used as foundations for marketing decision-making.

The terms *forecast* and *potential* are used in many different ways and are often confused. We use the following definitions:[22]

Potential: The maximum sales reasonably attainable under a given set of conditions within a specified period of time

Forecast: The amount of sales expected to be achieved under a set of conditions within a specified period of time

Thus, potential is an upper limit or ceiling on sales whereas a forecast is what you expect to sell. Both are circumscribed by the assumptions that the market conditions remain stable (what economists call the *ceteris paribus* condition, or "all else remaining equal") and that the numbers produced are good only for a specified period of time (e.g., a forecast for the year 2000). The managers at Dannon would be very interested in both market potential and forecasted sales. Potential gives them some estimate of whether there is growth left in the market, whereas the forecast helps them to plan manufacturing and distribution.

Market Potential

Market potential is one of the most difficult quantities to estimate because of the problems in developing a concrete number that people can agree on. Part of this difficulty results from the mechanics of the calculation, but part of it results from confusion over the notion of a ceiling or maximum amount that can be sold. Because estimates of market potential often bear little resemblance to current sales figures, these numbers are often viewed with skepticism.

However, market potential estimates have considerable value to marketing managers. They can be used to allocate resources over a product line so that products with the greatest potential receive more money for their marketing efforts. This may make more sense than allocating simply on the basis of current sales, which is a myopic approach. Products with higher estimated levels of market potential may also be given more aggressive objectives to achieve. As we will see in Chapter 10, estimates of market potential assist the sales manager in developing sales territories, assigning salespeople to those territories, and setting appropriate quotas. Depending on the situation, it may make more sense to develop territories that have equal potential so that the salespeople have equivalent chances of performing well and earning bonuses. An important use of market potential is strategic: When there is a large gap between actual and potential sales, the marketing manager should ask, "Why is there such a big difference?" Often, such ruminations can lead to innovations in packaging, choosing new segments, or other activities that narrow the gap between a product category's actual and potential sales.

The general approach for estimating market potential has three steps:

1. *Determine the potential buyers or users of the product.* Using either primary or secondary marketing research information or judgment, the marketing manager must first establish who are the potential buyers of the product. These potential buyers should be defined broadly as any person or organization that has a need for the product, the resources to use the product, and the ability to pay for it. In fact, it might actually be easier to start with all of the end buyer "units" and then subtract those who cannot buy the product. For example, apartment dwellers are not potential buyers of lawnmowers, diabetics are not potential customers for food products containing sugar, and law firms are not potential customers for supercomputers. This part of the analysis can be done judgmentally and often relies on the expertise and experience of the marketing manager.

2. *Determine how many individual customers are in the potential groups of buyers defined in step 1.* At this stage, the manager must use basic data such as how many households there are in a particular country, how many people live in apartments, and what percentage of the population has diabetes.

3. *Estimate the potential purchasing or usage rate.* This can be done by taking the average purchasing rate determined by surveys or other research or by assuming that the potential usage rate is characterized by heavy buyers. This latter approach assumes that all buyers of the category could potentially consume as much as heavy buyers.

The estimate of market potential is simply the product of step 2 times step 3, that is, the number of potential customers times their potential buying rate.

An illustration of this method applied to the market for disposable diapers for babies in the United States is shown in Table 4–8. The answer to step 1 begins with all babies between the ages of 0 and 2.5 years (the average age of toilet training). Babies who are allergic to the lining should be subtracted from this total. Assume that research shows that 5% of all babies have such an allergy. Data obtained from the National Center for Health Statistics show that there were 3,952,767 births in the United States in 1994, or approximately 4 million (high degrees of precision are unnecessary for potential calculations). The current infant mortality rate in the United States is about 1%, leaving about 3,960,000 babies who can potentially wear disposable diapers. Subtracting another 5% leaves 3,762,000 babies. Data from Mediamark Research[23] show that the heaviest users go through 9 or more diapers per day (assume 10), the heaviest medium users 7, and the heaviest light users 3. Assuming that the heaviest users are 0–1 years old, the medium users are 1–2, and the light users are 2–3 (and only half the children 2–3 years old will need diapers at all), then the total market potential is 69,221,364 diapers per day, or 25,265,797,860 diapers per year! This compares to actual sales of over 500 million units.

Note that in calculating the market potential for disposable diapers, you do not subtract out the number of babies using cloth diapers. Unless they are allergic to the lining, they are part of the potential market for disposables because their parents *could* buy them but they are not. It is up to marketing managers to induce the switching. ◆

Table 4–8 Market Potential Illustration

Disposable Diapers in the United States

Step 1: Who are the potential consumers?
   Babies 0–2.5 years old less those who are allergic to the liner and other materials

Step 2: How many are there?
   Facts: 4 million births annually, an annual 1% mortality rate, and 5% allergic incidence or 3,762,000 0–1 years old, 3,724,380 1–2 years old, and 3,687,136 2–3 years old

Step 3: How much can they consume?
   0–1: 10 diapers per day
   1–2: 7 diapers per day
   2–3: 3 diapers per day

Market potential:
   0–1 years old   3,762,000 × 10   = 37,620,000
   1–2 years old   3,724,380 × 7   = 26,070,660
   2–3 years old   (3,687,136 × 3)/2* = 5,530,704

   Total/day   = 69,221,364

   or   = 25,265,797,860 diapers per year

---

*Assumes one-half of the children 2–3 years old are toilet-trained and therefore do not need diapers.

The important insights from the calculation of market potential come from the steps of the analysis. In the first stages, the marketing manager must consider who the potential customers are. This activity creates a broadened perspective that often carries beyond the current boundaries of the target marketing efforts of the major competitors. For example, by considering that children might be potential consumers of seeds, Burpee developed a program aimed at creating young gardeners. The second insight comes from step 3, a consideration of the potential purchasing rate. One way to increase sales is to get customers to buy more. This can be done with innovative and larger package sizes, promotions, or product enhancements. For example, when videocassette recorders were first introduced, who suspected that families would eventually own 2, 3, or more of them? Therefore, the benefit from going through the market potential exercise is that the marketing manager often obtains a better understanding of two new routes to sales growth: new, untapped segments and greater per capita purchasing quantities.

Forecasting

Consider the data shown in Table 4–9 on sales of personal computers (PCs) in the United States from 1984 to 1996. Assume these data were available to a marketing manager in 1997. The market has obviously grown rapidly, with an average growth rate of 10.8% between 1984 and 1996 and an average of 20% in the 1993–1996 period. Suppose you are the marketing manager for Toshiba's PC line and you are interested in further penetrating the U.S. market. Your laptop computers have been very successful but, overall, you are in eighth position in the market, trailing IBM, Compaq, Dell, and others by a wide margin. However, Toshiba, a Japanese company, is a world leader in electronics, with $50 billion in sales. Your superiors have indicated that your marketing plan should have an objective of achieving a fifth-place position by the end of 1998.

Table 4–9 U.S. Sales of Personal Computers (1984–1996)

Year	Sales (000's)	Year	Sales (000's)
1984	7,719	1991	11,535
1985	7,925	1992	12,442
1986	8,130	1993	15,714
1987	8,778	1994	18,571
1988	9,425	1995	22,857
1989	10,027	1996	25,714
1990	10,628		

Sources: "Dell Computer Corporation," Harvard Business School case #9-596-058, and Neal Templin (1996), "Veteran PC customers spur mail-order boom," *The Wall Street Journal*, July 17, p. B1.

This is obviously a challenge. The marketing plan you must create is outlined in Chapter 2. A key part of the situation analysis is developing some predictions or forecasts for a variety of market conditions that will exist in the U.S. market in the rest of 1997 and beyond. These include the following:

- A forecast of the likely consumer trends in adopting PCs in the home.
- A forecast of the actions competitors will take.
- Predictions about the economic climate. Because PCs are expensive, interest rates, employment rates, and other macroeconomic conditions are important indicators of the health of PC sales.
- Predictions about corporate buyers' attitudes towards technology changes.

These important questions must be addressed for 1997 and every year for which marketing plans are developed. In addition, the Toshiba marketing manager is interested in forecasts of specific quantities such as sales, market share, and profits. Sales forecasts are essential for production planning. Producing too few units results in retail shortages and opportunities for potential customers to buy competitors' products. Producing too many units increases inventory holding costs and often results in price cutting, lowering profit margins. Sales forecasts are also important for budgeting purposes. Part of the marketing plan is to develop a pro forma income statement. The top line of the statement, sales revenue, is produced from forecasted sales. Managers also like to do **scenario planning,** asking "what-if" questions. As a result, forecasts of alternative outcomes based on different assumptions about advertising spending, price levels, and competitor actions are important parts of planning.

Therefore, forecasting in general and sales forecasting in particular are important marketing research activities. Many different forecasting methods are available.[24] As Table 4–10 shows, we divide the methods into four types: **judgment methods,** which rely on pure opinion; **counting methods,** which use customer data; **time-series methods,** which use the kind of sales data shown in Table 4–9; and **association/causal methods,** which try to develop statistical models relating market factors to sales.[25] The remainder of this chapter focuses on further defining and describing these various forecasting methods.

Judgmental Methods

Naïve Extrapolation **Naïve extrapolation** simply takes the most current sales and adds a judgmentally determined *x*%, where *x* is the estimated percentage change in sales. For

Table 4–10 Summary of Forecasting Methods

Dimensions	Judgement				Counting	
	Naïve Extrapolation	**Sales Force**	**Executive Opinion**	**Delphi**	**Market Testing**	**Market Survey**
Time span	Short/medium term	Short/medium term	Short/medium term	Medium/long	Medium	Medium
Urgency	Rapid turnaround	Fast turnaround	Depends whether inside or outside company	Needs time	Needs time	Needs time
Quantitative skills needed	Minimal	Minimal	Minimal	Minimal	Moderate level	Yes
Financial resources	Very low	Low	Could be high if outside experts used	Could get high	High	High
Past data needed	Some	Not necessary	Not necessary	Not necessary	Not necessary	Not necessary
Accuracy	Limited	Highly variable	Poor if one individual; better if a group	Best under dynamic conditions	Good for new products	Limited

Time Series			Association/Causal			
Moving Average	**Exponential Smoothing**	**Extrapolation**	**Correlation**	**Regression**	**Leading Indicators**	**Econometric**
Short/medium	Short/medium	Short/medium/long	Short/medium/long	Short/medium/long	Short/medium/long	Short/medium/long
Fast turnaround	Fast turnaround	Fast turnaround	Fast turnaround	Moderately fast	Moderately fast	Needs time
Minimal	Minimal	Basic skills	Basic skills	Basic skills	Basic skills	High level
Low	Low	Low	Moderate	Moderate/high	Moderate	High
Necessary	Necessary	Necessary	Necessary	Necessary	Necessary	Necessary
Good only in stable environment	Good in short run	Good for trends, stable time series	Highly variable	Can be accurate if explained variance is high	Moderately accurate at best	Best in stable environment

Source: David M. Georgoff and Robert G. Murdick, "Manager's guide to forecasting," *Harvard Business Review*, January–February 1986, pp. 110–120.

example, given the PC sales level of 25,714,000 in 1996, the manager would have to determine what percentage to add to it to predict sales in 1997. This could be the most recent growth figure (12.5%), the average of the last 4 years (20%), or a percentage based on the recent growth figures modified by some other information.

Sales Force In the **sales force method of forecasting,** a marketing manager would ask the salespeople calling on retail and corporate accounts to form their own forecasts of the sales in their territories. These would be summed to provide an overall forecast. This approach is usually justified by the fact that the sales force is close to customers and is therefore in a good position to understand buying habits. On the other hand, salespeople might underestimate sales if their quotas are based on forecasts or be overly optimistic to impress the sales manager.

Executive Opinion In the **executive opinion method of forecasting,** the marketing manager might simply rely on his or her own opinion to predict sales based on experience and other qualitative knowledge gained from reading trade publications and talking to industry representatives at trade shows. Alternatively, the manager might consult with internal or external experts. There are consultants who specialize in different industries and provide a variety of forecasts (such as the Gartner Group and Intelliquest for computers).

Delphi Method The **Delphi method of forecasting** is implemented by forming a jury of experts from a diverse population. For video games, this might include consultants, marketing managers, and distributors or retailers. These people are sent a questionnaire and asked to provide an estimate of 1999 sales and a justification for the number. The answers are collated by the company or a research firm and the information redistributed to the panel members. Given the other members' responses and their reasoning, the members are asked to revise their estimates. Usually, the second round produces convergence on a number. This method is also useful to forecast the demand for new products and technologies for which there are no available data.

Counting Methods

Market Testing The **market testing method of forecasting** uses primary data collection methods to predict sales. Focus groups, in-depth interviews, or other methods are used to estimate the likely demand for a product. This method is often used in new product forecasting. A marketing manager would be unlikely to use this approach to forecast market or brand demand but might use it for a new model that was being launched.

Market Surveys In many cases, companies use the **market survey method of forecasting,** using purchase intention questions, for example, to attempt to predict demand. The surveys often use a 10-point scale, with 1 meaning nearly certain not to purchase and 10 meaning nearly certain to purchase. The company or research firm must estimate the cutoff for counting the response as a forecasted sale. The Toshiba manager could administer this survey to a sample of households to estimate consumer demand, to purchasing agents in companies to estimate corporate demand, and to retailers and distributors to estimate sales through various channels.

Time-Series Methods

Moving Averages The **moving averages method of forecasting** is a simple method for taking the data shown in Table 4–9 and using averages of historical sales figures to make a forecast. The researcher must decide how many years (or, in general, periods) of data will be used to form the forecast. Assuming a 3-year moving average, the forecast for 1996 would use the average of sales from 1993, 1994, and 1995: 19,047,333 units. The forecast for 1997 would drop the 1993 sales figure and add the 1996 sales figure, for an average of 22,381,666 units. Obviously, the merits of the method are its ease of implementation and low cost. On the downside, any sales series must adjust for trends or the forecasts will always be behind (rising trend) or ahead (falling trend).

Exponential Smoothing   The **exponential smoothing method of forecasting** also relies on the historical sales data and is slightly more complicated than the moving average. The formula for a simple exponentially smoothed forecast is

$$PS_{t+1} = aS_t + (1 - a)PS_t$$

where PS is the predicted sales in a period and S is the actual sales. In other words, an exponentially smoothed forecast for period $t + 1$ is a combination of the current period's sales and the current period's forecast. The smoothing parameter a is between 0 and 1 and can be empirically determined from the historical sales data. Exponential smoothing is close to moving average forecasting, but it includes exponentially declining weights on the past sales values, as opposed to the latter's equal-weighted scheme. Assuming a high value of $a = .9$ (because of the rapid changes in sales, making recent sales more important) and the moving average forecast for 1996 of 19,047,333 units, the 1997 forecast would be $.9 \times 25,714,000 + .1 \times 19,047,333 = 25,047,333$ which will be closer to the actual number than the moving average forecast.

Extrapolation   It is basic human nature to linearly extrapolate data. When a baseball player has an outstanding early season, announcers and writers always say "At this pace, he will hit . . ." The assumption is that he will keep up the same pace. The same holds for sales forecasting. Figure 4–5 shows a graph of the PC sales data over time. Time-series extrapolation simply extends the line into the future. This can be done by calculating the slope of the line; the data from 1992 on seem particularly appropriate. Alternatively, if you are familiar with regression analysis, you could analyze the following simple regression:

$$S = a + b\text{Time}$$

where Time is simply the numbers 1–13 for each time period. The parameter b is the slope of the line through all the data observations.[26] If this calculation is done for the PC data (using an Excel spreadsheet), the estimate of b is 1,388,700, or an average change of 1,388,700 units per year. The estimate of a, the spot where the line crosses the y-axis, is

Figure 4–5

PC Sales Graph

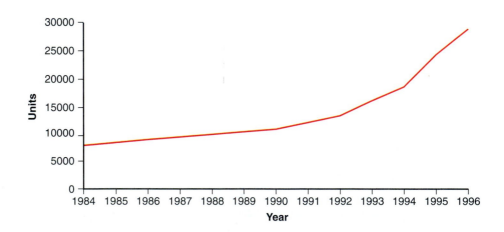

3,314,800. Therefore, the forecast for 1997 would then be 3,314,800 + 1,388,700 × 14 (the next year), or 22,756,000 units.[27] More sophisticated forms of extrapolation could be used, such as a variety of nonlinear approaches. Linear extrapolation can be dangerous, particularly in a fast-growing category, because a forecast of continued growth is assured.

Association/Causal Methods

Correlation A correlation is a number between −1 and +1 indicating the relationship between two variables. If one variable is sales, the correlation would indicate the strength of the association between sales and the other variable chosen. A high positive correlation (near 1) indicates that as the variable changes, sales change at approximately the same rate. Although the correlation itself does not produce a forecast, the **correlation method of forecasting** can be useful for detecting variables that are indicators of changes in sales.

Regression Analysis **Regression analysis** is a generalization of the time-series extrapolation model that includes independent variables other than time. Normally, the marketing manager selects variables that he or she believes have a causal effect on sales, such as price, advertising, demographic, and macroeconomic variables. For example, in the PC market, the variables predicting market demand might include average price, marketing effort such as advertising and the number of distribution channels, and the subscription levels of America Online and other Internet service providers, which might have a secondary demand effect on PC sales.

Leading Indicators Economists use certain macroeconomic variables to forecast changes in the economy. When changes in these variables occur before changes in the economy and they are thought to cause those changes, they are called **leading indicators.** One such indicator for PCs might be investment in computer networks, which ultimately leads to PC purchases. Other leading indicators might be measures of the general health of the U.S. economy.

Econometric Models **Econometric models** are large-scale, multiple-equation regression models that are rarely used in product forecasting. They are often used to predict the performance of a country's economy or a particularly large business sector such as the demand for all manufactured goods.

A Tip

It has been found that taking the average of a set of forecasts using disparate methods outperforms any one approach. This finding is intuitive: Diversification of forecasts, as in a portfolio of stocks, reduces the unique risk associated with any one approach. Because most forecasts are judgment based, checking a forecast with some other method is a good idea. For example, using expert judgment, Jupiter Communications, a well-known Internet research firm, forecasts that consumers will spend $443 million buying clothing on-line by the year 2000. I leave it to the readers of this book to check the accuracy of this forecast.

EXECUTIVE SUMMARY

Key learning points in this chapter include the following:

- Marketing research is critical to developing a marketing plan and, therefore, to an understanding of the market in which your product or service competes. It is impossible to develop a sound marketing strategy without some form of marketing research.

- There are two kinds of marketing research information. Primary data are those that are collected specifically with your research topic in mind; secondary data were initially collected for some other reason.
- It is always advisable to begin a marketing research project by searching for useful secondary sources of information.
- Secondary sources of information can be internal or external to the organization. A significant amount of useful external information can be found on the Internet.
- Primary data sources include informal sources, qualitative sources such as focus groups, and quantitative sources such as surveys, panels, and experiments.
- Market potential is the maximum amount of sales obtainable in a product category at a point in time. Estimates of market potential guide the marketing manager in exploring potential new segments and new ways to increase consumption rates.
- Forecasts are made for expected sales, profit, market share, technology, or other data of interest. A variety of methods for developing forecasts include judgmental, counting (customer data–based), time series (historical sales data), and association/causal (identifying key factors affecting sales). It is always useful to take the average of a set of forecasts developed using disparate techniques.

CHAPTER QUESTIONS

1. Go to your business library and compile a list of its secondary sources of information that are useful to marketing managers. What else do you believe is needed?
2. Suppose that McDonald's was considering bringing a new kind of hamburger to its stores. What kind of research would it need to do in order to have some confidence that the new product would sell well?
3. Suppose that Microsoft was introducing a new operating system to replace Windows 98. What kind of research would it need to do in order to have confidence that the new software would sell well?
4. What are the tradeoffs between all the kinds of research described in this chapter? Suppose you worked for a small startup company with a small research budget. Which of these kinds of research would be most valuable?
5. Other than forecasting sales, what other uses are there for forecasting methods?

Integrated Case

Application Exercises:
Marketing Research in the Personal Computer Industry

1. Go to your library and develop a list of resources that would be beneficial for developing a marketing plan for a company's product line of PCs. Be specific; do not simply list "government documents."
2. Make a list of five aspects of consumer buying and usage behavior about which you would like to learn. Ask about ten of your friends and acquaintances to be part of a focus group. Moderate the focus group so that your aspects of consumer behavior are addressed. Write a report summarizing the findings.
3. Based on your focus group results and any other topics of interest, develop a list of research objectives for a survey. Based on this list, draft a short survey. Administer the survey to 25 people, analyze the results, and write a brief report.

4. Choose a country and estimate the market potential for home computers in that country.
5. Update the sales information shown in Table 4–9. Check on the forecasts developed in this chapter. Forecast sales for the year after the last year of data available using three different methods. Compare the forecasts, explaining why you think the results differ.

FURTHER READING

Readers interested in more details about the various marketing research methods should consult the following two textbooks: V. Kumar, David A. Aaker, and George S. Day (1999), *Essentials of Marketing Research* (New York: Wiley), and Donald R. Lehmann, Sunil Gupta, and Joel H. Steckel (1998), *Marketing Research* (Reading, MA: Addison-Wesley). A useful article describing methods of researching international markets is Lambeth Hochwald (1998), "Are you smart enough to sell globally?" *Sales and Marketing Management,* July, pp. 53–56.

Consumer Behavior and Analysis

5

CHAPTER BRIEF

In this chapter, the reader will learn how to analyze buyers in consumer markets. The key learning points include the following:

The concept and activity of market segmentation
Issues in implementing market segmentation strategies
Understanding why consumers make purchase decisions, that is, the motives behind buying behavior
Understanding how consumers make purchase decisions, that is, the mechanism used to make purchases
The importance of understanding where and when consumers purchase

Club Méditerranée, better known as Club Med, began as a sports association in France in 1950.[1] Founded by a former member of the Belgian Olympic team and some of his friends, the first Club Med was a vacation village in Majorca, Spain, with an initial membership of 2,500. It was a village of tents where members slept in sleeping bags and assisted in cooking meals and cleaning. There was a staff of five sports instructors.

A vacation at a Club Med was (and is) a unique experience. It allowed vacationers, generally city-dwellers, to escape from the routine of their daily lives. Each Club Med location offered its own society free of the need for money, with very casual dress and no telephones, radios, or newspapers. People could mingle freely without the societal and class barriers that often separated them in their normal lives. The employees were also unusual; called *gentil organisateurs* (GOs), or "nice organizers," they provided service to the vacationers (*gentil membres* [GMs], or "nice members") and acted as sports instructors, entertainers, and confidants, generally behaving as GMs. No tipping was allowed. Because of this free and open atmosphere, Club Med became closely identified with a swinging, hedonistic lifestyle.

By the mid-1970s, Club Med operated 77 villages in 24 countries, with 19 ski villages, 35 summer villages, 26 year-round villages, and 2 winter seaside villages (some villages served several purposes), and was the largest vacation organization of its kind. Over 500,000 people visited the villages yearly; nearly half were French, 18% from North and Central America, and about 25% from other Western European countries. By the late 1980s, visitors had increased to 1.8 million each year and there were 114 villages in 37 countries.

However, problems arose in the 1980s and have continued to this day. Vacationers who went to Club Med in the 1970s as singles had children in the 1980s. The Club Med image, firmly etched in prospective customers' minds, was inconsistent with what families were looking for. When Club Med changed many of its locations to be more hospitable to children, they were not what singles were looking for. Increased concern about AIDS, more competitors (e.g., cruises), and significant demand for more intellectually oriented vacations also contributed to Club Med's financial losses in the 1990s.

To improve its market position, Club Med clearly needs to study its customers. The company needs to understand the following:

- Who are the customers visiting its various locations? Who are the customers who are not going to Club Med but taking vacations? Who are the customers who have gone to Club Med once but not returned?
- What are the various types of customers looking for when they take vacations in general and at Club Med in particular?
- What criteria do people use in choosing vacations?
- Do customers use travel agents or make the reservations themselves?
- Which types of customers travel at different times of the year?

The marketing research methods described in Chapter 4 are used to analyze one of the key external constituents a marketing manager must consider in developing a marketing plan and strategy: customers. A customer analysis is one of the key building blocks on which the strategy rests; no strategy can be developed without an up-to-date understanding of customer behavior. Besides being essential to applying the customer targets part of the strategic framework developed in Chapter 3 (see the marketing strategy diagram), a customer analysis is fundamental to the market and customer orientations described in Chapter 1.

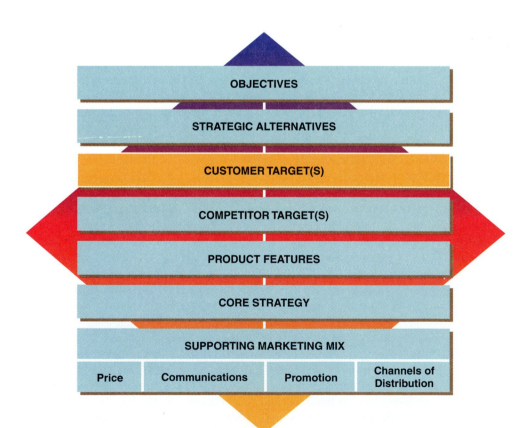

A customer analysis addresses five questions that are the focus of this chapter:

- *Who* are the current and potential customers for the product or service?
- *Why* do they buy?
- *How* do they make purchasing decisions?
- *Where* do they buy the product or service, that is, what channels of distribution are used?
- *When* do they buy?

The objective is to develop a complete picture of customer behavior in the relevant product category or market.

Keep in mind that a customer analysis should include more than just current customers. Although it is certainly important to understand your current customer base as well as you can, several other groups are important as well:

- Analyzing competitors' customers may help you to understand why they are buying competitors' products instead of yours and provides some ideas for stimulating brand switching.
- Analyzing former customers helps you to understand weaknesses in your product or service operations.
- Analyzing people who have never purchased the product helps you to understand how to expand the market and achieve sales closer to market potential.

Thus, in this chapter we use the term *customer* in a general sense to refer to the four possible types of customers and all the concepts developed apply to all potential customers. In addition, we focus on analyzing consumers, individuals, and households purchasing products and services.[2]

WHO ARE THE CONSUMERS?

The analysis required to answer this question addresses one of the key principles in marketing: **market segmentation.** Market segmentation breaks mass markets into segments that have different buying habits. In grouping customers by many different variables or characteristics, we acknowledge that customers are different and that they should be treated differently in terms of marketing variables such as advertising and often in terms of product attributes. In other words, two questions that help to determine whether a particular segmentation scheme is useful are (1) Do the people in different segments behave differently toward the product or service? and (2) Would we use different marketing elements (price, communications, etc.) with the different segments?

There are many examples of how segmentation is applied in marketing. Diet cola brands such as Diet Coke and Diet Pepsi exist for consumers who want the attributes of a cola but also want a low-calorie drink. Special prices are often used as inducements for particular market segments. For example, matinee movie prices attract customers during the lower-volume daytime period. Airlines in Asia offer special prices by age, race, and gender; Air India has a "ladies' fare" program offering 33% discounts to women traveling between India and shopping destinations such as Dubai, Hong Kong, and Singapore.[3] Different hotels serve different kinds of travelers, including budget-minded, family, extended stay, and luxury travelers. Thus, the concept of market segmentation has become ubiquitous in marketing.

It is important to separate the act of segmenting the market from the act of choosing which segment or segments to pursue actively. The former, the topic of this part of this chapter, is where the marketing manager considers the many different possible ways to segment the market for the product. In doing this, the manager often uses both secondary and primary marketing research (discussed in Chapter 4) to develop profiles of the customers and their buying habits. The act of choosing which segments to pursue is called selecting the **target market** and is part of the marketing strategy covered in Chapter 3.

The concept of segmentation is important because it implies an understanding that customers are heterogeneous. The idea that only some customers might be interested in your product and are worth targeting is also important because it has implications for marketing efficiency and effectiveness. A segmentation approach to the market rather than a mass marketing approach (i.e., marketing to all customers and letting the purchasers self-select) is efficient because money is spent only on those whom the manager has determined are potential customers. Thus, less money is wasted on customers who have a low probability of buying the product, which is important in an era when budgets are being tightened. At the same time, segmentation is more effective than mass marketing because of the tailored nature of the programs. For example, toothpaste users tend to seek decay prevention, teeth whitening, or social (breath-related) benefits. A mass marketing approach would develop one product and one communications program that attempted to bundle all benefits simultaneously. As a result, none of the segments would necessarily be satisfied because the typical consumer in each would not feel that the product was right for him or her. A segmentation approach would develop separate advertising campaigns focusing on each benefit in media used by the members of each segment. Although this approach can be expensive, the overall response in terms of sales will be better because the sum of the three segments' responses to communications that are tailored to their needs will be greater than if the same amount is spent on a mass market campaign.

Interestingly, in some situations, single-customer segments make sense. The first situation is one in which the number of customers is small. For example, an Amway sales representative considers potential customers one at a time. The second situation is the current trend toward one-to-one marketing or **mass customization.**[4] In this case, even when there are too many customers to treat each one separately, companies attempt to give the customer the perception that he or she is being treated as a unique segment. This is done through information technology. It can be through an information technology link to a manufacturing facility, such as Levi Strauss's system for custom-fitting women's jeans. Some companies create a database of information from previous transactions and use that information to create a custom-tailored feel for the next transaction. For example, Ritz-Carlton hotels keep electronic files on customer tastes and use the information to make the experience feel unique. Note that it is still necessary to understand how the segments are different and to treat them differently. For example, why does Levi Strauss custom-fit jeans for women (and now men) but not children?

Although I will cover mass customization more fully in Chapter 12, a brief illustration will show that delivering products to segments of one person or organization is rapidly becoming common.

Dow Jones, publisher of *The Wall Street Journal,* has seen the competition for suppliers of business information intensify dramatically. Not only are the traditional business weeklies (*Business Week*) and newspapers (*Barrons*) still thriving, but others, such as the distinctively pink-colored *Financial Times,* are stepping up their global marketing efforts.[5] Looking for new markets in which to expand, the managers of the *Journal* decided to target younger people who are interested in business and investing but who do not read daily newspapers. Thus, the company developed a new online version of the paper that extended the daily paper but added two unique features:

A current trend among companies today is one-to-one marketing, or mass customization. Each customer who visits the Prescriptives counter can buy custom-blended makeup suited to her own unique profile. (Francis Hogan/Electronic Publishing Services Inc.)

personalization and interactivity. Thus, *The Wall Street Journal Interactive Edition* was born in the spring of 1996.

Subscribers to the new edition provide information to the company that permit the customization of material to the particular subscriber. Thus, the "Personal Journal" section provides a customized selection of news and feature articles that match the interests of the particular subscriber. In addition, customers can create up to five different personal profiles and track separate stock portfolios for each by placing the information in separate folders. Each folder can be customized to different business sectors. As a result, one folder can track the performance of stocks and companies in the utilities sector and another can do the same in technology. In addition, articles in the paper are stored in the appropriate folders. The company is continually investing in its ability to personalize the site to the individual reader, thus taking a mass-produced product and creating it for a segment of one—the essence of mass customization. ◆

Segmentation Variables

The task facing the marketing manager is to identify variables that describe the customers in terms of their inherent characteristics, called **descriptors,** and to link those variables to customer behavior toward the product or service. Both kinds of information are needed. For example, it is insufficient to note that 50% of the population are women and 50% are men; what is useful is to know that *50% of the purchasers of your product* are women and 50% are men. This information links characteristics to behavior.

The kinds of variables that usually serve as descriptors are shown in Table 5–1. As can be seen, they fall into three major categories:

- Geographic. The underlying rationale is that tastes vary by part of the world, part of a country, or even between cities and rural areas.
- Demographic. Income, age, occupation, education, race, and other variables have all been found to distinguish between different kinds of consumer buying habits.
- Psychographic. These variables characterize the psychological differences between people in terms of lifestyles, personalities, and social class. People with identical demographic profiles can have quite different personalities and lifestyle interests and, hence, different interests in products and services.

Table 5–1 Consumer Market Segmentation Variables

Descriptor Variables

Geographic

Region	Pacific, Mountain, West North Central, West South Central, East North Central, East South Central, South Atlantic, Middle Atlantic, New England
City or Metro size	Under 4,999, 5,000–19,999, 20,000–49,999, 50,000–99,999, 100,000–249,999, 250,000–499,999, 500,000–999,999, 1,000,000–3,999,999, 4,000,000 or over
Density	Urban, suburban, rural
Climate	Northern, southern

Demographic

Age	Under 6, 6–11, 12–19, 20–34, 35–49, 50–64, 65+
Family size	1–2, 3–4, 5+
Family life cycle	Young, single; young, married, no children; young, married, youngest child under 6; young, married, youngest child 6 or over; older, married, with children; older, married, no children under 18; older, single; other
Gender	Male, female
Income	Under $9,999, $10,000–$14,999, $15,000–19,999, $20,000–$29,999, $30,000–$49,999, $50,000–$99,999, $100,000 and over
Occupation	Professional and technical; managers, officials, and proprietors; clerical, sales; craftspeople; forepersons; operatives; farmers; retired; students; homemakers; unemployed
Education	Grade school or less; some high school; high school graduate; some college; college graduate
Religion	Catholic, Protestant, Jewish, Muslim, Hindu, other
Race	White, Black, Asian
Generation	Baby boomers, Generation X
Nationality	North American, South American, British, French, German, Italian, Japanese
Social class	Lower lowers, upper lowers, working class, middle class, upper middles, lower uppers, upper uppers

Psychographic

Lifestyle	Straights, swingers, longhairs
Personality	Compulsive, gregarious, authoritarian, ambitious

Source: Philip Kotler (1997), *Marketing Management,* 9th ed. (Upper Saddle River, NJ: Prentice Hall), p. 257.

For example, Club Med would use country of origin (U.S., Europe, etc.), demographics (young marrieds without kids, single, families), and psychographics (hedonists, extroverts) to help target likely prospects.

The kinds of behavioral variables that can be used to form segments are shown in Table 5–2. The most popular variables are benefits and usage rate. Usage rate or quan-

Table 5–2 Consumer Market Segmentation Variables

Behavioral Variables

Occasions	Regular occasion, special occasion
Benefits	Quality, service, economy, speed
User status	Nonuser, ex-user, potential user, first-time user, regular user
Usage rate	Light user, medium user, heavy user
Loyalty status	None, medium, strong, absolute
Buyer readiness stage	Unaware, aware, informed, interested, desirous, intending to buy
Attitude toward product	Enthusiastic, positive, indifferent, negative, hostile

Source: Philip Kotler (1997), *Marketing Management*, 9th ed. (Upper Saddle River, NJ: Prentice Hall), p. 257.

tity is obviously important to a marketing manager because it measures how the consumer is actually behaving. Each purchasing level generates its own set of questions. Are heavy users already saturated or is there more potential in that group? Can medium users be bumped up to the heavy group? Are light users simply brand switchers? Benefit segmentation is a useful way to segment because it relates fundamentally to why people buy products and recognizes the fact that consumers buy the same product for many different reasons.

One example of geographic segmentation is shown in Fig. 5–1. This figure shows the differences between the United States, China, and India in ownership rates and household conveniences. These data are useful for demonstrating the market potential (or the difficulty in marketing) for a variety of products directly or indirectly related to those shown.

Demographic variables cover a wide variety of household descriptors. A currently popular age-related type of segmentation, called **cohort analysis,** develops profiles of each generation. This type of analysis is illustrated in Fig. 5–2. Much is being made about the

Figure 5–1

Global Differences: India, China, and the United States

Source: Miriam Jordan (1996), "Marketing gurus say: in India, think cheap, lose the cold cereal," *The Wall Street Journal,* October 11, p. A7.

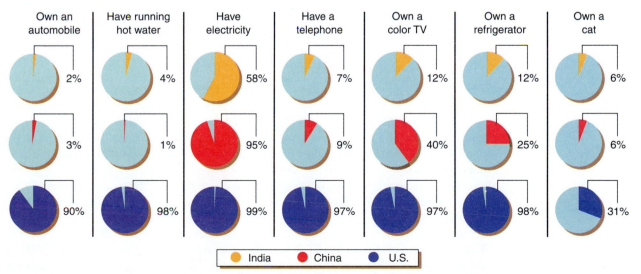

THE DEPRESSION COHORT
(the G.I. generation)

Born: 1912-21
Age in '95: 74 to 83
% of adult population: 7% (13 million)
Money motto: Save for a rainy day.
Sex mindset: Intolerant
Favorite music: Big Band

People who were starting out in the Depression era were scarred in ways that remain with them today—especially when it comes to financial matters like spending, saving, and debt. The Depression cohort was also the first to be truly influenced by contemporary media: radio and especially motion pictures.

THE WORLD WAR II COHORT
(the Depression generation)

Born: 1922-27
Age in '95: 68 to 73
% of adult population: 6% (11 million)
Money motto: Save a lot, spend a little.
Sex mindset: Ambivalent
Favorite music: Swing

People who came of age in the Forties were unified by the shared experience of a common enemy and a common goal. Consequently, this group became intensely romantic. A sense of self-denial that long outlived the war is especially strong among the 16 million veterans and their families.

THE POSTWAR COHORT
(the silent generation)

Born: 1928-45
Age in '95: 50 to 67
% of adult population: 21% (41 million)
Money motto: Save some, spend some.
Sex mindset: Repressive
Favorite music: Frank Sinatra

Members of this 18-year cohort, the war babies, benefited from a long period of economic growth and relative social tranquility. But global unrest and the threat of nuclear attack sparked a need to alleviate uncertainty in everyday life. The youngest subset, called the cool generation, were the first to dig folk rock.

THE BOOMERS I COHORT
(the Woodstock generation)

Born: 1946-54
Age in '95: 41 to 49
% of adult population: 17% (33 million)
Money motto: Spend, borrow, spend.
Sex mindset: Permissive
Favorite music: Rock & roll

Vietnam is the demarcation point between leading-edge and trailing-edge boomers. The Kennedy and King assassinations signaled an end to the status quo and galvanized this vast cohort. Still, early boomers continued to experience economic good times and want a lifestyle at least as good as their predecessors'.

THE BOOMERS II COHORT
(zoomers)

Born: 1955-65
Age in '95: 30 to 40
% of adult population: 25% (49 million)
Money motto: Spend, borrow, spend.
Sex mindset: Permissive
Favorite music: Rock & roll

It all changed after Watergate. The idealistic fervor of youth disappeared. Instead, the later boomers exhibited a narcissistic preoccupation that manifested itself in things like the self-help movement. In this dawning age of downward mobility, debt as a means of maintaining a lifestyle made sense.

THE GENERATION X COHORT
(baby-busters)

Born: 1966-76
Age in '95: 19 to 29
% of adult population: 21% (41 million)
Money motto: Spend? Save? What?
Sex mindset: Confused
Favorite music: Grunge, rap retro

The slacker set has nothing to hang on to. The latchkey kids of divorce and day care are searching for anchors with their seemingly contradictory "retro" behavior: the resurgence of proms, coming-out parties, and fraternities. Their political conservatism is motivated by a "What's in it for me?" cynicism.

Figure 5–2

Age Cohorts in the United States

Source: Faye Rice (1995), "Making generational marketing come of age," *Fortune,* June 26, pp. 110–114.

Generation X cohort and how different it is from its predecessors, the Baby Boomers. Consider also Table 5–3, which shows the differences in purchase incidence of a variety of products between African Americans, Hispanics, and Asian Americans. Some product categories such as ready-to-eat cereal, frozen vegetables, deodorants, and canned soups show some remarkable differences, giving only partial information about how heterogeneous the U.S. population is.

There are several well-known approaches to developing psychographic profiles of consumers. One of these is Global Scan, developed by advertising agency Backer Spielvogel & Bates Worldwide.[6] Global Scan measures a wide variety of attitudes and consumer values and matches them against media use, viewing habits, product use, and buying patterns. The company typically surveys 1,000 people in countries around the world and 3,500 in the United States. Figure 5–3 shows the different Global Scan psychographic segments

Table 5–3 Ethnic Differences in Consumption

Product	African American	Hispanics	Asian American
Regular coffee	54%	72%	49%
Decaffeinated coffee	19	20	13
Regular carbonated soft drink	71	77	70
Diet carbonated soft drink	23	20	12
Fruit juice/nectar	68	78	73
Ready-to-eat cereal	72	78	44
Shampoo	76	93	89
Conditioner	52	61	59
Toothpaste	92	95	93
Frozen vegetables	40	21	17
Bath soaps	95	97	89
Deodorants	84	89	26
Dishwashing detergent	86	88	79
Canned soups	53	32	36
Powdered cleansers	57	53	46
Fabric softener	67	81	51
Liquid cleaners	61	57	43
Toilet paper	95	95	93
Bleach	76	73	57
White rice	73	89	90
Packaged cheese	53	65	39
Packaged sliced meats	39	55	43
Potato chips	52	36	41
Underwear	63	66	66
Packaged cookies	46	42	44
Analgesics/headache remedies	60	80	48
Peanut butter	54	31	51
Beer	31	38	44
Condoms	16	9	12

Source: *Brandweek* (1995), July 17, p. 28.

and how they vary between Japan, the United States, and the United Kingdom. The groups are as follows:

- Strivers: Young people (median age 31) who live hectic, time-pressured lives. They strive hard for success. They are materialistic, seek pleasure, and demand instant gratification.
- Achievers: They have achieved some of the success that strivers aim for. They are affluent, assertive, and upward bound. They are very status conscious and buy for quality and are slightly older than strivers.
- Pressured: This group cuts across age groups and is composed mainly of women who face constant financial and family pressure. They do not enjoy life as much as they could and feel generally downtrodden.
- Adapters: These are older people who maintain time-honored values but keep an open mind. They live comfortably in a changing world.
- Traditionals: They hold onto the oldest values of their countries and cultures. They resist change and prefer routines and familiar products.

Figure 5–3

Global Scan Segments in Three Countries

Source: American Demographics (1991), *Going Global: International Psychographics* (Ithaca, NY: American Demographics Books).

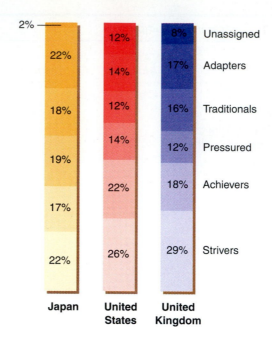

As can be seen in Fig. 5–3, the sizes of the psychographic segments vary somewhat between countries.

A second popular scheme for dividing a country's population into psychographic groups is SRI International's VALS2 (Values and Lifestyles). Based on questions like those shown in Fig. 5–4, the VALS2 groups are the following:[7]

- Actualizers (9.8% of the U.S. population): These are successful, sophisticated, and active people with high self-esteem and significant resources. Image is important to these people.
- Fulfilleds (11.0%): Mature, satisfied, comfortable people who value order, knowledge, and responsibility. Most are well educated and are in or have recently retired from professional occupations. They are conservative, practical consumers.
- Experiencers (11.8%): These people are young, vital, enthusiastic, impulsive, and rebellious and seek variety and excitement. They are avid consumers and spend much of their money on clothing, fast food, music, movies, and video.
- Achievers (15.6%): They are successful career people who feel in control of their lives. They are committed to work and family and buy established, prestige products and services.
- Believers (16.5%): These are conservative, conventional people whose beliefs revolve around family, church, community, and their country. They are conservative consumers favoring national products and established brands.
- Strivers (13.8%): They are striving to find a place in life. They are unsure about themselves and low in socioeconomic status. They feel that they do not have enough money.
- Makers (10.8%): These are practical people who have constructive skills and value self-sufficiency. They experience the world by working on it (e.g., fixing their cars). Makers are politically conservative, suspicious of new ideas, and resentful of government intrusion on individual rights.

Figure 5–4

Sample VALS2
Questions

We are interested in the attitudes that describe you as a person. For each of the following statements, please indicate how much you agree or disagree with that statement as a description of you. There are no right or wrong answers—just answers that describe you best.

7. I am often interested in theories.
⊙ Strongly disagree ○ Slightly disagree ○ Slightly agree ○ Strongly agree

8. I like outrageous people and things.
⊙ Strongly disagree ○ Slightly disagree ○ Slightly agree ○ Strongly agree

9. I like a lot of variety in my life.
⊙ Strongly disagree ○ Slightly disagree ○ Slightly agree ○ Strongly agree

10. I like to make things I can use every day.
⊙ Strongly disagree ○ Slightly disagree ○ Slightly agree ○ Strongly agree

11. I follow the latest trends and fashions.
⊙ Strongly disagree ○ Slightly disagree ○ Slightly agree ○ Strongly agree

12. Just as the Bible says, the world literally was created in six days.
⊙ Strongly disagree ○ Slightly disagree ○ Slightly agree ○ Strongly agree

13. I like being in charge of a group.
⊙ Strongly disagree ○ Slightly disagree ○ Slightly agree ○ Strongly agree

14. I like to learn about art, culture, and history.
⊙ Strongly disagree ○ Slightly disagree ○ Slightly agree ○ Strongly agree

15. I often crave excitement.
⊙ Strongly disagree ○ Slightly disagree ○ Slightly agree ○ Strongly agree

16. I am really interested only in a few things.
⊙ Strongly disagree ○ Slightly disagree ○ Slightly agree ○ Strongly agree

17. I would rather make something than buy it.
⊙ Strongly disagree ○ Slightly disagree ○ Slightly agree ○ Strongly agree

18. I dress more fashionably than most people.
⊙ Strongly disagree ○ Slightly disagree ○ Slightly agree ○ Strongly agree

19. The Federal government should encourage prayers in public schools.
⊙ Strongly disagree ○ Slightly disagree ○ Slightly agree ○ Strongly agree

20. I have more ability than most people.
⊙ Strongly disagree ○ Slightly disagree ○ Slightly agree ○ Strongly agree

- Strugglers (10.7%): They are poor, ill-educated, low-skilled, and elderly, with concerns about security and safety. They are cautious consumers.

When matched against purchasing and media habits, psychographics can provide useful information about the consumers of a product or service that goes beyond demographic information.

A final illustration is the segmentation scheme devised by Forrester Research, Inc., a well-known technology consultant. They divide consumers into 10 groups through the use of what they call Technographics.[8] As can be seen in Fig. 5–5, the groups range from Fast

Figure 5–5

How Tech Customers Stack Up

Source: Forrester Research Inc.

How Tech Customers Stack Up

	Career	Family	Entertainment
Optimists	**Fast Forwards** These consumers are the biggest spenders, and they're early adopters of new technology for home, office, and personal use.	**New Age Nurturers** Also big spenders, but focused on technology for home uses, such as a family PC.	**Mouse Potatoes** They like the on-line world for entertainment and are willing to spend for the latest in techno-tainment.
Optimists	**Techno-Strivers** Use technology from cell phones and pagers to on-line services primarily to gain a career edge.	**Digital Hopefuls** Families with a limited budget but still interested in new technology. Good candidates for the under-$1,000 PC.	**Gadget-Grabbers** They also favor on-line entertainment but have less cash to spend on it.
Pessimists	**Hand-Shakers** Older consumers, typically managers, who don't touch their computers at work. They leave that to younger assistants.	**Traditionalists** Willing to use technology but slow to upgrade. Not convinced upgrades and other add-ons are worth paying for.	**Media Junkies** Seek entertainment and can't find much of it on-line. Prefer TV and other older media.
Sidelined Citizens: Not interested in technology.			

Legend: More affluent / Less affluent

Forwards, who are early adopters of technology for a wide variety of uses, to Sidelined Citizens at the other end of the technology adoption spectrum.

Marketing managers are interested in behavioral variables such as usage rate and degree of loyalty. However, Enterprise Rent-A-Car segments its markets based on another behavioral variable: occasion.[9] It may be a surprise to learn that Enterprise is larger than Hertz in the United States in terms of the size of its fleet and the number of locations. Enterprise specializes in renting cars to people whose car has been wrecked or stolen and totally ignores the airport rental business. Thus, they have focused much of their business on a market segment that is supported by insurance companies. The rest is focused on another occasion segment ignored by the major companies: the local business for customers who need a car for errands or short trips.

Traditionally, the first two descriptor categories, geographic and demographic variables, plus behavioral data on usage, have been used to form segments. However, more and more, marketing managers are combining psychographic and a variety of usage measures to better understand their target groups. These new kinds of segments cut across broad demographic groups. For example, Colgate-Palmolive introduced its new Total brand of toothpaste into the United States in 1997. In addition to the usual cavity-fighting and breath-freshening properties, the product has an ingredient, triclosan, that combats gingivitis. This unique combination of benefits also comes with a higher price tag. The prime target for the product are "orally aware" consumers who have an above-average interest in their oral health (psychographic), are heavy users of toothcare products in general, and visit their dentists regularly (both behavioral). This segment is very broad in terms of income and age, traditional demographic groups.[10]

Marketing Research Implications: Data Collection

To collect information of the type described in this section, the marketing manager can use either primary or secondary data. It is common for the manager to use a survey designed in-house or by a marketing research firm to better understand the customer base. Although the questions would cover a range of topics, these surveys include requests for descriptive information that falls into the categories shown in Table 5–1. In addition, the surveys try to obtain behavioral data indicating quantities purchased and other information. You are likely to have good data on your own customers; however, information on noncustomers requires using external sources of information.

A major source of secondary information on market segments is syndicated data. These data cover a large number of different product categories and are sold to companies requesting the reports.

One common syndicated source of information for consumer products and services is produced by Mediamark Research, Inc. (MRI) and its main competitor, Simmons Market Research Bureau (SMRB). The kinds of data produced by the two firms are shown in Table 5–4. In this case, the data are from MRI and cover the credit card category in 1996. The data are obtained by administering questionnaires to large samples of U.S. households. The responses to the surveys are extrapolated to the general population. As can be seen, the rows represent demographic and geographic variables and the columns represent behavioral variables—in this case, ownership of a particular credit card. The numbers in the "Total U.S." column represent the total number of adults in the United States in that particular row. For example, in 1996, there were 24,848,000 18- to 24-year-old adults in the United States. The numbers in column A represent the number of owners of a particular credit card in the row segment. Thus, 624,000 18- to 24-year-old adults carried an American Express Green card. Column B (% Down) indicates what percentage of Green card holders are in the particular segment. Thus, 10.6% of all Green card holders are 18–24 years old. The number in column C indicates the percentage in the segment who are Green card holders; thus, 2.5% of all 18- to 24-year-old adults hold the Green card. An important column is labeled "Index." This gives the relative incidence of Green card holders in the segment compared to the overall percentage holding the Green card. In this case, because 3.1% of all adults hold the card (the top number in column C) and 2.5% of 18- to 24-year-old adults hold the card, the index is 2.5/3.1 multiplied by 100, or 82. A quick glance in the "Index" column shows which segments have a disproportionately greater tendency to hold a card than the overall U.S. population does for that card. Thus, good segments for the Green card are adults who graduated college (Index = 213), 45- to 54-year-old adults (Index = 131), people holding professional and executive jobs (Index = 199 and 203, respectively), those with a household income of $75,000 or more (Index = 227), and people who live in New England (Index = 182). To contrast, the Discover card indexes tend to be more evenly distributed over the categories, indicating that its holders come from a wider variety of demographic groups and geographic locations. ◆

A second kind of syndicated data links together census data and purchasing data to form psychographic-like segments. Perhaps the best known of these systems is Claritas's PRIZM system. Claritas analyzes several dozen demographic variables, including household composition, income, employment, education, ethnicity, and housing, and has developed 62 separate clusters each with a distinctive name that describes its members. They include the following:

- Blue-Blood Estates: America's wealthiest suburbs, populated by upper-upper-class executives, mainly white.

Table 5–4 MRI Credit Card Data

Base: Adults	Total U.S. '000	American Express Green				Discover				Visa Regular/Classic			
		A '000	B % Down	C % Across	D Index	A '000	B % Down	C % Across	D Index	A '000	B % Down	C % Across	D Index
All adults	191,663	5,864	100.0	3.1	100	30,128	100.0	15.7	100	49,544	100.0	25.8	100
Men	91,780	3,265	55.7	3.6	116	14,766	49.0	16.1	102	25,536	51.5	27.8	108
Women	99,882	2,599	44.3	2.6	85	15,362	51.0	15.4	98	24,008	48.5	24.0	93
Household heads	117,261	3,902	66.5	3.3	109	17,801	59.1	15.2	97	31,322	63.2	26.7	103
Homemakers	118,895	3,442	58.7	2.9	95	18,594	61.7	15.6	99	29,287	59.1	24.6	95
Graduated college	39,600	2,577	43.9	6.5	213	8,632	28.6	21.8	139	13,827	27.9	34.9	135
Attended college	51,083	1,705	29.1	3.3	109	8,843	29.4	17.3	110	15,047	30.4	29.5	114
Graduated high school	64,414	1,204	20.5	1.9	61	9,937	33.0	15.4	98	15,539	31.4	24.1	93
Did not graduate high school	36,567	*379	6.5	1.0	34	2,717	9.0	7.4	47	5,130	10.4	14.0	54
18–24	24,848	624	10.6	2.5	82	2,335	7.8	9.4	60	5,679	11.5	22.9	88
25–34	42,530	1,404	23.9	3.3	108	6,894	22.9	16.2	103	10,954	22.1	25.8	100
35–44	41,652	1,539	26.2	3.7	121	7,497	24.9	18.0	114	12,232	24.7	29.4	114
45–54	29,737	1,187	20.2	4.0	131	5,827	19.3	19.6	125	8,510	17.2	28.6	111
55–64	21,537	639	10.9	3.0	97	4,011	13.3	18.6	118	5,980	12.1	27.8	107
65 or over	31,359	471	8.0	1.5	49	3,564	11.8	11.4	72	6,190	12.5	19.7	76
18–34	67,378	2,028	34.6	3.0	98	9,229	30.6	13.7	87	16,633	33.6	24.7	95
18–49	125,542	4,207	71.7	3.4	110	20,199	67.0	16.1	102	33,569	67.8	26.7	103
25–54	113,920	4,130	70.4	3.6	118	20,218	67.1	17.7	113	31,696	64.0	27.8	108
Employed full time	104,602	4,370	74.5	4.2	137	19,336	64.2	18.5	118	32,199	65.0	30.8	119
Part time	18,438	535	9.1	2.9	95	3,286	10.9	17.8	113	4,976	10.0	27.0	104
Sole wage earner	33,616	1,274	21.7	3.8	124	5,450	18.1	16.2	103	9,625	19.4	28.6	111
Not employed	68,622	960	16.4	1.4	46	7,506	24.9	10.9	70	12,370	25.0	18.0	70
Professional	18,645	1,138	19.4	6.1	199	4,034	13.4	21.6	138	6,720	13.6	36.0	139
Executive/Admin./Managerial	17,299	1,075	18.3	6.2	203	3,985	13.2	23.0	147	6,162	12.4	35.6	138
Clerical/Sales/Technical	36,128	1,506	25.7	4.2	136	7,179	23.8	19.9	126	10,722	21.6	29.7	115
Precision/Crafts/Repair	13,592	347	5.9	2.6	84	2,220	7.4	16.3	104	4,154	8.4	30.6	118
Other employed	37,376	838	14.3	2.2	73	5,204	17.3	13.9	89	9,416	19.0	25.2	97
H/D income $75,000 or more	30,884	2,141	36.5	6.9	227	6,470	21.5	20.9	133	10,218	20.6	33.1	128
$60,000 - 74,999	18,628	977	16.7	5.2	171	4,006	13.3	21.5	137	6,546	13.2	35.1	136
$50,000 - 59,999	17,867	759	12.9	4.2	139	3,843	12.8	21.5	137	5,709	11.5	32.0	124
$40,000 - 49,999	21,774	525	9.0	2.4	79	4,496	14.9	20.6	131	6,688	13.5	30.7	119
$30,000 - 39,999	26,273	749	12.8	2.9	93	4,223	14.0	16.1	102	7,254	14.6	27.6	107
$20,000 - 29,999	29,109	399	6.8	1.4	45	3,796	12.6	13.0	83	6,549	13.2	22.5	87
$10,000 - 19,999	28,635	*254	4.3	0.9	29	2,310	7.7	8.1	51	4,735	9.6	16.5	64
Less than $10,000	18,491	*61	1.0	0.3	11	984	3.3	5.3	34	1,845	3.7	10.0	39

Census region: North East	39,523	1,919	32.7	4.9	159	7,346	24.4	18.6	118	10,462	21.1	26.5	102
North Central	45,204	892	15.2	2.0	65	8,830	29.3	19.5	124	13,350	26.9	29.5	114
South	66,230	1,936	33.0	2.9	96	8,182	27.2	12.4	79	13,830	27.9	20.9	81
West	40,706	1,117	19.0	2.7	90	5,770	19.2	14.2	90	11,901	24.0	29.2	113
Marketing reg.: New England	10,306	574	9.8	5.6	182	1,970	6.5	19.1	122	2,865	5.8	27.8	108
Middle Atlantic	33,365	1,420	24.2	4.3	139	5,828	19.3	17.5	111	8,465	17.1	25.4	98
East Central	25,685	*410	7.0	1.6	52	4,764	15.8	18.5	118	7,274	14.7	28.3	110
West Central	29,116	654	11.1	2.2	73	5,412	18.0	18.6	118	8,738	17.6	30.0	116
South East	36,576	842	14.4	2.3	75	3,923	13.0	10.7	68	7,252	14.6	19.8	77
South West	20,968	946	16.1	4.5	148	3,102	10.3	14.8	94	4,594	9.3	21.9	85
Pacific	35,648	1,017	17.3	2.9	93	5,129	17.0	14.4	92	10,357	20.9	29.1	112
County size A	78,926	3,688	62.9	4.7	153	13,403	44.5	17.0	108	21,229	42.8	26.9	104
County size B	57,057	1,479	25.2	2.6	85	9,408	31.2	16.5	105	15,859	32.0	27.8	108
County size C	27,313	*413	7.0	1.5	49	4,052	13.5	14.8	94	5,953	12.0	21.8	84
County size D	28,367	*285	4.9	1.0	33	3,264	10.8	11.5	73	6,503	13.1	22.9	89
MSA central city	61,417	2,000	34.1	3.3	106	9,299	30.9	15.1	96	16,351	33.0	26.6	103
MSA suburban	92,855	3,492	59.6	3.8	123	16,548	54.9	17.8	113	24,898	50.3	26.8	104
Non-MSA	37,391	*372	6.3	1.0	33	4,281	14.2	11.4	73	8,295	16.7	22.2	86
Single	42,982	1,418	24.2	3.3	108	5,028	16.7	11.7	74	9,994	20.2	23.3	90
Married	112,978	3,658	62.4	3.2	106	20,741	68.8	18.4	117	32,214	65.0	28.5	110
Other	35,703	788	13.4	2.2	72	4,358	14.5	12.2	78	7,337	14.8	20.5	79
Parents	67,202	2,042	34.8	3.0	99	10,753	35.7	16.0	102	17,671	35.7	26.3	102
Working parents	51,532	1,903	32.5	3.7	121	9,006	29.9	17.5	111	15,321	30.9	29.7	115
Household size: 1 person	24,108	600	10.2	2.5	81	2,862	9.5	11.9	76	5,393	10.9	22.4	87
2 persons	61,450	1,879	32.0	3.1	100	10,549	35.0	17.2	109	16,569	33.4	27.0	104
3 or more	106,105	3,385	57.7	3.2	104	16,717	55.5	15.8	100	27,583	55.7	26.0	101
Any child in household	79,549	2,290	39.0	2.9	94	12,197	40.5	15.3	98	20,148	40.7	25.3	98
Under 2 years	15,302	*362	6.2	2.4	77	2,234	7.4	14.6	93	3,382	6.8	22.1	85
2–5 years	31,074	889	15.2	2.9	94	4,365	14.5	14.0	89	7,659	15.5	24.6	95
6–11 years	35,450	997	17.0	2.8	92	5,371	17.8	15.2	96	9,094	18.4	25.7	99
12–17 years	35,996	1,107	18.9	3.3	101	5,702	18.9	15.8	101	9,103	18.4	25.3	98
White	162,526	5,339	91.0	3.3	107	27,944	92.8	17.2	109	45,514	91.9	28.0	108
Black	21,957	*391	6.7	1.8	58	1,305	4.3	5.9	38	2,475	5.0	11.3	44
Spanish speaking	14,144	*327	5.6	2.3	75	1,683	5.6	11.9	76	3,250	6.6	23.0	89
Home owned	127,498	4,337	74.0	3.4	111	22,824	75.8	17.9	114	36,344	73.4	28.5	110

*Indicates small sample size.

Source: Mediamark Research, Inc.

- Gray Collars: Inner suburbs populated by aging couples with high-school educations who work in blue-collar jobs. These are concentrated in the Great Lakes industrial region.
- Hard Scrabble: The country's poorest areas, from Appalachia to the Colorado Rockies and from the Texas border to the Dakotas. Most are white and aging and many have only a grade-school education.

What is interesting is how the groups vary in terms of consumption of various products and services. For example, people in the Blue-Blood Estates group are more than six times as likely to buy imported beer than those in the Hard Scrabble group. Because the data are known by ZIP codes (no individual household data are used), PRIZM can be very useful for a direct mail campaign. Similar services are offered by Equifax's MicroVision, Strategic Mapping's ClusterPLUS 2000, and a joint product between SRI International and Market Statistics called GeoVALS, which develops geographic maps of the locations of the members of the different VALS2 groups.

Club Med could use such services in the following way. The company could take the demographic data it already collects about its customers and overlay it onto, say, the PRIZM clusters. Because PRIZM clusters are identified by ZIP codes, very targeted direct mail catalogs can be constructed and mailed to appropriate households. For example, urban singles with high disposable income levels can be mailed brochures highlighting only the sites most appealing to singles.

It should be noted that the syndicated research studies can show only what has happened in the past. It may be inaccurate to extrapolate from these data to the potential of a particular segment because the segments may reflect only historical marketing patterns of the companies in the market. For example, the fact that Table 5–4 shows disproportionately high Green card ownership in the New England region may only reflect American Express's marketing efforts that have targeted that area. Primary research is more capable of determining potential by asking appropriate questions that probe possible future behavior.

Marketing Research Implications: Developing Target Markets

Market segmentation is an intuitively appealing process; it makes a great deal of sense to try to find different segments of the market that are more interested in your product than others or develop products specifically for those segments. At the same time, given the myriad ways of segmenting markets, the task of determining which segments are better than others is daunting. This is the job of determining on which segments you should focus—the selection of target markets (see the complete marketing strategy diagram). Selecting target markets moves segmentation away from the purely descriptive (i.e., developing what are called buyer/nonbuyer profiles) to the strategic aspects of marketing in which marketing managers pursue particular groups of customers.

One criterion that should always be applied is parsimony. Although having a large number of segments sounds appealing because you can capture most of the differences between customers, it is expensive and inefficient to pursue too many segments. If the segments are different in terms of their behavior toward your product and they should receive different levels of marketing, a budget stretched over too many segments results in an insufficient concentration of resources in any one segment. It is very expensive to develop advertising and promotion programs for a large number of different target audiences.

Although it is not possible to generalize about the appropriate number of segments to pursue, the following criteria can be applied to a particular scheme or way to segment the market:

- Does the segmentation scheme explain differences in purchasing behavior or some other related variable (e.g., membership in different loyalty groups)? The basic issue to explore is whether the segmentation variable (say, income) explains purchasing behavior better than another variable (say, VALS2 groups). This can be done by considering the behavior as a dependent variable and the segmentation variables as independent variables in a framework like the following:

$$\text{Behavior} = f \text{ (segmentation variables)}$$

Several statistical approaches can be used to determine the strength (in a statistical sense) of the relationship between the variables and purchasing behavior. The marketing manager could then choose that variable (e.g., income) and particular levels of that variable (e.g., households earning $75,000 or more per year) that have the strongest association with the behavioral variable of interest.

For example, the MRI data shown in Table 5–4 can be analyzed using an "eyeball" approach. Again using the American Express Green card owners as an illustration, the behavioral or dependent variable of interest is simply ownership versus nonownership. The independent variables are the demographics on the left side of the table. The variables that explain the most variance in ownership are those that have the greatest variation in their index numbers.[11] Thus, on a judgmental basis, the four most useful variables appear to be education level, occupation, income, and geography. You probably would also want to compare these variables to others, such as psychographics, which would be collected using another method.

- What is the segment size? It is clear that segmenting the market into too many groups results in some that are too small to be economically viable. Thus, one criterion for a particular scheme or level of a variable is whether it is of sufficient size in terms of number of customers, sales revenue, or potential profit to be worth targeting.
- What is the segment's growth rate? A marketing manager might prefer growth, indicating future revenues, over current size.
- Are any particular environmental factors associated with the segment? This would include factors such as regulatory, social, cultural, economic, or other exogenous factors. For example, targeting health-conscious consumers might make sense if there is a particular health boom in the country to which the product or service is being marketed. An industrial products company might not consider marketing to a government segment if the marketing manager thinks that there is too much bureaucracy involved with getting orders or becoming a supplier places too many constraints on them (e.g., pricing, other countries with which they can do business).
- What is your potential competitive position? You might choose to ignore a lucrative segment if a competitor is well entrenched or if you decide that you cannot offer a product that has a competitive advantage over what is already being offered.

Therefore, the marketing manager's job is to not only develop alternative segmentation schemes but to also determine which of a large number of alternatives are most appropriate for the product or service.

◆ Illustration: Harley Davidson

One of the true success stories in American business is the motorcycle manufacturer Harley Davidson.[12] Since 1990, sales of Harley Davidson motorcycles and parts and accessories have increased 15% per year and are constrained by production capacity. Even with cash, the purchaser of a new Harley may have to wait up to 2 years to take delivery. Although the motorcycles cost about $15,000 new, customers who have their orders in the queue can sell their undelivered motorcycles for $20,000.

This was not always the case. The company was very successful from its beginnings in 1903 as a manufacturer of large, heavy motorcycles until the late 1950s. When Honda introduced its small motorcycles in the United States in 1959, all other manufacturers including Harley were caught napping because they believed that the fad for such small motorcycles would be short-lived. Harley was acquired by several firms that sought to increase its share by expanding production. However, they had significant quality control problems and their share of the heavyweight bike segment declined from 80% in 1973 to around 30% in 1980. The company was able to right itself after senior management purchased it from its last owner, AMF.

Harley's success resulted from a confluence of environmental changes in the United States and around the world. Harleys are seen as more than just motorcycles. They represent America, Hollywood, masculinity, and a number of other icons. In addition, with the increased number of affluent Baby Boomers, there are more than enough customers for the product. The company has successfully created brand loyalty through its image and its Harley Owners' Groups (HOGS).

Because of the current excess demand for its products, Harley's problem is not identifying new market segments to pursue for further growth. The company has done an excellent job of focusing its products at the heavyweight end of the market. However, the company, like many, is very interested in understanding its existing customer base in order to develop new services such as membership programs and ancillary merchandise. The image of the typical Harley owner is a hard-core gang biker. If the customer base is more diverse, then certain programs tailored to such a group would not appeal to all owners. Increased competition has also made maintaining and building the Harley image more important.

In 1994, a survey was administered to a national U.S. sample of registered owners. Of 2,500 questionnaires mailed, 761 responses were obtained, for a return rate of 30.4%. This is a fairly high response rate for a mail survey, indicating that nonresponse bias is likely to be low. The questionnaire included the following:

- 72 motorcycle lifestyle statements (a 1–5 scale, from not at all descriptive to extremely descriptive)
- 78 general lifestyle statements (same scale)
- 33 behavioral questions measuring frequency of participating in various activities as well as magazine readership and television viewing (1–5 scale, from not at all to extremely often)
- Demographics

Table 5–5 Harley Davidson Segmentation Study/ Lifestyle Factors

At-One-Ness	Passenger Preference
Hard Core	In the Dirt
Always in the Saddle	Wear Leathers
Trick Bike Modifications	Solitary Rider
Harley Zeal	Time Poor Rider
Ride Fast and Hard	

Source: William R. Swinyard (1996), "The hard core and zen riders of Harley Davidson: a market-driven segmentation analysis," *Journal of Targeting, Measurement and Analysis for Marketing*, 4 (June), pp. 337–362.

The responses to the lifestyle questions were subjected to a multivariate statistical approach called **factor analysis,** which reduces the 72 questions (in the case of the motorcycle lifestyle questions) to a fewer underlying factors based on the correlations of the responses to the questions. For example, two of the questions were as follows:

"I would like to do 'gang' biker things."
"Sometimes I feel like an outlaw."

One would expect that the responses to these two questions on the 1–5 scale would be similar across respondents. Thus, they do not measure different, independent underlying traits but really one. The analysis of the 72 questions revealed 11 different underlying lifestyle dimensions; these are shown in Table 5–5.

A score was created for each respondent based on his or her answers to the questions in the 11 dimensions. Using another statistical method, cluster analysis, and the scores on the 11 dimensions, the respondents were grouped into six owner segments based on similarities of their scores on the dimensions. These are shown in Table 5–6. The averages of the demographic variables for each segment are shown in Table 5–7.

Table 5–6 Harley Davidson Segmentation Scheme

Psychographic Segments

Tour Gliders
I like long-distance touring bikes.
I use my bike for touring.
My bike is made more for comfort than for speed.
I love to ride long distances. To me, 500 miles is a short trip.
I like bikes with plastic farings and engine covers.

Dream Riders
Most of the time, my motorcycle is just parked.
I like wearing a helmet when I ride.
I don't know many other people who ride motorcycles.
My bike is pretty much stock.
I use my bike mainly for short trips around town.

Hard Core
Some people would call me and my friends "outlaws."
I have spent lots on speed modifications for my bike.
Sometimes I feel like an "outlaw."
Some people would call me a "dirty biker."
I think it's true that "real men" wear black.

Hog Heaven
When I'm on my bike, people seem to be admiring me.
I really believe that cars are confining, like a cage.
Women admire my motorcycle.
When I ride I feel like an Old Wild West cowboy.
I feel close to other motorcyclists I see on the road.

Zen Riders
I like dirt bikes.
When I'm on my bike, people seem to be admiring me.
I like the attention I get when I'm on my bike.
Most of the time, my motorcycle is just parked.
I get excited about motocross or scrambling.

Live to Ride
I love to ride long distances. To me, 500 miles is a short trip.
Motorcycles are a total lifestyle to me.
Riding, to me, is often a magical experience.
It's true that I live to ride and ride to live.
My bike is everything to me.

Table 5–7 Harley Davidson Segmentation Scheme

Segment Descriptor and Behavioral Variables

Characteristic	Tour Gliders	Dream Riders	Hard Core	Hog Heaven	Zen Riders	Live to Ride
Relative size of segment	13.8%	39.8%	9.7%	8.7%	20.3%	7.6%
Summary of demographics						
Average owner age	42.6	42.9	36.2	39.2	36.9	36.6
Sex male	93.8%	95.1%	93.5%	85.4%	94.7%	91.7%
Married	60.0%	68.5%	51.1%	56.1%	75.0%	58.3%
Number of children at home	1.3	1.2	1.0	1.2	1.2	1.2
Education: college graduate	15.4%	24.7%	8.7%	7.3%	19.8%	25.0%
Income of $50,000 and over						
Personal	29.7%	30.2%	4.4%	31.7%	26.3%	25.0%
Household	50.8%	52.0%	26.6%	41.0%	55.4%	55.5%
Average Income						
Personal	$40,438	$40,087	$27,389	$34,744	$38,816	$33,667
Household	$46,563	$46,500	$34,944	$40,397	$47,435	$44,222
Occupation: professional/managerial	21.5%	30.1%	0.0%	26.8%	19.8%	29.4%
Summary of motorcycle ownership						
Motorcycle is 1991 or newer	24.6%	30.7%	7.3%	22.0%	28.7%	15.2%
Owned motorcycle under 2 years	16.7%	22.7%	10.3%	35.5%	30.4%	30.3%
Bought motorcycle new	40.0%	50.0%	15.2%	45.0%	33.0%	55.9%
Model year of principal Harley	1985.9	1985.8	1980.5	1986.2	1983.6	1985.7
This is their first motorcycle	1.5%	9.0%	15.9%	19.5%	9.4%	2.8%
No. of motorcycles owned	9.06	5.34	6.3	6.82	5.7	9.77
No. of Harleys owned	4.74	1.63	2.85	2.13	1.44	2.12
Money spent on motorcycle for						
Purchase of motorcycle	$9,048	$7,460	$5,082	$6,631	$6,966	$8,976
Parts/accessories this year	$690	$322	$1,260	$321	$767	$860
Parts/accessories in total	$1,571	$1,426	$3,233	$2,419	$1,734	$2,483
Estimated value of motorcycle today	$10,066	$8,414	$8,062	$8,591	$8,827	$10,342
Riding per year						
Number of miles	7,351	3,675	7,099	5,051	4,169	9,662
Number of days	188	109	187	148	112	214
Number riding years	24.1	20.2	16.5	16.9	18	17.7
Type of motorcycle they ride						
Touring	39.0%	16.4%	0.0%	7.9%	12.6%	31.3%
Full dress	18.6%	18.6%	11.4%	10.5%	14.9%	18.9%
Cruiser	23.8%	26.0%	36.4%	29.0%	28.7%	31.3%
Sportster	5.1%	30.5%	29.5%	52.6%	35.6%	0.0%
Other type	13.6%	8.5%	22.7%	0.0%	8.0%	18.8%

As can be seen, the six segments are quite different from each other, both psychographically and demographically:

- Tour Gliders: 14% of the sample, they like to use their bikes for long trips. Compared to the other segments, they are somewhat older, more likely to be married, upper income, more professional, and veteran motorcycle owners, particularly Harleys.
- Hard Core: These are the archetypal Harley owners. Perhaps surprisingly, they are only 9.7% of the sample. Compared to the others, they are younger, less likely to be

married, less educated, lower income, and own an older motorcycle. These are the outlaws (or people who would like to feel that way).

- Zen Riders: To these 20%, riding a motorcycle is a spiritual experience. They are young, most likely to be married, educated, upper income, and tend to use their bikes less than others.

From the company's standpoint, the behavioral data in Table 5–7 are particularly interesting. Note the differences in the money spent on parts and accessories, the model of bike owned, and the percentage who bought their motorcycle new. The survey gives the company a very good idea about which group to target for different kinds of products and services. For example, the Hard Core and Zen Riders are the poorest targets for upgrading to new motorcycles because they have the lowest incidence of new purchases. The best target for new bikes is the Dream Rider segment because they have a very high incidence of buying new models and are the largest segment (40% of the sample). However, the Hard Core segment spends by far the most on accessories and parts (although it is a small group).

Thus, as we discussed in the section on developing target markets, this illustration highlights the need to consider a variety of factors in determining which segments to target for various products. Although we discussed briefly the tradeoff between the size of the segment and the potential purchasing power, measured by the different segments' past behavior, characteristics such as segment growth and degree of competition must also be taken into consideration. In addition, it has been assumed that the psychographic approach shown is the best way to segment the market. As we noted earlier, it is important to consider a variety of segmentation schemes and compare them on their differential abilities to explain past behavior and to satisfy the other criteria for a good target segment.   ◆

WHY DO CONSUMERS BUY?

As we noted at the beginning of this chapter, a customer analysis also must address the question, "Why do customers buy the product or service?" A simplified model of the steps in the purchase process for any kind of product or service is shown in Fig. 5–6.[13] The first step in any kind of purchasing behavior is need recognition, or reasons why people make purchases (we explore the other steps in Fig. 5–6 later in this chapter). A consumer realizes that his car is old and worn out and realizes that it is more economical to purchase a new one than to continue to repair the old one. Needs can be recognized by the potential customer, or someone else—a friend, a salesperson—can make the customer more aware of the need.[14]

Consider the famous hierarchy of needs posited by Abraham Maslow.[15] He theorized five ordered levels of human needs:

- Physiological: basic human needs such as food, sleep, and water
- Safety: physical safety from injury, job security, and financial security
- Social: friendship, affection, acceptance by reference groups
- Ego: success, self-esteem, prestige
- Self-actualization: achieving one's potential, self-fulfillment

These are obviously most relevant to consumer products and services. A product could be marketed to satisfy several of the needs simultaneously. For example, in the automobile illustration, the consumer may seek a sporty car that satisfies both a transportation and an ego need.

Although Maslow's hierarchy is an interesting way to characterize why people buy products, it is not very specific and does not describe why most industrial or business-to-business purchases are made. A better way to think about what motivates people to purchase

Figure 5–6

Simplified Customer
Behavior Model

Source: William D. Wells and
David Prensky (1996),
Consumer Behavior (New
York: Wiley).

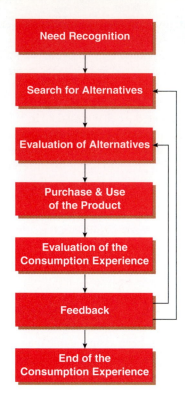

products and services is to think of them as offering not physical attributes but benefits, as we discussed in Chapter 1. That is, the sole reason for a consumer to purchase is to obtain the benefits the purchase delivers.

Thus, one of the jobs of the marketing manager is to translate characteristics into product benefits. This can be done using managerial judgment or marketing research. In particular, focus groups that permit depth research (e.g., clinical focus groups, as discussed in Chapter 4) are useful because they encourage customers to develop lists of benefits they obtain from products. However, surveys or other marketing research methods can also be used.

The Minute Rice advertisement shown in Fig. 5–7 is a good example of communications focusing on product benefits rather than features. There is no mention of product attributes (fluffiness, texture, flavor, calories). Only two key attributes of the product are mentioned: speed of preparation (perfect rice in 5 minutes) and flexibility (can be used in a variety of meals). The reasons for buying the product are simple, direct, and clear. Thus, benefits are useful as a communication device that addresses the reasons customers want to buy the product. Again, consumers do not buy product features; they buy products and services for the benefits they provide.

It is particularly important to develop an analysis of benefits by market segment. The framework shown in Table 5–8 is useful for conceptualizing how benefits sought can vary between market segments. The basic approach is to form a matrix with a segment-by-benefit format.

Consider British recreational vehicle manufacturer Land Rover.[16] Table 5–8 shows their approach to segmenting the U.S. market by demographic variables and nine benefits. The numbers in the table represent mean importance ratings[17] on a five-point scale where 1 = not at all important and 5 = extremely important (differences of .3 or greater are significant at the 95% level). The company first established

Table 5–8 Sport Utility Vehicles

Benefits by Segment

| | Key Demographic Groups | | | | | | | |
| | Age | | Gender | | Kids | | Household Income | |
	Under 40	Over 40	Males	Females	Kids	No Kids	<$100,000	>$100,000
Quality	4.4	4.5	4.4	4.5	4.5	4.4	4.5	4.4
Safety	4.2	4.4	4.1	4.5	4.4	4.3	4.3	4.4
Performance	4.2	4.2	4.2	4.3	4.2	4.2	4.2	4.2
Off-road capability	4.2	4.0	4.0	4.1	4.0	4.1	4.0	4.1
Aesthetics	4.1	4.0	4.0	4.1	4.0	4.1	4.0	4.2
Comfort/convenience	4.0	4.1	3.9	4.2	4.1	3.8	4.0	4.0
Service factors	4.0	4.0	4.0	4.3	4.0	4.0	4.0	3.9
Economics	4.0	4.0	3.8	4.1	4.3	3.9	4.0	3.4
Status/image	3.0	2.8	2.8	2.9	2.9	2.7	2.9	3.2

Numbers shown represent mean importance ratings as measured on five-point scale where 1 = not at all important and 5 = extremely important.

This ad for Rembrandt's Dazzling White toothpaste and bleaching gel clearly appeals to the consumer's basic motive for buying such a product: It claims to whiten teeth dramatically. Rather than explaining what product features support this claim (e.g., a special formula), this ad campaign focuses on the benefits of the product for the consumer. (Copyright DEN-MAT CORP.)

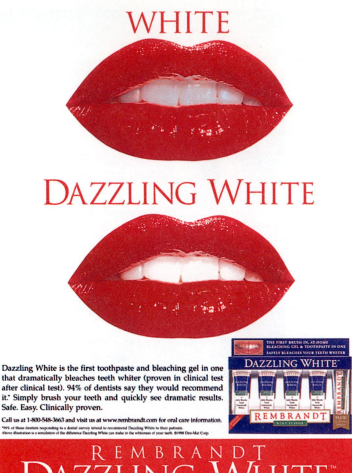

(using a marketing research consulting firm) that these were the key benefits used by sport utility vehicle (SUV) customers in evaluating different brands. Although many of the differences are not significant, it is clear that for all the segments, product quality (durability, manufacturer reputation, reliability) is the most important benefit and status/image the least. In addition, safety tends to rate higher than the other benefits. Some notable differences between segment levels are that women value safety, comfort/convenience, service, and economics (total cost of ownership) more than men; survey respondents with children rated comfort/convenience and economics higher than those without children; and households with income below $100,000 rated economics higher and status/image lower than households with income above $100,000. ◆

It is important for marketing managers to "benefitize" their products and services to appeal to the basic motives for making purchases. In addition, the analysis of customer benefits should be done at the market segment level so products and communication programs can be tailored to segment needs.

HOW DO CONSUMERS MAKE PURCHASE DECISIONS?

Referring back to the beginning of this chapter, the third key question that a marketing manager must ask in performing a customer analysis is "How do customers make their purchase decisions?" In this section, we explore some of the ways in which purchasing decisions are made.

Search for Alternatives

As Fig. 5–6 shows, following the need recognition stage of the buying process, the customer is hypothesized to search for alternative products that deliver the desired benefits. In general, customers use two sources of information: internal and external.

Internal sources of information are those that are retrieved from memory. Examples are as follows:

- Past experiences with products
- Past conversations with experts
- Old magazine articles such as those in *Consumer Reports*

Any source of information that has already been obtained and is recalled is an internal source.

New sources of information that the customer obtains from the environment after establishing the need are considered external sources of information. For example, after establishing the need to take a vacation, a consumer will not only retrieve information from memory such as the level of satisfaction with other places she has visited, but may also seek out or be exposed to the following:

- Advice from a travel agent
- Articles in travel magazines
- Recommendations from friends and relatives
- Advertisements

Thus, there is overlap between internal and external sources; the difference is in the timing of the receipt of information.

Although it is clear that many external sources of information are provided by the marketing manager, it should not be assumed that you cannot affect internal or other external sources of information such as recommendations. Long-term memory can be stimulated by any kind of information. For example, advertisements for a particular personal computer brand can emphasize the historical reliability and customer service record of the company, which not only provides external information to new buyers or those who might switch from another brand but can also stimulate positive associations for a buyer who already has the brand. Word-of-mouth recommendations can also be stimulated both personally (by giving incentives to old customers to recommend and sign up new customers) and electronically (through user groups or other Internet-based discussions).

It is difficult to predict how much information search will occur. Economic theory predicts that rational customers will collect information only to the point at which the marginal benefit of obtaining the information in terms of incremental value to making a choice equals the marginal cost. However, because much of the information in the environment can be collected at very low cost (e.g., the passive viewing of a television commercial), economic theory is not very predictive in this case. The amount of information collected will vary by some variables that you would expect: expertise in a product category, how recently a purchase was made, and the importance of the purchase to the customer. Thus, the information search will be more extensive for expensive products and services that are purchased infrequently, such as durables (TVs, video cameras, automobiles), significant long-term investments (stocks, satellite TV dishes and service), and capital investments made by companies (copying machines, mainframe computers, factory automation software).

What Happens Next?

As a result of the search for alternatives through internal and external information sources, customers form three different sets of options:

- The **evoked or consideration set.** This is the set of products from which the customer will choose to purchase. Although the brands in the set may have different underlying probabilities of being chosen, all of the brands have at least a nonzero probability.
- The **inert set.** This is the set of products that the customer has no intention of buying or has no information about. These brands have a zero probability of being chosen.
- The **purchase set.** This is the set of products the customer has actually chosen within a specified period of time.

Clearly, although being in many purchase sets is the best situation of all, before purchase can even occur, the marketing manager must get the product into as many evoked or consideration sets as possible (i.e., move the product from the inert set to active consideration). For example, Club Med's marketing managers must ensure that when people are thinking of a vacation, they include Club Med in the set of options they are considering. For new products and those with low awareness (i.e., those in most consumers' inert sets), the manager must devote a large portion of the marketing budget to making customers aware that the product exists. When awareness is not low, the problem is probably related to performance, quality, or image.

Primary data collection will inform you about the status of your product in these sets. One approach is to do pure awareness research. This can be done using aided or unaided recall. In the latter case, the researcher simply asks the respondent to list any brands he or she has heard of in the target product category. With aided recall, the respondent is given a list from which to choose brands. However, this kind of research may not always be a good guide to how many evoked sets contain your brand because the feeling about the brand could be negative rather than positive. As a result, the questionnaire may contain more direct questions about whether the respondent would consider buying the brand or the company's product on a subsequent purchase occasion.

It is interesting to note that information collected about the purchase set is only partial information because it does not contain any indication about other brands or options considered. For frequently purchased products, scanner panel data provide information about the purchase set but not the evoked/consideration set. It is useful to have both kinds of information because the evoked set is a better indication of potential competition than the purchase set, particularly if the latter demonstrates considerable brand loyalty.

Evaluating Options in the Consideration Set

Following the purchase process shown in Fig. 5–6 and logic, the next task facing the customer is to make a choice from the evoked set.[18] A way to conceptualize this part of the decision-making process is to consider that all products and services can be decomposed into their attributes or benefits (hereafter simply called attributes) that customers want to obtain by purchasing the product. For example, we can use the list in the left column of Table 5–8 to generate the set of attributes customers of SUVs use to choose among brands. This forms the basis for a popular model of decision-making called the **multiattribute model.**

In order to understand how customers develop choices from the evoked set using this model, two kinds of information are required. First, we require information about how useful or important each attribute is to the customer in making a brand choice, or how important each attribute is relative to the others. These are called importance weights or importance rankings. The second kind of information required is how customers perceive the brands in the evoked set in terms of their attributes.

The model raises four key questions:

- Which attributes do customers use to define a product?
- How do we determine how much of each attribute a brand possesses?
- How are the importance weights determined?
- How do customers combine the information from the previous two questions to make choices?

The marketing manager must first determine the set of attributes customers use in making purchase decisions. This can be done using managerial judgment (not recommended because of the bias introduced), focus groups, or more systematic survey research. In this stage of the research, the questions asked are usually open-ended to elicit from the customers or potential customers the attributes they consider for purchasing brands in the category.

Assuming that the manager has collected the set of attributes used, the second question to be addressed is how customers perceive the different brands on these attributes. It is critical that to understand how customers make purchasing decisions, you must appreciate the differences between their perceptions and reality (i.e., the "true" values of the attributes for each brand): *the former drive purchasing behavior, not the latter*. For example, perhaps Consumer's Union or some government agency has determined that the Chevy Blazer is the safest SUV on the market. Although this may be the reality, consumers in the market for an SUV may believe that the Jeep Cherokee is the safest, based on information from advertising, friends, or other external or internal sources.

How do you measure these perceptions? The most common way is to ask a sample of customers questions of the following type:[19] "Please rate the described brands on the following set of characteristics on a 1–10 scale, where 1 is poor and 10 is excellent."

The results of this survey for a sample of SUV customers are shown in Table 5–9 for eight of the nine attributes used in Table 5–8 (the Land Rover Defender was not yet introduced at the time of the survey). As can be seen, there are substantial differences in the average perceptions of the SUV brands across the eight attributes. For example, the Kia Sportage rates only 4.5 in quality, whereas the Ford Explorer rates 7.4. In addition, it would be helpful to break this down by the segments used in Table 5–8, such as age and gender. An extremely helpful picture of the relative position of the Land Rover Discovery is shown in Fig. 5–8. This figure breaks down the eight major attributes into their components, giving the manager a very quick and useful view of the relative perceptual advantages and disadvantages. Compared to the average SUV, the Discovery is perceived to be high in quality and off-road capabilities but low in aesthetics (particularly styling) and economics.

The importance weights are determined in a similar fashion. For example, using a survey approach, we can ask the following question: "Please rate the following attributes on a 1–7 scale, where 1 is very unimportant and 7 is very important in terms of how important each attribute is to you in making a decision about which sport utility vehicle to purchase." Alternatively, respondents could be asked to simply rank order the nine attributes shown in Table 5–8 from most to least important. As shown in the table, this particular study used a five-point scale. ◆

Table 5–9 Sport Utility Vehicles

Perceptions

	Quality	Safety	Perfor-mance	Off-Road Capability	Aesthetics	Comfort/Convenience	Economics	Status/Image
Total all makes	6.7	6.8	6.5	6.7	6.8	6.7	5.8	5.9
Chevy Blazer Full-Size	6.7	7.1	6.7	7.2	6.8	7.1	5.5	5.9
Chevy Blazer S-10	6.7	6.9	6.7	6.8	7.0	7.0	5.9	5.9
Ford Bronco	6.6	6.9	6.4	6.9	6.5	6.7	5.6	5.4
Ford Explorer	7.4	7.4	7.1	7.1	7.5	7.6	6.1	6.8
Geo Tracker	5.4	5.0	5.2	4.5	6.1	5.0	6.3	3.8
GMC Jimmy	6.5	6.8	6.5	6.7	6.8	6.7	5.8	5.7
GMC Yukon	6.4	6.7	6.2	6.8	6.5	6.6	5.3	5.9
Honda Passport	7.1	6.7	6.6	6.3	7.1	6.8	5.9	6.3
Isuzu Rodeo	6.4	6.5	6.1	6.0	6.7	6.3	5.9	5.2
Isuzu Trooper	6.3	6.4	6.1	6.1	6.2	6.5	5.8	5.3
Jeep Wrangler	6.4	6.5	6.0	6.8	6.8	5.7	5.8	4.6
Jeep Cherokee	7.1	7.3	6.9	7.1	7.2	7.3	6.0	6.4
Jeep Grand Cherokee	7.2	7.4	7.2	7.2	7.5	7.5	5.6	7.4
Kia Sportage	4.5	4.5	4.3	4.3	5.2	4.8	5.2	3.5
Land Rover Defender	NA	NA	NA	NA	NA	NA	NA	NA
Land Rover Discovery	7.4	7.6	6.4	7.4	6.5	6.9	4.9	6.9
Land Rover Range Rover	7.3	7.4	6.5	7.2	6.4	6.8	4.7	7.0
Mitsubishi Montero	6.1	6.2	5.8	5.9	5.8	6.3	5.4	5.3
Nissan Pathfinder	7.1	7.0	6.6	6.7	7.1	6.9	6.1	5.9
Olds Bravada	6.5	6.6	6.6	6.5	6.7	7.0	5.4	6.7
Suzuki Sidekick	5.3	4.9	5.2	4.4	6.0	4.8	6.2	3.8
Toyota 4Runner	7.4	7.3	6.6	7.0	7.2	6.8	5.9	6.1
Toyota Land Cruiser	7.1	7.0	6.3	6.9	6.4	6.7	5.2	6.1

Note: Mean differences in excess of .5 significant at 95% confidence level. Mean ratings on 10-point scale where 1 = poor and 10 = excellent, as provided by those very/somewhat familiar with the brand. Benefits "aggregate" or average multiple survey items tapping each domain. Benefits are ordered from left to right in terms of overall importance in SUV purchase.

Source: Allison-Fisher, Inc., Image Barometer, 2nd Quarter, 1994.

There are many other approaches to obtaining attribute perceptions and importance weight information.[20] No matter how it is obtained, information on perceptions and attribute importance is critical to understanding how your customers are making decisions.

Looking back at the four questions of the multiattribute model, the final—but least important—question concerns how customers combine the attribute perceptions and importance weights to make purchasing decisions. Perhaps the most obvious way to combine the information is to simply create a score for each brand based on a sum of the perceptions of the attributes weighted by the importance weights. This is called a **compensatory model** because a low score on one attribute can be compensated for by a higher score on another. Using the data from Tables 5–8 and 5–9, the weighted scores for the Chevy Blazer Full-Size and the Jeep Wrangler for the under-40 segment are 201.2 (4.4 × 6.7 for quality + 4.2 × 7.1 for safety, etc.) and 196.9 (4.4 × 6.4 for quality + 4.2 × 6.5 for safety, etc.), respectively. Thus, based on the compensatory model, the average under-40 consumer would be predicted to buy the Chevy Blazer. By performing the calculations for each brand, this kind of approach can be used to forecast sales and market shares.[21]

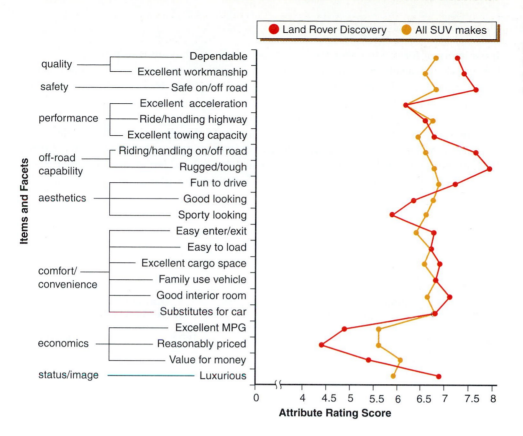

Figure 5–8

Perceptual
Comparisons:
Discovery Versus
Competition

Postpurchase Behavior

After the purchase is made, the buyer "consumes" the product or the service. It is important to note that, from Fig. 5–6, the buyer's purchase experiences or evaluation of the consumption of the product become part of the internal memory search. Good experiences create favorable memories and enhance the likelihood of future purchases. For frequently purchased products, repeat buying is critical to success because there are not enough new, untapped buyers to sustain a low-priced product for long. For high-priced, infrequently purchased products, good experiences lead to favorable word-of-mouth and increased chances of buying the same product again (or other products that the company markets). Bad experiences increase the probability that the product will not be repurchased and that the customer will not speak kindly of it to other potential buyers.

How does this evaluation process work? A central concept is that before consumption, customers form *expectations* about the product's performance and the benefits that it will provide. These expectations are developed based on the information the customer has collected from the prior search activities. During and after consumption, customers evaluate the product or service relative to these expectations; products that meet or exceed expectations receive a favorable postpurchase evaluation and the opposite reaction results for those that do not achieve the expected levels.[22] An herbicide sold to farmers based on its ability to kill insects without significant environmental damage creates those performance expectations. The farmer will analyze the results of applying the herbicide and mentally compare these results to the promises made by the salesperson or the distributor. Future purchases are highly dependent on this postpurchase evaluation.

WHERE DO CUSTOMERS BUY?

It is important for you to understand where customers are buying your product or service, that is, what channels of distribution are the most popular and what are the trends. These data can be obtained from secondary sources, usually industry trade publications or, if the former are unavailable, surveys.

Table 5–10 shows the sales of major appliances (televisions, refrigerators, washing machines, etc.) in the United States for 1996 and 1997 as well as the top 10 retailers. The two largest outlets for these products are electronics/appliance stores and mass merchants. It is interesting to note the significant increase in dollar sales at home improvement centers, department stores, and home furnishing stores at the expense of mass merchants, although

Table 5–10 Major Appliance Sales by Retail Outlet

Major appliance retail sales by type of outlet

	Estimated Major Appliance Sales in Millions			Number of Stores with Major Appliances		
	1997	**1996**	**Change**	**1997**	**1996**	**Change**
Department stores	$ 10.0	$ 9.0	11.1%	27	26	3.8%
Electronics/appliance stores	4,039.1	3,858.8	4.7	1,751	1,610	8.8
Home furnishings stores	485.2	437.8	10.8	1,390	1,314	5.8
Home improvement centers	611.0	470.0	30.0	420	380	10.5
Mass merchants	5,518.0	5,485.0	0.6	1,477	1,561	−5.4
Warehouse clubs	80.0	75.0	6.7	205	198	3.5
Other types	104.2	112.0	−7.0	221	214	3.3
Total registry	**$10,847.5**	**$10,447.6**	**3.8%**	**5,491**	**5,303**	**3.5%**

Source: *Twice* (1998), Nov. 23, p.26.

Major Appliance Retailers

Rank 1996 Revised	Store Type	Store Name	Estimated CE Sales Change in millions		Change 1996/1997	Number of Stores(c)	
			1997	**Revised 1996**		**1997**	**Revised 1996**
1	EA/N	Best Buy	$7,604.9	$6,835.3	11.3%	284	272
2	EA/N	Circuit City	6,808.5	5,863.0	16.1	556	480
3	CS	CompUSA	5,069.9	4,254.0	19.2	148	122
4	EO/L	RadioShack	3,215.7	3,101.1	3.7	6,904	6,869
5	MM	Sears	3,200.0	2,700.0	18.5	840	815
7	HO	Office Depot	2,996.0	2,480.0	20.8	612	570
6	MM	Wal-Mart	2,900.0	2,650.0	9.4	2,362	2,304
8	MM	Target Stores	2,700.0	2,300.0	17.4	797	736
9	MM	Kmart	2,235.0	2,230.0	0.2	2,136	2,141
11	HO	OfficeMax	1,905.0	1,625.0	17.2	713	564

Key to Store Types: EA/N: Electronics/Appliance stores/Multi-Regional; CS: Computer store; EO/L: Electronics only stores/More than 5 stores; MM: Mass merchants; HO: Home office stores

Source: *Twice* (1998), Nov. 23, p. 10.

the department store category has the smallest sales volume. Some of the growth in sales in the home improvement centers is obviously caused by the large percentage increase in the number of outlets selling major appliances, however. The more sales by specific chains help marketers in these product categories understand who's hot and who's not.

Like the MRI data presented earlier in this chapter, data showing where customers buy provide a good snapshot of current customer behavior but do not necessarily indicate where potential growth could emerge. For example, MCI recently signed an agreement with Amway for the latter's salespeople to market MCI's long-distance services door-to-door with the other Amway products (this deal was copied by AT&T signing a similar agreement with Shaklee). Current data on where customers sign up for long-distance telephone service would not show the door-to-door channel as capturing significant sales, but it may in the future.

WHEN DO CUSTOMERS BUY?

The final question to address is that of purchase timing. For each market segment, it is important to understand when they purchase your product or service in terms of

- Time of day (e.g., fast food, utilities, long-distance telephone service)
- Day of week (e.g., retail shopping, movies)
- Month or season (e.g., products purchased from firm capital budgets, seasonal products such as ice cream, soft drinks, and cold remedies)
- Cycles defined in years (e.g., durable good replacement cycles, products tied to economic conditions)

Timing issues affect both marketing and operations personnel. Because communications in media such as radio, television, the Internet, and print can be timed precisely, demand can be generated by placing the communications near the appropriate time of demand. For example, it is common to see advertisements for cold remedies before winter to get consumers to stock up before they actually need to use the product. Channels of distribution must have sufficient stocks of products when demand occurs. Seasonal patterns in demand can wreak havoc with product schedules and personnel management. Thus, some products attempt to smooth out seasonal fluctuations or other timing patterns by attempting to build demand in what have traditionally been off-peak periods. For example, the antacid Tums was repositioned to be perceived as a calcium additive as well. This changed the timing of consumption from primarily nighttime to any time of the day.

◆ Illustration: Mango

The launch of a new cellular phone in Israel shows how many elements of consumer behavior discussed in this chapter come together to develop a unique value proposition.[23] The brand, Mango, was launched in 1996 in market where there was only one competitor, Cellcom, that was being positioned as a medium-priced model aiming at middle-class adult buyers.

Mango was launched by Pelephone Communications, Ltd., and targeted the youth market. Not only was there no cellular phone targeting this segment, research showed that there was high market potential from exposure to telecommunication products, MTV, and international brands. Thus, the company decided that the primary target for a new phone would be teens aged 13–20, a group striving for freedom and control over their lives while seeking to be "in." A secondary target group was parents who needed to keep in touch with their children.

TUMS Brand Antacid/Calcium Supplement has repositioned itself to build additional consumer demand. The marketing campaign for TUMS antacids/supplements emphasizes that the product is an excellent source of absorbable calcium as well as an antacid. This marketing strategy positions the product as something to be taken every day, regardless of whether one's stomach is upset. (Courtesy of Smith Kline Beecham)

The company did a considerable amount of marketing research before the launch, including perceptual maps (see Chapter 3) containing all brands and products in the Israeli communication market as well as a future trend analysis. This led to the creation of a unique product targeting this age segment: a cellular phone limited to receiving calls, thus requiring no billing. Outgoing calls were limited to one number placed in the memory or to calls placed on a calling card. The phone had a very stylish design and was available in a wide range of colors (similar to the very successful Swatch brand of watches).

The implementation of the marketing strategy was consistent with the underlying behavior of the target audience. The product was available in location where many teens shop: a chain of pharmacies selling products like sunglasses, makeup, and other products popular with this age group. The price was 30% lower than the main competitor's. The communication program was very hip and creative. It was wildly successful: The brand had 52% of the market within 5 months as teens waited in line to buy the product.

Thus, Mango was successful because the marketing managers understood most of the key questions discussed in this chapter:

- They knew who the key buyers were.
- They knew the kinds of benefits teens are looking for in products.
- They understood the purchasing process, particularly the key attributes and how important they are to this group.
- They understood where this target group likes to shop.

EXECUTIVE SUMMARY

Key learning points in the chapter include the following:

- The main elements of understanding customers include *who* they are, *why* they buy, *how* they make purchase decisions, *where* they purchase, and *when* they buy.
- In understanding who customers are, you need to collect descriptive information about them and their buying behavior. It is important to develop links between the two to identify the best market segments to pursue.
- The basis of understanding why customers buy is knowing what benefits customers are seeking. This analysis should be conducted at the market segment level because benefits sought can vary between segments.
- The buying process (how?) for consumers is very complex. A simplified model of the process is that consumers search for alternatives that satisfy the motivation for buying, develop a consideration or evoked set of acceptable brands from which the purchase will be made, evaluate the options in the consideration set, and exhibit postpurchase behavior in terms of satisfaction that feeds back into the customer's information set.
- To determine where customers buy, you need to understand which channels of distribution are being used by the target customers and how they are changing.
- When customers are buying is defined by time of day, month/season, or buying cycle.

CHAPTER QUESTIONS

1. Think of a product or service that is mass marketed and one that focuses on one or more particular segments. How does the development of marketing strategy differ in the two cases?
2. For a product of your own choosing, pick one logical variable (e.g., age) that can be used to segment the market. Now, add a second variable (e.g., gender), so that customers have to satisfy the categories of both variables simultaneously (e.g., 18- to 24-year-old women). Now add a third variable. How many possible segments can you identify from a combination of the three variables? What implications does this have for the marketing manager?
3. Visit the VALS2 Web site and find out in which psychographic group you fall. Ask the questions to a couple of acquaintances in different age groups (mother, uncle, younger sister, etc.) and classify them as well. Would you have guessed that they would be in those groups?
4. Write a list of physical characteristics for a product. Take each characteristic and indicate what benefits it provides to a customer. How would an advertisement reflect this information?
5. What are the challenges in marketing products that are highly seasonal? Pick some examples to illustrate.

Application Exercises: Consumer Behavior in the PC Industry

Integrated
Case

1. Pick a country. Develop a variety of alternative ways to segment the consumer market for personal computers in that country.
2. Using either secondary or primary data (e.g., a small focus group), develop a matrix of consumer benefits sought by segment (from question 1). That is, put the various

segments on the left side of a matrix and the benefits across the top. Place check marks in the boxes of the matrix indicating how that segment values the benefit.

3. Going back to the matrix developed in question 2, develop a set of importance weights for each segment for each benefit sought.

4. Visit a local computer retailer. Observe consumer behavior at point of purchase, i.e., how many brands do they consider, how knowledgeable they are, how long they spend, and any other aspects of the buying process you wish.

5. Develop a report summarizing your findings. This report should include a comprehensive perspective on consumer behavior toward PCs.

FURTHER READING

The marketing research books listed at the end of Chapter 4 are good sources for researching consumers' attribute perceptions and importance weights. A good book on market segmentation approaches is Art Weinstein (1994), *Market Segmentation*, 2nd ed. (Chicago: Probus). Two fundamental books on buyer behavior are John A. Howard (1989), *Consumer Behavior in Marketing Strategy* (Englewood Cliffs, NJ: Prentice Hall); and James R. Bettman (1979), *An Information Processing Theory of Consumer Choice* (Reading, MA: Addison-Wesley).

Organizational Buying Behavior

6

CHAPTER BRIEF

The purpose of this chapter is to compare organizational or industrial buying behavior with the consumer behavior studied in Chapter 5. Purchasers in companies or other organizations use different criteria to make buying decisions than do individuals and families. Key learning points include the following:

The key differences between consumer and industrial marketing
Market segmentation for marketing to organizations
Understanding why organizational buyers make decisions
Understanding the mechanism used by organizations to make purchasing decisions, or how such decisions are made
The importance of knowing where and when such purchases are made

Neurogen Laboratories Inc. (renamed Symbus Technology in 1991) began in 1988 as a Boston-based institute focusing on research on neural networks.[1] Neural networks are computer programs that simulate how the brain works. Conventional computers are programmed to perform specific tasks repeatedly. Computers based on neural networks are programmed to learn from experience and deduce the correct course of action, as humans do.

The company could have developed products in one of two directions: robotic control and pattern recognition. In robotic control, the neural networks guide how the robots work. Because neural networks are adaptive, robots guided by such software are more versatile than normal robots because they can change their activities as needed. In pattern recognition applications, neural networks use computer imaging technology to identify a variety of objects, from diseased human organs to military targets.

Neurogen decided to apply its technology to pattern recognition and developed the first software to recognize handwriting, particularly handwritten numbers that are "segmented," not touching another digit. The company developed a product called Inscript, a collection of off-the-shelf semiconductors on a PC board together with Neurogen's proprietary software. Added to any computer scanner, Inscript could read virtually any handwritten digit at the rate of 15 characters per second.

Now that the company had a product, the problem was to find a market.[2] An obvious application of Inscript was to the form-processing industry. Billions of checks are written every year, charge slips are signed with numbers on them, and endless numbers of forms for taxes, insurance claims, ZIP codes on envelopes, and other uses make the form-processing

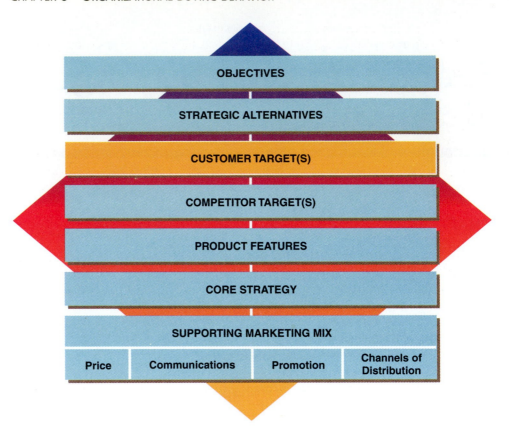

industry very large. The old approach to processing forms, using human labor, was very boring, time-consuming, error-prone, and expensive. If companies could transform the numbers on these forms into electronic digits for processing, money and time would be saved and accuracy increased.

Although companies such as IBM had spent many years working on handwritten character recognition, no solution had been found. Neurogen, an infant company, seemed to have found the solution and at a reasonable price. The PC board, software, and customer support cost only $60,000. In addition, the purchase was a one-time expense with a short payback period, depending on the application and volume processed.

Unlike Club Med, discussed in Chapter 5, Neurogen had no customers. The company knew that there were seven major markets for its product: banking, insurance, sales ordering, credit card companies, mutual funds, the U.S. Postal Service, and the Internal Revenue Service. The latter two are well-defined customers but the others are large, diverse industries about which Neurogen knew little.

The many questions Neurogen needed to address include the following:

- Within the banking, insurance, sales ordering, credit card, and mutual fund industries, which customers were the best targets for Inscript?
- In addition, did other possible market segments have a need for the product?
- Within the targeted companies, what purchasing process was used; that is, how were decisions made? Who were the decision-makers?
- How did these decision-makers vary in terms of the attributes and benefits they were seeking in a handwriting recognition product?

- Where might customers choose to buy the product?
- Were particular times of year better than others for attempting to sell the product?

The set of questions facing the Neurogen managers is basically the same as those facing the Club Med manager: *Who* are the customers? *Why* do they buy? *How* do they make purchasing decisions? *Where* do they purchase the product? *When* do they buy? Answers to these questions are critical to the development of a marketing strategy (see the marketing strategy diagram). There are two major differences, however. First, the Neurogen customer base is composed of companies, not individuals purchasing the product for their own use. When a firm markets a product or service to another organization, it is called **organizational marketing** or **industrial marketing.** Organizational marketing normally is targeted not toward an individual but toward a group of individuals collectively involved in the purchase decision. This group is usually called a **buying center.** This is a very important distinction between industrial and consumer marketing because the dynamics of group decision-making are very different from an individual consumer's decision-making process; the different people in a buying center often have different needs.[3]

In this chapter, we cover organizational buying behavior and show how the general questions addressed in Chapter 5 apply to industrial markets.

INDUSTRIAL VERSUS CONSUMER MARKETING

Although the basic marketing strategy framework holds for both consumer and industrial products, there are several differences between industrial or organizational buying and consumer purchasing behavior.[4]

Derived Demand

In many cases, the demand for an industrial product is derived from underlying consumer demand. An adhesive marketing manager sells her product to companies making toys, computers, televisions, and other products earmarked for consumer use. The demand for Neurogen's pattern recognition software is derived from the demand in the credit card, mutual fund, and other industries. Thus, industrial customers usually base their purchasing decisions on expectations or forecasts of the demand for their products. This means that the forward-looking company selling to industrial markets is concerned about both possible changes in buying behavior for its product and changes in the underlying consumer markets. In other words, even industrial marketers must be concerned about consumer behavior.

In some cases, the notion of derived demand is more subtle. The networking hardware made by Cisco Systems is not used as a component of a product that is sold to consumers. However, Cisco may sell its products to Hasbro, the toy manufacturer, as part of Hasbro's attempt to improve its information technology. Despite the fact that Cisco's routers and hubs are not toy parts, the company's success selling to Hasbro and other toy manufacturers is still driven by the underlying demand for toys. That is, if the toy business is bad, toy companies are unlikely to make big investments in information technology. Business services usually fall into this category; Waste Management's disposal services obviously are not used by their customers as factors of production, but the demand for such services may be affected by the health of their customers' businesses.

Product Complexity

Industrial products are normally more complex than consumer products. This has several implications for relationships with customers. First, it often means that industrial companies are more likely to be product focused rather than customer or market focused (recall our discussion in Chapter 1 about the differences). For example, Neurogen developed its software before identifying the markets to which it could be applied. Engineers and manufacturing personnel often have greater importance in industrial companies; such companies have to work harder to focus on customers rather than products. Second, increased product complexity means that product benefits and features are communicated differently. Few industrial marketers advertise on television because it does not enable them to explain complex products that are being purchased on the basis of how they work rather than how they look. Because of the need for more detailed communications, industrial marketers are heavy users of print media (e.g., trade magazines), personal selling, and the Internet.

Buyer–Seller Interdependence

With many consumer products, particularly low-cost supermarket or discount store items, the customer purchases the product and interacts little with the company.[5] However, with industrial products, the customer depends on its suppliers for its operation and, ultimately, its success in terms of profitability. The seller is part of the buyer's **supply chain** and must provide timely inventory replenishment, service and maintenance, spare parts, and efficient order handling. In other words, the economic success of the business-to-business marketer depends on the economic success of its customers.

Buying Process Complexity

As noted in the introduction to this chapter, industrial companies such as Neurogen sell to customers' buying centers. In this case, a variety of people with different backgrounds, valuations of product benefits and attributes, and attitudes toward the seller are all involved in the buying process. Many other factors also contribute to this complexity. Different kinds

For industrial products, the buyer–seller relationship does not end with the purchase decision. Instead, the buyer continues to rely on the supplier for the efficient operation of the product. In the case of this photocopier, service and maintenance are essential parts of the purchase decision. (Kevin Wilton/Corbis)

of organizations purchase in different ways. For example, some companies have centralized purchasing functions, in which all suppliers must work with one office, whereas others decentralize purchasing to divisions or product management. Some products are very technical, so that both parties must work together to finalize the product specifications to meet the buyer's specific needs. Many industrial purchases involve huge sums of money, so the purchasing cycle, or the length of time it takes to make a decision, can last several years.

WHO ARE THE CUSTOMERS?

Market segmentation is as important in industrial marketing as it is in the marketing of consumer goods and services. Although most industrial markets are not mass markets because of the more specialized nature of their products, the basic customer characteristics that make segmentation useful—different buying behavior and thus a different marketing mix for different groups of customers—are the same. For example, a marketing manager for an adhesive manufacturer may find that some of the potential customers find price to be very important and others need fast delivery. In this case, segmenting the market may enable the sales force to emphasize the different factors when calling on customers in the two segments, and the company can tailor its operations and marketing mix to suit each one. Alternatively, the manager may decide that because of cost considerations, there is no way to serve the price-sensitive segment. As in consumer markets, market segmentation is more effective and efficient for industrial marketers than simply trying to market the product in the same way to all customers.

Given a particular segmentation scheme, industrial companies often develop different products for the segments. For example, package delivery company UPS segments its market by how fast the customer needs to receive the package and tailors delivery options to that need, with higher prices being charged for quicker delivery. The company offers 10 options to meet these needs: Sonic Air (same day), Next Day by 8 A.M., Next Day by 10:30 A.M., Next Day by 3 P.M., Next Day (Saturday), Worldwide Express (next day anywhere in the world), 2nd Day (by noon), 2nd Day Air (any time), 3 Day, and Ground.

Segmentation Variables

As with consumer products, the organizational marketing manager must determine the variables that describe the customers in terms of their characteristics (called descriptors) and some kind of link between those variables and customer behavior toward the product or service.

Industrial marketers can use most of the same behavioral variables as consumer marketers. Table 5–2 presented a list of some of the most frequently used behavioral variables. Segments can be created based on benefits (e.g., service, speed of delivery), user status (e.g., past buyer versus new buyer), different levels of purchasing (e.g., heavy, medium, light), and even attitudes.

One set of descriptor variables for industrial marketing segmentation is shown in Table 6–1. These variables are divided into five categories:

- Demographics. Buyers of industrial products can be segmented by basic descriptors such as company size, industry type, geographic location, and number of employees.
- Operating variables. A second group of potential segmenting variables includes dimensions of the customer's operations, such as what technologies the customer is currently using and how many of your services or products they need.
- Purchasing approaches. You can also segment the market by variables related to the purchasing process and your existing relationship to the company. For example, a

---

Table 6–1 Market Segmentation Variables for Business Markets

Demographic

Industry: Which industries should we focus on?
Company size: What size companies should we focus on?
Location: What geographic areas should we focus on?

Operating Variables

Technology: What customer technologies should we focus on?
User/nonuser status: Should we focus on heavy, medium, or light users or nonusers?
Customer capabilities: Should we focus on customers needing many or few services?

Purchasing Approaches

Purchasing function organization: Should we focus on companies with highly
    centralized or decentralized purchasing organizations?
Power structure: Should we focus on companies that are engineering dominated?
    Financially dominated?
Nature of existing relationships: Should we focus on companies with which we
    have strong relationships or simply go after the most desirable companies?
General purchase policies: Should we focus on companies that prefer leasing?
    Service contracts? Systems purchases? Sealed bidding?
Purchasing criteria: Should we focus on companies that are seeking quality?
    Service? Price?

Situational Factors

Urgency: Should we focus on companies that need quick delivery or service?
Specific application: Should we focus on certain applications of our product rather
    than all applications?
Size of order: Should we focus on large or small orders?

Personal Characteristics

Buyer–seller similarity: Should we focus on companies whose people and values are
    similar to ours?
Attitudes toward risk: Should we focus on risk-taking or risk-avoiding customers?
Loyalty: Should we focus on companies that show high loyalty to their suppliers?

Source: Philip Kotler (1997), *Marketing Management,* 9th ed., (Upper Saddle River, NJ: Prentice Hall),
p. 267.

---

segment could be defined based on customers that use a bidding process versus those that do not or those that have centralized purchasing versus those that delegate purchasing authority throughout the organization.

- Situational factors. These include the customer's delivery speed needs, order size needs, and particular uses of the product.
- Personal characteristics. Although you are marketing your products to a business, the personal characteristics of the buyers can be used as segmentation criteria. For example, an organization's attitudes toward risk might help you determine whether it is likely to be an early purchaser of a new technology.

One use of such variables is shown in Table 6–2. This segmentation scheme is used by a company manufacturing medical diagnostic equipment used by research labs in universities, pharmaceutical companies, and research institutes. Clearly, industry descriptors

Table 6–2 Market Segmentation Scheme

Medical Equipment Manufacturer

	Number of Samples Processed	
Number of Researchers	Many researchers each with a few samples to process	Many researchers each with many samples
	Few researchers each with a few samples to process	Few researchers each with many samples

could be used to break the market up into segments. However, an alternative approach shown in the table is to classify current and potential customers by the number of researchers using the equipment and the number of samples processed by the researchers. This results in a four-box separation of customers into different groups characterized by demographic and operating variables. The assumption that must be verified is that the four groups actually behave differently, seek different benefits, and therefore need different products and information.

A second example, drawn from the DuPont product Kevlar, is shown in Table 6–3. This segmentation scheme is a combination of demographic (industry type and manufacturer versus end user) and a situational factor (current material used that would be replaced by Kevlar). Although it may look as if the scheme results in a large number of segments (56), not all combinations of the variables exist and the company would not choose to focus on many segments at once. DuPont could also segment the market by other variables, including product benefits.[6] For fishing boat owners, Kevlar's lightness

Table 6–3 Kevlar Segmentation Scheme

Present Material Applications	User Identity							
	Tires		Armament		Gaskets		Marine	
	Manu-facturer	End User	Manu-facturer	End User	Manu-facturer	End User	Manu-facturer	End User
Asbestos								
Plastic								
Fiberglass								
Steel								
Lead								
Polyester								
Nylon								

A company might choose to segment a market in many possible ways. In marketing Kevlar, DuPont has elected to segment the market by emphasizing the product's many benefits; this particular product–information pamphlet emphasizes Kevlar's durability and strength, which make it a superior material for use in protective gear. (Robin Adshead; The Military Picture Library/Corbis)

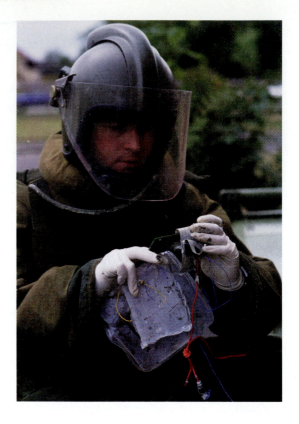

could lower fuel consumption and increase speed. For aircraft designers, Kevlar has a high strength-to-weight ratio. In industrial plant applications, Kevlar could replace asbestos used for packing pumps.

A second set of descriptor variables is based on the different kinds of purchases made by organizations, sometimes called **buy classes.**[7] These are shown in Table 6–4. **Straight rebuys** are routine purchases from the same suppliers used in the past. **Modified rebuys**

Table 6–4 Different Types of Organizational Purchases

Purchase Type	Complexity	Time Frame	Number of Suppliers	Applications
Straight rebuy	Simple	Short	One	Frequently purchased routine purchases such as printer toner
Modified rebuy	Moderate	Medium	Few	Routine purchases that have changed in some way such as air travel (new fares, flights, channels)
New task purchase	Complex	Long	Many	Expensive, seldom-purchased products

Source: J. Paul Peter and James H. Donnelly, Jr. (1997), *A Preface to Marketing Management* (Burr Ridge, IL: Irwin), p. 75.

characterize purchasing situations in which something has changed since the last purchase, such as a new potential supplier or a large change in the price levels. A **new task purchase** is made when the purchasing situation is unusual or occurs infrequently.

The marketing tasks differ between the purchasing situations. In the straight rebuy case, the current supplier is in an advantageous position because the buying process is likely to be automatic. The supplier's task is to maintain a good relationship with the customer and focus on timely deliveries at the expected quality levels. The job of the potential supplier who would like to break the straight rebuy is difficult; strong reasons to switch must be presented. If the purchasing situation has changed in some way, as in the modified rebuy case, new suppliers have more opportunity to present their cases. Some information will be collected by the customer about alternatives, so the current suppliers must realize that the repurchase situation is not automatic. In new task purchase situations, the purchasing process is a new one. For example, if Air France is in the market for new jet aircraft, it will open the bidding to the major worldwide vendors, Airbus and Boeing. The selling process is long and complex and Air France will seek extensive information.

Marketing Research Implications: Data Collection

As in consumer behavior analysis, data useful for developing market segments can be collected either via primary or secondary methods. Industrial product companies can either do their own in-house surveys or commission a marketing research firm to study the customers in a market. Because marketing research budgets in industrial companies are usually lower than in consumer product companies, such research is often done on a shoestring, with judgment often replacing hard data. This is unfortunate because primary data are proprietary to the company and can give it an edge in the marketplace, whereas secondary data are generally available to any company.

Because industrial product companies do not spend much money on primary research, they tend to use syndicated studies or other secondary studies more often. Government studies segmenting industries by Standard Industrial Classification (SIC) code are popular around the world, although SIC codes are not very useful at a particular industry level. Sometimes studies are conducted by trade associations, which distribute the data to all firms in the industry. Alternatively, consulting firms specializing in different industries conduct analyses that can be used for segmentation purposes. Examples are Dataquest and IntelliQuest, which specialize in the computer industry.

Figure 6–1 is an illustration of a report generated by the trade magazine *Computerworld* on the computer workstation market. The report focuses on what the company calls

Rank	Base	Vendor Mindshare		Loyal Vulnerable Lost
1	729	16%	IBM	76% / 17% / 7%
2	714	15%	Sun	75% / 19% / 6%
3	694	15%	Compaq	76% / 18% / 6%
4	544	12%	HP	75% / 20% / 5%
5	523	11%	Dell	78% / 18% / 4%
	1,434	31%	All Others	71% / 22% / 7%
	4,638	100%	All Vendors	75% / 22% / 6%

Figure 6–1

Workstation Brand MindShare, February 1997 through January 1998

Source: Computerworld Market MindShare Report, January 1998.

MindShare, a measure based on companies' commitment to specific brands. Of particular interest for segmentation purposes are the data on percentage of customers of each brand shown that are loyal, vulnerable (potential switchers to another brand), or lost, a scheme based on a behavioral variable. Although there is not much variation in the numbers, this trichotomy represents a way of segmenting the market, and the data on the three groups would be very useful to track over time. In other words, customers in each group should be treated differently from a strategic perspective, a requirement for a particular segmentation scheme. However, without any descriptor variables, the companies do not know which industry or particular customers to focus on.

Marketing Research Implications: Developing Target Markets

As is the case for consumer markets, the challenge facing the marketing manager of industrial products and services is to move beyond the profiling of alternative segments to actively pursuing one or more segments as part of the marketing strategy (see the marketing strategy diagram). Even if there were customers in each of the 56 alternative segments shown in the DuPont illustration (Table 6–3), it would not be feasible to focus on each one, except in the cases where the number of customers in each cell was very small. Thus, parsimony is also important in industrial marketing because it is inefficient to pursue too many segments.

Again, the criteria used to determine whether a particular segmentation scheme is useful are the following:

- Does the segmentation scheme explain differences in the behavioral variable of interest (e.g., purchase quantity)? For example, does industry classification explain differences in behavior better than the customer purchasing approach used?
- How many customers are there in the segment?
- What is the segment's forecasted growth rate?
- Are there particular environmental factors associated with the segment (e.g., regulatory, social) that make the segment more or less attractive?
- What is your potential competitive position in the segment?

◆ Illustration: Signode Industries

The Packaging Division of Signode Industries, Inc., now part of Illinois Tool Works Inc., is a manufacturer of steel and plastic strapping used by businesses to bind products for shipping.[8] A typical application of its products is to seal the box in which a washing machine is being shipped or to bind together a shipment of lumber. The strapping is applied using a hand tool or, if the strapping is applied at the end of an assembly line, a custom-designed power strapping machine.

In 1985 steel strapping and the machines used to apply the strapping made up 59% of the division's revenues. Steel strapping was specified in terms of size (width of the strapping) and grade (thickness and strength). The three standard grades of strapping were Apex (used in packages and corrugated boxes), Box Band Magnus (BBM, used to bind bricks and medium-weight packages), and Heavy Duty Magnus (HDM, used to bind rolls of steel).

Signode segmented its markets using some the variables described in this chapter. Table 6–5 shows its customer base divided into four groups (National, Large, Midrange, and Small) based on annual purchasing volume. Although this is useful information, segmenting by volume alone, a behavioral variable, does not provide us with any information

Table 6–5 Signode's Market Segmentation

Segment	Annual Volume	Shipping Quantity
National	Over $23,000	Carload (20 tons)
Large	$8,000–23,000	Carload or truckload (13 tons)
Midrange	$3,500–8,000	Less than truckload
Small	Under $3,500	Skid (0.6 ton)

Source: Rowland T. Moriarty, Jr. (1985), "Signode Industries, Inc. (A)," Harvard Business School case #9-586-059, p. 5.

about who the customers are in the different volume groups. In other words, it would be helpful to attempt to relate a descriptor variable such as industry or SIC code to see whether there is any relationship between different industry membership and volume. The marketing manager could use this information to target trade journals in different industries with print ads about Signode's products.

Table 6–6 provides additional information about these four segments. The top half of the table gives some idea about the relative size, changes in Signode's share from 1977 to 1983, profitability, how much sales time is devoted to each segment, and each segment's preferences for the three main grades of steel strapping. The National Accounts are a large portion of the market and Signode has a large share of their business, but the profit margins are the lowest. The reverse is true for the small accounts. The large accounts also use the heaviest strapping (HDM), whereas the smaller accounts use more Apex. Some of these data are corroborated by the table in the lower part of the table. As can be seen, the large accounts are fewest in number but make up a very large portion of the sales. They are also the most price-sensitive. The account migration data are interesting; Signode has been successful in getting smaller accounts to increase their purchases, but there is a large amount of account "churn" in each of the three segments (National and Large accounts are merged in this table), with about as many accounts lost as gained from 1982 to 1983.

Data linking a descriptor variable, industry membership, to some behavioral variables are shown in Table 6–7. The left side of the table shows the relationship of industry to Signode's share in that industry and how that has changed from 1977 to 1983. Relative to its overall share (52%), Signode's performance is well above average in the cotton and brick industries, nearly average in the primary metals, forest products, and paper industries, and well below average in the metal service and synthetic fibers industries. Of some concern is Signode's recent performance in the largest two markets, primary metals (18% of the overall market) and forest products (12%). In both segments, Signode's share has declined over the past 6 years.

A very interesting way to look at customers is shown in Fig. 6–2. In this figure, the top 164 national accounts were plotted on two dimensions: cost to serve and price paid. You would expect that a plot of this type would result in a 45-degree line sloping up to the right; that is, the customers that are the most expensive to serve also pay the highest prices. In other words, customers who demand higher levels of service should be charged the highest prices, and, assuming that the service has value to them, they should be willing to pay for

Table 6–6 Signode Sales Data

Sales Volume, Contribution, and Product Use by Account Size

	Small	Midrange	Large	National Accounts	Total
Sales Volume and Contribution					
% of total strapping market	19%	22%	23%	36%	100%
Signode share 1977	35	44	45	55	50
Signode share 1983	25	34	39	54	40
Contribution	54	42	34	28	36
% of sales time	12	35	20	33	100
Product Use					
Apex	62	46	23	20	
Box Band Magnus	16	21	40	30	
Heavy Duty Magnus	22	32	35	45	
Custom strapping	0	1	2	5	
	100%	100%	100%	100%	

Note: These estimates were provided by the industry specialists and reflect the lack of agreement within Signode regarding true market share by segment and product line. Thus, the numbers do not necessarily agree with all data in the case text.

Signode Strapping Sales by Account Size

	Purchase Size		
	Small (Skid: 0.6 ton)	**Midrange (Truckload: 13 tons)**	**Large* (Carload: 20 tons)**
1983 sales ($000)	$14,000	$29,200	$89,800
% of strapping sold	11%	23%	66%
Tons shipped	13,412	31,875	103,307
Average price per ton	$1,043	$916	$869
Number of customers	21,550	3,609	1,428
Account Migration, 1982–1983			
% of increase from lower size		22%	23%
Number of new customers	9,435	648	132
Number of lost customers	9,177	669	136

*Includes the 250 national accounts.

Source: Rowland T. Moriarty, Jr. (1985), "Signode Industries, Inc. (A)," Harvard Business School case #9-586-059, p. 13.

it. Signode clearly did not understand this relationship well. One group of customers, those in the lower right quadrant, are obviously very happy because they are getting high levels of service without paying for it. On the other hand, customers in the upper left quadrant are either unhappy or unaware that they are paying high prices without receiving commensurate service. These customers could easily be lost to competitors. A drawback of this figure is that the two dimensions are behavioral variables. Signode either has to identify the accounts individually and treat each as a segment or attempt to find a general pattern using some descriptor such as industry or company size. ◆

Table 6-7 Signode Segmentation by Industry

Industry	% of Total Market	Signode's 1977 Share	Signode's 1983 Share	Product Usage		
				Apex	BBM	HDM
Primary metals	18.0%	50%	42%	9%	12%	79%
Forest products	12.0	50	47	26	46	28
Paper	5.6	48	48	62	14	24
Metal service	3.9	39	37	14	28	58
Synthetic fibers	3.9	26	31	7	85	8
Cotton	3.3	98	98	0	0	100
Brick	3.1	86	82	0	100	0
Transportation	2.2	40	39	56	18	26
	52.0%					

Source: Rowland T. Moriarty, Jr. (1985), "Signode Industries, Inc. (A)," Harvard Business School case #9-586-059, p. 14.

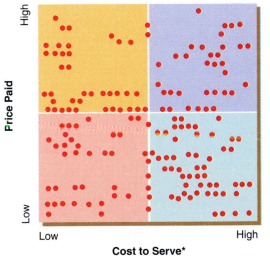

Figure 6–2

Signode's Top 164 National Accounts

Source: Rowland T. Moriarty, Jr. (1985), "Signode Industries, Inc. (A)," Harvard Business School case #9-586-059, p. 14.

Note: A similar scattergram (distribution of accounts) was found for Signode's top 1,200 accounts.

* Cost to serve includes sales expense, unbilled repair, parts, tools, and application and engineering services.

WHY DO CUSTOMERS BUY?

As we noted at the beginning of this chapter, a customer analysis also must address the question, "Why do customers buy the product or service?" A simplified model of how business-to-business customers make purchase decisions is shown in Table 6–8.[9] The first step is need recognition, or understanding why customers make purchase decisions.

The event that sets the purchasing or procurement process in motion within organizations can be internal or external. In the latter case, a supplier company attempts to anticipate the company's need through targeted communications, often made by a salesperson.

Table 6–8 Organizational Buying Stages

1. Identify need
2. Determine characteristics
3. Establish specifications
4. Identify potential sources
5. Request proposals
6. Evaluate proposals
7. Select supplier
8. Make postpurchase evaluation

There are two points in the first phase in the buying process at which these internal and external motivators have impact. The first is the recognition that a problem exists. This recognition could be stimulated by something as simple as a low supply of a part. Alternatively, a salesperson or an advertisement from a potential supplier could alert the buyer to the possibility that the product being currently used is technologically inferior to the new one being offered. This need must be stimulated by or communicated to someone in the buying organization who can influence whether a purchase is made. Otherwise, the problem recognized simply dies. The second part to this phase is that once a problem has been recognized, the buying organization must become aware that the solution to the problem lies with a purchase. Only then does the need become activated, resulting ultimately in a purchase from a supplier. It is possible that the part low in inventory can be supplied by another division's inventory. Or the company may not be able to afford the new product or service.

This need recognition phase varies somewhat between the different buy classes introduced earlier in the chapter. In the new task situation, the purchasing organization realizes that the problem cannot be solved without buying something new. For example, a company may decide that it needs to upgrade its document-copying capabilities. The company could purchase a new version of its existing copier, buy new copying technology, or decide to outsource its copying to a service firm. In the last case, this is a new task. For this need to arise, a senior manager must be aware that such outsourcing options exist and that the company can save money through that option. This manager would need to be exposed to this idea through a service company salesperson, an advertisement, or perhaps an informal source such as another business acquaintance. In other words, more effort by both external and internal parties is necessary for need recognition in a new task situation.

Straight rebuy situations are fairly straightforward because they are mainly a matter of reordering something that is purchased routinely (e.g., paper clips) and the need occurs when inventory is low. An example of a modified rebuy situation would be upgrading the existing copier to take advantage of new technology. In this case, the need for such an upgrade would not be as straightforward as the straight rebuy situation but not as complex as the new task. The manager in charge would be generally aware that new technology is available, but would have to research alternatives to determine what decision to make.

Like consumer purchases, industrial customers' purchasing decisions are benefit driven. Although industrial product purchases are more likely to be based on features rather than benefits because of the technical nature of the products, industrial buyers are very bottom-line oriented. Even industrial products must be sold on the basis of benefits; the key benefit is usually how much more money the customer can make with your product than with a competitor's.

Figure 6–3
Xerox Advertisement
Xerox Corporation

Most advertisements in trade magazines are very feature or specs (product specifications) oriented. Matrices comparing one product's specs to those of a set of competitors are very common. This is usually done because the targets for the trade ads are the technical people involved with the sale. However, the smart industrial marketer understands that somewhere in the buying center is a manager who is interested in the profitability of the purchase.

Figure 6–3 is an illustration of a benefit-oriented industrial product advertisement. The ad is from *Forbes,* so it is targeted toward senior, nontechnical managers. The focus of the ad is not on the technical aspects of the product, the Xerox Document Centre, but on the convenience of being able to go from digital to paper seamlessly and without leaving your desk. This translates to more workplace efficiency and greater productivity.

HOW DO CUSTOMERS MAKE PURCHASE DECISIONS?

The third key question a marketing manager must ask in order to understand industrial buying behavior is "How do customers make their purchase decisions?" In this section, we explore some of the ways in which such purchasing decisions are made.

The Buying Center

As we noted earlier in the chapter, when marketing a product to an organization, it is vital to understand that many players are involved in the purchase decision:

- The initiator. This is the person who first recognizes the need for the product or service.
- The influencers. These are people who influence the decision about which supplier is chosen.
- The decider. This is the person in the organization who has the ultimate authority for a "go–no-go" decision.
- The purchaser. This person actually authorizes payment for the product.
- The users. These people actually use the product.

This framework has many important implications. Like the market segments described earlier in this chapter, these microsegments, or different entities involved in the buying process, have different needs and seek different benefits. Thus, in the selling process, whether by direct sales or other channels, you must know not only that the particular organization is different from others in different segments, but that the different individuals must be the focus of different marketing approaches, perhaps even different value propositions.

 For example, let us return to the company that is seeking to purchase a new document copying system.[10] Because of the wide variety of people affected by copiers, different people occupy several of the buying roles:

- The initiator could be the office manager who is seeking a more powerful copier, either one that is similar to other machines already in use (to minimize the amount of training necessary) or one with new features that are important to the particular work being done. These new features may represent technological improvements in copying systems. Office managers are typically concerned about office productivity and throughput, or the amount of work produced.
- The influencers could include the office manager and the information system manager. The latter would be interested in compatibility issues with current hardware platforms used in the company, particularly if the new copying system must integrate with networked personal computers (see Fig. 6–3).
- The decider would be a more senior manager in the company. This person would be concerned with price and with the expected performance improvements.
- The purchaser might be a purchasing agent whose main concerns are terms of sale, installation timing, and after-sale support.
- The users would be the secretaries and other office personnel who use the new system in their work. The users are interested in ease of use, the quality of the interface and manuals, the ease of sharing documents, and similar features.

Thus, each person occupying the different buying roles can have very different needs and seek different benefits, which dictate how your company markets to the particular organization. ◆

Therefore, it is critical for a company marketing to organizations to understand the patterns of influence in each customer organization. A good salesperson understands this and seeks to identify the key decision makers and influencers and tailor his or her message to them. However, a second implication of the buying roles framework is that it may not be possible for a single salesperson or channel to be used to reach a customer, particularly a large one. Often, several approaches to communicating with customers are used at the different levels of the customer organization. For example, a junior salesperson is more likely to be focused on the user and influencers whereas a more senior salesperson would focus on the decision-maker, who is likely to be at a parallel level of authority.

Semiconductor manufacturers selling microprocessors to companies making products such as PCs, cellular phones, toys, and defense-related products must tailor the specifications (specs) of their chips to their customers' products. For example, a talking doll needs a chip with a particular processing capability (not very high in this case), power consumption, and size. Nearly every product using a microprocessor has different requirements.

Although this may be a straightforward observation, it is not always so clear who decides which processor to use in a particular product; many people can be involved in the purchase decision. Most companies have purchasing agents who actually write the checks to the suppliers. In this particular case, testing engineers evaluate different semi-conductors for a variety of technical factors such as cycle rate (the speed with which a device can form a complete cycle or operation such as reading or writing information).

Of particular importance in many purchasing situations are design engineers. The job of the design engineer is to find products that fit the basic product's specifications. Thus, the design engineer for a cellular phone is not as concerned about the technical aspects of the microprocessor (she can ask the testing engineer for a list of suppliers that have products meeting that need) as she is about whether the supplier's semi-conductor meets the design specifications of the product.

Recognizing that the design engineer was the key decision-maker for many of its customers, National Semiconductor designed their Web site to meet this need.[11] Focus group research determined that design engineers did not want fancy graphics at the Web site. Instead, they wanted to search for products whose performance parameters met their criteria, scan abstracts of data sheets, download the ones in which they were interested, and order samples. This should also be done quickly and easily.

National created the Web site (see Fig. 6–4) to meet these needs by designing four search tools. One is called a parametric search engine; using this, the design engineer can fill in a table with the design parameters of interest and the chips fitting those parameters are listed quickly. The engineer can also search for appropriate devices

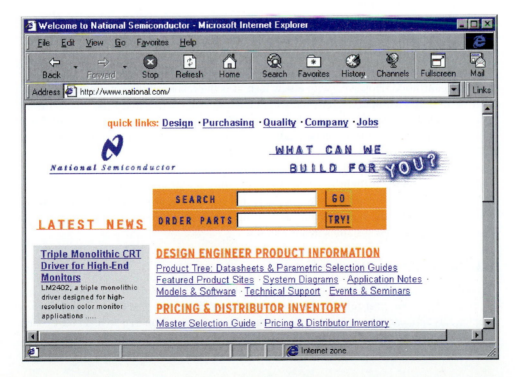

Figure 6–4

National Semiconductor Web Site

Courtesy of National Semiconductor.

through a text-based search. He or she can also look through system diagrams (e.g., the diagram of how semiconductors are used in air bag systems). Finally, the entire catalog of 8,000 National products is on-line.

Interestingly, the National Semiconductor Web site can be contrasted with Intel's. Because Intel has spent millions of dollars getting customers to request products with their chips inside, its Web site is more consumer-oriented than National's design-engineer focused site. ◆

The Buying Process

As Table 6–8 shows, following need recognition, there are seven stages in the buying process that ultimately lead to a purchase.

Determine the Characteristics

After the need has been ascertained, the next step in the buying sequence is to determine the characteristics of the product or service needed as specifically as possible (i.e., how should the problem be solved?). Usually, this stage is stated in terms of benefits rather than specific characteristics. Typical questions asked are "What application requirements must be met?" and "What types of goods or services should be considered?" In some cases, this analysis can be done internally, particularly for straight rebuy situations. However, for new task purchases, it may be difficult for the customer to know what options are available for consideration. In this case, it is critical for the company to make contact with the buyer as early as possible to deliver information about the different options available.

Continuing the copier illustration, at this stage of the buying process, the buying center would consider what benefits they would like to have from a new system. Candidates include faster copying capabilities, lower costs of the consumables (e.g., paper, toner), better sorting, quieter operation, and the ability to send documents directly from PCs to copiers.

Establish Specifications

This stage entails the translation of the needs into specific product features and characteristics. The result of this stage is a particular option or set of options from which price, delivery, system compatibility, and other characteristics can be determined. Again, with a straight or modified rebuy situation, this can usually be done in-house, depending on the size of the buying organization. However, with a new task, it is the responsibility of the selling organization to help customers determine what characteristics will satisfy the general need expressed. Often, companies need help even if the buying center members do not ask for it openly. At this stage, the sale can be made or lost, and it is crucial to understand the needs of the different people involved with making the decision.

In the document-copying case, the company may use the staff from its current document-copying center to help draw up specifications for products that meet the needs expressed in the previous stage. It is very likely that salespeople from Xerox, Ricoh, Canon, IBM, and other potential suppliers will start sniffing around for a possible sale because word about such acquisitions usually spreads quickly.

Search for and Qualify Potential Suppliers

The selling organization must ensure that it is on the buyer's list of potential suppliers. This list can be based on past relationships or reputation. The term *evoked set,* introduced in Chapter 5, is applicable here. In other words, the selling organization tries to be in the evoked set of as many customers as possible.

The objective of this phase of the buying process is for the buyer not only to have a list of potential suppliers, but to identify those who are *qualified*—a subset of the total list. To be on this list (also called the consideration set, as in Chapter 5), a potential selling company must not only carry the needed product or sell the service, but also satisfy other criteria set forth by the customer. These criteria might include financial soundness, an impressive customer base, or a track record of on-time delivery.

The company seeking a new document-copying system forms the list from the well-known companies listed earlier plus its current suppliers. These companies are so prominent that qualifying them is unnecessary. However, suppose the buying center is considering the option of outsourcing copying to a service company that will run its document center. In this case, a new task purchasing situation, the company may have to do its own research to identify potential suppliers. In addition, because the service companies may not be as well established as the companies actually selling or leasing copiers, some qualifying of the prospective suppliers may be necessary.

Request Proposals

The normal procedure once a list of qualified suppliers is formed is to send out a request for proposals (RFP) to potential suppliers. In their proposals, the suppliers indicate what products or services they propose to meet the needs and specifications of the buyer. Other terms of the proposal include price, delivery date, and any other aspects of the potential contract that are relevant. Thus, the company seeking a new copying system would send RFPs to all of the companies on its qualified list, seeking bids for the sale. However, in many cases, the RFP process is not so formal and the customer simply gives a number of companies a general idea of what it wants. RFPs usually are unnecessary for straight repurchase situations. In those cases, customers simply reorder from their current supplier.

Evaluate Proposals and Select a Supplier

After the customer receives the proposals, the buying center deliberates over the alternatives and makes a choice. Although not every member of the center has decision-making authority, all members normally have input into the final decision.

The multiattribute model described in Chapter 5 for evaluating options in a consideration set can be applied to this stage of the buying process. Three parts of the multiattribute model are used to determine which option to choose:

- The relevant attributes of the product being considered
- Perceptions or evaluations by each member of the buying center concerning how much each attribute is possessed by the products or services being considered
- How important each attribute is to the members of the buying center

These data can be assembled in a matrix like that shown in Table 6–9. Each member of the buying center has a set of importance weights (W) for each attribute (A). In addition, the buying center member has a set of evaluations or perceptions (P) of each product in the qualified list on each attribute. Using the approach described in Chapter 5, each center member forms a score for each product by multiplying the weight of the attribute by the perception or evaluation of the product's attribute and adding up the scores over all of the attributes. The product with the highest score on this index should be most preferred by that center member. Each center member bases his or her preference for a supplier on this combination of perceptions, evaluations, and importance weights. The final choice is the outcome of discussion and negotiation.

Table 6–10 applies the conceptual framework shown in Table 6–9 to the copier decision in a simplified form. We assume that there are only four key attributes: speed of the copier,

Table 6–9 Buying Center Decision-Making

Attribute	Buying Center Member 1		Buying Center Member 2		. . .
	Weight	$P_1, P_2, \ldots$	Weight	$P_1, P_2, \ldots$	
A_1					
A_2					
A_3					
.					
.					
.					

Note: Ps represent perceptions of each center member on each attribute for brands 1, 2, . . .

overall cost (price plus consumables), reliability, and company reputation. The first three can be measured objectively, so there is no variation between scores given by the office manager and purchasing manager. However, reputation is subjective and can therefore be evaluated differently by members of the buying center. The importance weights assigned to each attribute differ by the position held by the two center members. The office manager places the highest values on speed and reliability because those affect office productivity. The purchasing manager values cost the most because she is partially responsible for corporate profitability. Reliability, which affects cost, is also important. Speed is unimportant to this person. As can be seen, the overall evaluations between the two brands, Xerox and Canon, differ by center member. Even if these calculations are not done explicitly in this manner, buying center members implicitly consider these factors in reaching their recommended purchase.

Perform Postpurchase Evaluation

Because of the strong relationship between a supplier and a customer in industrial marketing contexts, information normally flows readily between the parties. Whether the infor-

Table 6–10 Buying Center Decision-Making

Copier Illustration

Attribute*	Office Manager			Purchasing Manager		
	Weight	Xerox	Canon	Weight	Xerox	Canon
Speed	.5	6	5	0	6	5
Cost	.1	2	5	.5	2	5
Reliability	.3	5	4	.3	5	4
Company Reputation	.1	7	4	.2	4	6
		$5.4^{\dagger}$	4.6		3.3	4.9

*Measured on a 1–7 scale where 7 is best (or lowest cost).
†The sum of $(.5 \times 6) + (.1 \times 2) + (.3 \times 5) + (.1 \times 7)$.

mation is transmitted to a supplier's salesperson or senior manager, the selling company is constantly informed about how its product is performing. If there is no such information flow, the seller should initiate such contact and demand feedback because the goal is to establish a long-term relationship. Obviously, the buyer will evaluate this relationship with the supplier when the time comes to make another purchase or give a recommendation about the supplier to another company.

External and Internal Influences on Purchasing Behavior

In addition to the steps listed in Table 6–8, a number of external and internal factors influence the decision-making process made by buying centers. These include the following:

- Environmental factors. Legal, cultural, political, economic, competitive, and other factors affect purchasing decisions.
- Organizational characteristics. These include the size of the company making the purchase decision, its level of technology, and the internal reward system.
- Characteristics of the individuals in the group. Participants in the decision-making process can differ in terms of education, motivation, personality, experience, and degree of risk-taking.
- Characteristics of the group as a whole. These include size, authority, leadership, and group structure.

WHERE DO CUSTOMERS BUY?

As is the case for consumer products, it is important for you to understand where customers are buying your industrial product or service. Of particular importance are changes in buying patterns that could signal new channels of distribution in which you have to invest.

Traditionally, the sales force and industrial distributors have been the most popular distribution channels for industrial products.[12] However, there has been considerable growth in direct marketing (direct mail, telemarketing) and the Internet as channels of distribution. For example, W.W. Grainger, the world's largest distributor of industrial and commercial equipment and supplies, has an on-line catalogue providing access to more than 189,000 items. It is estimated that nearly 80% of the value of Internet commerce involves business-to-business transactions, with the possibility of the total dollar value increasing to $300 billion by the year 2002.[13] There is a general trend toward disintermediation, or the elimination of intermediate buyers in the channels of distribution as improvements in information technology directly link manufacturers and service providers with their customers.

WHEN DO CUSTOMERS BUY?

The final question to address is "When do industrial customers buy?" Generally there is little interest in time of day or week in the industrial marketing arena. However, two key factors affect industrial purchasing:

- The customers' fiscal years. Generally, companies have more money in their purchasing budgets at the beginning of the fiscal year than near the end.
- General economic cycles. Producers of capital goods, very expensive industrial products such as mainframe computers and generators, are sensitive to economic

The Internet is fast becoming a popular distribution channel for industrial products. W.W. Grainger offers 190,000 items from its inventory of industrial and commercial equipment and supplies via its on-line catalogue. (Courtesy of W.W. Grainger, Inc.)

fluctuations. In many cases, these purchases are postponed until the relevant economy improves.

Thus, an important part of analyzing organizational buying behavior is taking these timing issues into account when developing marketing strategies.

EXECUTIVE SUMMARY

Key learning points in this chapter include the following:

- Analyzing industrial buying behavior involves addressing the same questions as you would in a consumer analysis: Who are the customers? Why do they buy? How do they make purchase decisions? Where do they buy? When do they buy?
- Differences between industrial and consumer buying behavior include the fact that demand for industrial products is often derived from underlying demand for consumer products and industrial products have greater product complexity, greater buyer–seller interdependence, and a more complicated buying process.
- Variables used for segmenting industrial markets fall into the same basic two categories as for consumer variables: descriptors, or variables describing the customer (e.g., company size), and behavioral variables such as degree of loyalty or purchase quantity.
- To understand why customers buy, you need to know how industrial buyers recognize that they have a need for a new product or service. This need is generated either internally (e.g., company personnel) or externally (e.g., a supplier's salesperson).
- To understand how customers buy, it is critical to recognize that industrial purchases are made by a buying center, or a group of individuals composed of the purchase initiator, influencer, decider, purchaser, and user.
- The buying process is composed of seven steps: determining the product need, identifying product characteristics, establishing specifications, identifying qualified suppliers, requesting proposals from potential suppliers, evaluating the proposals, choosing the supplier, and providing postpurchase feedback to the supplier.
- Where industrial purchases are made is changing to include greater use of the Internet and direct marketing.
- When purchases are made depends on corporate budgeting and business cycles.

CHAPTER QUESTIONS

1. Why is the notion of derived demand so important for companies selling products and services to other organizations? Can you think of an example in which an industrial company has benefited from changes in end-consumer demand? Suffered?
2. Go to the library and look at government documents that provide sales information by SIC code. Become familiar with the different levels of specificity of the codes. How useful are the data for a marketing manager? What are their limitations?
3. Choose an industrial product and try to guess the buying center for customers of that product. What is the customer behavior for a typical member in each group, expressed in terms of the basic customer behavior questions (Why? How? etc.)?

4. Suppose that you are hired as a salesperson for a company that sells the product in question 3. How do you find out who occupies each buying role in the center? How do you use the information from question 3 to do your job?

5. Go to a Web site for a company selling business-to-business products or services. Compare this Web site to one selling consumer products or services. What are the differences? To whom is each targeted?

Integrated Case

Application Exercises: Customer Behavior for the PC Industry

1. Interview a manager at a large company of your own choosing (use your judgment concerning the company size). In this interview, try to determine who occupies the different buying roles (e.g., initiator) for the purchases of personal computers and what buying process is used.

2. Using either the same person or one of the people in the buying roles, develop a matrix based on Table 6–9 or 6–10 to help determine the attributes used in making a decision and the importance weights for the different members of the buying center on those attributes.

3. Repeat exercises 1 and 2 for a small business. Compare the results from the large and small businesses.

4. Find a local PC retailer that deals with businesses and consumers (many stores sell to both kinds of customers). Interview a manager at the store about the differences in selling to the two groups.

5. Summarize these exercises in a report focusing on the implications of your findings for a PC manufacturer developing its marketing strategy.

FURTHER READING

The literature on how organizations make buying decisions is not nearly as extensive as that on consumers. Besides the references in the chapter endnotes, the following two books are most often consulted: E. Raymond Corey (1976), *Industrial Marketing: Cases and Concepts,* 2nd ed. (Englewood Cliffs, NJ: Prentice Hall); and Michael D. Hutt and Thomas W. Speh (1995), *Business Marketing Management,* 5th ed. (Chicago: Dryden). A book focusing on marketing research for industrial markets is William E. Cox, Jr. (1979), *Industrial Marketing Research* (New York: Wiley).

Market Structure and Competitor Analysis

7

CHAPTER BRIEF

The purpose of this chapter is to introduce the notion of competitor orientation. Although customer focus has received considerable attention in the marketing literature, the 1990s have seen an increased emphasis on understanding competitors and predicting their moves. The main learning points in this chapter are the following:

Performing a market structure analysis, which identifies your major competitors
Performing a competitor analysis
Alternative sources of information for analyzing competitors
Using game theory in the development of competitive strategy

Coca-Cola and Pepsi-Cola are two brands competing against each other in nearly every part of the world.[1] Coke was formulated in 1886 by Dr. John Pemberton, a pharmacist in Atlanta, Georgia, and quickly grew to be one of the best-known brands in the world. Pepsi was developed in 1893 in Bern, North Carolina, by Caleb Bradham, also a pharmacist. Unlike Coke, Pepsi struggled in its early days, nearly going bankrupt several times. Its first major inroad against Coke was in the early 1930s, when it offered its 12-ounce bottle for 5¢, whereas Coke was selling its famous 6.5-ounce bottle for the same price. Pepsi's radio advertising theme, "Twice as much for a nickel, too. Pepsi-Cola is the one for you," was rated in 1940 as the second best-known song in the United States behind the national anthem.

This was the beginning of what have become to be known as the cola wars, although Pepsi has consistently been the underdog. This has resulted in Pepsi usually being the leader in terms of new concepts and marketing programs. In the 1950s, 1960s, and 1970s, Pepsi innovated in the following ways:

- The company stressed the growing phenomenon of supermarket sales while Coke continued to emphasize its traditional strongholds of fountain sales (e.g., restaurants, bars, movie theaters), vending machines, and small retail stores.
- Pepsi was the first to introduce a large bottle size, 24 ounces, to capture family consumption.
- The company expanded its product line to include Diet Pepsi, Mountain Dew (a lemon–lime drink), and Pepsi Light.

Coke fought back through advertising, matching Pepsi's use of larger bottle sizes, using cans, and introducing new products such as Sprite (a lemon–lime drink); diet drinks Tab,

Fresca, and diet Sprite; and Mr. Pibb (a drink tasting like Dr Pepper). However, the company refused to use the Coke name on any product other than the flagship brand.

Two significant events in the 1970s and 1980s continued this emphasis on strong, head-to-head competition. The first was the 1974 Pepsi "Challenge," a nationally advertised blind taste test demonstrating that people preferred Pepsi's taste to Coke's. The Challenge was highlighted in store displays, communications to bottlers and other channel members, and in-store Challenge booths, where supermarket customers could take the challenge while shopping. Coke responded by discounting in selected geographic markets.

The second major event is now part of marketing folklore. Coke discovered in marketing research studies that younger consumers, obviously a key target market, preferred a somewhat sweeter drink, somewhat like Pepsi. Coke's sales were suffering. As a result, in April 1985, Coke announced that it would change the formula of its nearly 100-year-old brand. The announcement created an uproar; surveys indicated that over 90% of Americans heard about the change within 24 hours and that 70% had tried the new formula within the first month of its introduction. Consumers were very upset with this loss of a tradition; Pepsi was delighted and felt that it had won the cola wars. In July 1985, Coke reintroduced the old formula as Coke Classic while the new formula continued to be sold as Coke. This strategy was short-lived; in January 1986, Classic became regular Coke again and New Coke disappeared.

In the late 1990s, several factors affected the cola wars. First, many alternative beverages are competing for the ability to quench a drinker's thirst. These include ready-to-drink teas, shelf-stable juices, sport drinks, bottled waters, all-natural sodas, and the traditional competitor, beer. Brands such as Snapple, Gatorade, Perrier, Arizona, and others are very popular with consumers. Second, Pepsi's corporate diversification into snack foods (Frito Lay) and particularly restaurants (Pizza Hut, Kentucky Fried Chicken, Taco Bell) has taken management attention and resources away from soft drinks.[2] In addition, fast-food growth has slowed and the business is more capital intensive.[3] Third, untapped markets such as China and Muslim countries in which alcohol is forbidden are exploding. Coca-Cola is well positioned to capitalize on these growth opportunities because of its vast network of bottlers and marketing muscle. To give you some idea of the market potential left for Coke, the per capita consumption of Coke in the United States is 363 servings per person per year, in Mexico it is 332, but in France it is only 74 and in China it is less than 10. Finally, in 1998, Pepsi, becoming frustrated with its inability to compete with Coke in fountain sales and its widening deficit in market share (44% for Coke versus 31% for Pepsi), filed an antitrust lawsuit against Coke, claiming the latter has frozen it out of selling soft drinks in independently owned restaurants and movie theaters.

This illustration shows the importance of several analyses critical to development of the marketing plan (Table 2–1), the marketing strategy (see the marketing strategy diagram), and the marketing manager's job:

- Defining the competition is important in determining which other products are competing against yours for the same customer benefit (e.g., soft drinks versus bottled waters).
- Studying competitors is crucial to understanding how to develop a value proposition and make appropriate pricing, advertising, channel, and similar tactical decisions. Coke must understand Pepsi's corporate and brand strategies to calculate how to react.
- Rather than simply reacting to your competitors' moves, it is beneficial to anticipate them and act in a preemptory fashion. This requires strategic thinking.

As was clear from the Cadillac illustration in Chapter 2, the marketing manager's job is difficult because of the large number of changes in the external environment that must be considered and anticipated. In Chapters 5 and 6, methods for analyzing one element of the

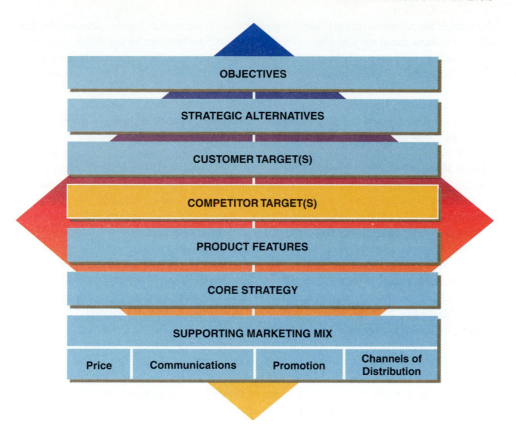

external environment—customers—were discussed. In this chapter, we focus on the competition. Note that this is an integral part of the marketing strategy shown in the marketing strategy diagram. The major topics discussed in this chapter include the following:

- Market structure. It is important to understand the nature of competition in the market in which you compete. A **market structure analysis** will identify the competitors for your product or service.
- The strengths and weaknesses of the competitors and their current and likely future strategies. This is usually called **competitor analysis.**
- The development of competitive strategy in the late 1990s rests heavily on notions of game theory, a way of structuring likely competitor moves, anticipating them, and developing preemptive moves. Some basic aspects of game theory are described at the end of this chapter.

MARKET STRUCTURE ANALYSIS

Definitions

The purpose of a market structure analysis is to enable the marketing manager to understand who the competition is. Misidentification of the competitive set can have a serious impact on the success of a marketing plan, especially in the long run. Overlooking an important competitive threat can be disastrous. For example, for many years the Swiss controlled the market for premium watches and Timex dominated the market for inexpensive watches. When Japanese firms such as Casio developed electronic watches in the 1970s, they were not viewed as a threat or serious competition in either business. Today, both Timex and Swiss firms offer electronic models, and only the strong success of the Swatch brand of inexpensive fashion watches has saved the Swiss watch industry. Coke and Pepsi have consistently underestimated the strength of their competitors in non–soft-drink categories.

Ambiguous definition of the competition also creates uncertainty and ambiguity in market-related statistics such as market share. This leaves open the possible manipulation of market boundaries, particularly when compensation or allocation decisions are at stake. Market share is defined as "us/(us + them)." We can undoubtedly measure the dollar sales for "us"; however, who are "them"? The marketing manager can make his or her market share seem large by including as few competing products or services as possible in the denominator. This trick is useful when it comes time to be evaluated for a bonus, but is not helpful for understanding the market from the customer's perspective.

For example, assume than an objective for a subnotebook computer (weighing four pounds with a hard disk drive but no floppy disk drive) is to gain 10% market share. The ability to achieve this objective depends on whether the market is defined as all subnotebooks, all portable computers (subnotebooks plus notebooks and laptops with floppy drives and perhaps CD-ROM drives), all portable Windows 95–based computers, all desktop computers plus portables, and so on.

Several different terms are used in defining a market. Figure 7–1 shows one possible set of definitions in a product–industry hierarchy. As can be seen in the figure, you might call all houseware products the **industry.** One particular product segment of that industry, food preparation appliances, defines the set of products more narrowly and coffee makers form what is usually called a **product class** or **product category.** Specific alternative cof-

Figure 7–1

Product–Industry Hierarchy

Source: George S. Day (1990), *Market Driven Strategy* (New York: Free Press), p. 97.

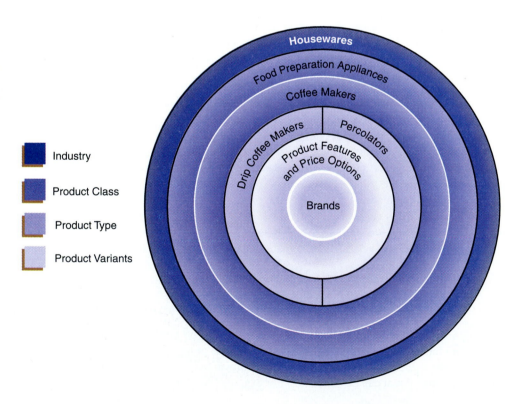

■ Industry

■ Product Class

■ Product Type

■ Product Variants

fee makers, percolators, drip coffee makers, espresso machines, and so on are **product types.** Different specific combinations of features within each product type are **product variants** and **brands.**

Competition can be defined clearly at every level of the hierarchy shown in Fig. 7–1. The number of competitors grows as you go up the hierarchy. However, the terms *industry* and *product class* do not get at the heart of competition or market definition. A good definition of an industry is the following:[4]

> An industry should be recognizable as a group of products that are close substitutes to buyers, are available to a common group of buyers, and are distant substitutes for all products not included in the industry.

The key part of this definition is the fact that competition is defined by the customer, not by the marketing manager; after all, it is the customer who determines whether two products or services compete against each other.

An alternative way to define the competition that better incorporates the customer's perspective is shown in Fig. 7–2. The narrowest definition of competition that results in the fewest competitors would include only products or services of the same product type. This is called **product form competition.** For a drip coffee machine brand, the narrowest way to define competition would be to include only the other brands of drip coffee makers. Although there may be some product variations such as capacity, the most direct competitors are the brands that look like yours. Another example of product form competition is Diet Coke versus Diet Pepsi because both are diet colas.

This narrow definition might be useful in the short run because these brands are your most serious competitors on a day-to-day basis. It is also a convenient definition of competition because it mimics the way commercial data services (e.g., A.C. Nielsen) often measure market shares. However, this narrow definition may set an industry standard for looking at competition and market shares in a way that does not represent the true underlying competitive dynamics. Thus, the product form view, though perhaps providing the set of the closest competitors, is too narrow for a longer-run view of competition.

Figure 7–2

Levels of Competition: Drip Coffee Makers

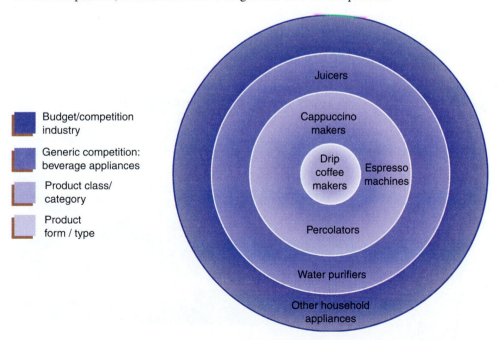

Budget/competition industry

Generic competition: beverage appliances

Product class/ category

Product form / type

Juicers

Cappuccino makers

Drip coffee makers

Espresso machines

Percolators

Water purifiers

Other household appliances

The second level of competition shown in Fig. 7–2 is based on products that have similar features and provide the same basic function. This type of competition, called **product class or product category competition,** is more inclusive because more brands are considered to be competitors. In the current example, this means that the drip coffee machine would face competition not only from other drip machines (product form competition) but also from percolators, espresso machines, and cappuccino makers.

The third level of competition shown in Fig. 7–2 incorporates the customer's notions of substitutability. At this level, competition is defined as the products or services that the customer views as fulfilling the same need. In the present example, the need, broadly defined, could be for a machine that makes beverages at home. This implies that other brands of machines creating beverages, such as juicers and water purifiers, would be competition. This level of competition is called **generic competition.**

This is a critical way to think about competition. Many products and services compete generically because they satisfy the same need. For example, think of business communications. There are many ways for two managers to communicate with each other: in person (requiring air or some other mode of travel), phone, e-mail, fax, teleconferencing, overnight mail, and regular mail. Do brands of orange juice compete against soft drink brands? When a person is thirsty, there are many ways to satisfy that need. The Coca-Cola company figured that the average person requires 64 ounces of liquid per day. They also calculated that around the world, Coca-Cola supplies less than 2 ounces per person per day. Former chairman Roberto Goizueta responded, "We remain resolutely focused on going after the other 62."[5]

The point is that there is a critical difference between generically defined competitors and product form or product category competition. The latter two are inward oriented, whereas generic competition is outward oriented. Product form and product category competitors are defined by products that look like yours. Generic competitors are defined by looking outside the firm to the customers. After all, the customer determines what products and services solve the problem at hand. Although in some cases there may be a limited number of ways to solve the same problem or provide the same benefit, in most instances focusing on the physical product alone ignores viable competitors.

The final level of competition shown in Fig. 7–2 is the most general, but very important for products such as drip coffee makers. Many products and services are discretionary items purchased from the same general budget. Assuming that drip coffee makers cost around $50, there are many other discretionary items a person may want to purchase with

Products that satisfy the same need but are not direct competitors are said to be generic competitors. The person in this photo has chosen a particular brand of bottled water to quench her thirst. She might have selected another brand of bottled water (a direct competitor), but she also could have selected another type of beverage altogether (orange juice, cola, iced tea, lemonade) and satisfied her thirst with a generic competitor. (Jean Pierre Lescouret/Corbis)

that money. Referring again to Fig. 7–1, many of these items may come from the same industry (in this case, housewares). A person shopping in a department store in the housewares area faces many other discretionary items for the home that are unrelated to making coffee or quenching a thirst. Products such as pots and pans and knives may find their way into the shopping basket and could be viewed as substitutable in the budget. This kind of competition is called **budget competition.**

This four-level model of competition has significant implications for developing product strategy because a different set of tasks must be accomplished at each level of competition for a product or service to be successful in the market. At each level, part of the marketing manager's job is fairly clear: Convince the customer that your company's version of the product, your brand, is better than the others. In other words, your most direct competitors are other brands of a similar product form. What differs at each level is how much additional marketing has to be done beyond touting your own brand's advantages. At the product form level, when the competition is viewed as consisting only of other products with similar features, marketing activities directly aimed at the similar competitors are all that is required. However, the problem becomes more complex as the competitor set grows. At the product category level, you must also convince customers that the product form is the best in the product category (i.e., a drip coffee maker is better than a percolator or espresso machine). At the generic competition level, you must also convince customers that the product category solution to the customer's problem (the benefit derived from the product category) is superior to the solution provided by other product categories (i.e., a coffee maker is better than a juicer). This is the same problem you face at the budget level (i.e., a coffee maker is better than a new set of knives).

It is also important to note that as you move from product form toward budget competition, customer targets also begin to change. Product form competition involves battling for exactly the same customers in terms of who they are and why they buy. As the focus moves outward in the concentric circle model of Fig. 7–2, both who your customers are and why they buy begin to differ as the need to be satisfied becomes more general. Because the key to success in business is obtaining and keeping customers, the most crucial form of competition is generally product form competition, in which competition occurs for the same customers. On the other hand, generic competition can destroy entire product categories when a major innovation occurs, so it also requires attention, especially for long-run planning.

A good example of cross-category competition is currently occurring in the breakfast market in the United States. If you work for Kellogg or General Mills, you normally think of your most important competition as being between cereal brands and flavor categories. However, the annual volume of cereal shipments fell 1% in the 12 months ending December 1998, after 40 years of 3% annual growth. The problem for the cereal manufacturers is the growth in "portable" breakfasts such as bagels and muffins, which are more convenient. Thus, the cereal manufacturers clearly face increased generic competition and have reduced prices dramatically to cope with it. Interestingly, a large amount of the growth in cereal sales over the previous 10 years had come at the expense of another generic competitor: eggs.[6]

Proctor & Gamble has changed the way it looks at the clothes-cleaning market by redefining the industry and taking a larger perspective.[7] The company markets products that clean one out of every two loads of laundry washed in U.S. homes. However, not content to wash clothes in washing machines, the company also wants people to use its products to clean coats, curtains, and upholstery. Thus, in 1998 P&G introduced Fabreze, a "fabric refresher," and test marketed a home dry-cleaning kit.

Selling laundry soap has become a difficult business. An estimated 98% of all U.S. households already use detergents, so there is little growth left from noncustomers. In addition, consumers are doing less laundry: The average family washes 7.0 loads of laundry per week, down from 7.7 loads in 1988.

One form of competition that often goes unrecognized is generic competition. Breakfast cereal manufacturers are facing increased generic competition from other breakfast food categories that are more portable, such as breakfast bars, bagels, and muffins. This New York City bagel shop represents a growing form of cross-category competition for the cereal manufacturing industry. (Thomas Kelly/Corbis)

Thus, managers of the North American laundry and cleaning products business took another look at the home cleaning market. Using a product category definition, P&G holds 51% of the $4-billion U.S. laundry detergent market. However, if the market is redefined in a more generic form to consider substitutes, P&G holds just 20% of the $10-billion clothes cleaning market. The potential for market share growth is considerably greater when you hold 20% of the market than when you hold 51% of it.

As a result of this market redefinition, P&G dedicated 20% of their employees to developing new products, compared to 4% a few years before. In addition to the two new products mentioned earlier, the company is looking at a variety of new product ideas aimed at cleaning all the textiles in a home. ◆

Measurement Issues

The preceding section begs the question of how the sets of competitors are formed, particularly for generic competitors. Product form and product category competitors can be determined from observation and external data sources. In particular, government documents provide valuable information about product form and category competitors, without disclosing the individual firms involved.

Table 7–1 shows some Standard Industrial Classification (SIC) categories. The numbers of digits in the classification scheme are roughly equivalent to the top three tiers of Fig. 7–1. The two-digit category, Industrial Machinery and Equipment, defines the industry. The three-digit categories, such as Engines and Turbines, occupy a higher level of specificity; the four-digit categories, such as Oil Field Machinery, provide narrower definitions such as product class or type information. These definitions of different levels of competition are useful, although your own definitions would be tailored to the specific product or service. However, the risk of using what might be an inappropriate classification scheme is offset by the vast amounts of information collected by the government that are categorized by SIC code.

As mentioned earlier in this chapter, consulting firms, trade associations, professional publications, and other organizations may supply their own category or industry definitions, which become the basis for managerial decision-making. For example, Table 7–2 has descriptive data on the twelve major on-line stock trading services. These are essentially product category data. There is no breakdown by product form (on-line versus full-service brokers, for example). In addition, no extrapolation to generic or budget competition is pos-

Table 7–1 SIC Concentration Statistics, 1992

SIC	Industry	Largest 4	Largest 8
35	Industrial machinery and equipment		
351	Engines and turbines		
3511	Turbines	79%	92%
3519	Internal combustion engines	56	75
3523	Farm machines and equipment	47	53
353	Construction and related machinery		
3524	Lawn and garden equipment	62	79
3531	Construction machinery	42	53
3532	Mining machinery	30	45
3533	Oil field machinery	37	51
3534	Elevators and moving stairways	57	67
3535	Conveyors	14	23
3536	Hoists, cranes, and monorails	29	46
3537	Industrial trucks and tractors	40	50
354	Metalworking machines		
3541	Machine tools (metal cutting)	35	46
3542	Machine tools (metal forming)	21	36
3543	Industrial patterns	10	16
3544	Special dies, tools, jigs, fixtures	3	5
3545	Machine tool accessories	17	24

Source: U.S. Bureau of the Census, *1992 Census of Manufacturers*.

sible. Investment vehicles other than stocks (e.g., real estate, jewelry, antique cars) are generic competitors, and there are many other things on which you could spend several thousand dollars rather than stocks (e.g., an MBA degree, a new car, a Club Med vacation). Although the data shown in Table 7–2 are interesting (and typical), they do little to help a marketing manager identify the competition. Even worse, dependence on data such as those in Table 7–2 could lead you to misidentify the key competitors in a particular product form.

Economists often use **cross-elasticity of demand** as an indicator of substitutability. Cross-elasticity is the percentage change in one product's sales due to a percentage change in a marketing variable for another product, such as price. If a cross-elasticity with respect to price is positive (a product's sales decline when another product's price drops), the two products in question are considered to be competitive. The major problem with this approach is interpreting the cross-elasticities. For example, a cross-price elasticity of 2.0 implies that a 1% drop in a competitor's price causes your sales to drop by 2%. However, this assumes that you do not react to the price cut. The interpretation also assumes that the market is not changing in any way (e.g., no new brands or changes in product design). In addition, a positive cross-elasticity does not imply cause and effect; that is, you cannot be certain that the price decline (increase) of a product actually caused the other product's sales to decline (increase).

The most difficult kinds of competition to assess are generic and budget because they cannot be observed readily and competitors may be numerous. In determining these kinds of competition, customer judgments are essential. This makes sense because both kinds of competition are based on how customers, not managers, view the world.

Many approaches for customer-based assessments of competition are available.[8] An example of such an approach is substitution in use.[9] This method estimates the degree of competitiveness through judged similarity of products in usage contexts. The typical data

Table 7–2 On-Line Trading Industry Facts: 1998

Comparing the 12 largest on-line brokers[1]

Firm	Address	Price	Products
Charles Schwab	www.schwab.com	$29.95 up to 1,000 shares	Stocks, corporate bonds and U.S. Treasurys, mutual funds, options
Fidelity Investments	www.fidelity.com	$25 for market orders, $30 for limit orders up to 1,000 shares[2]	Stocks, U.S. Treasurys, municipal bonds, mutual funds, options
DLJdirect	www.dljdirect.com	$20 up to 1,000 shares	Stocks, U.S. Treasurys, mutual funds, options
E*Trade	www.etrade.com	$14.95 market orders, $19.95 limit orders up to 5,000 shares	Stocks, bonds (U.S. Treasurys, municipal, corporate and agency bonds), mutual funds, options
Waterhouse Investor Services	www.waterhouse.com	$12 up to 5,000 shares	Stocks, mutual funds, options
Ameritrade	www.ameritrade.com	$8 market orders, $13 limit orders, unlimited shares	Stocks, mutual funds, options
Quick & Reilly	www.quick-reilly.com	$14.95 market orders, $19.95 limit orders up to 5,000 shares	Stocks, U.S. Treasurys, mutual funds, options
Datek Online	www.datek.com	$9.99 up to 5,000 shares	Stocks and mutual funds
Suretrade	www.suretrade.com	$7.95 up to 5,000 shares	Stocks, U.S. Treasurys, mutual funds, options
Discover Brokerage Direct	www.dbdirect.com	$14.95 market orders, $19.95 limit orders up to 5,000 shares	Stocks, U.S. Treasurys, mutual funds, options
Dreyfus Brokerage Services	www.edreyfus.com	$15, unlimited shares	Stocks, mutual funds, options
National Discount Brokers	www.ndb.com	$14.75 market orders, $19.75 limit orders	Stocks, mutual funds

[1]Ranked by number of on-line accounts as of year-end 1997, according to Credit Suisse First Boston.
[2]Cost is $14.95 for market orders, $19.95 for limit orders, up to 1,000 shares, for customers trading 12 or more times a year.
[3]Some shares of preferred-stock deals from various firms.
Sources: *Credit Suisse First Boston; the firms*

Phone Help	Banking Services	IPO Access	Institutional Research	Real-Time Stock Quotes
24 hours a day, 7 days a week	Check writing, credit/debit cards	Yes	No	200 free quotes plus 100 for each order
24 hours a day, 7 days a week	Check writing, credit/debit cards	Yes	Salomon Smith Barney research	Unlimited free quotes
7 a.m. to 1 a.m. Eastern time weekdays; 8 a.m. to 10 p.m. weekends	Check writing, debit/credit cards	Yes	DLJ research	100 free quotes plus 100 for each order; also 500 quotes for $19.95
8 a.m. to midnight Eastern time weekdays	Check writing, credit cards, mortgages	Yes	BancAmerica Robertson Stephens research	Unlimited free quotes
24 hours a day, 7 days a week	Check writing, credit/debit cards	No[3]	No	100 free quotes plus 100 for each order; 100 quotes for $5
5 a.m. to 9 p.m. Central time weekdays	Check writing, debit cards	No	No	100 free quotes plus 100 with each order
24 hours a day, 7 days a week	Check writing, credit cards	Yes	No	100 free quotes plus 100 for each order; unlimited quotes for $29.95 a month
8 a.m. to 7 p.m. Eastern time weekdays	None	No	No	Unlimited free quotes
7 a.m. to 6 p.m. Eastern time weekdays	Check writing	Yes	No	100 free quotes a day, plus one quote for each order; unlimited quotes for $29.95 per month
24 hours a day, 7 days a week	None	No	Morgan Stanley, Dean Witter research	Unlimited free quotes
9 a.m. to 7 p.m. Eastern time weekdays	None	No	No	Free with five or more equity trades a month; or unlimited quotes for $708 a year or $79 a month
7 a.m. to 8:30 p.m. Eastern time weekdays	Check writing, credit cards	No	No	100 free quotes plus 100 with each order

collection approach is to use focus groups. First, customers list all possible uses and contexts for a target product or brand. Next, either the original sample or a fresh sample of respondents list other products or brands that provide the same benefits or uses and rate their appropriateness for the different contexts or use occasions. This method can produce a large number of generic competitors or even budget competitors. However, its strength is that the method uses direct input from customers about what products and services they view as substitutes for different purchase or usage contexts.

COMPETITOR ANALYSIS

Training employees to collect and analyze information about competitors is one of the hottest areas of executive education. The Society of Competitive Intelligence Professionals (SCIP) has grown from a few dozen members in 1986 to over 6,000 today. Companies such as Kellogg, IBM, Microsoft, and Intel have hired ex–CIA officers and other professionals to help them better understand their competitors and predict their likely future strategies. Thus, like the market structure analysis just discussed, competitor analysis is a critical part of the situation analysis of the marketing plan.[10]

A framework for competitor analysis is shown in Fig. 7–3. The bottom line of a competitor analysis is a forecast of their likely future strategies (the circle in Fig. 7–3). In most cases, it is impossible to know what the competitors in your market will do in the future. However, the purpose of this part of the situation analysis is to force you to be proactive in the marketplace, anticipating where competitors are headed and developing appropriate strategies. Without the forecasting aspect of competitor analysis, you are always reacting to where competitors have been rather than where they are going.

The main parts of a competitor analysis are the following:

- A determination of the competitors' major objectives. It is useful to know whether they are pursuing growth (sales volume, market share) objectives or profit-related objectives.

Figure 7–3

Competitor Analysis Framework

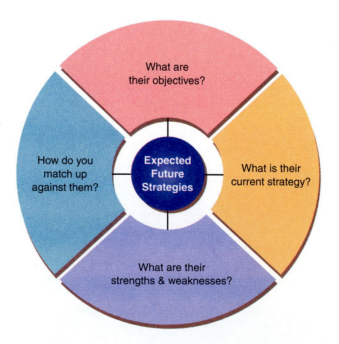

- An assessment of their current marketing strategies. This includes the segments pursued, how they are positioning the products or services, their value propositions, and the marketing mix.
- An assessment of their strengths and weaknesses. These can be evaluated on a number of dimensions, particularly the key success factors in the market.
- An internal analysis of your firm's strengths and weaknesses relative to the competitors. In other words, how do you match up against them?

Key Objectives

In Chapter 3, we discussed the importance of the objective as setting the overall direction for the marketing strategy. Thus, determining the competitors' objectives gives us a good idea about their current and perhaps future strategies. It usually does not take much research to uncover the objective. Sensitivity to competitors' actions, through observation, salesperson call reports, and many other resources, is the key.

Suppose you learn that a competitor is going to be aggressively pursuing a market share objective at the expense of short-term profits. This strategy would not be unusual for a new product in the market or a foreign competitor attempting to establish a beachhead in a local market. In this case, a cut in price, increased advertising expenditures, increased promotional activity to end customers and distributors, or increased distribution expenses are likely to occur. In other words, a rival marketing manager who is trying to expand a brand's market share will spend money on market development–related activities or price reductions.

Brands pursuing a profit objective at the expense of some share loss (usually called a harvest objective if the ultimate intention is to drop the product) would be marketed in the opposite way. An increase in a competitor's price, decreases in marketing budgets, and so on can be interpreted as a retreat (though perhaps only temporary) from active and aggressive competition in the market.

An important factor in this assessment of competitors' objectives is whether a competitor is publicly owned, privately held, or government controlled or owned. Because privately owned firms do not have to account to stock analysts, long-term profits may be more important than showing consistent positive quarterly returns. A good example of this kind of company is Cargill, the largest privately owned company in the world, which deals in commodities such as grain. Government-controlled firms may have objectives such as maintaining employment, providing service, or facilitating currency exchange. Some of the largest automobile companies in the world, such as Fiat (Italy) and Peugeot (France), have been unprofitable for many years because of high labor costs resulting from their countries' need to keep workers employed.

An interesting variant of the impact of private ownership on objectives occurs if the privatization resulted from a leveraged buyout (LBO). Even though the company is private, it is often more interested in profits and cash flow to pay down debt than it is in plowing money into activities that will help gain market share. An excellent example is the well-publicized LBO by Kohlberg Kravis Roberts & Company (KKR) of RJR Nabisco in 1988. Because of the large debt load the company assumed, many of RJR's brands became vulnerable to competitors, who took advantage of the opportunity to pursue market share gains. These competitors included Philip Morris in tobacco products (because RJR was reluctant to enter the low-price cigarette category) and competitors in snack foods, who took advantage of large cuts in advertising and promotion expenditures for RJR's Ritz crackers and Planters nut products. As of 1995, RJR was free of KKR, and began an attempt to regain the market share lost to Philip Morris, particularly for its flagship Winston cigarette brand.[11]

Estimates of competitors' objectives important information for marketing strategy development. A brand that is aggressive in its pursuit of market share must be viewed as a different kind of competitor than one that is attempting primarily to maximize profits. The latter would clearly be more vulnerable to you; you would probably want to avoid an expensive confrontation with the former.

Competitor Strategies

The marketing strategy diagram shows the elements of a complete marketing strategy. Other than the objectives, the major elements of the strategy that the marketing manager must monitor are the segments pursued (customer targets), the competitor targets, product features, the core strategy, and the supporting marketing mix.

Customer and Competitor Targets

How can the marketing manager determine the customer and competitor targets? For industrial products and services, three sources of information are useful: product sales literature, your own sales force, and trade advertising. The text of the sales literature may give information about the kinds of customers for whom the product is best suited and may also mention direct competitors by name. Your sales force should also be able to collect information from informal contacts, trade show discussions, and the like. The media in which the trade advertising is placed can be analyzed for their target markets by obtaining readership information from your advertising agency, information services such as Simmons Market Research Bureau or MRI, or the media themselves. For consumer products, media advertising is the best way to track the segmentation strategy and the competitor targets. As with industrial advertising, tracking services can identify the target customers by examining the audiences who view, read, or listen to the medium in which a competitor's ad appears. The copy of the ads themselves can be analyzed for competitor target information.

Product Features

Although we saw earlier in the book that customers buy benefits (i.e., what products and services can do for them, not product attributes), it is still useful to create a matrix of all comparative feature data. You can use this matrix to get a quick visual snapshot of how you compare to the competition, which you can use as part of the marketing strategy. Table 7–3 shows a product feature matrix (mid-1998) for eight handheld personal computer models.

Core Strategies

You can assess competitors' core strategies by studying their marketing communications. What you are looking for is how they are positioning their products in the market, how they are differentiating themselves, and, in sum, what is their value proposition.

An example of how this can be done is the advertisement shown in Fig. 7–4 for the Honda Passport, a four-wheel-drive sport utility vehicle. This is a crowded category (see Table 5–9 for other models) and many other manufacturers are interested in the Passport's positioning. The value proposition is clearly oriented toward the ability to use the car off the road and its ruggedness. Whether it works is not really the point (you can be the judge). What is important to the Honda marketing people is a competitor's positioning so they can take it into account in their own strategy formulation.

Table 7–3 Handheld PC Features

Reviewed units
Sidebar units*

Products listed in review order by category

Yes ■ No ▨

	Apple MessagePad 2100	AT&T PocketNet Service	Casio Cassiopeia A-20	Franklin Rex-3-DS PC Companion	Geofox-One Professional	HP 620LX Palmtop PC	Nokia 9000i Communicator	Psion Series 5 Handheld Computer
Price of tested configuration	$1,150 street	Telephone, $300 street; data access service, $29.99 per month	$600 street	$180 street	$799 direct	$900 street	$900 street	$600 street
Processor type/speed	StrongARM SA-110/162 MHz	N/A	Hitachi SH3/ 80 MHz	8-bit RISC/ 4.3 MHz	ARM-7 CL-PS7110/ 18.4 MHz	Hitachi SH3/ 75 MHz	Intel 386/ 24 MHz	ARM 7100/ 18 MHz
Operating system	Newton 2.1	N/A	Windows CE 2.0	Proprietary	EPOC32	Windows CE 2.0	Geoworks Geos 3.0	EPOC32
Dimensions (HWD, in inches)	1.1 × 4.7 × 8.3	1.2 × 2.2 × 6.1	1.0 × 7.3 × 3.1	0.3 × 3.8 × 2.1	0.8 × 7.4 × 4.7	1.4 × 7.8 × 4.1	1.5 × 6.5 × 2.5	0.9 × 6.7 × 3.5
Weight with batteries	22.4 oz.	9.6 oz.	15.2 oz.	1.4 oz.	13.7 oz.	20.6 oz.	14.0 oz.	12.5 oz.
Spacing on built-in QWERTY keyboard	N/A	N/A	12.0 mm	N/A	14.0 mm	13.0 mm	13.8 mm	14.3 mm
Speaker/ Microphone/ Digital audio recorder	■ ■ ■	▨ ▨ ▨	■ ■ ■	▨ ▨ ▨	■ ■ ■	■ ■ ■	■ ■ ■	■ ■ ■
Memory								
Installed/max-imum RAM	8MB/8MB	N/A	8MB/8MB	288K/288K	16MB/16MB	16MB/26MB	8MB/8MB	8MB/30MB
Installed/max-imum ROM	8MB/8MB	N/A	8MB/8MB	128K/128K	8MB/8MB	10MB/10MB	N/A	6MB/6MB

(continued)

Table 7–3 (Continued)

Reviewed units
Sidebar units*

Products listed in review order by category

Yes ■   No ▨

	Apple MessagePad 2100	AT&T PocketNet Service	Casio Cassiopeia A-20	Franklin Rex-3-DS PC Companion	Geofox-One Professional	HP 620LX Palmtop PC	Nokia 9000i Communicator	Psion Series 5 Handheld Computer
Display								
Resolution	480 × 320 pixels	4 lines × 12 characters	640 × 240 pixels	160 × 98 pixels	640 × 320 pixels	640 × 240 pixels	640 × 200 pixels	640 × 240 pixels
Dimensions (HW, in inches)	4.9 × 3.3	0.9 × 1.6	2.5 × 6.2	1.3 × 2.1	3.2 × 6.1	2.5 × 6.5	4.5 × 1.4	2.0 × 5.3
Number of colors or shades of gray	16 shades of gray	1 shade of gray	4 shades of gray	2 shades of gray	16 shades of gray	256 colors	8 shades of gray	16 shades of gray
Backlight	■	■	■	▨	■	■	▨	■
Input/Output								
Serial interface/VGA out/Compact card slot	▨ / ▨ / ■	▨ / ■	▨ / ■	▨ / ▨ / ■	▨ / ▨ / ■	■ / ■ / ■	▨ / ▨ / ■	■ / ▨ / ■
Built-in PC Card slots	Two Type II	None	One Type II	None	One Type II	One Type II	None	None
Communication								
Built-in software or hardware modem	None	Hardware	None	None	None	None	Software	None
Built-in modem speed in Kbps (data/fax)	N/A	19.2/19.2	N/A	N/A	33.6/14.4	N/A	9.6/9.6	N/A
IrDA port	■	▨	■	▨	■	■	■	■

Power

	Four AA alkaline batteries	Nickel hydride rechargeable battery pack	Two AA alkaline batteries	Two CR-2025 lithium ion watch batteries	Two AA alkaline batteries	Lithium ion battery pack	Two lithium ion batteries	Two AA alkaline batteries
Batteries	Four AA alkaline batteries	Nickel hydride rechargeable battery pack	Two AA alkaline batteries	Two CR-2025 lithium ion watch batteries	Two AA alkaline batteries	Lithium ion battery pack	Two lithium ion batteries	Two AA alkaline batteries
Rated battery life	24 hours	In use, 1.5 hours; standby, 9 hours; off, 55 hours	25 hours	6 months	25 hours	5.5 hours	In use 3.5 hours; standby, 35 hours; off, 1 week	35 hours
Battery charging time	N/A	30 minutes	N/A	N/A	N/A	4 hours	2.5 hours	N/A

Service and Support

	Four AA alkaline batteries	Nickel hydride rechargeable battery pack	Two AA alkaline batteries	Two CR-2025 lithium ion watch batteries	Two AA alkaline batteries	Lithium ion battery pack	Two lithium ion batteries	Two AA alkaline batteries
24-hour, 7-day live technical support	▪	◼	▪	▪	▪	▪	◼	▪
Standard warranty on parts/labor	1 year/1 year	90 days/90 days	1 year/1 year	2 years/2 years	3 years/3 years	1 year/1 year	1 year/1 year	1 year/1 year
One year on-site service included	▪	▪	▪	▪	▪	▪	◼	▪
24-hour turnaround for parts replacement	▪	▪	▪	▪	▪	▪	▪	▪

*These are preproduction units discussed in "Lightweight Newcomers Add Heavyweight Features."

N/A—Not applicable: The product does not have this feature.

NOTHING PICKS UP DIRT FASTER.

If you can see beyond the Passport's rugged good looks, you will appreciate its shift-on-the-fly 4-wheel drive and 190-horsepower V6 engine. ⓗ H O N D A

Supporting Marketing Mix

The mix provides insight into the basic strategy of the competitor and specific tactical decisions. These decisions are what customers observe in the marketplace; they are not exposed to and do not particularly care about a product's marketing strategy. However, customers are exposed to price, advertising, and other marketing mix elements. The areas to consider are the following:

- Price. Price is a highly visible element of a competitor's marketing mix; therefore, it raises several questions. If a brand's differential advantage is price based, is the list price uniform in all markets? If the strategy is quality based, what is the price differential claimed? Are discounts being offered? If so, to whom? What is the pattern of price changes over time?
- Communications. What advertising media are being used? What creative activities? Sales promotion activities such as price promotions, coupons, and other deals are important to track.
- Distribution. What kinds of selling approaches are being used? What are the sales commission rates? Have there been any changes in the distribution channels?
- Product or service capabilities. Product features have already been discussed; a comparison of customer service operations and capabilities is also useful.

Competitor Strengths and Weaknesses

To assess the strengths and weakness of a competitor, a table of the kind shown in Table 7–4 can be used. This table breaks down the information required to perform this assessment into five major categories:

- The ability of the competitor to conceive and design new products. This dimension of the analysis evaluates the new product introduction record of each competitor as well as their resources devoted to this effort. Clearly, a firm with a high ability to develop new products is a serious long-term threat in a market.

Table 7–4 Competitor Capabilities Matrix

	Firm/Product				
	A	**B**	**C**	**D**	**Our Product**
Conceive and design					
Technical resources					
Human resources					
Funding					
Produce					
Physical resources					
Human resources					
Market					
Sales force					
Distribution					
Service and sales policies					
Advertising					
Human resources					
Funding					
Finance					
Debt					
Liquidity					
Cash flow					
Budget system					
Manage					
Key people					
Decision process					
Planning					
Staffing					
Organization structure					

- The ability of each competitor to produce the product or deliver the service. A firm operating at capacity to produce a product is not as much of a threat to increase sales or share in the short run as is a firm that has slack capacity, assuming a substantial amount of time is required to bring new capacity on-line. Product quality issues are also important here.
- The ability to market. How aggressive and inventive are the firms in marketing their products? Do they have access to distribution channels? A competitor could have strong product development capabilities and slack capacity but be ineffective at marketing.
- The ability to finance. Limited financial resources hamper effective competition. Companies with highly publicized financial problems become vulnerable to competitors.
- The ability to manage. You can better understand competitor moves by studying the backgrounds of the competitors' managers. For example, someone just brought in to manage a product or a business who has a reputation as a cost-conscious operation-oriented person is likely to continue that behavior in his or her new job.

Details about the kind of information you might want to collect are shown in Table 7–5.

Table 7–5 Examples of Competitor Information to Collect

A. Ability to conceive and design
   1. Technical resources
      a. Concepts
      b. Patents and copyrights
      c. Technological sophistication
      d. Technical integration
   2. Human resources
      a. Key people and skills
      b. Use of external technical groups
   3. R&D funding
      a. Total
      b. Percentage of sales
      c. Consistency over time
      d. Internally generated
      e. Government supplied
   4. Technological strategy
      a. Specialization
      b. Competence
      c. Source of capability
      d. Timing: initiate versus imitate
   5. Management processes
      a. TQM
      b. House of Quality

B. Ability to produce
   1. Physical resources
      a. Capacity
      b. Plant
         i. Size
         ii. Location
         iii. Age
      c. Equipment
         i. Automation
         ii. Maintenance
         iii. Flexibility
   d. Processes
      i. Uniqueness
      ii. Flexibility
   e. Degree of integration
   2. Human resources
      a. Key people and skills
      b. Work force
         i. Skills mix
         ii. Union
   3. Suppliers
      a. Capacity
      b. Quality
      c. Commitment

C. Ability to market
   1. Sales force
      a. Skills
      b. Size
      c. Type
      d. Location
   2. Distribution network
      a. Skills
      b. Type
   3. Service and sales policies
   4. Advertising
      a. Skills
      b. Type
   5. Human resources
      a. Key people
      b. Turnover
   6. Funding
      a. Total
      b. Consistency over time
      c. Percentage of sales
      d. Reward system

D. Ability to finance
   1. Long term
      a. Debt/equity ratio
      b. Cost of debt
   2. Short term
      a. Cash or equivalent
      b. Line of credit
      c. Type of debt
      d. Cost of debt
   3. Liquidity
   4. Cash flow
      a. Days of receivables
      b. Inventory turnover
      c. Accounting practices
   5. Human resources
      a. Key people
      b. Turnover
   6. System
      a. Budgeting
      b. Forecasting
      c. Controlling

E. Ability to manage
   1. Key people
      a. Objectives and priorities
      b. Values
      c. Reward systems
   2. Decision making
      a. Location
      b. Type
      c. Speed
   3. Planning
      a. Type
      b. Emphasis
      c. Time span
   4. Staffing
      a. Longevity and turnover
      b. Experience
      c. Replacement policies
   5. Organization
      a. Centralization
      b. Functions
      c. Use of staff

Note that in Table 7–4 there is a column labeled "Our Product." You also have to do an honest self-analysis of your strengths and weaknesses by assessing your capabilities on the same dimensions as the competition. This is not easy to do; most managers feel that they are stronger than they really are on many of these dimensions. However, the analysis loses considerable value if the assessment is not accurate.

There are two ways to summarize the information from the analysis of strengths and weaknesses. One way is to first determine four to six key success factors for your market (e.g., strong distribution, excellent product quality). The competitors, including your company, can be rated on these factors. The format of the analysis could follow Table 7–6. This method provides an overview of the strongest companies or products in the market and shows what it takes to be successful in a particular market.

Table 7–6 Differential Competitor Advantage Analysis

Critical Success Factors	Firm/Product					Our Product
	A	B	C	D	E	
1						
2						
3						
4						
5						
Overall rating						

A second way to summarize the data is to use a classic format usually called a strengths, weaknesses, opportunities, and threats (SWOT) analysis. A SWOT analysis focuses only on your business and follows Fig. 7–5. Each quadrant of the figure contains a summary of the different components of the analysis, based on the competitive assessment and other information covered in this chapter. It is particularly important to examine the opportunities and threats.

Expected Future Strategies

As we noted earlier in the chapter, the bottom line of the competitor analysis is a forecast of their likely marketing strategies over the next year, the typical marketing planning horizon.

One approach does not involve forecasting at all: Sometimes competitors come right out and tell you what their future strategy will be. For example, in a 1992 article in the publication *Business Marketing,* the vice president of corporate marketing for the computer company Unisys indicated that the key segments they were going to pursue in the future were companies in the financial service, airline, and telecommunication industries as well as government contracts.[12] Closely scanning trade and general business publications often turns up nuggets like this one.

Figure 7–5

SWOT Analysis

Table 7–7 Three Scenarios

Scenario I: Gradual Adjustment

U.S. dollar remains weak, resulting in limited foreign sourcing. The product undergoes minor technological change without any strong patents or innovations. The U.S. economy grows at moderate pace, averaging about 3% per annum in GNP growth. Union power keeps declining without major strikes. Customers remain interested in high service.

Scenario II: High Turbulence

Major customers experience budgetary pressures from declining tax base. A strong U.S. dollar reduces exports and stimulates foreign products to enter the U.S. market. Overseas component sourcing and assembly increase. Product remains simple to manufacture.

Scenario III: Tough Times

Technological changes make the product very simple to produce. The U.S. dollar is very strong, causing stiff competition even at home. Furthermore, customers become increasingly more price sensitive and want less service. Some buy directly from overseas producers, bypassing the dealer network entirely.

Source: Paul J. H. Schoemaker (1991), "When and how to use scenario planning: a heuristic approach with illustration," *Journal of Forecasting*, 10, pp. 549–564.

Most of the time, however, you will not be as lucky as Unisys's competitors were in 1993. An alternative approach is to use the trend forecasting method described in Chapter 4, in which historical sales data were extrapolated into the future. You can do the same with competitors' marketing strategies by identifying a trend in their past actions and extrapolating it into the future.

A third approach to forecasting competitors' actions is to simulate them. For example, at many companies managers are given data about the competitors in their market. Then, they are divided into groups and asked to role-play the competition. In other words, they are asked, "If you were Company A, what would your marketing strategy be next year?" Using these simulated strategies, the company can formulate a strategy that accounts for reasoned forecasts of the competitors' actions.

A somewhat more sophisticated, long-term version of this simulation is called **scenario planning.**[13] In this analysis, alternative scenarios of the future are created, based on the structural aspects of the industry and competitor information. They are particularly useful as the basis for planning in uncertain environments, when data are scarce, and when many non-quantifiable factors affect outcomes in the market. Thus, fast-moving industries such as technology-based ones are particularly good applications for scenario planning, as are products that are subject to global political and economic forces, such as petroleum. Examples of brief scenarios are shown in Table 7–7. After a considerable discussion, the marketing manager would choose one scenario as the most likely and base his or her marketing plans on it. The analysis is somewhat similar to exploring "what-if" questions by using spreadsheet software.

WHERE DO WE GET THE INFORMATION?

Like the general marketing data sources listed in Table 4–2, information about the market is classified as primary or secondary. Many of the library sources mentioned in Chapter 4 provide the kinds of data that will help you perform the analyses described in this chapter.

A complete list of all kinds of sources is beyond the scope of this book.[14] However, some are particularly good for collecting information about competitors.

Secondary Sources

Some of the best secondary sources of information are the following:

- Internal sources. It is convenient to begin the search with internal queries about the existence of old marketing plans, market research studies, sales management call reports, and other documents.
- Annual reports. Although these are created only for publicly held companies (Dun & Bradstreet supplies what are called D&Bs on privately held firms) and they tend to be public relations oriented, you can comb through the report and find interesting financial information, plant locations, and general strategic thrusts from a corporate perspective. Public reporting documents at the line-of-business level, known as 10K statements, are more useful.
- Patent and trademark filings. These are available from on-line companies such as CompuServe and from MicroPatent, whose six–CD-ROM set, called MarkSearch, contains the text and images from the more than 1.5 million trademarks registered in the United States since 1884.
- General business and trade publications. As we have noted throughout this chapter, much information can be obtained from publications that are widely distributed (e.g., *Business Week,* the *Wall Street Journal*) or from those that are targeted towards specific industries (e.g., *Progressive Grocer, Marketing Computers, Twice* [for consumer electronics]).
- Consultants. Some organizations specialize in collecting information about particular markets. For example, FIND/SVP distributes a bimonthly catalog of available reports. The January/February 1998 issue offered a 227-page report on the market for bakery snacks. The report, costing $1,595, contains an analysis of marketing and new product trends, forecasts of the size of the U.S. market through the year 2001, and a close look at the market strategies of the major manufacturers.
- Trade associations. Most companies are members of trade associations; a list of such associations is available at most business libraries. These associations are usually formed for public relations or lobbying purposes, but they often perform market research for the member firms, which may provide industry data on market shares, price levels, and so on.
- Help wanted ads. A casual examination of the want ads in the *Wall Street Journal* or the *Financial Times* shows that companies disclose a good deal of information about their new products, areas of emphasis, job qualifications and standards, new plant or facility locations, and other information. It is useful to scan the Monster Board, the Online Career Center, and similar Internet-based job posting services.
- Electronic data services. The Web has a number of sites that are of particular interest for this kind of analysis. Some of them offer free information and others are subscription based:[15]

    Hoover's Online: Income statement and balance sheet numbers for 2,500 public companies.

    Cyberstocks: Links to information on companies that are prominent in Internet-related industries.

    Dun & Bradstreet's Online Access: Short reports on 10 million U.S. companies, many of them privately held.

> Ecola's 24-Hour Newsstand: Links to the Web sites of more than 2,000 newspapers, business journals, magazines, and computer publications.
>
> American Demographics: Provides demographic data as well as a directory of marketing consultants.
>
> Competitive Intelligence Guide: Sleuthing tips along with an "Internet Intelligence Index."

The biggest of all of these services is DIALOG, which offers access to such databases as Port Import Export Reporting Service (PIERS), the *Financial Times,* Moody's, press releases by more than 10,000 U.S. corporations, and much more.

Primary Sources

Special studies of the market will always be available from consultants who focus on particular industries. Other primary sources are as follows:

- Sales force and customers. Because salespeople interact with customers, including distributors, on a regular basis, they are in an excellent position to find out about competitor sales pitches, pricing, and many other aspects of their activity. Companies on the edge of technology use information from the sales force to make quick updates of their marketing data. With notebook computers and modems, salespeople can make their calls, complete call reports electronically, and send the information back to the local office or headquarters. On-line databases are immediately updated and ready to be viewed by marketing managers.
- Employees. Some companies train their employees to be vigilant about collecting market information. Like the salesperson call report, data collected by even non-marketing employees can be added to a corporate database.
- Suppliers. Often, suppliers are willing to give information about competitors' shipments to impress potential new customers.
- Trade shows. Company representatives often attempt to obtain information at competitors' booths. Peeks at new products and sales literature are always valuable.
- Reverse engineering or sampling competitors' products. If the product of interest is manufactured, you can buy the competitor's product and take it apart to study its costs, technology, and other strengths and weaknesses. If it's a service such as banking, open a small account and examine the competitor's statements and other information they send.
- Plant tours. Although many companies do not allow nonemployees into their manufacturing facilities, it is sometimes possible to obtain competitor information in this manner.[16]
- Internet newsgroups. On-line discussion groups have been formed to discuss almost everything, including companies, their products, and their strategies. A search of Dejanews shows what discussion groups exist in different categories.

COMPETITIVE STRATEGY: SOME GAME THEORY NOTIONS

As noted earlier in this chapter, one of the purposes of performing a competitor analysis is to anticipate a competitor's likely future strategies. A way of more formally (i.e., analytically) incorporating this anticipation into your decision-making is the use of a mathematical approach called **game theory.**[17] Game theory was invented by John von Neumann and Oskar Morgenstern to account for the interdependence of economic actors (e.g., marketing managers); interdependence occurs when the outcomes of a firm's actions depend on the actions of a competitor. It is also assumed that conflicts of interest exist in that the competitors differ in what they want to do and they cannot actively collude. Noncooperative game theory seeks to predict the behavior of rational, intelligent firms competing independently.[18]

The simplest form of a game requires three elements:

- A list of participants or players
- For each player, a list of strategies
- For each combination of strategies each player can use, a **payoff matrix** indicating the rewards and costs received by each player

Consider the pricing game shown in Fig. 7–6. The two players here are two managers, A and B. The strategies are to keep the product at the current price of $200 or increase it to $300. The payoffs are in the four boxes; for example, if both managers maintain the current price of $200, each will make $8,000 in profit. It is also assumed that the two managers move simultaneously rather than sequentially.

You should be able to immediately see two general benefits of thinking in game theory terms. First, you are forced to conceptualize the competitor's possible moves. Second, you must consider the financial (or other, such as market share) outcomes under the different scenarios. Thus, without even "solving" the game, there are important benefits to thinking strategically along game theory lines.

Solutions to game theory models require you to determine the game's equilibrium. The most common form of equilibrium is called the **Nash equilibrium.** A Nash equilibrium has the following properties:

A Nash equilibrium is a list of strategies, one for each player, with the property that no manager wants to unilaterally change his or her strategy. In other words, for each manager, its strategy in the equilibrium is the best response to the others' strategies in the equilibrium.

B's Strategies

	$200	$300
$200	$8K, $8K* (1)	$13K, $4K (2)
$300	$4k, $13K (3)	$10K, $10K (4)

A's Strategies

*The first number in each cell is A's payoff;
the second number in each cell is B's payoff.

Figure 7–6

A Pricing Game
Source: K. Sridhar Moorthy (1985), "Using game theory to model competition," *Journal of Marketing Research,* 22 (August), p. 264.

Let's try to work toward the equilibrium intuitively. Clearly, the best outcome for manager A is to keep the current price of $200 and have B charge $300 (this gives her $13,000 in profit). The best solution for manager B is to keep the price of $200 and have A charge $300. Thus, we have the conflict of interest necessary for a noncooperative game. The best collusive outcome is for both to charge $300; this results in the greatest total profits, $20,000, or $4,000 more than if A and B keep the prices the same. However, this collusive outcome is not an equilibrium because B has a financial incentive of $3,000 to move from box 4 to box 3 (i.e., not change her price). Likewise, boxes 2 and 3 are not equilibria. In box 2, B has an incentive to move to lower the price. In box 3, A has an incentive to lower the price. Box 1 is the equilibrium; neither manager has an incentive to increase the price. Therefore, the prediction is that both firms will keep prices at $200.[19]

This kind of game, in which competition leads to a less-than-optimum outcome for both managers, is called a **prisoner's dilemma game.** It is seen often in highly competitive industries. For example, you might wonder why Coke and Pepsi continue to run sales promotions and compete so strongly on price. Clearly, the best solution would be for neither to promote (box 4 in Fig. 7–6), which would jointly maximize their profits. However, both are worried that if they stop promoting while the other does not (boxes 2 and 3), they will suffer. As a result, the equilibrium is heavy promotion by both (box 1) and lower total profits. A similar situation holds for the airline industry, particularly on certain routes that are served by low-cost airlines such as Southwest. Prisoner's dilemma games also apply to advertising expenditures: Both competitors are afraid to reduce expenditures for fear of falling into box 2 or 3. Thus, the predictions of even this simple form of game theory are very consistent with what you see in practice.[20]

We can extend game theory notions to include the concept of leader–follower. In this case, one manager chooses to make the first move and the other follows. This is often the case in industries in which one company has historically chosen to be the first in changing price or making some other marketing mix or strategic decision. For example, U.S. Steel used to be the first company in the steel industry to raise prices to the industry's major customers, such as the automobile companies.

An example of this kind of game is shown in Fig. 7–7. In this case, we assume that A is typically the leader and B is the follower. In leader–follower games, the decisions are still made at the same time but the managers consider the market reactions from the perspective of A moving first. Manager A will not choose to raise the price to $300 because she sees that B's optimal move is to price at $200 no matter what she does. B's strategy is to charge $200 no matter what A does (again, A's strategy is not observable at this point). The $200/$200

Figure 7–7

A Leader–Follower Game

Source: K. Sridhar Moorthy (1985), "Using game theory to model competition," *Journal of Marketing Research*, 22 (August), p. 264.

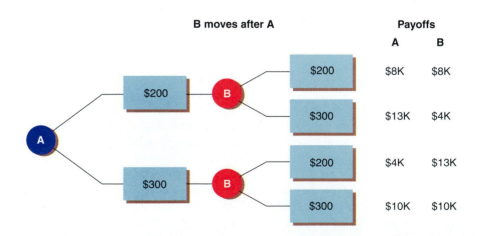

solution is an equilibrium because if B is going to choose $200 no matter what A does, A will choose $200 because it means $4,000 more in profits. At the same time, if A is going to choose $200, B does best by choosing $200. Although the equilibrium is the same as for the simultaneous game shown in Fig. 7–6, there is no guarantee that this will happen in general.

As we noted earlier, the central importance of game theory is the disciplined thinking it imposes on managers. However, other applications besides those already mentioned can benefit from this kind of thinking. For example, game theory thinking is well suited to decisions about new product entrants. The main issues are as follows:

- Is there a first-mover advantage?
- Can entry be deterred by an incumbent in the market? How?
- What is the incumbent's (entrant's) optimal defensive (entry) strategy?

Game theory has also been applied to model manufacturer–retailer relations in a channel system. Unlike competitors, who have a natural conflict of interest over customers, channel members are supposed to be cooperative. However, by assuming that each party acts independently, one can use game theory to obtain channel coordination rules.

Management consultants have latched onto game theory in their work. One consultant offers the following advice for applying game theory:[21]

- Industries with four or fewer significant competitors offer the best potential for using game theory because with a small number of competitors, it is easier to envision the possible strategies and payoff matrix. In addition, larger firms have more to gain through its application.
- If there are few purchases but each is large (mainframe computers, jet engines), competition is more intense and there is more value to thinking strategically.
- The same holds in an industry whose costs are largely fixed, such as airlines and financial services.
- Situations involving competitive bidding are excellent applications for game theory because it is crucial to strategize about bidding competitors.

In general, industries subject to strong competition (see the industry structure analysis earlier in the chapter) tend to be fertile application areas for game theory and strategic thinking.

EXECUTIVE SUMMARY

The key concepts covered in this chapter are the following:

- A market structure analysis attempts to assess current and potential competition.
- Most marketing managers can identify the competitors that are the most direct (i.e., those that physically look like their product or service). However, a broad view of competition should include a consideration of other organizations that are attempting to satisfy the same set of needs and benefits as your product does.
- Once you have completed a marketing structure analysis, you should analyze the most critical competitors identified to better understand their objectives, strategies, strengths, and weaknesses and to predict their likely future strategies.
- Information for analyzing competitors can come from both primary and secondary sources; the Internet is a prime secondary source.

- The game theory concept of equilibrium can help you strategically apply your expectations of competitors' likely future actions and their impact on market outcomes such as profits and market share.

CHAPTER QUESTIONS

1. Most marketing managers consider their product form or product category competitors to be the most serious threats. What are the pros and cons of this perspective?
2. Choose a product or a service. How would you design a research study to better understand the generic competitors for this product?
3. In most cases, competitors are viewed as being undesirable; that is, fewer competitors are better than more. Can you think of situations in which having competitors can help you?
4. What are the limitations to the game theory approach to understanding competitive strategy?
5. Other than the Coke/Pepsi illustration used in the book, have you observed any other markets in which the competitors appeared to be acting strategically in the game theory sense?

Integrated Case

Application Exercises: Market Structure and Competitor Analysis in the PC Industry

1. Pick a PC brand. Develop an assessment of the competition for that brand using Fig. 7–2 as a guide.
2. What are the implications of your answer to question 1 for the advertising of this brand? What are the implications for the company's sales force? (Hint: Consider the communication implications of the competition at each level.)
3. Pick two competitors for your focal brand. Based on this set of three brands, collect secondary data to develop a competitor analysis by answering the following questions:
   a. What are the two competitors' objectives?
   b. What are their current strategies?
   c. What are their capabilities (include your brand)?
   d. Based on your answer to (c), what are the relative strengths and weaknesses of the three brands?
   e. What is your best guess about the two competitors' likely future strategies?

FURTHER READING

Two good books on the topic of market definition are Derek F. Abell (1980), *Defining the Business: The Starting Point of Strategic Planning* (Englewood Cliffs, NJ: Prentice Hall); and Art Weinstein (1998), *Defining Your Market* (New York: Haworth). Many books give a more detailed look at competitor analysis. One is Timothy W. Powell (1993), *Analyzing Your Competition* (New York: FIND/SVP). An economics approach is provided by Sharon M. Oster (1994), *Modern Competitive Analysis* (New York: Oxford University Press). An excellent book applying game theory concepts to business strategy is Adam M. Brandenburger and Barry J. Nalebuff (1996), *Competition* (New York: Doubleday).

Communications and Advertising Strategy

8

CHAPTER BRIEF

The purpose of this chapter is to introduce the concept of integrated marketing communications (IMC) and explain how to develop advertising strategy within an IMC program. After reading this chapter, the reader should understand the following:

The basic model of communication between sender and receiver and how technology is changing that model

The elements of an IMC program

Setting advertising goals and selecting target audiences

Developing message strategies

Key elements of media planning

How advertising budgets are set

Alternative approaches for evaluating advertising spending

T he Land Rover Discovery was launched in the United States in 1994.[1] The Discovery was introduced in the United Kingdom in 1989 as the third brand in the Land Rover product line. The original Land Rover, developed in the late 1940s and modified as the Defender, was traditionally positioned as a rugged, off-road four-wheel-drive vehicle that evoked the feelings of an African safari. The Range Rover, first introduced in 1970, was developed to be an upscale version of the Land Rover, a sport utility vehicle (SUV) was both rugged and luxurious as well. The Range Rover was not sold in the United States until Land Rover North America (LRNA) was formed in 1986. It maintained the safari image but with more class and a higher price (over $50,000) than the Defender, which was priced in the high $20,000s. Land Rover had been very successful in developing a strong image and brand identity centered around a particular lifestyle: individualism, authenticity, freedom, adventure, guts, and supremacy.

The Discovery was born out of necessity. In the mid-1980s, the Japanese successfully identified a new SUV leisure segment in Europe that was broken into two distinct groups: young, affluent, childless adults looking to make a statement about their image and accomplishments, and more conservative buyers (who were more interested in functional aspects of the car) such as families and older traditionalists. Land Rover had not explicitly targeted either of these groups with its two models, the Land Rover (Defender from 1992) and the Range Rover; the former targeted the off-road and ruggedness benefit segment and the latter was very high-priced for young couples and families. In addition, in the early 1990s products targeting the latter segment were being introduced into the U.S. market at a rapid pace, with nearly every major automobile company having at least one model. The Discovery was introduced with a combination of an attractive price ($28,500) and the Land Rover heritage.

By late 1994, the Discovery was very successful, with prospective buyers facing waiting lists at the dealers. However, management decided to dramatically increase the overall LRNA sales objectives to 40,000 units per year for all models from the roughly 5,000 LRNA was selling at the time. This was going to be very difficult to do in the United States, given the rapid rise of the SUV category. Several brands, such as the Jeep Cherokee and Ford Explorer, sold over 300,000 units per year and every major automobile manufacturer either had a model or was planning to introduce one shortly (even Mercedes). In order to increase consumer awareness of the Discovery and differentiate it from the competition, LRNA developed a communication campaign involving several components. First, an advertising campaign promoting the car to both families and couples without children was used (see Fig. 8–1). Second, LRNA considered using a mix of corporate sponsorships and PR activities such as the "24 hours of Aspen," a car race, support of equestrian trials and polo matches, and sponsorship of the Virginia Cup Tennis Challenge. A third program involved what they called "experience" marketing programs. These included the Land Rover Driving Academy in Colorado, which gave specialized off-road driving instruction to Land Rover owners. Other communication activities included an owner newsletter and a Web site. LRNA also considered a variety of promotional efforts such as a treasure hunt designed to highlight attributes such as storage capacity and off-road capabilities. Finally, they developed a retail concept, Land Rover Centres: LRNA dealers would have Land Rover branded merchandise (outdoor clothing, watches), accessories (roof racks, bike carriers), off-road equipment (e.g., winches), and adventure travel arrangements.

In considering the adoption of an overall communications program for the Discovery, LRNA marketing managers had to consider the following:

- Have all the possible communication activities been considered?
- Are they well integrated; that is, are they sending a consistent message to the consumers?
- Is the advertising strategy appropriate for the Discovery?
- How much money should be allocated for the various communication activities?
- What new communication options exist (e.g., the Internet)?

In the marketing strategy diagram, it can be seen that a complete marketing strategy involves first a strategic part (with a selection of target segments and a core strategy involving the differential advantage and value proposition) and then a tactical or implementation part involving the marketing mix (price, advertising, channels of distribution, and promotion). In other words, you must first develop the general strategy and then make decisions about how to implement that strategy using devices that are visible to customers.

This chapter is about communications and advertising management. Although most people think only of advertising when we discuss communications, all elements of the marketing mix deliver a message to potential customers. The act of running a sales promotion may indicate to some customers that the list price is too high and must be lowered. Some customers may interpret a promotion as a sign of lower quality. Price is also a communication tool: A high price relative to competition means something different from a discount price. The product's package delivers messages. The fact that one brand can be purchased only in exclusive outlets can also be interpreted as a sign of quality. Sponsorship of a professional golf tournament reaches a particular segment and communicates that product's or

Protect your family from the most dangerous animals on earth.

For over 40 years Land Rovers have stood up to irate water buffalo and outmaneuvered entire stampedes.

So there's much to be said for the new Discovery when confronted by the automotive wildlife on Canada's roads.

It was the first family 4x4 to come with dual airbags.

What's more, with its superior ABS and permanent 4-wheel drive, the Discovery provides security that goes well beyond the front seats.

Particularly with our steel inner body cage and massive 14-gauge chassis surrounding your son, daughter, and golden retriever.

What's all the more extraordinary is

that the Discovery can provide this kind of security on virtually any kind of terrain. From Amazon trails submerged in water to the sands of the Kalahari, not to mention, the mud-covered lot at the little league field.

Why not call 1-800-FINE 4WD for more information?

Starting at around $41,900,* it's rather modestly priced.

Especially for a vehicle intended to keep a family of seven, a family of seven.

Land Rovers have survived jungles, swamps, even the Kalahari. But this?

Seat kicking, upholstery trouncing, and all-out mud slopping.

Such indulgences are perfect for the new Discovery from Land Rover.

Available dual sunroofs and folding jump seats make for an enormously spacious interior, seating a family of seven comfortably, wherever you go.

And you can go wherever.

It is, after all, a Land Rover.

Along with features such as permanent four-wheel drive, a 3.9 liter V-8

engine, and resilient coil spring suspension, it comes with a history of astounding driving accomplishments.

Surely it could take your kids to school in a blizzard. Actually, with a

7700 pound towing capacity in low range, it could take the bus.

What's more, the Discovery is the first 4x4 ever to have dual airbags. Along with its ABS system, side door beams, and steel inner body cage, it's a great place to have children.

Why not call 1-800-FINE 4WD for the nearest dealer? Starting at just under $29,000,* it's great for the one place known as the most challenging a vehicle has to endure: Suburbia.

Figure 8–1

Land Rover Discovery
Introductory
Advertising

Courtesy of Land Rover
North America, Inc.

How to prepare the Discovery for the jungles of Madagascar.

What can you possibly do to make the new Discovery from Land Rover any better?

It already has a 14-gauge steel chassis, steel frame, and phenomenally-resilient coil spring suspension, all of which enable it to drive through places where the only other vehicles you'll see are helicopters.

It also already comes with almost 70 cubic feet of interior space.

That's almost enough room for a whole Malagasy little league team.

And it already has a high level of security. Aside from its steel inner

body cage, side door beams, ABS, and permanent four-wheel drive, the Discovery is the first 4x4 ever to have dual airbags.

So why not call 1-800-FINE 4WD for the nearest dealer?

At just around $29,000,* it's an astonishingly capable vehicle. Realize though, that even the Discovery can't drive beyond a certain point:

"E."

service's interests in appealing to that segment. The sales force obviously directly communicates with customers.

Therefore, before describing the details of implementing a marketing strategy through the marketing mix, we provide the reader with some background in communication theory and discuss how the decisions you make affect your target customers. Forward-looking

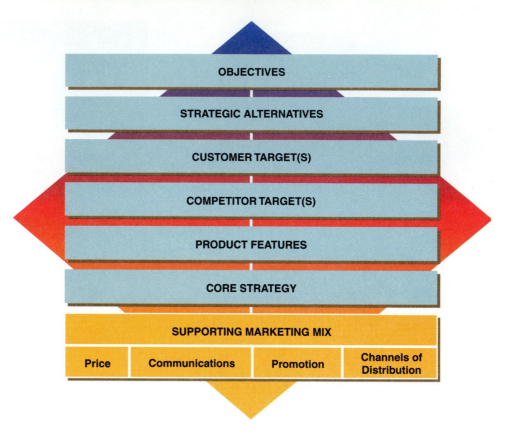

organizations are stressing a concept called **integrated marketing communications** (IMC), in which the marketing manager does not think of all the elements of the marketing mix as communicating separate messages; these messages are coordinated to reinforce what each is saying and to prevent customer confusion from conflicting messages. In other words, the decisions about the marketing mix must be made in concert, which makes developing a strategy before making implementation decisions even more important because the strategy provides the value proposition, which is the basis for all communications to customers.

COMMUNICATIONS

A basic communication model is shown in Fig. 8–2.[2] The two major participants in the communication process are the sender (the source of the communication) and the receiver. In marketing, these are typically the marketer and the customer. The sender uses some kind of medium or channel to communicate the message; this is represented in the middle of the figure. The sender decides how to send the message through an encoding process, which could be the creative part of an advertisement or Web site. The receiver (customer) interprets or decodes the message and decides what an appropriate response is. The receiver may also provide feedback or information to the sender. Finally, noise may interrupt or disrupt the communication process. For example, a person watching a television commercial at home may be distracted by a crying baby.

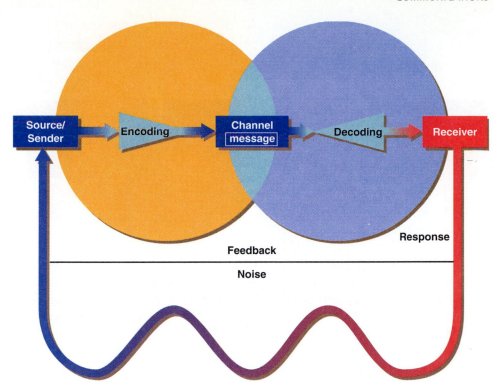

Figure 8–2

Model of the
Communication
Process

Source: George E. Belch and
Michael A. Belch (1993),
*Introduction to Advertising and
Promotion* (Homewood, IL:
Irwin).

Thus, the communication process starts when the source decides what kind of words, symbols, or pictures to use to encode the message. In some cases, the source could be the company; in others, it may be a spokesperson (e.g., Michael Jordan for Nike). The sender's objective is to encode the message in a way that resonates with the target audience. This obviously requires some marketing research to uncover what kinds of messages are appropriate for the audience.

Of particular importance to the marketer are the different channels or media that can be used. A distinction can be drawn between **personal** and **nonpersonal channels of communication.** The former include direct contacts such as a sales force or salespeople in a retail channel. Personal channels also include face-to-face interactions between customers, or what is called word-of-mouth communication. Such communications are critically important for the diffusion of new products and entertainment such as movies. It is therefore important to understand that customers can be attracted by messages directed to them or by an indirect approach in which opinion leaders or other buyers talk to other prospective customers. Nonpersonal channels are often called mass media and include television, newspapers, radio, direct mail, billboards, magazines, and the Internet.

A large portion of marketing communication is focused on the mass media. Figure 8–3 shows a modified version of the general communication model shown in Fig. 8–2.[3] The basic feature of this model is the one-to-many aspect of mass communication: The marketer is attempting to send persuasive communications to a large group of people. Thus, in this model the firm sends content or a message through a medium to a large number of potential customers.

A notable feature of this model is that there is no interaction between customers and firms. This concept of passive customers is incorrect because customers have always participated in personal channels of communication and have given feedback to companies in

Figure 8–3

Traditional Mass Marketing Communication Model

Source: Donna L. Hoffman and Thomas P. Novak (1996), "Marketing in hypermedia computer-mediated environments: conceptual foundations," *Journal of Marketing*, 60 (July), p. 52.

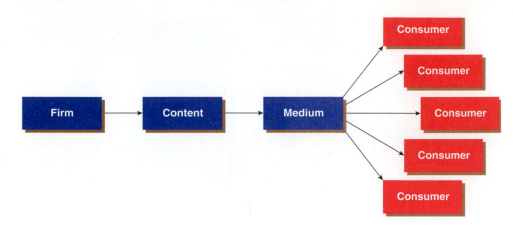

the form of complaints and responses to surveys. However, these channels have traditionally been slow, making it difficult for companies to be proactive.

In the current electronic environment, with Internet and Web technology, customers can communicate with each other easily and quickly. The speed with which news of Intel's 1994 problem with the Pentium processor spread through the user population and then to the general population astounded even Intel. In addition, customers can provide feedback to companies in real time rather than with a substantial delay. This feedback often comes from user groups who form their own electronic clubs (called listservs), can form a collective opinion, and supply information very quickly about new or developing products. These brand communities can be very active and influential.

For example, Saab owners, who tend to like the quirky nature of the cars (and are perhaps quirky themselves), have several very active user groups. They trade opinions about

As the spokesperson for Jell-O gelatin, Bill Cosby plays a key role in the company's marketing communications. Cosby's well-known rapport with young children makes him an ideal figure to connect with this product's target audience of moms and kids. (Michell Gerber/Corbis)

This trendy cyber cafe is just one example of how technology is changing marketing communications. Unlike traditional channels of communication, Internet and Web technology allow customers to provide companies with feedback in real time and share product-related problems and concerns with other customers easily and quickly. (Kevin Fleming/Corbis)

new product designs and service centers, and are generally very active participants in their groups. A new product idea was scratched when the user groups banded together to protest.[4]

This kind of environment is captured by the model shown in Fig. 8–4. In today's environment, marketing managers must be aware of the speed with which communications flow through the system and that a considerable amount of word-of-mouth can be generated in special interest user groups. A number of interesting questions emerge from this conceptualization of marketing communications:

- As the marketing manager, how do you manage these brand communities? If marketing-related communications are being transmitted in these groups, it can be potentially damaging to let negative information go without a response.
- What are the ethical dimensions of these kinds of communications? For example, a competitor's employee could pose as an owner and spread unfavorable information about a brand.
- In this kind of electronic back-and-forth, who really is the sender and who is the receiver? It is not always clear who is initiating the communications and who is marketing ideas to whom.

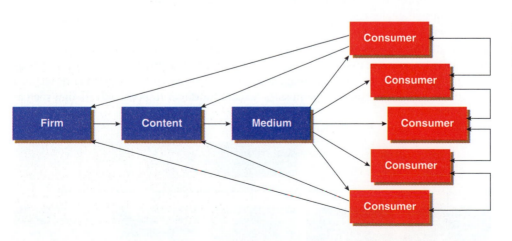

Figure 8–4

Modified Mass Communication Model

A final aspect of Fig. 8–4 is the interaction between the customers and the content. In this kind of environment,[5] the customer can create the content. For example, at the Web site for Firefly, users provide information about their preferences for movies and other descriptive information about themselves. The content is then customized based on this information; movies are recommended and advertising is targeted based on the member's supplied data. Thus, the interaction between the customer and the medium creates user-specific content.

INTEGRATED MARKETING COMMUNICATIONS

As we noted earlier in this chapter, the objective of an integrated approach to marketing communications is to ensure that all the elements of the communications mix are coordinated with the marketing strategy, delivering the same underlying positioning and value proposition to the target segment. Although different tools are used to accomplish the overall marketing objective, the job of the marketing manager is to aid this coordination by linking the various people and agencies involved.

Elements of the communications mix are shown in Fig. 8–5 and a spending breakdown is shown in Table 8–1. Although not all elements of the mix are used for every product or service, each has its own strengths and weaknesses and the marketing manager can use this complementarity to accomplish the marketing objective. Most of these elements are covered in more detail in later chapters of this book.

Advertising

Advertising has traditionally been defined as any paid form of nonpersonal communication about an organization, product, service, or idea by an identified sponsor.[6] However, advertising is no longer nonpersonal because it can depend greatly on interactions between an individual customer and the organization.

Advertising has several important advantages over other elements of the communications mix. It offers a fair amount of control over what you can say to potential customers. Advertising can also reach a large number of customers efficiently. Although it may cost hundreds of thousands of dollars to put a spot on a national television program, that program is probably reaching millions of potential customers; no other communications program can reach so many customers so quickly and at such a low cost per customer. Advertising is also flexible in that many different kinds of images and symbols can be presented. Copy strategies can be humorous, serious, or emotional, show the product in action, and explicitly compare your product to a competitor's.

Advertising also has drawbacks. It is difficult to evaluate the effectiveness of advertising, particularly because it is usually used to build sales in the long term by achieving other intermediate objectives in the short run (e.g., awareness). Because advertising rarely results in a measurable and observable change in sales (except for direct response advertising such as

Figure 8–5

Elements of the
Communication Mix

Table 8–1 Marketing Communications Expenditures

Consumer Versus Business-to-Business Products

	Percentage of the Communications Budget	
	Consumer	Business-to-Business
Television	45.1%	2.7%
Print advertising	14.5	27.4
Literature, coupons, point of purchase	16.2	9.3
Direct mail	6.4	27.1
Radio	5.6	0.8
Catalogs	4.1	10.7
Public relations	3.1	5.3
Trade shows	2.0	12.9
Out-of-home media	1.7	0.5
Dealer/distribution materials	1.3	3.3

Source: Cyndee Miller (1996), "Marketing industry report: who's spending what on biz-to-biz marketing?" *Marketing News*, January 1, p. 1; "Marketing industry report: consumer marketers spend most of their money on communications," *Marketing News*, March 11, p. 1.

infomercials, or extended TV commercials), you often wonder what you are getting for your money. In addition, advertising, especially TV advertising, can be very expensive and make it difficult for a small company or any company with a small budget to make much of an impact in the market. Much advertising in mass media (TV and general audience magazines, for example) is wasted because it is not the best communications element for targeting a specific audience directly. Many people outside the target audience see the ads, which may not be problematic except when products such as tobacco and alcohol (which are subject to legal age restrictions for purchase) are advertised. Advertising can be ignored or the signal disrupted by noise (see Fig. 8–2). Finally, customers are bombarded with ads in the United States and other Western countries; this makes it difficult for your message to get through the clutter.

Direct Marketing

Direct marketing is any communication form that sends messages directly to a target market with the anticipation of an immediate or short-term response. There are many ways to implement direct marketing. **Telemarketing** uses the telephone to reach potential customers. **Direct mail marketing** involves sending letters or catalogues. Some companies such as Amway, Mary Kay, and Tupperware have differentiated themselves from competition using a **direct sales** approach in which friends and neighbors are used as the sales force. Direct marketing also uses the Internet; some companies send e-mails to potential customers indicating that they have a special offer. Many companies rely exclusively on direct marketing as the main form of communication; others include it as one component of the communications mix. It is used extensively in both consumer and business-to-business marketing contexts.

The main advantage of direct marketing is clear: You can focus on your target and deliver a message intended only for that target. As a result, there is little waste in this customization process. In addition, the effectiveness of a direct mail campaign is easy to evaluate because the response comes quickly after the date of the promotion or not at all. In many societies, high levels of disposable income and interest in shopping convenience have made shopping through catalogues very popular.

However, many customers are put off by direct marketing efforts. Too many calls at home make customers wary of telemarketers. In many countries, the activities of such direct marketers are restricted. Many people's daily mail is full of direct mail pieces—what many people call junk mail—thus making it difficult for your message to get through the clutter. Response rates to direct marketing can be very low.

Sales Promotion

Sales promotion involves communication activities that provide extra incentives to customers or the sales force to achieve a short-term objective. **Consumer-oriented promotions** include devices such as coupons, point-of-purchase savings, sweepstakes, rebates, and free samples. Many promotions are oriented toward the channels of distribution, including the sales force; these are called **trade promotions.** The objective of trade promotions is to get the channels to carry the product and promote it. These include sales contests, quantity discounts, and training programs.

The advantage of such promotions is that they can generate a measurable short-term sales response. Sales promotion is much more effective than advertising in this regard. Sampling (free sample) programs are very effective for inducing trial of new products. Promotions such as coupons delivered in a magazine can complement an advertising campaign by reinforcing a brand name. They are also effective in getting customers to repeat purchase or buy a larger size. Trade promotions are essential to gaining shelf space in retail outlets.

A disadvantage of sales promotion is that it is always focused on price. As a result, customers can be induced to become more price sensitive and deal loyal (loyal to the brand that is on some kind of promotion) rather than brand loyal. In some ways, it actually works against advertising, which is more focused on building brand equity. Customers can also begin to expect sales promotions and delay purchases until a rebate or some other special deal is offered. Finally, most studies of the effects of sales promotion show the results to be short lived.

Publicity and Public Relations

Unlike advertising, **public relations** (PR) and publicity are communications for which the sponsoring organization does not pay. PR normally takes the form of an article in a magazine or newspaper or in any other form of nonpersonal news distribution. Often, companies employ PR firms or agencies to make sure that articles and other news favorable to the company are placed in media to which a variety of constituents (e.g., customers, stockholders, legislators) are exposed.

The main advantage of PR is that it comes from a supposedly unbiased source. It therefore has more credibility than advertising, which everyone knows is intended to promote the product or service. In addition, other than the cost of the PR agency, it is inexpensive.

The problem with PR is that the sponsoring company has little control over it. You cannot control the placement of the item in a publication, what is said about you, or any other aspect of PR. In addition, PR can be negative. If your company is accused of sexual discrimination in hiring and promotion practices, this is likely to damage your reputation. In these cases, PR firms usually attempt to limit the problem by taking damage control measures such as releasing favorable information about the company.

Personal Selling

Personal selling is the use of face-to-face communications between seller and buyer. For companies marketing business-to-business products and services, this is often the largest part of the marketing budget. Salespeople can target their messages to customers and the personal interaction permits them to respond to customer questions on the spot. In addition, more information can be communicated through a salesperson–customer encounter than would be possible through advertising or other mass communication approaches. This makes personal selling particularly appropriate for very expensive and complex products and services.

The major drawback of personal selling is the expense. Training and compensating salespeople is expensive. In addition, even with the best training programs, it is difficult for the marketing or sales manager to control what happens in the sales encounter. For example, a training program that focuses on marketing the product on a quality basis can fall apart if the sales force sells on price instead.

Miscellaneous Communications Activities

A number of other communications activities are important parts of the communications mix. A product's package can deliver a variety of messages to customers, including price, nutrition, ingredients, information about how to use it, and other recipes. In some industries, trade shows (large convocations where sellers, buyers, and suppliers congregate) are important ways to communicate with potential customers and demonstrate new products. Some companies sponsor events such as golf and tennis tournaments, which are intended to target customers who attend and watch them. Companies pay movie companies to place their brands in scenes so that millions of viewers can see them on the big screen.

A good example of a miscellaneous communications activity is the money spent by LRNA on the Land Rover Centre concept mentioned at the beginning of the chapter. The brand's image as a rugged, outdoor four-wheel-drive SUV is enhanced by these centers, which have a hunting-lodge look and a driving demonstration course. Forty of these centers have been built, with 70% containing the demonstration course. The course offers customers the opportunity to drive the vehicle on a 40-degree incline, demonstrating how stable the ride is. The outdoorsy feel is enhanced by the sales associates wearing khaki safari clothing.

Illustration: Amdahl Corporation

For more than 20 years, Amdahl Corporation was very successful selling IBM-compatible mainframe computers.[7] Founded by ex-IBMer Gene Amdahl, the company's mission was to take advantage of the huge installed base of IBM mainframes and use that to its advantage with lower prices.

However, in 1993, because of the increasingly smaller but more powerful computers used by most business customers, as well as a significant shift to networked personal computers running from servers rather than mainframes, the company lost $580 million on $1.7 billion in revenues.

As a result, the company shifted its marketing strategy away from selling IBM-compatible mainframes and peripheral equipment to selling services. In particular, they are trying to leverage their experience in mission-critical computing by abandoning their dependence on customers having IBM mainframes. They help customers prevent and resolve problems with hardware, networking performance, overall system availability, security, and backup for any hardware platform. This change has resulted in a sales mix that is now about 60% services (mainframe maintenance, services, and software) and 40% hardware.

Because of the new strategy, they also needed a new communications program to introduce customers to their new emphasis on selling services, not hardware. Aimed at current customers, the advertising campaign (see Fig. 8–6) uses a variety of provocative themes such as "End Segregation," focusing on the arbitrary separation of data within a company.

Figure 8–6

Amdahl
Advertisement

Amdahl Corporate Branding
Campaign by Dazai
Advertising, Inc. San Jose,
CA 1996.

To support the advertising campaign, designed to position Amdahl as a reliable supplier of both services and hardware, the company instituted a communications program designed to be integrated with the print advertising campaign. This included direct mail and telemarketing campaigns as well as a PR campaign (see the press release in Fig. 8–7). ◆

◆ Illustration: M&M Mars

M&M Mars is using a variety of communication devices to launch its new M&M's Crispy, candy-coated milk chocolate surrounding a crispy rice center.[8] The launch of the new brand is being supported by a $50-million advertising budget, more than 75 million free samples, and 100 million coupons offering free products. The tagline for the rollout is "The Feeding Frenzy Has Begun," which was appropriate in the initial stages because the company could not make enough to fill the demand.

The advertising began with the 1999 Super Bowl commercials and ran for 36 weeks. The commercials introduced the nervous-looking Orange M&M animated character who hangs out with Red and Yellow. The advertising campaign also uses radio and print media. Radio spots are played in the top 100 markets, and the print campaign featured ads in magazines such as *Rolling Stone, Entertainment, People,* and *TV Guide.*

Specifics about the coupons and other promotional support include the following:

- 15 million samples distributed in specially marked packages of cereals such as General Mills Honey Nut Cheerios and Frosted Cheerios
- College campuses and high schools were hit with 10 million samples
- 50 million samples were given away at "impulse" locations (e.g., supermarkets)
- Two full-page free-standing inserts (FSIs) in newspapers offered a free single pack.
- 2 million free sample coupons were distributed in M&M packs and boxes of Kudos
- The product was featured in the M&M/Mars Web page.

The objective of the integrated communication program was to increase M&M's sales more than 7% over the 1998 figure of more than $337 million. ◆

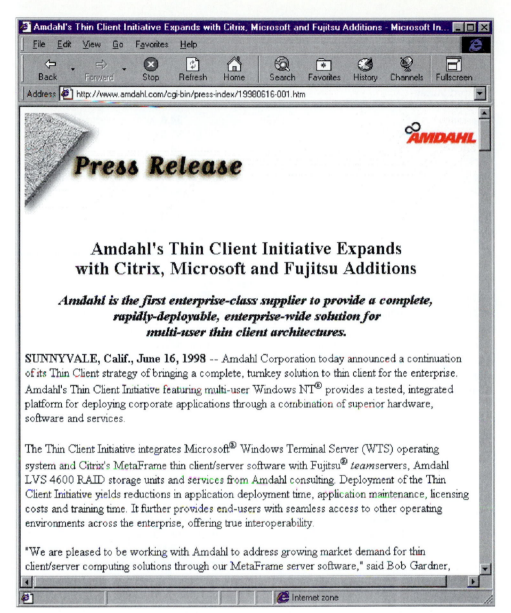

Figure 8–7

Amdahl Press Release

Courtesy of Amdahl

ADVERTISING MANAGEMENT

Advertising is a major expense for marketing managers worldwide and a big business. In 1998, about $112 billion was spent on advertising in the United States, $38 billion in Japan, and $22 billion in Germany.[9] Table 8–2 lists the advertising expenditures for the top 10 countries and the percentage spent on TV and newspapers, the media constituting the greatest expenditures. To give you some idea of the amount of money spent on advertising by company, Table 8–3 breaks down advertising spending by major consumer brands and Table 8–4 does the same for business-to-business advertising.

Often, for consumer products, marketing managers think of advertising spending in the context of how much to spend on both advertising and sales promotion. Table 8–1 shows that, for these kinds of products, advertising and promotion (television, print advertising,

Table 8–2 Top 10 Global Advertisers (by country)

	Spending ($ billion)	TV	Newspapers
United States	112.4	39.0%	36.1%
Japan	37.9	45.5	27.5
Germany	22.3	24.6	43.1
United Kingdom	18.9	31.8	35.9
France	10.6	34.5	23.3
Brazil	10.1	60.8	22.1
Italy	7.2	54.8	21.5
Spain	5.2	38.5	33.8
Australia	5.1	35.3	41.5
Canada	4.9	36.0	40.7

Source: Juliana Koranteng (1998), "To global ad markets," *Ad Age International*, May 11, pp. 15-19.

literature, radio, and out-of-home media) are over 80% of the communication budget. In recent years, the percentage of the advertising and promotion budget spent on advertising has declined as more money has been devoted to promotion, particularly promotion oriented toward trade or distribution channels. In 1993, 52% of the advertising and promotion budget went to trade promotion and 28% to media advertising. In 1995, spending on trade promotion jumped to 58% of the advertising and promotion budget and media advertising declined to 23% (consumer-oriented promotion remained virtually level).

Advertising decision-making has six stages:

1. Target audience selection
2. Goal setting
3. Message strategy

Table 8–3 Leading Consumer Product Advertisers in 1997

Company	Total U.S. Ad Spending ($ millions)
General Motors	$3,087.4
Proctor & Gamble	2,743.2
Philip Morris	2,137.8
Chrysler	1,532.4
Ford Motor Co.	1,281.8
Sears, Roebuck	1,262.0
Walt Disney	1,249.7
PepsiCo	1,244.7
Diageo*	1,206.6
McDonald's	1,041.7

*Diageo is the merged company of Grand Metropolitan (e.g., Burger King, Pillsbury) and Guinness.

Source: *Advertising Age* (1998), September 28, p. s4.

Table 8–4 Leading Business-to-Business Advertisers in 1997

Company	Total U.S. Ad Spending ($ millions)
AT&T	$210.4
IBM	199.8
Microsoft	176.7
Compaq	172.5
MCI	168.7
Hewlett-Packard	127.6
Sprint	115.2
American Express	76.7
Canon	76.5
3M Corp.	75.9

Source: *Business Marketing* (1998), September, p. 19.

4. Media planning
5. Budget setting
6. Measurement of advertising effects

Selecting the Target Audience

In general, this decision follows directly from the marketing strategy. As we showed in Chapter 3, the selection of target markets is a critical step following the statement of marketing objectives, and follows an extensive analysis of the various segmentation options. The target audiences for advertising include the segments you have decided are the keys to your marketing strategy.

However, advertising could include noncustomer targets. Some advertising, particularly corporate advertising, is targeted toward potential investors, regulators, channel members, employees, or other relevant constituents. Thus, although customers are the most logical targets and the ones that should receive the most resources, you should consider other relevant audiences as well.

Setting Advertising Goals

Clearly, the reason companies advertise is to increase sales and profits, if not in the short run, then in the long run. You might wonder why sales increases would not be the obvious goal for advertising to accomplish.

The problem is that many factors in the environment affect sales, not just advertising. If a great new advertising campaign is adopted, sales could actually decline if the competitor lowers its price to the point at which many customers respond. Alternatively, the company may not have discovered the appropriate channels, packaging, or other elements of the marketing mix that affect customer response in the marketplace. Changes in customer purchasing habits or other kinds of behavioral shifts can also affect sales of a product. Thus, it is inappropriate to place a sales goal on advertising alone when many things a company and the competition can do, as well as changes in the environment, ultimately affect sales. The exception to this rule is direct response advertising in which a toll-free telephone number is given for immediate reaction by the customer. This kind of advertising is actually a hybrid of traditional advertising and direct marketing.

This dilemma creates a tension between the firm and the advertising agency. The former is interested in getting a measurable return on its investment in advertising and the latter does not want to be held to sales as a short-term goal. The marketing manager should know that, for the most part, advertising can be effective in building sales, but only to the extent that the complete marketing strategy is appropriate, given the competition and the environment, and that it takes time for advertising to be successful. Therefore, although some advertising agencies are compensated for achieving sales goals, the majority are evaluated on the basis of more intermediate goals.

These intermediate goals are based on models of how advertising creates a customer response. A few of the most popular models of how advertising works are shown in Fig. 8–8. Although the details of the models vary, they all have three basic stages of movement from a low level to a high level of response:

1. The lowest level of response is the cognitive stage. This is the act of thinking about the product; no feeling towards it have been aroused. At this level of response, customers are becoming aware of the product and developing knowledge of the product's attributes and benefits.
2. A higher level of response is the affective stage. At this level, the customer has gone beyond mere knowledge of the product and has begun to develop attitudes, preferences, and perhaps interest (although the customer could develop negative rather than positive affect).
3. The final stage is behavior. This could be purchase but also other kinds of behavior such as visiting a retailer to see a product demonstration or returning a reply card in a magazine for more information about the product.

Figure 8–8

Models of the Advertising Response Process

Source: George E. Belch and Michael A. Belch (1993), *Introduction to Advertising and Promotion* (Homewood, IL: Irwin), p. 199.

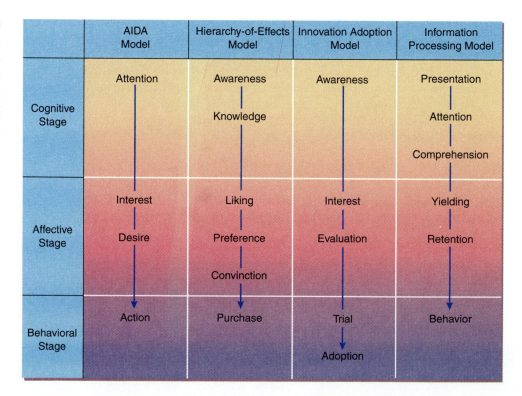

	AIDA Model	Hierarchy-of-Effects Model	Innovation Adoption Model	Information Processing Model
Cognitive Stage	Attention	Awareness Knowledge	Awareness	Presentation Attention Comprehension
Affective Stage	Interest Desire	Liking Preference Convinction	Interest Evaluation	Yielding Retention
Behavioral Stage	Action	Purchase	Trial Adoption	Behavior

All of the models in Fig. 8–8 are hierarchical models in that they posit customers moving up a ladder of interest about the product. They are useful conceptualizations of how customers react to communications because they recognize that customers could be in various readiness states. The models also imply a set of tasks that persuasive communications such as advertising must perform, from first informing the customers that the product exists to the point of getting the customer to move from favorable attitudes to taking some actions. There is no intended timing of the movement from stage to stage; it could occur over several years in the case of an expensive and complex product to virtually simultaneously in the case of a new product introduced in a supermarket.[10]

The importance of these hierarchical models is that they provide some valuable objectives for advertising short of sales. An obvious objective can be simple awareness that the product exists. This is clearly a good objective for a new product (establishing awareness) or one for which research has determined that the awareness level is too low (increasing awareness). If marketing research finds that awareness is high but few potential customers perceive the product favorably, you can use affective objectives such as building brand preference or positioning in ways consistent with the marketing strategy. Nonsales behavior objectives such as trial (for new products or those with low trial rates) and repeat purchasing are also possible.

The choice of objective can be considered in the context of the product life cycle. Figure 8–9 shows how these goals might change over time. When a product category is new, the focus is on educating customers about the features of the product and, if appropriate, its relative advantage over the product it is replacing. For example, when Proctor & Gamble launched its Pampers brand of disposable diapers in 1966 (the product had been in test market since 1962), consumers had to be educated about the advantages of the product over cloth diapers and diaper services. In the early and late growth stages of the life cycle, more competition has entered and there is a concomitant need to stress product differences and brand superiority. Thus, the advertising objectives are more likely to be affective, except for any new brands entering at this stage. Finally, at the maturity stage, competition is intense and the products are fairly similar in terms of their characteristics. At this stage, image (affective) and brand loyalty (behavior) become very important.

Developing the Message Strategy

The marketing manager should always be involved in determining the objectives of advertising. After all, you have developed the marketing strategy and are in the best position to

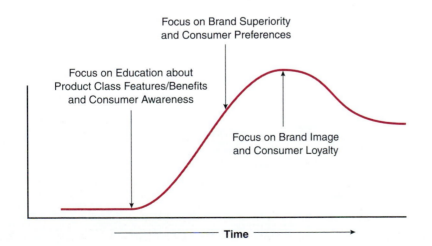

Figure 8–9

Advertising Goals over the Product Life Cycle

know what communications are required to achieve the overall marketing objectives and persuasively communicate the value proposition to the target markets.

However, choosing the best way to attain advertising objectives is the creative part of advertising. This is usually the terrain of the advertising agency, which employs professionals who try to develop the art of advertising, the actual executions that customers see in the media.

In some cases, the advertising focuses on product attributes, following the multiattribute model described in Chapter 5. Product attribute-focused advertising can try to

- Influence the attributes used by customers in evaluating the competitive offerings in a product category
- Change the perceptions of some of your product's attributes
- Change the perceptions of some of a competitor's product's attributes
- Increase or decrease the importance weights of the product attributes

This kind of advertising is used in product categories in which there are real, physical differences between products that can be captured in an advertisement.

An example of this kind of advertising is shown in Fig. 8–10. In this ad for the Land Rover Discovery, several attribute-related messages are being conveyed. First, Land Rover

Figure 8–10

Land Rover Advertisement

Courtesy of Land Rover North America Inc.

is influencing the attributes customer use to choose an SUV and their importance weights by listing only 12 of the many attributes possible (Alpine windows and headlamp washers have not traditionally been on car buyers' lists of the most important attributes sought). Second, perceptions of both the Land Rover and the two competitors explicitly listed, the Jeep Grand Cherokee Limited and the Ford Explorer Limited, are also affected. By comparing the more expensive versions of the Grand Cherokee and the Explorer, Land Rover is trying to make these brands appear to be more expensive than people thought.

In other cases, the advertising focuses almost exclusively on imagery and symbols and eschews reference to product attributes. Much television advertising uses this kind of an approach because images are more easily remembered in a short commercial than facts. Product categories in which it is difficult to establish tangible differential advantages often use image-oriented advertising. Also, this kind of advertising can be used when a marketing manager wants to position a product or service in a certain way in the customer's mind.

Different approaches to creating advertising or appeals can be classified more specifically in the following ways.[11]

Informational or Rational Appeals

Informational appeals focus on the functional or practical aspects of the product. These messages emphasize facts, learning, and persuasion. The job of this kind of advertising is to persuade the target audience that the brand being advertised satisfies their needs better than the competition. This kind of advertising also may communicate to the audience the value proposition, or what some in the advertising industry call the unique selling proposition. An example of this kind of advertising is shown in Fig. 8–11. This ad is from a company called UUNET, a subsidiary of MCI WorldCom that provides networking hardware to connect companies to the Internet. Because Internet connections are becoming increasingly important for companies, the reliability of such products is critical. As you can see from the bold text, the unique selling proposition is the 100% Internet service availability guarantee. The attempt is to create a rational appeal to potential customers who are concerned about losing access to the Internet.

Informational appeals can be of several general types:

- Feature appeals. Like the ads in Figs. 8–10 and 8–11, these appeals focus on the dominant attributes or characteristics of the product or service. These ads tend to implicitly use the multiattribute model of decision making.
- Competitive advantage appeals. These ads make either a direct or indirect claim of superiority against a targeted or general class of competitors.
- Favorable price appeal. In these ads, price is the dominant factor. This approach would obviously not be used by the marketer who is trying to differentiate the product on the basis of a dimension other than price because in that case, the price is likely to be higher than the competition's.
- News appeals. These are advertisements in which some kind of announcement about the product dominates copy.
- Product or service popularity appeals. In these ads, the copy touts how popular the product is among the target audience. Because it is popular, the advertisement implies, it must follow that the product is of high quality or has outstanding value.

Emotional Appeals

As the name implies, **emotional appeals** are intended to tap an underlying psychological aspect of the purchase decision. Many advertisements for consumer products and even some

business-to-business products use humor, fear, and sex to try to achieve their objectives. Such advertising may stimulate greater memory of the ad (known as recall) and more liking of the brand. An example of an emotional ad tapping underlying psychological constructs is the Johnnie Walker Black Label scotch ad shown in Fig. 8–12. This ad is an attempt to communicate a sense of style associated with being a "gentleman." This image is reinforced by the well-dressed character in top hat and tails.

Within the two broad categories of appeals, informational and emotional, are a variety of different tactical or execution approaches. These are specific approaches taken by advertisers to communicate their messages:

- Straight-sell or factual message
- Scientific/technical evidence
- Product demonstration
- Comparisons
- Testimonials
- Slice of life, in which a customer's problem is shown and the product is given as the solution
- Animation
- Personality symbols

Enjoy Black Label Responsibly. Johnnie Walker Black Label, Blended Scotch Whisky. Imported 12 Year Old. 43% Alc./Vol. (86 Proof) ©1997 Schieffelin & Somerset Co., New York, N.Y.

Figure 8–12

Johnnie Walker
Advertisement

Courtesy of Schieffelin and
Somerset Co.

- Fantasy
- Dramatization
- Humor

Evaluating Message Copy

Marketing managers often are not involved with the development of the actual advertising copy; that task is delegated to in-house or agency creative specialists. However, you must be heavily involved with testing the advertising copy (or at least be aware that testing should be done) before committing a substantial amount of money to it. Many variables are usually testable (the spokesperson, the message itself, the execution, media, and other factors).

Laboratory Tests

Figure 8–13 is a classification of the different methods used for pretesting and posttesting advertising.[12] Pretests are measures taken before implementation of the campaign, and a posttest is an evaluation of the advertising after it has been developed but before it has been rolled out nationally or internationally. In laboratory tests, people are brought to a particular location, where they are shown ads and asked to respond to them. The advantage of lab tests is that the researcher can carefully control the environment without distractions to the respondent and manipulate several different aspects of the advertising. The disadvantage is that the situation is not realistic; the respondent provides

Figure 8–13

Classification of Copy-Testing Methods

Source: George E. Belch and Michael A. Belch (1993), *Introduction to Advertising and Promotion* (Homewood, IL: Irwin).

	Advertising-related test (reception or response to the message itself and its contents)	**Product-related test** (impact of message on product awareness, liking, intention to buy, or use)

Laboratory measures (respondent aware of testing and measurement process)	**Cell I**
	
	Pretesting procedures
	 1. Consumer jury
	 2. Portfolio test
	 3. Readability tests
	 4. Physiological measures
	  Eye camera
	  Galvanic skin response
	  Electrodermal response
		Cell II
		
		Pretesting procedures
		 1. Theater tests
		 2. Trailer tests
		 3. Laboratory stores

Real world measures (respondent unaware of testing and measurement process)	**Cell III** Pretesting procedures 1. Dummy advertising vehicles 2. Inquiry tests 3. On-the-air tests Posttesting procedures 1. Recognition tests 2. Recall tests 3. Association measures 4. Combination measures	**Cell IV** Pretesting and posttesting procedures 1. Pre- and posttests 2. Sales tests 3. Minimarket tests

answers in an unnatural environment. Field tests provide real-world measures because they are conducted under natural viewing conditions. Their advantages and disadvantages are the mirror image of those of lab tests: The environment is realistic, but the researcher cannot absolutely control other variables that might affect response to the ad, such as a competitor's ad, noise from children, or other distractions.

This billboard ad for Camel Lights cigarettes illustrates an emotional appeal approach. The company's use of an animated character with a hip image has been challenged as a thinly disguised attempt to target the juvenile market by appealing to their desire to look cool and suggesting that smoking is harmless. (Joel Rogers/Corbis)

Consumer Jury The most common form of testing for advertising concepts is the use of focus groups. TV advertising concepts are usually presented as storyboards, rough pictures with captions showing the "story" that will be told in the ad (obviously, for radio ads, only words are used). For magazine or other print formats, actual executions are shown; multimedia technology allows for the use of more realistic ads.

Portfolio Tests In this approach, respondents are shown both control and test ads. After viewing the portfolio, respondents are asked what information they recall from the ads and which they liked best. The ads with the highest recall and liking are considered to be the most effective.

Readability Tests Readability of the copy of a print ad can be determined by counting the number of syllables per 100 words, the length of sentences, and other structural aspects of the copy. The results provide a sense of the reading skill needed to comprehend an ad, which should match that of the target audience, and are then compared to norms obtained from successful ads.

Physiological Methods A more scientific approach to assessing advertisements involves techniques that measure involuntary physical responses to the ad. These include the following:

- Pupil dilation. Pupilometers measure dilation (an activity related to action or arousal) and constriction (conservation of energy).
- GSR/EDR (galvanic skin response/electrodermal response). Response to a stimulus activates sweat glands; this activity can be measured using electrodes attached to the skin.
- Eye tracking. Viewers are asked to watch or read an ad while a sensor beams infrared light at their eyes. This can measure how much of an ad is being read, what part of the ad is attracting attention, and the sequence of reading and attention.

Theater Tests This is a widely used method for pretesting TV commercials. The service is sold by companies such as Advertising Research Services and Advertising Control for Television. Participants in theater tests are recruited by phone, shopping mall intercepts, and direct mail. A television show or some other entertainment is provided in a movie theater–like facility with commercial breaks ("trailer" tests use smaller, mobile facilities near shopping malls). The show is used so that the respondents do not focus solely on the commercials; a cover story might inform them that the TV show is a pilot for a new network or cable series. After viewing the ads, the participants are asked questions about recall, attitude, interest, and other behavioral responses.

Laboratory Stores In this testing procedure, the researcher attempts to simulate a shopping environment by setting up a supermarket–like shopping shelf with real brands. Respondents are shown advertising copy and make actual brand choices. A popular supplier of this kind of testing is Research Systems Corporation, with its ARS Persuasion copy-testing system.

Real-World Measures

Dummy Advertising Vehicles Researchers construct dummy magazines with regular editorial matter, regular ads, and a set of test ads. The magazines are distributed to a random sample of homes in a predetermined geographic area. After being asked to read the magazine as they normally would, the consumers in the sample are interviewed on the editorial content as well as the test ads.

Inquiry Tests These are also used for print ads. The marketing manager or advertising agency can track the number of inquiries generated from an ad that has a direct-response toll-free phone number or a reader inquiry card attached. In industrial marketing, the use of "bingo" cards, response cards that have numbered holes corresponding to the numbered ads in the magazine, is very common.

On-the-Air/Recall Tests Information Resources, Inc. (IRI), Burke Marketing Research, ASI Market Research, Nelson, and others sell this kind of service. A real TV ad (one of perhaps several executions being tested) is inserted in a TV program in one or more test markets. Consumers are then contacted and asked whether they saw the ad; if so, they are asked further questions about recall of copy points, brand, and the like. The services differ somewhat in the questions asked and how the sample is recruited. Gallup & Robinson, for example, recruits subjects, who are asked in advance to watch the particular show on which the test ad is being run.

Recognition Tests This is the most widely used method for posttesting print ads and is closely associated with Starch INRA Hooper's through-the-book method. With this approach, a researcher interviews respondents at home or at work by first asking whether they have read a particular issue of a magazine and, if so, going through the issue to obtain information about whether the respondents have seen the ad, how much of it they have read, and how much they recall. The Starch method and the resulting Starch scores are used to track and evaluate complete campaigns.

Sales/Minimarket Tests In some areas of the United States IRI has created what they call BehaviorScan markets, in which a city is wired with two separate TV cables. This split-cable arrangement allows advertisers to manipulate the ad copy by showing one execution on the test cable, and keeping the current copy on the control cable. The programming is otherwise identical. A sample of households on both cables is enlisted to have their purchases electronically scanned at supermarkets, drug stores, discount stores, and convenience stores. By comparing the purchase rates between the two samples, an advertiser can determine whether the ad copy on the test cable stimulated more purchases than the ad shown to the control group. This method is limited to ads for frequently purchased consumer goods with sales objectives.

Selecting Media

Choosing the media to use for advertising is becoming more difficult with the rapid growth of alternative media beyond the traditional network (national) and spot (local) TV, radio, newspaper, print (magazine), and outdoor (billboards, where legally permitted) media. The emergence of cable television and the Web has created two new major media; several minor media (e.g., CD-ROMs, supermarket floors, bathroom stalls, shopping carts) are also being explored. In addition, as shown in Table 8–2, for products and services marketed globally, media decisions may vary by country because of differences in media habits, customs, regulations, and other local factors.

There are three main aspects to media planning:

- Selecting the appropriate media for the advertising campaign
- Selecting specific vehicles within each medium
- Scheduling the advertising

These three kinds of decisions are used to create a media plan, which is a detailed document showing the precise scheduling of all the advertising over a planning horizon. Thus, given an available advertising budget, the decision is how to allocate it across media types, then within each medium, and finally over the appropriate time period.

Media Selection

The alternative media have various advantages and disadvantages. We will focus only on the major ones.

Television As noted earlier in this chapter, TV can reach many people quickly and efficiently. It is also the best medium for action and image advertising. However, unless you have a large budget, the production and media costs for TV are enormous, which puts it out of the range of many companies. In addition, it is difficult to narrowly target an audience with TV because of the wide range of people who watch it. Except for extended infomercials, TV is not good for factual (informational) copy because of the speed with which data flash by the screen, combined with a general lack of attentiveness of audiences. Finally, with the high penetration rate of VCRs in many countries, it is easy to tape a show and then fast-forward through the commercials.

Magazines and Newspapers (Print) Print is much better for complicated messages. In addition, print has archival value because it can be stored. Consider the aged magazines in doctors' offices; the ads in those magazines are still gaining exposure long after the month or week in which they were published. Magazines are better than newspapers for color reproduction. Print is better for targeting specific audiences than TV, and magazines are better than newspaper, which is more limited to specific sections (e.g., sports, entertainment). Print, like spot TV, can also reach geographically defined target segments.

Radio Radio is an excellent medium because of its low cost, attentive audience, and creative flexibility. Of course, product demonstrations are not possible. Radio, like TV, can reach audiences quickly, unlike the lag in publication dates with print (except for daily newspapers). Radio is also excellent for targeting specific audiences; each radio station has its own marketing strategy aimed at a particular market and you can thus choose to advertise on particular stations fitting your segment profiles.

Outdoor Billboards are a good medium for reminder and image advertising, but the images can be fleeting as you drive by. They are obviously poor for extended messages. Outdoor advertising tends to be used by product categories for which access to other media has been legally denied (e.g., tobacco, alcohol in the United States). Most countries and geographic areas impose legal limits on the use of outdoor advertising, either banning it entirely, limiting its locations and size, or restricting the products that can use it. For example, Australia has banned cigarette advertising on billboards.

Cable TV Cable is a nice hybrid of radio and television because it has the best features of both. Like radio, it is inexpensive and reaches targeted audiences; each cable channel (e.g., MTV) is generally designed around a theme and an audience that can be accessed easily. It has all the creative flexibility of TV. The main drawback is that the number of viewers for many of the channels is very low because of the large number of alternatives.

The World Wide Web Because of the explosion of consumer use of the Web, advertisers have begun to look at it as a viable medium. There are two types of ads on the Web: a company's own Web site, which serves a variety of functions (e.g., advertising, customer service, distribution channel, sales), and an ad posted on another company's site. Most of the latter are simple static banner ads that create awareness and, if clicked, often take you to the advertiser's site. However, the creative options are increasing all the time and continuous-motion ads are becoming more common. The advertising expenditures are still very small relative to other media (only $2 billion in 1998, according to the Internet Advertising Bureau). However, the Web, like radio and cable TV, has a very well-defined target audience; the main users are affluent, well-educated men and women. This ability to target has been aided by companies such as DoubleClick, Inc. that count the hits received by sites, analyze the people visiting the site (by their software, Internet addresses, and browsing habits), and guess what kinds of products they are interested in buying. Most importantly, Web advertising offers a level of interactivity that no other medium can. For example, a few of the very creative approaches to interactive advertising are the following:

- Click-to-Video ads let users click on a banner ad and view commercials played through their TV sets.
- RingMeNow allows users to type in a telephone number into a banner ad field, triggering an immediate or scheduled toll-free callback.
- Enliven produced an interactive ad for Amazon.com that offered Web surfers an instant excerpt printout of Tom Wolfe's *A Man in Full.*

As a result, advertising expenditures on the Web are expected to increase dramatically.

Choosing the Specific Vehicles

The budget allocation decision within a specific medium is driven by two major factors: a set of statistics describing each vehicle (e.g., in terms of how many people read or watch, the cost) and the appropriateness of the vehicle for the product being advertised.

Analyzing Media   Trying to match target audiences to vehicles typically leads to a comparison of efficiency in reaching desirable audiences. An important number is cost per thousand (CPM), the ratio of the unit cost to the number of thousands of total audience. CPM is a measure of the efficiency of a vehicle; obviously, lower CPMs are better. Even more importantly, the CPM for the target segment shows the vehicle's efficiency for the important group the advertiser is trying to reach, defined by the demographics the client is targeting.

For television, a popular counting measure is the gross rating point (GRP). The number of GRPs attained by a TV schedule is the product of the reach (the percentage of the potential target audience that are tuned in to the commercial) and the frequency (the number of times the commercial is aired). Therefore, a commercial shown four times on a show reaching 20% of the target audience would attain 80 GRPs.

Ratings and circulation data (such as Arbitron's radio audience ratings, Nielsen's TV ratings, Standard Rate and Data Services, Audit Bureau of Circulations, and Simmons's magazine audience measurements) are vital inputs to decisions and consequently are hotly contested measures. A.C. Nielsen, in particular, has come under fire by the TV networks for allegedly underestimating their audiences by changing their sampling approach to households. Smaller audience estimates mean lower advertising prices and thus decreased revenues and profits.[13] At all times, your focus should be on cost per thousand relevant readers, listeners, or viewers (i.e., the cost per thousand in the target market).

Despite Nielsen's problems, it is important to recognize that CPM or GRP numbers may also overstate actual ad readers or viewers. Most people do not read the many pages of ads that fill the fronts of magazines, study inserts in newspapers, or even stay in the room during TV ads. Hence, adjusting total audience to likely readership or viewership levels is very important. This is why Nielsen has spent millions of dollars improving its TV viewing methodology by introducing "peoplemeters" so subjects can record when they are actually in the room viewing the TV.

One important aspect of targeting spending is product use. A number of services rate media vehicles by product usage. Therefore, for strategies targeting heavy users of a product, CPM can be weighted by such usage.

Another important aspect of choosing media vehicles is regional differentiation. Not only does product usage vary by region and country, but so do features and cultural preferences. Therefore, even though regional vehicles may cost more in a CPM sense, it is often desirable to focus on certain regions (especially if your share or distribution levels varies regionally) and use somewhat different messages and media by region or country.

Contextual Fit It is important to choose vehicles that are a good fit for the product or service being marketed. Contextual fit falls into two subcategories: media fit and program and ad context. The media fit issues are fairly obvious: It is difficult to demonstrate operation of a machine on the radio, incorporate music or other sounds in print media, or provide detailed information that will be recalled in radio or TV ads.

A more subtle level of fit involves the context of the ad, including both the program and other ads. Product fit involves the interaction between the product image and the image of the vehicle. For example, even if professional wrestling delivers upscale viewers at a competitive CPM, does it make sense to advertise upscale products (e.g., the Land Rover Discovery) between matches? This issue is magnified if a vehicle airs controversial topics that can lead to a backlash or even a boycott against advertisers.

The interaction of the image of the immediate context is also relevant. For example, a humorous ad may lose its effect if placed in the context of a comedy show or a series of eight other humorous ads. In a serious vehicle, it may be perceived as tasteless. Although it is impossible to control or predict exactly which other commercials will run during a particular TV commercial break, educated guesses are both possible and recommended. Competitive effects are serious when many products in the same category advertise close together, with the result being that many consumers cannot distinguish their claims from one another.

Duplication and Wearout Depending on the advertising objective, duplication (multiple exposures to the same ad) may be either desirable or undesirable. Apparently competing vehicles commonly duplicate audiences; for example, a large amount of overlap occurs among readers of *Fortune, Forbes,* and *Business Week.* Multiple exposures of the same ad are usually necessary for attaining objectives. However, customers might tire of exactly the same message fairly quickly, although evidence seems to suggest that this is less a problem for complex messages than for simple ones. In contrast, some evidence suggests that varying copy slightly, though somewhat expensive, slows down ad wearout.[14] Although the number of possible combinations of vehicles makes thorough analysis difficult (though not impossible, given increased computer power), a reasonable sense can be achieved by estimating the unduplicated audience of each vehicle and, when reach is the objective, concentrating on vehicles with large unduplicated audiences.

Scheduling Advertising

After selecting the appropriate vehicles, the next decision is the actual timing or sequencing of the ads. This decision is based on how your advertising objective responds to the proposed advertising and how much decay is expected when the advertising is not present. Three basic patterns of advertising can be used over a proscribed time period:

- Flighting, which alternates a burst of advertising with a period of no advertising
- A continuous pattern of advertising evenly distributed over the period

- Pulsing, or a basic level of advertising combined with regularly scheduled bursts of advertising

Research has not convincingly demonstrated that one spending pattern is best in meeting all the advertising objectives that can be set. One well-known experimental study found that flighting or pulsing led to a higher temporary peak in recall whereas a continuous pattern produced higher total recall.[15]

Another factor affecting advertising timing is the seasonality of the sales of the product or service. Timing is affected strongly by the target audience. For example, retail stores make decisions about ski equipment purchases long before consumers do; likewise, dealers make decisions about purchasing industrial goods long before their customers do. In addition, issues of immediate relevance (which suggests advertising during the buying season) and clutter (which may argue for off-season advertising) have an impact on timing. Alternatively, for seasonal products such as cold remedies, a leading spending pattern is sometimes used that delivers messages before the major usage season (fall and winter) to get consumers to stock up on a brand.

In most cases, specialized media companies use sophisticated computer programs to place ads in the most appropriate medium, within the budget allocated, that meets the advertiser's objectives. A new approach for TV scheduling called media optimizing takes advantage of the latest Nielsen TV viewing data based on their "peoplemeter" technology, which provides real-time information to companies and their media planners. Peoplemeters attached to TVs are turned on and off when people enter and leave the room and thus provide more accurate measures of actual TV viewing. The meters electronically deliver the viewing data instantly, thus providing the most up-to-date information possible.[16]

 Recall from Chapter 5 the illustration of the introduction of the Mango cellular phone in Israel.[17] The phone was introduced by Pelephone Communications, Ltd. targeting teens aged 13–20, with a secondary target group being the teens' parents trying to keep contact with their children. Its key features are that the phone is generally limited to receiving calls, with only one outgoing phone number programmed into memory (or calls could be made to a calling card number and then to any phone number). Thus, no monthly billing is necessary. The introductory price was 30% below other cellular phone prices, it was introduced in a variety of colors, and it was sold in a chain of pharmacies popular with the target group.

The communication objective for the introductory advertising campaign was to position it as the "Swatch" of cellular phones.[18] The marketing managers wanted to build purchase consideration and desire for the product (both cognitive and affective objectives, as shown in Fig. 8–8) in the target audience. For the secondary target (parents), the product was marketed as a solution for keeping contact with their children without having a bill at the end of the month.

The media strategy used outdoor (billboards, posters) as a teaser campaign, followed by newspapers and youth magazines. The billboards and posters saturated Tel Aviv, especially around schools, universities, and youth hangouts. The newspaper advertising provided product feature information and supported the image and targeted both groups (teens, parents). After the teaser campaign, TV was used, 80% on prime-time programs appealing to both families and teens and the rest on shows that targeted teens.

The creative strategy was of the MTV variety: hip, cool, fashionable, yet sophisticated. The ads used Generation X language and the appropriate look. The rational message of "Cellular Phone With No Bill" and the emotional messages of freedom and control combined to implement Mango's positioning. This combination of rational and emotional appeals was important not only to support the Mango brand but to also differentiate Mango from the other Pelephone brands targeted to businesspeople. ◆

Budgeting

Because of the large amounts of money involved and the importance of advertising to marketers, one of the most important jobs of the marketing manager is to determine how much to spend. Setting advertising budgets has an immediate impact on costs and longer-term effects on sales. Consequently, advertising is just as much an investment as R&D and new plants and equipment. Like spending on R&D, spending on advertising has a long history and a weak record for measuring effectiveness precisely.

A crucial distinction exists between viewing advertising spending as an investment and viewing it as an expense. Investments are expected to generate returns over a long period of time. Often, when advertising is viewed as an expense, the budget is cut near the end of a quarter or fiscal year to achieve a profit target. In contrast, marketing-oriented firms view advertising as a long-term investment in the brand.[19]

Figure 8–14 shows examples of successful investments in brands. The two graphs show a positive relationship between advertising investment (measured as cumulative advertising

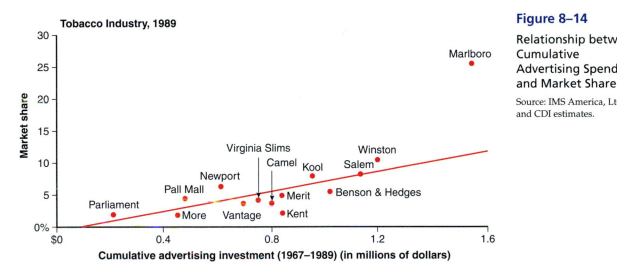

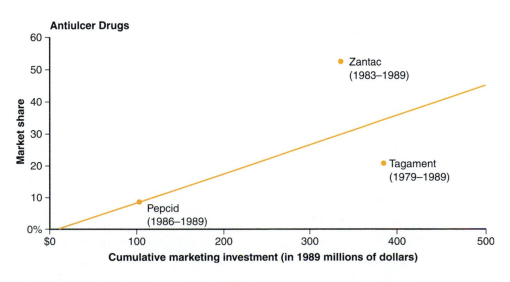

Figure 8–14

Relationship between Cumulative Advertising Spending and Market Share

Source: IMS America, Ltd., and CDI estimates.

spending) and market share for the tobacco and antiulcer drug categories. Consistent investment in advertising for products can lead to a superior market position.

The following are the most commonly used methods for setting advertising budgets.

Objective and Task

Budgeting by advertising objectives and the tasks needed to achieve those objectives is a logically appealing approach in that the marketing manager first determines the advertising objectives to be achieved (e.g., target audience, awareness), and then chooses a media plan to reach those goals. The sum of the costs of the media vehicles needed to achieve the objectives becomes a budget. In practice, the budget that results from this process is usually used as a starting point for negotiating within the organization as financial constraints and the needs of other products become a part of the overall budgeting process.

Percentage of Sales

The manager using the percentage-of-sales method approaches advertising as a cost to be borne and selects a percentage of sales, either past or expected, to devote to advertising. This method seems to turn normal causal thinking—that advertising causes sales—on its head. Whether based on past or expected sales, it is clear that poorly performing brands will subsequently get lower budgets, lower sales, lower budgets again, and so on if one applies this approach mindlessly, without adjusting the percentage appropriately. By using a percentage, the method views advertising almost as a variable cost, like raw materials or direct labor.

Table 8–5 shows advertising-to-sales ratios by industry for 1998. Although this table is not meant to imply that all the companies in these industries use some kind of percentage-of-sales method for setting ad budgets, the ratio for a product's industry category or SIC code is a useful starting point for trying to assemble a budget from scratch. The range of the ratios is quite large; the highest advertising-to-sales ratio is for dolls and stuffed toys (SIC 3942) at 14.6%; the smallest one is steel works and blast furnaces (SIC 3312) at 0.1%.

Competitive Parity

This approach to budgeting attempts to spend at levels proportional to the competition's spending. One argument for the competitive parity method is based on the efficient market hypothesis developed in finance: Firms that survive tend to be those with more optimal budgets, so the survivors' budgets may offer an estimate of the optimal level in a competitive market. In other words, a successful competitor may have a better idea of how much to spend than you do.

A useful way to implement this method is to consider share of advertising dollars spent in the product category, also known as share of voice (SOV), rather than absolute advertising dollars, and compare SOV to market share. Although small-share brands tend to focus on profit taking and large-share brands on investing in future profits, to maintain a presence in the market, the former must usually have higher SOVs than market shares in order to rise above the clutter and get their messages out. Conversely, large-share brands gain economies of scale with large advertising budgets, which enable them to purchase large blocks of media time or space. Therefore, they can normally have SOVs lower than their market shares. One study found that the breakeven share level, at which SOV can be the same as market share, is between 19% and 21%. Above that market share level, you can spend proportionately less on advertising; below that level, you should spend more.[20]

Table 8–5 1998 Advertising-to-Sales Ratios for the 200 Largest Ad Spending Industries

Industry	SIC No.	Ad Dollars as Percent of Sales	Ad Dollars as Percent of Margin	Predicted '99 Ad Growth Rate (%)
Accident & health insurance	6321	0.7	7.9	9.4
Agricultural chemicals	2870	10.3	31.3	18.4
Agricultural production-crops	0100	1.5	5.5	6.0
Air courier services	4513	1.3	10.3	5.9
Air transport, scheduled	4512	1.2	8.2	2.9
Air-cond, heating, refrig eq	3585	1.8	6.7	6.4
Amusement & recreation svcs	7900	2.6	8.2	41.3
Apparel & other finished pds	2300	5.3	13.8	10.4
Apparel and accessory stores	5600	4.2	9.8	9.4
Auto and home supply stores	5531	1.4	4.3	11.1
Auto dealers, gas stations	5500	2.7	15.3	48.4
Auto rent & lease, no drivers	7510	1.9	4.7	5.9
Bakery products	2050	3.0	4.9	9.6
Beverages	2080	7.7	12.7	−2.2
Biological pds, ex diagnstics	2836	1.5	2.3	8.8
Blank books, binders, bookbind	2780	8.5	14.5	5.6
Bldg matl, hardwr, garden-retl	5200	4.3	12.1	11.4
Books: pubg, pubg & printing	2731	11.7	20.9	−3.2
Brdwoven fabric mill, cotton	2211	1.3	8.3	2.7
Btld & can soft drinks, water	2086	4.9	10.1	9.7
Business services, nec	7389	1.1	2.6	14.5
Cable and other pay TV svcs	4841	0.8	1.7	21.0
Can fruit, veg, presrv, jam, jel	2033	1.4	5.1	5.7
Can, frozn, presrv fruit & veg	2030	3.6	8.0	2.1
Catalog, mail-order houses	5961	8.7	28.2	9.2
Chemicals & allied products	2800	1.9	4.4	−1.6
Cigarettes	2111	8.2	15.0	−3.2
Cmp and cmp software stores	5734	0.8	5.3	16.5
Cmp integrated sys design	7373	1.6	3.7	10.3
Cmp processing, data prep svc	7374	1.1	2.7	10.3
Cmp programming, data process	7370	0.9	2.2	19.8
Commercial printing	2750	8.0	24.7	10.0
Communications equip, nec	3669	3.1	7.6	0.6
Computer & office equipment	3570	1.9	5.4	8.8
Computer communication equip	3576	2.3	3.8	16.8
Computer peripheral eq, nec	3577	2.8	6.1	8.6
Computer storage devices	3572	1.9	6.8	17.8
Computers & software-whsl	5045	0.3	3.4	5.3
Construction machinery and eq	3531	0.5	1.4	8.9
Convenience stores	5412	0.6	1.5	1.1
Convrt papr, paprbrd, ex boxes	2670	2.9	6.8	11.7
Cookies and crackers	2052	3.1	5.9	5.8
Cutlery, handtools, gen hrdwr	3420	11.2	20.8	13.5
Dairy products	2020	4.9	9.9	7.8
Dental equipment & supplies	3843	1.6	3.1	12.5
Department stores	5311	3.3	10.7	6.2
Distilled and blended liquor	2085	11.9	20.7	10.6
Dolls and stuffed toys	3942	14.6	28.3	10.4
Drugs & proprietary stores	5912	0.9	3.2	9.2
Drugs & proprietary-whsl	5122	1.1	8.1	13.4

(continued)

Table 8–5 (Continued)

Industry	SIC No.	Ad Dollars as Percent of Sales	Ad Dollars as Percent of Margin	Predicted '99 Ad Growth Rate (%)
Eating and drinking places	5810	5.0	36.3	−18.0
Eating places	5812	4.3	19.7	7.3
Educational services	8200	5.4	16.2	8.9
Elec meas & test instruments	3825	3.5	6.8	8.4
Electr, oth elec eq, ex cmp	3600	1.5	6.0	−7.8
Electrical housewares and fans	3634	5.5	16.9	6.8
Electric lighting, wiring eq	3640	2.7	7.4	6.2
Electrical indl apparatus	3620	2.0	4.5	22.4
Electromedical apparatus	3845	1.1	1.7	11.5
Electronic comp, accessories	3670	2.4	6.2	−4.7
Electronic computers	3571	1.6	5.2	12.3
Electronic parts, eq-whsl, nec	5065	0.8	4.6	3.9
Engr, acc, resh, mgmt, rel svcs	8700	1.7	5.6	26.5
Equip rental & leasing, nec	7359	4.2	8.7	59.8
Family clothing stores	5651	2.9	8.6	13.4
Farm machinery and equipment	3523	1.0	3.6	4.9
Fire, marine, casualty ins	6331	0.7	5.6	6.4
Food and kindred products	2000	10.5	24.6	3.8
Food stores	5400	4.8	10.8	18.1
Footwear, except rubber	3140	3.9	9.5	11.5
Furniture stores	5712	7.1	17.2	10.0
Games, toys, chid veh, ex dolls	3944	12.8	22.2	5.1
Gen med & surgical hospitals	8062	1.1	6.6	19.0
General indl mach & eq, nec	3569	1.1	2.8	13.2
Glass, glasswr-pressed, blown	3220	1.2	2.2	−15.8
Grain mill products	2040	8.4	16.0	−11.6
Greeting cards	2771	2.7	4.0	3.4
Groceries & related pds-whsl	5140	2.7	83.7	8.2
Groceries, general line-whsl	5141	0.2	2.2	-0.4
Grocery stores	5411	0.9	3.4	1.8
Gskets, hose, bitng-rubr, plstc	3050	1.1	3.6	7.9
Hardwr, plumb, heat eq-whsl	5070	2.1	36.3	6.5
Health services	8000	6.8	21.0	20.9
Heating eq, plumbing fixture	3430	7.0	15.5	−15.2
Help supply services	7363	0.8	3.8	8.7
Hobby, toy and game shops	5945	3.9	12.6	7.1
Home furniture & equip store	5700	2.7	6.9	12.5
Hospital & medical svc plans	6324	1.1	5.2	23.7
Hotels and motels	7011	3.4	10.9	20.0
Household appliances	3630	2.5	8.3	4.0
Household audio & video eq	3651	4.2	14.6	5.5
Household furniture	2510	7.9	26.5	18.0
Ice cream & frozen desserts	2024	4.2	14.6	0.0
In vitro, in vivo diagnostics	2835	1.4	2.6	2.6
Indl coml fans, blowrs, oth eq	3564	2.4	7.4	14.2
Indl inorganic chemicals	2810	0.2	0.6	−24.7
Indl trucks, tractors, trailrs	3537	1.7	7.8	5.2
Industrial measurement instr	3823	0.9	2.1	12.4
Industrial organic chemicals	2860	1.1	3.1	3.6
Investment advice	6282	4.5	14.2	14.0

Table 8–5 (Continued)

Industry	SIC No.	Ad Dollars as Percent of Sales	Ad Dollars as Percent of Margin	Predicted '99 Ad Growth Rate (%)
Jewelry stores	5944	4.8	11.2	10.1
Knit outerwear mills	2253	3.3	10.0	6.0
Knitting mills	2250	4.7	16.1	1.8
Lab analytical instruments	3826	1.8	3.3	8.5
Lawn, garden tractors, equip	3524	3.3	8.1	4.7
Leather and leather products	3100	5.4	11.7	0.7
Lumber & oth bldg matl-retl	5211	0.7	2.6	11.6
Lumber and wood pds, ex furn	2400	0.3	1.9	5.1
Machine tools, metal cutting	3541	1.0	2.8	6.6
Malt beverages	2082	8.3	17.0	2.3
Management services	8741	0.8	4.3	11.1
Manifold business forms	2761	11.6	20.9	−1.7
Meas & controlling dev, nec	3829	2.1	4.8	15.5
Meat packing plants	2011	6.0	24.6	4.8
Membership sport & rec clubs	7997	6.8	18.7	−0.9
Mens, boys frnsh, work clthng	2320	2.8	6.5	8.5
Metal working machinery & eq	3540	3.6	9.5	−3.8
Millwork, veneer, plywood	2430	3.6	10.5	10.3
Misc amusement & rec service	7990	3.3	8.5	11.1
Misc business services	7380	0.9	1.7	5.4
Misc elec machy, eq, supplies	3690	3.5	9.3	10.2
Misc food preps, kindred pds	2090	3.1	9.5	11.7
Misc furniture & fixtures	2590	1.0	2.6	8.4
Misc general mdse stores	5399	3.7	16.2	−4.5
Misc indl, coml, machy and eq	3590	1.5	3.8	−0.9
Misc manufacturing industries	3990	3.6	7.4	11.2
Misc nondurable goods-whsl	5190	1.3	6.1	−26.2
Misc shopping goods stores	5940	2.9	10.7	13.0
Misc transportation equip	3790	5.0	18.1	1.7
Mortgage bankers & loans corr	6162	3.6	6.0	19.3
Motion pic, videotape prodtn	7812	9.7	22.5	18.4
Motion pict, videotape distr	7822	8.4	19.4	−19.8
Motion picture theaters	7830	2.9	14.7	9.1
Motor vehicle part, accessory	3714	1.2	4.7	3.9
Motor vehicles & car bodies	3711	2.7	12.7	5.5
Motorcycles, bicycles & parts	3751	1.6	5.3	10.6
Newspaper: pubg, pubg & print	2711	4.4	15.8	9.7
Office furniture, ex wood	2522	0.8	1.8	11.2
Office machines, nec	3579	0.3	1.0	7.9
Operative builders	1531	1.3	12.0	12.0
Ophthalmic goods	3851	8.2	12.6	11.5
Ortho, prosth, surg appl, suply	3842	2.0	3.7	7.7
Paints, varnishes, lacquers	2851	3.0	6.9	12.5
Paper mills	2621	2.0	4.8	−2.6
Patent owners and lessors	6794	10.8	21.7	12.9
Pens, pencils, oth artist matl	3950	7.2	16.2	−1.4
Perfume, cosmetic, toilet prep	2844	11.9	19.2	6.7
Periodical: pubg, pubg & print	2721	7.0	14.2	1.5
Personal credit institutions	6141	1.2	2.4	18.8
Personal services	7200	14.2	26.5	18.6

(continued)

Table 8–5 (Continued)

Industry	SIC No.	Ad Dollars as Percent of Sales	Ad Dollars as Percent of Margin	Predicted '99 Ad Growth Rate (%)
Petroleum refining	2911	1.0	4.3	6.8
Pharmaceutical preparations	2834	5.5	7.8	8.9
Phone comm ex radiotelephone	4813	2.5	5.4	11.9
Phono recrds, audio tape, disk	3652	9.4	17.7	3.7
Photographic equip & supply	3861	3.9	7.8	8.4
Plastic, synth matls; ex glass	2820	1.2	4.0	1.7
Plastic products, nec	3089	10.6	28.9	−0.3
Plastics, resins, elastomers	2821	0.8	3.0	−19.4
Poultry slaughter & process	2015	2.6	18.2	7.8
Prepackaged software	7372	3.8	5.2	14.2
Racing, incl track operations	7948	3.2	7.9	18.6
Radio broadcasting stations	4832	6.0	20.0	28.4
Radio, TV broadcast, comm eq	3663	0.9	2.3	8.4
Radio, TV, cons electr stores	5731	3.7	15.4	16.5
Radiotelephone communication	4812	4.3	9.8	24.2
Real estate agents & mgrs	6531	2.4	8.5	18.2
Real estate investment trust	6798	2.3	4.6	12.0
Record and tape stores	5735	1.1	3.1	−0.5
Refrig & service ind machine	3580	2.2	6.4	10.0
Retail stores, nec	5990	3.7	9.6	17.1
Rubber and plastics footwear	3021	8.7	21.1	13.4
Security brokers & dealers	6211	1.7	3.1	16.7
Semiconductor, related device	3674	2.3	4.4	9.3
Ship and boat bldg & repairing	3730	2.7	8.4	8.4
Shoe stores	5661	2.7	7.9	3.4
Skilled nursing care fac	8051	3.1	18.6	6.0
Soap, detergent, toilet preps	2840	11.2	23.0	4.1
Spec outpatient facility, nec	8093	0.9	2.7	20.9
Special clean, polish preps	2842	13.1	22.3	7.5
Special industry machinery	3550	2.1	6.1	10.8
Sporting & athletic gds, nec	3949	4.1	10.7	12.4
Steel works & blast furnaces	3312	0.1	0.6	9.5
Structural clay products	3250	0.8	12.8	6.3
Sugar & confectionery prods	2060	14.2	31.8	4.4
Surgical, med instr, apparatus	3841	1.5	2.4	11.5
Svcs to dwellings, oth bldgs	7340	1.5	8.3	−1.7
Tele & telegraph apparatus	3661	1.0	2.9	6.6
Television broadcast station	4833	1.9	5.7	10.4
Tires and inner tubes	3011	1.8	6.4	0.1
Tobacco products	2100	4.5	6.3	8.9
Unsupp plastics film & sheet	3081	3.8	12.3	11.6
Variety stores	5331	1.8	7.9	6.0
Video tape rental	7841	3.8	12.5	5.7
Watches, clocks and parts	3873	14.4	25.4	13.1
Water transportation	4400	4.1	10.2	11.9
Wine, brandy & brandy spirits	2084	11.2	19.0	7.6
Wmns, miss, chld, infnt undgrmt	2340	8.9	20.7	−3.4
Women's clothing stores	5621	1.8	4.9	5.0
Womens, misses, jrs outerwear	2330	3.0	9.2	−3.2
Wood hshld furn, ex upholsrd	2511	3.3	9.9	7.9

Source: *Advertising Age*, June 29, 1998, p. 22.

Affordability

The affordability method is the ultimate in "advertising as a cost of doing business" thinking and is similar in spirit to the percentage-of-sales method. If you use this method, you select an advertising budget that, together with projected sales, price, and other costs, results in an acceptable income statement and profit level. Unfortunately, like the percentage-of-sales method, as advertising becomes less affordable because a brand is doing poorly, the role of advertising may become more important. In addition, projected sales should be a function of the level of advertising and should therefore vary with different budgets.

Experimentation

With this approach, you try different levels of spending, either in different regions or in more controlled settings, and monitor the results. You then use the results to select among different advertising budgets and plans. Experimentation is increasing in popularity and represents a step toward using a more scientific approach to setting budgets.[21]

The case of the sugar substitute Equal highlights the use of experimentation for setting advertising budgets.[22] Managers for Equal used information from an IRI BehaviorScan split-cable TV market to test alternative advertising budgets rather than testing copy as described earlier in this chapter. When the brand was introduced, the marketing manager tried two levels of media spending: $3.8 million and $5.7 million (extrapolated from the BehaviorScan market to national levels). After a 20-week test, there was no significant difference between Equal purchasing rates by households on the two cables. Thus, the lower spending level was chosen as being more appropriate. ◆

Decision Calculus

Computerized decision support systems (DSSs) such as ADBUDG[23] help structure budget decisions systematically. Managers provide subjective inputs about, for example, the sales or share impact of increasing or decreasing advertising spending by different levels (25%, 50%, and 100%, for example). A computer program then estimates likely customer response to various advertising spending levels and calculates the optimal spending amount. Although using subjective data alone produces results that may be hard to sell to others in the organization, DSSs that combine judgment with real data have facilitated decision-making and promise to be more useful in the future.

Surveys of companies' advertising budgeting practices have shown varying percentages devoted to the different methods, but the top three methods used are consistently objective and task, affordability, and percentage of anticipated sales.[24]

Measuring Advertising Effects

Given the amount of money spent on advertising, it is surprising how little effort is spent assessing whether it is meeting the stated objectives. Volumes have been written on topics such as copy testing with focus groups and in theater settings; however, as we discussed earlier in this chapter, these two methods tend to be used for making decisions about different copy strategies rather than for postimplementation assessment.

Tracking Studies

Conventional tracking studies are surveys that ask respondents two kinds of questions. One type is "top of mind," or, more technically, unaided recall, in which the respondent is asked whether he or she can recall seeing an ad for the brand. For example, the respondent might be asked, "Have you seen the advertising campaign that prominently features frogs?" If the answer is *yes,* this technique follows up the question with a request to repeat the main copy points to determine comprehension. If the respondent indicates that the campaign is for Budweiser beer and features the frogs croaking "Bud-weis-er," then the campaign gets high marks. Attitudinal questions might also be asked. The second type of survey uses aided recall: "Have you seen the Budweiser beer campaign featuring frogs croaking 'Bud-weis-er'?" This method detects information not actively in memory that can be important when primed at the point of purchase. Not surprisingly, the numbers produced by aided recall are much larger than those produced by unaided recall.

These studies then track the responses over time, often at constant time intervals, using either the same sample of respondents (a panel) or a different, randomly selected group. The manager can then view how awareness, comprehension, or interest builds, plateaus, or never gets off the ground. Often the percentages obtained from these studies are also compared to norms derived from previous advertising campaigns.

If the advertising objective is more behavioral in nature, tracking studies may also follow sales, inquiries, repeat purchases, or other measures over time. If the manager notes when a new campaign starts, the measures can simply be plotted and inspected for any movement. The major problem with this kind of tracking is similar to the problem with using sales as an advertising goal: It is difficult to attribute movement in sales solely to advertising, given the other aspects of the marketing mix as well as competitors' moves.

Experimentation

In addition to its use in setting budgets and evaluating potential advertising copy, experimentation as a means of assessing advertising effectiveness has a long tradition in marketing. Unfortunately, field experiments—using real products in an actual setting—are costly and time-consuming because they involve manipulating different levels of marketing variables in different sales territories, in different stores, or to different groups of customers for an extended period of time to detect any effects of the manipulated variable. Moreover, field experiments are politically difficult from an organizational perspective, for although it is easy to get a regional manager to accept an increased advertising budget (or price cut), it is hard to obtain acceptance for a decreased budget.

Most experiments focus on sales-related advertising objectives. A comprehensive analysis of 389 split-cable TV experiments found that the average elasticity for new products was higher than for established products, 26% versus 5%. The researchers also found that an examination of successful advertising spending tests (as opposed to copy tests) showed that about two-thirds of the original increase persisted in the year after advertising returned to normal levels and one-third persisted into the second year. They also found that most of the increase was caused by greater purchases of the product per household rather than an increase in the percentage of households that buy the product (penetration), suggesting that the advertising reminded or encouraged consumers to do something they were already inclined to do.[25]

Linking Objectives to Incremental Contribution

A financially oriented approach to evaluating advertising effectiveness attempts to draw a direct link from the advertising objectives to the contribution resulting from the advertising.[26] An illustration of this approach for a luxury sports sedan is shown in Table 8–6. It assumes that you have set quantitative, measurable objectives for the advertising. Suppose you have set goals of a 10% improvement in the perception of style, 5% in performance, and 5% in sportiness, for an average improvement of 6.7% over the three dimensions. Assume that there is a multiplier of 1.5 (perhaps based on prior marketing research) from

Table 8–6 From Objectives to Incremental Contribution

Example: Luxury sports sedan

Change in perceptions		6.7%	
Impact on consideration	× 15	10.0%	Increase in consideration
Conversion to showroom visits	× 0.5	5.0%	Increased probability of showroom visit
Closing rate on showroom visits	× 0.10	0.5%	Increase probability of purchase
Size of segment	× 500,000	2,500	Incremental cars sold
Marginal contribution per car	× $5,000	$12.5m	Net incremental contribution from advertising to segment

Source: Naras Eechembadi (1994), "Does advertising work?" *The McKinsey Quarterly*, no. 3, p. 124.

perception improvement to increase in the number of buyers who will consider buying the car, hence the 10% increase in consideration shown in the table. Also, experience tells us that 50% of the increase in consideration actually results in a showroom visit and 10% of those visits result in a sale. Thus, the advertising has increased the probability of purchase by 0.5%. If the segment size is 500,000 people and the profit contribution per car is $5,000, the incremental contribution from the advertising is $12.5 million. This figure can then be compared to the cost of the advertising.

Past Sales and Advertising

An approach to evaluating advertising effectiveness is to use historical data and statistical methods to estimate the relationship between advertising spending and market response variables such as sales or market share. The statistical methods used are normally regression or some other advanced econometric technique. For example, given past levels of sales and advertising, you could estimate the following equation:

$$\text{Sales} = a + b\text{Adv}$$

where a and b are unknown parameters that are estimated from the data. Although this postulates a very simple (and probably incorrect) linear relationship between sales and advertising, the statistical significance of b tells you whether advertising spending levels are importantly related to changes in sales over time. More sophisticated models enable you to incorporate other marketing mix variables besides advertising, and nonlinear relationships permit the estimation of elasticities, competition, and interactions (e.g., the effects advertising might have on price sensitivity).

A number of studies done in this tradition have yielded some generalizable results.[27] Averaging across 128 studies, it appears that the average elasticity of current advertising on current sales is about 22% (that is, a 100% increase in advertising leads to a 22% change in sales); the carryover effect (the elasticity of the impact of current advertising on future sales) is about 47%, indicating that the long-run impact is more important than its immediate effect.[28]

Measuring the Effectiveness of Web Advertising

In principle, all of the methods described in this chapter can be used to measure the effectiveness of advertising on the Web through banner ads or visits ("traffic") to Web sites designed to have a heavy communications component. However, because of the small amount of advertising and the low incidence of Web usage in the general population, it is unlikely that conventional approaches to measuring advertising effectiveness will detect any signal from the marketplace that would be useful to marketers using the Web.

As substitutes for more traditional approaches, a number of different services have been introduced that attempt to measure the effectiveness of Web advertising and sites. Most Web advertising is intended to get users to visit the site. Thus, much of the focus has been on the sites themselves. It is easiest to measure hits, or the number of visits made. It is also possible to analyze "clickthrough" data, which show how many pages at a site a user visited and how long the visit was. What is more difficult to measure is the impression the site made. The services listed here focus largely on hits and differ in the technology used.[29]

I/Pro With an investment from A.C. Nielsen, this service is the best-known and most widely recognized name in Web measurement. The I/Pro service I/Count measures how long users stay at a site, the number of visits to each page, and the "clickstream," the previous and subsequent sites visited.

NetCount This service is similar to I/Pro but has a better measurement system for determining whether a user simply viewed the ad on the page or actually clicked on it. Others in the Web site measurement field include Accrue, Intersé, Business Publications Audit, and the Audit Bureau of Circulations.

EXECUTIVE SUMMARY

The main concepts of this chapter are the following:

- Underlying marketing communications decisions are theories about how communications flow from sender to receiver.
- The concept of integrated marketing communications (IMC) has become central to the communication strategies of companies in the 1990s. The idea is that all communication activities, including advertising, promotion, and personal selling, must be coordinated in order to send a consistent message to customers.
- There are six aspects to managing advertising: selecting the target audience, choosing the appropriate goals for advertising to achieve, deciding what message strategy is most appropriate for the product or service being marketed, selecting media and developing a media plan, setting the budget, and evaluating or measuring the effectiveness of the advertising.
- Web sites and banner ads are unique forms of advertising in terms of design and evaluation.

CHAPTER QUESTIONS

1. Consider the notion of a brand community developed in this chapter. How would you go about creating one for a brand; that is, what specific steps would you take?

2. Integrated marketing communication (IMC) is a very important concept in marketing. What are the barriers to a marketing manager's implementation of IMC? If IMC is not achieved, what is the impact on the marketing strategy?

3. Find two different ads: one with an emotional appeal and one with a rational appeal. How would you design an advertisement for each of the two products with the opposite appeal?

4. Consider two different products: an industrial product and a consumer product. How would the media for these products differ? What would affect the advertising scheduling for these two products?

5. Suppose that a new communication program is being developed for your school. What would be the goals of this program? What information would you collect to measure the effectiveness of the program?

Integrated Case

Application Exercises: Communication in the PC Industry

1. Collect as many print ads for a PC manufacturer as you can. Consider the other elements of the communications mix; develop a sketch of several other communication activities and how they would be integrated with the print advertising.

2. Following the six steps indicated in the chapter for developing an advertising campaign, choose one of the major PC brands and develop a campaign targeting the consumer market.

3. Do the same as question 2 for the business-to-business market.

4. Evaluate the print ads you have collected in question 1. Do you think they work? You will have to make some assumptions about the target audience (find the demographics for the magazines) and the goal of the advertising.

5. Collect information on the market shares and advertising spending levels of several of the major PC manufacturers (the latter can be obtained from *Bureau of Advertising Research/Leading National Advertisers,* available in most business libraries). Compare the market shares and share-of-voice figures. What do you conclude?

6. Go to the various Web sites of the major PC manufacturers. Evaluate their effectiveness as communication vehicles.

FURTHER READING

A good recent review of the literature on advertising effectiveness is Demetrios Vakratsas and Tim Ambler (1999), "How advertising works: what do we really know?" *Journal of Marketing,* 63 (January), pp. 26–43. Other than the books referenced in the chapter, two good books on advertising and promotion are John R. Rossiter and Larry Percy (1997), *Advertising and Promotion Management,* 2nd ed. (New York: McGraw-Hill); and Gerard J. Tellis (1998), *Advertising and Sales Promotion Strategy* (Reading, MA: Addison-Wesley). Those interested in advertising should also read the *Journal of Advertising Research* and *Advertising Age.*

Channels of Distribution 9

CHAPTER BRIEF

The purpose of this chapter is to introduce methods of distributing products and services to customers. Key learning points include the following:

The functions of channels of distribution

Key factors affecting the choice among alternative channel structures

Channel options

Managing channels of distribution, particularly resolving conflicts between channel members

Special topics in channels of distribution, including the Web, changes in supermarket retailing, and multilevel marketing

Direct marketing

After World War II, the large Japanese beer company Dai-Nippon was broken up into two regional breweries, Asahi and Sapporo.[1] This left Kirin the only national beer brewer in Japan and, as a result of this advantage, the company occupied nearly two-thirds of the Japanese beer market in 1976. This market dominance continued into the early 1990s; as shown in Fig. 9–1, in 1991, Kirin held nearly 50% of the Japanese beer market whereas Asahi held only 24%. However, by 1997 Kirin's dominance had eroded to the point; its share had dropped to 43% and Asahi's rose to 33% (Fig. 9–1 shows earlier comparison data from 1996). What happened?

Traditionally, Kirin tailored its manufacturing and marketing to the fact that Japanese beer consumers liked their beer fresh. As a result, Kirin built its breweries near big towns, concentrated on making high-quality beer, and distributed its products through liquor shops and restaurants, normally small, "mom and pop" outlets.

Three major changes led to the erosion of Kirin's position. One change was a shift in consumption from bottles to cans. Because they take up less space, cans are cheaper to stock. In addition, sales through vending machines, which use cans, increased dramatically. Almost half of all beer sold in Japan is now in cans, up from 17% in 1985. Kirin was late in investing in canning technology. A second change is related to changes in consumer preferences. In 1986, Asahi launched its tremendously successful Asahi Super Dry, a "dry" beer that Kirin has had difficulty matching.

A third reason for Asahi's ascendance is distribution related. There has been a revolution in Japanese retailing; large supermarkets and discount stores now sell 40% of all the beer consumed in Japan. In 1989, this figure was only 10%. Asahi concentrated on these

Figure 9–1

Japanese Beer Market

Source: "How Kirin lost its
sparkle," *The Economist*,
September 14, 1996, p. 66.

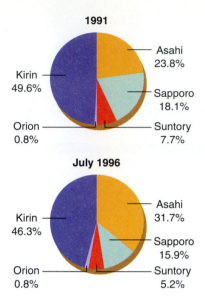

large stores while Kirin continued to focus on the small shops that had been its tradition. In addition, many of the small liquor stores on which Kirin focused its distribution strategy are being converted into convenience stores. Because the stores now sell many more items besides liquor, space is even more scarce than it was before. This gives further advantage to Asahi, which invested in canning technology much earlier than Kirin.

As this illustration shows, distribution is a key element of the marketing mix and an important part of the marketing strategy (see the marketing strategy diagram). Key questions that must be addressed when making channel decisions are the following:

- What system of channel members works best for your product or service? Should you sell directly to customers or use intermediaries such as retailers and wholesalers?
- How can you use the channel system to perform important tasks such as physical distribution and marketing research?
- How do you manage channel members who have business and personal goals different from yours?
- How do you motivate the channel members to carry and promote your product?
- How can you use emerging channels such as the Internet and hybrid systems (combining several alternative channel structures) to capture sales when the customers are changing?

These questions and others are addressed in this chapter.

THE IMPORTANCE OF CHANNELS OF DISTRIBUTION

The importance of **channels of distribution** in the marketing mix is simple: Customers must have access to your product or service to be able to purchase it. The purpose of a system of distribution channels is to provide an efficient means of getting your products to customers and customers to your products. All companies use channels of distribution, whether they sell directly to end customers using a sales force or use a multilevel system made up of many different entities.

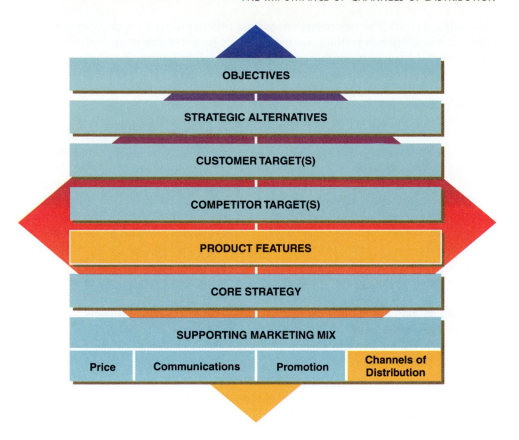

In many people's minds, channels imply physical distribution, or what is usually called logistics. They may assume that the concept of channels does not apply to services. However, it is clear that companies marketing services must solve the same distribution problems as those that market tangible products. Thus, airlines use company-owned telephone or direct channels to allow customers to make reservations directly. Banks have retail branches.

One way to think of channels of distribution is as a value-added chain. This concept is shown in Fig. 9–2. The beginning of the chain consists of suppliers that provide raw materials, labor, technology, or other factors of production. The firm then uses channels or intermediaries that enable customers to gain access to the product or service. These intermediaries are used only if they add value to the system and are compensated for the added value. In other words, Proctor & Gamble would not use wholesalers and supermarkets if they did not believe that the value of these two intermediaries' services was worth the cost.[2]

A more subtle point made by Fig. 9–2 is that channels of distribution are customers, just like end customers such as consumers. Noncaptive channels (i.e., those not owned by the company) must be convinced to carry your products, just as end customers must be convinced to buy them.[3] The marketing manager attracts noncaptive channels in two ways. First, you must use a variety of promotional devices to induce channels to carry your product and motivate them to sell it. A common myth is that a channel is primarily an agency for the physical

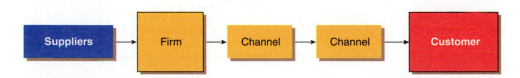

Figure 9–2

The Value-Added Chain of Distribution Channels

distribution of goods. This misconception seriously underestimates the importance of the marketing activities channels perform. Second, you must realize that channels want to distribute your product only to the extent that their customers want the product. Retailers or other distributors want to be assured that you will spend sufficient money and pay attention to getting the customers to want your brand. These two activities draw an important distinction between two kinds of basic activities of channel management: push (getting channels to carry and sell the product) and pull (motivating customers to ask for your brand by name).

A final point made by Fig. 9–2 is that channel members are an extension of the firm, but not a substitute. Particularly in the case of independent, noncaptive channel members, customers may associate problems in the channel with you even if they are not your fault. For example, a customer may buy a Packard Bell personal computer at CompUSA and have problems setting it up or learning to use it. Much of this difficulty may stem from inadequate information provided by CompUSA (the channel). However, the image of the manufacturer, Packard Bell, may be negatively affected by problems created by the retailer.

This issue relates to another common myth about channels: that the channel stops at the loading platform and what happens afterward is the buyer's responsibility. This is clearly false. It is in the best interests of the company to motivate the channels to act in both of their interests. Thus, in the CompUSA example, it is in the best interest of Packard Bell to invest in training programs for CompUSA employees to ensure that end customers are satisfied with their purchases.

Technical definitions of marketing intermediaries are provided in Table 9–1 and some general channel structures for industrial and consumer products are shown in Fig. 9–3.

Table 9–1 Major Types of Marketing Intermediaries

Middleman: an independent business concern that operates as a link between producers and ultimate consumers or industrial buyers.

Merchant middleman: a middleman who buys the goods outright and takes title to them.

Agent: a business unit that negotiates purchases or sales but does not take title to the goods in which it deals.

Wholesaler: a merchant establishment operated by a concern that is engaged primarily in buying, taking title to, usually storing and physically handling goods in large quantities, and reselling the goods (usually in smaller quantities) to retail or to industrial or business users.

Retailer: a merchant middleman who is engaged primarily in selling to ultimate consumers.

Broker: a middleman who serves as a go-between for the buyer or seller. The broker assumes no title risks, usually does not have physical custody of products, and is not seen as a permanent representative of the buyer or seller.

Manufacturers' agent: an agent who generally operates on an extended contractual basis, often sells within an exclusive territory, handles noncompeting but related lines of goods, and has limited authority with regard to prices and terms of sale.

Distributor: a wholesale middleman, especially in lines where selective or exclusive distribution is common at the wholesaler level in which the manufacturer expects strong promotional support; often a synonym for *wholesaler*.

Jobber: a middleman who buys from manufacturers and sells to retailers; a wholesaler.

Facilitating agent: a business that assists in the performance of distribution tasks other than buying, selling, and transferring title (e.g., transportation companies, warehouses).

Source: Based on Peter D. Bennett, ed. (1995), *Dictionary of Marketing Terms*, 2nd ed. (Chicago: American Marketing Association).

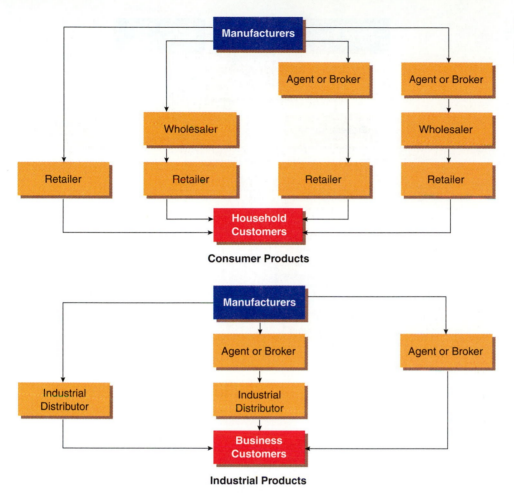

Figure 9–3
Alternative Channel
Systems

A more concrete example, from the food service disposable industry (e.g., paper cups, napkins), is shown in Fig. 9–4. As can be seen, the channel system is complex, involving many kinds of participants:

- A direct sales force
- Brokers or agents
- Wholesalers
- A company-owned distribution center
- Industrial/institutional buyers
- Cash-and-carry outlets (small, limited-function wholesalers that may also be open to consumers)
- Small, independent distributors

Note that we use the term *system* to describe distribution channel networks. The marketing manager must think in terms of maximizing profits for or meeting the goals of the entire system. You become successful only if your channel members are successful. Because the ultimate goal is to get a customer to choose your brand, your job is to design and manage the system to attract customers profitably.

You can look at channel decisions from two perspectives. The natural perspective involves planning how to best design and manage a system for your products and services.

Figure 9–4

Channel System for a
Manufacturer of Food
Service Disposables

Source: Center for Research
and Education in
Wholesaling, University of
North Florida, 1994.

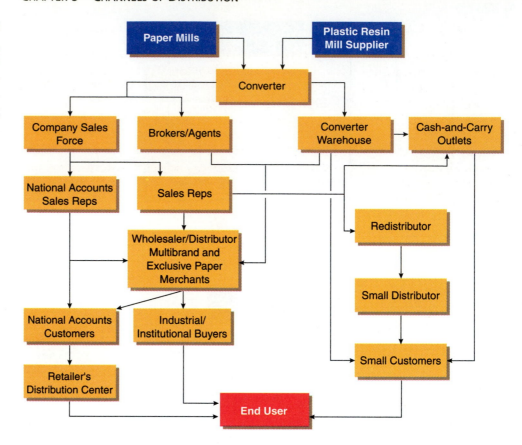

Another perspective involves planning how to make money acting as a distributor for another product. Because channel members are compensated for their value-added services, you might take advantage of access to particular market segments or other expertise. Some examples of this are the following:

- Pacific Bell has traditionally marketed its services through direct, company-owned channels. However, in California, the company has enlisted Fry's Electronics to sell integrated service digital network (ISDN) service.
- IBM has agreed to sell computer storage devices made by Storage Technology Corp. (StorageTek). Thus, IBM makes additional profits and fills a hole in its product line.
- AT&T is selling long-distance service through Shaklee, a company that sells nutritional supplements, personal care, and other products on a door-to-door basis. Shaklee has better access to ethnic and non–English-speaking communities than AT&T would have through its normal direct mail and telemarketing approaches. Likewise, MCI is selling its services through Amway.

Thus, Fry's, IBM, Shaklee, and Amway add products and profit that they would not otherwise have.

CHANNEL DYNAMICS

Another common myth about channel systems is that once they are designed, the basic structure does not change (of course, individual retailers or wholesalers may). This is simply not true; channel structures must adapt to changes in the environment. In addition, innovation in distribution can create new marketing opportunities.

The Japanese beer industry highlighted at the beginning of the chapter is a good example of how channels of distribution can change over time. The personal computer industry is another. Traditionally, mainframe and minicomputers have been sold through direct sales forces. These channels were used during the early days of the personal computer industry (the 1970s). However, new distribution channels also developed. Computer retailers became widespread, dominated by companies such as ComputerLand and Businessland. These retailers targeted both households and small businesses, sold hardware as well as software, and gave service and instruction to novice users.

A critical change in the market occurred in the mid-1980s: Customer knowledge about PCs grew as the novelty factor wore off, and increased numbers of competitors made price and availability the most highly valued product attributes. The change in the market resulted in three major changes in distribution channels. First, a new channel developed consisting of mass resellers. Second, mail order has become a very large and important channel. For example, Dell sold over $12 billion worth of personal computers worldwide in 1997 and is the fastest-growing computer brand in Europe, selling mainly through direct mail.[4] In contrast, Dell's efforts to use conventional retail channels have been unsuccessful. Third, we have seen the growth of computer superstores such as CompUSA and Soft Warehouse. Finally, the Internet has grown as a virtual retail site. Table 9–2 shows PC sales by distribution channel and demonstrates dramatically how the sales have changed over time.

Is the PC category unique? No. In consumer electronics, the same shift has occurred, from small stores with personalized service to large superstores such as Circuit City. Likewise, large office equipment retailers such as Staples and Office Depot have grown dramatically. In hardware, it is Home Depot.

Why has this happened? Although a number of factors underlie the changes in channels in these examples, the key reason is that customers have changed. In particular, as the products sold through a channel structure mature, customer knowledge of product variants, attributes, and technology also increases. Many computer buyers are now on their second, third, or fourth PC. Home stereo component systems, developed by Pioneer in the 1960s,

Table 9–2 PC Sales Volumes by Channel (% shipped)

	Direct Sales	Direct Response	Value-Added Resellers	Dealers	Computer Superstores	Mass Merchants	Consumer Electronics
1984	15.0	10.0	10.0	60.0	0	2.0	3.0
1987	10.4	13.1	12.3	56.8	0	3.4	4.1
1988	9.5	14.2	13.4	55.1	0	3.6	4.1
1990	8.3	14.6	14.9	51.2	1.5	5.0	4.5
1992	5.1	16.1	15.5	44.7	4.9	8.6	5.1
1994	3.9	14.2	16.2	42.0	8.5	9.6	5.6

Source: Das Narayendas and V. Kasturi Rangan (1996), "Dell Computer Corporation," Harvard Business School case #9-596-058.

Toys are yet another example of a product category being overtaken by "superstore" distribution channels like this FAO Schwartz Superstore. Armed with increased product knowledge, today's customers have a lesser need for the personalized service that characterizes some of the more traditional distribution channels. (Lynn Goldsmith/Corbis)

are not novelties anymore. As customer knowledge increases, their information needs change and often decrease, so the need for personalized service also decreases. This change leads to an increase in sales through outlets (direct mail, discount stores, superstores) that do not provide such information but do offer wide product lines and low prices. In sum, channels must evolve as the customers evolve.

Differential advantage can also be obtained through channel structure decisions that deviate from conventional wisdom. Direct-distribution consumer packaged goods companies such as Avon in cosmetics and Amway in household cleaning products (and the aforementioned Shaklee) chose to avoid the conventional retail channels, supermarkets and drugstores, used by their competitors. Almost any economic analysis would show how expensive it is to sell detergents door-to-door. However, these companies found that some segments of the population enjoy their personal approach to selling these low-priced products, and they have created very large niches for themselves throughout the world.[5] In the United Kingdom, the Korean company Daewoo Group eschews traditional car dealerships and instead sells from a chain of automotive accessory stores, Halfords. The company salespeople are in booths inside the stores and cars for test driving are in the stores' lots. Halfords handles service. This arrangement permitted Daewoo to instantly build a retail network with more than 120 outlets.

Other examples of differential advantage through distribution channels are:

- Virtual Vineyards sells wine only through its Web site.
- Calyx & Corolla sells flowers by mail.
- Several software companies, including Oracle, McAfee Associates, and Netscape, sell their products through downloading from the Internet.
- Coors distributes its beer only in refrigerated trucks so that the beer remains cold and fresh from the plant to the retailer.
- Gateway 2000, the direct marketing personal computer company, has introduced its Destination model, a PC for the living room with a 31-inch monitor that doubles as a TV, into retail channels CompUSA and the Wiz. However, there is only one floor model; a customer orders a customized model, the order is sent to their South Dakota manufacturing facility, and the store takes delivery and then sets up the machine in purchasers' homes.
- A company called Direct Casket allows customers to buy caskets directly from the company using a combination of traditional showrooms, a toll-free phone number, and the Internet.

CHANNEL FUNCTIONS

Channel members provide a wide variety of functions and services for a firm. Although not every member of the system performs each service, the decision about what channel structure to use is based on a matching of company and customer needs, who can satisfy them best, and how much the firm is willing to pay for them.

Marketing Research

Because channel members often have direct contact with customers, it is an ideal situation for collecting information about customer and competitor behavior. Salespeople can include such information on their call report forms. Market research surveys can be distributed at retail outlets. Telemarketing representatives can not only book orders but ask additional questions such as "Where did you first hear about us?"

Communications

An important role of the channels is to communicate information about the product or service to customers. In supermarkets, for example, end-of-aisle displays can be used to feature a brand. Sales literature and product brochures are distributed through wholesalers and retailers. In some cases, the channel may develop independent marketing programs. For example, a local hardware store may run a print ad in a newspaper featuring a particular manufacturer's lawnmower. In this case, the store would be partially or fully reimbursed for the cost of the ad through cooperative (co-op) advertising.

Contact

Some channel members seek out and interact with customers. Independent agents and wholesalers develop retail accounts for products.

Matching/Customizing

A valuable service provided by the channels is matching or attempting to tailor the product to a customer's needs. For example, automobile dealers try to match customers' desires for particular colors and option packages. Wholesalers try to deliver products to customers in lot sizes that match their needs.

Negotiation

In many cases, the channels also negotiate the final price. This is obviously true for the automobile dealers, although many dealers are moving to a one-price, no-negotiation system. An important job of a salesperson is to work with the customer and his or her superiors on the transaction price.

Physical Distribution

For products with physical characteristics, channels also provide basic logistical services. For example, Proctor & Gamble distributes its products through wholesalers, whose job is to supply the supermarket regional warehouses (for large chains, Proctor & Gamble may ship directly to the warehouses). Ultimately, the products have to get to the supermarkets.

Financing

For durable goods such as TVs and video cameras, an advantage of using a retail system is that the burden of financing falls on the retailers rather than the manufacturers. Thus, Philips, Sony, Matsushita, and other manufacturers do not have to be concerned about how customers pay for their products. Wholesalers may establish credit programs, leasing schedules, or other means of customer financing.

Risk-Taking

When the distribution system is characterized by the channel members purchasing and therefore taking title to the products, risk is shifted from the manufacturer to the channel members. This is why both push and pull programs are important. Pull programs such as customer-focused communications help to reduce channel risk; in fact, distributors usually require them before agreeing to carry the product.

Service

Channels can also provide repair service, answer customers' questions about how to use the product, and provide warranty support. Often, this service supplements a company's own service operation. For example, Sony has regional service centers throughout the world. However, consumer electronics retailers also service Sony products to make it more convenient for customers and to reach geographic areas that the service centers do not.

Relationship Management

As we noted earlier, the channel is often an extension of the firm, the organization the customer sees when gaining access to the product or service. Thus, the channel member can enhance (or harm) the quality of the relationship between the selling firm and the customer. For example, a retailer can enable a customer to sign up for a loyalty program.

Product Assembly

For some products, the channel may actually be part of the manufacturing process, performing assembly or other "finishing" parts of the process. An example is IBM's recent deal with its biggest distributor, Inacom. Inacom has traditionally shipped finished IBM PCs to large corporate customers. However, a wholesaler who wanted to answer every customer need would have to stock 2,200 combinations of components and features. Inacom built a new $20-million plant to build PCs from IBM-supplied parts. This will cut down total system time (from order to delivery) from 2 days to 4 hours and reduce the overall costs by 10%.[6]

Framework for Choosing among Channels

A matrix like that shown in Table 9–3 can be used to help determine which alternatives are most attractive at a given time. For example, you can assign a set of weights to the importance of the different functions provided. You then rate each channel option on, say, a 1 to 7 scale, evaluating the ability of the option to provide the function. By multiplying the importance weight of the function by the channel evaluation and adding across all the functions, you can give each channel a score. Although you should not rely solely on a mechanical scoring procedure for making important decisions such as which channels to use, the process of assigning the importance weights and assessing how the different channel options perform the functions shown in Table 9–3 is very useful.

Table 9–3 Channel Function Analysis

	Channel			Internal	
	Representative	Wholesaler	Retailer	Sales Force	Direct: Phone, Mail, Internet
Marketing research					
Communications					
Contact					
Matching/customizing					
Negotiation					
Physical distribution					
Financing					
Risk-taking					
Service					
Relationship management					
Product Assembly					
Overall attractiveness					

Table 9–3 can also be used to assess the characteristics of a current channel structure. By putting your current channel members across the top of the table and then indicating which channels are doing a good job at performing the functions, you obtain a nice picture of whether the system is performing all the essential services for your product.

FACTORS AFFECTING THE CHANNEL SYSTEM

Customer Behavior

A careful analysis of customer behavior, as described in Chapters 5 and 6, leads to a better understanding of what kind of channel structure is necessary to satisfy the different segments. One question of the customer analysis, "Where do they buy?" helps in understanding current purchasing patterns. However, this does not necessarily help you redesign the channel structure because it does not indicate whether customers are satisfied with current access to your products and whether it could be improved. Electrolux, the Swedish manufacturer of vacuum cleaners, has discovered that people are reluctant to buy products from door-to-door salespeople. Electrolux has introduced specialty retail stores in shopping malls as a result. As we noted earlier in this chapter, channels must be designed with the customer in mind. Thus, understanding the other customer analysis questions (*who, why, how,* and *when*) are vital inputs to the channel structure decision.

A good example of the need to structure channels around customer needs is Coors's and Kirin's distribution systems, designed around customers' perceived need for fresh beer. By starting with a key consumer need, the two companies built their logistics to satisfy that need by relocating plants, using refrigerated delivery trucks, and working with retailers to ensure that the beer remained refrigerated and fresh.

Table 9–4 shows an analysis of primary consumer wants and needs that drove Saturn's distribution system design. It is clear from the eventual design of the system that the middle section of the table, "Buying Wants and Needs," had a significant impact. Consumers they studied wanted a fair price, a fair negotiation process, convenience, honest and courteous

---

Table 9–4 Consumer Wants and Needs Driving the Saturn Distribution System

---

Shopping wants and needs
  High-quality information
    Comprehensive, including competitors
    Accurate, credible, objective
    Current
    Easy to understand and compare
  Comfortable, convenient access to information
    Low pressure, nonthreatening
  Evaluation assistance
Buying wants and needs
  Fair price
  Fair negotiation process
    Free of pressure
    Easy to understand, all costs clear
    Free of deception, dishonesty
  Convenience
  Honest, courteous treatment
  Inventory availability
Service wants and needs
  Quality of work
    Do right the first time
    Use high-quality parts
    Guarantee quality of work
  Convenience
  Timeliness
  Honest, courteous treatment
  Diagnose and recommend needed repairs accurately and honestly
  Fair price

Source: Presentation at Northwestern University by Saturn executives in May 1992.

---

treatment, and inventory availability. A key shopping want or need was lack of pressure and a nonthreatening environment. Thus, Saturn's No Hassle/No Haggle policy and well-known low-pressure environment fit the needs very well.

The rapid growth of automated teller machines (ATMs) reflects a shift in distribution channels by banks to account for changes in customer behavior. The increased convenience of ATMs took advantage of an increase in the number of dual-career couples and increased technological awareness of the populations around the world, along with an increase in the value of the time that had been previously spent in line in the banks.

Competitors

As we noted earlier in this chapter, a key reason for picking a particular channel system is to differentiate your product or service from the competition. In this sense, the product includes service, packaging, and the place of purchase. Therefore, even though Amway's floor cleaner may not be any better than Unilever's, the personal selling

Southwest Airlines has redesigned its channel structure to satisfy customers' wants and needs—in this case, the desire for low-fare, no-frills, friendly flying. To serve this need, Southwest introduced its ticketless travel system, which has been highly successful. (Courtesy of Southwest Airlines)

approach adds a dimension to the product that differentiates it from those purchased in retail outlets.

In other words, in choosing the channel structure it is important to include the competitor's channels in the competitor analysis. These channels are part of the competitor's marketing strategy. The key decision you have to make is whether to emulate it (because that's what customers expect) or to try something new and different. If the segment of customers who want the "new and different" channel is too small, then it would be difficult to be profitable by changing your channels in that direction. The only way Calyx & Corolla can be successful selling flowers by mail order is if the convenience segment is large enough. Otherwise, the traditional system of flower distribution and retailing will prevail.

Competitive distribution structures can differ in the same market. In electronics distribution, the two major competitors are Hamilton-Avnet and Arrow. Hamilton believes that customers want local delivery, so they have inventory at more than 50 locations around the United States. Arrow takes a different path: They have a few central locations but promise to ship overnight.

The Marketing Strategy

Clearly, as a result of the customer and competitor analysis (and the environmental scan), the marketing strategy developed has a large impact on the channel structure. As we noted in Chapter 3, the value chain can be used to determine various bases for differential advantage:

- Inbound logistics
- Operations
- Outbound logistics
- Marketing and sales
- Service

Each of these factors has implications for the channel structure. If you are the marketing manager for Steinway and you differentiate on the materials you use to make the pianos (inbound logistics), you have a high price and a few, exclusive distributors. Federal Express differentiated itself by having the most efficient operation in the package delivery industry. Their distribution setup included using their own planes, so that every package stayed in their own system. Wal-Mart sustains low prices by having the most efficient system for providing stock information to their warehouses and replenishing supply (operations and outbound logistics). Companies such as Amway, Tupperware, and Mary Kay Cosmetics differentiate on the basis of door-to-door as opposed to retail sales (outbound logistics, marketing). Lexus differentiates itself from other luxury car brands by its slavish devotion to high levels of customer service, which is manifested by the investment they make in their retailer's facilities and parts distribution.

Although flexible and dynamic, channel systems cannot be as easily changed as a marketing strategy. Thus, the key to linking the marketing strategy to the distribution channels is through the value proposition, that is, the core or basic way you intend to differentiate your product from the competition. Normally, the value proposition does not change as often as implementation or marketing mix issues do.

Resources

It is obviously critical for products to have distribution; no one can buy something that is not available. However, particularly with new products or an existing product being launched in a new market domestically or overseas, the amount budgeted for channels may be lower initially. For example, when the Japanese copier company Savin entered the U.S. market, they used independent agents to sell their products rather than setting up their own direct sales force. Why would they do this? Because agents are compensated only when they sell, based on a negotiated commission rate, the channel costs become variable costs rather than fixed. This method may be important when demand for the product is uncertain. If the product becomes successful, further investments are made in consolidating the market position. Thus, if resources invested in the product are insufficient to create a captive distribution system, you should look for lower-cost alternatives to give customers access to your products.

Clearly, resources are always a constraint. It makes little sense for every brand to invest in a fully company-owned system down to the retail level. IBM developed its own retail stores in the 1980s. However, the company quickly discovered that it is expensive to develop and market a retail network and that was not the company's strength. At some point, most companies have to make a hard decision about how much of the channel system to own and how much of it should include indirect or noncompany components.

CHANNEL OPTIONS

Direct and Indirect Channels

Channel selection is often thought of as two sequential decisions. First, you have to decide whether to use direct (e.g., sales force) or indirect customer contact (e.g., wholesalers, retailers).[7] Then you have to select particular channels within each group.

At one time, the tradeoff between the two was clear. Direct channels tended to imply a sales force. The main advantages of a sales force is that it is under your control and dedicated to your company's products. You can train the salespeople to deliver a particular message to potential customers and change that message when the marketing strategy changes. The downside to the sales force is that it is expensive to train and maintain it and its reach is limited by its size. Indirect channels can reach more customers and perform functions that the sales force cannot (see Table 9–3). However, as we discuss later in this chapter, they are not necessarily working exclusively for you. This loss of control is important; when you are not controlling the message given to customers, you must depend on the channel to deliver one that is consistent with your strategy.

Today, the limited reach of the direct sales channel is somewhat mitigated by the widespread use of telemarketing and direct mail. Both of these methods can reach large numbers of customers efficiently. You can control the messages as well. However, some functions that may be necessary for the product or service you are trying to market cannot be performed by these two methods.

The choice between direct and indirect channels, like any other decision, ultimately rests on the relative profitability of the two methods. How much is it worth to use distributors to give customers access to your products and services? Direct appears to be better than indirect in the following cases:

- Information needs are high because of technical complexity or for other reasons.
- Product customization is important.
- Quality assurance matters.
- Purchase orders are large.
- Transportation and storage are complex.[8]

In contrast, the following cases tend to lead to the use of indirect channels:

- One-stop shopping for many products is important.
- Availability is important.
- After-sale service is important.

However, it is clear that companies have gained differential advantage by violating some of these general guidelines. For example, the personal computer companies such as Dell and Gateway 2000 that use direct mail violate the above guidelines because after-sale service is very important for computers.

Another factor to consider in choosing between direct and indirect channels is the level of commitment you might expect to obtain from potential intermediaries. Channel members must be motivated to sell your product when they have multiple products to sell. Even when a significant amount of pull money has been promised, there is no guarantee about the dedication you can get from noncaptive channel members. From your perspective, you use multiple channels to get your product or service to customers and the focus is on your company's product alone. However, from the channel member's perspective, she or he has products from multiple companies to sell and is not necessarily focused on yours (unless the channel carries noncompeting product lines).

How do you get higher commitment from an indirect channel other than through promises of money directed at the end customer? Of course, higher profit margins are important. Giving the channel member exclusive rights to distribute or sell the product in a particular geographic area is another approach. For example, Paul Mitchell hair products are sold only through beauty salons, so they know that they will not have to compete with drug stores or other retail outlets. Providing sales training programs, promotions such as cooperative advertising plans, and sales contests are other ways to gain commitment from indirect, independent channels.

Another factor in the decision between direct and indirect channels is customer loyalty. For some kinds of products, the customer builds loyalty to the channel member rather than to the company. This loyalty can pose a long-term problem if the channel member drops the product. For example, customers are often more loyal to their stockbrokers than to the brokerage firm. As a result, if the broker leaves Merrill Lynch and joins Paine Webber, the customer will often shift his or her business along with the broker.

Sometimes the choice between direct and indirect channels is based on the likelihood that the channel member will compete with your product. Most channel members are in business solely to act as an intermediary between firms and customers. However, sometimes channel members become competitors. Store brands or private labels are examples of channel–manufacturer competition and during the early 1990s they gained share at the expense of national brands. The Gap started by selling Levi's jeans and other similar leisure wear. However, The Gap switched to selling its own brand of jeans and eventually dropped Levi Strauss as a supplier.

Finally, advances in information technology are disrupting the channel structure of many industries. Not only are more channels (such as electronic shopping services and telemarketing) being added to the channel mix, but in some circumstances, channels are being bypassed. This is a key issue in the expansion of the Internet, a channel discussed later in this chapter.

Multiple-Channel Systems

Most **multiple-channel systems,** like those shown in Figs. 9–3 and 9–4, use a combination of direct and indirect channels. For example, a common approach is to use direct sales for large national or international accounts and a wholesaler for smaller accounts for which direct sales are not cost-effective. Or, a company may use a direct sales force to sell to intermediaries such as wholesalers.

The main problems with using a variety of channels are the following:

- Coordination and management issues become more important. A particular problem is confusion about who should receive a commission on a sale or how it should be divided when several channel members are involved. For example, a distributor may provide a lead on a sale that is then closed by a salesperson.
- Loss of control can be frustrating. The marketing manager can exert control over captive channel members but not independent ones.

A particular problem occurs when a customer can buy a product at several different channels for different prices.[9] A consumer interested in buying a camera can try out various models at a local camera shop and then purchase it from a mail order company at a lower price. Although the channels are intended to focus on different segments of the market (service sensitive versus price sensitive, as we showed in Chapters 5 and 6) segments are not always so distinctly separated and there is considerable overlap and movement between them.

This problem is illustrated in Fig. 9–5. The problem is the area between the price-sensitive and service-sensitive customers, those who wear different hats on different pur-

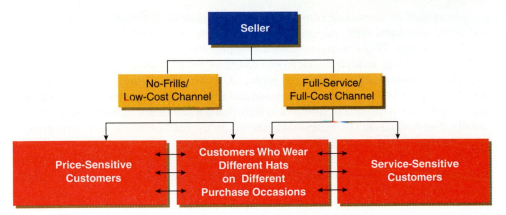

Figure 9–5

Multiple Channels

Source: V. Kasturi Rangan (1994), "Reorienting channels of distribution," Harvard Business School case #9-594-118, p. 7.

chase occasions. If the local store offers sufficient service to warrant the price, the customer will still patronize it. For example, the camera store owner may service the cameras bought in his store and provide occasional tutorials on improving photos or other specialized advice that the mail order firm does not provide.

◆ Illustration: Ingersoll-Rand

Ingersoll-Rand is one of the leading firms in the stationary air compressor industry.[10] Compressed air has a wide range of applications, from powering tools and other machinery (plant air), powering and controlling pneumatic systems in certain types of equipment (special machinery), and supplying air for manufacturing processes (process air). In the mid-1980s, the company marketed three types of compressors: reciprocating, rotary screw, and centrifugal.

The company used four different kinds of channels for marketing its products:

- A direct sales force. The sales force was responsible for sales to users of all centrifugal compressors, rotary compressors above 450 horsepower, and reciprocating compressors above 250 horsepower. The sales force sold directly to Ingersoll-Rand's largest customers.
- Independent distributors. These channel members sold reciprocating compressors below 250 horsepower and rotary compressors below 450 horsepower. These distributors sold mainly to smaller customers. The rationale was that these customers were more numerous and geographically dispersed, so it made more economic sense to use independent distributors rather than the direct sales force.
- Company-owned air centers. These were similar to the independent distributors but had territories that did not overlap. Independent distributors and air centers sold identical Ingersoll-Rand products and accessories at identical prices. However, the former carried other manufacturers' lines, but the air centers carried only Ingersoll-Rand products.
- Manufacturers' representatives. These people were charged with selling the do-it-yourself (DIY) products, mainly reciprocating compressors less than 5 horsepower. These products were sold through consumer channels such as hardware stores.

Besides the economic advantages of using channels other than direct sales, the multiple-channel design was motivated by underlying differences in segment buying behavior. Large customers such as automobile companies required a great deal of technical sophistication and coordination and their requests for price quotations contained detailed specifications that had to be met. These customers tended to require the largest machines, had longer selling cycles requiring multiple contacts, and had large buying centers (see Chapter 6), with multiple people involved in the decision process. Customers requiring smaller machines did not require as much technical assistance and had fewer people involved with the decision but needed faster delivery and parts availability that a wider dealer network could provide. Finally, customers using air compressors for filling their tires could satisfy their needs at local retailers.

Thus, this is a good example of a company selling a large product line to multiple segments; both economics and segment needs drove the design of the channel of distribution system. ◆

Hybrid Systems

A modification of the multiple-channel system is the **hybrid system.**[11] In a hybrid system, rather than serving different segments, the channel members perform complementary functions, often for the same customer. Some channel members may do the customer contacting, for example, while others perform service functions. The purpose of a hybrid system is to permit specialization and thereby improve levels of performance for the different complementary functions. Figure 9–6 shows this kind of system.

As shown in this figure, the key difference between hybrid and more conventional multiple-channel systems is that hybrids are more horizontal; that is, tasks are parceled out among the channel members. In a conventional system, often the tasks are vertical: As each member of the channel gets the product, it performs some function and then gives it to the next member.

A more detailed view of a hybrid system is given in Fig. 9–7. The channels vary in the tasks they perform; these tasks include generating the lead, qualifying sales leads, presale marketing, closing the sale, postsale service, and account management (maintaining relations with an existing account). The various methods and channels that can be used to accomplish these tasks are listed down the side of the figure. In this example, direct mail is used to generate leads; telemarketing to qualify leads, for presale activity, and postsale service; and direct sales to close the deal and manage the account once the sale is made. The grid can also be useful for identifying points of overlap and conflict in a channel system.

Figure 9–6

Hybrid Channel Design

Source: V. Kasturi Rangan (1994), "Reorienting channels of distribution," Harvard Business School case #9-594-118.

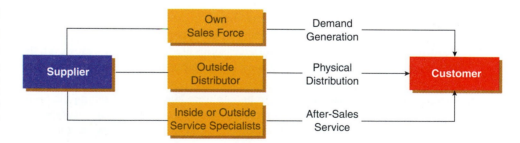

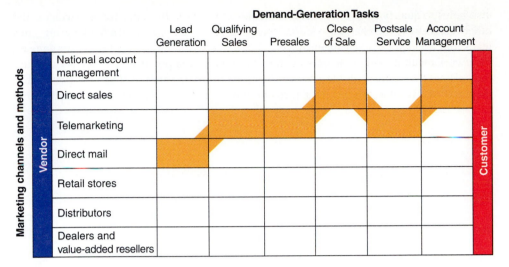

Figure 9–7

Example of a Hybrid Channel System

Source: Rowland Moriarty and Ursula Moran (1990), "The hybrid grid: the elements of a hybrid marketing system," *Harvard Business Review,* November–December.

◆ Illustration: Digital Equipment Company

Digital Equipment Company (DEC) made its reputation selling minicomputers, most notably its well-known VAX computers.[12] While computer companies such as Hewlett-Packard, Sun, and IBM found other models for their channel systems, DEC stuck to the expensive direct sales approach. This approach has become increasingly inefficient as prices for computer workstations and personal computers have dropped precipitously over the last several years.

The new model of channel relationships that DEC's competitors began to use was partnerships with system integrators, value-added resellers (VARs), and distributors. Not only is this system more economical than a direct sales force, but it also enables computer companies to better satisfy customer needs by offering solutions to their system or computing problems rather than simply selling products. DEC's direct sales approach gave salespeople little incentive to work with these kinds of resellers because they received no compensation for turning potential customers over to resellers. In addition, when the company did establish partnerships, DEC occasionally forced salespeople to push their own proprietary solutions over those of its partners.

The lack of success was even more frustrating to DEC because the company held a technological lead with the introduction of its Alpha chip, considered to be the fastest in the market, which should have given them the lead in computer workstations. Unfortunately, because of DEC's channel problems, Sun, Silicon Graphics, Hewlett-Packard, and IBM were much more successful with less advanced technology.

In mid-1994, DEC decided to rebuild its channel structure. Traditional direct salespeople still sell to large national accounts such as government agencies. However, part of the sales force was assigned to work directly with channel partners to find sales leads and make sales. An important part of their hybrid channel strategy was the 1996 opening of a sophisticated call center that performs a number of functions. The center answers partner and customer technical and marketing questions. It also captures end-user information that can be useful to future sales and relationship-building. However, the center also helps to qualify sales leads and then hands them off to the sales force, partners, and other members of the channel system. Nearly 400 DEC employees track incoming sales leads and do a quick assessment of the caller's needs and budget. A telecoverage team then works with the other channel members to discuss the prospect's needs. As a result, the partner's meeting with the prospect is much more productive. The new system has increased the volume of sales done through non–sales force channels from 42% in 1995 to 58% in 1996.   ◆

CHANNEL POWER AND MANAGEMENT

In this chapter, we have described a variety of channel arrangements you can use to structure a system. However, for every channel system you will encounter a different set of problems in managing the system and maximizing profits, market share, or whatever objective you have set.

Channel Power

Because of the many goals that exist within channels and because few marketing managers consider channel members as customers, members of a channel system are unlikely to coordinate their activities spontaneously; it usually takes a crisis to bring solutions to channel conflicts. It takes **channel power** to coordinate activities in a system:

> Power is the ability of one channel member to get another channel member to do what it otherwise would not have done.[13]

What factors affect who has the power in a channel relationship? Channel members are likely to have significant bargaining power over the marketing manager in the following cases:

- The channel's sales volume is large relative to the product's total sales volume. In this case, channel members with high sales volumes are going to be more effective in extracting terms such as delivery and push promotions.
- The product is not well differentiated from competitors. If the product is perceived to be a commodity by customers, then channel members can play your product against others; that is, they can appear to be (or actually be) indifferent to keeping your brand on the shelf.
- The channel has low switching costs (i.e., it is easy to find an alternative to replace your product).
- The channel poses a credible threat of backward integration or competition with you. A good example is the increase in private labels sold by supermarkets in the United States and Europe. This is one reason supermarkets have increased their power in their relationships with manufacturers.
- The channel has better information than you about market conditions. This can happen when channels are very good at collecting market information and using it to their advantage.

This latter point has become very important in channel relationships, particularly with the significant inroads information technology has made in many industries. The trendsetter in this area was the U.S. retailer Wal-Mart, whose business model is based on using computers to manage inventory and provide the right product mix in every store based on local tastes. Wal-Mart single-handedly changed the balance of power in retailing by forcing large suppliers, even Proctor & Gamble, to live by its rules and by having other retailers and industries follow that model. For example, if you break the windshield of your car, your insurance company will probably ask you to dial the toll-free phone number of a national network of auto glass installers. The local glass companies that are not connected are bypassed in this application of information technology. Travel, health, music, and many other industries have been dramatically affected by a shift in power between elements of the distribution system as computers and communication networks change long-standing supplier–buyer relationships. The impacts have been to eliminate intermediaries, collapse or shorten inefficient supply chains, and allow customers and companies to be linked directly.[14]

Retail marketing in the United States has changed dramatically as Wal-Mart's strategy has spawned a large number of "category killers," or large retailers selling products in a particular product category at a discount. Examples are Home Depot (hardware), Toys 'R' Us, Office Depot (office equipment), Circuit City (consumer electronics), Take Good Care (health care products), Sneaker Stadium (running shoes), and CarMax (used cars). They all rely on information-intensive operations to keep costs down and ensure the lowest prices. They also deal directly with companies producing the products to eliminate the intermediaries. Obviously, the category killers pose a significant threat to smaller retailers. Category killers have been so successful in changing the landscape of retailing that in some parts of the country, local retailers have enlisted the help of politicians to keep them out. The biggest problem facing these megaretailers is how to keep from competing against themselves.

On occasion, channel power is manifested in obvious hardball tactics. Toys 'R' Us has warned toy manufacturers that it might not carry some of their product lines if the lines are also sold to warehouse clubs that sell those products at a discount. Because of the power Toys 'R' Us has in the industry, large companies such as Mattel and Hasbro exclude warehouse clubs from some of their toy lines. This policy caught the eye of the Federal Trade Commission, which argued that such a policy had the effect of raising prices to consumers.[15]

Channel Management

Channel Conflict

Managing a channel system usually involves resolving conflicts in which one member of the system believes that another member is impeding its ability to achieve its goals. Such conflict is characterized by the different levels of intensity, frequency, and importance of the disputes that arise. Figure 9–8 illustrates these levels of conflict and divides them into three increasingly fractious intensities.

The three major sources of conflict are the following:[16]

- Goal divergence. Clearly, your objective and the objectives of channel members can differ. You may be rewarded on the basis of worldwide market share but the local retailer stocking your product wants to make enough money to send her kids to college and retire comfortably. Often, the sales force is rewarded on a commission basis, wants to sell quantity, and is willing to be flexible on price, whereas your strategy is high quality, high price.
- Domain dissensus. Conflict can arise when the perception of who owns a particular domain differs between channel participants. The domains can be
  The population to be served.
  The territory to be covered.
  The functions or duties to be performed.
  The technology to be employed in marketing (e.g., who is responsible for attaching coupons to packages?).

Figure 9–8

Levels of Conflict between Manufacturers and Channel Members

Source: Allen J. Magrath and Kenneth G. Hardy (1988), "A strategic framework for diagnosing manufacturer–reseller conflict," Marketing Science Institute report no. 88-101 (Cambridge, MA: Marketing Science Institute), p. 3.

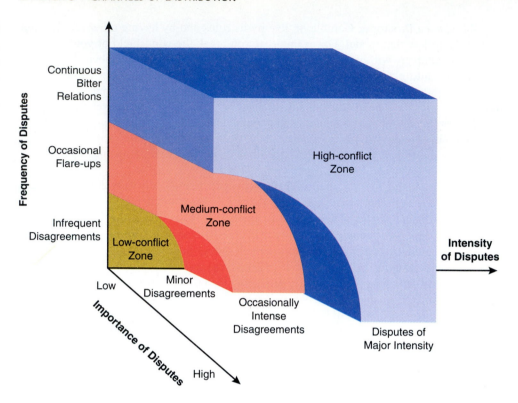

- Differing perceptions of reality. This is a basic human frailty; one side believes it has been wronged and the other believes it has acted in good faith. For example, a retailer may not think that the manufacturer's support in terms of cooperative advertising and training is sufficient while the manufacturer believes that it is offering the same level to that retailer as to others that have been successful.
- Misuse of power. Supermarkets that have gained power now charge fees for stocking products, called slotting allowances. This is a nuisance for large companies but a big problem for small ones trying to break into that channel. In Florida, Disney does not allow tour operators who work with rival Universal to distribute tickets to Disney World.

As noted earlier in this chapter, the domain issue is particularly a problem with multiple channels. The camera retailer is upset that customers can come into his store, try the camera, obtain advice, and purchase the same model at a discount electronics store or by mail order. The retailer feels that the manufacturer is not protecting him. Similarly, Hallmark traditionally distributed its cards through specialty card shops. However, because it has lost market share to competition at discount stores, supermarkets, and drug stores, the company decided in late 1996 to sell Hallmark-branded cards to mass merchandisers such as Wal-Mart, Kmart, and Kroger. This has angered many owners of the card shops, who formerly had the exclusive right to sell Hallmark cards and other merchandise. In 1996, Luxottica, an Italian manufacturer of eyeglass frames, bought the world's biggest optical chain, LensCrafters. That put the company directly into competition with the retailers who formerly sold their frames; many dropped the brand and U.S. sales declined as a result. Apple Computer announced in 1997 that it will take orders for its personal computers through its Web site, putting it in conflict with its traditional retailers.

Conflict Resolution

The conflict arising in channel systems can be resolved in many different ways. The basic approach is to determine where such conflict exists, then try to understand the channel members' concerns. This approach requires research on the channels (remember that they are customers). You can do this by talking to channel managers, employees, the sales force, or any other person who has contact with the channels. Understanding the channel members' concerns requires sensitivity. Once you know the locus and source of the problem, you can devise an effective remedy. Even then, however, you may only make progress toward solving the problem.

Let's return to the Hallmark situation. There are two sources of conflict. The first is goal divergence. Hallmark wants to increase its U.S. sales and profits; the card shop owners want the same, but for their stores only, not across all possible outlets. Hallmark's original "solution" to its problem created conflict between the card shops and discounters. The company then devised a two-part solution. The first part was to launch a new product line called Expressions from Hallmark, which is priced lower and sold only in the discount stores. The card shops still get the premium Hallmark brand. The second part of the solution was to launch a $175-million advertising campaign promoting its Gold Crown retail stores.[17]

The first part of their solution—demarcating products and product variants or brands by channels—is a common one. Such a strategy makes it more difficult for the camera shopper to use the camera specialist only for information. For example, if Nikon sells its better products only through specialty stores, the information seeker cannot purchase a similar model at a discounter or through mail order. Similarly, golf club lines are usually demarcated between pro shops and sporting goods stores.

A second example of conflict resolution is how Holly Farms Corp. handled a problem with a new chicken product it developed in 1987.[18] The company developed a roasted chicken that was very successfully test marketed (up to 90% of those trying said they would repurchase) and rolled out nationally. However, it failed for distribution reasons: Grocers complained that it had a short shelf life and they would not reorder any until their existing supplies had been exhausted. The chicken had a shelf life of 14 days but it took 9 to get it from the plant to supermarkets. Grocers could not sell their inventories within 5 days. Grocers also complained that Holly Farms did not educate the meat managers on how to deal with the product. After seeking advice from the supermarkets and further product development, the company lengthened the shelf life from 5 to 10 days by packing the chickens in nitrogen rather than air and giving the product its own distribution system to shorten the logistical part of the problem. The company also shifted a considerable amount of money out of TV advertising and into in-store demonstrations and promotions.

As a final example, let us return to the Ingersoll-Rand case discussed earlier. The company used four channels to distribute its air compressors: direct sales, independent distributors, company-owned air centers, and manufacturers' representatives. Even though the channels appeared to be defined clearly, sometimes they competed directly with each other. A salesperson might submit a bid on a 400-horsepower compressor while a distributor would submit a bid to the same customer for two 200-horsepower machines. For smaller compressors, distributors and air centers competed with the manufacturers' representatives for the under-5-horsepower compressors. To reduce interchannel competition, Ingersoll-Rand introduced its Full Partner Program, in which commissions were given for referrals as well as sales. For example, if a direct salesperson referred an inquiry to a distributor or an air center, she or he would get a 1% commission if a sale was made and 2% if the salesperson actively assisted in the sale.

Thus, from these illustrations, we have seen four ways to resolve conflict:

- Demarcating product lines (i.e., separating product offerings by channel to help reduce domain problems)
- Working with the channel members to develop joint solutions
- Putting more money into push and pull activities
- Developing financial arrangements such as commissions and higher margins

Channel power can also be used as a conflict resolution tool. If such power exists, the channel member can influence another channel member's behavior. Power sources can be converted into persuasion through the following

- Threats
- Legalistic pleas
- Promises
- Requests
- Recommendations
- Information exchange[19]

Of course, not all of these approaches will work; their success depends largely on how the channel member with the power chooses to exercise it.

SOME SPECIAL TOPICS IN CHANNELS OF DISTRIBUTION

Using the Web

Although the Internet serves a variety of nonselling purposes such as product information and customer service, its greatest strength lies in its ability to give customers direct access to products and services. Although estimates vary, in 1998 consumers spent $10 billion shopping on the Web, about $4 million in the fourth quarter holiday season alone.[20] Nearly half of this was spent on computer hardware and software, with travel coming in second (16%) and books, music, and entertainment third (13%). Business-to-business sales via the Internet are considerably higher; it is estimated that $43 billion was spent on-line in industrial marketing contexts.[21]

There are several models for using the Web as a channel. In many cases, Web channels develop incremental business for the companies sponsoring the sites. However, there is also potential for increased channel conflict, particularly from the domain perspective.

Stand-Alone Sites

Many Web sites are stand-alone sites; that is, the company uses the direct marketing approach offered by the Web as its only channel of distribution. The sites often offer a new channel to other companies. An example of this approach is Virtual Vineyards, which sells wines from small California vineyards, along with specialty foods and accessories. Virtual Vineyards supplements the vineyards' normal channels of distribution (direct sales to restaurants or sales at their vineyard tasting rooms). Another example is CUC International's Netmarket, which features its Shoppers Advantage service, allowing customers to purchase name-brand consumer products at discounts. This service expands the suppliers' channels, but unlike the Virtual Vineyards site, it entails a potential domain problem for the suppliers because Shoppers Advantage is a competing channel for their retailers. E*Trade is the company's only channel for discount brokerage services.

The Mall Approach

Some sites approximate shopping malls by selling space to other small Web sites. This approach enables customers to shop from a large number of different vendors at one virtual location. An example is Industry.net, which provides a mall for manufacturers and resellers of business equipment and services. Many of these clients use other channels as well. For consumer products, Netmart is a Web host that features chat rooms and Web sites from other small companies and organizations.

Electronic Catalogues

These are often simply Internet-based versions of catalogues that are also sent via direct mail. For example, Land's End posts its catalogue on its Web site. In addition to what is offered in the catalogue, the site offers specials on overstocks, sometimes by live bidding.

Company-Owned Sites

Some sites are sponsored by companies and both supplement and compete with existing channels. For example, Toshiba's site provides product information on its personal computers as well as the names of stores where you can purchase them, such as Best Buy, CompUSA, Computer City, and Circuit City.

Channel conflict is a particularly important issue for company-owned sites. For example, at the Hewlett-Packard Web site, buyers of medical equipment can purchase the same ultrasound machines and electrodes that traditionally have been sold through their own sales force and other distributors. In November 1998, Proctor & Gamble opened a Web site for its Hugo Boss men's and women's fragrance line. Consumers who click on a Web ad can purchase products for direct delivery to their homes, which obviously puts the site in conflict with traditional upscale department stores that also sell the products. Some companies such as the Finnish cellular phone company Nokia have avoided selling on the Web in order to maintain good relations with their distributors. Because Web marketing is fairly new, it is unclear how this issue will ultimately be resolved. However, the problem is growing larger.

Brokers

Some sites simply match buyers and sellers. An excellent example is Auto-by-Tel. At this site, prospective buyers of new cars input the model and features they want. Automobile dealers that have paid to be part of the system receive the information and then bid on the car. The buyer simply walks into the dealer with the best price, buys the car, and leaves. Auto-by-Tel can also arrange financing. Estimates are that 10–15% of cars bought in the United States in 1998 were purchased this way, with predictions that up to 25% will eventually be sold outside of traditional dealers. The implications of this channel are profound for automobile dealers; only the most efficient and technologically advanced dealers will survive.

Incremental Channels

Some sites are incremental to captive channels; that is, they do not compete with independent channel members. The site Hot Hot Hot sells spicy sauces and complements its retail outlet in Pasadena, California. The Charles Schwab e-Schwab site complements Schwab's other channels including phone. Dell Computer sells about $1 million worth of computers each day through its Web site and 80% of the customers are new to the company.[22]

Some Supermarket Issues

With the increased power retailers have obtained in the distribution channel system, particularly for grocery items, the difference between manufacturers' and retailers' perspectives is magnified. Retailers' scarce resource is their selling space, and they care less about how a particular brand is selling than what is happening to the sales of a product category, department, or store as a whole. Of course, the reverse is true for manufacturers.

This category perspective can be coupled with the data explosion that has given retailers, manufacturers, and data suppliers a microscope with which to analyze the performance of different product categories in different parts of the country, different parts of a state, and different areas within a city. To optimize their product mix, retailers want to offer the appropriate brands in a category, and they want the mix of brands and product varieties to be appropriate for the ethnic and socioeconomic composition of the shopping areas in which particular stores are located.

Thus, in the early 1990s, the **category management** concept was introduced. In category management, product categories are considered to be the business units that should be customized on a store-by-store basis to satisfy customer needs. Retailers have category managers who are empowered to operate their categories as separate businesses.

Under a category management system, manufacturers must be concerned about meeting not only their objectives but also the retailer's. Within the manufacturer's organization, the product management, sales, and marketing research organizations must work as a team because typically a salesperson sells a large number of a company's products, managed by an equivalently large number of product managers. Salespeople work closely with product managers, and marketing research managers and management information specialists provide information to both marketing and sales. Interestingly, in this era of category management, the salesperson is really the key person because she or he is the link between marketing managers interested mainly in their brands and retailers interested mainly in their categories. The job of the salesperson in this environment is to become intimately familiar with the needs of both the retailer and the customer so that he or she can adapt the company's offerings to the needs of a particular store.

Some companies have developed their own category management systems to aid retailers. Figure 9–9 is an Anheuser-Busch advertisement for its category management system, Eagle Eye Micromarketing. Clearly, category leaders such as Anheuser-Busch are very interested in helping the retailers manage their categories, which helps manufacturers consolidate and enhance their own positions.

Another development in supermarket retailing is the increased need to control costs and operate efficiently to compete with category killers. This need to be efficient has driven category management and created two new concepts: *efficient consumer response* **(ECR)** and the *continuous replenishment program* **(CRP).**[23] ECR is the process of reducing costs throughout the entire distribution system, resulting in lower prices and increased consumer demand. Part of this process is CRP, in which the members of the supply chain partner with supermarkets.

In CRP, retailers, wholesalers, and marketing managers work together to attempt to forecast demand accurately; these forecasts drive the electronic inventory replenishment system. When it works, CRP can reduce inventories at both the retail and warehouse levels by 15–60%. The difficult part is getting manufacturers and retailers to work together because

Figure 9–9

Advertisement for Anheuser-Busch's Category Management System

Anheuser-Busch Advertisement

both must be open about their strategies and performance. When they do not work together, third-party consultants try to predict sales in particular markets by counting individual stock keeping units (SKUs).

Philip Morris's Kraft unit is a leader in ECR and CRP. By combining the sales forces from Kraft, General Foods, and Oscar Mayer Foods into one, they have combined as many as nine invoices per customer to a single invoice. In addition, by 1996, more than $500 million of Kraft's sales were made using electronic reordering systems developed through CPR programs.

Multilevel Marketing

Amway, Mary Kay, Tupperware, and many other product and service lines are sold using multilevel or network marketing distribution systems. Even products such as personal computers (Hand Technologies, Inc.) are being sold this way. The concept behind the system is simple: People recruit other people, who recruit others, and so on, to sell the products. Part of the commission on each sale is transmitted through the system so that the person at the top of the pyramid can receive substantial income by managing the network.

The use of the term *pyramid* is unfortunate because multilevel selling has been linked to illegal pyramid schemes that have bilked people out of their money. Though legal and very successful, these systems still have image problems. One problem is that some systems force salespeople or distributors to purchase a significant amount of inventory in advance. Another is that the amount of sales that actually occur is far less than that promised (how many relatives do you have?); the riches some people have made rarely accrue to the average distributor. Thus, many network marketing systems are plagued by high turnover and shattered dreams.

However, network marketing does offer individuals the opportunity to make extra money and perhaps manage their own businesses. In addition, in the last several years, the industry has tried hard to reverse its negative image. In 1992, the Direct Selling Association adopted a new ethics policy that forces members to buy inventory back from distributors for at least 90% of the purchase price. Many managers, displaced through corporate downsizing programs, have joined these organizations, bringing an element of professionalism that was previously missing. Courses are being taught on the subject. Perhaps most importantly, many have been very successful. A look at the *Inc.* 500 shows that many of the fastest-growing small companies in the United States use this kind of distribution system. It is estimated that all such network organizations generated sales of nearly $20 billion in 1996.

An example is the long-distance phone company Excel (now part of Teleglobe Inc.).[24] Excel is the fifth largest long-distance company in the United States, with over 4 million customers and 1996 revenues of $1.4 billion. The company purchases capacity from the phone companies and resells it to customers at a discount. The top salesperson in the company earns over $1 million per month, which motivates many of Excel's 1 million distributors. However, the average distributor has only four customers and one is the salesperson him- or herself, so the annual turnover rate is 80%. That is because the average monthly long-distance bill is $28 and the commission rate at the bottom of the network is 2%. Thus, a salesperson with only four customers earns just over $20 per year. Those higher up in the network also collect commissions on what their distributors sell and bonuses when the distributors sign up new customers. ◆

DIRECT MARKETING

One of the strongest trends in marketing has been toward **direct marketing.** Direct marketing is most often associated with traditional methods such as direct mail (often called junk mail) and telemarketing. However, it also includes Internet-based marketing as well as radio, TV (e.g., "infomercials"), and teleconferencing. In general, direct marketing includes any method of distribution that gives the customer access to the firm's products and services without any other intermediaries (generally, direct marketing excludes the sales force). It is sometimes called direct response advertising because the intention is to get the customer to respond immediately to a communication. Direct marketing is thus a hybrid of a channel and communication device.

The following statistics will give you some idea of the reach of direct marketing.[25] In the United States, total direct marketing sales were about $1.2 trillion in 1997. Of this amount, 46% was for business-to-business and the remainder for consumer products and services; $244 billion was from telemarketing and nearly $150 billion from direct mail. Companies spent nearly $60 billion on outbound telemarketing services (in which the company calls the customer) in 1996, a 36% increase from 1991. E-mail is also becoming a major tool in the direct marketing industry. Forrester Research predicts that by 2002, 250 billion solicited commercial e-mail (SCE) messages will be sent per year.[26] Although you might think that direct marketing is most useful for small-ticket items, some more expensive products are also sold in this way. Witness the use of the Neiman-Marcus catalogue to sell items worth thousands of dollars and more. In addition, in 1994, IBM attempted to sell its low-end mainframe computers via its IBM Direct operation.

Why has there been such an increase in the use of direct response methods? Two events, occurring simultaneously, have driven this trend. First, in an era where cost control is of paramount importance, direct marketing can be used to make the channel system more efficient. For example, direct mail can be used to reach prospects that would be too expensive to reach with a sales force because of their disparate geographic locations or low purchase rates. As we showed earlier in this chapter, mail or phone also can be used to complement other channel activities in a hybrid channel system. Second, an effective direct marketing operation relies heavily on an excellent database of customer names, addresses, and phone numbers. Companies have been making significant investments in databases for direct marketing and for building and maintaining customer relationships.[27] Improvements in computer technology and data mining software (programs that sift through vast amounts of customer information) have made it easier to use direct marketing and have resulted in greater efficiency of this channel and higher profits.

The three keys to successful telemarketing are the following:[28]

- The list. Demographic targeting, beginning with a good list of prospects, can increase the success rate by as much as 60%. Lists can come from in-house sources (names accumulated from direct mail, trade shows, and print advertising responses maintained on a database in your firm), companies such as Dun & Bradstreet and Donnelly (which compile lists of prospects with particular characteristics), and response lists accumulated from magazine subscriptions or catalogue buyers, which can be purchased from a list broker.
- The offer. There must be a compelling reason for the customer to buy over the phone. The reason can be a significant discount from the normal price or, more often, the offer of a product or service that cannot be purchased elsewhere. This offer must be stated early in the conversation and communicated clearly.
- Integrity. There is considerable perceived risk when buying over the phone. The telemarketer must reduce this risk through devices such as money-back guarantees or a well-known brand name.

For a successful direct mail effort, the following guidelines also apply:[29]

- The copy. In general, longer copy (the text of the direct mail letter) is better because it gives you the opportunity to inform and persuade. The letter should be as long as it takes to communicate your product's benefits. However, you have about 4 minutes to convince the reader that the offer is worth buying. Words, sentences, and paragraphs should be kept short, with a friendly tone.
- Layout/design. Decisions about typeface, colors, graphic elements, personalized addressing, and other visual elements should be considered carefully. Format is very important because direct mail is often screened, particularly in a business-to-business context.

It is clear that we should expect to see more direct marketing tools in the future.

◆ Illustration: Mercedes-Benz

Mercedes-Benz introduced its $35,000 M-class sport utility vehicle (SUV) in the fall of 1997.[30] Although the SUV category has become very popular and dealers were clamoring for competitive entry, Mercedes took some time to decide whether to have such a model and finally decided to build it in Alabama. In an interesting twist, the company hoped to presell the entire 35,000-car U.S. allotment via direct mail.

Why direct mail? First, traditional marketing using advertising has become very expensive. Second, Mercedes wanted a campaign that would inspire more yearning for the car than a traditional campaign could. As we noted earlier, a direct mail piece can be fairly long and use a variety of media including photos and CD-ROMs. Such media give the prospective customer a better feeling for the new car than a print or TV advertising campaign.

Working with New York–based Rapp Collins Worldwide, Mercedes took 500,000 names from their lists and lists of other SUV owners. They asked these people to participate in a 2-year dialogue-by-mail with Mercedes that would precede the introduction of the car. Of the 500,000 people, 70,000 agreed. Mercedes added other names, to create a list of 135,000 prospects. Two mailings were sent; the first contained a survey asking about customer preferences in styling, safety, and other features. Based on the stated preferences, the follow-up letter focused on these features, comparing the Mercedes SUV to the competition and emphasizing the features of the Mercedes that were consistent with customer preferences.

Mercedes spent $12 million on the direct mail campaign. It had such an impact that more than 1,000 buyers in Texas contacted their local dealers and put down deposits. This campaign, combined with other marketing efforts, led to the presale of a significant number of the cars.

◆ Illustration: ON Technology

ON Technology is a Cambridge, Massachusetts software company selling two major product lines: communication software (e.g., Meeting Maker and DaVinci eMAIL), and network management tools.[31] Over the years, the company has relied almost exclusively on direct marketing, developing significant expertise in direct marketing and database development.

Typically, its direct marketing program includes three to five pieces. The first mailing is a bingo card (a response card on which the customer circles or otherwise marks a product information request on a grid, with numbers keyed to other product offerings). This card offers a free 30-day software trial. Simultaneously, the prospects are contacted 15–18 times by phone and e-mail. The bingo cards have a typical response rate of 2–3%.

When the card comes back, the potential user (typically a network administrator) receives a copy of the software and a free ON Tech t-shirt. The "trialer" is then contacted via phone asking whether she or he needs assistance installing or configuring the program. About 15% of the trialers actually install the software. The trialers are then sent another mailing, including a list of product features, frequently asked questions (FAQs), other relevant information, and reprints of favorable reviews and articles. The trialers then receive another call, called the "feature walk," in which ON Tech ensures that the trialer understands the features of the product and offers explanations where necessary. A final mailing attempts to close the deal.

The database is maintained and managed by Edith Roman Associates in New York and includes 300,000 networking professionals. This database is supplemented by mailing lists from high-tech magazines.

The direct marketing system was recently tested by the release of ON Guard, an Internet firewall (security) product priced at $7,500 and aimed at small to mid-sized companies. It is competitive with Cisco Systems, whose product can be bundled with its local-area network routers, and Microsoft and 3Com are developing similar products. The product achieved a market share of more than 30% in its first year. To supplement the direct mail and telemarketing campaigns, ON Tech set up the Firewall Center on its Web site, dedicated to providing general information about Internet firewalls to potential customers. ◆

These illustrations from two industries representing completely different products and customers show how direct marketing can be an important complement to other forms of communication.

EXECUTIVE SUMMARY

The topics covered in this chapter include the following:

- The distribution channel system gives customers access to your products and services and is a value chain in which different members of the system add value and are compensated accordingly.
- There are many different channel structures; no one channel system is appropriate for every industry, product category, or firm.
- The channel structure depends on customer and competitor behavior, the marketing strategy used, and the resources available. Channel systems can evolve over time as these elements change.
- Channel members perform a wide variety of functions for the system.
- A common decision sequence is to first choose between direct and indirect channel systems and then choose particular channel members.
- Hybrid channel systems include a number of different channel types that complement one another and perform different tasks to obtain a sale.
- Channel power enables a channel member to exert some authority to get another member to do something it would not otherwise do on its own.
- Channel management involves maintaining good relationships and resolving conflict between channel members.
- Conflict can be resolved by demarcating products between channel members, helping the channel members to achieve their goals, and offering more push and pull money.
- New channel opportunities are arising from the emergence of Web-based marketing, changes in the supermarket retailing (category management, efficient consumer response [ECR], and continuous replenishment programs [CRPs]), and multilevel or network marketing.
- Direct marketing is probably the fastest-growing channel. Direct mail and telemarketing are most popular, but direct response TV, radio, and other media are also popular.

CHAPTER QUESTIONS

1. Develop two examples of companies that are using other companies as distributors (such as Pacific Bell using Fry's Electronics for ISDN service). What benefits are the original companies receiving in these two cases?
2. Besides the illustrations in this chapter, give an example of another industry that has witnessed substantial change in channels of distribution. What are the fundamental reasons (e.g., consumer behavior, competition) for this change?
3. An executive at a large package delivery company has complained that by shifting some of its business to independent channel members, the company has "lost control of the

customer." What do you think he means by this statement? Why does he consider this to be bad for the company?

4. Levi Strauss sells the same products, Levi's, Dockers, and Slates, to multiple channels of distribution, from high-image (Bloomingdale's) to low-image (Sears, Mervyns) outlets. What would you suggest as a distribution strategy so that the company can better differentiate its product by channel and not suffer brand confusion problems?

5. What are the pros and cons of using the Web as a distribution channel? Are there some situations where it should not be a part of the channel mix?

Integrated Case

Application Exercises: Distribution Channels in the PC Industry

Continuing the PC industry case, complete the following exercises:

1. Using Fig. 9–3 as a model, choose a PC manufacturer and sketch out its channel of distribution system.

2. Given the current market trends in the PC industry, determine whether your answer to exercise 1 is the ideal distribution channel structure for the company. If not, develop a new recommendation.

3. Select a PC manufacturer and show how the company takes (or could take) advantage of the different functions channel members perform.

4. Choose a company that uses both direct and indirect channels of distribution. Develop a system that minimizes channel conflict and gives the different channel members incentives to sell as much of the brand as possible.

5. Go to the Web sites of three different PC vendors. Compare and critique the sites as channels.

FURTHER READING

The best book in this area is the one by Stern et al. referenced in the chapter. An alternative reference is Bert Rosenbloom (1995), *Marketing Channels: A Management View,* 5th ed. (Fort Worth, TX: Dryden). A good reference on direct marketing is Edward L. Nash (1995), *Direct Marketing: Strategy, Planning, Execution* (New York: McGraw-Hill).

Personal Selling

10

CHAPTER BRIEF

The purpose of this chapter is to introduce some of the major issues in managing the personal selling process. After reading this chapter, the student will have learned the following:

How the sales force fits into the marketing organization

The major jobs of a salesperson

Managing the sales force in terms of improving performance, designing sales territories, determining sales force size, and assigning salespeople to territories

Setting sales quotas

Issues in sales force compensation

The impact of technology on sales management

GE Capital, a division of General Electric Company, started during the 1930s by providing financing to customers purchasing GE appliances.[1] The division now provides a wide range of financial services in five sectors: equipment management, consumer services, specialized financing, midmarket financing, and specialty insurance. The sectors include 28 distinct businesses, including Penske Truck Leasing, GE Capital Mortgage Services, and GE Capital Consumer Financial Services. Since 1988, GE Capital's net income has grown at an average rate of 18% per year, with over $40 billion of revenues in 1998. Although some of this growth has come from acquiring new businesses, much of it has been internal growth: developing new business through its sales force. This group was rated the best sales force in the United States in 1998 by *Sales & Marketing Management.*

How has GE Capital's sales force been so successful? First, the sales force is large (about 14,000 salespeople). Second, the company has an excellent mentoring program in which senior sales representatives guide junior reps through learning the selling process and working with customers. Third, GE Capital's salespeople have strong customer orientation; industry experts rate them highly in terms of their abilities to listen to customers, respond to their needs, and develop long-term relationships. Finally, the company strongly believes in continuous training.

For example, the division has developed its "Find More, Win More, Keep More" (FWK) program, designed to gain more business from both new and existing customers. "Find More" means constantly looking for new customer segments to penetrate. "Win More" means getting more business from existing customers instead of letting them go to competitors for some of their financing business. "Keep More" means putting significant effort into retaining the best customers.

At the same time, GE Capital faces the same problems faced by any other company that has a sales force:

- Recruiting and selecting the sales force
- Training, evaluating, and supervising the sales force
- Motivating the sales force and setting quotas
- Assigning the appropriate geographic territories and customer accounts to each salesperson

As mentioned earlier in this book, personal selling and sales force management fulfill several important marketing tasks. First, it was noted in Chapter 8 that the sales force is part of the communications mix. The sales force must be given the tools and training to implement the marketing strategy and integrate its efforts with the rest of the communication programs. In Chapter 9, we discussed the sales force as a channel of distribution, a direct channel to the customer. Clearly, the sales force satisfies the major criterion for a channel: It gives customers access to the firm's products and services.

Therefore, the sales force has a dual role in the implementation of the marketing strategy (see the marketing strategy diagram). The salesperson not only communicates information about the product or service and delivers the key value proposition to the customer, but also attempts to complete the transaction with the end customer (a key role of some channels). In addition, many companies spend a significant sum of money on sales force activities. Table 10–1 shows the 10 largest sales forces in the U.S. manufacturing sector. The resources spent training, motivating, and rewarding these salespeople

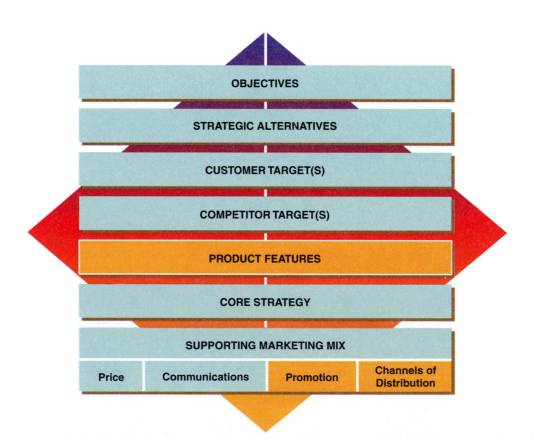

Table 10–1 Ten Largest Sales Forces in the United States Manufacturing Sector, 1997

Rank	Company	Estimated Number of Salespeople
1	Sara Lee	29,000
2	IBM	16,000
3	PepsiCo	15,000
4	International Paper	13,225
5	General Electric	12,800
6	Interstate Bakeries	10,863
7	SBC Communications	10,403
8	Philip Morris	10,000
9	Sysco	9,582
10	Microsoft	9,346

Source: *Selling Power* (1997), September, p. 42.

rival or surpass the money spent on other channels and types of communication. It is therefore natural that this chapter follows discussions of communication and channels of distribution.

There are different titles used in sales management depending on the level of the organization. Figure 10–1 shows the different titles typically used in a midsized sales organization. The vice president of marketing or sales heads the sales organization. Most of the other titles describe job responsibilities defined by the size of the geographic territory covered (national, regional, and district sales managers). The largest part of the organization is made up of the field sales representatives, or reps.

Although we will not cover all of the issues a particular sales manager has to deal with, this chapter should give you a good sense of the diversity of the salesperson's and sales manager's jobs. Because there are many different titles and duties assumed by the people within a sales force and because they vary across companies and industries, in this chapter we will cover the general area of sales management, rather than focusing on one particular organizational level.

Figure 10–1

Sales Force Organization in a Medium–Sized Firm

Source: Douglas J. Dalrymple and William L. Cron (1988), *Sales Management*, 6th ed. (New York: Wiley), p. 6.

THE SALES FORCE AND THE MARKETING ORGANIZATION

In Chapter 2, the marketing manager's job was defined and some aspects of marketing organizations illustrated (see Figs. 2–1 through 2–5). The relationship between sales and marketing organizations is unusual. Although you might think that the sales organization would be part of marketing because the sales force helps to implement the marketing strategy, sales organizations are often separate and powerful entities within companies. In such firms, marketing is viewed as providing a support function (advertising, selling materials, trade shows) to sales.

Figure 10–2 shows the organizational structure of Adobe Systems Inc., a computer software company. The product marketing group includes product managers responsible for putting together marketing strategies and programs for products such as Acrobat (text formatting), Photoshop (imaging), Persuasion (presentations), and Pagemaker (desktop publishing). In this organization, product marketing is different from marketing in that the latter is more tactical in nature; that is, marketing offers support to product managers by planning promotional events, designing trade show displays, and so on. In this case, the sales organization is separate from marketing. The sales force is responsible not only for calling on corporate customers but also for channel merchandising (handling relationships and other matters with distributors).

Types of Sales Organizations

There are three kinds of sales organization structures. One structure is organized around product lines. The product/product sales organization sells a product or product line to all markets and often coexists with a product-focused organization. A disadvantage of this structure is that a customer may be called on by several salespeople from the same company.

Figure 10–2

Adobe Systems
Marketing
Organization

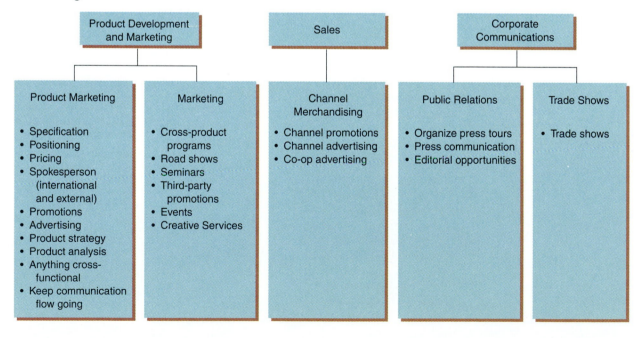

An example of the product/product structure is shown in Fig. 10–3, which shows the organizational structure for Hewlett-Packard's Medical Products Group (MPG).[2] MPG sells a variety of products, including patient monitoring systems, operating room systems, peri-natal monitoring devices, and clinical information systems. On the right side of the chart is the U.S. Field Operations, with different national sales managers (NSMs) for the different product groups within MPG. The Imaging Systems Division (ISY), which manufactures ultrasound devices for cardiologists and vascular surgeons, has its own sales force and national sales manager, as do the other three product groups. The ISY sales force only sells the products made by that division.

A second type of organization is a market/market system, in which the marketing organization is aligned by market segment, as is the sales force. In this case, the sales force sells the entire product line to customers in the segment. An illustration of this kind of organization is shown in Fig. 10–4.[3] MCI's U.S. marketing operations are organized by geographic market segments. In each geographic territory, the sales force is responsible for selling all telecommunications services to the customers.

A third organizational form is called product/market. In this case, the company has a product management structure but the sales force sells all products marketed by a division to a single market. An example of this kind of structure is the General Foods dessert division shown in Fig. 2–2. In this case, there are individual product managers for Jell-O Gelatin, Jell-O Pudding Pops, and other products, but the sales force for the desserts division is responsible for selling all of the division's products to the national supermarket chains.

Figure 10–3

Hewlett-Packard Medical Products Group Organization Chart, 1992

Source: Frank V. Cespedes (1994), "Hewlett-Packard imaging systems division: Sonos 100 C/F introduction," Harvard Business School case #9-593-080, p. 18.

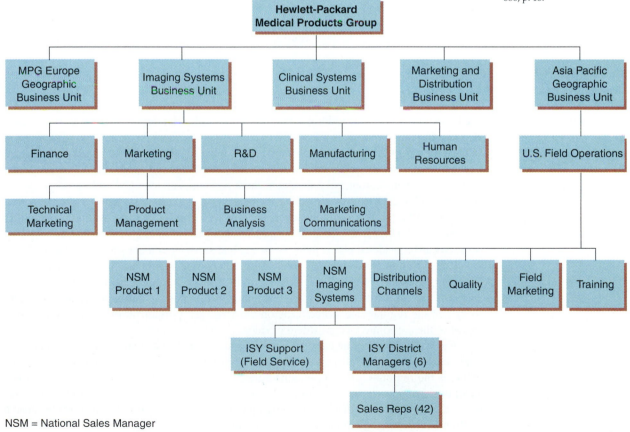

NSM = National Sales Manager

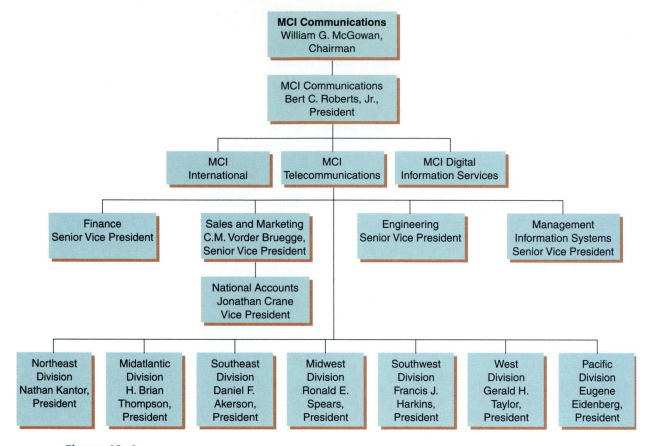

Figure 10–4

MCI Communications Corporation Organizational Chart, 1986

Source: MCI Communications Corporation: National Accounts Program, Harvard Business School case #9-593-044, p. 15.

National/Key Accounts Organizations

Many companies have an additional layer of salespeople who deal with the largest accounts. Because in many companies a few large corporate accounts make up a large percentage of sales, a higher level of attention to their business makes good sense. For example, a national study done in 1990 showed that 50% of the sales of the firms surveyed were accounted for by only 10% of their customers.[4] National account personnel are charged with developing new accounts and maintaining existing ones; the latter is particularly important for long-term relationship-building. Key account managers become very familiar with a customer's operations and problems and are in an excellent position to satisfy the customer's needs. In addition, such positions are considered plums in the company and serve as a career goal for the sales force.

It is common for companies to establish a separate organization to deal with major accounts. As shown in Fig. 10–5, there are four common ways to organize the key account sales force. The most common form of organization is for the national/key account sales force and the regular sales force to be on the same level organizationally and for both to report to the corporate vice president of sales.

The ways in which the national account and regional sales teams interact can vary. In some cases, the national account team calls on national or international headquarters, whereas the regional salespeople concentrate on the local offices. In others, the national account manager acts as a coordinator for the regional team. With either kind of arrangement, there are often difficulties dividing up the commissions earned from sales because it is often unclear who contributed the most to the sale.

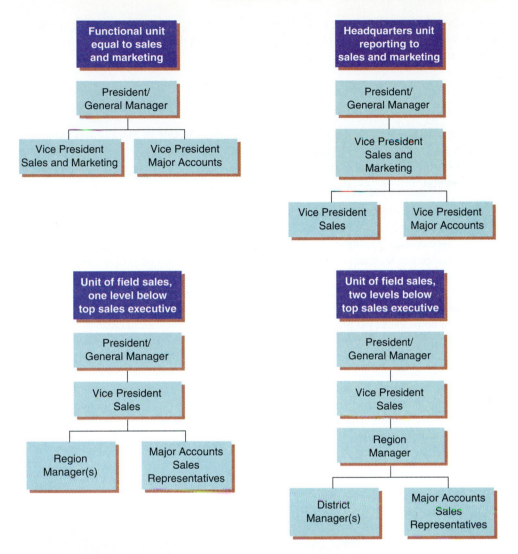

Figure 10–5

Ways to Organize National Account Sales Forces

Source: Gilbert A. Churchill, Jr., Neil M. Ford, and Orville C. Walker, Jr. (1993), *Sales Force Management*, 4th ed. (Homewood, IL: Irwin), p. 157.

◆ Illustration: Marriott Lodging

Marriott Lodging's key account managers (KAMs) handle three to six major accounts.[5] These KAMs report to the vice president of sales, who reports to the senior vice president of sales and marketing. Each KAM is the main contact point between Marriott and the customer (e.g., large corporate clients) and is responsible for developing long-term relationships with the customers assigned to him or her. The KAMs are compensated by a combination of salary (70%) plus bonus (30%). The bonus is based on a combination of revenue targets and the quality of the relationships established.

The advantage of focusing on individual customers is that the KAM assigned to an account gets to know the customer's business very well. Marriott KAMs are expected to use on-line newspapers and other resources to research customer financial data, industry trends, and anything related to the customer's business. The objective is to be proactive and recommend money-saving ideas to customers to help them reengineer their travel processes. Of course, these ideas include recommending a mix of Marriott hotels across the spectrum from full-service to economy. The KAM system is working so well that in many accounts, a 1-percentage-point increase in Marriott's market share in that account is worth $1 million in incremental revenue.   ◆

WHAT DOES A SALESPERSON DO?

Obviously, a salesperson is rewarded on her or his ability to sell, or close orders from customers.[6] However, this overall task of selling does not adequately describe the different kinds of selling that occurs in business. A common way of classifying selling situations is the following:

- Response selling. In this situation, the salesperson is basically an order taker; the customer initiates the sale and gives the order to the salesperson.
- Trade selling. This kind of selling includes order taking, but also entails responsibilities such as making sure the stock is adequately displayed on shelves, setting up displays, providing demonstrations, and other activities sometimes called merchandising.
- Missionary selling. In this kind of selling, the salesperson attempts to influence the decision maker rather than the user or purchasing agent. The missionary salesperson helps the buyer promote the product to internal or external customers.
- Technical selling. In many industries, the salesperson also acts as a technical consultant to the purchaser. For this to be successful, the salesperson must have strong technical training. For example, the Hewlett-Packard salespeople in the Imaging Systems Division must be knowledgeable about the latest developments in ultrasound and other medical imaging technologies.
- Creative selling. This method involves developing new customers and maintaining old ones by investing a considerable amount of time in understanding buyers' needs and wants.

In any personal selling relationship, the salesperson must establish and maintain rapport with the customer. In addition, some kinds of selling require technical training and significant knowledge of the particular industry. This pharmaceutical salesperson has good communication skills, but he also must have strong technical training and be knowledgeable about the latest developments in the drug industry. (David J. Sams/Picture Network International)

A salesperson performs a wide variety of activities, including the following:

- Planning the sales call. The good salesperson spends a considerable amount of time planning the call. This planning includes using information provided by the company and past sales calls about competition (both the salesperson's and the customer's), the economic, technological, political, and social environment, and the product or service. Today, preparation also involves learning how to use the latest technology in giving presentations.
- Traveling to the customer site and making the call.
- Filling out the call report. This involves a detailed examination of what happened during the call, "win–loss" reports on new business won or customers lost, any information picked up about competition such as their prices, and any other market intelligence.
- Postcall analysis. The good salesperson analyzes what happened, talks with his or her supervisor, and collects feedback about the call that can be used in future efforts.
- Communicating with the customer. It has been said that after a sale is made, for the seller, it is the end of the process; for the buyer, it is only the beginning.[7] Thus, the good salesperson knows that establishing and maintaining rapport with the customer is necessary for future business. Even if no sale is made or a sale is lost, communicating with customers or potential customers is vital.

Thus, there are different kinds of sales jobs and different tasks to perform.

DIRECTING THE SALES FORCE

Determinants of Performance

What factors contribute to the success of a salesperson? Like other resources such as advertising and promotion, money spent on the sales force is expected to produce revenues and profits. As a result, companies are always interested in improving the performance of their sales forces. It is important for the marketing manager to develop a better understanding of the factors that contribute to a salesperson's success in order to help improve one person's performance or the performance of a group of salespeople.

A number of models have been developed to help explain performance.[8] Figure 10–6 shows one such model. As can be seen, performance is a result of both internal or individual factors and external factors. We review these factors in more detail here.

Internal Factors

The salesperson's motivation is a basic force behind how much effort he or she devotes to the job (planning sales calls, following up on customer questions, filling out reports) and how he or she responds to different kinds of incentives. Clearly, the sales force is motivated by financial incentives such as commissions on sales, salary guarantees, and bonuses. However, salespeople can also be motivated by sales meetings and contests, education and training, and information about the company and its plans.

In a way, the marketing manager must understand what motivates his or her salespeople, just as the manager would have to know what motivates his or her customers to buy. Different salespeople are motivated by different factors. For example, a salesperson who has been with a company for many years may be more motivated to sell from

Figure 10–6

Determinants of
Sales Force
Performance

Source: Rolph E. Anderson,
Joseph F. Hair, Jr., and Alan
Bush (1992), *Professional Sales
Management*, 2nd ed. (New
York: McGraw-Hill).

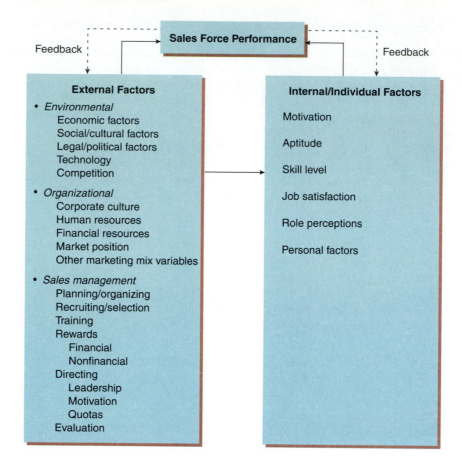

company loyalty than is a younger salesperson who is looking to develop a track record
for future career moves. Some salespeople (like people in general) are more motivated
by money than others. Thus, it is critical to understand what motivates each salesperson
on the force.

Salesperson performance is also affected by their aptitude for selling, or their natural
ability to sell. It is generally thought that some people are born salespeople and others are
not. However, this implies that selling skills cannot be taught, which is not true. At the same
time, some aspects of aptitude, such as empathy and persuasiveness, cannot be taught easily and give one person an edge over another.

Aptitude is a person's natural ability. Acquired skill is also important for a good salesperson. As we just noted, good selling skills can be taught. There are many courses available,
both within companies and offered by specialized firms, that can teach aspiring and experienced salespeople how to improve their communications, negotiation, closing, and other skills
involved with personal selling. In addition, in technical selling situations, selling skill is
enhanced by continuous updating of the scientific knowledge relevant to the product.

Not surprisingly, higher levels of job satisfaction have been found to be positively correlated with salesperson performance. Research has found that satisfaction is related to both
intrinsic and extrinsic motivation. Intrinsic motivation comes from within and is related to
the satisfaction a salesperson obtains from the different aspects of the job, such as being on
the road and meeting people. Extrinsic satisfaction is derived from rewards such as promotions, salary increases, and sales contests.

Understanding what motivates a salesperson is critical in managing sales performance. Some salespeople may be motivated by financial incentives; others, like this salesperson, may be motivated by sales contests and public recognition of superior performance by coworkers. (Owen Frankin/Corbis)

The salesperson also needs to understand both his or her superior's expectations and the kind of selling that is necessary to be successful. This knowledge is called role perception. For example, if the sales manager expects the salesperson to spend half of his or her time taking care of the stock on the shelves and the salesperson thinks that is a minor part of the job, this mismatch in expectations will lead to lower performance.

Finally, personal factors such as gender, attractiveness, education level, and other factors are often related to success in particular industries.

External Factors

A major set of factors affecting performance are environmental. These factors are derived from the marketing plan described in Chapter 2. Included are the following:

- Customers. Obviously, changes in customers' tastes, buying behavior, and their own competitive conditions make the salesperson's job more difficult.
- Competitors. Tracking the competition is important for successful selling. This involves more than prices (the usual focus of salespeople); it also involves changes in their strategies, financial condition, product line, and other factors.
- The industry environment. Changes in technology, social changes, economic shifts, regulation, and politics affect the job.

In general, the wise salesperson obtains the product or product line marketing plan and absorbs the information in the situation analysis.

Although some people seem to be born with a natural aptitude for selling, important selling skills can be taught. Personal selling courses such as this one often focus on improving skills such as negotiation and closing and involve some amount of role play. (Bob Rowan/Corbis)

A second set of external factors relate to the organization. The salesperson's success is affected by a number of factors internal to the company for which he or she works. For example, it is easier to sell if the products are market leaders. Conversely, the market position is affected by the sales force's efforts. Poor market position is not necessarily caused by unsuccessful marketing strategies. An important factor is the amount of financial resources a company puts into sales efforts. Sales force performance is likely to improve as more money is spent on higher salaries, better incentives, better training, and selling aids. High-quality personnel and a culture that supports personal selling efforts also help.

The quality of the sales management also directly affects the performance of the sales force. This quality is affected by the amount of resources the company spends on sales management. However, it is also affected by the kind of people who occupy key sales management posts. They affect the organization by selecting capable salespeople, designing effective reward systems, and motivating salespeople.

Thus, sales force performance is affected by many factors, both individual or internal and external. Senior marketing management must understand these factors and optimize them.

DESIGNING SALES TERRITORIES

A **sales territory** is a group of present and potential customers assigned to a salesperson. In most cases, as the term implies, sales territories are geographic areas selected to minimize travel time between accounts and delineate clearly which person is responsible for a particular account.

Designing sales territories is a very important part of sales management. Territories that are not balanced in terms of potential sales can be demoralizing to the salespeople assigned to them. An insufficient number of territories means salespeople spend too much time traveling and not enough time selling. Too many territories means lower income and salespeople fighting over the geographic boundaries. This latter problem is particularly important to GE Capital as they increase the size of their sales force. GE's sales force is very aggressive and used to be rewarded with significant bonuses for exceeding their sales quotas. If territories are shrunk, reps may wonder how they will meet their ever-increasing quotas with fewer potential customers.

There are three major interrelated decisions concerning sales territories:

- Deciding how many salespeople to have
- Designing the territories
- Allocating selling effort to the accounts

Determining the Size of the Sales Force

Three major methods are used to estimate the sales force needed.

Breakdown Method

The **breakdown method** is a very simple method that assumes an average productivity level for each salesperson. The number of salespeople needed can be computed from the following equation:

$$n = s/p$$

where n = the number of salespeople needed, s = the forecasted sales, and p = the average sales per salesperson. Therefore, a company expecting to sell $100 million worth of goods in 1998 with a sales force currently averaging $5 million per salesperson needs 20 people.

The major problem with this method is similar to using the percentage of expected sales to set advertising budgets (see Chapter 8). This formula assumes that the number of salespeople is determined by the expected sales level when, in fact, the opposite is also true. That is, in many cases sales could be increased with more salespeople.

Using the "average" salesperson does not account for other factors. These include variations in territory potential, the mix of experienced and inexperienced salespeople if there is turnover, and other factors. In addition, the number is highly dependent on an accurate forecast for sales. As we noted in Chapter 4, forecasting sales accurately is highly problematic in most cases.

Workload Method

The **workload method** is based on the ability to calculate the total amount of work necessary to serve the entire market. The number of salespeople required is the total workload calculated divided by the amount of work the average salesperson is expected to handle. Six steps required to implement this method:

1. Classify all the firm's customers into categories. It is common to divide the set of customers into three categories, based on the amount of sales for which they account (other criteria could be used as well). For example, you might classify your customers into A, B, and C customers based on an analysis of the distribution of sales. Customers classified as A might be the top 25%, B the next 50%, and C the bottom 25%. Even better, the assignment could be based on sales potential rather than actual sales.
2. Determine the frequency with which each type of account should be called upon and the necessary length of each call. For example, based on experience and judgment, the following data might be used:

   Class A: 12 times/year × 120 minutes/call = 1,440 minutes, or 24 hours
   Class B: 6 times/year × 60 minutes/call = 360 minutes, or 6 hours
   Class C: 2 times/year × 30 minutes/call = 60 minutes, or 1 hour

3. Calculate the workload necessary to cover the entire market. Let us assume that there are 200 A customers, 400 B customers, and 200 C customers. Then the total workload necessary would be the following:

Class A: 200 customers × 24 hours = 4,800 hours
Class B: 400 customers × 6 hours = 2,400 hours
Class C: 200 customers × 1 hour = 200 hours

or a total of 7,400 hours.

4. Determine the time available for each salesperson. Assume for this illustration that the typical salesperson works 48 weeks each year (4 weeks of vacation) for 50 hours each week. This gives a total of 2,400 hours per year for selling.

5. Allocate the salesperson's time by task. As we noted earlier in this chapter, the salesperson has activities other than selling (planning, writing up call reports) that take time. Suppose that selling is only 50% of the salesperson's time; this leaves 1,200 hours that can be allocated to selling.

6. Calculate the number of salespeople needed. This is simply the workload of 7,400 hours divided by the 1,200 hours available or 6.17 (rounded to 7) salespeople.

This method makes intuitive sense and is more logically appealing than the breakdown method. However, it also makes several assumptions that may not hold. Different accounts within a class may require different amounts of effort. For example, a class A account that has been active for many years may require little time, whereas a new account may require a great deal. Also, different salespeople operate with varying amounts of efficiency and can allocate more or less time for traveling, planning, and other activities.

Marginal Economic Method

Basic microeconomics teaches us that we should allocate a resource up to the point where the marginal revenue obtained from an additional unit of the resource equals the marginal cost. If we recast this method in terms of profit, particularly contribution margin (the amount of revenue that goes to cover fixed costs), it is very appealing. Suppose that it costs $60,000 to hire a salesperson; based on this approach, salespeople should be hired as long as they can sell enough to generate $60,001 in contribution margin (much more in sales, depending on the variable margin rate). The $1 in contribution generated was previously unavailable and would go towards covering fixed costs.[9]

Although this **marginal economic method** sounds theoretically appealing, it is more difficult to implement than the other two because it is difficult to know what the "marginal" salesperson can generate in sales. In addition, the marginal sales volume will decrease as additional salespeople are added because the remaining customers are more difficult than those who are already buying your product or service.

Designing Sales Territories

The steps involved in designing sales territories are shown in Fig. 10–7.

1. Select the control unit. This is the basic geographic unit that will be used to form the territories. The most common units are (in decreasing size) countries, states, counties, cities/Standard Metropolitan Statistical Areas (SMSAs), ZIP codes, and blocks. Obviously, the control unit varies by the kind of product or service. For a consumer product sold door-to-door, neighborhood by neighborhood, through Mary Kay or other multi-level selling companies, blocks would be appropriate. For nuclear power plants, coun-

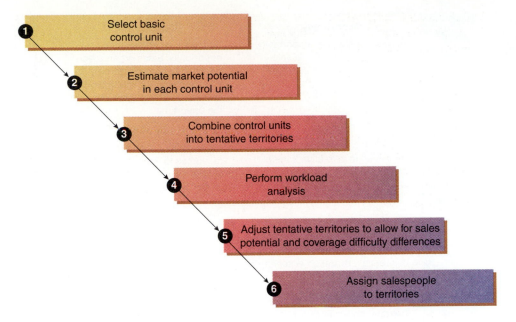

Figure 10–7

Territory Design

Source: Gilbert A. Churchill, Jr., Neil M. Ford, and Orville C. Walker, Jr. (1993), *Sales Force Management*, 4th ed. (Homewood, IL: Irwin), p. 239.

tries would probably be more relevant. Of course, most products are somewhere in between those two extreme examples.

2. Estimate the market potential in each basic geographic unit. The methods described in Chapter 4 can be used.

3. Form tentative territories. To do this, contiguous geographic units should be combined so as to make the territories equal in market potential. This is only a first pass at the territory design. The number of territories should be based on calculations of the appropriate number of salespeople (note that this assumes the assignment of one salesperson per territory).

4. The fourth step is to calculate the workload for each of the tentative territories. The tentative territories formed in step 3 may be close to each other in market potential but may differ significantly in terms of workload. The first part of the workload analysis is to determine the distribution of accounts by their size (based on actual revenues, potential, or some other measure). However, in this case the analysis must be done at a micro level, that is, account by account. Subsequently, each account must be assessed for the amount of time necessary to serve it. A potential account would be allocated more time because more selling effort is needed to create a new account than to maintain an existing one. An account planning matrix like the one shown in Fig. 10–8 could be used to prioritize the accounts and determine the effort needed to service each one. The total workload can then be computed for each territory.

5. Adjust the tentative territories. The workload analysis (and any other relevant information) is then used to adjust the initial solution to territory design. Again, adjustments should be contiguous so that salespeople do not waste time traveling through another salesperson's territory.

6. Assign salespeople to territories. This step is more difficult than it sounds. Salespeople have varying abilities and fit better with different kinds of accounts. Some are better at developing new accounts, some are better at maintaining relationships; some are better with smaller accounts, some with larger. There are also personal aspects that must be considered. A salesperson who was born and raised on the West Coast may not be interested in moving to the Southeast.

Figure 10–8

Account Planning
Matrix

Source: Gilbert A. Churchill,
Jr., Neil M. Ford, and Orville
C. Walker, Jr. (1993), *Sales
Force Management,* 4th ed.
(Homewood, IL: Irwin),
p. 249.

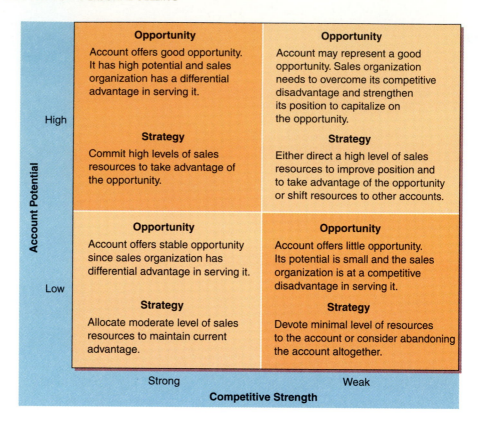

◆ **Illustration: Syntex Corporation**

Syntex Corporation is an international life sciences company that develops, manufactures, and markets a wide range of health and personal care products.[10] Syntex Laboratories is the U.S. human pharmaceutical sales subsidiary. A main product line is anti-inflammatory drugs to treat arthritis, analgesics for pain, oral contraceptives, a variety of topical products for skin diseases, and other related products.

Syntex's major products include Naprosyn, used to treat arthritis; Anaprox, an analgesic; Lidex and Synalar, topical steroid creams for skin inflammations; Norinyl, an oral contraceptive; and Nasalide, a steroid nasal spray for treating hay fever and other allergies. The success of these drugs propelled the division to account for 46% of the total corporate sales.

In ethical or prescription pharmaceutical sales, often called detailing, the target customers are normally physicians who prescribe the drugs for their patients.[11] This is a difficult job because appointments are hard to obtain and the competition is fierce. Pharmaceutical salespeople distribute samples and provide physicians with clinical information about the performance of their products. They also provide information about recommended dosage levels and thus must be a credible source of such information. As in any salesperson's job, the major decisions to make are which physicians to visit, how often to visit them, and what information to present.

At the time of this illustration, the vice president for sales at Syntex oversaw 6 regional and 47 district sales managers as well as 433 general sales representatives. The major decisions he had to make were how many salespeople to have, their geographic allocation, call frequency, allocation of sales calls across physician specialties, and which products to feature during the calls. To help do this, the company used a version of a model called CALLPLAN.[12] The model was used to calculate the optimal amount of sales effort needed for the different products and specialties and the different contribution margin opportunities available for different sizes of the sales force. One version of the model was used to allocate sales calls to specialties and the other was used to determine the appropriate number of sales presentations for each product.

To help do this, a sales response curve was estimated for each brand. The sales force was asked to estimate the sales level that would be expected compared to the present level under the following conditions:

- No sales effort
- One-half of the current sales effort
- 50% more effort
- A saturation level of effort

The result was a sales response curve like that shown in Fig. 10–9.

Figure 10–9 shows two hypothetical sales response curves for two brands, A and B. The basic idea comes from microeconomics: An additional salesperson should be assigned to pursue the customer that provides the greatest incremental contribution to profit. Suppose that the company has three salespeople assigned to brand A and two to B. Using Fig. 10–9, to which brand should the first new rep be assigned? If the rep is assigned to A, the incremental profit is $100; if assigned to B, it is about $75. Thus, the first new rep should be assigned to A. Where should a second be assigned? The marginal contribution obtained from going from four to five reps is only about $50. Thus, the second new rep should be assigned to B. This process would continue until no incremental profit was obtained from hiring another salesperson for either product.

The application of the model to Syntex data showed that the sales force should be increased to over 700 representatives and that this would produce more than $7 million in additional profits. The analysis is based on a combination of managerial judgment and statistical modeling. However, the company had been previously using very informal, simplified analyses.

Computer analyses for territory design and salesperson assignment are common today. These programs combine sophisticated geographic mapping capabilities with optimization

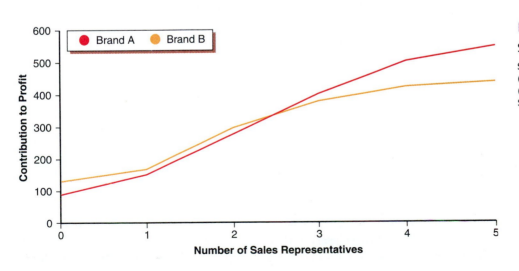

Figure 10–9

Sales Response Curve

Source: Darral G. Clarke (1983), "Syntex Laboratories (A)," Harvard Business School case #9-584-033, p. 12.

algorithms. An example of such software is CallMax, sold by Metron, Inc.'s TerrAlign group. The CallMax program

- Automatically generates optimal calling plans for the field sales force
- Minimizes distance between calls
- Calculates call frequency requirements for customers
- Balances the weekly calls across customers

SETTING SALES QUOTAS

Sales quotas are specific goals that salespeople have to meet. Clearly, quotas are needed to provide an incentive and a benchmark that distinguishes between excellent and less than excellent performance. Quotas also help sales and other managers to evaluate the performance of individual salespeople. They are usually part of the compensation scheme; exceeding one's quota usually means some kind of bonus, either in money or some other reward (vacations, merchandise). There are four different kinds of quotas.

Sales Volume–Based

The most commonly used quota is based on sales volume, in dollars or units sold. Quotas could be based on total sales volume or on individual product or product line sales. The latter criterion is particularly useful when new products are introduced because salespeople are more inclined to sell proven winners than uncertain products. Monetary quotas are easy to understand but may give extra incentives to sell higher-priced items, which may not necessarily produce the most profits.

Financially Based Quotas

These quotas normally are stated in terms of profit margins (gross or net). Such quotas steer the salespeople toward the products and services that are the most profitable to the company rather than those that are the highest priced or easiest to sell. A problem with this kind of quota is that it is more difficult for the salesperson to know where she or he stands in relation to the quota than when sales volume–based quotas are used. Profit margins can be manipulated by accounting procedures, which are mysterious to most marketing personnel.

Activity-Based Quotas

These quotas are based on the different activities that must be performed by a salesperson. Activity-based quotas could be based on

- Number of customers called on
- Number of demonstrations made
- Number of new accounts established
- Customer satisfaction indices[13]

Combinations

Although activity-based quotas help the sales force to do its job, most of these quotas are used in conjunction with a monetary or volume quota. Often, different quotas are used simultaneously. For example, the GE Credit FWK program described earlier in this chapter forms the basis for the development of quotas. The sales reps are compensated on both sales and activity-based achievement. The difficulty with such a system is that it becomes more difficult for the salesperson to determine how well she or he is doing in meeting the quota.

COMPENSATION

Figure 10–10 shows the different components of potential compensation and their objectives. The basic form of compensation is normally salary plus commission. A **commission** is a payment based directly on a sale or some other activity. For example, the sale of a $10,000 pump might mean a 1% or $100 commission to the salesperson. **Salary** is the basic amount of money paid regularly to the salesperson. Other forms of compensation are available to sales managers. **Incentive payments** are monetary awards for special performance. They are usually given in recognition of particularly outstanding sales performance, such as a President's Circle of the top 1% of the salespeople in a company. **Sales contests** are competitions to achieve some short-term goal (e.g., the introduction of a new product).

The most common decision to be made by a sales or senior marketing manager is what combination of salary and commission to use. A sales force could be paid on straight (100%) salary, straight commission, or some combination of both.

Straight Salary

This kind of compensation scheme is useful when management is more interested in long-term goals than simply selling as much volume as possible. For example, today, because of the increased recognition that long-term customer relationships are more profitable than simple transactions, more time is spent on relationship-building activities than in past years. Much of the time spent relationship-building does not generate immediate revenue. In addition, other activities such as competitor analysis and market research are valuable investments of time that do not generate revenue. If management wants to encourage such activities, straight salary is more logical than commissions. Another instance in which straight salary makes sense is one in which the products and services have long selling cycles. It takes several

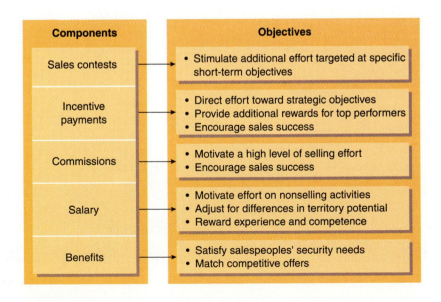

Figure 10–10

Components and Objectives of Compensation Plans

Source: Gilbert A. Churchill, Jr., Neil M. Ford, and Orville C. Walker, Jr. (1993), *Sales Force Management*, 4th ed. (Homewood, IL: Irwin), p. 581.

years for Boeing salespeople to close a deal to sell airplanes to British Airways. Similarly, large construction projects, nuclear power plants, supercomputers, and other products take a long time to sell. In such cases, compensation based largely on commission would not work well. Finally, straight salary is often used for new salespeople, who are unlikely to generate substantial sales in the short run. The challenge with compensation schemes based largely on salary is to tie salary increases to performance.

Straight Commission

Clearly, commissions give salespeople incentives to sell because there is a direct relationship between income and performance. Such a scheme also rewards the best performers; under-performing salespeople do not receive as much income. Commission schemes are also easy to manage because the payments are tied directly to visible performance. In addition, commission programs can be targeted; new products that are important to the company can be awarded higher commissions than existing products. However, in general, straight commission programs give management little control over what the sales force does because each salesperson will try to maximize his or her income in his or her own way; this usually means that activities that do not result directly in a sale are ignored. Such programs can also be discouraging during a period when the company's products are not selling well. Commission-based compensation schemes can be difficult to implement when a national accounts program overlaps with a local sales force. There are often problems allocating the commissions between the relevant parties when a sale is made. Finally, straight commission schemes produce fluctuating incomes for the sales force. In practice, there are few straight commission selling jobs. Many are found in the multilevel marketing industry (e.g., Amway, Mary Kay).

Combination Plans

Most compensation schemes combine salary and additional financial incentives (commissions or bonuses). These plans provide some incentive to perform nonrevenue activ-

For products that have long selling cycles, such as this airplane, a straight salary compensation scheme is most desirable for the salesperson. In these situations, the salesperson focuses on relationship–building activities rather than sales volume. (George Hall/-Corbis)

ities and a base, secure level of income while still rewarding the best performers above the rest.

Whatever compensation scheme is used, a sales force is an expensive way to communicate with customers. Based on 1998 data, the average cost of a sales call is $156.71, including compensation, benefits, and travel and entertainment expenses. This cost varies by industry type:

Manufacturing	$218.00
Services	184.34
Distribution	101.54
Retail	91.02[14]

CONTROLLING AND EVALUATING THE SALES FORCE

The sales manager must perform some kind of analysis of sales force performance. Many objective or quantitative measures can be used in this evaluation.[15] Table 10–2 shows some of the more typical ratios of input and output measures that can be used.

There are two types of output measures:

- Orders. Of importance are the number and size of the orders obtained.
- Accounts. Typically measured are the number of active, new, lost, prospective, and overdue accounts.

There are several kinds of input measures:

- Sales calls
- Time efficiency (how many calls per day the salesperson makes)
- Expenses
- Time spent on nonselling activities

Numbers are important but they do not tell the whole story. Without further investigation, the sales or marketing manager sees the results but not the process. Understanding the process is critical to a better understanding of the results and therefore provides a blueprint for change.

As a result, subjective or qualitative measures are also used to evaluate sales force performance. An evaluator uses a rating scale to evaluate each salesperson on the following dimensions:

- Sales. This includes not just sales volume, which can be measured using external metrics, but how well the person is doing with different kinds of accounts and the whole product line.
- Job knowledge. Does the person understand the role of a salesperson in the company? Does the salesperson understand the company's policies and products?
- Management of the sales territory. This rates how well the salesperson manages his or her time, completes call reports, and so on.
- Customer and company relations. The salesperson must have good relationships with customers and internal personnel (shipping, product management).
- Personal characteristics.

Table 10–2 Common Ratios Used to Evaluate Salespeople

Expense ratios

- Sales expense ratio $\quad = \quad \dfrac{\text{Expenses}}{\text{Sales}}$

- Cost per call ratio $\quad = \quad \dfrac{\text{Total costs}}{\text{Number of calls}}$

Account development and servicing ratios

- Account penetration ratio $\quad = \quad \dfrac{\text{Accounts sold}}{\text{Total accounts available}}$

- New account conversion ratio $\quad = \quad \dfrac{\text{Number of new accounts}}{\text{Total number of accounts}}$

- Lost account ratio $\quad = \quad \dfrac{\text{Prior accounts not sold}}{\text{Total number of accounts}}$

- Sales per account ratio $\quad = \quad \dfrac{\text{Sales dollar volume}}{\text{Total number of accounts}}$

- Average order size ratio $\quad = \quad \dfrac{\text{Sales dollar volume}}{\text{Total number of orders}}$

- Order cancellation ratio $\quad = \quad \dfrac{\text{Number of cancelled orders}}{\text{Total number of orders}}$

Call activity or productivity

- Calls per day ratio $\quad = \quad \dfrac{\text{Number of calls}}{\text{Number of days worked}}$

- Calls per account ratio $\quad = \quad \dfrac{\text{Number of calls}}{\text{Number of accounts}}$

- Planned call ratio $\quad = \quad \dfrac{\text{Number of planned calls}}{\text{Total number of calls}}$

- Order per call (hit) ratio $\quad = \quad \dfrac{\text{Number of orders}}{\text{Total number of calls}}$

Source: Gilbert A. Churchill, Jr., Neil M. Ford, and Orville C. Walker, Jr. (1993), *Sales Force Management*, 4th ed. (Homewood, IL: Irwin), p. 765.

THE CHANGING NATURE OF THE SALES FORCE

The Impact of Technology

The hot topic in sales management in the late 1990s is sales force automation (SFA). The typical salesperson today is not the classic Willy Loman from *Death of a Salesman*. Today, the successful salesperson is highly skilled in using technological tools that enable her or him to work with prospective customers in an efficient way to solve problems. These include computers, information systems, and efficient communication links from the field to the home office. Investments in such technology invariably pay off in increased sales and return on investment.[16]

This travel agent illustrates the changing nature of today's sales force. Today's salesperson is highly skilled in using technology to work more efficiently and effectively. (Roger Ressmeyer/Corbis)

This reengineering of sales, called **virtual selling,** has occurred for several reasons:[17]

- The personal selling job has become more complex and it is getting more difficult to make a sale. This is because products in some industries have become more complex (mainly in technology-based industries). The notion of a salesperson trotting around with a product catalog has virtually disappeared.
- Customers have become more knowledgeable about what they want, but they also need guidance and advice about what products and services would help them the most.
- Corporations are becoming increasingly flat, with fewer middle managers providing product information for more senior managers. Salespeople are thus being called on to provide more information directly to decision-makers. This flattening phenomenon is also hitting sales forces.
- Intensifying global competition means more pressure at the point of sale.
- Demand for productivity improvements from all parts of the organization, including sales, has increased.

Ideally, the virtual selling organization would have the features shown in Table 10–3. Although these are worthwhile goals, few companies are anywhere near achieving all of them. However, many have made substantial progress toward fully automating their sales forces.

For example, Nordstrom Valves supplies pipeline valves to the oil and natural gas industries.[18] Their market position is at the high-price, high-quality end of the market and the main job of their sales force is to convince customers that it is worth it to pay the price premium of 15–25% over the competition.[19] Before computerization, Nordstrom's 20 salespeople had to perform complicated engineering calculations for each customer showing how the company's lower-maintenance and longer-warrantied products actually saved them money over the life cycle. Today, using a laptop computer, the salespeople can plug in a customer's specifications and instantly produce the same life cycle cost estimates. The color demonstration can be shown on the computer or projected onto a large screen using a video projection system. As a result, the customer very quickly sees the price justification and substantial time is saved, which can be used to make more sales calls. ◆

Table 10–3 The Virtual Selling Organization

- Equips salespeople with all of their leads, prospects, and contacts
- Provides the facility to track, record, and communicate all the history of an opportunity or account
- Supports team selling and workgroup collaboration
- Facilitates work flow and routing for approvals
- Provides access to all relevant information on products, price, competitors, and decision issues
- Incorporates support for unique selling methods and processes that support sales cycle tracking and analysis
- Provides salespeople with the ability to create custom presentations and on-demand, customized sales literature
- Enables the salesperson to find the best combination of products and services based on a customer's unique profile
- Empowers the salesperson to make his or her own decisions, develop custom contracts and proposals, and, acting as the customer's advocate, organize ad hoc interdepartmental company teams
- Offers on-line sales training on sales processes and new products and services
- Automates the administrative tasks of recording, tracking, and reporting salespeople's appointments, activities, correspondence, literature fulfillment, expenses, and forecasts
- Creates closed-loop marketing and sales systems that ensure complete traceability from marketing spending on lead generation through sales closure, product shipment, and customer support

Source: Thomas M. Siebel and Michael S. Malone (1996), *Virtual Selling* (New York: Free Press), pp. 13–14.

SFA can also help companies deliver more value to the customer. The sales force for a truck manufacturer asks each potential customer for what kinds of jobs they need a new truck and what kinds of loads they will be hauling.[20] On a laptop computer, a salesperson can examine maps of the truck routes and determine the grades of the hills along the routes. Based on this and other information, the salesperson can recommend the appropriate model and features on the spot and even recommend financing options. The truck company is also planning to phase out preprinted brochures and replace them with materials that can be printed out on the spot when requested.

Special-purpose computer software has also been developed to help salespeople perform standard activities. For example, contact management software tracks different kinds of information, from what happened on the last sales call with a customer to birthdays and other special events. For companies with large product lines, order configuration software keeps track of pricing structures and technical specifications so that the field salespeople are always up to date. This frees the rep from having to carry around volumes of literature or memorize large numbers of facts. Companies such as Siebel Systems have developed sophisticated computer software that automates a large number of tasks and lets the salesperson focus on selling rather than administration and data collection.

In general, the expansion of the Internet and improved information systems have made it much easier for salespeople to do their homework before calling on a customer. Using a laptop computer with a modem, a rep can quickly go to competitors' Web pages and find relevant product and marketing information. As noted in Chapter 7, companies that automate the call reporting system have a wealth of on-line data about customers' habits and the competition.

Some companies are also using technology in the compensation area. For example, IBM's North America business division has established an intranet for its 9,000 salespeople that allows them to compute an up-to-the-minute figure for their total compensation, including bonus.[21] The salesperson inputs his or her personal identification information and is led to another screen, where the rep selects his or her particular incentive plan. The salesperson can then determine what impact his or her performance will have on the specific compensation plan. IBM hopes that this system will motivate salespeople to achieve their sales goals.

◆ Illustration: Lanier Worldwide

Lanier Worldwide, a subsidiary of Harris Corporation, is one of the world's largest providers of document management systems, services, and support, with 1998 revenues of $1.3 billion.[22] In 1995, Lanier managers faced a problem: The cost of getting and placing an order for any of its office equipment was averaging $27 per order, substantially higher than the figure of $3 that came from research conducted in similar firms.

Lanier managers discovered that there were three reasons for this discrepancy:

- All orders were taken and processed manually.
- The information on customers was often inaccurate and duplicative.
- Because the sales force lacked modern sales tools to help generate leads and make sales, the turnover rate among the sales force was 120% in 1996.

The manual order entry and processing caused a high error rate and delayed the fulfillment of orders because the sales force was quoting inaccurate prices, necessitating manual correction by back-office personnel. Inaccurate records on what customers had purchased led to free service being given to customers who may not have deserved it. High turnover rates of salespeople eroded records of the customer base as they left with the index cards on which they had recorded customer data. Profitability of product lines was impossible to compute.

The new Lanier system was developed in three phases:

- Phase one: The company introduced its Market Encyclopedia System to provide the sales force with the tools needed to make customer presentations. It contains the sales and marketing information Lanier used to distribute in hard copy every week, including technical specifications on all its products and services, price and performance comparisons with competitors' products, and information on trends in the industry. It also provides video clips and slides that sales representatives can use to make different types of presentations.
- Phase two: The company created its Opportunity Management System, a lead qualification process. The system gives the sales force access to a list of more than 10 million names of managers at U.S. companies, with details on the companies and the types of equipment they have purchased in the past. The system also provides a checklist of steps each sales rep should take to move from the lead stage to closing the deal. When a sale is completed, an order form is generated for the customer's signature.
- Phase three: The Zero Defect Order system builds and prices the system that meets the customer's needs, including all required and optional equipment and accessories. The system permits the rep to give discounts, but also indicates at what point a discount will reduce his or her sales commission.

The financial benefits of the new system appeared quickly. Lanier achieved $48 million in cost savings in the first year through higher productivity because sales force turnover fell from 120% to 50% and free service was given only to customers who warranted it. In addition, the cost per order dropped from $27 to $15–16. The system has generated important information for the company. Lanier's managers can now perform a profitability analysis of each national account, which enables them to tailor compensation and add or subtract resources on an account-by-account basis. In addition, the company can track profits by product segment. For example, Lanier discovered that the profit margins on its analog copier business are increasing when they thought they were decreasing. ◆

The Salesperson's Job

It is clear that the salesperson's job has changed considerably. The success of General Motors's Saturn division shows how eliminating haggling from the traditionally unpleasant car-buying process can work. A division of American Express, American Express Financial Advisors (AEFA), has shifted from a traditional hard-sell, cold-calling method for selling mutual funds and insurance to an emphasis on building long-term relationships with clients. As a result, the former commission-only pay structure was abandoned for a system that rewards on the basis of customer satisfaction.

One vision of how the sales organization is being reinvented sees the new organization being driven by eight forces:[23]

- Relationship-building. The salesperson is on the front line of contact with customers. The new sales organization has much more of a long-term customer orientation than has been the case historically. (We will spend much more time on this topic in Chapter 13.)
- Fostering change. Two major changes have occurred in sales organizations. First, they have become more horizontal, flatter, and more focused on the basic components of the company's value proposition. Second, there is an increasing trend toward organizing along market segments, away from product-focused organizations.
- Gaining commitment through teams. DuPont uses teams composed of employees from research, manufacturing, and sales for planning new products.
- Coaching vs. commanding. This refers to a shift in sales management style to a more collegial, tutoring approach.
- Keeping score. Besides traditional sales volume measures, sales force performance is now being evaluated on the basis of customer satisfaction, customer retention, and share of customer purchases.
- New ways of reaching customers. As we noted in Chapter 9, the expanding number of channels of distribution has changed the nature of the selling business. The hybrid system shown in Fig. 9–7 shows how some of the activities formerly assumed by salespeople are now handled by telemarketing, for example.
- Removing performance hurdles. New sales organizations are doing a better job of assigning salespeople to territories that do not constrain their performance (i.e., territories with low potential or too many accounts for adequate coverage).
- Leveraging technology. As noted earlier, sales organizations today must take advantage of the latest technological advances for better and more profitable customer contacts.

EXECUTIVE SUMMARY

The main points of this chapter include the following:

- The sales force has a dual role in the implementation of the marketing strategy: It is both part of the communication mix and a distribution channel (i.e., a way to give customers access to the product or service).
- The sales force can be organized in a variety of ways depending on how product or marketing management is organized. A national or key accounts organization is a layer on top of the usual sales organization that deals with the company's largest accounts.
- Both internal (e.g., motivation) and external (e.g., the competitive environment) factors affect a salesperson's performance.
- Three important decisions that must be made by the sales manager are the size of the sales force, the design of sales territories, and the assignment of salespeople to the territories.
- Sales quotas or goals provide key incentives. Quotas are based on sales volume, financial indicators such as profit margins, or activities such as the number of customer calls.
- The most common form of compensation plan for salespeople is a combination of salary and financial incentives such as bonuses or commissions.
- Technology is changing the nature of the salesperson's job, particularly the use of laptop computers, which enable the representative to make better sales presentations and deliver more value to customers.

CHAPTER QUESTIONS

1. It is sometimes said that salespeople should be familiar with their customers' marketing plans (e.g., understanding the customers' competitors and customers). Of what use would this information be to the salesperson?
2. Considering the different tasks a salesperson must perform, how is the job different for an automobile salesperson and a representative selling a computer system?
3. What products or services would be most appropriate for implementing the three different approaches to determining sales force size described in this chapter? Be specific.
4. Besides the criteria for assigning salespeople to territories described in the book, what other factors should be taken into account?
5. How should the increased use of technology in the salesperson's job affect companies' recruiting and hiring practices? What are the benefits of having a sales force that is sophisticated in its use of technology?

Application Exercises: Sales Management in the PC Industry

Integrated Case

1. Choose a PC company that distributes its products through several channels, including direct sales to large corporate customers (use your analysis from Chapter 9) and retail.

Design an appropriate compensation scheme for the salespeople in the corporate customer segment, given the presence of the other channels.

2. What would be an appropriate design for this company's sales force?
3. What factors should be considered in designing sales territories for this company in the United States? In Europe? In Asia?
4. Develop a questionnaire that could be used to interview and evaluate the company's sales force that calls directly on large corporate customers.

FURTHER READING

Readers interested in keeping up with the latest developments in sales management should read *Sales & Marketing Management* regularly. A good source on building relationships for selling purposes is Regis McKenna (1991), *Relationship Marketing* (Reading, MA: Addison-Wesley). Further information on national account programs can be found in the *Guidebook for Major Account Management Practices,* Vols. 1–3 (Chicago: National Account Management Association).

Pricing

11

CHAPTER BRIEF

The purpose of this chapter is to introduce the concepts involved with strategic price-setting. Key areas of learning are the following:

The need for consistency between price and the marketing strategy
The concept of perceived value and how it is critical to setting price
Integrating competition and costs into the pricing decision
Deciding how much of the strategic pricing gap between cost and perceived value to capture
Specific pricing tactics such as product line pricing, value pricing, and competing against private labels
How the Internet is affecting pricing decisions

The ready-to-eat (RTE) breakfast cereal industry has been battered by a number of different forces in the 1990s.[1] First, private-label brands sold under supermarket chain and other brand names have made serious dents in national brand market shares. For example, Kellogg's total market share in the category dropped from 35% in 1993 to 32% in 1998. The number-two company, General Mills, dropped from 27% to 24% over the same period. Because the total category sales in 1998 were about $8 billion, this represents $240 million in lost revenues for each company. In addition, the category has seen breakfast habits in the United States change from RTE cereals to bagels and cookie-like products such as Kellogg's own Nutri-Grain bars as carbohydrate substitutes. Sales in foreign countries have not taken up the slack because it is very difficult to change cultural habits about breakfast, which, in most countries, do not include products like Cheerios.

The category tried price cuts in 1996. Philip Morris's Post subsidiary, the number-three company in the market, cut its prices 20% across the board to defend against the private labels and other products. Kellogg's followed with a 19% cut on two-thirds of its brands. General Mills, with two of the most popular brands (Cheerios and Wheaties), did not immediately follow the price cutting, but eventually decided to drop prices by 11%, less than the other leading manufacturers.

In 1997, General Mills decided to actually raise prices by an average of 2.6%. By 1998, the two top General Mills brands, Cheerios and Wheaties, averaged $3.26 a box, 17% more than the industry average and 57% more than the private labels. To support these brands and their price differentials, General Mills spends 33 cents of every revenue dollar on marketing, 3 cents more than the competition. Unfortunately, the price hikes have led to decreasing shares for its brands.

No decision worries a marketing manager more than the appropriate price to charge customers because for most product categories, price is the marketing variable customers react to more than any other. Price is an observable component of the product that results in consumers purchasing or not purchasing it and at the same time directly affects margin per unit sold. Other components of the marketing mix are important, of course, because they must work together to create a unified brand image and produce sales. However, price most often makes or breaks the transaction.

The pricing decision is most often viewed as a way to recover costs; that is, you must determine what price to charge beyond your costs of making the product or delivering the service in order to make a profit. For example, many companies try to calculate their costs and then add a standard markup to get a target return on investment. This strategy is very common in retailing, where the store manager simply marks up the product delivered from the supplier.

However, it is clear that a price developed in this way may not be an optimal price when the customer is taken into consideration.[2] The price could be higher than customers are willing to pay for that product. If the product is priced too low, the company loses potential profits.

As we will see later in this chapter, costs do matter in setting price; you would not want to price a product below cost, at least for long. However, the customer is also an important consideration, specifically in terms of **customer value:** what a product or service is worth to the customer. As a marketing manager, you must remember that the customer generally does not know or care what your costs are; what is important is whether the product delivers an appropriate amount of value for the price being paid. Thus, the purpose of price is not just to recover costs but to also capture the perceived value of the product in the mind of the customer.[3]

Therefore, in this chapter we will cover the various aspects of decision-making involved with setting price. The major factors affecting price are the following:

- Your marketing strategy
- Relative customer value
- Competition
- Your costs

A framework for price-setting is developed in which the key decision is how much of the gap between cost and customer value the firm can keep. In addition, some specific pricing tactics and the impact of the Internet on pricing decisions are described.

THE ROLE OF MARKETING STRATEGY IN PRICING

As we discussed in Chapter 3, you first design the marketing strategy and *then* the implementation of the strategy, the marketing mix (see the marketing strategy diagram). Thus, a key point is that the price must be consistent with the marketing strategy. The marketing strategy consists primarily of the market segmentation and core strategy, positioning, and value proposition decisions. Strategy decisions do not lead to a specific price-setting rule; rather, they give general guidelines for whether a price should be low or high.

 For example, the short-sleeved sport shirts sold under the Izod label (the crocodile, not alligator) are very popular. At one time, the company was independent and marketed the product to upscale, fashion- and image-conscious consumers. The shirts

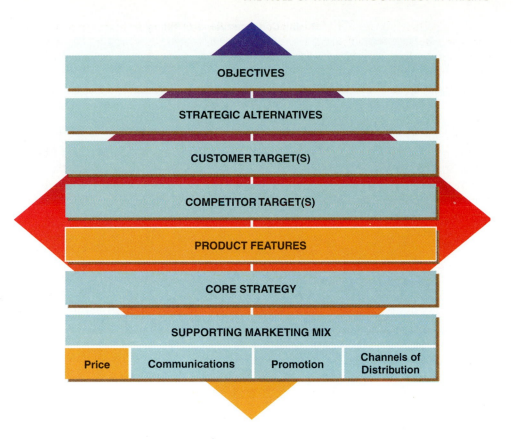

were sold in many colors and extensively distributed in department stores such as Macy's. The marketing strategy and mix were consistent and the price was concomitantly high.

Izod was subsequently bought by packaged goods company General Mills. The company believed that the brand had substantial growth opportunities beyond the targeted segments (i.e., market development opportunities; see Fig. 3–3). To reach these other segments, the channels of distribution were widened and the price reduced; discount stores began selling the Izod shirts. Unfortunately, reaching the new market segments produced a mismatch between the strategy and the marketing mix. The upscale segment simply stopped buying the shirts and fled to competitors such as Ralph Lauren's Polo. Eventually, General Mills divested Izod and it has gone back to its former successful strategy, including opening up its own exclusive retail stores. ◆

The market segmentation decision affects price because prices can vary widely over segments. Economists call this **price discrimination:** charging different prices to segments according to their price elasticity or sensitivity. Prices can also vary over segments if the products or services vary in quality. In business-to-business markets, prices may vary by customer size and ability to obtain quantity discounts from the supplier. Airline ticket prices vary not just by class of service (coach, business, first), but also by when the ticket is purchased (e.g., 21-day advance purchases versus the same day).

An example of such price variation in a product category is shown in Fig. 11–1. Such variations within a category are called **price bands or tiers.**[4] Figure 11–1 shows the price variation in the ice cream market. A statistical distribution of prices is shown in each band, indicating that there is not only variation across bands but also some variation within bands

Figure 11–1

The Ice Cream
Price Band

Elliot B. Ross (1984),
"Making money with
proactive pricing," *Harvard
Business Review*,
November–December,
pp. 145–155.

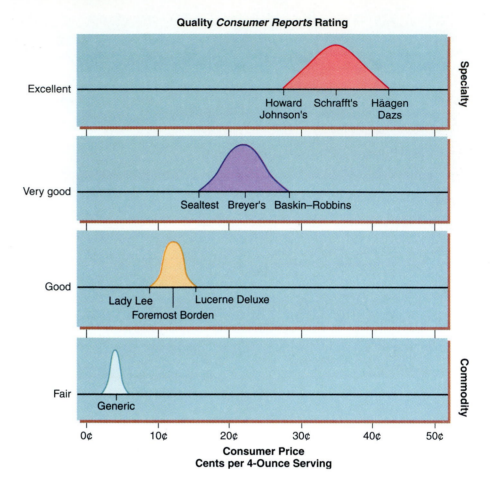

Quality *Consumer Reports* Rating

**Consumer Price
Cents per 4-Ounce Serving**

or segments of products. The wider the distribution, the more price variation exists within a band. As the price distributions show, there is a positive relationship between price and quality (as measured by *Consumer Reports*). The most intraband variation appears in the highest-quality tier.

Why does such variation exist within bands or tiers? For both industrial and consumer products, there seem to be several reasons. First, customers become loyal to certain products or suppliers; they tend to rate price lower than other factors such as reliability and speed of delivery. This makes them less price sensitive. Second, in some industries, price visibility is low; that is, the price charged is less obvious than it is at supermarkets or other retailers, where the price is marked on the item. For many industrial products, the list price is only the basis from which discounts that vary among customers are given. This method creates more transaction price variability. Third, competitive intensity can vary among segments; the larger the number of suppliers, the narrower the price band because more competition implies greater convergence on a standard price. Finally, some categories have large numbers of product variants because many options are available or because the supplier wants to fill the channel and keep competitors from getting shelf space.

Thus, the marketing manager has to understand the price sensitivity of the different target markets to set the appropriate price. However, as these illustrations show, there may be significant price variations even within a particular segment. In sum, the marketing strategy dictates the pricing policies that can be used at any given time.

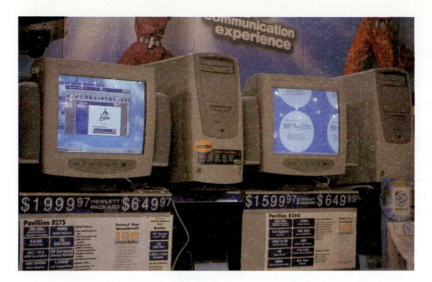

A good deal of price variation exists in the PC market. These two Hewlett-Packard PCs represent two different price bands or tiers. As the product information cards show, the higher–priced PC offers more features and benefits. (Bonnie Kamin/Photo Edit)

PERCEIVED VALUE

Customer Value

Customer value is a measure of how much a customer is willing to pay for a product or service. Economists call this concept the **reservation price,** the most someone is willing to pay for a product (or the price at which the product is eliminated from the customer's budget). Every customer, whether consumer or business, has a psychological concept of such a price. People receive price information and then assess whether it is good or bad. They compare the price being charged with the perceived value or benefits they would derive from purchasing it.

Despite the use of the term *perceived value,* there is no such single quantity in the marketplace. Customer value is unique to the individual customer. Therefore, when we use the term *perceived* or *customer value,* we refer to an average or typical value for a particular market segment or target market.

In addition, perceived value is always relative. Although the absolute level of perceived value of your product is important, in order to use the concept to set a price, it is also important to know how customers value competing options.

Here, we explicitly consider three possible relationships among perceived value, price, and cost, ignoring competition for the present:[5]

Perceived value > price > cost.
Price > perceived value > cost.
Price > cost > perceived value.

Note that in all three situations, we assume that price is greater than cost.

Perceived Value > Price > Cost

In this case, the marketing manager has set a price, either intentionally or mistakenly, below what customers would be willing to pay for the product or service. From the customer's standpoint, the product is a bargain. It is difficult to determine whether the low price is a mistake because customers do not usually write to you and thank you for pricing your product so low. In some cases, the fact that you have priced it below customer value will result in shortages and present a production and distribution problem.

You may underprice a product intentionally, for strategic reasons discussed later in this chapter. Strategically pricing below customer value is often called value pricing, or attempting to provide an exceptionally good value to the customer. This term should be distinguished from *pricing to value,* which means setting a price at the level you have determined to represent the customer's perceived value for your product.

A good example of value pricing is the Mazda Miata, introduced in 1990. Mazda's objective was to introduce a two-seat convertible with few power options and luxurious details. This throwback to the 1950s, a simple car with a sporty feel, was introduced at a price of $16,000 to $18,000. However, demand for the Miata was so high during the first few months after it was introduced that prices of $25,000 in the used-car sections of newspapers were common. Customers were buying the cars and quickly reselling them to make a significant profit. Clearly, Mazda could have charged more for the Miata. Perhaps company managers underestimated the demand for the car. However, they probably knew this craze was a short-term aberration and believed that the original price was more consistent with their long-term marketing strategy for the car. Also, high initial prices that are later reduced play havoc with the used-car market. Customers who paid the high price and tried to sell the cars later would find no demand for them because people could buy a new car for less than a used one. The pricing strategy did create a large amount of publicity, which helped create awareness and perhaps some preference for the car. Interestingly, this low entry price strategy was copied by BMW and Porsche with their own roadster entries, the Z3 and the Boxster. Also, Audi recently chose to price its European model A3is substantially lower than competing models from BMW and Mercedes while promoting the fact that the car has similar features.[6]

A lack of understanding of customer value eventually caused Western Pacific Airlines (see the opening case in Chapter 3) to file for bankruptcy.[7] As you might recall, Western Pacific was founded to compete for the growing Rocky Mountain business by locating its hub in Colorado Springs rather than the pricier and more competitive Denver International

One pricing strategy involves intentionally underpricing a product to provide an exceptionally good value for the customer. The introduction of the Porsche Boxster is a good example of such value pricing. Although high customer demand suggested that the car could have been priced much higher, the low entry price created significant publicity and consumer awareness. (David Young Wolff/Photo Edit)

Airport. When flights began in 1995, their average one-way ticket price was $75, compared to incumbents' round-trip fares of $250–300 from Colorado Springs. The airline was losing money on this fare and did not realize that by providing superior value to customers who wanted to avoid Denver, it could have charged a higher price after it was established, closer to the $250–300 other airlines had been charging before Western Pacific entered the market. Thus, bargain prices can result in business failure.

In some cases, setting a price below value is not intentional and simple consumer mania takes over. For example, when Nokia introduced its stylish 8810 mobile phone in Hong Kong, it was priced at HK$7,400. However, demand for it was so strong that retailers marked it up as high as HK$12,800, with some buyers indicating willingness to pay as much as HK$20,000.[8]

Price > Perceived Value > Cost

In this unfortunate situation, the manager has set a price that is higher than the target market is willing to pay. The customer looks at this situation as a bad deal and, unless the company has a monopoly or some other kind of market power, does not buy. Customers let you know that there is a problem by not buying. Waiting for customer reaction is an expensive form of marketing research, however, because the customers may have bought another brand and are out of the market for some time. The solution is obvious: Some kind of downward price adjustment or increase in customer value is necessary. However, without knowing the perceived value or willingness to pay, you do not know how far to lower price. In this case, the competitor often serves as the reference point.

Consumer interest can affect prices. These Tickle Me Elmo toys are priced much higher than the Tickle Me toys based on other Sesame Street characters. The popularity of the Elmo character during a particular selling season created huge demand-and inflated prices-for that toy. (Spencer Grant/Photo Edit)

Price reductions in response to lower perceived value are very common. Proctor & Gamble has taken a value-pricing approach to marketing many of its products, given the substantial inroads private labels have made in some product categories. Although their approach has resulted partially from an interest in reducing promotional expenses, it is also a recognition that the price-perceived value gap between national and private-label brands has decreased over the last 10 years or so. In 1997, McDonald's introduced Campaign 55, which featured substantial price reductions rotated over its different sandwiches (the 55 refers to 1955, the year the chain was founded). The price reductions made by the cereal manufacturers in 1996 also represented a move toward bringing price in line with perceived value.

Price > Cost > Perceived Value

This scenario clearly represents a failure. Usually, such products are weeded out in the new product development process. If not, they are ultimately withdrawn from the market. For example, the Yugoslavian-made car Yugo was withdrawn from the U.S. market because it received such negative reviews in publications such as *Consumer Reports* that customer value fell even below the manufacturing and marketing costs. One Cadillac dealer even offered to give a Yugo free to new Cadillac buyers.

A Framework

The need to understand customer-perceived value or willingness to pay is illustrated in Fig. 11–2, which shows the creation of a strategic pricing gap. The cost used by the marketing manager as a basis for pricing is the floor of the gap; you would not price below that cost.[9] The target segment's willingness to pay is the ceiling; you cannot price above that because the segment would not buy above that price. Therefore, your task is to figure out how much of the difference between value and cost you want to keep for yourself or share with the channel structure. It is important to understand that by understanding customer value, you can make this decision proactively. If you do not understand customer value, the market will help you make the calculation, often at great expense to you.

Figure 11–2

Strategic Pricing Gap

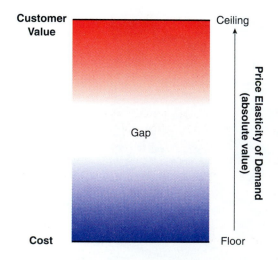

Price Elasticity

An important concept from economics is the **price elasticity of demand** (see also Chapter 7). The formula for the price elasticity is the following:

$$E = \% \text{ change in demand} / \% \text{ change in price}$$

Thus, if price is reduced by 2% and demand increases by 3%, $E = -1.5$; if price increases by 3% and demand decreases by 2%, $E = -0.67$. If $|E| < 1.0$, the product category is called price inelastic because the change in demand is less than the change in price.[10] If $|E| > 1.0$, the category is price elastic.

The relationship of price elasticity to customer value is shown in Fig. 11–2. If the product's price is low so that there is a considerable amount of value left for the customer (a good deal), a price increase or decrease will not have much impact. However, as the price gets closer to customer value, price elasticity (sensitivity) increases as the point at which the customer will not buy at all draws near. Thus, the vertical arrow on the right side of Fig. 11–2 indicates that price elasticity increases as the firm captures more of the value for itself and leaves less for the customer. It is also likely that as price gets closer to the value line, the asymmetry between price increases and decreases grows larger. That is, if customer value is $2.00 and price is $1.98, a $.01 price increase is likely to decrease sales more than a similar price decrease will increase sales.

Price elasticity is thus an indirect measure of customer value in that a manager can determine how close his or her brand is to the customer value point through planned price experimentation or market reactions to price changes. For example, when General Mills raised its cereal prices by an average of 2.6% in 1997, sales dropped 11% in the following quarter. This implied price elasticity of −4.23 indicated that the cereal prices were very close to the customer value point. An analysis across a large number of frequently purchased product categories showed the average price elasticity to be −2.5, again reflecting the fact that prices are probably closer to relative customer value than cost.[11] Studies of the retail gasoline market generally show price inelastic demand. However, significantly higher gas prices closer to customer value probably would not be welcomed by government policy-makers and consumer interest groups.

Calculating Customer Value

Although it is clearly an important concept, it is not easy to calculate customers' willingness to pay or customer value. Price elasticities give only a hint at how close or far you are from customer value. Some methods used to obtain more precise estimates are described here.

Calculating Value-in-Use

Particularly for industrial products, a useful way to estimate customer value is through a method called **value-in-use.** In this approach, the benefits of the product are put in monetary terms such as time savings, less use of materials, or less downtime. To implement the procedure, you first select a reference product, usually either the product the customer is currently using or a competitor's product. Second, you calculate the incremental monetary benefit to the customer of using the product or brand in question. Assuming it is positive, this incremental monetary benefit describes the range of prices obtainable. In terms of Fig. 11–2, pricing to the limit of the incremental benefit gives all the value to you, pricing to capture none of the incremental benefit gives it all to the customer, and in-between prices share the economic benefit.

Figure 11–3 shows one approach to the value-in-use calculation.[12] The bar on the far left is the reference product, *Y.* Assume that the reference product cost (i.e., the initial price) is $300. Also assume that the company that produces it incurs start-up costs of $200 (e.g., training) and postpurchase costs of $500 (e.g., maintenance). Together, these costs are called life cycle costs and recognize that the cost of buying a product often goes far beyond the acquisition cost.

Your product, *X,* is represented in the next bar. It is assumed product *X* has $100 less in both start-up and postpurchase costs. It is also assumed that the product offers approximately $100 more in value through additional features (e.g., energy savings). Therefore, if the customer is willing to pay $300 for product *Y,* then the customer should be willing to pay $300 more ($200 in reduced life cycle costs plus $100 extra value) for product *X.* The third bar assumes that the variable cost of $300 is the floor; the incremental dollar value to the customer is $600 (this is called the economic value to the customer, or EVC, in Fig. 11–3). The difference, $300, is the amount the product manager has to play with in setting price. This difference is the supplier's competitive advantage. The last bar shows one hypothetical split of the $300 pricing range. One such split leaves $125 for the customer and $175 for you.

An attractive feature of this approach is that the analysis provides valuable information for the salesperson to use in trying to close the sale. In this case, the salesperson can explicitly quantify the incremental economic benefit to the customer and show that the company is willing to give a "discount" of $125 from the true economic value. Because industrial buyers like to be shown how they can make a greater profit by choosing one product over another, this information should be quite persuasive.

The method shown in Fig. 11–3 can be applied to both products and services. A trend in business is to purchase a service from an outside vendor to replace the company's operation, a strategy known as **outsourcing.** For example, rather than operating the company cafeteria itself, a company might subcontract the operation to a food service company that specializes in such work. Other examples include General Motors paying PPG Industries to operate its automobile painting facilities and IBM contracting with Federal Express to act as a warehousing agent around the world. In these cases, the agents whose services are purchased can use the cost of the company providing the service itself as a reference prod-

Figure 11–3

The Economic Value Concept

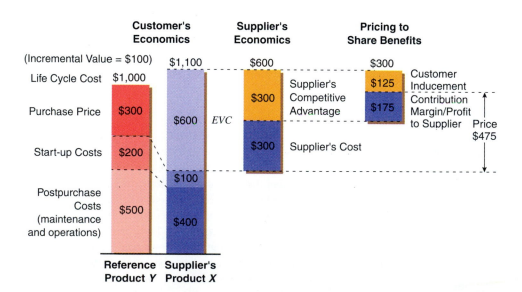

uct. Even if it is more expensive to pay the agent for these services than for the company to provide the service itself, benefits such as better use of employee time and company capital, improved productivity, and better technology can be quantified and shown to produce value to potential customers.

This method works well with products and services for which the economic benefits can be quantified. It is applicable for many consumer products. For example, General Electric can determine how much more to charge for an energy-saving refrigerator than for a competitor's model that is less energy-efficient by calculating the average electricity savings over the lifetime of the product. Even products such as disposable diapers have some economic benefits over diaper services in terms of time savings. For many consumer products, though, benefits cannot be stated in economic terms and this method has limited usefulness.

Survey-Based Methods

When economic-based approaches do not work, you can use some survey method to obtain willingness to pay information from customers. A variety of such methods have been developed. The problem with survey-based methods is that it is very difficult to get accurate information from pencil-and-paper exercises about what a customer might do in a buying situation. Although this problem is typical of marketing research, it is particularly a problem for pricing research, where people often give inaccurate responses about how much they are willing to pay.

For example, the following question is often used in surveys: "Please check the box next to the price you are willing to pay for this product." There is very little incentive for respondents to check anything but the box with the lowest price. Thus, survey-based pricing research must use more subtle approaches to the problem.

Table 11–1 shows a 1995 study that asked the following question of business customers of personal computers: "How much more are you willing to pay for Brand X compared to a no-name clone?"[13] These results were compared to those of a similar study done in 1993. The survey results are striking in that they not only estimate how much more or less one manufacturer can price its line relative to competitors but also show how the customer values of some brands decreased and others increased between 1993 and 1995. It is obvious that IBM can charge more than others. It is also obvious that DEC and AST were in big trouble in 1995; in fact, shortly after the survey, DEC pulled out of the personal computer market.

Table 11–1 What Buyers Will Pay for PC Brands

Question: "How much more are you willing to pay for Brand X compared to a no-name clone?"

Brand	1993	1995
IBM	$364	$339
Compaq	301	318
Apple	264	182
DEC	198	10
AST	176	17
Dell	161	230
Hewlett-Packard	145	260

Source: Reprinted by permission of *The Wall Street Journal*, © 1995 Dow Jones & Company, Inc. All Rights Reserved Worldwide.

One way to determine the appropriate price for a product or service is to conduct a pencil-and-paper survey. Although it is not the ideal research method for pricing research because everyone is likely to select the lowest price, subtly worded questions can overcome this limitation to some degree. (Rhoda Sydney/Photo Edit)

The **dollarmetric method** creates a scale that puts responses in monetary terms. Table 11–2 applies and analyzes a dollarmetric scale for soft drinks. This example analyzes five brands—Coke, Pepsi, 7UP, Dr Pepper, and Fresca—to determine what should be the relative prices of the brands. Consumers are given the brands in pairs. The respondent first chooses which of the two brands she or he prefers. Next, the respondent indicates how much extra she or he would be willing to pay to get a six-pack of the preferred brand.[14] The marketing manager then analyzes the data by summing the differences, positive and negative, in each brand comparison. As the bottom of Table 11–2 shows, for this customer, a six-pack of Coke is worth 2 cents more than Pepsi, 8 cents more than 7UP, 5 cents more than Dr Pepper, and 12 cents more than Fresca. If these results held up over a national sample, they would give some indication of the price difference Coke could maintain over the competing brands.

Three illustrations of estimating customer value show how marketing research methods can be used in practice to estimate customer willingness-to-pay.

◆ Illustration: Hewlett-Packard

In 1990, Hewlett-Packard (HP) developed a new test instrument and wanted to find an appropriate pricing level.[15] The company realized that asking direct questions about willingness to pay was not likely to produce accurate responses. As a result, it developed a catalog that included competing products and the new product. HP then hired a marketing research firm to conduct the study and disguise who was collecting the data to avoid biasing responses. Potential customers were randomly assigned to different groups and each group received the same brochure, except that the price for the HP instrument varied. Because all

Table 11–2 Dollarmetric Example

Pair of Brands (more preferred brand underlined)	Amount Extra Willing to Pay to Get a Six-Pack of the More Preferred Brand (cents)
Coke, Pepsi	2
Coke, 7UP	8
Coke, Dr Pepper	5
Coke, Fresca	12
Pepsi, 7UP	6
Pepsi, Dr Pepper	3
Pepsi, Fresca	10
7UP, Dr Pepper	3
7UP, Fresca	4
Dr Pepper, Fresca	7

Analysis

Coke + 2 (versus Pepsi) + 8 (versus 7UP) + 5 (versus Dr Pepper) + 12 (versus Fresca)	= 27
Pepsi − 2 + 6 + 3 + 10	= 17
7UP − 8 − 6 − 3 + 4	= −13
Dr Pepper − 5 − 3 + 3 + 7	= 2
Fresca − 12 − 10 − 4 − 7	= −33

other factors were controlled, the only difference in response had to be due to price. The customers were then asked to indicate which product they would choose, thus simulating the buying experience. Interestingly, HP managers found that as they increased price, demand went up. They priced the instrument thousands of dollars higher than they had planned. ◆

◆ Illustration: Rocket Science Inc.

A second illustration is from the company Rocket Science Inc., which makes games played over the Internet.[16] The company developed a Dungeons and Dragons-style role-playing game that they give away for free. You can find yourself in a dangerous situation such as facing a mortal enemy or a fierce-looking dragon, but you are defenseless because your weapon has been lost or you do not have any protective clothing. You notice a weapon lying on the ground or a suit of protective armor. The catch is that you have to pay to rent the equipment. For example, the armor costs $.05. The company has determined appropriate prices by observing perceived value in real time. If equipment is not rented at the posted price, the company drops the price. If it is very popular, the price is raised. Willingness to pay for the defensive equipment becomes the key to pricing. ◆

◆ Illustration: Rolling Rock Beer

The venerable Rolling Rock beer brand, owned by Labatt USA, was considering changing its traditional green bottle with a paper label to a more jazzy-looking bottle with a variety of white-painted labels.[17] Although the brand had a long tradition and a stable base of drinkers, its sales were declining because of inroads made by microbrewed and more contemporary brands. An important question that had to be addressed, along with general preferences for the new labels, was how much consumers would be willing to pay for Rolling Rock with the new labels.

The Labatt managers recruited consumers at shopping malls and other venues to view actual shelf sets of beer at every price range. The consumers were given money to spend in the form of chips; they were exposed to the old Rolling Rock bottles (old graphics and paper labels) and the new packages (two new painted graphics) at different prices and asked to allocate their next 10 purchases over Rolling Rock and the other brands in the test. Not only did the new packages gain customer approval, but consumers consistently indicated that they would be willing to pay more for the brand in the new packages. In three regions, the Northeast, Southeast, and West, purchase intent among Rolling Rock users increased dramatically at prices 20 cents higher per six-pack and at prices 40 cents higher.   ◆

Using the Perceived Value Concept

Marketing managers can use the concept of perceived value by considering a functional relationship among market share, perceived value, and price:

$$\text{Market share} = f(\text{perceived value/price})$$

As an application of this relationship, consider an observed decline in the market share of a product. How can this trend be reversed? Usually, the immediate response is a decrease in the denominator, that is, a price cut (through list price or a price promotion). Cutting the price is certainly one way to bring the relationship between perceived value and price back into balance. However, there is another way: You can attempt to increase the perceived value of the product.

The increase in perceived value can be accomplished in a variety of ways, linked to the differentiation approaches discussed in Chapter 3:

- Improve the product itself by increasing actual quality or offering better service or longer warranty period.
- Advertise to enhance the product's image.
- Institute value-added services such as technical support or financing.
- Improve the sales effort by training the sales force to sell value rather than price.

Notice that the numerator and denominator are not independent; that is, for some product categories, perceived value may be a function of price. In this case, lowering price may not actually produce the increase or stabilization in share desired because the functional relationship will not change: A lower price results in lower perceived quality. In fact, increasing price may raise perceived quality. Even if the increase in perceived quality does not rise proportionately more than the increase in price, it will mean higher profits at the same market share level.

Although reducing price is the most common way to regain market share losses (recall the McDonald's, Proctor & Gamble, and breakfast cereal examples used earlier in the chapter), it is actually much more expensive than adding value because the lower resulting profit margin must be multiplied by old number of units sold to estimate the investment that may or may not be recovered by increased sales volume. It has been found that a 3% price cut by the average Standard & Poor's (S&P) 1000 company reduces profit margins from 8.1% to 5.1%, a drop of 37%. In addition, McKinsey consultants estimate that the average S&P

company would need a 12% increase in sales volume to offset a 3% price cut.[18] Note that activities designed to raise perceived value can cost considerably less. How much does it cost to improve sales training procedures? How expensive is it to offer improved customer service? Value-enhancing activities are not free, but they are usually fixed costs that can be spread over a large volume, as opposed to per-unit reductions in margins. This is the approach taken by General Mills. They are using a combination of higher prices and increased marketing expenditures to regain market share, with the latter an attempt to sell the increased customer value associated with their brands.

A good example of this value-adding approach to pricing was provided by biotechnology firm Genentech in 1990.[19] In 1987, the firm introduced a drug called tissue plasminogen activator (TPA) that clears blood clots. At $2,220 per dose, the product is quite important to the company. In March 1990, a study was released showing that the drug was no more effective than an alternative, streptokinase, that sold for only $220 per dose. However, months later, Genentech was still selling TPA for $2,220 per dose. How? First, it trained its sales force to aggressively point out some of the limitations of the damaging study. Second, it temporarily gave hospital pharmacies a longer period in which to pay for TPA, thus encouraging them to stock up on the drug. Clearly, the costs of these two moves were far less than the cost of dropping the price of the product. ◆

COMPETITION AND PRICING

So far, the discussion about setting price has described two key elements of the marketing manager's thinking: the marketing strategy and the value customers place on the product. The first is obviously an internal factor because the marketing manager has control over the marketing strategy. The second is one of the external elements affecting all decisions: customers.

A third critical element in pricing decisions is the competition. Competitors' prices act as a reference point, either explicitly (as shown in the value computations earlier in this chapter) or implicitly as a way to assess the price of the product in question. Competitors' prices do not necessarily represent willingness to pay because the set of possible prices or marketing strategies may have been limited; that is, the competitors may not have an accurate idea of customers' willingness to pay.

Competitors' Costs

Marketing managers cannot make intelligent pricing decisions without having some estimate of the relative cost positions held by competitors. Even better are estimates of the actual costs. An understanding of the cost structure of the market provides at least two types of help. First, assuming that no brand would be priced below variable cost, cost estimates provide you with an idea of how low some competitors can price. This can be very useful in a price battle in which prices are going down. Second, cost estimates give you some idea of the margins in the category or industry. Using data on sales volume, which are usually easy to obtain, and information on marketing program costs, you can then estimate total profits. This can be important information in forecasting the likelihood that a product will stay in the market or estimating the amount of money a competitor has to put behind the brand strategy.

Costs can be estimated in several ways. A common approach for manufactured products is to use reverse engineering (see Chapter 7) to analyze the cost structure. You should purchase competitors' products and take them apart, studying the costs of the components and packaging. For many products, managers can readily identify components and their

Figure 11–4

Market Share Versus
Price and Cost

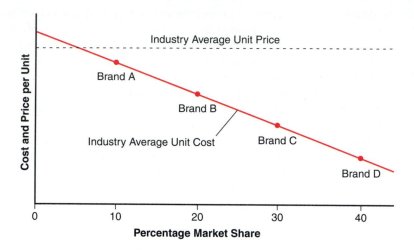

costs in the market. If a component is proprietary, such as a custom microprocessor in a computer, the cost can be estimated by engineers or other personnel.

Another way to estimate costs, or at least margins, is to use publicly available data on the competitors. Based on annual reports, 10K statements, and the like, you can ascertain average margins. These can be assumed to apply directly to the cost estimation, especially if the product is a big component of total sales or if, as is often the case, the company tends to use a cost plus percent markup pricing strategy.

Particularly for manufactured products (although it has been found to apply to some services as well), it is possible to understand current costs and forecast future costs through the use of the experience curve.[20] The experience curve phenomenon applies to certain products for which repetitive production of larger and larger amounts and concomitant investment in new manufacturing equipment systematically reduce costs over time. The conventional functional relationship assumed in experience curve economics is that costs (adjusted for inflation) are a decreasing function of accumulated experience, or production volume. Figure 11–4 shows an example of the experience curve phenomenon. In this case, experience is approximated by market share. Costs (and prices) are shown to be correlated with market share: The larger the share, the lower the costs. If you can construct a plot like that shown in Fig. 11–4 and statistically estimate the implied relationship between share and costs, you can forecast future relative cost positions under different assumptions of brand shares.

The costs of delivering services are more difficult to estimate. Because the costs associated with service products such as labor and office space are largely fixed, you can estimate relative cost positions by examining the number of employees, looking at efficiency ratios such as sales per employee, and assessing other similar measures. Again, it is particularly useful to understand the cost structure by becoming a customer of a competitor's service.

THE ROLE OF COSTS

We suggested earlier in this chapter that costs should have little to do with the pricing decision other than to act as a floor or lower limit for price (see Fig. 11–2). In a non–market-driven firm, full cost (variable costs plus some allocation for overhead) plus some target margin is used to set price. This approach totally ignores the customer: The resulting price may be either above or below what the customer is willing to pay for the product.

Other problems exist with using costs to set price. First, there are at least four different kinds of costs to consider. Development costs are expenses involved in bringing new products to market. Often these costs are spread out over many years and sometimes different products. Should price be set to recover these costs and, if so, in what time period? In some industries such as pharmaceuticals, patent protection allows companies to set the prices of prescription drugs high initially to recover development costs and then reduce them when the drugs come off patent and the generics enter the category. However, if there is no legal way to keep competitors out of the market, these costs must be viewed as sunk costs that do not affect decision making after the product is introduced into the market. Otherwise, the resulting price may be above customers' perceived value. A second kind of cost is overhead costs such as the corporate jet and the president's salary. These costs must ultimately be covered by revenues from individual products, but they are not associated with any one product. Often, the mechanism used to allocate these overhead costs among products is arbitrary and bears no relationship to how individual products use overhead or whether they would change if the product were withdrawn from the market. A third kind of cost is direct fixed costs. These costs, such as the marketing manager's salary and product-related advertising and promotion, are associated with individual products but do not vary with sales volume. Finally, there are variable costs, the per-unit costs of making the product or delivering the service. Of course, these must be recovered by the price.

Therefore, one problem with using costs to set price is that several kinds of costs are related in different ways to an individual product. When costs are used as the basis for setting price, you should ask "Which costs?" Are they costs related to marketing the product or product line or are they costs over which you have no control? Using price as a cost-recovery mechanism can lead to a mismatch between price and customers' perceptions of value for your product or service.

A second problem with using costs to set price, particularly variable or unit costs, is that they may be a function of volume (e.g., the experience curve) and, as a result, may be difficult to know in advance when developing marketing plans. Even if this is not the case, unit costs may be related to the use of capacity, which is also uncertain.

In most instances, customers do not really care what the firm's costs are; as Drucker puts it, "Customers do not see it as their job to ensure manufacturers a profit."[21] Using cost increases to justify raising price generates little sympathy from customers, particularly industrial customers, because the price increase has just raised their costs, which they may not be able to pass along to their customers.

Costs do play an important role in pricing: In the new product development process, the projected costs (however defined) and price determine whether a product is forecasted to be sufficiently profitable to be introduced. This issue is covered more completely in Chapter 17.

DECIDING HOW MUCH OF THE STRATEGIC PRICING GAP TO CAPTURE

Using Fig. 11–2 as the conceptual foundation, the key pricing decision becomes how much of the customer value to keep or give away. The factors involved in this decision are shown in Fig. 11–5.

Figure 11–5

Factors in the Pricing
Decision

Pricing Objectives

Your pricing policy can accomplish many different objectives for your product.

Penetration Pricing

Penetration pricing or market share pricing entails giving most of the value to the customer and keeping a small margin. The objective is to gain as much market share as possible. It is often used as part of an entry strategy for a new product and is particularly useful for preventing competitive entry. First, there is less of the market for the competition to get if you have been successful in penetrating the market. Second, the economics of entry look less attractive if the price levels are low. Penetration pricing is also appropriate when experience or scale effects lead to a favorable volume–cost relationship and when a large segment of the potential customer base is price sensitive.

There are some drawbacks to penetration pricing. It should not be used in a product category when there is a price–perceived quality relationship unless the marketing strategy is at the low end of perceived quality. In addition, if the product has a strong competitive advantage, this advantage is dissipated by pricing at an unusually low level. Another limitation of penetration pricing is that it is always more acceptable to customers to reduce price than to raise it. This limits the flexibility of this pricing approach in some situations.[22]

Skimming

The opposite of penetration pricing is **skimming or prestige pricing.** Skimming gives more of the cost–value gap to you than to the customer. This strategy is appropriate in a variety of situations. If there is a strong price–perceived quality relationship (e.g., wine) and the value proposition includes a positioning of the product at the high end of the market, this objective makes sense. It is also a reasonable objective when there is little chance of competition in the near future; however, the higher the price, the higher the margins (holding costs constant, of course) and thus the greater the chance that competition will enter because their economic calculations will look better. Skimming is also a good objective when costs are not related to volume and managers are therefore less concerned about building significant market share.

Finally, as we noted in Chapter 3, skimming makes sense early in the product life cycle because the early adopters of a new technology are normally price insensitive.

Return on Sales or Investment Pricing

Return on sales or investment pricing implies that you can set a price that delivers the rate of return demanded by senior management. As a result, investment pricing ignores both customer value and the competition. It is useful only when the product has a monopoly or near monopoly position so that the market will produce the needed sales volume at the price you set. This is typical of the pricing of regulated utilities such as gas and electricity.

Pricing for Stability

Sometimes customers for industrial products are as concerned about price stability as they are about actual price levels. This is because it is difficult to develop profit forecasts and long-range plans when prices for products and services that constitute a substantial portion of the buyer's costs fluctuate dramatically. Telephone rates for large users such as telemarketing firms and banks fall into this category. Such customers expect rates to rise over time. However, significant price hikes at random intervals play havoc with their planning processes. As a result, these firms would rather pay a somewhat higher average rate than be subjected to constant fluctuations. Forward contracts on raw materials play this role in many manufacturing industries.

Competitive Pricing

Competitive pricing describes a situation in which you try to price at the market average or match a particular brand's price. This is appropriate when customers have not been persuaded that significant differences exist among the competitors and that they view the product as a commodity. It may also be necessary in a category with high fixed costs because any loss of sales volume drives down sales and generates less revenue to cover those costs.

Psychological Aspects of Price

Customers actively process price information; that is, they consider the price they observe and make judgments about whether it is fair, whether it is a good deal, or whether it signals information about product quality. They also continually assess prices based on prior purchasing experience, formal communications (e.g., advertising) and informal communications (e.g., friends and neighbors), and point-of-purchase lists of prices and use those assessments in the ultimate purchasing decision. This is consistent with price being a communication vehicle as well as a revenue generator. Three key concepts related to the psychological aspects of price are reference prices, the price–perceived quality relationship, and price points.

Reference Prices

A **reference price** is any standard of comparison against which a potential transaction or purchase price is compared. In a retailing setting, the reference price is often listed on the sales tag as the "original" price from which subsequent markdowns have been made. This kind of reference price is an external reference price; an internal reference price is a mental price used to assess an observed price. Internal reference prices are formed from advertising, past purchasing experience, and so on and are often called perceived prices because the customer considers them the actual prices of the products in a category.

Reference prices can have a significant impact on brand choice for both durable and nondurable products.[23] In particular, when the observed price is higher than the reference price (the internal concept of reference price), it can decrease sales because the customer perceives this difference as an unpleasant surprise. For example, the large price increases for cars in the 1970s created what became known as a sticker shock when consumer reference prices for cars were significantly lower than the prices they saw in the showroom. A happier situation occurs when the observed price is below the reference price. This happens when a brand a consumer might buy anyway is being promoted at a lower price. Interestingly, several studies have found that the unpleasant surprises have a greater impact on purchasing probabilities than the pleasant ones.

The concept of reference price has important implications for marketing managers. Consider a brand that has been price promoted for several weeks. The customer will begin to replace the normal price with the promoted price as the reference point. Then, when the brand returns to the regular price, the customer may perceive the change as an increase in price and interpret it negatively.

A second important concept of reference price is expected future price. This is a particularly important concept for any product that experiences significant price changes over time. The airline industry has had protracted fare wars in which the prices of some flights fell rapidly in short periods of time. Some segments of fliers, such as business travelers, are unaffected by changes in fares because they do not have discretion about when they fly. However, fliers who do have discretion, such as people who are traveling for pleasure or have flexible schedules, simply wait for prices to drop further before booking. Price cutting merely exacerbates the airlines' problems because sales are low while discretionary travelers wait for the fares to drop even further. The same situation results from rebate programs in the automobile industry. Why purchase a car while a rebate war is in progress? Why not wait to see whether further price cuts are possible? Finally, new consumer durables are also subject to this phenomenon. Whenever a new Intel microprocessor is introduced and new personal computer models are developed for it, the prices are initially high but drop predictably. Discretionary purchasers can simply wait until the prices decrease further. The problem is predictability: If you create a predictable pricing pattern, you should not underestimate customers' abilities to process the information and make decisions based on their personal forecasts of future prices.

Relationship between Price and Perceived Quality

In some situations, contrary to standard microeconomic theory, a higher price can lead to higher rather than lower demand. This occurs when price is used to signal that the product is of high quality.

One reason such a relationship exists is for exclusivity or prestige. A high price means that fewer customers can afford it. Rolex could charge substantially less for its watches and still make a profit. However, because few consumers can afford thousands of dollars for a watch, few will own a Rolex, which is how their owners want it.

A second example of a strong price–perceived quality relationship occurs when a product's quality is difficult to assess before purchasing or difficult to assess at all. These products are often called experience goods (if you have to try the product before assessing its quality) or credence goods (if even after you have purchased and used the product or service, the quality is hard to evaluate). Examples of the former are most services, such as haircuts and legal advice. Examples of credence goods are car repairs such as brake servicing (the consumer cannot actually see what happened) and wine (only experts can distinguish between different levels of quality).

The major implication for marketing managers in this situation is that the price must be consistent with the marketing strategy. If customer research shows a significant correlation between price and perceived quality, a value proposition stressing quality or value-added features requires a concomitant high price. An exotic vodka supported with a highly creative advertising campaign (e.g., Absolut) cannot be priced at $1.99 per bottle without striking a discordant feeling in the (presumably) upscale consumer.

Psychological Price Points

In some cases, somewhat artificial price levels or price points distinguish between different market segments (see the discussion of the ice cream market earlier in the chapter). In these situations, seemingly minor differences in price that separate price levels defined, say, by the number of digits, can have (or at least are believed to have) a large impact on customer perception of how expensive a product is. For example, in the personal computer industry, a significant price point appears to be $1,000. This level is thought to separate the current buyers of personal computers from the mass market that has not yet purchased one. As a result, in 1999, a large number of companies such as Compaq, Packard Bell-NEC, AST, Apple, and clones like Monorail offered well-equipped models at $999 or less.[24]

An interesting and related phenomenon in pricing is the use of odd prices for many goods. Odd prices are just below an even number. For example, many prices end in $.99; many higher-priced items are $499 or even $24,999, for example. Clearly, many managers feel that the right-most digits of a price have a significant impact on customer decision making.[25]

Stage of the Product Life Cycle

In Chapter 3, the product life cycle was shown to have an important impact on the strategic choices available to the marketing manager. Not surprisingly, the method used to set prices can also change over the life cycle. Table 11–3 illustrates how DuPont approaches pricing with the life cycle in mind. The company simplifies the life cycle to three generic stages: sole supplier (introductory phase), competitive penetration (early and late growth), and shared stability, commodity competition, and withdrawal (maturity and decline). Particularly interesting is the focus for pricing decisions over the life cycle. When little competition exists, focus is on the customer and value is stressed. Notice that there is no mention of variable or investment costs that must be recovered. When competition enters, focus is on both customers and competitors. Thus, customer value is still important but how competitors will react is also addressed. Finally, in the late stages of the product category, the focus shifts toward competitors and costs to determine whether remaining in the market makes economic sense. There, profitability analysis is the key.

Another way to look at the impact of the product life cycle is through experience curve pricing. Figure 11–6 shows three different pricing scenarios. Increases in industry cumulative volume represent movement along the product life cycle. One possible pricing pattern, A, is strict experience curve pricing, with price declines as costs decline;

Table 11–3 DuPont Pricing over the Product Life Cycle

Competitive Cycle Stage	Focus of Attention	Pricing Method
Sole supplier	Customers	Value-in-use Perceived value
Competitive penetration	Customers Competitors	Reaction analysis
Shared stability Commodity competition Withdrawal	Competition and costs	Profitability analysis

Figure 11–6

Experience
Curve-Based Pricing
Patterns over the
Product Life Cycle

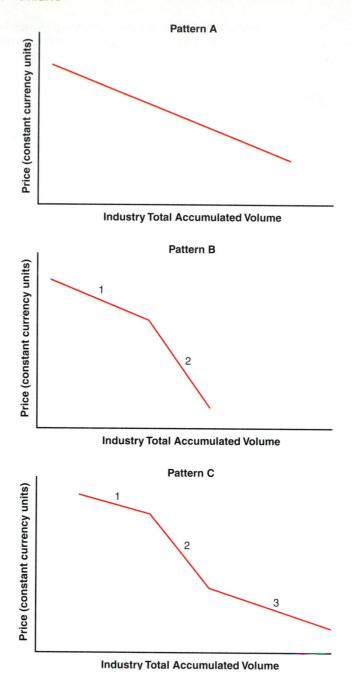

sometimes prices drop even in anticipation of the resulting cost decreases with increased
volume. This approach is usually an attempt to maintain a low price strategy over the
entire life cycle and maximize market share (penetration). In pattern B, the manager keeps
margins up for a period of time because there is little competition (segment 1 of the curve
is flatter than segment 2) and then drops price more rapidly as competition enters later in
the life cycle. In pattern C, the manager reacts twice: first when competition enters (seg-

ment 2 is again steeper than segment 1) and again when competition drops out (segment 3 is flatter than segment 2). Thus, under this last pricing pattern, margins are high in the early phase of the life cycle, drop due to competition, and then rise again after a category shakeout occurs.

Industry Conditions

Different aspects of the industry situation should also be considered when setting price:

- Threat of new entrants. The likelihood of new entrants into a category has an important effect on price. If the likelihood is low (barriers to entry are high), higher price levels can be sustained. If new entrants are possible, either from within the industry or from outside, lower prices help to protect the market position from potential erosion and make the profit potential of the market look worse for new product entries.
- Power of buyers/suppliers. High buyer power obviously tends to depress prices as it puts more pressure on the product to deliver a good value/price ratio. If suppliers have high power, they will often charge higher prices for goods or services supplied, whether raw materials, labor, or anything else. High supplier power thus raises the floor beneath which prices cannot be set.
- Rivalry. High industry rivalry clearly tends to be manifested in strong price competition.
- Pressure from substitutes. Like the threat of entry, the more available potential substitute technologies or solutions to customer problems are and the more value they offer, the greater the chance that price competition will exist. For example, Sony and Sega beat Nintendo to the market with advanced video game systems in 1996. However, when Nintendo introduced its 64-bit system near the end of 1996, the prices of the Sony and Sega models dropped significantly.
- Unused capacity. This concept is particularly important in a high-fixed-cost, high-contribution-margin (price minus variable cost) product category. These markets are characterized by some of the most vicious price battles because there is plenty of margin to give and the products must generate revenues to cover fixed costs. An excellent example of this kind of situation is the airline industry. Where markets are unregulated, price competition between airlines is intense (consider any market where Southwest Airlines competes).

Who Is the Decision Maker?

In industrial product markets, you must ensure that the price eventually set is consistent with the needs of the people in the buying organization who influence the purchasing decision.[26] In Chapter 6, we discussed the importance of understanding the roles different people play in the purchasing process and of recognizing that their needs differ. This is important for making pricing decisions. For example, suppose you sell a component such as a hard disk drive. A gatekeeper for the sale of the drive may be a design engineer. This person has to be convinced that the value offered by your drive is favorable for the product that will include the drive. The price itself is somewhat less important than the benefit or value. The people involved in developing specifications for the new product may be more interested in life cycle costs if they are being judged on the profitability of the product over, say, a 10-year period. Purchasing managers are evaluated on their abilities to keep cost variances down and may avoid suppliers who try to raise prices at a rate greater than inflation.

SPECIFIC PRICING TACTICS

Product Line Pricing

One common pricing task you face is how to set prices for a closely related set of products or a product line. For example, one problem would be how to price a line of personal computers that vary in microprocessor speed. Other variations are sizes of a TV screen, size of containers, and other features. A different problem is how to price complementary products such as a copier and toner or razors and blades.

Price Bundling

One approach is **price bundling,** which takes a set of products, offers them to customers in a package, and usually prices the package lower than the sum of the individual components. For example, home stereo systems are commonly offered in a rack system consisting of a turntable, an amplifier, a cassette player, a tuner, and a CD player in an attractive case. This bundle of items, often composed of models that are slow sellers, is usually specially priced to eliminate inventory. A similar example is packages of options in autos.

An alternative approach takes the opposite view. Sometimes the bundle can be priced *higher* than the sum of the components because it is attractive or convenient and thus adds value. A good example is McDonald's Happy Meal, which is targeted toward children. Any parent who computes the sum of the hamburger, french fries, and drink would find that she or he is paying a considerable sum for the toy and the package.

A different way to look at the issue is by unbundling. Some companies offer pre-designed packages of features and services that include components some customers do not need. For example, a telecommunication system might come with a standard service contract some customers may not find attractive because they already have considerable on-site technical help; alternatively, a "value" meal may come with unwanted french fries. In such cases, you could seek ways to unbundle the product package to allow customers to choose what they want to pay for.

For example, the San Luis Sourdough Company sells one-pound loaves of sourdough bread to supermarkets using a three-tier pricing policy.[27] Level 1 prices the bread at $.97 per loaf for supermarkets that are happy to have the bread simply dropped off. If the store wants to be able to return day-old bread for credit—level 2—the cost is $1.02 per loaf. If the store wants the company to accept returns, stock the shelves, and place bar codes on the packages, this level 3 service costs $1.05 per loaf. Thus, the company has cleverly unbundled its service levels so customers can choose the level that fits their needs and level of value.   ◆

Product-Line Pricing

The **product-line pricing** approach involves offering both a high-priced and low-priced brand. This is a classic strategy used by Proctor & Gamble. The objective is to have brands at multiple price tiers, such as Crest at the premium level and Gleem at a lower price. This strategy ensures that the company covers most customer segments. When the intent is to offer a brand that is slightly higher in price and one that is lower in price than a competitor, the strategy is called bracketing the competition. The obvious objective is to give customers little reason to buy the competitor.

Complementary Pricing

Complementary pricing applies to products that are used together when one of the products is a consumable that must be replenished continually. Two good examples are razors and blades (the consumable) and cameras and film (the consumable). Gillette prices razors rather modestly but makes huge margins on the blades. Similarly, the prices for Polaroid instant cameras are rather low compared to those for 35-mm cameras but the film is more expensive. This kind of pricing is useful only when there is limited competition for the consumables. Unlike Kodak and Fuji, which compete fiercely for the 35-mm film market, Polaroid dominates the market for instant film. Also, the replacement market for automobile parts (called the "aftermarket") is huge and composed mainly of companies that do not manufacture cars. Thus, premium pricing for parts cannot be used for the do-it-yourself mechanic segment.

Complementary pricing is also used for services that have fixed and variable components to price. Two examples are private golf clubs and telephone service. Both have a fixed monthly fee and a variable usage fee. Such complementary pricing can be a creative way to keep the marginal costs to customers low ("pennies a day") while retaining a continuous stream of revenue.

Value Pricing

Value pricing has been a key phrase in pricing during the 1990s. Although the term has never really been defined, it has been used by airlines, hotels, rental car agencies, supermarkets, and various other companies, usually for consumer products. The originator of the concept may have been Taco Bell. In 1990, Taco Bell developed a value menu that offered several items, such as tacos, for very low prices. The company was very successful in making inroads against other fast-food chains, which subsequently caused McDonald's and others to offer value-priced items. The sustained recession of the early 1990s caused other products to pick up the concept.

It is important to clarify the distinction between value pricing and pricing to value. As we have described in this chapter, pricing to value relies on estimates of the dollar value

Value pricing is used by many retail companies and has become common in fast-food restaurants. In addition to the menu of regularly priced items, most fast-food chains feature a value menu, with several items priced very low. Customers respond favorably to this strategy, being satisfied that they have gotten a good deal. (Spencer Grant/Photo Edit)

customers place on products and, when coupled with an estimate of the variable costs of producing a product or delivering a service, determines the range of possible prices that can be charged. Value pricing gives the customer most of the value–cost difference, that is, a "good deal." However, the term *value pricing* is not the same as penetration pricing. Penetration pricing implies low price alone. Value pricing is related to customer expectations: It gives customers more value than they expect for the price paid. This does *not* necessarily imply low price. Thus, value pricing is consistent with pricing at less than customer value, but it is accompanied by communications, packaging, and other elements of the marketing mix that indicate a high level of quality.

A good example of a product that was value priced while being priced high is the Lexus 400 at its introduction. The car cost around $40,000, which is not the low end of the market. However, the brand was very successful because it offered the kinds of luxury, features, and service for which some European manufacturers charged much more. Again, value pricing does not imply inexpensive, only that what you get represents more net value than other available options. At about $50,000 today, the Lexus is less value priced and represents Toyota's ability to capture more of the customer value through its prior success in the market. However, the 1999 Camry, at under $20,000, is considered an outstanding value and has been marketed that way.[28]

Differential Pricing

The key strategic decision of which customers to target recognizes that potential customers' behavior is heterogeneous. This heterogeneity can be reflected in price in various ways.

Direct Price Discrimination

Price discrimination to end customers, though unpopular with consumer advocacy groups, is not always illegal, and it is done all the time.[29] Witness the senior citizen discounts given at movie theaters or the quantity discounts on personal computers given to large customers. The theory is that price discrimination maximizes products' profits by charging each market segment the price that maximizes profit from that segment because of different price elasticities of demand. However, in practice, it is difficult to implement a price discrimination policy, particularly in consumer markets, because of the fragmentation of the customer base and the existence of firms that buy at one segment's low prices and resell to others (such as consolidators of airline tickets).

One way to implement price discrimination is through target delivery of coupons or other discount mechanisms by direct mail (recall the discussion in Chapter 8). Given the quality of databases available today, it is easy to identify households that have the highest probability of buying the product and need a price inducement. Direct mail companies send coupons from a variety of manufacturers to households, often using a name for the program such as Carol Wright.

Second Market Discounting

A useful pricing strategy when excess production exists is called **second market discounting.** With this policy, you sell the extra production at a discount to a market separate from the main market. As long as the product is sold at a price greater than variable cost, the contribution margin produced can help cover corporate overhead. Some examples of secondary markets are generic drugs, private-label brands, and foreign markets.

Periodic Discounting

Periodic discounting varies price over time. It is appropriate when some customers are willing to pay a higher price to have the product or service during a particular time period. For example, utilities such as electricity and telephone service use peak load pricing policies that charge more during the heaviest usage periods, partly to encourage off-peak usage. Clothing retailers mark down items that are slow sellers; those who want an item when it is first introduced pay a higher price. Theater tickets cost more on weekends.

Flat-Rate Versus Variable-Rate Pricing

An approach to differential pricing that is often used in services is to offer customers a choice between a fixed price and a variable usage fee (with perhaps a low fixed portion). The **flat-rate versus variable-rate pricing** concept allows customers to choose the option that best suits their level of usage. This became an important issue for the Internet service provider America Online, which initially priced its service at $9.95 per month plus a usage fee for e-mail and Web access beyond a prescribed limit. In early 1997, the company suddenly switched all its users to a flat rate of $19.95 per month. Although this was a good deal for heavy users (such as small businesses that used AOL as their primary Internet service provider), light users, a large portion of AOL's customer base, were outraged. Ultimately, the company was forced by its subscribers and public opinion to offer customers a choice between the two and allow customers to switch between the programs whenever they want.

Competing against Private Labels

Private labels—or "own" brands, as they are sometimes called because they are often a retailer's captive brand name—are ubiquitous. Virtually all supermarket chains sell private-label brands. In addition, many nonfood retailers such as department stores sell own brands.

Private-label brands have penetrated most retail product categories. This creates pricing issues for national-label brands because private labels are specifically created to provide lower-priced competition. As this supermarket aisle illustrates, for most types of cereals customers can choose between national and private-label brands. (Rick Brady/Uniphoto)

For example, Sears has a large number of private labels: Kenmore appliances, Craftsman tools, DieHard car batteries, Fieldmaster outdoor apparel, Laura Scott women's clothes, Nice Touch Promise pantyhose, and Freeze Frame junior clothing, among others.

Although doing battle with private labels clearly is a strategic issue, it is also a pricing issue because a major justification for private labels' existence is to produce a lower-priced competitor to national brands.[30] Product categories that private labels have successfully penetrated usually have two characteristics: There is a large price-sensitive segment, and no lower-priced entries exist in the category, except perhaps a no-name generic option. Thus, consumers pay a large premium for buying national brands. Generally, this means that national brand marketing managers have made pricing decisions that keep much of the difference between variable cost and customer value for themselves. Supermarket categories experiencing significant private-label growth include cold cereal, bottled water, dog food, coffee, chewing gum, and condensed soup. These categories historically have had high prices and fat profit margins (an exception is coffee, which usually has only high prices).

How should you defend your brands against the incursion of private labels? One obvious way is to reduce the price gap to the point where consumers are willing to pay and therefore value the brand name. However, as we already said, this is an expensive solution and one to which you should not immediately gravitate. Other ways to battle back are the following:[31]

- Add value in ways discussed earlier in this chapter.
- Develop new market segments that are less price sensitive.
- Build stronger relationships with the channels of distribution.
- Prune product lines of sizes or flavors that are not generating profits for the retailer.
- Raise the barriers to entry for private labels by investing in better customer databases and retention programs (information technology).

The key to fighting the price-oriented private labels is not making a knee-jerk reaction to compete on price but instead exploring other options. As described earlier in this chapter, General Mills has taken the value-added approach in its battle with private-label cereals.

PRICING AND THE INTERNET

Although many Web sites are trying to offer customized services and products that avoid competing on the basis of price, others are focusing on offering low prices for different product categories. For example, BuyComp.com, started in 1996, advertised itself as having the lowest prices for computer products. After changing its name to Buy.com and expanding its product line to include books and videos (the company plans to continue expanding), it now spends a considerable amount on advertising, touting its site as having "The lowest prices on Earth."

If you do not think you are getting the lowest prices at a given Web site, the Web enables you to compare prices quickly and easily; a few clicks on the mouse can save considerable time over visits to retail stores or multiple phone calls. Some Web sites do your bidding and price comparisons for you. These include Compare.Net (see Fig. 11–7) and PriceScan. If you are interested in the lowest price for, say, a particular model of a digital camera, Pricescan lists the prices offered for that model at a variety of Web sites, with links directly to the sites with the lowest prices. Easy price comparisons and the lack of highly persuasive communications make it difficult for a company selling on the Web to develop higher customer value and concomitant higher prices and profit margins for Web-based transactions.

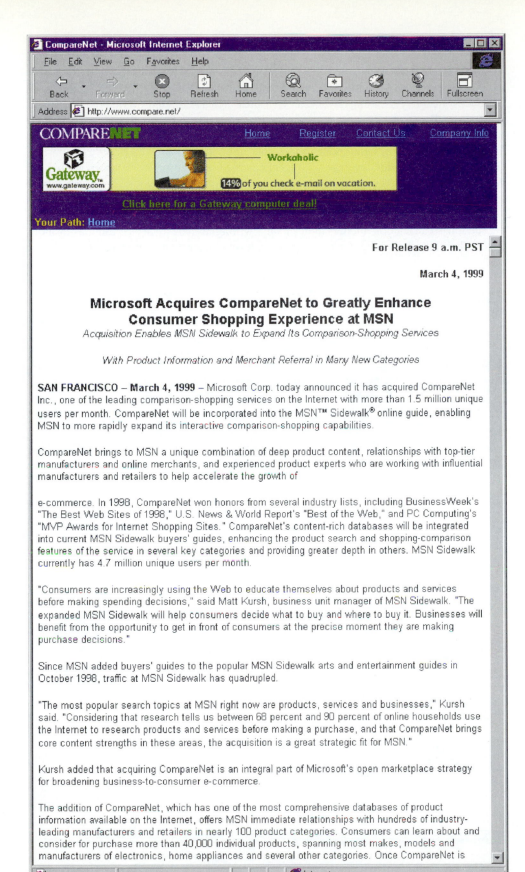

Figure 11–7

Compare.Net Web
Site

CompareNet

An industry that has been rocked by the Web is automobile retailing. Sites such as Auto-by-Tel (see Fig. 11–8), Microsoft Carpoint, and Autoweb.com provide the ultimate in convenience for car buyers. First, buyers can visit sites such as Edmunds to find out how much dealers actually pay for the cars. Armed with this information, buyers then go to these Web sites and invite retailers who are linked to the sites to electronically bid on car models with their specifications. These bid prices and costs can be used to actually order a car on-line and finance it or provide leverage with local car dealers. Industry observers note that the Web has revolutionized car buying and may eventually spell the demise of the traditional car retailer carrying large amounts of expensive inventory.[32]

One particular market pricing mechanism that has become very popular on the Web is the auction. At an auction, bidders indicate their willingness to pay in a continuous fashion, upping their bids until either the price rises to a level greater than their reservation price or

Figure 11–8

Auto-by-Tel Web Site

Courtesy of Autobytel

they win. In auctions, prices are determined by supply and demand at a particular time. The Internet has spawned a large number of sites on which sellers run electronic auctions to sell merchandise.[33] Market clearing prices reflect more accurately underlying customer value than do normal fixed prices. The main advantage of the Web as an auction site is the size of the audience. People from all over the world converge on these sites to create active markets in all kinds of goods and services. Examples include the following:

- The biggest and hottest of them all, eBay has been a phenomenal success as the flea market and garage sale on the Web. The company matches buyers and sellers of anything from Pez dispensers to baseball cards.
- Onsale runs seven live auctions each week in which people bid on goods purchased as surplus from companies at low prices. Since the site opened in 1995, more than 4 million bids have been placed.
- Aucnet is a used-car auction.
- Narrowline.com is an electronic exchange for Net advertising bringing together media buyers with Web sites looking to sell available advertising space.
- Priceline sells mortgages, cars, and airline tickets.

The on-line auction market is predicted by some to reach $4 billion by 2001.[34]

The Web is also enabling sellers to price discriminate efficiently. A company called Personify has developed software that lets a Web-based seller identify individual visitors to its Web site and then, by studying the clickstream (the way the customer navigates through the site) target the shoppers for specific products and prices. If the buyer behaves like a price-sensitive customer (e.g., one who compares a number of products without making a purchase), the customer might be offered a lower price. In addition, vendors such as CDnow e-mail certain buyers a special Web site address with lower prices.[35]

The long-term effect of the Web on prices is difficult to predict. On one hand, buyers can compare products and prices quickly and easily, thus driving down prices and margins. On the other hand, buyers give up detailed information about themselves and their purchasing habits, enabling sellers to tailor products and services to their needs. This customization and the increased convenience of shopping on the Web should result in the opportunity to charge higher prices. Complicating matters are studies that show that the so-called bargains on the Web are not always exactly as expected.[36] It is easy to see that pricing on the Web can result in varying prices for the same product over time and between individuals, a big change from traditional fixed prices. Even if the eventual outcome of these conflicting forces is unknown, the current implications for pricing are enormous.

EXECUTIVE SUMMARY

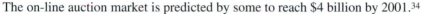

The main points of this chapter include the following:

- The purpose of price is to recover customer-perceived value for your product or service, not to recover costs.
- The four main components of a price are the marketing strategy, customer value or willingness to pay, competitors' prices, and your costs.
- As part of the marketing mix, price must be consistent with the marketing strategy in that it accounts for the target segment's price sensitivity and the value proposition.

- Customer value is the monetary value a customer places on your product. You can measure customer value directly by calculating the monetary benefits of your product or service or by using survey approaches.
- It is important to understand the competitors' cost structures as well as their past pricing practices.
- Price should always be set greater than variable costs. However, cost-based pricing is difficult to implement because there are many kinds of costs (variable, direct fixed, indirect fixed, development).
- The gap between variable costs and customer value is the strategic pricing gap.
- How much of the strategic pricing gap to capture is determined by your pricing objectives, psychological aspects of price, the stage of the product life cycle, industry conditions, and the decision-making structure within the buying organization.
- There are a variety of pricing tactics: product line decisions, value pricing, and differential pricing, or using different prices in different market segments.
- Developing a pricing strategy to compete with private labels is important for marketing managers in many industries. Although you can reduce price, you can also approach the problem in a number of other ways, particularly by adding value.
- The Internet is having an important impact on how customers find price information and use price to make buying decisions and on how final prices are determined.

CHAPTER QUESTIONS

1. Why is the marketing strategy so important to the pricing decision? Can you think of some examples in which the strategy and the price appear to be inconsistent?
2. Find other illustrations of companies that have set prices lower than customer value. Do you think they were set that way intentionally? If so, why?
3. Suppose your company had just developed a new TV set that had WebTV (currently, a separate unit attaching to a TV that, with a phone jack, allows you to surf the Internet using your TV screen as a monitor) built into it. What steps would you go through to determine how much more you would charge (if anything) for such a TV over the stand-alone price?
4. What other products and services exhibit a strong correlation between price and perceived quality? Are marketing strategies different for such products than for those for which there is no such natural relationship?
5. What are the implications for consumer welfare (i.e., privacy, safety) of the proliferation of auction sites on the Web? Are there any regulatory implications?

Integrated Case

Application Exercises: Pricing in the PC Market

1. Create a price band diagram (as shown in Fig. 11–1) for the PC industry.
2. Consider the willingness-to-pay information in Table 11–1. Construct a survey to update the information to the present time. What does this tell you about the value of the different brands?
3. Using the information developed in exercise 2 and the current price information obtained in exercise 1, develop an analysis of the pricing policies of the major PC manufacturers. Which are pricing above customer value? Which are pricing below customer value? Is market performance (i.e., market share) consistent with the answers to these questions?

4. Visit a local PC retailer (e.g., Best Buy, CompUSA) and examine the retail pricing policies used by different companies. In particular, how are the different product variations priced for each company? How competitive are the pricing policies? What do the salespeople say about the price–quality relationships for the different brands?

FURTHER READING

Other than the Nagle/Holden book referred to in this chapter, two other good books on pricing are Robert J. Dolan and Hermann Simon (1996), *Power Pricing* (New York: Free Press); and Kent B. Monroe (1990), *Pricing: Making Profitable Decisions,* 2nd ed. (New York: McGraw-Hill). Understanding customer value for industrial products is nicely explained by James C. Anderson and James A. Narus (1998), "Business marketing: understand what customers value," *Harvard Business Review,* 76 (November–December), pp. 53–65.

Sales Promotion

12

CHAPTER BRIEF

The purpose of this chapter is to introduce the various aspects of sales promotion decision-making. After reading this chapter, the student should have learned the following:

How sales promotion differs from advertising and other modes of communication
The different types of sales promotions available to the marketing manager
Differences between customer, trade, and retailer-oriented promotions
Issues in the development of promotional strategy and objective-setting
Allocating money between advertising and sales promotion
Electronic commerce implications for sales promotion

Binney & Smith, a small company based in Easton, Pennsylvania, makes one of the world's most popular items for children: Crayola brand crayons.[1] Since 1903, the company has produced the product that kids and parents adore, although the latter sometimes have problems cleaning up after the fun has ended.[2] The name *Crayola* came from Mrs. Binney, who combined the French word *crayon,* meaning "stick" or "pencil," with the suffix *ola,* for "oily." The product is made of petroleum-based paraffin wax and nontoxic color pigments. Crayolas come in 104 colors, and more than two billion are produced each year. The colorful Crayola Web page shown in Fig. 12–1 gives some indication of the kinds of services the company provides to children and their parents as part of their brand community-building efforts.

In the late 1990s, despite having a 98% unaided brand awareness among consumers, Crayola's sales were declining because of three major changes in the environment. First, company executives acknowledged that compared to video games and personal computers, Crayolas are somewhat lacking in excitement and technological innovation. The last big change in the product was made in the early 1950s, when a sharpener was added to the box. Second, sales of the standard 64-count boxes had dropped sharply as promotional efforts focused on the larger 96-count boxes. Third, for the first time, a competitor was appearing in the rather sleepy product category. Scientists at Purdue University discovered a way to make crayons out of soybean oil. Prang Fun Pro Crayons, made by Dixon Ticonderoga, were introduced in 1997 and positioned as a more environmentally friendly product. The company claims that they are safer for children, are nontoxic, glide smoother, and have brighter colors.

Figure 12–1

Crayola Web Site

Crayola, chevron and
serpentine designs are
registered trademarks;
rainbow/swash design is
a trademark of Binney &
Smith, used with permission.

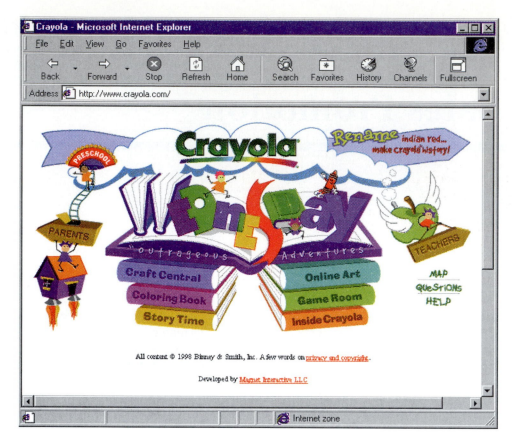

The many issues facing Crayola's marketing managers include the following:

- How can the company encourage its distributors and retailers to continue to carry the Crayola brand and give it as much shelf space if its sales continue to decline?
- How much money should be spent on various communication activities?
- How can the company revitalize sales of the traditional 64-count boxes?
- How can the managers create some excitement about a rather unexciting product?
- How can sales of the Crayola brand be revitalized, in both the short and the long term?

The marketing communications program most commonly involved with these issues is **sales promotion,** usually just called promotion. A definition of promotion is the following:[3]

> Sales promotion is an action-focused marketing event whose purpose is to have a direct impact on the behavior of the firm's customers.

This definition can be broken down to shed some light on specific promotional activities and their purposes:

- Sales promotions are action focused. They are intended to get customers to take action. This is perhaps their most distinguishing feature. In addition, they normally attempt to get customers to take action within a limited period of time. For example, coupons are intended to get customers to purchase the brand by the expiration date.

- Promotions are marketing events. More precisely, they are discrete programs with well-defined beginning and starting dates that offer incentives to customers to purchase or use the product. A coupon campaign has a beginning or drop date as well as an expiration date; contests and sweepstakes also run over a limited period of time. Both are considered events.
- Sales promotions are intended to have a direct impact on behavior. As we noted in Chapter 8, advertising usually works through a series of steps or a hierarchy, from awareness to purchase. Promotions work directly on behavior. As a result, there is no question about how to evaluate the effectiveness of a promotional campaign or event: Sales is almost always the measure of effectiveness. Although coupons do affect consumers' psychological processes, the objective is purchase or trial, not attitude change.
- Sales promotions influence customers. It is important to note that customers include both end customers and any channel members or intermediaries. Thus, certain promotional devices are appropriate for getting consumers or other end customers to buy; others, such as quantity discounts, are targeted toward channel members.

To provide a better idea of how and when sales promotions are used, Fig. 12–2 shows a simplified channel structure in which the manufacturer sells to a channel (here a retailer), which in turn sells to the final customer (the consumer). In this situation, promotion falls into three categories:

- Customer promotion
- Promotion to the channels, or trade promotion
- Channel-originated promotion, or retailer promotion

Customer promotion comes directly to the customer from the manufacturer. Trade promotion, in contrast, is directed at intermediate channels of distribution in an attempt to get them to buy more of a product and to commit their own efforts (e.g., sales force) to move the product through the next channel and ultimately to the consumer. Channel-originated promotion events are run by the channel itself, either to the next channel in the distribution chain or to final customers.

Sales promotion is related in an important way to the distribution channel issues discussed in Chapter 9. Figure 9–2 shows the value-added chain used to develop the motivation for establishing a channel system. Promotion is used for both push and pull activities and is the primary vehicle for the former. Push activities give the intermediaries incentives

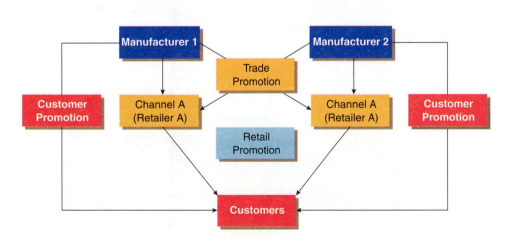

Figure 12–2

Simplified Channel and Promotional Structure

to carry and sell the product, whereas customer-oriented promotion gives customers a reason to come to the point of purchase and request the product.

Sales promotion is part of the implementation part of the marketing strategy (see the marketing strategy diagram) and part of the communications mix. Even though promotion is a short-term activity and often focuses on price, any messages communicated directly (e.g., in a print ad with a coupon) or indirectly (e.g., through a sales contest) must be integrated with the other communication vehicles and support the value proposition that is the core of the marketing strategy.

Figure 12–3 shows the changes in advertising and promotional spending for grocery items between 1986 and 1996. Since 1986, there has been a dramatic shift away from media advertising toward trade promotion, although the shares have stabilized since 1991. This change was caused by the increased power of the retail trade (discussed in Chapter 9), increased competition, and the mature state of many of these products (which increases the need for trade promotion to retain shelf space). The nearly 3:1 ratio of promotion to advertising reflects the short-term, sales-volume focus that pervaded the industry for many years. The recent stabilization and slight increase in advertising expenditures was probably caused by the significant emphasis on brand equity and brand-building by many companies.

Table 12–1 shows the amount of money spent on promotions in business-to-business markets in 1995. Although sales promotion is usually associated with consumer products, of all marketing and communication dollars spent in 1995, 16% were spent on business-to-business sales promotions and premium/incentive activities; even though some of this amount was for catalogs and other sales material, not what we consider sales promotion as defined earlier in this chapter, this is still a considerable amount. For example, when Microsoft launched its database software product, SQL Server 7, in January 1999, the company spent hundreds of millions

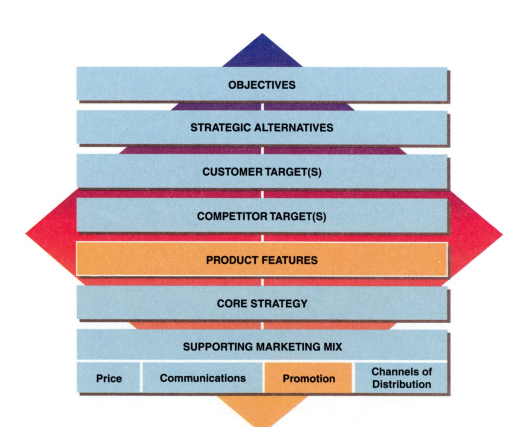

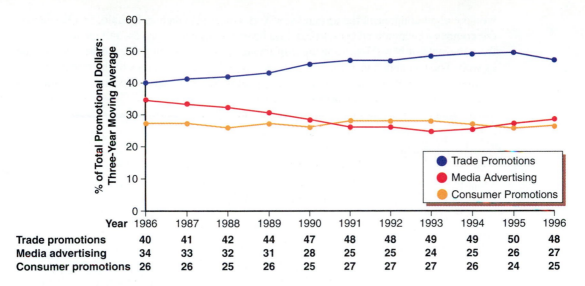

Year	1986	1987	1988	1989	1990	1991	1992	1993	1994	1995	1996
Trade promotions	40	41	42	44	47	48	48	49	49	50	48
Media advertising	34	33	32	31	28	25	25	24	25	26	27
Consumer promotions	26	26	25	26	25	27	27	27	26	24	25

Figure 12–3

Promotional and Advertising Spending for Groceries, 1986–1996

Source: Cox Direct (1997), *19th Annual Survey of Promotional Practices* (Largo, FL: Cox Direct).

of dollars for short-term promotions, including a 50% discount to any customer that dumped IBM, Oracle, Sybase, or Informix and 4 months of the services of one of its database experts.[4]

Even though there is heavy spending on sales promotions for both consumer and business-to-business products and services, there is considerable debate about their effectiveness and efficiency. For example, Proctor & Gamble is attempting to reduce its use of coupons because of their inefficiency (only 2% are redeemed) and costs of printing, distribution, and processing. Similarly, H.J. Heinz is attempting to reduce its dependence on price-focused communication activities (e.g., trade-oriented promotion) and make greater investments in advertising. Many companies complain about the problems of sales promotion but find it difficult to stop using it because customers have become used to the incentives. For example, when Proctor & Gamble announced in January 1996 that, as a test, it

Table 12–1 Business-to-Business Category Spending, 1995

	$ Billion	%
Sales force management*	11.9	22.9
Advertising	11.3	21.9
Direct marketing	6.3	12.3
Sales promotions	6.3	12.2
Trade shows	5.5	10.7
Public relations	2.6	5.1
Market research	2.5	4.7
Other	2.0	3.9
Premiums/Incentives	1.9	3.7
Online	1.4	2.6
Total	51.7	100.0

*Excludes compensation and commissions

Source: OutFront Marketing Study, *Business Marketing*, June 1996.

would end all coupons in the upstate New York cities of Syracuse, Buffalo, and Rochester, the company encountered boycotts, public hearings, signature drives, and an antitrust suit from the state of New York accusing it of trying to get other companies to stop couponing as well. The test ended in April 1997.[5] In addition, long-term studies of the effects of promotions show that consumers become more sensitive to price and promotions and less responsive to brand-building activities such as advertising.[6]

TYPES OF SALES PROMOTION

Table 12–2 provides a list of specific retailer, channel, and consumer promotions.[7] Figure 12–4 provides two examples of typical consumer promotions. The I Can't Believe It's Not Butter promotion offers the consumer a free scented candle with two proofs of purchase. In the other promotion, Reynolds is offering to make a donation to a well-known charity. Table 12–3 shows the kinds of consumer promotional events run in the major appliance industry. As can be seen, nearly all of the events are price oriented. Figure 12–5 shows a web site offering printable coupons for a large grocery chain, Price Chopper, as well as an offer for the chain's loyalty card giving consumers opportunities for discounts. These promotions are described in further detail here.

Table 12–2 Types of Promotions

Consumer Promotions	Trade Promotions	Retail promotions

I. Product based
  A. Additional volume or bonus pack
  B. Samples
    1. Central location (e.g., supermarkets)
    2. Direct (e.g., mail)
    3. Attachment (in- or on-pack)
    4. Media placed (clip-and-send coupons)
 	
II. Price based
  A. Sales price
  B. Coupons
    1. Central location (e.g., in-store)
    2. Direct (mail)
    3. Attachment (in- or on-pack)
    4. In media
  C. Refunds and rebates
  D. Financing terms
  E. Frequent users
 	
III. Premiums
 	
IV. Place-based promotions (displays)
 	
V. Games and sweepstakes
	I. Product based
	  A. Free goods
	  B. Consignment and return policy
	
	II. Price based
	  A. Buying allowances
	  B. Financial terms
	
	III. Place based
	  A. Slotting allowances
	  B. Display allowances
	  C. Warehousing and delivery assistance
	
	IV. Advertising and promotion based
	  A. Co-op advertising
	  B. Selling aids
	  C. Co-op selling
	
	V. Sales based
	  A. Bonuses and incentives
	  B. Contests and prizes
		I. Price cuts
		II. Displays
		III. Feature advertising
		IV. Free goods
		V. Retailer coupons
		VI. Contests and premiums

Consumer Promotions

Consumer promotions are used heavily by the packaged goods industry. Table 12–4 shows the results of a survey done to estimate the sales promotions used most often by these companies and how they changed between 1992 and 1996.

Price-Oriented Promotions

The dominant form of **price-oriented promotion** is **couponing.** In 1995, companies spent $8 billion distributing 292 billion coupons in the United States. Unfortunately, only 5.8 billion were redeemed. However, their use is widespread because nearly 90% of all U.S. households report using a grocery or some other coupon targeted toward supermarket products.[8] In addition, as Table 12–4 shows, 100% of the companies making items sold in supermarkets used coupons in 1996. Coupons are delivered to households by mail, in newspapers and magazines, in the stores at the point of purchase, at the checkout counter, and even electronically via the Internet.

With their high cost and a 2% redemption rate, why do marketers use coupons so heavily? There are two main reasons. First, coupons are a very effective way to target discounts and other incentives to particular households. Depending on how they are delivered, coupons permit marketing managers to price discriminate, that is, charge different prices to different households. For example, by combining a computer database of purchase histories with a direct mail program, marketers can target price-sensitive households. As any basic textbook in microeconomics shows, if consumer segments differ in price sensitivity, profits are

Table 12–3 Typical Promotional Events Held in the Major Appliance Industry

Brand	Program	Products	Dates
Admiral	Buy & Try promotion offers 40-day money-back guarantee with appliance purchases.	Selected washers, dryers, refrigerators, and ranges.	Through December.
Frigidaire	Frigidaire Savings Spectacular offers consumer rebates of up to $100 with selected purchases. Also, Vacation Sweepstakes offers 4-day/3-night vacation getaways to a choice of 80 resorts with purchases.	Savings Spectacular Selected Frigidaire and Frigidaire Gallery appliances. Sweepstakes Precision Wash dishwashers.	Savings Spectacular: October 13–November 9. Sweepstakes: Through December 31.
General Electric	Bring your Kitchen To Life promo offers consumer rebates of $20 to $100 with selected purchases. Also, free icemakers and water pitchers with purchases of selected refrigerators. GECAF offers no payments, no finance charges until April 1997 on appliance purchases.	Bring Your Kitchen To Life selected ranges, washers, dryers, microwave ovens, and dishwashers. Free icemakers/water pitchers. 12 refrigerators. Finance offer. Selected GE and GE Profile appliances.	Through December 1.
Kitchenaid	Cash-back offers with laundry appliance purchases, also, 6-month zero-percent financing on selected purchases.	Cash back. Selected laundry appliances. Finance offer. Selected dishwashers and compactors.	Cash-Back: November 24–December 28. Finance offer: November 3–December 14.
Maytag	Free icemakers offered with purchases of two refrigerator models. Also, consumer rebates of $20–100 on selected appliances.	Free icemaker. Refrigerator models RTD1900 and RTD2100. Rebate Selected dishwashers and refrigerators.	Free icemaker: Through December 15. Rebate: Through September 30.
Whirlpool	Consumer rebates of $20–$30 with appliance purchases. Also, 6-month zero-percent financing with purchases of selected cooking appliances.	Selected washers, dryers, and dishwashers. Finance offer. Selected freestanding gas and electric ranges and over-the-range microwave ovens.	Rebates: November 24–December 28. Finance offer: November 3–November 14.

Source: *Twice* (1996), October 7, p. 23.

maximized by charging high (regular retail) prices to price-insensitive customers and lower prices to price-sensitive customers. Second, coupons are very flexible in that they can achieve different kinds of goals. Some are simply discounts off regular price. Some discounts apply to larger sizes than the consumer normally buys. Some, such as the I Can't Believe It's Not Butter promotion shown in Fig. 12–4, encourage multiple-unit purchases with the promise of free gift. The many ways consumers obtain and use coupons are shown in Table 12–5 on page 338.

Table 12–4 Types of Consumer Promotions Used: 5-Year Comparison

Percentage of Respondents in Each Year

	1992	1993	1994	1995	1996
1. Couponing consumer direct	100%	100%	100%	97%	100%
2. Cents-off promotions	77	90	90	84	90
3. Sampling established products	66	78	78	72	90
4. In-store couponing	*	*	88	78	86
5. Sampling new products	73	84	75	72	86
6. Premium offers	69	78	70	56	79
7. Couponing in retailers' ads	65	88	90	84	76
8. Money-back offers and other refunds	88	80	85	66	76
9. Electronic retail promotions	*	*	83	56	72
10. Sweepstakes	61	63	70	63	69
11. Contests	47	51	48	44	52
12. Prepricing	41	51	55	44	48

* Not asked in this survey year.

Source: Cox Direct (1997), *19th Annual Survey of Promotional Practices.*

There are also several drawbacks to coupons. First, because they are so common, there is no way to gain a competitive advantage using a coupon program. In fact, many product categories are characterized by the prisoner's dilemma described in Chapter 7: No competitor will reduce the amount of couponing for fear of a precipitous drop in market share. Second, the response rates are very low, so the expense per redemption is high. Finally, there is considerable potential for fraud, ranging from counterfeiting to misredemption (merchants may intentionally or mistakenly take a coupon for the wrong brand).[9]

Manufacturers run many other price-oriented promotions. These include price, value, or bonus packs, which may offer larger sizes for the same price as a smaller size or two-for-one kinds of promotions in which the products are shrink-wrapped together. Refunds or money-back offers allow customers to get money back with proof of purchase. Automobile and consumer durable manufacturers use these kinds of programs extensively; called rebates in many cases, they offer substantial discounts from the normal retail price. Sometimes, these durable goods companies couch the discount in financing terms such as "no payments for 12 months" or simply lower financing rates. Even financial institutions provide such price-oriented deals to customers through special low-interest loans or reduced customer equity requirements.

Price-oriented promotions are obviously effective ways of motivating customers to buy your brand. However, such promotions may have negative effects on consumer behavior. First, price promotions can dilute brand equity because it is difficult to use advertising or other communications to trumpet the quality of your brand while you are discounting it. Second, product categories with frequent price promotions lead customers to be more price sensitive. For example, 1994 data show that in the ready-to-eat breakfast cereal category, 36% of all purchases were made using coupons and the average price discount from all price-oriented deals was 34%.[10] A third problem is that customers become accustomed to manufacturer deals and time their purchases to coincide with them. The astute car buyer knows that it is only a matter of time before almost any manufacturer starts to offer incentives; instead of buying now, why not wait? After a 2.8% decline in sales in the first quarter of 1998, cash rebates, low-interest financing, and cut-rate lease programs caused sales in the U.S. auto market to increase 6.3% in April. However, auto marketing managers witnessed a decline in sales as soon as the rebates and other financial incentives were dropped.[11]

Figure 12–5

Sample Retailer
Promotion

Price Chopper Supermarkets,
Schenectady, New York

**Figure 12–5
continued**

Sign Up For Your AdvantEdge Card Online...
and you can be eligible for great online features
and in-store frequent shopping awards!

Take AdvantEdge of Us!

*Get automatic savings
at checkout on
hundreds of
weekly offers!*

**The Price Chopper
Advant*Edge* Card.**

savings...

*It's all you need
to get savings and
convenience every
time you shop at
Price Chopper.*

convenience...

When you present your
Advant*Edge* Card to the
cashier, the discounts will
automatically be deducted
from your shopping total.
Just look at the bottom
of your receipt to see
your total
Advant*Edge* & manufacturers'
coupon/offer discounts.

Looking for more information
on the AdvantEdge Card and
our Frequent Shopper Program?

Go To Our...

- AdvantEdge Card
  sign-up
- AdvantEdge Card
  renew / update form

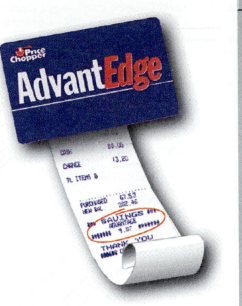

all the savings of coupons without the clipping

That's right.
You can take Advant*Edge* of
Price Chopper by getting
the Price Chopper
Advant*Edge* Card - it's the easy way
to save.
Just present your Price Chopper
AdvantEdge Card
at the checkout and
you'll get great savings on your favorite
national brands, and Price Chopper brand
They're highlighted in our weekly
circular and marked with special signing
in our stores.

see the savings on your register receipts

If you are already an AdvantEdge card customer but need a new card or need to
update the information for your card please click here!

recipes   our brand   good til'   new items   we know meat

Internet zone

Table 12–5 Coupon Distribution and Objectives

Media distributed

Freestanding insert. A leaflet of coupons for various products that can be inserted into a (usually Sunday) newspaper.

Run-of-press (ROP) newspaper. Coupons that appear on the actual pages of newspapers rather than being inserted as a separate page or section. Often these coupons appear in an advertisement for a brand (these are called in-ad coupons).

Sunday supplements. Coupons that appear on the pages of a newspaper Sunday supplement magazine such as *Parade* and *Family Weekly*.

Magazine. Coupons that appear in magazines other than Sunday supplements, such as *Better Housekeeping*. The coupons can be actually on a page, or attached using special tip-in or pop-up cards.

Direct mail

Coupons are mailed directly to consumers using the U.S. Postal Service. One mailing usually includes several coupons from various manufacturers, although much more expensive solo mailings are possible.

Package

On-package. The coupon appears on the outside of the package and can be used for a subsequent purchase.

Instantly redeemable. The coupon is on the outside of the package but can be removed easily and used on the current purchase.

In-package. The coupon is inside the package and can be used for a subsequent purchase.

Cross-ruff. The coupon is for another brand, manufactured wither by the same or a different firm. The coupon itself can be in or on package.

Retailer distributed

Retailer coupons. Coupons distributed by the retailer rather than the manufacturer. The coupons can be distributed by ROP newspaper, included in "Best Food Day" circulars, or handed out in the store.

Coupon-dispensing machines. Manufacturer coupons are distributed by a machine located in the store. The machine displays which coupons are available and the shopper specifies which coupons he or she wants.

Direct Sales Impact	Retail Trade Related	Integrate with Advertising and Other Promotions	Use as a Strategic Tool
Attract new triers	Gain in-store promotional support	Reinforce or enhance print media advertising	Preempt the competition
Attract brand switchers	Increase distribution	Synergize with other marketing instruments	Price discriminate
Increase category consumption	Motivate the sales force		Cushion a price increase
Maintain or enhance repeat purchase rates	More directly control retail price		Reach the appropriate target group
Defend market share			Gain trial for another product

Source: Robert C. Blattberg and Scott A. Neslin (1989), "Sales promotion: the long and the short of it," *Marketing Letters*, 1 (December), pp. 266, 269.

This store features a number of price–oriented promotions, a popular method of motivating shoppers to buy a particular brand. (Paul Almasy/Corbis)

Product-Oriented Promotions

Product-oriented promotions give away the product itself or a closely related product. Giving away the product for free is called **sampling.** Sampling is clearly useful when a new product or brand is being introduced. Free samples are delivered to the home via the mail or delivery, in supermarkets, and on the street. Not only are grocery items sampled, but computer hardware and software companies often give free copies of their products to select customers as beta test sites to help get any bugs out and stimulate early word of mouth.

Sampling has the obvious benefit of stimulating product trial because it gives the customer the opportunity to try the product for free. A survey has shown that sampling is much more effective than coupons, advertising, and games or contests in helping consumers evaluate products.[12] However, it does have some serious shortcomings. First, it is obviously very expensive (however, small trial packs may be sold at cost to afford the company some revenue). Second, a sampling program may not target the right potential customers; people who distribute free samples are not very discriminating about to whom they give the product. This is particularly a problem for tobacco companies because trial packs could be given illegally to teenagers under 18 years old.

A second kind of product-oriented promotion is **premiums.** These might be free merchandise provided with the purchase (e.g., the toy in a Cracker Jack box) or some free or reduced-price item for which the buyer has to send proof-of-purchase, with or without money. Some of these promotions are quite elaborate. The soft drink brand Mountain Dew sponsored a promotion focused on teenagers that offered a pager and free service for 12 months with a certain number of labels from 2-liter bottles. The company then paged the customers with a number they could call for reduced prices on a variety of teen-oriented merchandise sold by other vendors. These kinds of promotional programs are popular but have low response rates and uncertain impact on sales. In addition, in a world increasingly populated by such promotional events, it is becoming more difficult to find unique concepts.

Special Events

Contests and sweepstakes fall into this category of promotions. Every year, Publishers' Clearing House runs a sweepstakes in which the product being sold is magazine subscriptions but

McDonald's provides a premium in each of its Happy Meals for children, typically a small toy related to a newly released movie targeted at this age group. Although it is obviously popular with children, it is unclear whether the promotion has any impact on sales. (Phillip Gould/Corbis)

the main enticement is the opportunity to win a million dollars. Contests involve competition among consumers (for example, the first customer to name a song after hearing a few seconds of it on the radio wins a prize). These activities obviously create excitement and may get some new customers to try your brand. However, the response rate to these promotions is often low and they usually do not attract large numbers of entries. In addition, sweepstakes have a bad image because many consumers are suspicious about the prizes actually being awarded (by law, consumers can obtain a list of the winners) and whether they have a chance to win even if they do not buy the product (by law, they do).

Returning to our Crayola illustration, Binney & Smith ran an award-winning contest in 1997 called True Blue that resulted in a retail sales increase of 7%. The program asked children to locate eight new crayon colors inside specially marked boxes and invited them to nominate their favorite hero by drawing a picture, writing an essay, and dedicating one of the new colors to that hero. Eight winners were selected and offered free trips to the factory. The company received 10,000 entries with only one supporting print advertisement. ◆

Other special promotions are tie-ins to sports events and movies. Corporate sponsorships of tennis and golf tournaments, car races, and other events provide not only communication opportunities but also merchandise giveaways (i.e., sampling). Blockbuster movies are usually accompanied by merchandising involving toys at McDonald's. Such promotions stimulate interest in the movies and sales at the retailer or restaurant.

◆ Illustration: Beiersdorf

It was pointed out in Chapter 8 that any marketing mix elements that involve communication to the customer must be integrated not only with the marketing strategy but also with each other; this is the principle of integrated communications. Customer-oriented promotions must adhere to this principle.

Beiersdorf is a German skin-care product marketer; one of their major brands is Nivea.[13] In July 1995, the company launched a brand extension, Nivea Vital, in Germany and five surrounding countries. The brand was targeted toward women over the age of 50, a segment that had been ignored by cosmetics marketers in Europe. The launch included print and TV advertising featuring a model with gray hair and wrinkles, an unusual campaign that gained a considerable amount of public media attention (few campaigns, especially for cosmetics, use older models). The advertising program was supplemented with a direct mail campaign that included sending 55,000 women small packages showing pictures of the ads and containing samples, an explanation of the product and a survey. Within 15 months of the launch, Nivea Vital had 4.5% share of the $700-million German facial care market, significantly greater than Proctor & Gamble's Oil of Olay Vital and L'Oreal's Plenitude Revitalift. In addition, the brand did not divert any sales from the flagship Nivea brand, which is targeted to young women.   ◆

Trade Promotions

Like customer-oriented promotions, **trade promotions,** or incentives offered to the members of the channel system, can also be divided into groups based on their characteristics.

Product-based promotions include free goods and generous return policies. Return policies allow the channel to return unsold merchandise for a full or partial refund, reducing the risk of carrying the product.

Price deals include various volume discounts and allowances, as well as financing terms such as a long period of time before payment is due or below-market interest rates. The most commonly used trade promotions are off-invoice allowances. The purpose of an off-invoice allowance is to give the channel member a discount on orders for a fixed period of time. Sometimes, there is a performance requirement in which the channel member must sell a certain amount of the product during the promotion. Another variant of the allowance form of promotion is count-recount, which provides an allowance based on sales and is therefore given after the promotion period rather than before.

Place-based allowances are especially important for consumer packaged goods. Slotting allowances, which are payments to store chains for placing a product on a shelf, have become increasingly important as power has shifted from manufacturers to retailers. These fees, charged to manufacturers, have reduced the number of competitors in many product categories and have been particularly hard on small companies, for which the fees can become prohibitive. Display allowances compensate retailers for prominent display of goods. Often, the money a company spends to help the channel members sell their products is called market development funding.

Other promotions involve reducing inventory and transportation costs by warehousing the goods for the channel (as in just-in-time inventory) or paying all or part of delivery charges.

Providing selling assistance is also common. In addition to selling aids (such as brochures), companies often provide cooperative advertising money to retailers. In this arrangement, the company and the retailer share the expense of the retailer advertising the company's products in the local market. The retailer sends the company tear sheets of the print ads or the tapes of TV and radio ads to prove that the advertising was actually run, and the company reimburses the retailer for a percentage of the expense. Based on 1993 data, the most common arrangement is a 50–50 sharing and the second most common is the company paying 100% of the local expense; these two arrangements account for about 95% of all co-op contracts.[14] Manufacturers can also provide cooperative selling, in which their sales forces back up or refer leads to the channel's sales force.

Companies also offer a substantial amount of merchandising help to retailers to display and promote their products. An excellent example of a very effective sales tool is the egg-shaped display for L'Eggs hosiery. A more current example is the efforts by Zenith to help sell digital video disc (DVD) players put on the market in late 1996. Zenith arranged a countertop merchandising display stocked with two copies of six DVD movies at cost ($199) to demonstrate the video quality of the machines.

Finally, there are sales-based incentives, such as bonuses to the channel for meeting or exceeding a quota. Sales incentives can also take the more controversial (and in some cases, forbidden) form of direct prizes or bonuses (sometimes called "spiffs") to the channel's sales force.

Of all of the trade promotions mentioned, price-based ones carry the most risk to the company. In some cases, a company running a price-based promotion gives an incentive to the retailer to carry the product but also would like the retailer to pass some or all of the savings along to the end customer (the amount a retailer passes along to the customer is called the pass-through). By law, the company cannot force the retailer to do this. Therefore, in many instances price-oriented promotions simply result in the retailer or distributor "forward buying," or stocking up on the product at a discount while the promotion is running and then selling the inventory at the regular price. The company gains sales at the time the promotion is run, but this bump in the sales curve is temporary because the channel must sell the inventory eventually, resulting in lower sales by the company later. Only if the promotion has long-term effects (i.e., if a customer switches because of the promotion and continues to buy the brand) will the company be better off.

Retailer Promotions

Through **retailer promotions,** retailers often provide direct incentive to customers to buy. Most of these are simply the retail version of either the customer or channel promotions described previously. For example, a retailer can provide its own coupons or price reductions (see Fig. 12–5). In addition, retailers have embraced loyalty or continuity programs designed to get customers to be store loyal. In Fig. 12–5, some of the price reductions are available only to holders of the Price Chopper AdvantEdge Card. The customer's card is scanned in after the groceries have been scanned and the customer receives the discounts (in addition to any coupon discounts) on the spot.

Another form of retailer promotion is the special display. There are four general types of displays. End-of-aisle displays, or endcaps, are very popular and may feature an accompanying price cut. Displays in the front of the store are seen as the customer enters. Some displays are in the store aisles themselves. A fourth kind is a shelf "talker," a sign hanging on the shelf with information, usually about a special price. These special displays and other company-paid advertisements inside the store (e.g., announcements for contests and sweepstakes, information about recipes, etc.) are called **point-of-purchase** (POP) **advertising.**

Like the price-oriented promotions run by companies, retailer promotions can be effective in getting customers to increase their purchase quantities, switch brands, and change their purchase timing. Of course, retailers are focused more on their own stores than on the company's brands; company-distributed coupons can be redeemed at any retailer. However, these promotions have the same drawbacks as any price promotion. Although volume is generally increased, brand names can be diluted, brand loyalty eroded, and price sensitivity increased.

PROMOTION STRATEGY, OBJECTIVES, AND EVALUATION

Customer-Oriented Promotions

Strategic Issues

Because of the short-run nature of customer-oriented promotions and some of their problems (particularly those of price promotions), it may not be in a company's best interest to engage in heavy customer promotion spending. When a new product is being launched, customer-oriented promotions are critical to creating awareness and gaining customer trial, and are thus very valuable. Promotions for existing products have been found to have a large impact on sales and other objectives, but most evidence shows that these effects are temporary and are lost when a competitor retaliates with an in-kind promotion.

The promotion dilemma is similar to the prisoner's dilemma discussed in Chapter 7. If category sales are fixed—that is, if marketing expenditures do not increase primary demand and, in the short run, dropping expenditures does not cause demand to decrease to the benefit of other product categories—and marketing managers are interested in profits and margins rather than market share, all companies are obviously better off at a low level of expenditure. Short of collusion (which is illegal in the United States), however, cooperation is risky. As a result, because each participant is wary of losing market share, category promotional expenditures remain high. As a result, you should approach the use of price promotions with caution and an understanding of the costs as well as the benefits.

Objectives

As we noted earlier, promotion typically takes the short-run view. Even when the marketing manager has longer-term interests such as a sustained increase in market share, the operational objective of most promotions is to generate an immediate increase in sales. Recall the typical advertising objectives given in Fig. 8–9. These are based on hierarchy-of-effects models that postulate an increase in customer interest from awareness to interest to preference to purchase. Promotion can be directed toward any of these goals. However, Table 12–6 shows some goals that are particularly relevant for promotion.

For example, if awareness is a problem, a company can run a promotion such as a game or sweepstakes designed to increase awareness of a product rather than to increase immediate sales. Similarly, a company can run a tie-in promotion (for example, with a movie) that may improve brand image in addition to raising current sales. However, such relationship-building motives account for only a small percentage of promotion money spent.

By far the most common objective of a consumer promotion is a short-run transactional goal. The objective is usually stated in specific terms, such as "to increase sales 20% in the March–April time period." This statement should be qualified in two ways. First, you need to specify from what level sales should increase. Second, you must select the target customer. You can focus on getting current customers to buy more volume (expanding the market through a market penetration strategy), capturing occasional but not loyal customers (improving customer retention), or generating sales from current non-customers (market penetration

Table 12–6 Customer Promotion Objectives

I. Short-run (transactional)
   A. Current customers
      1. Buy more
      2. Be more loyal
      3. Buy now
   B. Occasional customers (brand switchers)
      1. Capture next purchase
   C. Non-customers
      1. Trial

II. Long-run (relationship building)
   A. Awareness enhancement
   B. Image enhancement

if customers are diverted from the competition or market development if they are new customers to the category). Many promotions focus on current customers, attempting to get them to buy more through a volume discount, to be more loyal (using coupons or frequent user programs), or to accelerate their purchases and buy soon (rebate-type promotions).

 Returning to the Crayola illustration, Binney & Smith wanted to increase sales of the 64-unit box. This turned into an objective for the True Blue contest. The contest included both the 96-count and 64-count boxes, whereas the 96-count boxes had received most of the promotional attention in previous years. In addition, the contest targeted consumers who were already familiar with the Crayola brand. ◆

Attracting occasional customers, typically through temporary price cuts such as coupons and rebates, is effective but also expensive. This expense not only produces lower margins on the sales to occasional customers, but may also lower margins on sales that would have been made in the absence of the promotion to occasional or regular customers. As a result, a major concern is how to target promotions to competitors' customers alone.[15] Promotions to noncustomers are generally used when a product is new (or "new and improved") or when there is a need to induce brand switching, as when the brand of interest has low market share. Promotions can be effective devices for generating such trial behavior. In a sense, targeting noncustomers implies a long-run relationship-building objective, not the usual short-term objective. However, most marketing managers will accept a short-term gain in switching and hope that product satisfaction leads to more purchases down the road.

Evaluating Customer Promotions

The most appropriate way to evaluate promotions is to develop measures consistent with the objectives that they are supposed to attain. A price promotion that increases sales 30% but fails to attract a substantial number of new customers may be a failure because it mainly rewarded existing customers when the goal was to obtain new ones.

The easiest approach to evaluating customer promotions is to look at the incremental results of the variable that has been set as the promotion's goal. This method provides a useful starting point, but may lead to an overestimate of the benefit of promotion because it ignores both where the sales come from and the long-run benefit of promotion.

A standard approach to measuring the impact of a sales promotion is tracking the before-and-after results. Assuming a sales objective for the promotion, Fig. 12–6 shows a typical tracking study, with point A on the horizontal axis representing the time when the promotion (e.g., a coupon drop) is given to end customers. Tracking studies such as these are common because the effects of a sales promotion often show up quickly.

Unfortunately, marketing managers tend to look at the shaded area above point A in Fig. 12–6 as the only measure of the impact of the promotion. This kind of simplistic analysis has several problems:

- The gain could be offset by the dip at point B, representing the possibility that consumers have merely increased their home inventories and will not need to buy again soon.
- The gain must be compared to a base amount: the amount of sales that would have been generated had the promotion not run. This baseline is difficult to calculate because it can change depending on time of year, competitive conditions, and other factors.
- The analysis does not account for other factors in the marketplace such as advertising and other promotions run simultaneously, sponsored by both the product in question and the competition.

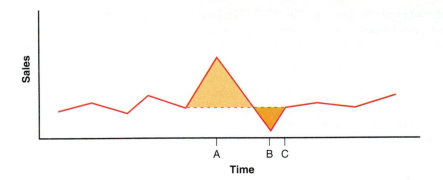

Figure 12–6

Evaluating Sales
Promotions: Tracking
Studies

Thus, although promotions are easier to analyze than advertising, there are still complicating factors.

Sales increases from customer-oriented promotions may reflect accelerated purchases by loyal buyers (who would have bought the brand anyway) rather than new sales volume from brand switchers. One approach to evaluating coupon promotions, for example, looks at purchase acceleration and brand switching as well as the impact of consumer promotions on regular purchasing.[16] A coupon can have several incremental impacts in the period in which the program is launched:

- Accelerated regular purchases: Regular buyers of the brand simply buy sooner.
- Accelerated captured purchases: Purchasers who would not have bought at the time or bought the promoted brand are persuaded to do both by the promotion.
- Unaccelerated regular purchases: Regular buyers use the coupon as a "bonus" price cut.
- Unaccelerated captured purchases: Purchasers of other brands switch to the promoted brand because of the promotion.

Obviously, accelerated and unaccelerated captured purchases are pluses for the marketing manager because they are new business. However, for unaccelerated regular purchases, the amount of the coupon (plus redemption costs) comes out of revenues. Accelerated regular purchases are potentially but not necessarily negative; if subsequent sales are depressed as a result of increased inventory, there is no benefit except for a slight time value of money advantage. If most of the purchases fall in this category, it would explain the postpromotion dip found in Fig. 12–6. One possible benefit of promotion is that captured buyers will remain loyal and purchase the promoted brand again later. It is also possible that purchase quantity could increase if the coupon was focused on larger package sizes. In any event, the point is that in evaluating such a program's effectiveness, it is necessary to estimate both the overall magnitude of the impact (i.e., sales) and the source of the additional sales.

Trade Promotion

Strategic Issues

As we noted in Fig. 12–3, trade promotion is the largest part of the advertising/promotion budget; most firms feel that such promotion expense is simply a cost of doing business. However, given its high cost, it is useful to approach trade promotion from a strategic perspective, with some ideas about when it may or may not be useful.

Such a framework is shown in Fig. 12–7. The two axes of the figure are the holding costs to the channel member (that is, how much it costs the channel member to hold inventory) and the promotional elasticity of the end customers. When holding costs and price elasticity are high, the manager should use trade deals. This is because the channel member will not want to keep a large inventory and the deal gives the member an incentive to stock the product. Given the price elasticity, the channel member will pass the savings on to customers to help clear the inventory. Paper products, soft drinks, and personal computers fit this cell. The lower-right-hand cell is straightforward: There is no incentive to trade deal when the channel member will simply forward buy to build inventory at a low cost and the customers are not interested in price promotions, so there will be no passthrough of the savings. An example of this kind of product is laxatives. Products with high holding costs and low price elasticities also should not have much trade promotion. It is clear that neither the channel member nor the company has an incentive in this cell. Produce items such as cheese and lettuce and bakery items fit this cell. With low holding costs and high elasticities, the channel will want deals for forward buying; there is also more likely to be passthrough of the deal because price elasticity is high. In addition, even if the company does not want to use trade deals in this situation, competition will probably force it anyway. This describes canned tuna and many other supermarket items that are not bulky and have low economic value.

Objectives

Common goals for trade promotions are shown in Table 12–7. Perhaps the most important trade promotions are those that motivate the channel member to market your product through advertising, selling, or display. By taking the channel member's perspective (see Chapter 9), you can see that the channel member will be more proactive in marketing the products or companies that are giving more incentives for doing so. Recall that both push and pull activities are necessary for a successful channel system. Promotional incentives are also given to the retailer's sales force; a recommendation by such a salesperson often affects a customer's purchase decision if the customer does not have a brand name in mind when entering the store. Some retail promotions are intended to load the retailer or channel member with inventory. This makes out-of-stocks less likely, gives the channel member an incen-

Figure 12–7

Strategies for Trade Dealing

Source: Robert C. Blattberg and Scott A. Neslin (1990), *Sales Promotion* (Englewood Cliffs, NJ: Prentice Hall).

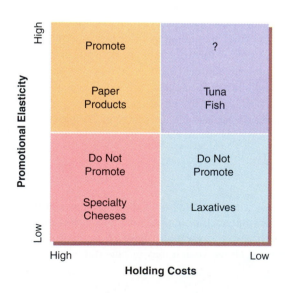

Table 12–7 Objectives of Trade Deals

Induce retailers to offer a price discount.

Induce retailers to display the brand.

Induce retailers to advertise the brand.

Offer incentives for the retailer's or dealer's sales force to push the brand to the customer.

Gain or maintain distribution for a model or item within the product line.

Gain or maintain distribution for the brand.

Load the retailer, dealer, or distributor with inventory to avoid out-of-stocks.

Shift inventory from the manufacturer to the channels of distribution and the consumer.

Avoid price reductions.

Defend the brand against competitors.

Induce price fluctuations into the market.

Finance retailer inventories.

Source: Robert C. Blattberg and Scott A. Neslin (1989), "Sales promotion: the long and the short of it," *Marketing Letters*, 1 (December), p. 314.

tive to push the product further down the channel system, may account for seasonal surges in demand, and reduces the manufacturer's holding costs.

A particularly important use of retail-oriented promotions is to gain or maintain distribution. When a new brand is introduced or when the product category is new, gaining distribution is critical to giving customers access to the product. When a product category is in the decline stage of the life cycle or when a brand's sales are declining, the channel member will begin to consider replacing it with a product that provides greater profit. In order to maintain the profit level of the product to the channel member and keep the product on the shelves, the marketing manager often uses price-oriented promotions to compensate for the decline in sales.

Evaluation

One approach to evaluating trade promotions is tracking before-and-after results. In this case, the baseline sales level is defined as the volume that would have been sold to the channel member in the absence of the promotion. Although it is subject to most of the same limitations of the analysis of customer promotions, one advantage in this context is that few other marketing mix elements target the channel members, so it is not necessary to separate the effects of different programs. For example, advertising normally targets end customers, not channel members.[17]

An important criterion for evaluating trade promotions is how often a retail promotion is run when the channel members receive some kind of deal. The company's sales force must convince retailers not to load up in inventory and pocket the discount, but to pass it along to end customers. Majers, a subsidiary of A.C. Nielsen, has a service that helps companies track passthrough from trade deals. Majers records all retail promotions in a geographic market for different consumer product categories. Reports indicating the company's share of promotion by retailer and for the total market are generated and used by the sales force to gain cooperation from retailers. These reports evaluate the performance of both the retailers and the sales force as well.

◆ **Illustration: Proctor & Gamble** ──────────────────────────

As a result of the strategy and objectives set by the marketing manager, a promotion plan or schedule for a planning period is developed. A template for such a plan is shown in Table 12–8. It is based on a new product introduction by Proctor & Gamble and it shows the range and number of kinds of promotions typically considered by a large packaged-goods company.[18] The consumer and trade promotion options for introducing the brand include the following:

- Trade allowances: The sales force advised the brand manager that a $2.70/case trade allowance on all sizes in the first 3 months was necessary to stimulate initial stocking, in-store displays, and newspaper feature advertising by the channels.
- Sampling: P&G considered sampling, particularly through the mail, to be the most effective trial-inducing promotion device.
- Couponing: The brand manager could mail them directly to the target audience, deliver them through a co-op program mailed with other product coupons, place them as freestanding newspaper inserts (FSIs), put them in magazine print ads, or offer them through Best Food Day (BFD) editions of local newspapers.
- Special pack promotions: Four options considered were trial-size packs (small containers the consumer bought at deep discounts), prepriced packs (trial-size packs of the smallest container), price packs (discounts offered in special displays), and bonus packs (extra detergent for a smaller-package price).
- Refunds: The brand manager could develop a program whereby consumers received money back for multiple purchases.
- Premiums: On or in pack (on or in the package), near-pack (displayed on a shelf near the product), free-in-mail (merchandise offered with proofs-of-purchase), and self-liquidators (consumers send in money for a premium, which covers the costs of the promotion).[19]
- Sweepstakes/contests.

In addition to the particular promotions that would be run, the brand manager has to be concerned with the timing of the promotions over the introductory year. The sales promotion plan template shown in Table 12–8 can be used to schedule the different promotions in the appropriate months and track their costs.   ◆

Retail Promotion

Because they are intended for end customers for the most part, retail promotions have the same strategic aspects, objectives, and measurement approaches as other end-customer promotions discussed earlier in this chapter. However, the focus of retail promotions is on the retail store or chain rather than a specific brand.

One unique feature of retail promotions is the impact they can have on purchasing decisions right in the store. The Point-of-Purchase Advertising Institute (POPAI) periodically studies the in-store habits of customers in mass merchandise stores and supermarkets. Their 1995 study found that 70% of supermarket shoppers and 74% of mass retailer shoppers chose purchases in the store, in what are often called impulse purchases. The categories most sensitive to POP advertising and displays are film/photofinishing, socks and underwear, dishwashing soaps, and cookies and crackers.[20]

A particularly interesting aspect of retail promotions is how they can interact with each other and with consumer promotions to create larger effects than each one would on its own. An example of such interactions between retail promotions is shown in Table 12–9. In this case, the retailer manipulates five retail promotions: a short-term price cut or discount, a special in-store display, a major newspaper ad for the brand, a smaller line ad and a display, and a major ad with a display. As can be seen, the base case is no price cut and no promotional activity for the brand (referred to in the table as merchandising). The sales performance of the brand in this base case is set to an index of 100. Across the top row of Table 12–9, the significant impact of increasingly larger price cuts by themselves (that is, with no accompanying nonprice promotions) can be found. The figure shows that, for this brand, offering a 10% discount increases sales 77% over the base case. Down the first column (no discounts), the impact of the separate merchandising policies and two pairs can also be seen. A special display with no price cut increases sales by only 13%, whereas a major ad increases sales by 85%. The inner figures of the table show the interaction effects between price cuts and merchandising. Whereas a major ad increases sales by 85% over the base case and a 10% price cut increases sales 77% when they are run separately, when both are in force together the increase in sales is a whopping 227%.[21]

PROMOTION BUDGETING

Setting a budget for sales promotion generally follows the same approaches discussed for setting advertising budgets (see Chapter 8). Again, the major distinction is between analytical methods (e.g., objective and task, optimization) and convenient guidelines (e.g., percentage of sales, competitive parity). However, two questions must be considered: How much money should be spent on the total advertising and promotion budget? Of this amount, how much should be spent on promotion?

Advertising and Promotion Budget

Seven conditions have been found to affect the total budget for advertising and sales promotion for manufactured products.[22] Companies spend more on advertising and promotion relative to sales under the following conditions:

- The product is standardized (as opposed to being produced or supplied to order).
- There are many end users.
- The typical purchase amount is small.
- Sales are made through channel intermediaries rather than directly to end users.
- The product is premium priced.
- The product line has a high contribution margin.
- The product or service has a small market share.

Note that the first four conditions are typical of consumer products and services; this is consistent with the fact that the marketing managers for these products spend much more money on sales promotion than do their counterparts managing business-to-business products and services.

Allocating Money between Advertising and Promotion

The second important question is how to allocate money between advertising and sales promotion. In organizations in which the overall marketing budget is set, rather than specific amounts for advertising or promotion (or other expenditures), this may be the most important question.

Table 12–8 Sales Promotion Plan

Event	Timing												Number of Average Weeks Volume	Cost
	Jan.	Feb.	March	April	May	June	July	Aug.	Sept.	Oct.	Nov.	Dec.		
Stocking allowance														
$/Physical case														
Trade allowance														
$/Statistical case														
Sampling														
6 oz.														
3 oz.														
1.5 oz.														
2 × 0.75 oz.														
Couponing														
Mail														
Single														
Co-op														
Extended														
FSI														
Single														
Full page co-op														
2/5 page co-op														
BFD														
Magazine														
Special pack														
Price pack														
Bonus pack														
Trial size														
Refund														
Print														
Point of sale														
Direct mail														
In- or on-pack														
Own brand														
Other brand														
Premium														
On- or in-pack														
Near-pack														
Free-in-mail														
Self-liquidator														
Partial liquidator														
Group promotion														

Source: John A. Quelch (1983), "Proctor & Gamble (B)," Harvard Business School case #9-584-048, p. 24.

Table 12–9 Sales Effect of Deal Discount, Feature Advertising, and Displays

	Discount			
	0%	**10%**	**20%**	**30%**
No merchandising	100	177	313	555
Display	113	201	356	631
Major ad	185	327	580	1028
Display and line ad	254	451	799	1414
Display and major ad	309	548	971	1719

100 = Base sales when no promotions occur.

Source: Robert C. Blattberg and Scott A. Neslin (1989), "Sales promotion: the long and the short of it," *Marketing Letters*, 1 (December), p. 83.

Several factors affect this allocation decision. First, the total amount of resources available has a major impact. If the marketing budget is small, major media advertising is usually not worthwhile unless the target market is local and can be reached by media such as radio and newspapers, because advertising usually needs to meet a minimum or threshold amount to have any impact at all. Beneath the threshold value, the money is wasted. In such cases, spending the money on sales promotion results in a greater market impact than advertising.

Second, customer factors affect allocation decisions. Knowing the behavior of customers can help you determine whether advertising or promotion makes more sense. One relevant aspect of customer behavior is the degree of brand loyalty. As noted earlier in this chapter, promotion money spent on a product or service exhibiting high levels of loyalty rewards primarily existing customers. Although this may be what the marketing manager wants to do, it is usually not the best way to spend the money. If customers are not very loyal, the marketing manager should try to understand whether their behavior is typical of the category; if so, there may be an opportunity to attract brand switchers with promotions. However, it is also possible that the product manager has created nonloyal customers through frequent price-based promotions, and thus all that happens is a temporary swapping of customers.

A second relevant aspect of consumer behavior is the type of decision required of them. If the product is complex and therefore requires a fair amount of information processing, more money should be spent on advertising because it is a better communication device. Alternatively, most sales promotion money is spent on product categories in which decision making is routine and involves little processing of information about the product.

The third factor affecting allocation decisions is whether advertising and promotion dollars highlight the unique aspects of the product, called **consumer franchise building (CFB).**[23] CFB activities are those that build brand equity, including advertising, sampling, couponing, and product demonstrations. Non-CFB activities focus on price alone and include trade promotions, short-term price deals, and refunds. In this approach, the marketing manager must track the following ratio:

$$\text{CFB ratio} = \text{CFB\$}/(\text{CFB\$} + \text{non-CFB\$})$$

The CFB ratio should stay above 50% or 55% for the brand to remain healthy. The concept behind CFB-based budgeting is obvious: Unless the marketing manager is careful, the funds spent on price-related activities that detract from brand equity and build price sensitivity can dominate the advertising and promotion budget.

SALES PROMOTION AND INFORMATION TECHNOLOGY

In-Store Information Technology

For supermarket and mass merchandiser shoppers, the combination of Universal Product Codes (bar codes) and improvements in information technology has produced a number of ways to deliver promotions directly to shoppers in the store.

The best example is Catalina Marketing Corporation's Marketing Services unit, which produces red-bordered coupons (with UPC codes) right at the cash register after a customer rings up the purchases. These coupons are tied to purchases that have been scanned as part of the customer's order. A company buys time on the coupon delivery system (say, one month) when coupons for its brand are produced and competitors' coupons are not.

For example, suppose you are the marketing manager for the number-two brand of peanut butter. Some steps you might follow to increase share are the following:

1. For a 12-week period, every scanned purchase of the number-one brand produces a high-value (say, $1) coupon for your brand.
2. When the $1 coupon for your brand is redeemed (scanned), a repeat purchase coupon for a slightly lower value (say, $.75) is issued. This helps to build continuity or repeat purchase.
3. Simultaneously, a medium-value coupon (say, $.50) is issued whenever a complementary product (for example, grape jelly) is purchased.
4. A six-month Checkout Direct program is then launched in which customers who use an ATM or check are tracked for their purchase frequency of peanut butter. Customers who purchase peanut butter every 6 weeks are given a coupon after shopping in the fifth week between purchases (i.e., the week before their forecasted regular purchase).

Using the Internet

There has been a proliferation of special deals offered through the Web. Typing in the keyword *coupon* at the Yahoo! search site produces over 500 sites where coupons can be obtained. Most of these electronic coupons can be printed on the user's laser or inkjet printer; Fig. 12–8 shows an example from a pizza restaurant.[24] A Web site that offers a number of coupons from different companies is www.coolsavings.com. Registered members can get discounts from companies such as Kids 'R' Us, T.J. Maxx, JC Penney, Kmart, and Northwest Airlines and enter a number of contests and sweepstakes.

An alternative is to run a contest or sweepstakes for Web site visitors. This has been done by a knitted sweater company, Blarney Woolen Mills. Figure 12–9 shows a 1999 sweepstakes co-sponsored by a number of companies with the prize being a trip to Ireland.

Obviously, the effectiveness of these promotions is limited by the number of users with access to the Web sites. Additionally, many of the coupon offers have to be found by the users. For example, to get Safeway supermarket coupons, the user has to visit the Safeway Web site. It would be better to offer the coupons through a linked content site because those sites get more traffic than most of the sites offering the coupons.

Figure 12–8

Electronic Coupon

Courtesy of VALUE
BOOK.com

However, because many sites require the user to register and provide an e-mail address, it is a simple matter to proactively offer special deals by sending messages to the registrant's mailbox.

EXECUTIVE SUMMARY

The main points of this chapter include the following:

- Sales promotion is generally focused on the short-term; promotional devices are the main tools marketing managers use to change customer behavior in the short run.
- There are three kinds of sales promotions: promotions run by companies targeting end customers, promotions run by companies targeting channel members, and promotions run by channel members, usually retailers, targeting end customers.
- Customer-focused promotions are most often price related (e.g., coupons), but may also involve the product (e.g., sampling) and special events (e.g., contests and sweepstakes). Customer promotions are incentives to buy the product, but can also increase purchase volume, induce customers to switch brands or use larger sizes, and achieve other purchase-related goals.
- Trade promotions are intended to give incentives to channel members to stock and promote the product. Like customer promotions, the vast majority are price related. However, some also give marketing assistance (e.g., co-op advertising).
- Retailer promotions involve both price and special displays and other forms of point-of-purchase (POP) advertising.

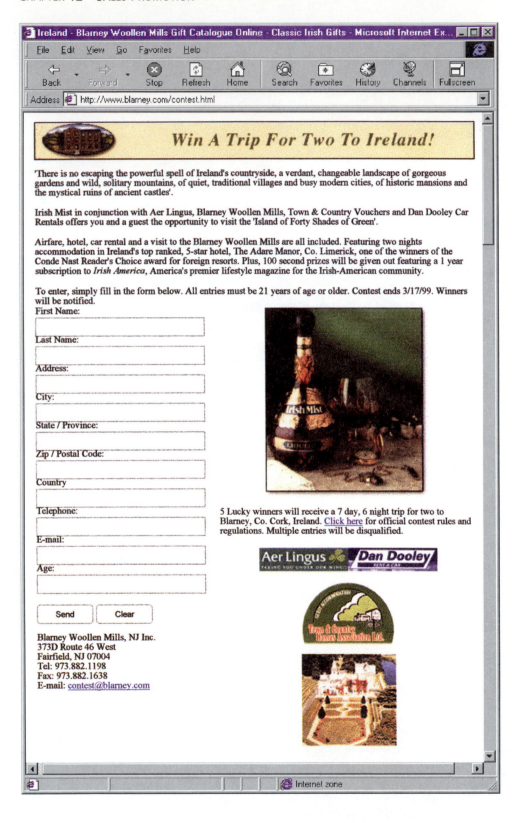

- The most popular way to evaluate the effectiveness of sales promotion is to track the goal of the promotion (e.g., sales volume) and compare the relevant data before and after the promotion is run. This approach does not control for other marketing factors that affect the data and can be confounded if multiple promotions are being run simultaneously.
- Increasing numbers of promotions are being run on the Web and delivered using information systems (e.g., point-of-purchase systems coordinated with bar-coded, scanned purchases).

CHAPTER QUESTIONS

1. How are advertising and sales promotion similar? Different? Which do you think is a more effective communication tool and why?
2. Are particular kinds of customer-oriented sales promotions more likely to have long-term effects on buying behavior than others?
3. Consider Fig. 12–7 ("Strategies for Trade Dealing"). What other products or services would fit into the four boxes?
4. Summarize the factors that affect the allocation of money between advertising and promotion. Considering the consumer franchise-building approach, when would you want the CFB ratio to be below the 50–55% recommended? When might you want it to be much higher?
5. A number of new in-store coupon delivery systems other than the Catalina system are being developed (e.g., freestanding kiosks). Compared to coupons delivered through the mail or newspapers and magazines, what kind of impact do you expect these coupons to have on consumer behavior other than simply inducing a one-time trial?

Application Exercises: Sales Promotion in the PC Industry

Integrated Case

1. Visit local computer retailers and talk to the salespeople, examine displays, and scan the rest of the retail environment. Make a note of any POP advertising and promotion for PC brands. Note which brands or models are sold through the retail channel.
2. Given the information you have accumulated in prior exercises, develop a set of objectives for both trade and customer promotion.
3. What kinds of promotions would achieve the objectives set in exercise 2?
4. How much money should a PC manufacturer spend on promotion and advertising (use your advertising data developed in the Chapter 8 exercises to help answer this)?
5. Develop a PC sales promotion plan like the one shown in Table 12–8.
6. Take the perspective of a retailer. What retail promotions would you use to sell more units of a particular brand?

FURTHER READING

The book by Gerard J. Tellis (1997), *Advertising and Sales Promotion Strategy* (Reading, MA: Addison-Wesley), provides supplemental reading for this chapter as for Chapter 8. The academic literature is very large in this area (see the Blattberg/Neslin book cited in the chapter, for example). For a paper on the psychological interpretation of coupons, see Priya Raghubir (1998), "Coupon value: a signal for price?" *Journal of Marketing Research,* 35 (August), pp. 316–324. A paper on an interesting variant of coupons, cross-ruff coupons (coupons on the package for one brand that are for redemption with the purchase of another brand), is Sanjay K. Dhar and Jagmohan S. Raju (1998), "The Effects of Cross-Ruff Coupons on Sales and Profits," *Management Science,* 44 (November), pp. 1501–1516.

Customer Relationship Management

13

CHAPTER BRIEF

The purpose of this chapter is to introduce concepts underlying the development and maintenance of long-term customer relationships. After reading this chapter, the student should understand the following:

The economics of customer loyalty (i.e., why long-term customer relationships are good business)
Measuring customer satisfaction
Developing strong customer service programs
Loyalty or frequency marketing programs
The growing importance of mass customization
Using marketing information systems to develop and maintain customer relationships

In 1997, Oura Oil had 35% of the retail market for gasoline in the Osaka, Japan area, with revenues of $210 million.[1] The company has built its market position by consistently providing a superior level of customer service.

When customers enter an Oura service station, they are constantly attended to by service employees dressed in clean, starched, white uniforms who bow and enthusiastically take care of their needs. These attendants pump the gas, clean the windows, taillights, and headlamps, check the tire pressure, and handle payment promptly and cheerfully. When the customer leaves, the attendant helps him or her enter the stream of traffic.

Although Oura has distinguished itself from its competitors with such service, because of several environmental factors the retail gasoline market in Japan is changing. First, after several years of suffering through a difficult economy, Japanese consumers are more price sensitive and more willing to trade superior service for lower prices. Second, hypermarkets (large discount chains with retail gas operations) have taken some customers from the higher-priced, service-oriented gasoline chains. Finally, in 1997 Japanese law changed to allow self-service pumps. This has lead to further price competition.

Japanese consumers are also changing. More retail gas customers are women because men, the traditional Japanese breadwinners, are using mass transportation. Employers have encouraged the movement to trains, subways, buses, and other forms of transportation in order to reduce pollution and road congestion. Though not directly affecting price sensitivity, this shift in the purchaser of gas changes the target for the marketing strategy.

Senior management in the company thinks that it should maintain its high level of service in the face of increasing price competition. Even if they introduce the new self-service pumps,

In today's competitive environment, long-term customer relationships are critical to business success. Some companies have been able to build their market positions by consistently providing superior customer service. At Oura Oil in Japan, service employees bow, serve customers with enthusiasm, and help them enter the stream of traffic when exiting. (Michael S. Yamashita/Corbis)

Oura cannot match the one-stop shopping for the large number of consumer goods that hypermarkets offer. Thus, a higher level of service is Oura's value proposition to the customer.

How can Oura continue to build its business in the face of such competition? How can the company compensate for its higher prices other than through service if the price-insensitive segment of the market and its traditional male target segment are shrinking?

Many companies are facing this problem today. Providers of frequently purchased products and services such as retail gasoline as well as less frequently purchased durable and industrial goods have attempted to build higher levels of customer satisfaction through the development of better relationships. These relationships are intended to increase repeat purchasing rates and therefore increase long-term sales and profits. This chapter discusses how you can create programs to achieve higher customer satisfaction and long-term customer loyalty.

What is the impact of low loyalty and high switching rates between products? The telecommunication industry is an excellent example. Consider the huge expense of getting customers to switch long-distance telephone suppliers in the United States. AT&T and MCI are among the largest users of direct marketing to attract switchers. Often, the switchers are customers who were their own customers in the past. This customer turnover (churn) rate is hurting cellular companies as well. The annual turnover in the U.S. wireless market was 36% in 1997, compared to 24% in 1994. It has been estimated that it costs a cellular company $300–$400 in discounts and marketing expenditures to sign up each subscriber; each percentage point increase in churn costs enough to reduce the total market value of the cellular companies by $150 million.[2]

Different perspectives on the buyer–seller relationship are shown in Fig. 13–1. Panel A of Fig. 13–1 is very much like the sales orientation discussed in Chapter 1. In this situation, the seller figures out a way to make the sale to the buyer, but the relationship between the two is at a distance because the seller has done little to try to understand the buyer's motivations and needs. The salesperson has used his or her creativity or personality to make the sale, not an understanding of the customer.

In panel B, the company selling the product or service has done a better job understanding the customer by getting "into" the buyer, determining enough about his or her needs to make the sale. This is the more traditional marketing concept or customer orientation.

However, neither concept is sufficient in today's globally competitive environment. Both can be characterized by the following:

For the seller, the sale is the end of the process; for the buyer, it's the beginning.[3]

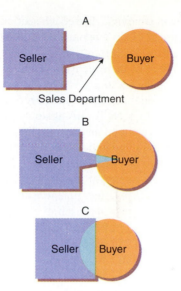

Figure 13–1

The Buyer–Seller Relationship

Source: Theodore Levitt (1986), *The Marketing Imagination* (New York: Free Press), pp. 113–114.

Oura Oil has followed the panel B model by understanding that the customer does not necessarily like stopping for gasoline; Oura has made the experience as pleasant as possible and developed some value-added services (e.g., cleaning the windows). However, the challenge to the company is to make the customer feel that the sale of gasoline at one particular time is not the end of the process but part of an ongoing relationship.

In today's competitive environment, where long-term relationships are critical to marketing and general business success, it takes more than the execution of the marketing concept to satisfy customers over a long period of time. Panel C illustrates the new model of relationship marketing. Here, the buyer and seller have become interdependent. Each party to the relationship depends on the other in some way.

A distinction has been made between different kinds of industrial buyer–seller relationships.[4] This distinction is applicable for all kinds of goods and services. **Transaction buyers** are those who are interested only in the purchase at hand. They may not be interested in a long-term relationship at all, or the sellers in the market may not have done a good job showing the customer the benefits of such a relationship. The former situation exists when a company sees the benefit in sharing the business between a number of suppliers. **Relationship customers** see the benefits of the interdependency shown in panel C of Fig. 13–1.

The previous chapters of this book focused on what might be called customer acquisition, or the ways marketing is normally used to obtain customers. In this chapter, the focus is on customer retention, or how to keep customers over the long term. This is the challenge facing many companies like Oura Oil.

THE ECONOMICS OF LOYALTY

A simple example demonstrates the economic power and importance of loyalty.

Several years ago, a passenger flying on a British Airways (BA) flight from London to San Francisco complained about being seated near the smoking rows in the coach section. Although there is much less in-flight smoking today than in previous years, many readers will identify with this traveler's complaint; being one or two rows from the smoking area on a 10-hour flight is more than annoying. The coach section was full and the dissatisfied customer was (or at least claimed to be) a regular BA customer. A simple solution would have been to move the customer to business class in an unobtrusive way (so other passengers do not get the same idea) because there were unoccupied seats in that section. My guess is that such a move would have gained a strongly loyal customer at a very low marginal cost (for business-class food). However, the BA personnel declined to move the passenger, who very loudly indicated that he would never fly BA again.

This example illustrates a very important concept: **lifetime customer value.** Compare the amount of revenue and profits that would be derived from the customer to the small incremental cost of moving him to business class. When you lose a customer for life, you are actually losing the (discounted) stream of income that passenger would have produced over his lifetime. In addition, how many other potential customers will he tell about it?

Compare that illustration to Lexus's approach to customer loyalty. A CEO unexpectedly received a $200 check from Lexus after a few customers had complained that the cars' original tires wore out too soon. This impressed the customer, who was very adamant in saying that he would be a Lexus customer for life—not for just the money, but for doing the right thing.[5]

Clearly, no company is going to have a 100% loyalty rate. As noted earlier, some customers have multiple vendors as company policy. In addition, if many customers are involved, it is impossible to satisfy all of them. However, the economic reasons for increasing the retention rate are compelling. Figure 13–2 shows the impact of a 5-percentage-point increase in retention on the net present value of a customer revenue stream for a variety of industries. For example, in the advertising agency industry, increasing its client retention rate from, say, 80 to 85% results in an increase of 95% in the net present value of the aver-

Figure 13–2

Impact of a 5-Percentage-Point Increase in Retention Rate on Customer Net Present Value

Source: Frederick F. Reichheld (1996), *The Loyalty Effect* (Boston: Harvard Business School Press), p. 37.

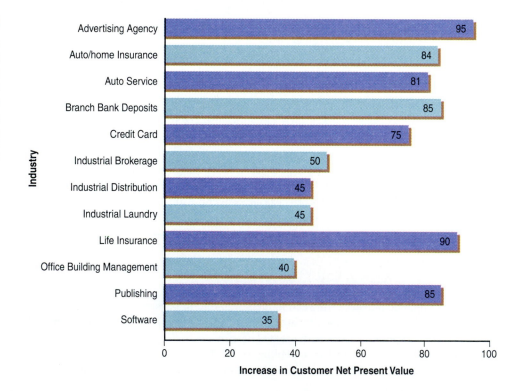

age customer's billings. This is for two reasons. First, what looks like a small difference in retention rates is greatly magnified over a long period of time. Second, retained customers are much more profitable than switchers.

Figure 13–3 breaks down the difference in profits. Loyal customers are more profitable because they stimulate revenue growth, are less expensive to serve, refer new customers to the company, and are often willing to pay a price premium. Let us look in more detail at the components of Fig. 13–3.

Acquisition Cost

Obviously, any new customer involves some incremental costs, called **acquisition costs.** For example, American Express must send a number of direct mail pieces or make tele-marketing pitches to obtain new customers. New customers of industrial equipment require more sales calls than existing ones. Thus, acquisition costs represent an initial loss for any customer.

Base Profit

This is simply the profit margin a company earns from an average customer. The longer a customer is retained, the longer the base profit is earned.

Revenue Growth

Retained customers have been found to increase their purchase quantities over time. This is an intuitive finding. Think about a store to which you have become more loyal over a period of time. It is likely that you not only shop there regularly, but that you also buy more items there. Alternatively, you might purchase life or home insurance from the company from which you purchase auto insurance.

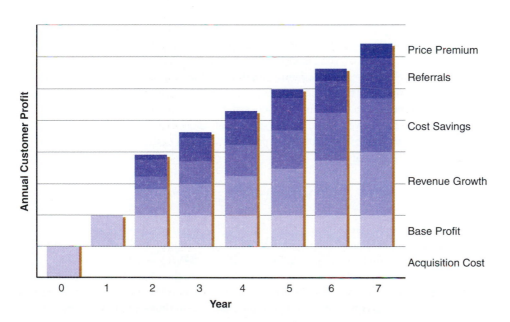

Figure 13–3

Why Loyal Customers Are More Profitable

Source: Frederick F. Reichheld (1996), *The Loyalty Effect* (Boston: Harvard Business School Press), p. 39.

Operating Costs

It has also been found that existing customers cost less to serve than new customers. The former have a better knowledge of the company's systems and procedures. For example, if you are a good customer of the direct mail clothing company Lands' End, you undoubtedly know how to fill out the form (fewer mistakes for the company to follow up on) and how to read the product descriptions (less time on the phone for customer service representatives).

Referrals

Good customers also talk to their friends and neighbors about your company. Additional business comes from favorable word of mouth by satisfied customers. This is a particularly good source of new business for service companies; as we will see in the next chapter, service quality is more difficult to ascertain before purchasing, so advice from someone who has tried the service and is satisfied with it is particularly important.

Price Premium

Loyal customers are often more price insensitive than customers who need a price inducement to switch or to become a new customer. When was the last time you checked the price of your favorite brand of toothpaste? Such loyal customers are getting significant customer value from using the product or service and are not concerned about price. Note that in the example discussed at the beginning of the chapter, Oura Oil does not have the lowest gasoline prices in the Osaka area.

The Total Effect

If you can collect hard information on all these components of the lifetime value of a customer, you can develop a picture of how valuable customer satisfaction and loyalty are to your business. Figure 13–4 is an illustration from the credit card industry showing the increase in value of an active account over 20 years. For example, the value of a customer who stays for 3 years is $98 ($178 in profit minus the $80 acquisition cost); if a credit card issuer can retain a customer for 5 years, the net profit is $264.

An interesting question is how much you would pay today to acquire an account, given the kind of information shown in Fig. 13–4. Suppose we knew that the average account remained active for 5 years. You should not be willing to pay $264 for that account today because the cash flows occur in the future and those dollars are worth less today because of the time value of money. The present value of a cash flow n years in the future is determined by the firm's discount rate, or opportunity cost of capital. This is the rate of return that the company could get if it invested the money in alternative opportunities rather than in obtaining a credit card customer. To calculate the present value of a cash flow n years in the future, use the following formula:

$$\text{Present Value}_n = \frac{\text{Cash flow}}{(1 + I)^n}$$

where I is the discount rate.

Therefore, the present value of a 5-year customer, assuming a 10% discount rate, is $40/(1 + .10) + $66/(1 + .10)^2 + $72/(1 + .10)^3 + $79/(1 + .10)^4 + $87/(1 + .10)^5 −$80, or $172.98. In other words, you should not pay more than $173 to acquire an account that you expect to retain for 5 years. Another way to look at these numbers is from a retention perspective. If a credit card customer in the third year indicates that he or she is think-

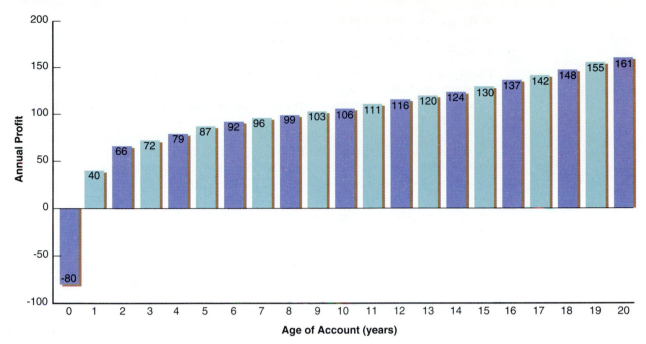

Figure 13–4

Customer Life Cycle Profit Pattern in the Credit Card Industry

Source: Frederick F. Reichheld (1996), *The Loyalty Effect* (Boston: Harvard Business School Press), p. 39.

ing about switching, the present value of the incremental profit for years 4 and 5 is $79/(1.10) + $87/(1.10)^2 (recall that we are in year 3 already) or $143.72. This gives you an idea of how much you would spend to retain that customer (for example, using a reduction in the interest rate on the card or adding benefits such as life insurance or lost card protection).[6]

Therefore, the economics of customer retention programs are compelling. Although there is some dispute about the effectiveness of different approaches to retaining customers (we will discuss this further later in the chapter), there is no doubt that it is more profitable to keep customers as long as possible rather than spending more and more to acquire new ones. In other words, it is cheaper to retain customers than to acquire new ones.

Fingerhut Corporation is a $2-billion company selling a variety of products for the home, including apparel, housewares, fitness equipment, sporting goods, and many other products.[7] Fingerhut is on the leading edge of lifetime customer value measurement. In its massive database, the company has collected more than 3,000 data elements per customer from data on purchasing behavior, preferences, and financial and credit data. Using sophisticated mathematical algorithms, the company has developed some of the world's most sophisticated models of lifetime value by projecting expected customer revenues and costs on an individual customer basis.

As you might expect, the company focuses a considerable amount of resources on its most productive customers (i.e., those who buy a lot). If you order a product by mail, you receive a phone call from a representative confirming the order and telling you when it will arrive. The representative will also ask you whether you are interested in being contacted about future products that match your interests, including special offers. The company also offers a personalized service called the birthday club that invites you to provide birthdays, dates, and interests for spouses, friends, children, and grandchildren. The company will call you when these dates are approaching to remind you of the special days and offer you customized merchandise. ◆

APPROACHES TO CUSTOMER RETENTION

Customer Satisfaction

Clearly, one of the requirements of customer loyalty is satisfaction. Satisfied customers are much more likely to repurchase and become good customers than dissatisfied customers. Many studies have shown a positive relationship between satisfaction, loyalty, and profitability.[8]

Spurred by the quality movement of the 1980s, the introduction of several very public competitions such as the Malcolm Baldrige Award for Quality, and well-publicized satisfaction surveys such as the one done by J.D. Power for automobiles, many companies around the world are investing substantial sums in measuring customer satisfaction and exploring its impact on their businesses. As a result, this has become a big business for research firms. By one estimate, up to one-third of all revenues generated by U.S. marketing research firms are from customer satisfaction surveys and analyses.

The basic customer satisfaction model is shown in Fig. 13–5. The model is often called an **expectation confirmation/disconfirmation model** because it presumes that levels of customer satisfaction with a product or service are determined by how well the product performs relative to what the customer expected. In the center of the figure is perceived customer satisfaction. The circle on the right is experienced quality, or how the product or service actually performed. To the left, the customer is assumed to form an expectation or prediction about the product's performance. This expectation is formed from a variety of sources of information, including advertising, word-of-mouth information from friends and relatives, and past experience with the product or product category. If the product meets or exceeds expectations, the customer is satisfied to different degrees. Obviously, if the product just meets expectations, satisfaction is less than if the product goes way beyond expectations. Any performance below expectations results in a dissatisfied customer.

Satisfaction can be measured in a number of ways. As in the multiattribute model shown in Chapter 5, the most common approach is to use a scale to compare satisfaction, along a number of product dimensions, with competition and expectations. Figure 13–6 shows several common scale types. Federal Express has been known to use the 101-point scale, General Electric uses the 10-point scale, and most other companies use a 4- or 5-point scale. For example, a satisfaction question for an airline might look like the following:

"How satisfied were you with the food (relative to your expectations)?"

Very dissatisfied   Very satisfied

    1   2   3   4   5

Figure 13–5

Customer Satisfaction Model

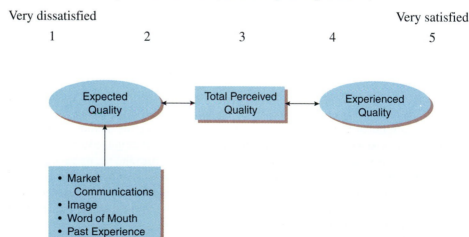

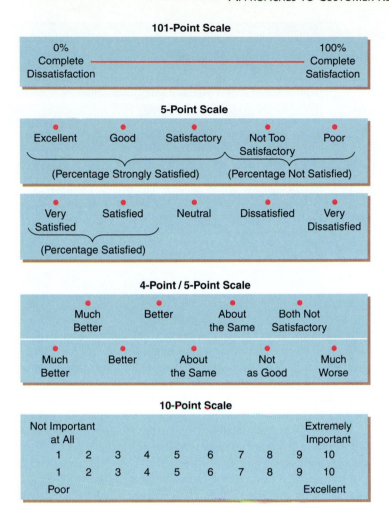

Figure 13–6

Customer Satisfaction Scales

Source: Mack Hanan and Peter Karp (1989), *Customer Satisfaction* (New York: AMACOM), p. 104.

After obtaining satisfaction measures on a number of attributes, the survey always contains an overall satisfaction question:

"Overall, how satisfied were you with the flight today?"

Very dissatisfied				Very satisfied
1	2	3	4	5

Most companies track these satisfaction measures over time and relative to competition in order to determine trends in different market segments or product areas.

Customer satisfaction surveys for products and services sold via the Web can be conducted quickly and easily using a service introduced in 1999 by CustomerSat.com. The Web site operator first designs the survey using a variety of questionnaire options provided at the CustomerSat.com site. The survey is then distributed by a pop-up window at the client's Web site. The frequency of the pop-up window can be adjusted to appear to every visitor or as few as 1 out of 100 visitors for sites that have heavy traffic. Reports based on the answers to the survey questions are generated and updated in real time for the client.

Often, rather than survey-based measures, satisfaction is measured using an objective indicator such as number of complaints. For example, Fig. 13–7 shows 1996 data from the

Figure 13–7

Customer
Satisfaction: Airline
Complaints per
100,000 Passengers,
January–September
1996

Source: Wendy Zellner (1997),
"Coffee, tea—and on-time
arrival," *Business Week*,
January 20, p. 30.

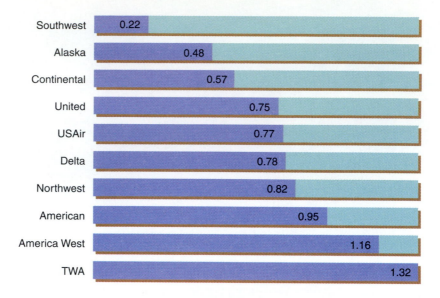

U.S. Department of Transportation on the number of complaints it receives per 100,000 passengers for the leading U.S. airlines. These complaints are not divided into the separate components of dissatisfaction (e.g., on-time record, food quality, service quality), but they still give indicate how the flying public views the airlines.

Interestingly, a large amount of evidence indicates that merely satisfying customers is not enough to keep them loyal to your company or product. In other words, although Fig. 13–6 implies that "excellent," "good," and "satisfactory" ratings all imply "strongly satisfied," there may be a real difference between those responses. Research by Xerox showed that totally satisfied customers (i.e., those choosing 5 on a 5-point scale) were six times more likely to repurchase Xerox products over the next 18 months than those that were only satisfied (i.e., those choosing 3 or 4 on the 5-point scale).[9] The biggest differences in loyalty between completely satisfied and merely satisfied customers have been found in the most highly competitive industries, such as automobiles and many services.

The relationship between satisfaction and loyalty is complex. One study identified four customer types based on their levels of satisfaction and loyalty:[10]

- Loyalist/Apostle: These customers are completely satisfied, have high loyalty, and are very supportive of the company. Apostles help you get new customers through referrals.
- Defector/Terrorist: They tend to be dissatisfied or somewhere in the middle, switch to competitors, and are unhappy with you. Terrorists spread negative word of mouth.
- Mercenary: They can have high satisfaction but high switching rates as well. Their commitment to you is low. They are usually price and promotion sensitive, and rarely stay with you long enough for them to be profitable.
- Hostage: These customers are stuck with you. They may be dissatisfied but they are highly loyal because there may not be a viable alternative. A good example is cable TV service. When an alternative surfaces (e.g., satellite TV), they switch.

Thus, Apostles and Mercenaries can be highly satisfied but exhibit totally different loyalty patterns. Likewise, Apostles and Hostages are both highly loyal, but for very different reasons. It is therefore critical to understand the context within which you are measuring satisfaction and loyalty.[11]

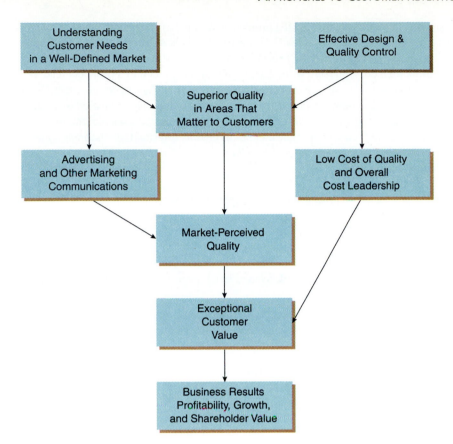

Figure 13–8

Customer Value
Management

Source: Bradley T. Gale
(1994), *Managing Customer
Value* (New York: Free Press),
p. 19.

Customer Value Management

As we just noted, having a satisfied customer is not sufficient for keeping them loyal to you over a long period of time. How do you completely satisfy customers?

One approach to completely satisfying customers is **customer value management.**[12] This approach is summarized in Fig. 13–8. As can be seen, a key to achieving exceptional customer value is a high level of perceived quality on the part of the market (i.e., the customers). This notion that perceived quality is positively related to profitability has been shown in many studies. Figure 13–9 shows the results of one study from the survey-based Profit

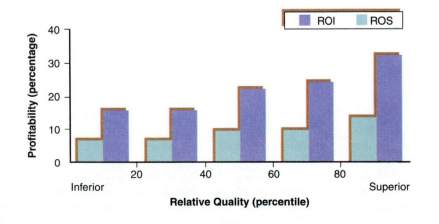

Figure 13–9

Relationship between
Perceived Quality and
Profits

Source: Robert D. Buzzell and
Bradley T. Gale (1987), *The
PIMS Principles* (New York:
Free Press), p. 107.

Impact of Market Strategies (PIMS) project, covering 3,000 strategic business units of manufacturing and service companies.[13] The vertical axis is return on sales (ROS) or return on investment (ROI). The horizontal axis is based on responses to the PIMS survey on how managers think their customers view the quality of their business unit's products relative to competition's. These responses are broken down into quartiles. As can be seen, there is a definite positive relationship between perceived quality and profitability, measured by both ROS and ROI. Note that the key here is *perceived* quality, not measured or actual quality.

In this context, customer value can be defined as offering the customer a high level of perceived quality at the right price relative to competition. In other words, using the equation from Chapter 11,

$$\text{Market share} = f(\text{perceived value/price})$$

Customer value for maximizing customer satisfaction can be seen as a favorable ratio or perceived value to price, whether value or price is high or low.

One way to quantify the advantage you have in a particular business over competition is to use the multiattribute model described in Chapter 5. Table 13–1 shows such an analy-

---

Table 13–1　Customer Value Analysis: Perdue Chickens

Quality Attributes	Importance Weights	Performance Scores		
		Perdue	Others	Ratio
Yellow bird	5	7	7	1.0
Meat-to-bone	10	6	6	1.0
No pinfeathers	15	5	5	1.0
Fresh	15	7	7	1.0
Availability	55	8	8	1.0
Brand image	0	6	6	1.0
	100			
Customer satisfaction score		7.15	7.15	
Market-perceived quality ratio				1.0

Performance Scores

Quality Attributes	Weight	Perdue	Avg. Comp.	Ratio	Weight Times Ratio
1	2	3	4	5 = 3/4	6 = 2 × 5
Yellow bird	10	8.1	7.2	1.13	11.3
Meat-to-bone	20	9.0	7.3	1.23	24.6
No pinfeathers	20	9.2	6.5	1.42	28.4
Fresh	15	8.0	8.0	1.00	15.0
Availability	10	8.0	8.0	1.00	10.0
Brand image	25	9.4	6.4	1.47	36.8
	100				126.1
Customer satisfaction		8.8	7.1		
Market-perceived quality ratio:					

Source: Bradley T. Gale (1994), *Managing Customer Value* (New York: Free Press), pp. 31, 33.

sis for Perdue Chickens. The analysis was conducted using the perceptions of members of a poultry association, not consumers. The top panel of the table shows the relative perceived value of Perdue and the competition before Frank Perdue revolutionized the processed chicken industry. As can be seen, Perdue had no quality advantage over the competitors (i.e., the market was considered to be a commodity market). However, the same analysis conducted in the early 1980s shows how Frank Perdue changed that industry. Note the changes in the importance weights on the attributes, most notably the dramatically increased weight placed on brand image. This is a direct result of the substantial amount of money Perdue spent on TV and print advertising (much of which featured Frank Perdue himself) hammering home the quality of Perdue's chickens. The other major change is the perceived quality advantage Perdue had over the competition.

From these quantitative results and information about how end customers trade off price and quality, a customer value map like those shown in Fig. 13–10 can be created. Relative prices can be calculated from market data. The market-perceived quality ratios are from the multiattribute analysis. The slope of the fair-value line is the relative importance weights

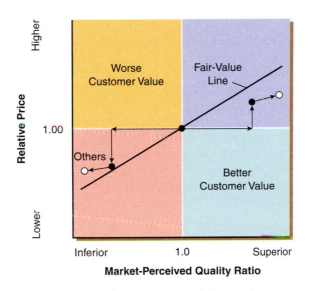

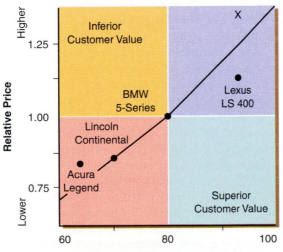

Figure 13–10

Customer Value Maps

Source: Bradley T. Gale (1994), *Managing Customer Value* (New York: Free Press), pp. 34, 46.

placed on price and quality. Brands or products below the fair-value line are in a strong position because they offer high perceived quality for the price. The opposite is true for brands or products above the line.

The top panel of Fig. 13–10 shows how Perdue stacked up against the other chicken producers. The large dot in the center shows the pre-Frank Perdue days (i.e., the implications of the top panel of Table 13–1). Prices were the same and no one had a perceived quality advantage. The black dots above and below the fair-value line represent the positions of Perdue and the competitors in the first years after the quality differentiation campaign began; the white circles are where the brands moved when Perdue became firmly established in the market.

The lower panel of Fig. 13–10 is based on the luxury car market in the early 1990s. This figure is consistent with the notion that you can be expensive but still considered to be a good value for the money. The Lexus LS 400, the most expensive car in the group, was perceived to offer the best quality for money; the lower-priced Acura Legend did not fare as well.[14]

The important question at this point is, "How do you use this information to manage customer value and retain customers?" The information from the multiattribute analyses (Table 13–1) is useful because it shows how and where the sources of competitive advantage or disadvantage are obtained on the relevant dimensions of quality. There are four other ways this information can be used:

- Use the information as a key driver of marketing strategies. The data from Table 13–1 become competitive advantages and part of the value proposition that is communicated to customers.
- Explain and communicate that information throughout the entire organization to focus on product and service improvements.
- Understand and manage the key business processes underlying the necessary improvements, such as customer service operations or delivery.
- Develop new product concepts that take advantage of opportunities shown by the analyses.

Customer Service

An important component of customer satisfaction is **customer service.** Although we will discuss the marketing of services in the next chapter, all products, whether manufactured or services, have a service component. Automobiles and computers must be repaired. Customers have questions about how to set up a VCR. Machinists need technical advice about how to operate a new lathe. The quality of these encounters can make or break a relationship with a customer. How many times have you sworn not to return to a restaurant or not to buy a product from a company that has delivered poor customer service?

Companies that market services know that the level of customer service delivered is equivalent to product quality. However, many companies in manufacturing businesses underestimate how important these service encounters are to customer loyalty. Although it is important that a personal computer works as advertised, for some consumers, it is equally important that the company provides helpful responses to questions and does not leave them waiting on the telephone to speak to a representative.

Thus, regardless of the type of product, the relationship between buyer and seller is only beginning when the purchase is made. The points of contact between buyer and seller are not all equal in importance. Those that are critical to the relationship are called moments of truth.[15] It is important for you to understand which customer contacts are sufficiently critical to the long-term relationship to be considered moments of truth for your business.

The key to using customer service to develop these long-term relationships is to view service as a way of differentiating your product from the competition. Figure 13–11 illustrates this differentiation effort. Consider the core product to be the basic attributes of the product or service. For a manufactured product, these would be the physical characteristics. For example, for a car, color, weight, gas mileage, and similar characteristics constitute the core product. The expected product is the core product plus any expectations about the product or service held by the target segment. Thus, the expected car would also feature a certain level of reliability, service from the dealer, prestige obtained from driving it, and so on.

How, then, do you use customer service to differentiate your products? Today, whether you are in a high-tech or low-tech business, all competitors in a market either offer or have the potential to offer equivalent core products. Thus, it is difficult to achieve differentiation based on product features and attributes. Also, simply meeting expectations is insufficient for maintaining buyer loyalty over an extended period of time. To differentiate, you need to reach a third level (shown in Fig. 13–11): the augmented product. In other words, you have to go beyond expectations by offering levels of customer service that competitors cannot match.

An example of this is Intuit, the company offering Quicken personal finance software (as well as Turbo Tax and other products). Although it is very successful in its category, Intuit is still very small compared to companies such as Microsoft, Corel, and IBM. Intuit has telephone operators who answer technical questions, as all other software vendors do. However, its technical support people take extra measures to satisfy customers. If they receive a complicated problem late on a Friday afternoon, the support specialists are likely to work on it over the weekend and call the customer back on Monday.   ◆

A second illustration is shown in Fig. 13–12. One of the biggest complaints consumers have in the area of customer service is automobile repairs. This figure shows how one dealer has managed to go beyond customer expectations and deliver outstanding customer service.

Finally, consumers in China are not used to high levels of product quality or service. However, appliance maker Haier Group Co. has differentiated itself from other Chinese brands as well as foreign manufacturers by offering outstanding service. Not only do the company's products meet international standards in physical product quality, but the company has invested in 12,500 sales and service centers and a toll-free hotline, the latter previously unknown in China. The company guarantees delivery or repair of its appliances within 24 hours and even went so far as to install an air conditioner at 4:30 A.M. on Chinese New Year's Day.[16]   ◆

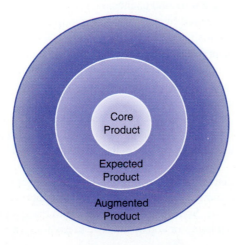

Figure 13–11

The Augmented Product

Source: Theodore Levitt (1980), "Marketing success through differentiation—of anything," *Harvard Business Review*, January–February.

Figure 13–12

Illustration of
Outstanding
Customer Service

Source: Bob Tasca (1996), *You Will Be Satisfied* (New York: HarperCollins), pp. 95–96.

Last summer at a little before 4:00 P.M. on a blisteringly hot Saturday, a tow truck pulled up in front of our service area at Tasca Lincoln-Mercury.

Behind it rode a small red, well-used Mercury Tracer. In the truck was an entire family, looking despondent—their holiday on Cape Cod seemed in jeopardy. There they were, stuck in Seekonk, Massachusetts, with a broken car, and who knew for how long? The kids grew increasingly fidgety. "Can you do anything for us?" the dad asked, his tone of voice revealing his frustration and disappointment. "I know it's late in the day, but you're the only place around here open for service." His voice trailed off.

He was right; it *was* late in the day and we *were* the only place open. That was just the problem. Our guys had been working since 7:00 that morning—sometimes in the direct sunlight. The temperature had reached ninety-five degrees and hadn't dropped much yet. Only one more hour to go, and they could drive home and relax with their families and friends. The service assistant who talked with the new customers looked at his team. "Well?"

The team leader responded, "I don't know; it's pretty late in the day, and the men are all tired, and we don't even know what's wrong with it. ... Okay, we'll take a look at it."

The word came back in less than twenty minutes. "Bad fuel pump—and we haven't got one in stock now. We just used the last one. Can't get more parts until Monday."

The kids really looked crestfallen now. A couple of the team members eyed them. "Hey," yelled one, "we got a used Tracer on the lot. We could cannibalize the pump."

"Let's go," yelled the team leader.

While they pushed one car and drove the other into the service bays, the service assistant explained the proposal to the family and asked for their approval to install a used part. They agreed. Twenty minutes later, their revived red Mercury Tracer sat happily idling in front of them. Time? 4:57. Time to go—for everybody.

I asked the team members later, "Would you have done it if it had taken more time?"

"Yeah," they said, "it was the look in those kids' eyes. We knew if we did it, it would make their day."

Some useful customer service principles are the following:[17]

- Service is the backbone of any business. If you do not satisfy the customer the first time, you may not get a second chance.
- Great service is measured by customer satisfaction. Profits will follow if your customers are highly satisfied.
- Compensation plans determine behavior. Thus, your compensation scheme should reward your workers for delivering high levels of service.
- Sales and service departments are complementary. Great service gives the sales department more to sell.
- The hours your service department is open send signals about your dedication to customer satisfaction. You should be open when your customer needs you.
- Service technicians should work together to solve customers' problems.

One way to differentiate through customer service is with service guarantees.[18] Guarantees not only offer the customer some assurance about product quality but also reinforce the brand image at the same time. Some examples are Domino Pizza's promise that you will get your pizza delivered in 30 minutes or you do not have to pay for it (now you receive a reduced-price coupon) and Lucky Supermarkets' offer of "Three's a Crowd" service that guarantees the opening of a new checkout station when any line has more than three people. Although their effectiveness varies, such guarantees can differentiate a product from the competition.

Another way to demonstrate excellence in customer service is through service recovery. Unfortunately, products do break down and there are often tense moments as services are delivered (e.g., the waiter spills soup on your dress). Thus, a critical moment for a company is when the product or service does not perform up to expectations or fails to work properly. How you react in such situations is crucial for maintaining customer relationships.

Effective service recovery demands significant training and the right people to do the job. When service recovery is necessary, customers are typically unhappy because some aspect of the product or service has failed. The people dealing with the situation must be compassionate and good listeners, as well as effective problem solvers. In 1997, because of its highly selective screening process focusing on interpersonal and empathy skills, Southwest Airlines sorted through 105,583 job applications to fill 3,006 positions.[19]

A company can also make capital investments to improve service recovery. For years, Microsoft served its corporate clients mainly using toll-free support lines and partnerships with other service companies. However, in 1995 the company announced plans to establish teams of service employees who would work 24 hours a day to get computers back up and running, visiting corporations in person if necessary. Some of these investments are Internet-based. MCI customers with PCs can monitor their accounts and pay their bills over the Web. In fall 1998, the company introduced a service in which their highest-spending customers can click on an icon to get a service representative to talk with as they continue surfing the Web.   ◆

Turning around a potential disaster can be a tremendous boost to loyalty. The British Airways anecdote earlier in this chapter was a lost opportunity.

In a more positive vein, an IBM account team was having difficulty overcoming the hostility of a potential major buyer of mainframe processors. Although the potential buyer did own several IBM processors, the company was not interested in buying any more or in buying peripheral equipment such as tape and disk drives. The account team's basic strategy was to build a new level of confidence from the lower levels of the company's organization that were key influences in the buying decision. Although they were having some success with this approach, one of the breakthrough events

Some companies have used customer service to develop long-term relationships and differentiate their products from the competition. This involves going beyond expectations and offering levels of customer service that competitors cannot match. Domino's Pizza offers a service guarantee that promises delivery of your pizza in 30 minutes or it's free. (Tony Freeman/Photo Edit)

that turned the account around was how they handled a failure of one of the installed IBM processors. A large number of IBM personnel worked around the clock to restore the system. Their efforts prompted a laudatory letter from the director of the company's information systems group and went a long way toward improving the relationship. Eventually, the team's efforts resulted in a larger order.[20] ◆

A company that differentiates itself from larger companies through its customer service is the Internet service provider (ISP) MindSpring Enterprises Inc.[21] Although it is considerably smaller than AOL, AT&T, and Microsoft Network, the company has over 600,000 customers, annual revenues of $100 million, and a market value of $1.5 billion. This is because of the following characteristics of its customer service:

- Its customer service centers handle more than 150,000 calls per month, with an average hold time of 3 minutes, 19 seconds, far below the norm for technology-based companies. In addition, its "abandon rate" (the percentage of callers who hang up from frustration) is only 4%.
- The company places a very high value on its customer service representatives by elevating the job status within the company. They also give fun titles to the personnel: Technical support experts are called "sports," customer service representatives are "smiles," and salespeople are "sailors."
- The company develops innovative tools to enable their "smiles" to help customers. One tool allows the representatives to monitor whether the customer has been able to get on-line successfully after the help session. If the customer is successful, the "smile" sends a congratulatory e-mail to the customer. If the customer has problems, the representative calls the customer back.

Loyalty Programs

One of the major trends in marketing in the 1990s is the tremendous growth in **loyalty programs** or, in general, **frequency marketing.** These are programs that encourage repeat purchasing through a formal program enrollment process and the distribution of benefits. The best example of such programs are the frequent-flier programs offered by every major airline in the world, where miles are accumulated and then exchanged for free travel or merchandise. The innovator was American Airlines, which started its AAdvantage program in 1981. A newsletter that follows loyalty programs is *Colloquy,* www.colloquy.com (see Fig. 13–13).

These programs have migrated to many different industries. Some examples are the following:

- Cracker Barrel, a restaurant chain with a country flavor, has its Cracker Barrel Old Country Store Neighborhood program where you earn one "neighborhood" point for every dollar spent at its stores. The points are redeemable at the stores.
- The retailer Pier 1 Imports has a Preferred Card program with three levels of benefits: basic (under $500 in annual spending), Gold ($500–$1,000), and Platinum (over $1,000 spent annually).
- Hallmark's Gold Crown Card program is targeted to customers of their Gold Crown retail stores. Customers receive points for money spent and greeting card purchases, which are redeemable for certificates of different monetary value. These certificates are spendable only in the Gold Crown stores.
- Sam Goody/Musicland retail music stores started the Replay program in 1992. To join, customers pay an annual membership fee of $9.95 and complete an application. When they make purchases and show their ID card, they accumulate points redeemable for

PROGRAM **SNAPSHOT**

Federated Department Stores
Family of Cards / Club Macy's

LAUNCH:
- Launched Fall 1997 "to recognize and reward loyal customers"

ENROLLMENT:
- Enrollment is automatic to all Macy's cardholders (no-annual fee credit applications are available at point of sale or customers may apply by calling a toll-free credit services number)

BENEFITS/STRUCTURE:
3 levels of membership (based on charge volume):
- Preferred Level (available to all cardholders):
  - No annual fee, "hassle free" returns and 10% off first day of card usage
  - Advance notice of sales and special events
  - Special shopping days
  - "Preferred customer status"
  - Flexible payment plans in selected departments
- Premier Level (must charge $500–$2499.99/year to qualify):
  - Preferred Level benefits
  - Quarterly personal communications with targeted offers
  - Exclusive 10–15% off Premier Days (3 times/year) with preferred savings coupons
  - Premier Club Visa (offered by invitation to Premier Level members who charge $1000–$2,499/year) includes:
    › Earn $25 Reward Certificates for free Macy's merchandise (get 3% toward Reward Certificates for every $1 charged at Macy's; get 1% toward Reward Certificates for every $1 charged elsewhere)
    › Periodic Double Reward events
    › Free gift wrap and free delivery certificates provided quarterly
    › Club Macy's "one2one" communications with exclusive offers
    › Purchasing power of 2 credit lines (Macy's and Visa)

- President's Club (must charge $2500+/year to qualify):
  - Unlimited free gift wrap on Macy's purchases
  - Free basic alterations on Macy's purchases
  - Free local delivery on Macy's purchases
  - Quarterly Club communications with special offers
  - Exclusive 10-15% off President's Club Days
  - Exclusive toll-free number
  - Club Macy's "one2one" communications with exclusive offers
  - President's Club Visa (offered by invitation to President's Club members) includes:
    ◦ Earn $25 Reward Certificates for free Macy's merchandise (get 3% toward Reward Certificates for every $1 charged at Macy's; get 1% toward Reward Certificates for every $1 charged elsewhere)
    ◦ Periodic Double Reward events
    ◦ Club Macy's "one2one" communications with exclusive offers
    ◦ Purchasing power of 2 credit lines (Macy's and Visa)
    ◦ Exclusive President's Club toll-free number

MEMBERSHIP SERVICES/COMMUNICATION:
- Preferred:
  - Toll-free customer services number
- Premier:
  - Quarterly personal communications with targeted offers
  - Club Macy's "one2one" communications with exclusive offers
- President's Club:
  - Above, plus Exclusive toll-free number

DATA COLLECTION:
- Credit application requires: Name, social security number, date of birth, employer, business phone, annual household income range, previous/permanent address

monetary-valued certificates. They also qualify for discounts on CDs and tapes. As of 1997, there were 600,000 members in the program, of which 50% were active.

- Another type of program is Volkswagen's VW Club, which attempts to build a community around the brand name by promoting a clublike, limited-membership feeling. Members pay a $25 fee and receive *Volkswagen World* magazine, a T-shirt, road atlas, decal, phone card, and discount offers on travel and recreation. Members can also obtain discounts on parts and service from local dealers.

- A small Spanish grocery chain, Plus, differentiates itself from other grocery chains through its loyalty card program; over 80% of its customers use the card.

Technology is changing the way these programs can operate. Most of them currently involve a special-purpose membership card or a co-branded Visa or MasterCard. The magnetic strip on the back of the card forwards data from the transactions to a separate information system, which tracks behavior and issues rewards. So-called smart cards have microprocessors built into them. These cards can store points accumulated from loyalty programs, which allows for more sophisticated multiple retailer programs to be developed. For example, in the United Kingdom, Shell has a program whereby points collected at Shell service stations can be converted into free gifts, flights, or movie tickets.[22]

These frequency or loyalty programs can have several problems:[23]

- Making the reward too high. Restaurant chain Chart House's program, the Aloha Club, offered free around-the-world trips to any member who ate in all 65 Chart House restaurants. Unfortunately, the company underestimated the zeal of its

Companies use loyalty programs to build long-term customer relationships. They encourage repeat purchasing by offering special benefits in exchange. One example is the Driver's Edge Visa card. Buyers accumulate points when they use the card for purchases; the points can be used for the purchase of a Ford vehicle. (Francis Hogan/Electronic Publishing Services Inc.)

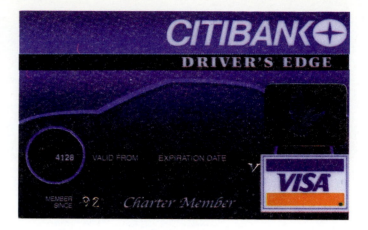

300,000 members; 41 members qualified, costing the company a considerable sum of money. Although the value of the program to the customer should exceed the cost of being a member, the programs should also be cost-effective.

- Ubiquity. There are so many programs that customers are rebelling against carrying all the cards. You should target your best customers with these programs and provide a compelling reason for joining.
- What kind of loyal customers are you actually getting? As we have noted in this chapter, it is possible to confuse loyalty with repeat purchasing. United Airlines has many repeat-purchasing customers in the San Francisco Bay Area because of its Premier frequent-flier program. At the same time, because United is the major carrier in the region, these customers are also "hostages" and are not necessarily attitudinally loyal to the company. Compare the failure of United's shuttle services in California with Southwest Airlines' tremendous success (although Southwest's frequent-flier program is less attractive than United's).
- Lack of inspiration. Many programs are simply copies of other programs. To be successful, the program must have a differential advantage over competitors' programs.
- Lack of communication with customers. Loyalty/frequency programs need to have a significant communication component to retain customer satisfaction.
- Insufficient analysis of the database. A large amount of information is produced from these programs about customer behavior. To maximize the value of these programs, these data must be mined for better market segmentation, targeting, and new product development.

 Let us return to the Oura Oil illustration. How has the company responded to the problems noted at the beginning of the chapter? Oura has established what it calls its Five-Up Club, a customer reward program for which a customer registers by completing a membership application containing demographic questions. Each club member receives a membership number, card, and gift on enrollment. As in other programs, members earn points as they buy gas, which can be redeemed for gift certificates or merchandise. The company will issue up to four cards per family and a family can pool its points to earn even better rewards. Customers who purchase over 5,000 gallons of gas per year receive a special card that entitles them to "super" service when they pull into an Oura station; attendants vacuum the interior of their car and refill their windshield-washer fluid for free. As of January 1997, the club had 170,000 members and about 80% of all purchases were recorded using the card.

Oura has gone beyond the rewards aspect of most programs. The company has sponsored a trip to an orchard where members can pick their own fruit, developed special interest clubs, and created an Internet site where members can chat with each other.

What are the results? At the end of 1996, Oura's gasoline sales were up 5% against 1995's sales for the same period, while total sales in the Osaka region decreased by 3%. Of course, it is difficult to determine whether the increase is solely due to the Five-Up Club. However, this is an excellent example of how loyalty programs can be successfully used to differentiate what is normally thought of as a commodity product. ◆

Loyalty programs are not just for consumer products and services. Bell Atlantic's Business Link loyalty program offers discounts, bonuses, and special benefits to targeted business customers based on call volume. About 80% of the eligible business customers enroll. The results? The account defection rate is up to 30% less for enrollees than for nonenrollees. Friedrich Grohe, a Germany-based manufacturer of kitchen and bathroom fittings, has a loyalty program with 1,500 members in Germany. Members pay $130 per year and attend product training to earn points, which can be redeemed for advertising and trade show booths designed and built by Grohe.[24]

Other Ideas

The notion of building relationships with customers is often thought of as the job of the sales force or other personnel related to marketing. From the customer's perspective, the concept of customer service does not necessarily imply marketing; in many cases, it may simply be the need to communicate with the company, to personalize it.

A successful program built on this idea was launched by Southwestern Bell Telephone Company in 1995.[25] The company began the Volunteer Ambassador program in which employees volunteer to establish relationships with designated customers. The objective is to put a face on the company and to let each customer know that Southwestern Bell cares about him or her and values the business. The ambassadors are drawn from a pool of nonsales employees, and each is assigned 5–10 customers whom they are expected to visit quarterly. The program started with 1,300 volunteers and expanded to 3,500 as of 1997. ◆

A good source of information about how to improve customer loyalty is to examine customers who defect. Marketing research studies often focus on your customers or potential customers; rarely are ex-customers analyzed. However, there may be more to learn from customers who have been lost than those who are loyal because the former can provide a number of ideas on how to improve the product or service, based on actual performance levels they deemed to low to continue as a customer.

An example is the MicroScan company, which manufactures advanced instruments used by medical laboratories to identify the microbes in patient cultures and determine which antibiotics would be most effective.[26] In 1990, the company (along with its main competitor, Vitek Systems) was growing rapidly as more and more customers were converting from manual systems to automated equipment. The company became interested in failure analysis and decided to seek out customers who had defected to competitors. In this industry, defection is often partial because companies often buy equipment from one supplier and consumables (e.g., test tubes, liquid agents for testing) from another. The company interviewed every totally lost customer and many of those who were only partial defectors and tried to determine the root cause of the defection. It was a very valuable exercise: The company found that there was concern about the reliability of their instruments, features of the equipment, and the attitudes held by the company toward customer problems. By paying attention to these problems, the company became the clear leader in the industry and has integrated this customer defection analysis into its standard business practices. ◆

MASS CUSTOMIZATION

Customer retention and loyalty are also being affected by a new marketing process called **mass customization.** Also called one-to-one (or simply 1–1) marketing, this is a process whereby a company takes a product or service that is widely marketed and perhaps offered in many different configurations and develops a system for customizing (or nearly customizing) it to each customer's specifications. This imparts a feeling that the product was made especially for the customer, an important affective (attitudinal) component of a buyer–seller relationship.[27] Because services can be and often are tailored to each customer, most of the focus of 1–1 marketing has been in the manufacturing sector, where a combination of information and flexible manufacturing technologies have enabled companies to personalize their products for customers.

Some examples of 1–1 marketing are the following:

- Levi Strauss will custom-fit women's jeans in selected U.S. locations. In the Personal Pair program, they let a customer try on some sample jeans and feed the information into a computer, which forwards the data to a factory. The jeans cost $10 more than the mass-produced variety. In fall 1998, the program was expanded to serve men and include more options.
- In a Custom Foot shoe store, the customer places his or her foot on an electronic scanner that measures the foot in 14 different ways. Next, working with a computer-image of the shoe, the customer chooses a shoe style, type and grade of leather, color, lining, and other features. The order is then sent to Italy for production and shipped back to the United States in 2–3 weeks. The shoes sell from $99 to $250.

Mass customization is a new marketing process that enables companies to attract and keep customers by offering products tailored to meet the needs of each customer. Levi Strauss's Personal Pair program offers an alternative to mass-produced jeans, allowing customers to have jeans made to fit their own unique measurements. (Francis Hogan/Electronic Publishing Services Inc.)

- MySki sells made-to-order skis on the Web, which allows them to produce for a market of one. The site allows customers to input their experience level, recommends some possible models, and then helps the customers design their own skis, including the graphics. It takes 14–30 days to receive them.
- Ross Controls is a major manufacturer of pneumatic valves, which force air through machine tools. The company has been turned into a custom manufacturer by training its engineers to be what the company calls "integrators." Integrators are company engineers who work hand-in-hand with customers to get their specifications for the valves and, using computer software, design and build the products in the company's automated machine shop. The custom-designed valves are sometimes delivered the next day.
- CompUSA, the computer retailer, announced in September 1997 that they were going into the custom-built PC business. Customers can walk into most CompUSA stores, build a made-to-order PC around a core product, and receive it at their homes within 5 business days.

There are four different approaches to mass customization:[28]

- Collaborative customizers talk to individual customers to help determine their needs, identify the exact product meeting those needs, and then make the customized product for them. This is the typical concept of mass customization represented by the examples just cited.
- Adaptive customizers offer one standard but customizable product that is designed so users can alter it to their own specifications. This would be appropriate when customers want the product to perform differently on different occasions.
- Cosmetic customizers present a standard product differently to different customers. An example would be a company that sells a product to different retail chains, each of which wants its own packaging, sizes, and other features.
- Transparent customizers provide each customer with unique products or services without telling them that the products have been customized for them. This is most useful when customers do not want to restate their needs repeatedly. Internet services such as Amazon.com produce customized recommendations for books to customers based on past purchases. These recommendations are sent via e-mail.

The commonality between the four kinds of mass customizers is that they all realize that customers are heterogeneous and want different combinations of product features and benefits. This recognition goes beyond market segmentation as mass customization engenders a feeling among customers that the company cares enough for them to develop products that precisely fit their needs. The desired outcome is a longer-term relationship than would be obtained using conventional marketing and manufacturing approaches.

A major application of the Web is for mass customization. Every time you visit a Web site, information about you is collected by that site and can be ultimately used to target specific messages. Some of this information is collected by what is called a cookie, a small tag of data inserted into your Web browser files that can identify you as a unique entity every time your return to the site that issued it. Figure 13–14 shows one application of this technology by Amazon.com, which customizes a list of recommended books to the customer's past purchasing behavior. Figure 13–15 shows one company's use of an approach that customizes Web sites to the customer. This site, My CDnow (see also My Yahoo and MyExcite), creates a new Web site personalized to each user.

Figure 13–14

Amazon.com
Customized Book
Recommendations

Courtesy of Amazon.com

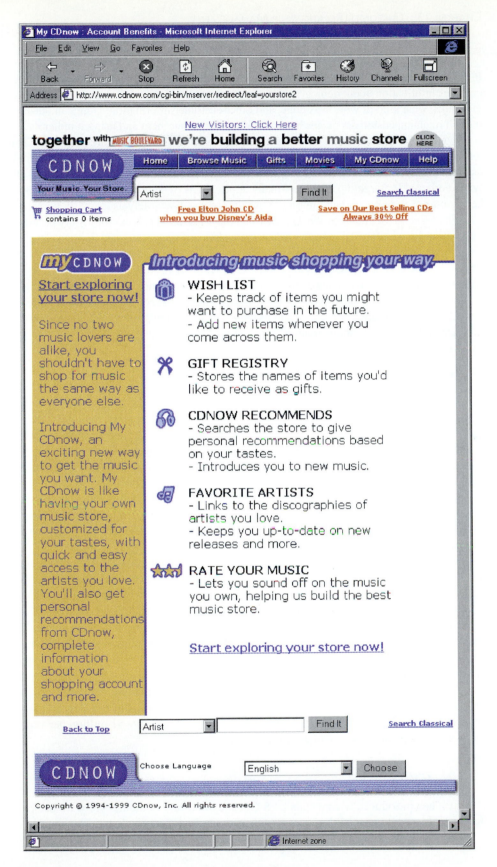

MARKETING INFORMATION SYSTEMS

It should be clear by now that the heart of any customer relationship program is a database that contains information about demographics, purchasing behavior, and, if appropriate, past service calls, what kind of work was done, and other customer information. Doing an outstanding job retaining customers means having information about them and using it judiciously.

This use of databases and database marketing is related to direct marketing (see Chapter 9) because the names, addresses, and other information in a customer database can be used to sell products and services. However, although the customer database is certainly analyzed and used for targeting purposes, many applications of databases for relationship marketing purposes go beyond attempting to use the information solely as the basis for selling.

The vehicles for obtaining the data are often the registration process for loyalty programs, transaction-based information from credit and loyalty cards, purchase data through electronic data interchange (EDI) systems, or corporate order-processing systems. As you might expect, many of these databases are enormous. For example, the data warehouse for British retailer Sainsbury requires 2–3 terabytes (trillion bytes) just to store 1 year's worth of data. The industry that supports these databases is also enormous. Consider the computer hardware, software (often called data-mining software), and trained staff needed to comb through a database of this size and develop recommendations for programs based on the analysis.

◆ **Illustration: Harrah's Entertainment**

Harrah's Entertainment Inc. has created one of the most comprehensive customer databases in the gambling industry with the advent of their Total Gold brand strategy.[29] Not only do they collect the basic kinds of demographic information, but they also have data on which restaurants you visited and what you ate, whether there were any problems with your room during your stay, and how much you gambled and at which games. As of 1998, the database has around 13 million customers, of whom 6 million are active (see Table 13–2).

Like many relationship marketing programs, Harrah's approach is based on a loyalty card on which customers can accumulate points redeemable for merchandise and services based on their gambling volume. Obviously, part of the rationale for the program is to get people to come back to Harrah's and gamble some more.

The advantage of the database program is that it allows Harrah's to do a much better job segmenting its market than they could do previously. Casinos have known their very best customers for a long time on a personal basis. These customers receive benefits such as free hotel rooms and extensive lines of credit. Although the big rollers have always been treated well, the large midsection of the gambling market has not been as identifiable. This large part of the market has traditionally received bulk mailings and general advertisements; personalized communications acknowledging their customer record will clearly have a much greater impact on the quality of the relationships.

A side benefit of the database is marketing efficiency. After merging the databases from the company's 16 casinos, managers found that 20% of the mailings of the *Harrah's World* newsletter were duplicative. The company estimates that it will save $1 million per year by merging the separate database operations. ◆

◆ **Illustration: UPS**

UPS has introduced what it calls UPS OnLine Solutions, computer software packages that permit its customers to gain access to data about their shipping habits worldwide (see

Table 13–2 Harrah's Total Gold Program

Enrollments

Membership is automatic for Harrah's *Gold Card* members.

Non *Gold Card* members self-select at point of sale and complete an enrollment application including name, address, and other interests such as slot tournaments, football, or sports.

Members must be 21 years or older to join.

Enrollment process includes an ID check in compliance with state regulations.

Benefits/structure

Members swipe their card through magnetic readers to earn points for slot play at any Harrah's location. (The card reader counts the amount of money put into play when inserting a coin or token or when pressing a credit button.)

The amount of play required to earn one point varies from city to city, but 40 points are worth a dollar at every Harrah's casino.

To earn rewards at table games, members show their cards to the Harrah's personnel, who reviews the member's past play at all Harrah's casinos, then rates the level of play and rewards the appropriate "complimentaries."

After earning 100 points during one casino trip, the member receives 25 bonus points, plus 25 bonus points for every additional 50 points earned during the same trip.

At 200 points, members can redeem points for cash, merchandise, food, lodging, or show tickets at any Harrah's casino, or save their points (up to a year) for a vacation to any Harrah's casino in the United States.

Free show ticket upon first visit to any Harrah's other than the one where the *Total Gold* card was obtained.

10% discount for purchases in Harrah's owned shops.

Preferred Reservations include priority access to rooms, shows, and events.

Additional benefits vary from property to property based on tracked play.

Co-branded Visa cardholders earn *Total Gold* points equal in value to 1% of all purchases made with the Visa card.

Member services/communication

Exclusive toll-free number.

Quarterly newsletter, *Harrah's World*, including points statement and information on new properties, big winner spotlights, and Harrah's merchandise.

Rewards are selected through ATM-like Total Rewards Kiosks that print Total Rewards Vouchers for instant redemption at any Harrah's casino.

Data collection

Enrollment application requests name, address, and other interests such as slot tournaments, football, or other sports.

Dollar increments up to $10,000 a day, average spending, and average spending by day, by week, and by trip.

Harrah's tracks about 65% of its customer base and in some areas tracks as much as 85% of total play.

Statistics/results

13 million members, 6 million of whom are active, 2.5 million of whom are highly active.

Cross-market visitation has increased by more than 80%.

Source: *Colloquy* (1998), 6, p. 5.

---

the advertisement in Fig. 13–16). Every package is turned into a "smart" package by the bar-coded shipping label used by the company. The contents and all the other information about the package (e.g., weight, destination) are put into a massive database, which the customer can access. Customers can then tap into the data and find out where they ship, what they are shipping, and how much it is costing.

Who benefits? Obviously, the company can better control inventory by knowing how much is necessary and being able to calculate warehousing costs. Customer service, production, and accounting also benefit. Finally, of course, UPS benefits. By showing customers the benefits of keeping their shipping with UPS, UPS increases customers' switching costs and concomitant loyalty. In addition, UPS can analyze the data themselves to help their marketing efforts. Thus, the customer database is valuable to both parties.   ◆

EXECUTIVE SUMMARY

The main points of this chapter include the following:

- The buyer–seller relationship does not end when a sale is made; buyers expect sellers to deliver services after the sale.
- The economic advantages of customer loyalty through long-term relationships are clear: increased profits derived from profit margins produced over the term of the relationship, increased revenues from greater purchase volume, lower costs of serving loyal customers, referrals to new customers, and price premiums (because loyal customers tend to be more insensitive to price).
- A key to long-term relationships is customer satisfaction. Completely satisfied customers are produced when companies go beyond customer expectations in the relationship.
- Another key to long-term relationships is managing customer value: the ratio of perceived value to price.
- Outstanding customer service is provided by going beyond the physical product or service attributes to the augmented product (that is, seeing that what you are selling is not just the product itself but the product and services you can offer to differentiate your product from competition).

- A popular way to maintain loyal customers is through loyalty or frequency programs. These programs reward customers for repeat purchases.
- Long-term relationships can also be established through mass customization, or 1–1 marketing, in which the customer sees the company as providing a product or service tailored to his or her needs.
- Relationship marketing is built on the foundation of a strong customer database.

CHAPTER QUESTIONS

1. Think of a recent example in which you were treated poorly by a company. Assuming you chose not to buy any more of that company's products or services, approximately what is the present value of the revenue that company has lost? (Assume the only lost revenue is from your purchases and not, for example, from your negative word-of-mouth.)
2. Consider the customer satisfaction model shown in Fig. 13–5. Why is it important for marketing managers to measure customer expectations as well as actual satisfaction from consumption or usage?
3. Think of a company that has provided great customer service to you recently. What did they do? How did they go beyond what you expected? What do companies have to do to get employees to deliver such service?
4. Are loyalty programs more likely to be successful for certain kinds of products and services than for others? Given the proliferation of loyalty programs, how can you differentiate your program from competitors' programs?
5. Mass customization or 1-1 marketing is considered to be the best way for Web-based businesses to be successful. Why can Web businesses implement mass customization more easily than businesses using conventional channels? Can you think of any reasons why mass-customized products and services could deliver lower levels of customer satisfaction than more mass-produced products?

Application Exercises: Relationship Management in the PC Industry

Integrated Case

Continuing the PC case, complete the following exercises:

1. Qualitatively assess the different factors contributing to the value of customer loyalty in the PC business. Use Fig. 13–3 as a guide. Do not try to put actual numbers in the categories.
2. For both the consumer and industrial markets, create a customer satisfaction program for a PC manufacturer.
3. Construct a customer value map for a PC manufacturer using information collected from other students or some other set of respondents. Using a set of four competitors, follow Table 13–1. First, determine the attributes, then the importance weights and brand values (use averages across the respondents). Construct the relative values using your PC manufacturer as the reference point. Using relative prices collected from some external source, the relative perceived quality data, and price–quality tradeoff information (use the latter data to construct the slope of the fair-value line), construct a value map. Your PC manufacturer should be at the (1.0, 1.0) coordinate.
4. Develop an outline of a loyalty program for your PC manufacturer.

FURTHER READING

A book that goes into the details of building a 1–1 marketing program is Don Peppers and Martha Rogers (1999), *The One to One Fieldbook: The Complete Toolkit for Implementing a 1 to 1 Marketing Program* (New York: Currency/Doubleday). Readers interested in keeping up with 1–1 examples should subscribe to the Peppers and Rogers electronically distributed newsletter, *Inside 1to1.* A good article on how to learn from service recovery situations is by Stephen S. Tax and Stephen W. Brown (1998), "Recovering and learning from service failure," *Sloan Management Review,* Fall, pp. 75–88.

Strategies for Service Markets

14

CHAPTER BRIEF

The purpose of this chapter is to introduce the differences between developing strategies for services versus manufactured products. Key areas of learning are as follows:

The nature of services and the characteristics that distinguish them from manufactured goods
The service quality model
Measuring the quality of services
Developing marketing strategies for services
Marketing mix decision-making for service businesses
How information technology affects the marketing of services

One of the largest investment brokerage firms in the U.S. in terms of number of offices is Edward Jones, based in St. Louis.[1] The company initially located its offices in rural and small towns but now has offices in metropolitan areas as well. In fact, the firm has more than 4,700 offices in the U.S. and through its affiliates in Canada and the U.K. The company is so successful and innovative that it is one of the few firms with which eminent consultant Peter Drucker has agreed to work.

What makes Edward Jones so successful in an industry where it is difficult to differentiate and develop a unique value proposition? Any broker working for any company can give clients access to a wide variety of financial instruments (e.g., mutual funds, options, commodities, stocks, and bonds). A key aspect to Edward Jones's success is its organizational structure. Each office is managed by an individual investment representative (IR) who is autonomous and can therefore be as entrepreneurial as he or she wants. Each IR can segment his or her market, develop communication programs, and determine employee work hours; in short, he or she has complete control over the operation of the office.

However, the key to its success is a constant focus on helping customers achieve their financial goals by asking the following questions continuously: What is our business? Who is our customer? What does the customer value? The company's IRs focus on long-term relationships and long-term investments rather than seeking high short-term returns, which carry a high level of risk. IRs do not sell their clients initial public offerings (IPOs), options, commodity futures, or penny stocks (stocks with share prices less than $1). They also do not have their own company-branded mutual funds, as other firms such as Charles Schwab do, because they believe that such funds present IRs with a potential conflict of interest.

What the company does offer clients (depending on their goals) are stocks in stable companies with high capitalization. They also recommend highly rated bonds and mutual funds with sound track records when appropriate. The IRs are rewarded for not churning customers' accounts (buying and selling often to generate commissions) through a trailing fee, an annual 0.25% commission for IRs who do not move clients' funds around from investment to investment. The company believes that its investment representatives should help customers understand their investments and feel comfortable with their investment decisions rather than focusing on short-term returns.

The company's marketing strategy is well represented by its Web site, shown in Fig. 14–1. The feel of the site is decidedly low-tech, with lettering in handwritten script and typewriter styles. The site has an individualized feel to it. Notice that one of the hot links is to "Neighborhood Branches"; this is obviously local rather than Wall Street. "Investment Solutions That Work" focuses on reliability rather than high risk.

Thus, two key elements of the Edward Jones value proposition are local investment advice and security and the close customer relationships.

This illustration shows some of the key differences between services and manufactured products. Products such as automobiles and computers can be touched, examined, and tested by customers before they are purchased. They exist before they are sold. Services are intangible and do not exist until the customer buys them. As a result, services are marketed based

Figure 14–1

Edward Jones
Web Site

Courtesy
of Edward Jones

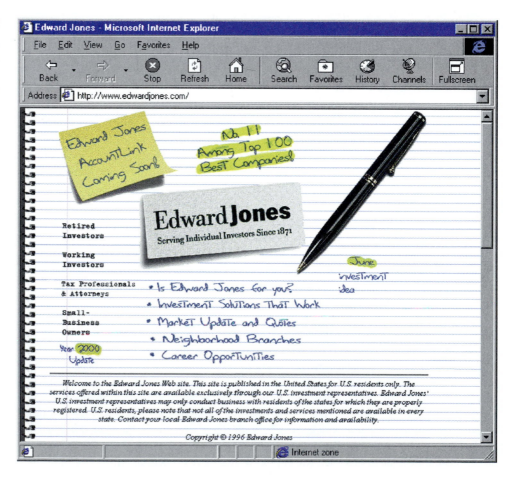

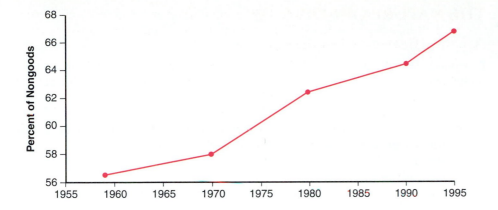

Figure 14–2

Services as a Percentage of the U.S. GNP

Source: Steven M. Shugan (1994), "Explanations for the growth of services," in R. Rust and R. Oliver, eds., *Service Quality: New Directions in Theory and Practice* (Thousand Oaks, CA: Sage), p. 226.

on assertions of what they can do for the customer because the customer cannot usually verify that before purchasing. Image and perception are crucial components of service marketing. In addition, many services have a strong human component. Because of the customers' interaction with the delivery or production of the service, quality is a critical component of service marketing. As a result, it is easy to see why Edward Jones has been so successful. Their promise—peace of mind—resonates with their target customers and they stress the importance of the human interactions with those customers.

Services now account for 70% of all jobs in the United States and increasing proportions of jobs in other industrialized nations. Figures 14–2 and 14–3 show the growth of services as a percentage of the U.S. GNP and in relation to manufacturing and agriculture jobs. Worldwide, many companies better known for their manufactured products are generating serious revenues from services. For example, nearly 25% of IBM's 1997 revenues were from services (e.g., consulting, computer facilities management); the similar figure for database company Oracle was 50%.[2] Although service marketing is not completely different from the marketing of manufactured goods, it is important to understand the differences.

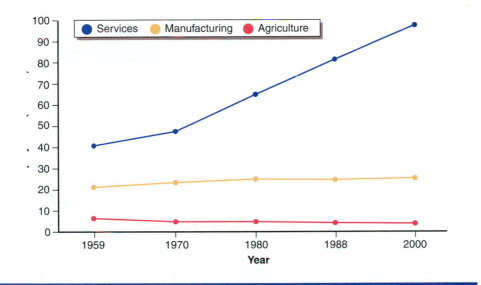

Figure 14–3

U.S. Employment by Sector

Source: Steven M. Shugan (1994), "Explanations for the growth of services," in R. Rust and R. Oliver, eds., *Service Quality: New Directions in Theory and Practice* (Thousand Oaks, CA: Sage), p. 227.

THE NATURE OF SERVICES

A Classification of Goods

Economists have developed a classification of different types of product attributes that is useful for understanding the differences between manufactured products and services.[3] The three major types of attributes are the following:

- Search attributes. These are characteristics of which the quality can be assessed before purchase. These are typical of manufactured products; for example, a consumer can assess the picture quality of a TV or an industrial purchaser can determine the strength of an adhesive.
- Experience attributes. These are characteristics of which the quality can be assessed only after purchase or during consumption. These are typical of services. For example, the quality of an airline's service is unknown before the customer purchases a ticket and takes a trip.
- Credence attributes. These are characteristics of which the quality may not be determined even after consumption because the customer lacks the expertise to make an evaluation. An example of such products is wine: Only the most knowledgeable consumers can tell the difference between a very good and an excellent wine.

Figure 14–4 displays goods and services on a continuum from search to credence attributes. As can be seen, manufactured goods are normally high in search attributes and most services are characterized by experience or credence qualities. The major implication of this typology is that services are more difficult to evaluate before purchase than manufactured products; this leads to a different evaluation process by customers and a different marketing strategy by the firm.

Figure 14–4

Continuum of Evaluation for Different Types of Products

Source: Valarie A. Zeithaml (1991), "How consumer evaluation processes differ between goods and services," in C. Lovelock, *Services Marketing*, 2nd ed. (Englewood Cliffs, NJ: Prentice Hall), p. 40.

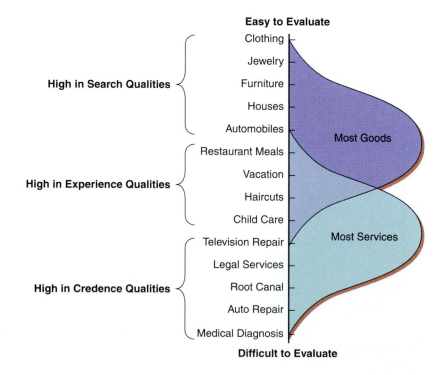

Characteristics of Services

Some of the basic characteristics of services are the following:

- Intangibility. The intangible nature of services and this impact on assessing service quality has been mentioned. A further implication of intangibility is the difficulty of inventorying services. In many cases, when a service is not performed at a particular time, the revenue is lost forever and cannot be recaptured. An example of this is when a Federal Express jet takes off with unfilled capacity. Although later planes may be filled, the lost revenue from the unfilled one is gone because the space cannot be held for later purchase. A similar situation exists with unfilled seats at a baseball stadium, slack time in an auto repair facility, and underused staff in an accounting firm. With respect to physical goods, TV sets not sold one day can still be sold the next.

- Nonstandardization. As noted earlier, many services are performed by humans. As a result, they can vary from purchase occasion to occasion. The haircut you get from a stylist in January can differ from the haircut you get in February, even from the same person. The service on a United Airlines flight from San Francisco to Boston can vary from trip to trip. Therefore, it is much more difficult to control quality for services than for manufactured products. Compare this situation with the quality control mechanisms that exist for autos and similar products; there is much greater uniformity from product to product.

- Inseparability of production and consumption. In many cases, services are produced and consumed simultaneously; that is, the customer is part of the production process. However, it has been said that services are performed, not produced, and the customer is part of the performance. The customer's involvement in service delivery increases the difficulty of standardizing services. The service quality is determined by this interaction, not simply by the quality of the service provider's efforts. For example, the excitement of a classroom discussion varies with the preparation by both the instructor and the students. If the students or the instructor are unprepared, the quality of the service is diminished.

SERVICE QUALITY

The Service Quality Model

How do customers determine whether they have received good service from a supplier? As noted earlier in this chapter, one characteristic of services is that because of their intangibility, perceptions play a greater role in assessing quality than they do with manufactured products. It is not an exaggeration to say that particularly with services, quality is how the customers perceive it.

Figure 13–5 showed the basic customer satisfaction model. The basis of both satisfaction and service quality is customer expectations: Customers evaluate the quality of a service in terms of what they expect to occur when the service is delivered. Figure 14–5 shows an expanded version of the model that includes several features unique to services. As before, quality is defined in terms of customer perceptions. The final stage of the transaction between the firm and the customer occurs when the customer assesses the quality of the service encounter. The right side of the figure describes the customer evaluation process during and after the service contact. The left side depicts the customer's prediction of what the service contact will be like, or the expectation.

Figure 14–5

A Model of
Perceived Quality

Source: Christian Grönroos
(1990), *Service Management
and Marketing* (Lexington,
MA: Lexington Books), p. 41.

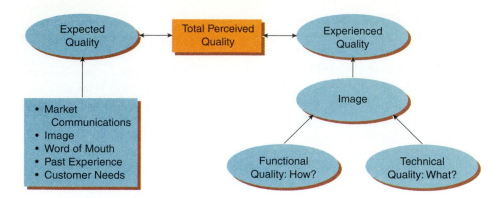

Expectations are based on a variety of information sources. A key source of information is the set of communications offered by the firm. These include advertising and brochures. Other sources of information include word-of-mouth communications from friends, relatives, suppliers, and others. Customer needs also affect expectations; if a software problem is important to the operation of a business, the customer will expect and hope to get a quick answer. Past experience with the company plays a key role. If a customer called a toll-free telephone number to solve a problem and had to wait several hours to get through because all the lines were busy, this experience will create an expectation of a similar experience in the future. This source of information is important when the customer has had some experience with a service provider. However, because services are intangible and difficult to sample before purchasing, new customers rely more on the other sources of information to form their expectations.

The experienced quality (shown on the right side of Fig. 14–5) results from an image or perception the customer forms after the service encounter. This perception of experienced quality is based on two components. The first component is the set of features or attributes of the service, or technical quality. In the computer software example, this would be the quality of the advice given. Functional quality is how the service is delivered, or the quality of the actual interaction with the company. This could include the friendliness of the telephone service person, how many rings it took before someone answered, and so on. This dimension of service quality reflects the fact that customers take a broad view of the quality of a service encounter.

Let us return to the Edward Jones illustration. When a client is new, she forms an expectation of the quality of the investment advice she will receive from recommendations from friends (word-of-mouth), the image the firm has developed based on its communications, and her needs (e.g., the establishment of a retirement account). After taking the advice of a Jones broker, the client experiences a certain degree of service quality, based on the returns of the retirement fund as well as her interactions with the broker and the information she receives, such as monthly. The client compares her expectations with the experienced quality and forms a perception of the actual quality of the service. If the client is not new but seeking to add to her investments already managed by Jones, then the expected quality is also based on the firm's past performance.

The Dimensions of Service Quality

Although there are many models of the different factors that affect service quality,[4] a parsimonious and well-known model contains the factors shown in Fig. 14–6:

- Reliability. This is the ability to perform the service dependably and accurately (i.e., deliver it as promised).

Figure 14–6

Dimensions of
Service Quality

Source: Valarie A. Zeithaml
and Mary Jo Bitner (1996),
Services Marketing (New York:
McGraw-Hill), p. 119.

- Responsiveness. This is the ability of the service provider to respond to the customer's needs on a timely basis.
- Assurance. This is the service provider's employees' knowledge and courtesy and the confidence they instill.
- Empathy. This is the high level of attention given to customers.
- Tangibles. Services do have attributes (e.g., interest rate, price), and the quality of a service depends on customers' perceptions of these attributes. Tangibles also include facilities, written materials, and other physical evidence of the service.

The importance of these dimensions of service quality is that service firms can use them for the purposes of differentiation and positioning. These uses are described more fully later in the chapter.

Gaps in Perceptions of Quality

Inevitably, a discrepancy will arise between the expectations formed about the service encounter and the experienced quality. As you might expect, customers who are upset with poor service tend to talk about it. As also might be expected, they talk more about negative experiences than positive ones.

This asymmetry of the effects of negative and positive discrepancies is theoretically justified by the well-known psychological phenomenon called **loss aversion.**[5] Figure 14–7 is a graphic representation of loss aversion. Losses are situations in which the expectations of service quality were higher than the realized quality. Gains are the opposite situation. The curve to the left of the vertical axis demonstrates that losses are more negatively valued than gains are positively valued. In other words, customers react more strongly to unexpectedly poor service than they do to unexpectedly good service.

Negative gaps in perceived service quality can be remedied in two ways. The marketing manager can either lower expectations or raise service quality through improved service features (technical quality) or higher-quality interactions (functional quality). Because expectations are difficult to manage and lowering customer expectations is not usually in the best long-term interest of the service provider, raising service quality is usually chosen. However, a good example of the former is the author's dentist, who consistently overestimates the

Figure 14–7

Loss Aversion of
Service Quality

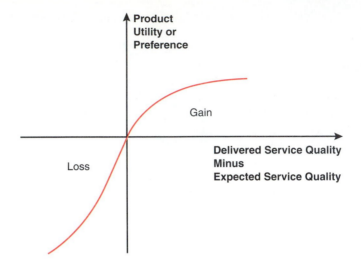

length of time it will take for the visit. Even though patients learn to expect that he will over-estimate the length of the visit, it is still a nice bonus when it actually happens. Financial service firms such as Edward Jones had to lower investors' expectations in late 1998, when the bull stock market that had been raging since the early 1990s began to cool down.

Positive gaps in perceived service quality can also be a problem because customers' expectations adapt over time. When a positive gap exists, the service provider must increase quality just to keep matching expectations. Consider Singapore Airlines. Singapore Airlines has consistently been recognized as the airline with the best service in the world. Of course, this is very pleasing to the company. However, it also creates potential problems because every passenger expects an almost magical experience from them. When that lofty expectation is not met, customers are disappointed even though the level of the service is still very high. A similar situation exists for popular restaurants and other services that generate strong word-of-mouth. Although this is a "problem" that most managers would love to have, it is still important to understand that customer expectations do drive their ultimate evaluations of quality.

Tavern on the Green is one of the hottest restaurants in New York City, renowned for its excellent quality and service. However, this reputation is a double-edged sword: Customer expectations can be raised to unrealistic levels. (Kelly/Mooney/Corbis)

We can categorize the major discrepancies between expectations and realizations into four general types of gaps:[6]

- The gap between customers' expectations and management perceptions. One key problem is that managers often think they know the bases on which customers form expectations but often are incorrect. Companies can remedy this problem by conducting focus groups for managers to attend and presenting them with more formal research results.
- The gap between management's perceptions and service quality specifications. Even when managers have a good understanding of how customers form expectations, they can find it difficult to apply their understanding to the design of the service operation. For example, knowing that computer software customers want quick response to phone calls is not enough; defining acceptable response time takes discussions with customers.
- The gap between service quality specifications and service delivery. Even if the previous gap is closed, marketing objectives will not necessarily be met. Simply setting the appropriate response time is still different from actually meeting the targets.
- The gap between service delivery and external communications. As Fig. 14–5 shows, communications with customers can have a powerful effect on expectation formation. As noted earlier, some of these are traditional communications such as advertising. Others are more personal; for example, how many times has a customer service person promised that a plumber or cable TV installer would be at your home at a particular hour and the person has been late?

Measuring Service Quality

Service quality cannot be measured in the way the quality of physical goods is measured. Manufacturers can use engineering or other physical metrics to assess quality as products come off the manufacturing line. By necessity, service quality is measured using a survey instrument administered to customers.

One of the most popular approaches to measuring service quality is the **SERVQUAL** instrument.[7] SERVQUAL is composed of questions about the five categories of service quality shown in Fig. 14–6 (tangibles, reliability, responsiveness, assurance, and empathy). Each customer surveyed completes one 22-question survey measuring expectations and then one survey for each company or product to measure actual competitor performance. The SERVQUAL score for a service is the difference between the perception of the dimension and the expectation. A company can then determine its quality of service on each of the five dimensions by taking the average score across the questions for that dimension and calculating an overall score. A weighted SERVQUAL score can also be calculated by asking the customer to give importance weights (summing to 1) on each of the five dimensions. Table 14–1 shows four tangible and four reliability questions. Besides using SERVQUAL to calculate service quality perceptions, managers can use it to track competition, examine differences among market segments, and track internal service performance.

Of course, high scores on service quality surveys do not guarantee satisfied customers. For example, in 1990 the General Accounting Office issued a report on a survey of 20 companies that had scored well in the 1988 and 1989 Baldrige competitions. One important result was that although responding managers said customer satisfaction levels had increased since then, customer retention remained almost unchanged.[8]

Table 14–1 Example of SERVQUAL Survey

	Strongly Disagree						Strongly Agree
1. Excellent _____ companies will have modern-looking equipment.	1	2	3	4	5	6	7
2. The physical facilities at excellent _____ companies will be visually appealing.	1	2	3	4	5	6	7
3. Employees at excellent _____ companies will be neat appearing.	1	2	3	4	5	6	7
4. Materials associated with the service (such as pamphlets or statements) will be visually appealing in an excellent _____ company.	1	2	3	4	5	6	7
5. When excellent _____ companies promise to do something by a certain time, they will do so.	1	2	3	4	5	6	7
6. When a customer has a problem, excellent _____ companies will show a sincere interest in solving it.	1	2	3	4	5	6	7
7. Excellent _____ companies will perform the service right the first time.	1	2	3	4	5	6	7
8. Excellent _____ companies will provide their services at the time they promise to do so.	1	2	3	4	5	6	7

Source: Reprinted with the permission of The Free Press, A Division of Simon & Schuster, from *Delivering Quality Service: Balancing Customer Perceptions and Expectations* by Valarie A. Zeithaml, A. Parasuraman, and Leonard L. Berry. Copyright © 1990 by The Free Press.

The Return on Quality

Despite the title of a popular book on quality,[9] it normally takes a significant investment to improve service quality. For example, Florida Power & Light spent millions of dollars competing for Japan's prestigious Deming Prize. However, the ensuing lack of attention to controlling the costs of the quality improvements upset the state's ratepayers, causing the quality program to be dismantled.

As a result, several authors have developed a **return on quality (ROQ)** approach based on the following philosophy:[10]

- Quality is an investment.
- Quality improvement efforts must be financially accountable.
- It is possible to spend too much on quality.
- Not all quality expenditures are equally valid.

The basic notion behind the ROQ approach is that managers are looking for improvements in actual customer behavior, such as increased loyalty, that generate a profit. The ROQ model is shown in Fig. 14–8.

The key to the approach is to break down satisfaction levels with an overall process into satisfaction levels with components of those processes. This allows a more targeted approach to investing in service quality because the company can invest in the areas that will deliver the greatest return. This ultimately leads to higher overall satisfaction and greater customer retention.

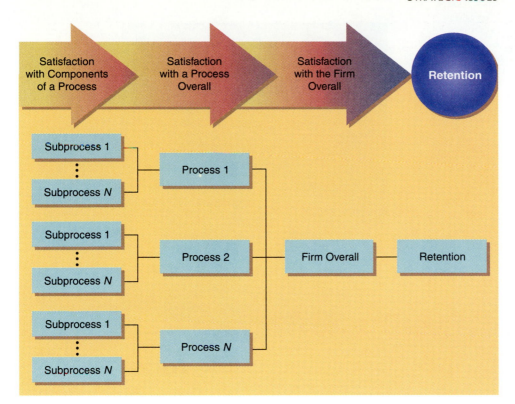

Figure 14–8

Linking Customer Satisfaction to Retention

Source: Roland T. Rust, Anthony J. Zahorik, and Timothy L. Keiningham (1994), *Return on Quality: Measuring the Financial Impact of Your Company's Quest for Quality* (Chicago: Probus).

For example, Marriott found that customers at full-service Marriotts wanted five things (processes): a great breakfast, fast check-in, fast check-out, clean rooms, and friendly service. Managers at the company then examined each process to see which subprocesses needed the most attention; that is, they gave each process the greatest leverage to increase customer satisfaction with the process and, ultimately, overall customer satisfaction. To improve breakfast service, the company speeded up service by hiring runners to bring the food to the servers; this allowed servers to be more attentive to customers. To improve check-in, the company established a system of allowing customers to register and get their room keys at the door, bypassing the front desk. For quicker check-out, the bill is slipped under the room doors at 4 A.M. and the customer just has to sign it.[11] ◆

STRATEGIC ISSUES
The Problem of Intangibility

We have noted several times in this chapter that services are intangible and, therefore, more difficult to evaluate. The challenge for a firm marketing services is to make the product tangible to the customer in order to facilitate the prepurchase evaluation and comparison to competitors.[12] Although it is possible to rely solely on image and positioning, customer reaction is more uncertain and idiosyncratic.

There are many examples of attempts to tangibilize services. Professional photographers show prospective customers books of their work. Landscape architects invite potential customers to drive by other houses for which they have constructed gardens or

trimmed trees. Advertising agencies send companies from whom they are soliciting work reels or books of their ads. Cruise operators send videotapes of happy vacationers with scenes from the ship and ports of call. Anything the marketing manager can do to make the service tangible to the potential customer reduces the amount of uncertainty involved with the purchase and increases the chances that the customer will choose you rather than the competitor.

Additionally, service providers can do a better job reminding customers of the excellent service they have received. Hotel cleaning personnel leave the strip of paper over the toilet seat, indicating that the bathroom has been sanitized. An executive at a computer company sent a letter to an information system manager, reminding the manager of all the free consulting services (e.g., evaluation of their accounts receivable system) the company had obtained over the course of the selling process. Intangibility can also mean invisibility; the challenge is to take a service that has been provided and remind the customer of what he or she has received. Many times, excellent service is taken for granted because the company has not done a good job of reminding customers of that excellent service.

One way to make a service tangible is to use sampling or other promotions to get customers to try the service at low cost or risk. New advertising agencies often send speculative creative work to companies with which they would like to develop a more permanent relationship. MBA programs usually offer prospective students the opportunity to sit in on classes to get a better feeling for the quality of the instruction and students.

The Problem of Low Barriers to Entry

Many service industries are characterized by low barriers to entry. This is particularly characteristic of professional services. It is common for law firms, stock brokerage firms

Figure 14–10

Sprint Advertisement

Sprint Bromiens

(e.g., Edward Jones), advertising agencies, consulting firms, and similar organizations to splinter, with several senior members of the original firm leaving to start their own. It is easy to obtain the credentials to become a travel or real estate agent and set up a business. Even telecommunication companies have started without any lines or repair personnel by merely purchasing excess capacity from existing companies and reselling long-distance and local services. New airlines often start up by renting used airplanes, purchasing landing rights at airports with unused capacity, hiring nonunion pilots and flight attendants, leasing maintenance services from other airlines, and using telephone or Internet-based reservation systems. Low barriers to entry create more competition, customer switching, employee turnover, and lower profits. The problem is exacerbated by the fact that many customers are loyal to the person in the company with whom they have had the most contact, rather than the company itself, and move with the employee to the new company.

Competition puts pressure on the company to develop a clear differential advantage and positioning in the marketplace. You can use the dimensions of service quality noted earlier in the chapter to differentiate your business from competition and effectively communicate or position the service.

- Reliability. An example of this positioning is shown in Fig. 14–9 in the advertisement for Tyco International's Fire & Security Services division. The message that the company is a supplier of reliable services comes through very clearly in its overall theme of protection.

- Responsiveness. An example of this positioning is shown in Fig. 14–10 in the advertisement for Sprint. Note the key words "consult" and "count on us." The text of the ad implies that Sprint is very responsive to the needs of rapidly growing businesses.
- Assurance. This aspect of service quality describes how the company inspires trust and confidence. The advertisement for Morrison & Foerster LLP shown in Fig. 14–11 is an attempt to position the firm as one you can trust if your business spans the globe.
- Tangibles. The ad for the Internet-based E*Trade (Fig. 14–12) emphasizes tangible features such as price and investor information.

An additional framework for thinking about differentiating services is the value chain shown in Fig. 3–7. Service companies can attempt to differentiate themselves from competition by emphasizing the following value chain:

- Inbound logistics. In the case of services, this focuses squarely on the quality of the employees. Because services are produced by people, product quality is directly related to staff quality and training.
- Operations. For service companies, the operation *is* the product. McDonald's quality is based on the extraordinary quality and consistency maintained throughout its restaurants. For Edward Jones, the operation is the one-person brokerage site. Federal Express's hub-and-spoke operation in Memphis is the key to its on-time record and high levels of customer satisfaction.
- Marketing and sales. As we have noted, because of the significant emphasis on image and positioning, strength in marketing is critical to success in service businesses. Because there are often few objective measures on which customers can compare competitors (other than price), marketing success often leads to success in the marketplace.

Figure 14–11

Morrison & Foerster
Advertisement

Photo: Uniphoto, Creative:
Bothwell Marketing, by:
Anne Bothwell, Agency for
Morrison & Foerster

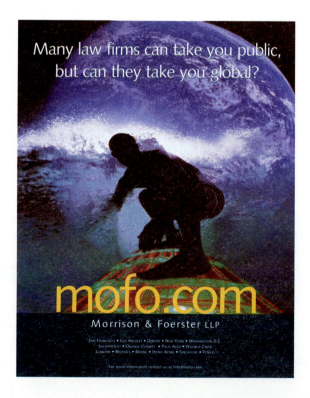

- Service. Service quality brings customers back for repeat business. Marketing can gain trial, but only customer satisfaction creates repeat purchasing. A large part of service quality is customer relationship-building (see Chapter 13) because so much of service marketing depends on personal relationships. We discuss the topic of service quality in more detail later in this chapter.

In general, these forces work together in service industries to create **reputation.** For professional services, reputation is the key asset because it is the basis for positive word-of-mouth and reduces the amount of uncertainty inherent in service products. Thus, reputation can be viewed as the sum of the competitive strategy components of excellence in employee recruiting (inbound logistics), service operations, marketing and sales, and service quality.

Service Design

Because services are intangible, they are difficult to describe and, therefore, to design and redesign if a new service is desired. Perhaps the best way to understand this is to think of design of a manufactured item. Physical goods can be blueprinted; that is, either on paper or using computer software, the physical nature of the product (width, length, circuitry design, etc.) can be described. As a result, physical product attributes can be shown, communicated, and understood easily.

Service blueprinting involves creating a flowchart that describes the flow of activity from the time the customer first contacts the service provider to the time the customer receives the service.[13]

An example of a service blueprint is shown in Fig. 14–13, a blueprint for a mail delivery service. The process or flow of the service begins when the customer calls the firm. The customer speaks with a customer service representative and then a variety of activities occur, culminating with the arrival of the package at its destination.

What is interesting about the figure is that the activities are broken down in three types. The first type, above the top line, are the parts involving customers: calling the company, giving the package for delivery, and receiving the package. The middle two types of activities describe customer contact points (what we called moments of truth in Chapter 13). Some of these contact points are observable to the customer, or "onstage"; these include the customer

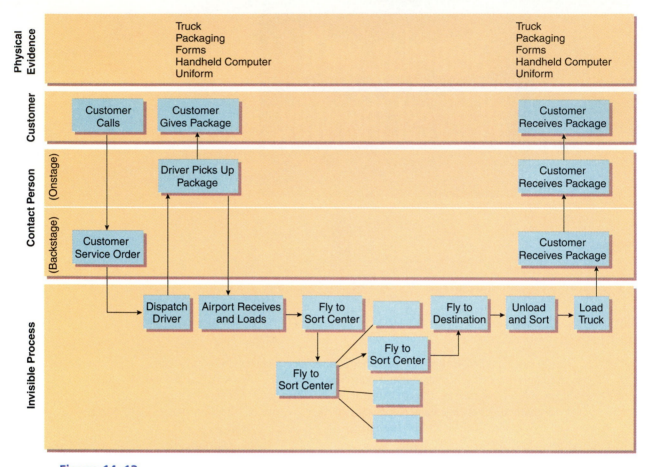

Figure 14–13

Express Mail Delivery Service Blueprint

Source: Valarie A. Zeithaml and Mary Jo Bitner (1996), *Services Marketing* (New York: McGraw-Hill), p. 281.

interactions with the drivers picking up and delivering the package. "Backstage" contact points are those in which the contact is not face-to-face; in this instance, this is limited to the person taking the order. If there were a problem with the delivery, a backstage contact would be with a customer service representative handling customer complaints or problems. For this service, much of the activity is below the third line, invisible to the customer.

These blueprints or flowcharts are extremely valuable to service companies. Perhaps the most valuable aspect of blueprints is simply the exercise of creating one. The act of creating a service flowchart forces you to put yourself in the shoes of the customer and thereby develop better insights about the service encounter. As a result, the moments of truth become clear. In addition, the key areas for potential service failure and thus the need for backup and recovery systems are highlighted. In Fig. 14–13, it is easy to see that each arrow involves a potential service failure, creating the need to think carefully about the process. When the customer calls the service center to place an order, how is she greeted? How many phone rings are acceptable? After the order is placed, the company needs a system to give the order efficiently and quickly to the dispatcher to get a driver to pick up the package. When the driver has the order and goes to the customer's home or place of work, how is the driver dressed? Is she or he polite and knowledgeable? These kinds of questions can be extended to the other boxes and arrows in the blueprint.

As a result, blueprints are useful tools for understanding the design of the service and for redesigning it. For example, Federal Express and UPS have information systems in place, so the large space in the top half of Fig. 14–13 between "Customer Gives Package" and "Customer Receives Package" could have a box labeled "Customer Tracks Package." Bar coding on each package enables the companies to know where every package is at a given time. Customers can input the package ID number using PC-based software or the companies' Web sites and obtain that location information for themselves.

◆ Illustration: Singapore Airlines

Although Singapore is only 25% of the size of the state of Rhode Island, Singapore Airlines is one of the world's 10 biggest airlines, as measured in international tons-kilometers of load carried.[14] The airline became successful by concentrating on marketing. The goal of the airline's management was to create an international airline with a distinctly Asian personality. At the top of the priority list was an emphasis on customer service; the company used the island's main natural resource—the natural hospitality of its people—as a competitive advantage. Through comfortable seating, free drinks and movie headsets, and the hospitality of its flight attendants, Singapore Airlines has set the world standard for international air travel quality.

In 1991, the airline was facing increased competition and improved service quality from several Western and Asian airlines, including Cathay Pacific, Japan Airlines, Thai International, and Malaysia Airlines. The challenge facing the company was how to continue to maintain the airline's outstanding reputation for customer service and technical innovation.

To better understand customer needs, the company undertook two activities. The first was a blueprinting operation. The result is shown in Fig. 14–14. Although the format is somewhat

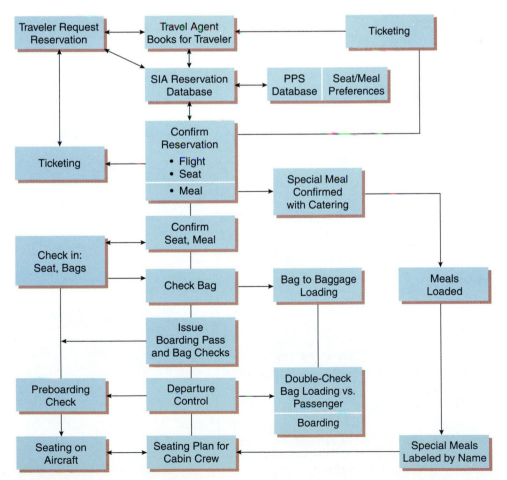

Figure 14–14

Singapore Airlines Service Blueprint

Source: Sandra Vandermerwe and Christopher H. Lovelock (1991), "Singapore Airlines: using technology for service excellence," IMD case #592-014-1, p. 20.

different from that of Fig. 14–13, it can be seen that the parts of the service operation visible to the customer are on the left part of the figure, and the internal aspects of the operation are on the right. This flowchart goes only up to the point where the customer is seated on the aircraft. In addition, the contact people are omitted.

A more thorough analysis of customer activities is shown in Fig. 14–15. Note that these activities are divided into three parts: preflight, in-flight, and postarrival. Singapore Airlines used this flowchart in two ways. First, each block in the activity sequence was separately analyzed from a customer service, moment-of-truth perspective. Second, the airline also evaluated each block to see where technological enhancements could improve their customers' experiences and provide additional ways to differentiate from the competition. ◆

Figure 14–15

Singapore Airlines: Detailed Customer Service Activities

Source: Sandra Vandermerwe and Christopher H. Lovelock (1991), "Singapore Airlines: using technology for service excellence," IMD case #592-014-1, pp. 21–23.

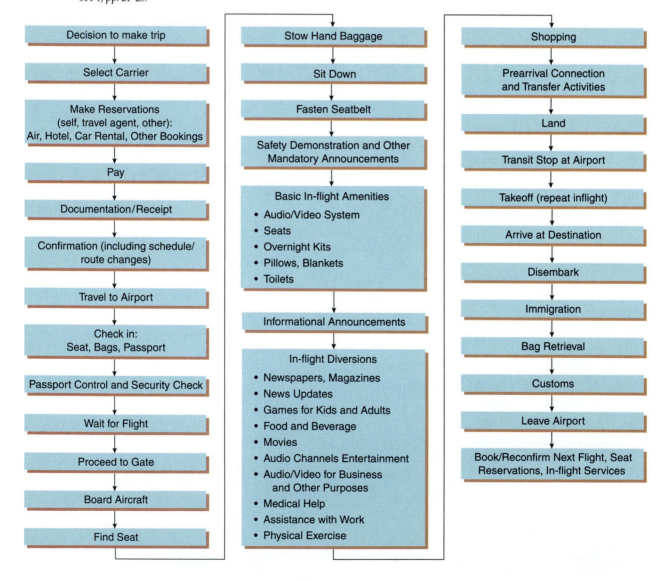

MARKETING MIX IMPLICATIONS
OF SERVICE MARKETING

In general, decisions on pricing, channels of distribution, and communications are made using the same general principles described earlier in this book, whether the product is a manufactured good or a service. However, a few subtle differences must be acknowledged.

Channels of Distribution

Because services are intangible, the notion of physical distribution channels does not apply. However, the general principle of channels offering customers access to the product does.

Because services are characterized by the inseparability of production and consumption, service organizations must be physically present when the service is delivered or engage others to be present. Recall the comparison of direct and indirect channels in Chapter 9. Any time the product leaves the producing company's hands and is put under the control of others, there is the potential for the independent channel member to do a less effective job marketing the product than the producer would. This is an even greater problem with services because they are often delivered by people. Nonstandardization of services increases when the service is being delivered by people who do not work for your company.

As a result, we can draw a distinction between the service principal (the company or person originating the service) and the service deliverer (the person or company that actually delivers the service to customers). As with physical goods, service deliverers or intermediaries can provide a number of benefits to the principal. Service deliverers can coproduce the service with the principal. For example, franchisees delivering automobile lubrication services (e.g., Jiffy Lube) execute the principal's concepts by operating the service centers and lubricating the cars (often other services are available as well). Service intermediaries also provide the customer with locations that make it easy to purchase services. Multiple Jiffy Lube outlets in a metropolitan area make it convenient for customers to purchase the lubricating services. These local retail outlets also promote the Jiffy Lube brand name and provide local presence for the service principal.

Because services are intangible, perishable, and generally not storable, services must be brought to the customer. That is, the service principal must design a channel structure that brings the customer and the provider together.

The three major approaches to service distribution are franchising, agents and brokers, and electronic channels.

Franchising

Franchising is an extremely popular form of retail service distribution covering a wide variety of consumer and business-to-business services. A franchise is a contractual agreement between originator of the service concept (the franchiser) and an individual or organization that provides retail distribution for the service (the franchisee). It works particularly well when the service can be standardized across disparate geographic locations. Elements of a typical franchise agreement are the following:[15]

- The nature of the service to be supplied by the franchiser
- The geographic territory within which the franchisee can market the service
- The percentage of the revenue generated by the franchisee that must be paid to the franchiser
- The length of the agreement
- The up-front fee paid by the franchisee to the franchiser

- The terms by which the franchisee agrees to operate and deliver the service
- An agreement by the franchisee not to sell another company's services
- The promotional support provided by the franchiser to help develop the franchisee's market
- The administrative and technical support provided by the franchiser
- The conditions under which the agreement can be terminated

Agents and Brokers

Many service companies use independent agents or brokers to sell their services. Well-known examples are the insurance and travel industries. As the discussion in Chapter 9 showed, there are tradeoffs with using these methods for distributing any kind of product. Major advantages include a wider distribution and the fact that agents and brokers know their local markets well. Disadvantages include the loss of control: It is very difficult to determine what agents and brokers are doing and what they are saying about your product.

Electronic Channels

The growth of the Internet has spawned many opportunities for distributing services. The financial services industry in particular has taken advantage of electronic channels through services such as home banking and stock brokerage. The advantage of electronic channels is their low cost and the ease of access (for those with Internet connections). For example, rather than using a large number of branch banks or automatic teller machines ("bricks and mortar"), customers of most major banks can now check their balances, move money between accounts, and pay bills using the banks' Web sites. The implications of the Internet and technology in general on service marketing are discussed more thoroughly later in this chapter.

Advertising

The role of communications in service delivery is shown in Fig. 14–5. As we have discussed, a key element of service quality evaluation is the assessment of the service relative to expectations. Advertising plays an important role in setting customer expectations. Therefore, marketing managers for services must be very careful not to promise what cannot be delivered. All communications targeted to customers should be examined in terms of how well

Franchising is a popular approach to service distribution. Across the United States, travelers know that they can expect the same standard of quality and service from franchises such as the Marriott Marquis. (Richard Hamilton Smith/Corbis)

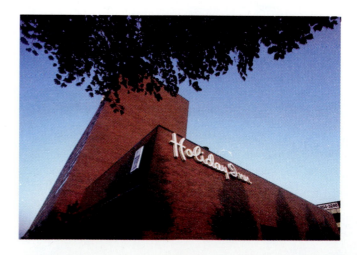

The financial services industry has taken advantage of the growth of the Internet by offering convenient on-line services and information related to personal banking, mortgages and loans, credit cards, investing, retirement planning, tax filing, and more. This home page for Citibank U.S. shows some of these on-line services. (Courtesy of Citibank)

they reflect reality; if you do not do this, the customer certainly will. The unique aspects of services discussed in this chapter have the following implications for advertising.[16]

First, service advertising should contain vivid information. Vivid information is more likely to hold the viewer's attention and excite the imagination. It also results in improved customer understanding of the service. Because service attributes are intangible, this improved understanding is critical to a customer's ability to evaluate the service's quality and to compare it to other options. Vividness can be achieved through three different strategies: attempts to make the service tangible; concrete, specific language; and dramatization. A good example of the latter is the series of American Express commercials featuring actor Karl Malden that demonstrated the value and security of American Express traveler's checks by showing the disasters that can befall travelers if they use a competitor's brand.

A problem customers face when purchasing a service is developing alternatives from which to make the final choice. The reason that this can be difficult is inherent in the way services are distributed. When a service is delivered through a franchise operation, there is only one choice at a particular location, unlike the normal assortment available from retailers of physical goods. Although some (e.g., travel agents) do offer competing services, many do not. Thus, a major problem facing service companies is how to get your brand into the customer's choice set.

The relevant communication goal is to have the customer connect your brand with the product category. This can be done with repetition or through an approach called interactive imagery. Imagery involves having customers visualize a concept or relationship. Interactive imagery integrates two items in some mutual or reciprocal action. This approach can be used to enhance vividness. The advertisement for Marriott shown in Fig. 14–16 is an example of this kind of imagery. In this ad, the interaction with the businesswoman and the craft dealers highlights the business traveler's ability to get work done and enjoy the local surroundings.

Finally, service attributes are experience or credence attributes, not search attributes. Therefore, prepurchase evaluation of services is difficult. One way to approach this problem is to highlight the behind-the-scenes rules, policies, and procedures that make the service provider the best option to choose. This helps to make the service tangible to customers and gives assurance that it will be of high quality. Alternatively, a marketing manager can use the ad to show the service actually in use. The advertising for Singapore Airlines' first-class service is an example of this approach. The picture of the very comfortable-looking passengers in the ads gives potential customers a sense of how great a trip on Singapore Airlines would be.

Pricing

Customers find service prices difficult to determine and compare. You cannot put price tags on services. The fact that services can be delivered in many different configurations make the task even more difficult. For example, try finding out a rate on a mortgage for a house. The combinations of terms (5, 15, 20, 30 years), amount of downpayment, points you are willing to pay (percentage of the loan amount paid as a fee to the mortgage originator), and myriad other options are nearly infinite. Try the same exercise with life insurance policies. Therefore, it is important to simplify your pricing policy as much as possible to eliminate customer confusion.

Figure 14–16

Marriott
Advertisement

Marriott International

More than with physical goods, price is often used as an indicator of service quality. This is because service quality is more difficult to ascertain. Thus, the pricing of services must be consistent with the overall strategy for the product. For example, if you decide to drop the price of your service but attempt to maintain a premium brand image through your communications and other elements of the service operation, customers will become confused or skeptical: If you are so good, why are you so cheap? Although consistency between the strategy and price is important for all products, in service businesses, where purchasing is driven so heavily by perceptions, it is critical.

In service industries, the role of the reference price is very important. As described in Chapter 11, a reference price is an internal standard against which observed prices are compared. Reference prices are based on both past experience in a product category (internal reference prices) and observed prices in the marketplace (external reference prices). Not only is price information more difficult to collect for services, but the large number of product alternatives can make price comparisons impossible. For example, for competing automobile insurance policies, the deductibles or other aspects of the policies often are slightly different, making exact price comparisons difficult. When a customer cannot use observed prices easily to make a purchase decision, internal reference price becomes more important as a way of simplifying the process.

To illustrate these two service pricing principles, the author recently decided to have the gutters of his house cleaned before the winter rains hit (fortunately, there is no snow in Berkeley). Obtaining prices for such services is very time-consuming because it entails waiting at home for the (uncertain) arrival of the service providers. Two companies gave bids, one much higher than the other. With little experience to draw upon, I calculated a reference price based simply on what seemed to be reasonable. Both bids were below this price, so they both remained in the running for the work. I then chose the higher of the two, figuring that the lower-priced company would skimp on the work somehow. ◆

THE IMPACT OF TECHNOLOGY ON SERVICE MARKETING

The rapid improvements in and diffusion of information technology and the use of the Internet have changed marketing in general and, specifically, service marketing for three main reasons:

- As mentioned earlier in the chapter, the use of the Internet has created a new channel of distribution ideally suited for certain kinds of services, particularly those involving financial transactions.
- Recall that an important feature of services is that because they are often delivered by people, their quality is variable both at one point in time and over time, (i.e., they are nonstandardized). Computerization, substituting capital for labor, provides uniform service delivery at a quality level people cannot match.
- As in all product categories, companies are looking for new ways to differentiate their products from competitors. Information technology and the Internet have provided powerful, tangible opportunities for such differentiation.

◆ **Illustration: Financial Services** ————————————————

Perhaps the best example of how an industry has used all three of these opportunities is the financial services industry.[17] In 1995, global spending on information technology in the financial services industry was nearly $100 billion; it is expected to reach $200 billion annually by the year 2005. Some of this expenditure is for building, expanding, and using customer databases that are based on financial transactions such as credit card purchases. Some is for expanding ATM networks so that banks can serve customer needs more efficiently. Much of the rest is for creating network server capacity for Internet-based activities such as stock transactions and bill paying.

There is uncertainty about the mechanism by which home banking and investing will occur. It is almost taken for granted that the mechanism will be computer based; that is, people will invest and bank through modem or other connections through a stand-alone or network PC. However, some industry observers who believe that the mechanism will be telephone based. After all, the household penetration rate of touch-tone telephones is far greater than that of PCs. In Britain, Direct Line became the dominant auto insurer within a few years using a phone-based system.

One major problem is the perceived lack of security for sensitive financial transactions on the sprawling Internet. A second problem is that the shift from labor to capital has given some smaller banks a market opportunity: They position themselves as the "human" bank in a valiant struggle against the giant, faceless competitors. For some market segments, that is an appealing strategy.

Some specific illustrations are given here.

Wells Fargo Bank

Since 1980, following the acquisition of two large California-based banks (Crocker and First Interstate), Wells Fargo has closed more traditional branch bank locations than it currently operates.[18] Rather than spending about $4 million to open a new branch, Wells prefers to spend $50,000 on a branch in a supermarket. The company's marketing strategy is simple: They are attempting to differentiate themselves on the basis of convenience and value.

Wells was the pioneer in lending using technology; by developing proprietary credit-rating and other computer programs, they became the largest small business lender in the United States. As early as 1996, the bank had 200,000 cyberaccounts (people and businesses banking through Intuit's Quicken, Microsoft Money, Prodigy, and its own Web site) and is the largest provider of Internet banking services. Wells now allows customers to apply for home equity loans on-line and receive a customized loan (or denial) in 3 seconds! The technology behind this includes real-time links to credit bureaus, databases with customer transaction histories and real estate property values, and software that can perform cash flow analyses. The bank uses similar software to make loans to small businesses. This is a big change for the bank, which used to turn away such loans as being too small and thus being unprofitable to process. By reducing the loan approval process from 4 days to 4 hours, the bank dramatically increased its share in that segment of the market. Although many of its competitors poke fun at the mistakes the bank has made in the drastic switch to computerization as well as the "inhuman" nature of its service, the company has a clear strategy and has staked out a large niche in a very competitive market.

Charles Schwab

Many people know Charles Schwab as one of the earliest discount stock brokers in the United States. The company has been extraordinarily successful in the new electronic commerce age. As of 1998, of the roughly 5 million active, on-line brokerage accounts in the United States, about one-third are with Schwab. Interestingly, there are cheaper alternatives; E*Trade (see Fig. 14–12) charges about 50% less than Schwab's e.Schwab service. However, because prices are so low and Schwab dominates the industry in customer service and reputation, the price difference does not seem to matter. Schwab's customers are technically sophisticated: 70% own PCs and 50% are hooked up to the Internet. To help more customers move to the Web, Schwab is putting Net-linked PCs in branches and offering training sessions, sometimes even in customers' homes. In order to stay on the leading edge, the company spends about 13% of its revenues on information technology.

Chase Manhattan Bank

In 1996, Chase spent $1.8 billion on information technology; among banks, only Citicorp outspent it. The bank has become expert at data mining, taking vast amounts of customer transaction data and "slicing and dicing" it in a variety of ways to help managers spot opportunities with both business and consumer segments. Chase has a 71% market share in middle-market (medium-sized companies) lending in the New York metropolitan area. A large part of this market dominance is due to its $20 million Relationship Management System, which lets its 1,000 lending officers access and update customer information on laptop computers while away from the office. The lending officers can quickly locate customers with more borrowing potential and can instantly calculate the profitability of each customer. Using a Windows-based PC system, retail (consumer) managers can analyze customer data and determine how profitable each product is at any time, as well as simulate what-ifs for possible product changes. In auto finance, Chase is third behind General Motors and Ford, with $11 billion in loans. In conjunction with IBM, Chase developed a proprietary touch-screen system that enables auto dealers to obtain customer loans in 5 to 10 minutes. ◆

EXECUTIVE SUMMARY

The main points of this chapter include the following:

- Most services can be characterized as having experience attributes (where product quality is determined only after usage) rather than search attributes (where product quality can be ascertained before purchase).
- The main characteristics of services are intangibility (lack of physical attributes), nonstandardization (because they are usually delivered by people), and inseparability of production and consumption.
- Service quality is defined by the service provider's reliability, responsiveness, assurance, empathy, and tangibles (service features or physical aspects of the service delivery).
- Service quality is assessed negatively when there is a gap between customer expectations and experienced quality.
- Service quality can be measured through the use of survey instruments such as SERVQUAL; the financial return on investments in service quality can also be evaluated.
- Some strategic issues in services marketing are tangibilizing the service to customers, combating low entry barriers, and using service blueprints to design services.
- New technologies on service marketing affect channels of distribution, improved standardization of service offerings, and the establishment of competitive advantage.

CHAPTER QUESTIONS

1. Consider the three kinds of attributes described in this chapter: search, experience, and credence. Which of these are most appropriate for services? What are the implications for marketing managers?

2. Recall the last time you had an unsatisfactory encounter with a service provider. Given dimensions of service quality discussed in the chapter, exactly where were the negative gaps between expectations and the actual service?

3. Pick two services, one consumer and one industrial. What can a company in each industry do to make its services more tangible to customers?

4. Develop a blueprint for the course registration process at your school or university. Where are the likely service failure points? Where can the school improve its service levels?

5. Suppose you have spent the first 5 years of your career working for Proctor & Gamble as the assistant, associate, or brand manager for Crest toothpaste. You apply for a job as a senior marketing manager for United Airlines. What have you learned at P&G that is applicable to airline marketing? What do you need to learn about airline marketing to be effective beyond the fact that airlines are different from toothpaste?

Integrated Case

Application Exercises: Service Marketing in the PC Industry

Although personal computers are obviously not services, a useful exercise is to consider how PC manufacturers can extend their businesses and brand names by developing and marketing services. An example from the mainframe computer category is IBM's extensive business developed from corporations' needs to move computer facilities.

1. Develop a service business for a PC manufacturer.
2. Develop a service blueprint for this new service (see Figs. 14–13 through 14–15).
3. Develop a marketing strategy for that new service business.
4. How does the strategy for the service business differ from the strategies developed for PC manufacturers?

FURTHER READING

A good background paper for service quality measurement is Terry Grapentine (1998/99), "The history and future of service quality assessment," *Marketing Research,* Winter/Spring, pp. 5–20. The *Journal of Service Research* is an excellent source for contemporary research on the marketing of services. An article on an interesting aspect of service marketing, why customers switch service providers, is Susan M. Keaveney (1995), "Customer switching behavior in service industries: an exploratory study," *Journal of Marketing,* 59 (April), pp. 71–82. For an article on pricing in service industries characterized by yield management policies (balancing capacity constraints with lost revenues from, for example, empty seats in a theater), see Ramarao Desiraju and Steven M. Shugan (1999), "Strategic service pricing and yield management," *Journal of Marketing,* 63 (January), pp. 44–56.

Strategies for Technology-Based Markets

15

CHAPTER BRIEF

The purpose of this chapter is to introduce the special nature of marketing technology-based products and services. Key areas of learning are the following:

Customer behavior factors affecting the adoption rate of new technologies
The diffusion of innovations model for understanding how consumers adopt new technologies over the product life cycle
Developing marketing strategies for high-technology products
Marketing mix decision-making

Rogers Communications, Inc., is a Canadian communication company with three main lines of business: cable television (35% of revenues and 48% of profits in 1995), wireless (e.g., cellular) communications (33% of revenues and 43% of profits), and multimedia (TV stations, newspapers, etc.).[1] The company is Canada's largest cable television and cellular phone operator.

In late 1995, the company launched a new service called The Wave, which would give home and business users access to the Internet via cable TV lines. This and similar products are called cable modems.[2] At the time, there were three different ways a user's computer could be connected to the Internet:

- A user could use a standard phone line with a modem and a subscription to an internet service provider (ISP), which would then connect the user to the Internet.
- Through local telephone companies, a user could subscribe to an integrated service digital network (ISDN), which, with a more expensive modem and an ISP, could connect at much faster speeds than a standard phone line.
- The fastest option available mainly through corporate links rather than through the home was fiberoptic cable or special copper wire.

Many alternative technologies for delivering the Internet to homes and businesses are being considered because of the convergence of the television, telephone, and computer industries. Although the vast majority of computer connections from the home are made by modem, because of the slow speed of conventional telephone lines it is clear that this technology will be superseded by one of the existing options or some other technology (possibly including new telephone technology), permitting much higher rates of Internet access. Both the technology to be used and the industry that will disseminate it are uncertain. The most likely candidates are phone (e.g., AT&T) and cable TV companies. However, any company with a pipeline into the home, including utility companies, are also candidates. In addition, a wide variety of wireless options are being considered, such as satellite TV.

Thus, in 1995, the issues facing Rogers Communications included the following:

- Consumer issues. Who are the likely customers for this new service? How much do they know about service features and benefits? How much are they willing to pay?
- Strategic issues. Assuming that the company chooses to launch the new service, what strategy should be used, skimming (high price, low market share) or penetration (low price, high market share)?
- Technology issues. Is there sufficient content on the Web to create derived demand for the new service? Particularly relevant for the home market, how fast will the market grow and to what penetration levels will personal computers grow? What will be the standard technology for connecting to the Internet? More broadly, will the Internet and the Web be superseded by some new technology?
- Competitive issues. Against which companies and substitute technologies will Rogers be competing?

The goal of this chapter is to focus on the marketing of technology-based products and services such as The Wave. It should be noted that technology itself exists not only in products, but also in processes and management. For example, even in what are thought to be low-tech products such as toothpaste, most companies are using the latest manufacturing and information technologies to make the products and manage the companies. This is necessary simply to remain competitive in the late twentieth century's globally competitive markets.

The emphasis here is on the products and services. However, it is difficult to define exactly what *high-tech* entails. Most products and services use advanced technology somewhere in the production process or in the product itself. A service delivered over cable TV to connect to the Internet might be considered high-tech. But what makes that service high-tech? Although many definitions of *high-tech* have been offered, a useful distinction between high-tech and low-tech products is made on the basis of two kinds of uncertainty: market and technological.[3]

There are many sources of market uncertainty. Customers are uncertain about a technology's potential uses and benefits. In the Rogers Communications situation, the value of having a high-speed connection to the Web and, in general, of the Web and the Internet, is unclear. Another kind of uncertainty is the lack of knowledge about the potential market size or the rate at which the technology will diffuse through the population. This makes estimating the profit potential of a new, technology-based product difficult to estimate. Market uncertainty also arises from how the product or service will have to adapt to changing technological standards. A good example is how personal computer companies had to adapt to changes in the size of floppy disks from $5\frac{1}{4}$ inch to $3\frac{1}{2}$ inch, with possible further changes to come. Thus, market uncertainty is the lack of knowledge about what the market wants.

Technological uncertainty is not knowing whether the technology can meet customer needs better than competing technologies. Perhaps the main source of uncertainty is whether the product or service will actually perform as promised; customers are skeptical about new technology and the hype that accompanies brand new products. Thus, a key problem for Rogers Communications is convincing homeowners that high-quality access to the Internet as well as TV shows can be delivered over the same line. Another source is the reliability of the new technology. New-generation jet aircraft are always tested thoroughly before they are sold to commercial airlines to reduce perceived reliability problems. The ability of a company to deliver a new high-tech product is always uncertain. When computer software companies announce new versions of their products, the promised delivery dates are usually met with skepticism on the part of customers because of the delays that are usually encountered (such software is often called vaporware). Particularly for corporate customers, an important source of uncertainty is technological obsolescence (how long the current technological standard is likely to last). The author can recall when PCs built with the 286 microprocessor (the IBM AT, for example) were promised to last for some time; these were made obsolete rather quickly by computers built with the 386 microprocessor. Companies worry about the size of investments to make in a technology and often delay purchasing until they are satisfied that they can amortize the investment over what they consider to be a reasonable period of time.

Thus, one definition of a **high-technology product market** is one in which both market and technology uncertainty are high. A key manifestation of a high-tech market is short product life cycles. They are shortened by technological innovation that often makes obsolete the previous version or all versions of the product. When product life cycles are short, there is considerably more pressure on marketing managers to make a profit as quickly as possible. Fine-tuning the product after it is introduced is not always possible. Thus, it is fairly common for high-tech products to be launched with bugs or defects.

Table 15–1 shows how short product life cycles can be. This table shows the introduction date, initial selling price, and technical capabilities of Intel microprocessors. Although other companies such as AMD also make these microprocessors, Intel is normally the innovator, and a switch in their technology largely means the end of the life cycle for the previous generation.[4] As can be seen, the life cycles average around 3 or 4 years.

Another characteristic of high-tech markets is that they are turbulent. Sales can go up or down rapidly. Companies are founded and disappear weekly. Managers become instantly wealthy on paper based on their stock holdings when their company goes public; this wealth can disappear almost as quickly when the stock price drops precipitously. Many companies bet on digital audiotape; now they are betting on digital video disks (DVDs). Large companies such as Lotus and Wang grow large and prosperous and then, because other companies leapfrog their technology (Microsoft's Excel versus Lotus 1-2-3) or because they make

Table 15–1 Changing Microprocessor Technology

Intel Chip	Date	Initial Cost	Transistors	Initial mips*
4004	11/71	$ 200	2,300	0.06
8008	4/72	300	3,500	0.06
8080	4/74	300	6,000	0.6
8086	6/78	360	29,000	0.3
8088	6/79	360	29,000	0.3
1286	2/82	360	134,000	0.9
1386	10/85	299	275,000	5.0
1486	4/89	950	1,200,000	20.0
Pentium	3/93	878	3,100,000	100.0
Pentium Pro	3/95	974	5,500,000	300.0
789[†]	1997	1,000	8,000,000	500.0
886[†]	2000	1,000	15,000,000	1,000.0
1286[†]	2011	N/A	1,000,000,000	100,000.0

*Million instructions per second. [†]Industry estimates.

Sources: Kleiner Perkins Caufield & Byers; Intel Corp.; Dataquest, Inc.

Figure 15–1

The Speed of Change

Source: Dallas Federal
Reserve Bank.

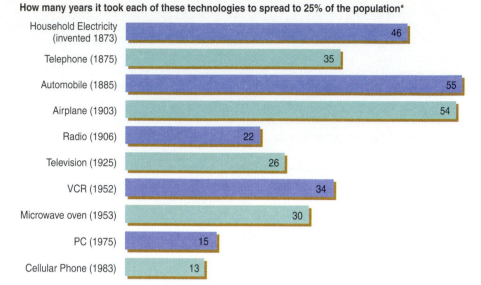

How many years it took each of these technologies to spread to 25% of the population*

Household Electricity (invented 1873)	46
Telephone (1875)	35
Automobile (1885)	55
Airplane (1903)	54
Radio (1906)	22
Television (1925)	26
VCR (1952)	34
Microwave oven (1953)	30
PC (1975)	15
Cellular Phone (1983)	13

*Defined as 25% of households, except for airplane, automobile, and cell phone.
Airplane: 25% of the 1996 level of air miles traveled per capita.
Automobile: The number of motor vehicles reached 25% of the number of people age 16 and older.
Cellular phone: The number of cellular phones reached 25% of the number of registered passenger automobiles.

the wrong technological bets (Wang's focus on stand-alone word processing systems), they virtually disappear. When economic times get difficult, high-tech products are often hurt by uncertainty about the soundness of the investment.[5]

Thus, the high-tech marketing world is fast-moving and exhilarating. In addition, the rate of adoption of new technologies is increasing, putting more pressure on companies to innovate or become obsolete. Figure 15–1 shows the increase in the diffusion of new technologies in the United States for selected products. Whereas it took 55 years for the automobile to penetrate 25% of the population, it has taken only 13 years for the same to occur for cellular phones. This rapid diffusion presents both opportunities and challenges to marketers. The rapid diffusion and shorter product life cycles means that the management of high-tech products is not just a game in which engineers try to outdo each other. Mature markets imply that segmentation, positioning, and sound execution of the marketing mix are as important as, if not more important than, having the latest and greatest technology.

CUSTOMER BEHAVIOR

Factors Affecting the Adoption Rate of New Technologies

From the customer's perspective, the unique problems associated with the marketing of technology-based products are concentrated largely in the earliest stages of the product life cycle. After the product category is established, in the late growth or maturity stage of the product life cycle, most products, whether high-tech or low-tech, become well known and are marketed in much the same way as other kinds of products and services. For example, when videocassette recorders were first marketed in the 1960s, customers had little idea about how to use them and why they would be worth buying. Today, VCRs are almost a commodity business, with strong price competition and multiple units in many households.

What factors affect the success rate of technology-based innovations? The most extensive analysis of how customers, both consumers and businesses, consider whether to adopt new technologies was conducted by Everett Rogers.[6] Rogers identified five key factors or attributes to explain why or why not customers adopt new technologies.

Relative Advantage

Relative advantage is simple but critical: A customer will adopt an innovation only if she or he considers it to be an improvement over the current product being used to satisfy the same need. Relative advantage can be stated in many different terms: economic, psychological, or utilitarian. Thus, the rate of acceptance or diffusion of an innovation throughout the population is increased by the innovation's relative advantage.

Consider the adoption of word processing systems (such as those sold by Wang in the 1970s) and word processing software. Clearly, a key relative advantage of this innovation was economic. Most readers will not remember the error-correcting and revision processes for manuscripts before word processing. Secretaries spent a great deal of time manually cutting and pasting. In addition, book production costs have dropped dramatically because most publishers can produce a book directly from the author's computer files. The benefits of new seed strains developed through biotechnological advances include increased yields of many crops and thus greater profits for farmers. Again, it can be seen that relative advantage is often economic.

Particularly for consumer products, relative advantage can be obtained from psychological benefits or status. Although the initial targets for cellular phones were businesspeople, many people with economic justification for the product bought them for the status conferred by the antenna on their cars. The initial purchasers of DVD players purchased not only the new technology itself but the ability to say that they are among the first in their neighborhoods to own one.

Relative advantage is also obtained from noneconomic, utilitarian benefits of new technologies. Although some consumers may have purchased cellular phones for their status, many others purchased them for the increased ability to stay in touch with children and baby-sitters. VCRs provide economic benefits by enabling people to watch movies at home at a lower price. They also allow consumers to time-shift TV viewing by taping programs and replaying them at more convenient times.

Compatibility

A second attribute of innovations that is evaluated by customers of new technologies is the **compatibility** of the innovation with existing systems, values and beliefs, or previously introduced ideas. Higher compatibility leads to faster adoption of innovation.

For example, the initial penetration rate of satellite TV dishes was very slow. The earliest dishes were large structures that occupied a large amount of outdoor space. Early adopters were people living on farms or in other rural areas where there was plenty of land; the dishes were incompatible with apartments and houses in urban areas. The sales of these systems increased rapidly in the late 1990s as technological improvements greatly reduced their size and thus made them compatible with more consumers' living conditions. ◆

Other products have succeeded by being compatible with customer knowledge or systems. The rapid penetration rate of cellular phones is at least partially related to the fact that although the technology was new, they were basically still telephones, a product with which customers were very familiar. The great success of Iomega's Zip and Jaz drives, computer disk drives holding large amounts of data, was influenced by the fact that the company made them compatible with existing personal computers. One of the advantages of The Wave is that cable TV is ubiquitous and well known to many customers.

Complexity

The perceived **complexity** of the innovation is negatively related to the success of an innovation. Simple innovations are clearly more likely to be adopted than those that require a significant amount of explanation about their use and benefits. One of the problems with the Apple Newton personal digital assistant was that it had too many features for most users. In addition, the handwriting recognition feature of the product was difficult to train to recognize the user's particular style.

Trialability

Trialability is the ability of potential users to try a product on a limited basis before adopting. Obviously, this is a particular problem for new technologies, where uncertainty about the product is high. It is also a problem for services; as we noted in Chapter 14, their inherent intangibility and experience attributes make prepurchase evaluation difficult.

Many high-tech companies handle this problem by establishing beta test sites for early versions of a product. Particularly large and influential customers are given prototypes to use in their organizations and generate feedback for the company. New services are tested by customers in realistic settings. For example, the cable modem network developed by @Home was first tested in Fremont, California, in residents' homes.

Observability

Observability is the degree to which an innovation and its results are visible to others. The cellular phone antenna makes the adoption of the phone observable to others and reinforces the idea that it is a useful innovation (in addition to the status aspect mentioned previously). German software firm SAP is the leader in enterprise application software, programs that manage a company's vital operations, from order-taking to manufacturing to accounting. The category has expanded dramatically as stories about the tremendous cost savings and efficiencies obtainable from such software have been published in most leading business publications and mentioned in numerous speeches around the world. In other words, the economic relative advantage has been enhanced because the innovation is more observable.

Potential for Network Externalities

The previous five aspects of innovations were promulgated by Rogers's work. Another factor that has been found to have a significant impact on the adoption of new technologies is the potential for **network externalities.** The concept behind network externalities is simple: For many products and services, the value of owning them increases as the number of owners increases.[7] The original concept was developed for telephone-like networks; clearly, the benefits from owning a phone increase as the number of owners increases. Thus, the attractiveness of many products is driven by how many others are "on the network." Examples include the telephone, on-line services such as America Online, video game systems (kids like to share games and bring them to friends' houses), and computer software. The importance of network externalities limits a company's ability to develop the market for a product or service because the markets for stand-alone products (i.e., those not subject to network externalities) normally develop more quickly.

◆ Illustration: Fax Machines

Perhaps the classic example of a product affected by network externalities is the fax machine. The first transmission of an image over a wire was performed by a Scot, Alexander Bain, in 1842.[8] However, the first commercial applications of facsimile transmissions did not occur until 1910, when news photos were transmitted over long distances. By the 1940s and 1950s, the main uses of fax technology were for transmitting weather maps, newspaper proofs, news photographs, and fingerprints. However, transmission speeds of about 10 minutes per page were too slow for commercial applications. In addition, there were no standards for the machines, so different manufacturers' devices could not communicate.

Although the machines continued to improve, the industry did not really take off until the Consultative Committee on Telegraph and Telephone (CCITT), an international standard-setting group, developed standards for fax machines in 1976. The CCITT developed the retroactive G1 standard to be compatible with the Xerox Telecopier launched in 1967, a machine that could transmit documents at a rate of a page every 4 to 6 minutes. The G2 standard, popularized by Matshushita around 1973, halved the transmission time of the G1. However, the G3 standard adopted in 1980, characterized by transmission speeds of 10–20 seconds per page, really created the market. In Japan, the first market to adopt fax machines in large quantities, the installed base went from 140,000 in 1980 to 1.1 million in 1985 and to 3 million in 1988. This growth resulted from several factors, including product improvements such as smaller machines that could sit easily on desks. However, it was also clearly related to the network aspect of the product: The more that were sold, the more valuable having one became.

The importance of network externalities is made even clearer by the failure of Federal Express's ZapMail facsimile service. Launched in 1983, ZapMail promised document-quality transmission, a big improvement over the chemically coated paper that was the standard of the time. However, the machines were proprietary and had to be leased from Federal Express. Because they could not communicate with existing fax machines, the success of the product depended entirely on how many were adopted. When few were, there was no incentive for users to adopt more. The company pulled the plug on ZapMail in 1986.[9] ◆

Perceived Risk

An important concept related to these factors affecting the adoption of new technologies is **perceived risk.** Perceived risk is the uncertainty involved with relative advantage, compatibility, complexity, trialability, observability, and potential for network externalities.

Perceived risk is defined as the extent to which the customer is uncertain about the consequences of an action.[10] Although perceived risk may be high in many different purchase situations, the high-tech environment is particularly susceptible to it. There are two components of perceived risk: uncertainty (the likelihood that certain outcomes might occur) and consequences (whether these outcomes will be positive or negative and how severe they might be).

Thus, the challenge for high-tech marketing managers is to reduce either the uncertainty or severity of possible negative consequences. The former can be done using the beta test sites described earlier. In addition, high-tech firms often employ application engineers, who work closely with customers to ensure that the product or service works in their environments. Offering extensive employee training is also a common strategy. Minimizing negative consequences can be accomplished through generous warranty and return policies or discounts on upgrades.

The Problem of High-Tech Versus High-Touch

Some observers believe that too much technology can overwhelm consumers, causing them to yearn for the "old days" and to reject some technological advances in products and services. This has come to be known as the problem of high-tech versus high-touch.[11] The occupation of bank teller has not disappeared; many people like the human interaction of going into a bank and having a person take care of their business. Despite the tremendous growth in Internet-based booksellers, Borders Books, a retailer with ample reading space and coffee bars, has also had significant growth. Many automobile models have dispensed with high-tech digital speedometers and other fancy gadgets and returned to basic analog instruments. The key message is that when dealing with products that have significant technology components, part of your marketing research must focus on whether more technology is perceived to be better by your target audience.

The Diffusion of Innovations

Customers react to the characteristics of innovations and perceived risk differently. Some customers are risk takers and some are risk averse. Some customers have the vision to see the relative advantage of a technological innovation earlier than others. In other words, some customers will adopt an innovation earlier than others. In addition, the rate of adoption of new technologies is highly dependent on how many customers are in this early adopter group; if this group grows, the technology is likely to be adopted by a large fraction of the potential user group. If the group stays small, the technology is not likely to be a successful product category.

Everett Rogers developed a very popular framework for understanding this process: the **diffusion of innovations.**[12] Figure 15–2 illustrates the sizes of different customer cohorts that typically buy new innovations at different stages of the innovation's life cycle. As can be seen in the figure, Rogers's model assumes that innovativeness, like many other human traits, is distributed normally throughout the population.

The basic idea behind the diffusion of innovations is that, like a disease or a new idea, the spread of the innovation is affected by the amount of "inoculation" that occurs from the first buyers. These first buyers, the **innovators,** try the product first. If they like it, they spread positive word-of-mouth about the product to later users who, in turn, also talk about it. Combined with the marketing efforts of the companies involved, the product then spreads through the population. The success of the product is ultimately determined by how favor-

Figure 15–2

Innovator Categories

Source: Everett M. Rogers (1995), *Diffusion of Innovations,* 4th ed. (New York: Free Press).

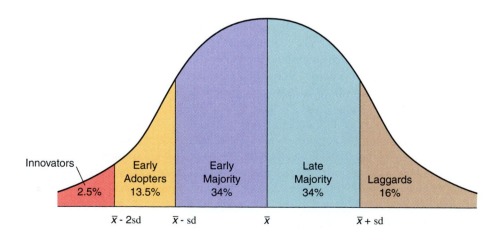

able the word-of-mouth is. That is, information from innovators and other early buyers about the product may reduce later buyers' perceived risk.

The symmetric decomposition of the complete life cycle shown in Fig. 15–2 is an ideal picture and applies mainly to completely new products. The percentages in each group may be different for each new technological development. However, a considerable amount of research has verified that there are five types of adopters:

- As we noted previously, the earliest customers for a new technology are called innovators. These customers have a high utility for being on the leading edge, are often technologists, are eager to try new ideas, and are generally venturesome. In addition, because they are most interested in being the first to own a new technological product, they are price insensitive. They are very valuable to companies because they help to get the bugs out of new products. In late 1997, people buying DVD players were the innovators. In industrial marketing situations, these customers are often called **lead users.**
- The next group of customers to adopt new products are **early adopters.** These customers are generally not interested in technology for its own sake, but are good at detecting the value of a new product and how it will enhance their lives or their businesses. Their value in high-technology markets is their vision in how the technology can actually satisfy customer benefits. Thus, this group is critical to making a new technologically based product successful. The satellite television industry is appealing to this group.
- A larger portion of the market are the **early majority.** These buyers are interested in new technology and gadgets but take a wait-and-see attitude to see whether the product is not a fad; they are basically pragmatists. The value of this group of customers is obvious: It is a large group and is necessary to attract for the product to be commercially viable. Cellular phone marketers and those marketing the newer digital phone technology are targeting this group.
- The **late majority** are similar to the early majority but are more conservative in terms of how much of an industry infrastructure must be built before they will buy. They want the product to be an established standard and require substantial levels of product support. VCRs and CD players are being purchased by this group of consumers.
- **Laggards** generally are not interested in new technology and are the last customers to buy, if they ever do. These are the technology skeptics. Even the penetration rates of televisions and telephones in the United States are not 100%!

The diffusion curve shown in Fig. 15–2 is a stylized version of how markets actually evolve. Not only do the actual percentages in each buyer group differ by product category, but at a given point in time, it is not necessarily clear which stage you are in. However, as we will show later in this chapter, the diffusion curve has important strategic implications for the marketing of high-tech products.

It is fairly obvious that the particular innovator group purchasing a product at a given point in time varies among different kinds of technologically based products depending on where they are in their product life cycles. Early technologies such as satellite television are appealing to a different group than microwave ovens. However, even for one product, the innovator group can vary across markets. Table 15–2 shows the penetration rates of mobile (mainly cellular) phones in different European countries. In countries such as Belgium and Greece, the product is appealing to innovators and early adopters, whereas in the Scandinavian countries, the high penetration rates indicate that mobile phones are well into the early majority group.

Table 15–2 Penetration Rates of Mobile Phones in Europe

Country	Penetration Rate
Greece	7.6%
Belgium	7.8
France	8.0
The Netherlands	9.6
Germany	9.9
Ireland	10.8
Austria	11.0
Spain	11.7
Portugal	12.3
Switzerland	12.6
UK	14.1
Italy	16.8
Denmark	29.8
Finland	32.5
Sweden	32.7
Norway	35.3

Source: *Financial Times* (1997), November 24, p. 11.

MARKETING STRATEGIES FOR HIGH-TECH PRODUCTS

The Chasm Model

The diffusion of innovations model assumes a smooth transition from one stage to the next.[13] A naïve view would be that all you have to do is to get some innovators to try your new product or service and, assuming you do not make any major mistakes and that you support the product with the normal amount of marketing, the momentum of the diffusion curve will lead you to success.

More specifically, you might assume that the following strategy would work:

- Use the technologists (innovators) to educate the visionaries (early adopters).
- Create satisfied visionaries so they can positively influence the pragmatists (early majority).
- Become profitable by serving the early majority well through high-quality products and excellent customer service.
- Gain some of the late majority by reducing costs and prices.
- Forget the laggards.

Of course, this is not true in general and less true in high-tech markets. A revised version of the diffusion curve is shown in Fig. 15–3. The gaps between the diffusion groups indicate the potential to lose momentum; the large gap between the early adopters and early majority is called the **chasm.**

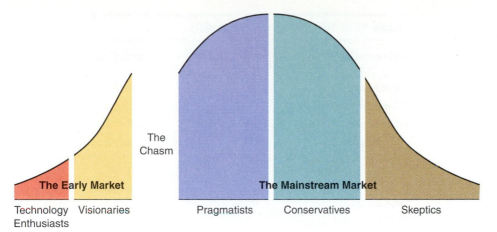

Figure 15–3

The Chasm Model

Source: Geoffrey A. Moore
(1995), *Inside the Tornado*
(New York: HarperBusiness),
p. 19.

The first small crack is between the innovators and the early adopters (between Technology Enthusiasts and Visionaries in Fig. 15–3). Recall that the innovators are venturesome and interested in technology. The main concern of early adopters is how the new technology will solve their problems. Thus, this crack in a high-tech market occurs when the innovating firms do not do a good job of showing how the technology can be put to good use.

There are a number of good examples of this problem. Home banking has been around for many years; nearly 50 U.S. banks were experimenting with it in 1983. In 1989, AT&T and Chemical Bank closed down their joint venture called Pronto after spending $100 million on it. Although home banking has been picking up because of increased use of the Internet, it still accounts for a miniscule proportion of banking transactions. The technology for videophones has existed for over 60 years. However, there is still no real commercial market for them, although the PC-based videoconferencing market is being adopted by some innovators. The development of laser disk players was a $500-million calamity for RCA because they could not sell the nonrecordable devices to more than a few risk-taking customers.

The second small crack in the diffusion curve occurs between the early and late majority (between Pragmatists and Conservatives in Fig. 15–3). In this case, the marketing task is to make sure that the technology can be understood easily by people who are inherently not technologists. This is the problem that faces PC makers; although 45% of U.S. households own PCs, getting the late majority to adopt involves making the computers very easy to set up and use. Thus, many companies ship their computers with CD-ROM disks that walk the buyer through the setup process. In addition, Microsoft's Windows 98 operating system is finally plug-'n'-play (much like Apple's computers have always been), which makes it much easier to add peripheral devices such as modems.

The major crack, between early adopters and the early majority, is called the chasm. The early majority wants the products to work and to enhance their lives or their profit margins. The challenge is how to move a high-tech product from the early market, made up of technology enthusiasts and visionaries (early adopters), to pragmatists in the mainstream market. This is not as easy as it sounds; Table 15–3 shows some of the differences between the two groups. Products and services that cannot make the transition fall into the chasm. Successful high-tech marketing management involves figuring out how to move from the more technology-focused early market to the pragmatic needs of the early majority, where sufficient sales volume can occur to sustain the product.

Table 15–3 Visionaries vs. Pragmatists

Visionaries	Pragmatists
Intuitive	Analytic
Support revolution	Support evolution
Contrarian	Conformist
Break away from the pack	Stay with the herd
Follow their own dictates	Consult with their colleagues
Take risks	Manage risks
Motivated by future opportunities	Motivated by present problems
Seek what is possible	Pursue what is probable

Source: Geoffrey A. Moore (1995), *Inside the Tornado* (New York: Harper Business), p. 18.

To successfully cross the chasm, we can fall back on the basic strategic principles we discussed in Chapter 3. In that chapter, it was noted that a successful marketing strategy involves targeting specific segments of customers and developing a value proposition for those segments. These concepts can be applied in a high-tech context: To appeal to the pragmatists, you must develop a specific application or general strategic approach (theme) that solves the needs of a sizable segment of the early majority. Preferably, this application or theme provides an entrée into other segments of the early majority that are not initially penetrated.

Some examples of the applications approach are the following:

- Apple Computer used desktop publishing to cross the chasm. Not only did they have their successful Macintosh and Laserwriter (printer) products, but they had the right partners in Adobe (PostScript) and Aldus (Pagemaker).
- Tandem Computers was founded to deliver fault-tolerant computing (i.e., computing capabilities that do not fail). Although there were a number of possible segments on which they could focus, the company decided to focus on automatic teller machine networks and on-line banking applications.
- Silicon Graphics (SGI) makes computer workstations and competes with Sun, IBM, and a variety of other companies. SGI crossed the chasm by focusing on high-end computer graphic applications, including special effects for movies and animation.

These are all examples of application segments or niches. An alternative approach is to try to pursue a thematic niche. For example, Oracle, the company that dominates the worldwide database market, chose as its theme to develop database software that would be portable across incompatible hardware platforms. Another example is 3Com's enormously successful Palm Pilot, the hand-held personal digital assistant (PDA). The themes of the Palm Pilot are ease of use and functionality. Although other PDAs (e.g., the Apple Newton)

A high-technology product being watched to see whether it will cross the chasm between early adopters and the early majority is a TV/Internet hybrid that allows users to surf the Net via their televisions. The best-known brand in this product category—and the one poised to cross the chasm first—is WebTV Plus from Microsoft. (Courtesy of Web TV Plus.)

preceded it to market, none was successful in crossing the chasm because of a lack of understanding what customers really wanted.

You should note that the application and thematic approaches to crossing the chasm are not the same as simply repositioning the product, something that can be done for any kind of product or service. The difference in the high-tech context is that the products had an initial market success based on the technology alone. As the products gained initial footholds in the market, the challenge became how to change the marketing from a technology sell to a benefits approach. This shift in emphasis is what makes high-tech marketing different.

As of the late 1990s, there are two high-tech products worth watching to see whether they can cross the chasm that is appropriate for their nascent industries. One product is the much-hyped network PC. Unlike normal PCs, network PCs do not have their own hard or floppy disk drives for storing data or programs. Instead, they are designed to be part of a network, with data and programs on a central computer or server. Only a few hundred thousand network PCs have been sold, compared to the hundreds of millions of PCs. The author is willing to bet that the chasm will not be crossed as the prices of more fully functional PCs are so low that a $500 network PC does not seem like a logical investment.[14]

The second category perched on the edge of the chasm consists of products that hook up to televisions and a phone line to provide Internet access. The best-known brand is WebTV, marketed by WebTV Networks, owned by Microsoft. In late 1997, the company launched WebTV Plus. The original WebTV was launched before Christmas 1996, with much fanfare and a $25-million marketing budget. However, only 150,000 units have been sold. The WebTV Plus product is priced at around $300 and lets users seamlessly jump from TV to a Web page and even view the two simultaneously. In addition, because users can download Web pages nightly to the unit's hard drive, access time is significantly reduced. The question that remains is whether people want to surf the Net when they can just watch TV. ◆

◆ Illustration: Baan Co.

Baan Co. is an enterprise application software company located in Menlo Park, California, and Putten, The Netherlands.[15] This kind of software integrates all of a company's operations, from raw material acquisition to accounts payable. Its main competitors are SAP (mentioned earlier in this chapter) and Oracle. Although it is dwarfed by SAP, which has 33% of the world market to its 5%, Baan's revenues have been increasing at an annual rate of 80% since 1994.

A sign that Baan Co. has moved its products from the early adopter, visionary, market segment to the more mainstream early majority market occurred when it signed a contract with Boeing in 1994. A customer of that size and with so much at stake in terms of product quality does not make such vendor decisions without believing that the company's product provides substantial benefits and that these benefits have been well established.

How has Baan crossed the chasm to reach mainstream customers such as Boeing? The product sold by its main competitor, SAP's R/3 software, requires expensive consultants to implement. In addition, users of R/3 need to forecast their needs years in advance because the program is difficult to change after it has been installed. Baan chose a thematic approach to crossing the chasm by making its product easier to install and modify, thus reducing a customer's dependency on consultants.   ◆

◆ Illustration: Netscape

One of the major success stories to emerge from the explosion of the World Wide Web was Netscape.[16] Since Netscape Navigator was released in 1994, it has held the lion's share of the Web browser market. As of 1999, despite Microsoft's vigorous attempts to dislodge it with its own product, Internet Explorer, Navigator still held 50% of the market.

When Netscape Navigator was released, the strategy was to get it on as many desktops as quickly as possible. As a result, the company made the browser easily accessible and also made Netscape's home page the default start page when a customer invoked the product to browse the Web. This strategy gained the company a large share of the innovator and early adopter market.

The problem remained about how to gain access to the larger early majority market, particularly with Microsoft's aggressive marketing approach, which involved including Internet Explorer in Windows 95 (Netscape charged for Navigator). The company took an application approach by making two strategic moves. First, Netscape decided to become the leader in selling Web server products. They acquired a company called Collabra, which developed a product that competed with Lotus's popular Notes groupware (software that permits managers in different locations to share and work on documents simultaneously). Collabra Server works on Web servers, whereas Notes still is limited to a company's local or wide area network. The second change was to focus on the consumer market, which they saw as offering a significant opportunity for growth and as a way to erode Microsoft's advantage.   ◆

Switching Costs and Lock-In

An important consideration in marketing high-technology products is that customers often make significant investments in these products that make it difficult for them to switch brands.[17] For example, it is difficult for a law firm to switch word-processing software because of the new training required and at least temporary loss of efficiency that would ensue. Costs of switching brands are called switching costs. Switching costs are good for sellers and bad for buyers.[18] Although switching costs are most typical of technology-based products, they exist for many other kinds of products and services. For example, one reason that consumers do not switch banks easily is the hassle (cost of time) to move accounts from one bank to another.

From the strategic perspective of a seller, the goal is to increase a buyer's switching costs to the point of lock-in, the point at which it is very costly for a buyer to switch brands. There are a number of ways you can try to lock in customers to your brand:

- Contractual commitments. These require the customer to buy from you. Normally, this will happen only if the buyer feels that the price is right, that there is some chance that the number of suppliers will diminish in the future, or that the product or service you are selling is unique. This can happen in markets for components such as hard disk drives or semiconductors.
- Durable purchases. This occurs when a customer makes a significant purchase (e.g., a mainframe computer) and needs the software and peripherals that are compatible with it. In the 1980s, Bell Atlantic invested $3 billion in AT&T's digital telecommunication switch, the 5ESS. The 5ESS required a proprietary operating system that only AT&T could provide. Thus, AT&T locked in Bell Atlantic.
- Brand-specific training. If you can train personnel to the point where it is too expensive to switch to another product, then the customer's switching costs increase significantly.
- Information and databases. When a customer invests significantly in a particular format for storing information and data, it is difficult to switch. This can happen with lower-priced consumer products as well. When CD players first came on the market, many music lovers had significant investments in tapes. The idea of starting all over with a new format did not kill the market for CD players but certainly did slow its penetration with older consumers.
- Loyalty programs. One of the main reasons that such programs have proliferated (see Chapter 13) is the potential ability of companies to lock in customers who would not buy a company's product or service for which they did not receive points of some kind.

The point here is that marketing managers in high-tech markets often seek to lock in customers by increasing switching costs.

Market Segmentation Issues

One of the interesting questions from a marketing strategy perspective is whether it is possible to identify customers in the different adoption groups and thus target them. The consumer group that has been the most studied is innovators.[19] Some traits have been associated with the tendency to be in that group:

- Higher income
- Higher education
- Youth
- Greater social mobility
- Venturesomeness
- Greater social participation
- High opinion leadership

Obviously, some of these factors (e.g., income) are observable demographic and socioeconomic variables. Others (e.g., social mobility) must be linked to demographics themselves in order for the people to be identified.

A more general conclusion is that innovators should really be characterized and identified on a category-by-category basis because there does not appear to be a generalized innovator type. In other words, one person can be an innovator with respect to stereo equipment but a laggard with respect to washing machines.

In industrial product markets, innovators and early adopters are often called lead users. Like innovators, lead users cannot be characterized easily. However, rather than attempting to define them by firm descriptor variables such as size or industry, we can define lead users by two behavioral characteristics:[20]

- They face needs that will be common in the marketplace, but they face them months or years before the rest of the marketplace does.
- They are positioned to benefit significantly by obtaining a solution to those needs.

Companies defined by the first characteristic are important customers because they have the same needs as most of the other potential customers, but because of their own innovativeness, they require innovations from their suppliers before the other companies. The second characteristic is important from a commercial perspective because customers who will gain economically from an innovation will invest more in it.

Identifying lead users is basically a task for marketing research. Questions must be designed to elicit information that can determine whether a customer fits the two characteristics of lead users.[21]

Positioning

As we noted in Chapter 3, product positioning involves communicating a point of difference to a target market. When the product is in the early stage of the life cycle, the major competition is the technology that is being replaced by the new one. Thus, when positioning a technology-based product to innovators and early adopters, logical bases for establishing differential advantage are the six attributes of innovations described earlier in this chapter:

- The relative advantage of the new technology
- Its compatibility with existing systems
- The lack of complexity
- Its high level of trialability
- The observability of the benefits
- The presence of network externalities

The advertisement in Fig. 15–4 is an example of a positioning strategy for a new technology-based product. In late 1997, several companies including Philips and Hewlett-Packard

Figure 15–4

Philips CD-ReWritable
Advertisement

Courtesy of Philips

introduced recordable CD-ROM drives for personal computers, which allow the user to write on the CD, much like a floppy disk or hard drive. The target market is already familiar with read-only CD-ROMs. The main aspects of the product's position appear to be the following:

- Relative advantages. It enables you to write, rather than simply read, CD-ROMs and has a high storage capacity.
- Compatibility. It plugs into an existing PC, and the disk you create can be read on conventional CD-ROM drives.
- Network externalities. Because it is compatible with existing conventional CD-ROM drives, you can take the CD-ROM you have created and send it to other computer users.

The advertisement in Fig. 15–5 is interesting because it is a new technological spin on an old concept: videophones. This ad focuses on compatibility (all you need is a standard phone line and a touch-tone phone), lack of complexity (no special wiring or a PC), and, importantly, observability. The ad does a great job highlighting the key ability of being able to see the person at the other end of the line. Note that the network externality issue is not mentioned: The person on the other end needs a ViaTV Desktop Videophone as well.

◆ Illustration: DNA Plant Technology Corporation

In 1994, two companies were providing bioengineered tomatoes to the marketplace.[22] DNA Plant Technology Corporation (DNAP) was a leader in agricultural biotechnology, applying a range of technologies involving classic plant breeding, molecular biology, and plant tissue culture to develop fruits and vegetables with characteristics that were valued by

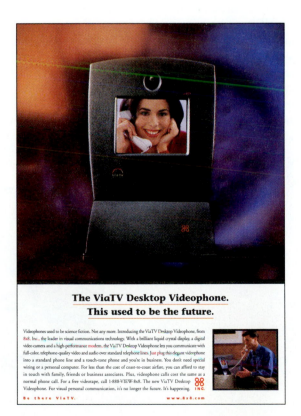

Figure 15–5

ViaTV Advertisement

Courtesy of 8 × 8 Inc.

consumers and food processors. In addition to tomatoes, DNAP was researching a long line of products that included sweeter, crunchier carrots, freeze-tolerant strawberries, longer-life bananas and pineapples, and seedless grape varieties. DNAP introduced its FreshWorld tomato in November 1993, and by October 1994 it was distributed by 1,000 grocery stores in five mid-Atlantic states.

DNAP's main competitor was Calgene, which introduced its Flavr Savr tomato, marketed under the MacGregor brand name in the Midwest in 1994. Calgene's entry strategy differed from DNAP's in that rather than relying on established channels of distribution, Calgene built or acquired businesses to facilitate the market entry of its genetically engineered products. Calgene Fresh was a wholly owned subsidiary for producing, distributing, and marketing their tomatoes.

Both companies faced a significant amount of perceived risk on the part of consumers. This risk was primary related to the fact that "bioengineered" meant little to the average consumer other than implying some kind of nonnatural production process. Such a positioning would clearly not be successful. Consumers were more dissatisfied with the fresh tomatoes sold in supermarkets than with any other produce item because of the industry emphasis on shelf life and firmness rather than flavor. However, given the high level of consumer knowledge about traditional vine-ripened tomatoes, DNAP's and Calgene's products faced significant perceptual hurdles to attract customers. Focusing on the new products' relative advantage, taste, both DNAP and Calgene positioned their brands as offering improved flavor, color, and texture over traditional tomatoes.   ◆

Positioning through Branding

As high-tech products mature, the marketing strategies used are very similar to those for any other product in the mature or decline stage of the life cycle. Customer knowledge is high, perceived brand differences are small, and the marketing tactics are heavily price and distribution oriented. VCRs, microwave ovens, computer modems, word processing software, and other products that at one time were technological innovations are now marketed like consumer packaged goods.

As a result, branding has become important even for high-tech products. As we noted in Chapter 3, brand names are often used to develop perceptual-based differential advantages. In many cases, what is being stressed is the corporate brand, but individual brands or families of brands have also been popular. An example of the latter is Hewlett-Packard's use of the LaserJet, InkJet, and OfficeJet names for their lines of printers.

Branding has become increasingly important for high-technology products that are now considered mainstream. Because consumers cannot differentiate easily among product attributes in this category, the brand name (such as the PhotoDisc brand of laptops, CDs, and cell phones) is a critical means of conveying differential advantages to the consumer. (PhotoDisc)

A characteristic of high-technology companies is that because they are usually founded and run by engineers, there is an inordinate focus on the technology and product features rather than the customer and the benefits sought. High-tech branding campaigns are attempts to deemphasize the products and their attributes and instead focus on broader goals. Some examples are the following:

- 3Com is the second-largest company selling computer networking products (behind Cisco Systems). The company has broadened its scope since acquiring U.S. Robotics, a large modem manufacturer, and the Palm Pilot, a fast-selling personal digital assistant. As a result, 3Com would like to associate its brand name with these new products along with their individual brand names (U.S. Robotics and Palm Pilot) and is spending $80 million to do so.
- Seagate Technology is one of the largest manufacturers of hard disk drives. These not only are sold to personal computer manufacturers to place inside their PCs, but are also sold on a retail basis for owners who want to replace their current drive or add another one. The company has begun a $50-million global TV, print, and Web campaign so it can be known as the company for finding the information you need.

One of the best arguments for developing a brand identity in high-tech marketing is made by companies that sell components or ingredients that are used inside other products and are invisible to the customer. An example is Seagate, whose largest market is selling to PC manufacturers (how many people know the brand of their hard disk drive?). Dolby creates sound-enhancing and filtering technology for stereos and other types of equipment. Branding a component can be valuable in establishing your own credibility as a supplier as well as lending your prestige to the product in which your product is placed, usually called the **original equipment manufacturer (OEM).** This is called cobranding.

The best example of cobranding in high-tech markets is the famous "Intel Inside" branding campaign developed by Dennis Carter at Intel Corporation.[23] Since the campaign was adopted in 1991, the company says that over $3 billion worth of advertisements have carried the "Intel Inside" logo (see Fig. 15–6 for an example). Interestingly, the motivation for developing the campaign was not cobranding.

Intel was founded in 1968 by computer industry legends Robert Noyce and Gordon Moore to produce memory products based on semiconductor technology. Intel is credited with inventing 16 of the 22 major breakthroughs in microelectronics between 1971 and 1981. Their major coup was IBM's selection of its 16-bit 8086 microprocessor for the IBM PC in 1980. The development and success of the 80286 for the AT, 80386, up through the current Pentium III have created a company with over $26 billion in sales.

In 1990, an Intel competitor, AMD, copied the 80386 and subsequently, the 80486 microprocessors. This copying is often called cloning. Although Intel sued AMD for copying their technology and AMD countersued Intel for antitrust violations, the eventual settlement allowed AMD (and other clone manufacturers such as Cyrix) to develop clones of Intel's chips. Thus, although Intel has always been the first to make technological advances in microprocessor technology, it does not take much time for clones to appear.

Intel's reaction was the development of the "Intel Inside" campaign. The idea actually has its origins in Japan, where PC manufacturers used the encircled words

"Intel in it" to indicate that their computers had the highly valued Intel microprocessor. Because this was the most important part of the computer, the logo reassured buyers that the OEM used high-quality components. This eventually led to the "Intel Inside" logo you see in many ads today.

The campaign is a co-op advertising program. Intel puts aside 6% of customers' spending on chips for use in ads containing the logo. Intel reimburses OEMs for half of the cost of TV ads and two-thirds the cost of print ads if they use the "Intel Inside" logo.

Has it worked? Intel has 95% of the market, but the competitors are significantly reducing the time it takes to clone Intel chips. In addition, because the clone manufacturers sell at lower prices, the PCs made using non-Intel chips are usually priced lower as well. The key is brand loyalty: Because 50% of customers coming into a store want a specific processor, developing a brand identity is important to success. In addition, recognition of the Intel brand name is very high (more than 90% for business purchasers and 70–80% for consumers). ◆

Handling Overlapping Technologies

Consider the sales data for Intel microprocessors shown in Fig. 15–7. As can be seen, the sales of the 386 processor began well before sales for the 286 had peaked; likewise, sales of the 486 began well before the 386 peaked. A problem for some technology-based markets is that technological developments overlap; that is, a new version of the technology is available before the market for the previous generation of the product is saturated. Note the use of the term *available;* a key strategic decision is when to introduce the new generation when the old version is still going strong because the sales of the new generation product are likely to divert sales from the old.

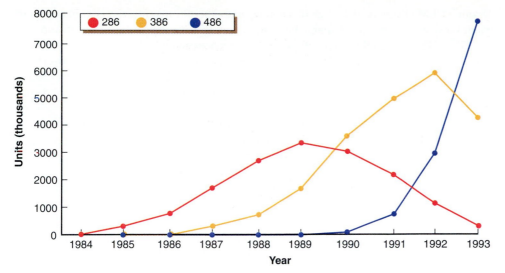

Figure 15–7

Industry Sales of Intel-Based Microprocessor Families

Source: InfoCorp.

Also, clone manufacturers may step in and begin to reduce the profitability of the old-generation market. This occurs because clone manufacturers inevitably charge low prices, which then cause the incumbent to drop its price. As a result, an interesting strategic situation exists with new technology and clones of the old technology.

Although it is difficult to characterize the general solution to this strategic problem, some research has shown that if the new-generation product is incremental (i.e., faster processing speed), then the optimal strategy is to follow a line extension strategy (i.e., have both the new and old products on the market simultaneously). This is exactly what Intel does; the company continues to market the previous generation for customers who do not want and are not willing to pay higher prices for the newer generation. In addition, the threat of competitive cloning activity requires the innovating company to continue to innovate. The only way to combat cloning companies is to beat them to market with newer technology-based products.[24]

MARKETING MIX ISSUES

Channels of Distribution

Marketing managers for technology-based products use all of the traditional channels of distribution: retailers, various middlemen, direct sales, telemarketing, and so on. The channel design and management issues discussed in Chapter 9 are therefore relevant to the marketing of these kinds of products and services.

What makes channel issues unique in this context are the use of two different kinds of intermediaries: OEMs and value-added resellers (VARs).

OEMs

A company typically uses OEMs when it is an ingredient in another company's products. For example, Canon is the world's largest manufacturer of the engines in laser printers (the part of the printer that produces the copies). Not only does Canon make the engines for its own brand of laser printers, but it also sells them to Hewlett-Packard as an OEM channel for its LaserJet line. Hard disk drive manufacturers such as Quantum and Seagate sell through OEM channels such as Dell, Compaq, and other PC manufacturers. Software companies also use the PC OEM channel because many PCs come bundled with software.

Table 15–4 highlights some of the differences between OEM and branded marketing for products such as hard disk drives. A branded product is sold on a stand-alone basis (rather than as an ingredient) to end customers. For example, as we noted earlier in this chapter, hard disk drives are sold through both OEM and regular retail (both mail order and computer store) channels.

The general characteristic of OEM marketing is that it is a technical sell, with you talking directly to engineers. The customer is interested in how your product fits into its laptop computer, printer, or other device. Thus, knowledge of technical aspects of the product is important. In addition, the sale is usually very price oriented because the customer has a good idea about your cost structure, and because your product is only an ingredient, the brand name is not generally visible ("Intel Inside" notwithstanding) and is therefore not a key selling point for obtaining a higher price. OEM selling is usually more like a traditional sales job versus the branded mass marketing approach. Terms of supply such as delivery quantities, timing, and quality are of paramount importance to the OEM. As a result, strong negotiation skills are required.

VARs

A **value-added reseller (VAR)** is an organization that buys products from a variety of vendors, assembles them in a package, and resells the package to specialized segments, often called vertical markets. For example, a VAR focusing on the law firm segment would purchase personal computers from a company, bundle together special software designed for client management and law firm accounting, and then sell the package as a turnkey (i.e., simply "turn the key" to start) system to customers. Similarly, a telephone company would work with companies selling local area network software (e.g., Novell) and hardware (e.g., Cisco) to design a system to install in large office buildings so the builder would be able to buy an external and internal data and phone system as a package. In this case, the phone company is a VAR to Novell and Cisco.

A difference between an OEM and a VAR is the number of ingredients: an OEM normally has a much larger number of suppliers, whereas the VAR has a few discrete components to its system. Occasionally, the components of a VAR system are identified to the customer. As a result, the VAR must be particularly sensitive about who is responsible for customer service. A law firm may experience a hardware problem with its customer management and accounting system. Who is responsible: the hardware company or the VAR? This is not usually a problem with an OEM channel; if a Compaq computer has a hard disk problem, the customer does not contact Seagate or Toshiba but Compaq.

Another difference between a VAR and OEM is that the former is more like a joint venture. Therefore, selling through a VAR is more like a partnership relationship than a supplier relationship. An OEM sale is usually the end of the transaction until the next supply is needed.[25] With a VAR, there are longer-term issues such as customer service and joint marketing. Companies using VARs as a key channel often spend a considerable amount of money working with the VARs to help them sell systems to customers.

Finally, companies selling through VARs also have well-established markets into which they can also sell by themselves. Thus, marketing managers for products using VARs also have to have significant branded marketing skills. Although some OEM products, such as hard drives, are also sold on a stand-alone basis to end customers, most are not. As a result, products sold through OEMs are significantly driven by derived demand; that is, their markets expand only to the extent that the markets for OEM products expand.

Table 15–4 OEM vs. Branded Marketing

OEM	Branded	OEM	Branded
Customer		**Competition**	
Heavy engineering influence	Not necessarily a technical sell	Similar product	Feature set differentiation
Cross-functional decision making	Individual decision-makers	Overlapping customer set	Narrow product line
$ Multimillion-dollar account size	Thousands of customers	Business won or lost at design-in	Alliances common
Horizontal market orientation	Vertical market orientation	Support and relationship key	Company and product awareness key
Promotion		**Cost**	
Executive selling	PR activities: articles, white papers	Many hidden costs	Large non–product related expenses
Key industry analysts and influencers	Advertising	Significant engineering effort in cost reduction	Product positioning and feature set drive product costs
Word-of-mouth	Events: trade shows and seminars	Customers often know your costs	Customers care about price, not cost
	Channel programs		
Pricing		**Communication**	
Usually cost based	Value based	Direct marketing and sales contact	PR and advertising play a major role
Negotiated by each OEM	Standard price lists and discount structure	Emphases on relationship building	Simple, clear messages
Detailed pricing schedules	Marketing ownership	Marketing effort spans several organizations	Marketing control
Senior executive involvement	Periodic pricing adjustments	Ongoing communication	Heavy competition for end-user attention
Frequent pricing action		**Summary**	
Product		Great general management training	More classic marketing
System component	A stand-alone product	Technical background a plus	Product knowledge required
Requirements often set by customer	Ease of use very important	Program management role	Convey market requirements internally
Close engineering coor-dination with customer	Market orientation and product position determine specification	Strong interpersonal skills, one-on-one selling	Strong communication skills
Integration testing a major element of sales cycle	Short evaluation cycle	Business creativity	Product and program creativity
Place		Know your customer's business	Know the vertical markets for your product
Direct sales dominate	Mix of indirect and direct sales channels	Sharp negotiating skills	Channel knowledge
Product fulfilled by manufacturer	Channels change with product life cycle	Execution drives success	Strategy and marketing intelligence
Account teams deliver service and support	Product fulfilled at several levels		

Source: Bill Rossi, Cisco Systems.

◆ Illustration: OEMs

Logitech is the leading maker of the devices with which users input data into personal computers (mice, trackballs, and joysticks, as well as color scanners and digital video cameras).[26] For many years since its founding in 1981, the company's name was barely known to consumers even though many used their products every day. The reason is that Logitech is the largest OEM supplier for mice, larger even than Microsoft, its main competitor. Logitech's customers (OEMs) put their own names on the mice. Its first big customer was Hewlett-Packard, with Olivetti and AT&T following soon thereafter. By 1997, the company was generating over $400 million in revenue, much of it coming from mice sold through these OEMs. In fact, 17 of the top 20 personal computer manufacturers bundle Logitech mice with their systems. In 1999, Logitech produced its 200 millionth mouse.

Logitech was successful in the OEM business for a number of reasons. Its first mouse was produced by Swiss watch company Depraz in 1982. Logitech secured the U.S. marketing rights to the product and developed the necessary software. However, after obtaining the OEM contract with Hewlett-Packard, the company realized that it could not meet Hewlett-Packard's price and quality requirements for an OEM supplier and decided to build its own, tailored for mass production. High levels of quality control in the manufacturing process led to other OEM contracts. In order to meet the increased quantity and price demands by the OEMs, Logitech opened a new manufacturing facility in Taiwan in 1986 and another in Ireland in 1988. In addition, the company developed a leading-edge reputation by simultaneously developing new technologies for pointing devices and incorporating some of these aspects into both their OEM and retail products. By 1992, 60% of the company's sales were from OEMs.   ◆

◆ Illustration: VARs

Artisoft has made the transition from hardware to software company.[27] Originally, the company made hardware for local area networks (LANs), competing with much larger companies such as 3Com and Cisco Systems. In 1994, the company decided to build the company around a single product, LANtastic, easy-to-use networking software designed for the small business market. The product has been very successful: It is the market leader in that segment, with an installed base of around 5 million users. It is the leader in the market for peer-to-peer networks, in which PCs are connected to each other. However, there are significantly larger competitors such as Novell (Novell Netware) and Microsoft (Microsoft NT) in the client/server market, which generally serves larger companies by linking users to each other through powerful, dedicated workstations or PCs called servers. Not surprisingly, these competitors have eyed the lucrative small business market and threatened LANtastic's market position.

The company has reacted by attempting to diversify its product line into other areas such as modem and phone line sharing software. However, its key asset is its reputation and installed base in the small business market. To fortify this position, Artisoft has placed a high priority on solidifying its relationship with VARs that sell into the small business market. These VARs are computer companies and distributors that sell systems bundled with LANtastic to this target group. About 60% of Artisoft's sales are through VARs, with the rest coming from mail order and retail. Artisoft uses 13,000 VARs and spends half of its marketing budget on building and maintaining relationships with them.

A considerable amount of this money is spent on supporting and training the VARs to sell LANtastic's upgrade from version 6.0 to 7.0. Artisoft has developed a program called

"Upgrade to the World," aimed at getting VARs to encourage customers to buy the upgrade. Artisoft provides customizable marketing tools such as customer mailers that the VARs can use to sell the software directly to their own customers. They have also developed a VAR certification program called the Artisoft Partner Alliance Program, which certifies VARs to sell software depending on their training and commitment to the products. ◆

Other Marketing Mix Variables

Communication Strategy

The communication strategy for high-tech products follows the adoption curve. As we mentioned earlier in the chapter, innovators are interested primarily in the technology. They are usually aware of its existence through the grapevine (i.e., trade shows and conferences). However, of particular importance is their role as an opinion leaders. They are very valuable because they can heavily influence early adopters to purchase, particularly by confirming that the product or service actually works. Word-of-mouth can be spread through beta test sites. Beta testing normally is done on the customer's premises. Potential buyers place great importance on seeing that a new system actually works (recall the importance of observability and trialability). In addition, marketing often works with public relations to ensure that new products are reviewed in technical magazines. Thus, the press is also an important opinion leader.

Later buyers have different communication needs. Early adopters and early majority buyers are more interested in the benefits of the product. Later buyers need information that reduces the perceived risk of the technology. For example, Motorola has launched a new $15-million TV, print, radio, and outdoor campaign promoting its new Beepware line of pagers. The intent is to demystify pagers and overcome the late majority's (and perhaps some of the early majority's) perception that pagers are only for businesspeople. Beepware is a pager/watch combination that helps to reduce perceived risk through a product (a watch) that is familiar to all people.

Price

It is common for high-tech products to follow a skimming strategy and to reduce prices over the life cycle. This makes sense in light of the different kinds of customers who purchase such products over time. In addition, because the product life cycles for high-tech products normally are short, there is less time to make a profit and, therefore, more pressure to keep prices high as long as possible. Innovators are price insensitive and are willing to pay high prices for the latest gadgets (i.e., their levels of customer value are high). However, customer value declines as the later purchasing groups enter the market. This is a very common occurrence for high-tech consumer durables. Video cameras, VCRs, CD players, PCs, and many other products exhibit a steady decline in price over time. Although some of this decline results from declining manufacturing costs, it is also driven by increased competition and the price sensitivity of purchasers later in the life cycle.

EXECUTIVE SUMMARY

The main points raised in this chapter are the following:

- Although it is difficult to clearly separate low from high-tech products, the latter are normally characterized by high levels of uncertainty in both markets (customer acceptance) and technology (will it work?).

- Factors affecting the adoption rate of technology include its relative advantage over the former technology, its compatibility with existing systems, the complexity of the innovation, its trialability, its observability (how observable the benefits are to the customer and to others), and its potential for network externalities (the effect of the number of other people on the system or using the product).
- Another factor affecting the adoption of high-tech products is customers' level of perceived risk.
- There are five categories of adopters of new technologies: innovators (those who purchase a product for the technology itself), early adopters (those who can see the benefits of the new technology earlier than others), the early majority (pragmatists who wait for the technology to be established), the late majority (very conservative buyers), and laggards (uninterested).
- The chasm is the potential gap between the time when early adopters and the early majority purchase.
- To cross the chasm and ultimately have a successful product or service, the marketing manager must target customers with a specific application or strategic approach (theme).
- Innovators do not have general characteristics and tend to vary over product categories.
- In industrial markets, lead users can be identified by behavioral characteristics: They face needs earlier than other companies in their industry and also stand to benefit the most by obtaining a solution to those needs.
- High-tech products can be positioned along the dimensions affecting product adoption (relative advantage, compatibility, etc.).
- A key distribution channel for ingredient products (semiconductors, hard disk drives) is original equipment manufacturers (OEMs), who make products in which the ingredient is a component.
- A key distribution channel for some products such as computer software is value-added resellers (VARs), who bundle the product with other products and sell them as a package to customers. Companies using VARs often develop partnerships in terms of joint marketing and training because the product is a more identifiable part of the package.

CHAPTER QUESTIONS

1. Consider two marketing managers: one who is in charge of the Intel Pentium III microprocessor and the other who markets a brand of Frito Lay potato chips. How are the jobs different? How are they similar?
2. As noted in this chapter, Microsoft is attempting to market WebTV, the device that attaches to your TV set and permits Web browsing. Apply the factors affecting the adoption rates of new technologies described in the chapter to this situation. Which are the most difficult to overcome? Which are the easiest?
3. Pick a technology-based product or service that currently has low sales. What are the possible ways that this product can cross the chasm?
4. Pick two technology-based products, one consumer and the other industrial. From the buyer's perspective, what are the potential switching costs? From the seller's perspective, how can the companies lock in customers?
5. Consider the discussion in Chapter 9 about how to manage channels of distribution. How are the channel management issues different for VARs and for OEMs?

Integrated
Case

Application Exercises: High-Tech Marketing and the PC Industry

Continuing the PC case, complete the following exercises:

1. Collect some advertisements from the early to mid-1980s for some PC brands. On what basis were PCs marketed (relative advantage, compatibility, etc.)?
2. Conduct a small research project to obtain a better understanding of how PCs are being used in the home.
3. Conduct a small research project to obtain a better understanding of why households that do not own them have not yet purchased.
4. Pick a business segment that uses PCs and specialized software. Develop a VAR program from the perspective of the manufacturer. Do the same from the perspective of the software company.
5. Looking at the components of an actual PC, find as many companies as possible using the PC manufacturer as an OEM. Try to find information about other channels the companies use.

FURTHER READING

A good book that discusses the unique aspects of marketing high-tech products (although the examples are a bit old) is William H. Davidow (1986), *Marketing High Technology* (New York: Free Press). More recent books on high-tech marketing include Eric Viardot (1998), *Successful Marketing Strategy for High Tech Firms,* 2nd ed. (Norwood, MA: Artech House). A book focusing on consumer buying behavior in high-tech product categories is Allan C. Reddy, ed. (1997), *The Emerging High-Tech Consumer* (Westport, CT: Greenwood).

Global Marketing Strategies

16

CHAPTER BRIEF

The purpose of this chapter is to introduce the issues involved with selling products and services outside of a home country. Key areas of learning are as follows:

The conceptual and practical differences between international and global marketing

Factors to consider in making decisions about whether to enter a particular foreign country or part of the world

Alternative entry strategies

Marketing strategy considerations such as the effects of culture on consumer behavior, product positioning decisions, and global branding

Global marketing considerations for channels of distribution, pricing, and advertising and promotion

The effects of the Internet on global marketing

F&P Gruppo is an Italian company marketing the Gallo brand of rice.[1] Focused on the production of value-added rice (rather than simply the commodity), the company is only one of a few companies in the world involved with the entire process, from growing and milling to packaging and marketing. The company is a privately held, family-owned company dating back five generations with production facilities in Italy, Germany, Argentina, and Uruguay. As of 1991, Gallo brand rice was sold throughout Europe and South America.

The Gallo brand name and the rooster logo were used across different geographic markets and product lines. In 1991, the company marketed white rice, parboiled (partly boiled) rice, and brown rice. Gruppo had also recently developed and introduced quick-cooking rice. The company had been very successful in most of the markets it had penetrated. In Italy, its market share was 21% (based on volume), and in Argentina, where the Gallo brand had been marketed since 1905, its share was 17.5%.

In 1992, the company was considering two important decisions. First, managers were considering expanding its small presence in Poland. Second, given its success in various countries around the world, managers were considering whether to undertake a significant international expansion outside its existing markets.

Some data on the country differences are shown in Table 16–1. Some qualitative differences between the markets were the following.

Table 16–1 Market Characteristics of Italy, Argentina, and Poland, 1990

	Italy	Argentina	Poland
Population (millions)	57.7	32.3	38.4
Age distribution: 0–14, 15–59, 60+	18%, 63%, 19%	30%, 57%, 13%	26%, 60%, 14%
Percentage urban population	67%	85%	60%
Annual population growth	0.1%	1.0%	0.4%
GNP per capita (US$)	15,652	2,134	2,500
Per capita expenditures on food (US$)	2,170	465	256
GDP breakdown: agricultural, industrial, services	4%, 33%, 63%	13%, 41%, 45%	14%, 36%, 50%
Inflation rate	6.5%	17%*	600%
Cereal imports (tons)	6,699	4	1,550
Rice is a major crop	Yes	Yes	No
Television set penetration	1 per 3.9 persons	1 per 4 persons	1 per 3.9 persons
Radio penetration	1 per 3.9 persons	1 per person	1 per 3.6 persons
Literacy rate	98%	92%	98%
Advertising expenditures per capita (US$)	116	13	N/A
Advertising expenditures: percentage breakdown by medium	Print = 59%	Print = 45%	N/A
	TV = 35%	TV = 31.3%	
	Radio = 2.5%	Radio = 8.8%	
	Cinema = 0.2%	Cinema = 0.8%	
	Outdoor = 3.3%	Outdoor = 14.1%	
Number of consumers per retail food outlet	182	1,318	724
Distribution concentration: percentage of retail sales through supermarkets	56%	56%	15%

*Argentina inflation rate estimated for first quarter 1992, down from 3,000% in 1989.

Source: John Quelch (1993), "Gallo Rice," Harvard Business School case #9-593-018, Table A.

ITALY

In Italy, rice is a staple of the diet; it is used by 98% of the population, and per capita consumption averages 5 kilograms per year. About 80% of the volume of branded rice products is sold through grocery stores, with 85% being white rice. Rice is seen as an alternative to pasta; consumer research shows that people view it as quick and easy to prepare, versatile, healthful, and easily digested.

In 1992, Gallo branded rice was sold to retailers through 60 agents and brokers who carried Gallo exclusively, rather than through a captive sales force. There were three product lines. Riso Gran Gallo was the white rice line sold in nine varieties, the Blond brand name was used for the parboiled products, and Grand Risi del Mondo was a super-premium line.

The competition was fragmented, with the four leading brands having only 45% of the market. The major competing brands were Flora (a French brand marketed by conglomerate BSN), Curti-Buitoni (marketed by Nestlé), and Scotti (a regional Italian firm). Private labels held 17% of the market and the rest was held by small, regional companies.

POLAND

In 1992, Poland was still suffering from the demise of communism in the late 1980s. Problems included inflation, low wages, and unemployment. However, new products from other European countries were entering the country and state-owned stores were being replaced by retail chains. In addition, consumers were becoming more sophisticated because of global communications and increased foreign travel, with the resulting exposure to better products and services. Rice distribution had been controlled by a state-owned company, Pewex, which had a network of about 800 stores, and purchases could be made only in dollars. In 1992, 70% of retail food sales were made at open markets and market halls, 15% at supermarkets, and 15% at small grocery stores.

Because rice had a poor, low-quality image, total rice consumption in Poland was only 2.3 kilograms per year, less than half the consumption in Italy. In addition, only 65% of the population used rice, mainly as an occasional substitute for potatoes. There was little knowledge of different types of rice and how to use it in recipes and little understanding of its nutritional value.

The Gallo brand had a small presence in Poland. It was sold in 200 Pewex stores and imported through a private distribution company founded by a former Pewex agent. The main branded competitor in Poland was Uncle Ben's, marketed by Mars Company. However, 95% of the market was unbranded white rice sold in paper bags.

The issues facing Gallo's marketing management were the following:

- Should they expand their presence in Poland, given that there might be other markets offering better opportunities for sales and future growth?
- How should they incorporate the differences in consumer behavior and cultural differences into their marketing plans?
- Which segments should they target and how should the Gallo brand, given its Italian heritage, be positioned and advertised?
- Should they even use the Gallo brand? What does the brand mean to Polish consumers?
- Given exchange rates and other cost and customer differences, what price should they charge?
- In a country with different marketing institutions and historical attitudes toward business, what distribution channels would be most effective?
- Beyond the Polish market, if the company chooses to expand the brand to more markets, should they use one brand name and positioning or different brand names and product positions for different markets or parts of the world?

Clearly, many of the decisions facing the marketing managers appear to be similar to those that have been discussed already in this book. What is different is that the context for the decision has moved from examining different strategic alternatives *within* a market to examining alternatives *between* markets that may be quite different from each other and from the original, focal market.

The focus of this chapter is marketing decision-making when you are entering new countries or regions of the world. This international orientation has been described by a number of terms that are often interpreted to mean the same thing: *global, international, multinational,* and *foreign marketing.* To be more precise, we can define such marketing in terms of the extent to which a company is involved with sales beyond its home market:[2]

- No direct foreign marketing. In this case, the company focuses the marketing of its product in the home market. Some units may be sold in overseas markets through importers who purchase the product and then sell it in their home market or through other mechanisms. However, this overseas distribution is not sought actively by the company.
- Infrequent foreign marketing. When a company has excess capacity, it may attempt to sell some of it in foreign markets. However, this is not a permanent strategy and the international sales disappear when the capacity normalizes.
- Regular foreign marketing. At this stage, the company has a permanent interest in foreign sales and produces enough to enter some international markets or establishes its services in a limited number of markets. The company may use specialized agents for distribution or its own channels in a few key markets.
- International marketing. These companies are fully committed to generating a large portion of company profits from nondomestic sources. Often, these multinational companies establish foreign subsidiaries with a significant presence in many markets.
- Global marketing. Although used widely, this term has come to mean a particular strategic approach to foreign markets.[3] Global marketers treat the whole world, including their domestic market, as one market. To contrast, multinational or international markets view the world as a series of different markets requiring separate marketing strategies in each. Global marketers attempt to standardize product features and positioning as much as possible around the world.

As you can see, there are different degrees to which a company decides to be involved with marketing to countries beyond its domestic market.

Once a company decides to move to the regular foreign marketing phase, decision-making becomes much more complex. To emphasize this point, consider the model shown in Fig. 16–1, which captures the forces affecting companies and products in international markets. Although these factors exist in any home market, it is easy to see that adding differences in many of these areas each time a new market is opened can create a giant headache for marketing managers. For example, when General Motors attempted to enter Japan, the managers found that customer tastes are different (the Japanese like smaller cars and prefer Japanese-made products), the competition uses different distri-

Figure 16–1

The International
Marketing
Environment

Source: Frank Bradley (1991),
*International Marketing
Strategy* (New York: Prentice
Hall), p. 7.

bution methods (door-to-door selling versus retail outlets), and the government levies high import duties to protect its own manufacturers, thus raising prices. Marketing in any new country brings new challenges in the form of differences in the eight forces noted in the figure.

Despite enticing estimates of potential demand, many of the forces shown in Fig. 16–1 combine to make success hard to achieve, particularly in emerging markets. Consider the following examples:

- China has proven to be a very difficult market in which to succeed. Despite successes such as Proctor & Gamble, several global automobile manufacturers such as Peugeot, Citroën, Volkswagen, Mercedes, and General Motors are either losing tremendous sums of money or have already bailed out.
- Foreign drug manufacturers in China have invested a considerable amount of money but are currently having problems with new restrictions on foreigners' ability to sell drugs and problems with protecting their patents.[4]
- Although overall car sales in Brazil have doubled over the past 5 years, Ford has had many problems, particularly with the launch of the Fiesta.[5]
- Many companies investing in India have had difficulties with the constantly changing economic policies pronounced by the government.
- The financial problems in southeast Asia in the late 1990s, beginning in Thailand in 1997, created a boom–bust cycle in the whole region.

Despite these difficulties, there is no doubt that the 1990s represent a huge expansion in companies seeking to market their products internationally. Many companies, from McDonald's to IBM to Sony to Daimler Benz, generate more sales from foreign markets than from their own domestic markets. The rapid expansion of the economies and consumer demand in many emerging markets such as China, Thailand, and Brazil have fueled the growth of the global economy. It is therefore critical to understand the factors that should be considered in developing marketing strategies for these foreign markets.

Rapid expansion of economies and increased consumer demand in emerging markets are fueling the growth of the global economy. As a result, an increasing number of companies are marketing their products internationally. This McDonald's outlet in the Middle East is just one example of this company's many global markets. (Christine Osborne/Corbis)

THE GLOBAL MARKETING DEBATE

The term *global marketing* is used in two ways: as a generic term encompassing any marketing activities outside a company's home market, and to refer to a standardization of the marketing strategies used to market a product around the world. Most books titled *Global Marketing* or chapters in marketing management books like this one use the term in the first sense. However, the second sense is a distinctly different approach to marketing than that implied by the basics of marketing strategy: that market segments (e.g., countries or parts of countries), if found to require different features, positioning, and marketing mix elements, should be treated differently.

The first person to call for a truly global approach to marketing was Theodore Levitt:[6]

> A powerful force drives the world toward a converging commonality, and that force is technology. It has proletarianized communication, transport, and travel. It has made isolated places and impoverished peoples eager for modernity's allurements. Almost everyone everywhere wants all the things they have heard about, seen, or experienced via the new technologies.
>
> Gone are accustomed differences in national or regional preference. Gone are the days when a company could sell last year's models—or lesser versions of advanced products—in the less-developed world. And gone are the days when prices, margins, and profits abroad were generally higher than at home.
>
> The globalization of markets is at hand. With that, the multinational commercial world nears its end, and so does the multinational corporation.

Levitt's view of the world in the early 1980s was one in which dramatically improved telecommunication enabled people in Africa to witness events occurring around the world and see products being consumed, whetting their appetites for such goods. In addition, large global companies were able to produce, distribute, and market on such a massive scale that they could sell for low prices anywhere.

Nowhere in the marketing industry was this approach embraced more completely than in the advertising agency business. The 1980s saw a wave of mergers creating superagencies that could service a client's business globally and ensure that the messages being communicated were as uniform as possible. This created an era of global brands. Examples of such global brands are Coke, McDonald's, Levi's, and Toyota.

The agency that most typified Levitt's model of global marketing was London-based Saatchi & Saatchi (S&S), which won the British Airways account in 1982.[7] S&S's rationale for global marketing was predicated on seven consumer-based factors:

- Consumer convergence. Differences between nations are often less than differences within nations. Upscale consumers in Paris have more in common with their counterparts in New York than with many other French people.
- Demographic convergence. Aging populations, falling birth rates, and increased female employment are common in industrialized countries.
- Decline of the nuclear family. Fewer traditional husband–wife households, fewer children per household, and improvements in the status of women are common occurrences around the world. This has led to more nontraditional meals and increased need for convenience.
- The changing role of women. The major trend here is increasing numbers of women working outside the home. Other related factors are higher divorce rates and lower marriage rates.
- Static populations. Population growth rates have stabilized and the population over 65 is increasing.

- Higher living standards. This creates a growing demand for consumer durables and more leisure.
- Cultural convergence. As noted earlier, global telecommunication has had an impact on consumer wants and needs worldwide. Teenagers in Tokyo, Hong Kong, London, and San Francisco dress and talk similarly and buy the same kinds of products.

With the world becoming more similar in so many ways, many brands and products can be marketed in a uniform way in all countries.

Almost immediately, Levitt's theory and the S&S approach provoked strong objections to this global marketing perspective.[8] The common complaint was that the concept of global marketing is the opposite of market or customer orientation; it is more similar to a product orientation. This is because it ignores a systematic analysis of customer behavior in each market, which may cause the appropriate strategy to be more localized. In fact, there are many intercountry and regional cultural differences that make global marketing difficult to implement (see the section on culture later in this chapter). Not only are there significant differences between countries and regions of the world, but most countries are heterogeneous themselves. Few consumer product companies entering the U.S. market would consider using one positioning strategy for the whole country. Likewise, why should there not be differences within Germany, Japan, or Argentina? As you saw in the introduction to this chapter, there are significant differences in the rice-consuming habits of Italians and Poles, despite the fact that both are what many consider simply Europeans.

Is global marketing "right" or "wrong"? As you might suspect, it depends on the particular product or service being marketed. It is never a waste of time to start with the hypothesis that you can market your product globally. There are obviously many advantages, ranging from manufacturing and operations (making the same product or having the same service operation) to marketing (using the same advertising campaign). Not only are efficiencies leading to lower costs important, but for products and services used by businesspeople or other travelers, having a unified image around the world is important. For example, the American Express image of safety is reassuring to people in cities around the world where their offices are located.

In addition, many of the observations made by Levitt and others about consumers in the world beginning to have similar tastes have merit. This is particularly true of younger consumers. In the Star Hill Mall in Kuala Lumpur, Malaysia, cellular phones made by Nokia, Motorola, Ericsson, and other companies are fast sellers, even at more than $150 each plus monthly charges. The target group is 18- to 25-year-olds. Advertisements touting other products are shown on MTV; 70 million households get MTV Brasil, MTV Latin America, MTV Mandarin, MTV Asia, or MTV India. A research study showed that even in poorer countries such as China, in the cities, the average child between 7 and 12 has $182 in spending money per year. In Thailand, Citibank has focused its attention on college students and young adults for its credit card business and has 500,000 credit cards in circulation.[9]

However, the phrase "think globally but act locally" is on the mark: It is always important to take the initial hypothesis of a global marketing strategy and test it against local conditions. Beyond changing the language of the TV commercials, this may also involve product modifications and new positioning strategies. In addition, some companies do not mind having different images in different countries. For example, several large Japanese companies such as Matshushita (Panasonic, National, Technics brands), Shiseido (cosmetics), and Nissan disdain global marketing altogether and would be considered international or multinational marketers because they tailor strategies for each country they enter.[10]

In other words, different degrees of standardization are appropriate because there is a continuum from what we have called international marketing (different strategies for each country) to pure global marketing (one unified strategy worldwide).[11] A key factor in whether a product can be marketed globally is the degree of scale economies or efficiencies that are obtainable. Large production volumes of products such as automobiles and televisions can result in significantly lower prices that local companies cannot match. Some companies do not have the management or financial resources to adapt products and marketing programs to each country. Perhaps most importantly, products that are not highly culture bound are more easily marketed globally. For example, most industrial products and products used outside the home, such as credit cards, fall into this category.

◆ Illustration: Orangina

The French soft drink Orangina embarked on a global marketing strategy in 1995.[12] In 1996, its sales grew by double digits to nearly $300 million worldwide. This occurred despite a 15% decline in beverage sales in many of its European markets. Nearly one-third of its sales are outside France, where its market share is second only to Coke's in the soft drink category.

The global campaign is consistent across all markets. Orangina had an image as a French drink; the international advertising campaign had female forms passionately dancing the lambada.[13] As a result, the campaign was considered too sexy for some of their conservative markets, such as those in Muslim countries. The new campaign is intended to bring out Orangina's unique spirit and feature: the only orange soft drink brand with real pulp (it has 14% pulp content). Because it has pulp, it must be shaken before being drunk. This point of difference is emphasized by the slogan "Shake me, shake me." As a result, the approach can be used in all of the product's 54 markets. The commercials are the same in all markets, with the voiceover in different languages. These are tailored to different customs and legal environments. In the litigious United States, the voiceover says "Shake it gently" to avoid someone shaking it so hard that the cap flies off and injures someone. In Britain, the voiceover says "For goodness shake," which reflects their fondness for playing on words. ◆

◆ Illustration: Tambrands

Tambrands' only product is the tampon brand Tampax.[14] It is the number-one brand in the world, but it is highly dependent on sales in the United States (45% of its total), where it has heavy competition from companies such as Playtex. In addition, 70% of women in the United States already use tampons. Thus, the company is looking to overseas markets for growth.

Because of cultural and religious sensitivities, prior tampon ads have typically shown active women, stressing the product's comfort. However, Tampax's marketing managers decided to take a riskier approach to the advertising but tailor part of the message to different countries. For example, in Brazil, many young women believe that they lose their virginity if they use tampons. In other countries with low usage rates, women feel squeamish about using the product.

In general, the company has divided the world into three clusters. Most women in Cluster One (the United States, the United Kingdom, and Australia) are already familiar with the product. In Cluster Two (France, Israel, South Africa), only 50% of women use tampons and although there is some concern about the virginity issue, the bigger fear is that it is an unnatural product. Cluster Three includes large countries such as China, Russia, and Brazil that have low usage rates and concerns similar to those in Cluster Two.

Thus, the advertising campaign has the common thread of women holding the readily identifiable blue box of Tampax and ending with the tagline "Tampax. Women Know." However, the rest of the message varies. In Brazil, the message is "Of course, you're not going to lose your virginity. That will happen in a much more romantic way." In China, the concern is about leakage. Thus, for this kind of product, a truly global marketing campaign is infeasible. ◆

STRATEGIC ISSUES

Market Entry Strategies

Normally, companies enter foreign markets using the sequence described earlier in this chapter: first with infrequent foreign marketing, then as an international marketer, and finally, if appropriate, as a global marketer. Thus, important decisions at early stages in this hierarchy of foreign involvement are as follows:

- The choice of which country or countries to enter
- The timing of the entry
- How to operate in these countries

The first two decisions are beyond the scope of this book.[15] Once the decision has been made to enter a country, from a marketing perspective, the most important decision is the mode of entry (i.e., whether to export using a local importing firm, license the product to a company, establish a joint venture, or use some other approach).

As shown in Fig. 16–2, five sets of factors should be considered when attempting to decide how to enter a new foreign market.[16] Three of these factors—country characteristics,

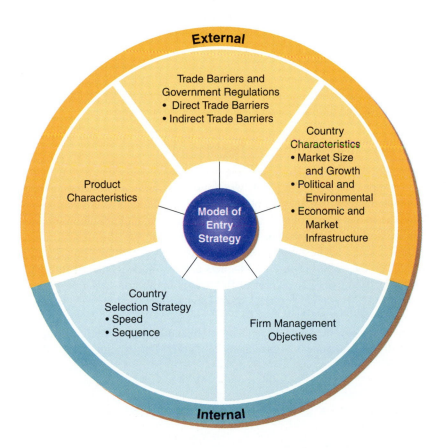

Figure 16–2

Factors Affecting Mode of Entry

Source: Susan P. Douglas and C. Samuel Craig (1995), *Global Marketing Strategy* (New York: McGraw-Hill), p. 147.

trade barriers and government regulations, and product market characteristics—are external to the firm and cannot be affected by you. The other two—the management's objectives and country selection strategy—are internal to your company.

Country Characteristics

A key characteristic is the market size and growth. Larger countries and those with higher growth rates are more likely to be seen as good places to make significant investments. Therefore, the idea of a wholly owned subsidiary or sales force in such a country would make more sense than one in a smaller country with lower growth prospects. In these latter markets, lower-cost approaches or those that are mainly variable costs (e.g., licensing, where payments must be made only when products are sold) are normally preferable.

Table 16–2 shows some economic indicators for a variety of countries. These numbers on per capita GNP, gross domestic product (GDP) growth rates, inflation, and interest rates give some information about the potential for market growth and some information about market size (higher per capita GNP should be positively correlated with market demand). However, these numbers do not include another measure of size: population. Thus, India's per capita GNP in 1995 was only $340, but there are nearly one billion Indians.

A second country factor is the political and environmental risk. Companies are understandably reluctant to make substantial investments in countries with high levels of political instability. Although many emerging markets have governments that are increasingly hospitable to business in general, it is unknown how long this attitude will last. For example, although Russia is a large, tempting market on most dimensions, in 1996 the communist candidate for president received 40% of the vote. That is worrying to managers considering making significant investments in the country. A similar potential problem exists for F&P Gruppo and their marketing plans for Poland. Table 16–3 shows some indicators related to this kind of risk, as manifested in long-term debt ratings.

The third country factor is the economic and market infrastructure. Using Russia as an example again, the internal telecommunication, road, and airline structure is much weaker than in developed countries. This is another drawback to making substantial investments in Russia and would lead to more joint or other lower-risk arrangements.

Trade Barriers and Government Regulations

The government of India used to restrict the percentage of an Indian firm owned by a foreign-based company to 49%. Coca-Cola withdrew from India in 1977, stating that it would not operate in country where it could not control the marketing and production of its products. When the Indian government loosened this regulation, Coke reentered India.

Countries often have laws that place restrictions on the abilities of companies to operate freely; some of these regulations target foreign companies. In some cases, tariffs or quotas on the import of foreign products and components make establishing local facilities more attractive. This is part of the reason many non-U.S. companies such as Nissan, Toyota, BMW, and Mercedes have opened large manufacturing plants in the United States.

In some instances, the trade barriers are more subtle. Many foreign companies complain about the restrictiveness of the Japanese market. For example, NTT, the Japanese

Table 16–2 Economic Indicators

The health of a country's economy is probably the key determinant of how well its stock market will perform. Countries with high levels of gross national product per capita tend to have less risky and more developed stock markets, and high rates of economic growth, low inflation, and low interest rates usually favor strong stock market returns.

	GNP Per Capita (US$, 1995)*	Real GDP Growth Rate Average 1990–95, In Percent[†]	Projected GDP Growth, 1997[‡]	Projected Inflation Rate, 1997[‡]	Short-Term Interest Rate (May–June)[§]
United States	$26,980	2.6%	3.0%	2.9%	5.81%
Level 1: Most Similar to United States					
Australia	$18,720	3.5%	3.2%	2.1%	5.25%
Canada	19,380	1.8	3.5	1.7	3.25
Denmark	29,890	2.0	2.7	2.5	3.68
France	24,990	1.0	2.4	1.6	3.43
Germany	27,510	N.A.	2.3	1.8	3.16
Ireland	14,710	4.7	6.3	2.2	6.31
Netherlands	24,000	1.8	3.0	2.7	3.26
New Zealand	14,340	3.6	3.7	1.9	6.84
Sweden	23,750	−0.1	2.0	2.3	4.37
Switzerland	40,630	0.1	0.7	1.0	1.42
United Kingdom	18,700	1.4	3.3	2.6	6.68
Level 2: Other Developed					
Austria	$26,890	1.9%	1.7%	1.9%	3.45%
Belgium	24,710	1.1	2.3	2.0	3.37
Finland	20,580	−0.5	4.4	1.3	3.08
Hong Kong	22,990	5.6	5.0	7.1	6.19
Italy	19,020	1.0	1.0	2.4	6.87
Japan	39,640	1.0	2.2	1.3	0.62
Norway	31,250	3.5	4.2	2.5	3.47
Singapore	26,730	8.7	6.6	1.8	3.69
Spain	13,580	1.1	2.8	2.5	5.20
Level 3: Mature Emerging Markets					
Argentina	$ 8,030	5.7%	5.0%	1.1%	6.25%
Brazil	3,640	2.7	4.5	8.0	20.84
Chile	4,160	7.3	5.8	6.0	9.25
Greece	8,210	1.1	3.0	6.9	10.05
Korea	9,700	7.2	5.6	4.4	12.50
Malaysia	3,890	8.7	8.0	3.8	8.18
Mexico	3,320	1.1	4.5	17.3	18.07
Philippines	1,050	2.3	6.3	6.5	11.17
Portugal	9,740	0.8	3.3	2.5	5.80
South Africa	3,160	0.6	2.2	10.2	16.36
Thailand	2,740	8.4	6.8	4.5	19.00

(continued)

Table 16–2 Economic Indicators (Continued)

	GNP Per Capita (US$, 1995)*	Real GDP Growth Rate Average 1990–95, In Percent[†]	Projected GDP Growth, 1997[‡]	Projected Inflation Rate, 1997[‡]	Short-Term Interest Rate (May–June)[§]
Level 4: Newly Emerging Markets					
China	$ 620	12.8%	9.5%	6.0%	N.A.
Colombia	1,910	4.6	3.4	18.0	23.12%
Czech Republic	3,870	−2.6	2.6	7.8	23.15
Hungary	4,120	−1.0	2.4	17.7	20.61
India	340	4.6	6.6	8.0	6.75
Indonesia	980	7.6	8.0	7.3	13.00
Israel	15,920	6.4	4.8	7.9	N.A.
Poland	2,790	2.4	5.0	15.3	20.78
Sri Lanka	700	4.8	N.A.	N.A.	N.A.
Taiwan	12,150	6.2*	6.0	3.4	5.25
Venezuela	3,020	2.4	3.9	46.6	20.15
Level 5: The Frontier					
Egypt	$ 790	1.3%	5.0%	6.2%	N.A.
Jordan	1,510	8.2	6.5	4.0	N.A.
Morocco	1,110	1.2	3.0	3.5	N.A.
Nigeria	260	1.6	4.7	14.1	N.A.
Pakistan	460	4.6	5.0	11.0	N.A.
Peru	2,310	5.3	5.0	9.9	15.6%
Russia	2,240	−9.8	2.0	15.0	N.A.
Turkey	2,780	3.2	3.9	75.0	71.6
Zimbabwe	540	1.0	N.A.	N.A.	N.A.

*1992–1995.

Sources: *International Finance Corp. Emerging Markets Database 1997 Factbook; Dow Jones & Co. [†]World Bank; Dow Jones & Co.
[‡]International Monetary Fund; Organization for Economic Cooperation and Development. [§]J.P. Morgan & Co.

telecommunication giant, claims that it has had open competition for suppliers for many years. However, the reality (at least according to potential non-Japanese suppliers) is that design specifications and other elements of the bidding process favor Japanese companies. When there is a serious problem with these informal barriers, it is often useful to enter a new market with a local partner that knows the ropes.

Product Market Characteristics

The physical characteristics of the product or service can affect how entry should be accomplished. Where it is very expensive to ship a product, local licensing or manufacturing arrangements are usually made rather than direct exporting. This is usually the case with soft drinks and beer, especially when the sales volumes are high. More expensive goods such as computers and watches are usually exported.

Table 16–3 Economic and Market Risk

Long-term debt ratings reflect a variety of economic and political risks; triple-A suggests the lowest risk. Expect bigger stock swings in markets with higher volatility. Correlation indicates how much diversification a foreign market offers U.S. investors. A correlation of 1 means the market moves in lockstep with the United States; zero means the market is unaffected by U.S. moves; a negative figure means the market moves in the opposite direction of the United States.

	Standard & Poor's Long-Term Foreign Currency Credit Rating	Moody's Long-Term Foreign Currency Credit Rating	Volatility (Annualized standard deviation; 5-yr. avg. as of 3/97)	Correlation with United States (5-yr. avg.)
United States	AAA	AAA	7.33%	1.00
Level 1: Most Similar to United States				
Australia	AA	Aa2	12.95%	0.44
Canada	AA+	Aa2	12.20	0.46
Denmark	AA+	Aa1	12.28	0.15
France	AAA	Aaa	11.68	0.32
Germany	AAA	Aaa	13.20	0.16
Ireland	AA	Aa1	N.A.	N.A.
Netherlands	AAA	Aaa	10.12	0.45
New Zealand	AA+	Aa1	14.93	0.31
Sweden	AA+	Aa3	16.09	0.43
Switzerland	AAA	Aaa	12.31	0.06
United Kingdom	AAA	Aaa	11.68	0.38
Level 2: Other Developed				
Austria	AAA	Aaa	11.43%	0.14
Belgium	AA+	Aa1	10.37	0.36
Finland	AA	Aa1	31.19	0.33
Hong Kong	A+	A3	31.95	0.39
Italy	AA	Aa3	22.06	0.10
Japan	AAA	Aaa	20.51	0.09
Norway	AAA	Aa1	17.14	0.42
Singapore	AAA	Aa1	13.00*	0.48*
Spain	AA	Aa2	18.41	0.39
Level 3: Mature Emerging Markets				
Argentina	BB	B1	33.98%	0.42
Brazil	BB–	B1	39.91	0.16
Chile	A–	Baa1	24.35	0.23
Greece	BBB–	Baa1	22.69	0.17
Korea	AA–	A1	25.39	0.00
Malaysia	A+	A1	23.69	0.25
Mexico	BB	Ba2	35.68	0.23
Philippines	BB+	Ba1	28.34	0.17
Portugal	AA–	Aa3	18.01	0.23
South Africa	BB+	Baa3	22.62	0.12
Thailand	A	A3	32.25	0.21

(continued)

Table 16–3 Economic and Market Risk (Continued)

	Standard & Poor's Long-Term Foreign Currency Credit Rating	Moody's Long-Term Foreign Currency Credit Rating	Volatility (Annualized standard deviation; 5-yr. avg. as of 3/97)	Correlation with United States (5-yr. avg.)
Level 4: Newly Emerging Markets				
China	BBB+	A3	24.35%	0.23
Colombia	BBB–	Baa3	25.39	–0.05
Czech Republic	A	Baa1	24.21	0.08
Hungary	BBB–	Baa3	40.81	0.35
India	BB+	Baa3	31.63	–0.05
Indonesia	BBB	Baa3	26.22	0.50
Israel	A–	A3	N.A.	N.A.
Poland	BBB–	Baa3	75.38	0.25
Sri Lanka	N.A.	N.A.	28.02	–0.05
Taiwan	AA+	Aa3	36.68	0.12
Venezuela	B+	Ba2	44.72	0.00
Level 5: The Frontier				
Egypt	BBB–	Ba2	N.A.	N.A.
Jordan	BB–	Ba3	13.54%	0.08
Morocco	N.A.	N.A.	N.A.	N.A.
Nigeria	N.A.	N.A.	65.16	–0.06
Pakistan	B+	B2	29.20	0.08
Peru	N.A.	B2	34.26	0.09
Russia	BB–	Ba2	N.A.	N.A.
Turkey	B	B1	61.97	0.04
Zimbabwe	N.A.	N.A.	31.38	0.13

*3-year average.

Sources: Standard & Poor's; Moody's Investors Service; International Finance Corp.; Ennis, Knupp & Associates.

Management Objectives

An internal factor is the company's commitment to international expansion. Often, companies with little interest and those that are risk-averse develop joint partnerships to minimize that risk. Those with more aggressive expansion objectives make larger investments in new markets.

Country Selection Strategies

The company's approach to country selection affects the entry strategy. If you enter a Level 1 country (see Tables 16–2 and 16–3), it should be easy to understand the impact of the other factors described in Fig. 16–2. Although the decision could be to invest or proceed cautiously, the decision is much better informed than for a Level 5 country. In this case, most companies choose to find local partners or another entry approach, minimizing risk. In addition, if the company is attempting to enter multiple markets simultaneously, the restrictions imposed by the expense of this multiple entry strategy could point to lower-cost, lower-risk options.

Modes of Operation

Figure 16–3 provides an overview of the strategic options for entering a new foreign market.

Exporting

This is the most common approach to entering international markets. **Indirect exporting** uses agents, trading companies, or other organizations to handle the process of moving the goods from the home market to the foreign country. The originating firm usually incurs little risk this way, particularly when the agent or the exporting organization assumes ownership of the goods. The tradeoff is that there is little control over how the product is marketed in the export country. In addition, the firm does not learn anything about the country to which the products are exported and thus gains little experience from which it can benefit later. In **cooperative exporting,** the company enters into a collaborative agreement with a host company to cooperate on marketing, distribution, or other necessary activities. An exporting company may enter into an agreement with a host company for the latter to sell its products through its sales force. This approach affords more control than indirect exporting. In **direct exporting,** the company establishes its own operations in the foreign country. This is more expensive and risky than the other approaches, but the exporting company has control over the marketing of its products and gains expertise in the local market over time.

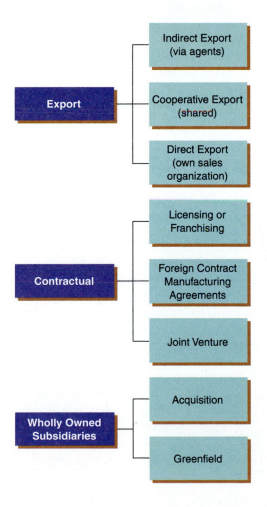

Figure 16–3

Modes of Operation

Source: Susan P. Douglas and C. Samuel Craig (1995), *Global Marketing Strategy* (New York: McGraw-Hill), p. 154.

Contracting

Three forms of contractual arrangements are popular in international marketing. In **contract manufacturing,** the company provides the necessary technology for the local firm to manufacture the product but does the marketing itself. An obvious benefit is that the company does not have to establish its own manufacturing facility. The major risk is that the local company might take the technology for itself. Although companies are protected from such behavior by U.S. courts, there is enough variability in how foreign companies are treated in other countries that this risk is still appreciable. In a **licensing agreement,** the firm receives a royalty fee (normally a percentage of sales) from the licensor in exchange for the latter's ability to use a patented technology, trademark, or brand name. Although this appears to be a low-risk option, the local firm may not do a very good job marketing the brand and may actually hurt its image. Licensing has become a very popular way to spread products with a brand name (e.g., Disney) or movie characters (e.g., *Star Wars*) around the world. In service industries, a similar arrangement to licensing is franchising (see Chapter 14).

A significant portion of contractual arrangements for international marketing are **joint ventures.** Joint ventures are a very effective way for a company to sell its products in foreign markets that are otherwise difficult to navigate. Many joint venture arrangements are possible, with different fractional ownership agreements. A joint venture is particularly attractive when the project is so huge that no company wants to assume all the risk. Examples are large infrastructure projects such as airports and dams, which often involve firms such as Bechtel and Swedish firm Asea Brown Boveri (ABB). Joint ventures are particularly popular for entering emerging markets, where the risks are great. The type of venture can vary by country, depending on local laws.[17]

However, most joint ventures fail. The most common problems are breakdowns in communication, goal conflicts, differences in culture, and disagreements about how to share profits.

◆ Illustration: Fuji Xerox

Many people consider the joint venture between Xerox and Fuji Photo Film, Fuji Xerox (FX), to be the most successful joint venture in history between an American and a Japanese company.[18] Interestingly, the Xerox partner in the joint venture, Rank Xerox, was itself a 50–50 joint venture between Xerox and Britain's Rank Organization. Rank Xerox manufactured copiers and other products developed by Xerox and marketed them worldwide except in the United States and Canada. FX was established in 1960 as a 50–50 joint venture with Rank Xerox and was originally intended to be only a marketing organization to sell xerographic products made by Fuji Photo Film based on Xerox patents. However, the Japanese government refused to approve a marketing-only agreement, so FX received exclusive rights to manufacture products through a subcontract with Fuji Photo Film. FX had the exclusive rights to sell the machines in Southeast Asia and Japan; Rank Xerox received a 5% royalty on sales and equally split the profits with Fuji Photo. See Table 16–4 for some of the aspects of the joint venture agreement that have evolved over time.

Over the years, FX evolved into a fully integrated operation with strong research, development, and production capabilities. Not only does Fuji Xerox design, build, and sell virtually all of its own products, but it supplies more than 90% of the small and midsize photocopiers sold by Xerox itself. Its annual revenue as of 1996 is about 45% of Xerox's (about $7.5 billion) and FX is growing more rapidly than the U.S. parent. It has become virtually independent of its parents, so much so that it is not viewed as a joint venture anymore but a stand-alone corporation.

Table 16–4 Major Agreements Between Xerox And Fuji Xerox

1960 Joint Enterprise Contract and Articles of Incorporation (1962)
Established equal ownership of FX by Rank Xerox and Fuji Photo Film
Defined FX's exclusive license to xerography in its territory:
  Japan, Taiwan, Philippines, the Koreas, Indonesia, Indochina
FX nonexclusive license to nonxerographic products in territory
Specifies terms of technology assistance
  Royalty due Rank Xerox: 5% of net sales of xerographic products

1976 Joint Enterprise Contract (JEC)
Agreement between Rank Xerox and Fuji photo Film, updating 1960 JEC
Specified Board of Directors composition
FX management to be appointed by Fuji Photo Film
Agreements on technology transfer, royalties, and transfer pricing
Identified matters requiring Xerox concurrence, including
  Financial policy, including major capital expenditures
  Business and operating plans
  Relations with third parties
  Sales outside of FX licensed territory

1976 Technological Assistance Contract (TAC)
10-year agreement between Xerox and Fuji Xerox
Revised technology assistance agreements of 1960, 1968, and 1971
Maintained 5% royalty on xerographic products

1978 R&D Reimbursement Agreement
Defines reimbursement to FX for R&D on FX products marketed by Xerox
  100–120% of design cost

1983 Technology Assistance Agreement (TAA)
10-year agreement between Xerox and Fuji Xerox
Replaced 1976 technology transfer agreements
Revised royalty rates:
  Basic Royalty on total FX revenue, plus
  Royalty on xerographic revenues to decline annually from 1983 to 1993

1983 Product Acquisition Policy
Provided guidelines for intercompany transfer pricing
Established concept of reciprocal manufacturing license fee (MLF), designed
to reimburse FX for development and manufacturing costs:
  Up to 25% markup on assembled machines supplied by FX
  Up to 20% markup on unit cost for FX machines assembled by XC
  Specific designs and services required by Xerox reimbursed 100%

1985 Procurement Policy
Provided guidelines for Xerox procurement in FX licensed territory:
  FX right to bid first
  Procurement from third party to be coordinated with FX

1986 Arrangements Strategy Agreement
Defined parameters for negotiating alliances with third parties

Source: Compiled from Xerox Corporation documents.

Why has this joint venture been successful when many others fail? Most observers claim that the autonomy granted FX from the beginning has been the key. Paul Allaire, Xerox's CEO, says that this autonomy, which created a strong presence in Japan, permitted Xerox to see competitive threats earlier and allowed them to better understand their development and manufacturing techniques. FX became the change agent within Xerox and helped the latter recover when it was threatened by Canon and other strong competitors in the 1970s.

Wholly Owned Subsidiaries

This is the do-it-yourself approach: establishing your own company-owned subsidiary in charge of manufacturing and marketing. This can be done by acquiring an existing local company. Alternatively, the subsidiary can be built from scratch. This is called the green-field approach. Obviously, both of these are very expensive and are normally considered only when the company is ready to make a significant investment and commitment to the local market.

Consumer Behavior: The Importance of Cultural Differences

In understanding customer behavior in different countries, the same questions addressed in Chapters 5 and 6 apply here. That is, it is always useful to ask "Who are the customers?" "Why do they buy?" and so on because there is no reason to believe that the same segments or attitudes will exist in other countries as exist in the home market for a product or service.

For example, consider Table 16–5, which contains information about consumer behavior toward beer and the Heineken brand. The top panel of the table shows the results of focus group responses of perceived correlates of beer taste. As you can see, there are significant differences between countries in the consumer perceptions of what factors have positive and negative correlations with beer quality. For example, Americans and Italians feel that a good aftertaste is an important factor, whereas Dutch and Germans do not like an aftertaste or consider it to be unimportant. Germans and Americans believe in positive price–perceived quality relationships, but the Dutch and Italians do not. With respect to the Heineken brand, Americans and Germans like the fact that the Heineken brand has been family brewed since 1863, whereas the Dutch and Italians do not value that fact, and, in fact, feel negatively about it. Germans and Americans also like the 100% malt characteristic, whereas the Dutch and Italians are indifferent to it.

The biggest issue facing companies wanting to market products in other countries is the fact that significant differences in culture can affect the way customers respond to the product and the marketing strategy. The sociocultural environment is composed of the factors shown in Fig. 16–4. Demographic factors include the population size, growth rate, age distribution, and geographic density. These data normally are readily available.

More difficult to obtain and idiosyncratic to the product category are the behavioral attributes: values and attitudes. These are usually determined by a country or region's culture, the ways of living built up by a group of people and transmitted through generations. The main elements of culture are the following:[19]

- Language
- Religion
- Values and attitudes
- Social organization
- Education
- Technology and material culture

Obviously, countries differ on these dimensions. Japan and Korea are more homogeneous than India and the United States. Thus, it may be possible to treat the first two as a segment,

Table 16–5 International Consumer Behavior

Heineken Beer

	Netherlands	Germany	Italy	USA	Average Eight Countries
Brand vision	−	+	+	−	−
Quality					
Two years Amsterdam training	+	+	+	+	+
24 quality checks	+	+	+	+	+
Bottles returned to Amsterdam	+	+	+	+	+
Brewing skills					
100% malt	0	+	0	+	0
Smooth taste	−	+	+	+	0
Pure taste	+	−	+	+	0
Matured longer	−	0	−	−	−
Tradition					
Family since 1863	−	+	−	+	0
Original recipe	+	+	0	+	+
Where beer was born	+	+	+	+	+
Availability					
More bars/more countries	+	0	−	0	0
Manufacturing					
Ingredients	−	+	−	−	−
Water quality	+	+	−	−	0
Scale of plant	+	+	−	+	+
Product					
Taste experience	+	+	+	+	+
Balanced taste	+	+	+	+	+
Aftertaste	−	−	+	+	0
Freshness	+	−	−	+	0
Foam	+	+	0	+	+
Drinkability	+	+	−	−	+
Day after	+	+	−	−	0
Marketing					
Price	−	+	−	+	0
Advertising	+	−	+	+	+
Packaging	−	+	+	+	+

A minus sign (−) indicates the factor is an unimportant or negative indicator of quality.

Source: John A. Quelch (1995), "Heineken N.V.: Global branding and advertising," Harvard Business School case #9-596-015, exhibits 6 and 8.

but the latter two cannot be treated that way. Table 16–6 describes the link between cultural factors and buying behavior in Japan.

Sensitivity to cultural differences is necessary for successful marketing of a product into a foreign country. It is not only important in understanding the end customer for consumer products, but is also essential in marketing industrial products and services, where there is considerable face-to-face interaction. Many guides exist to help keep you from embarrassing yourself and your company when abroad, and they are well worth studying.[20]

Figure 16–4

Elements of Culture

Source: Frank Bradley (1991), *International Marketing Strategy* (New York: Prentice Hall), p. 11.

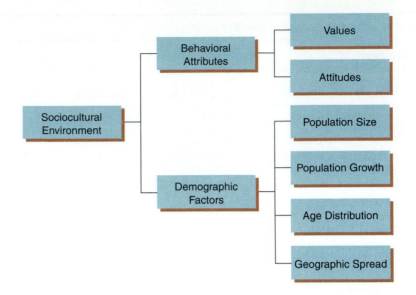

Product Positioning

Decisions about product positioning (i.e., which of a set of possible value propositions to communicate to customers) follow the customer analysis closely. As is the case in the home market, you must decide which segments to target and what value proposition is most compelling for that segment. The principles of product positioning do not change in an international context.

What does change is how the positioning strategy relates to the decision to develop separate marketing strategies for each country or region rather than a global marketing strategy. Based on our discussion in the previous section, you can see how difficult it is to implement a global positioning strategy when cultural differences are so pronounced around the world. Not only must the appropriate target markets match, but the value proposition must be similar in each country where the global campaign is implemented.

Some of the problems involve language. For example, Proctor & Gamble promoted its Vidal Sassoon brand of shampoo in many countries with the line that it gives the consumer a "salon-washed feeling." Unfortunately, in Poland, the expression translated as a "living room-washed feeling." There are many similar examples of how simple problems with translations impede a global positioning strategy.

Usually, the reasons it is difficult to position brands globally are more complex. Customers in one part of the world may not relate to the message because of cultural differences. Nike recognized that linking its image to global sports figures such as Michael Jordan would not work in Thailand, where success in sports is not viewed as positively as in other parts of the world. Their research showed that success in academics, music, and the arts is as highly valued. Thus, they have positioned their products based on the theme "a passion to excel in all walks of life."[21]

◆ Illustration: Saatchi & Saatchi

Before Saatchi & Saatchi assumed the British Airways account, the airline was positioned differently around the world because local advertising agencies had more control over the local content of the advertising. For example, in the United States, the airline mar-

Table 16–6 Understanding the Modern Japanese Consumer

Here are seven important points to remember about the new Japanese consumer.

First, the new Japanese consumer wants ways to save time. The capsule hotel, in which guests sleep in cubicles stacked one on top of the other, exists as an inexpensive alternative for those who don't want to take the long 2- to 3-hour train ride home. Moreover, 24-hour golf ranges, tennis courts, and convenience stores exist to expand the use of time when offices have closed for the day.

Second, the new Japanese consumer wants to purchase only those goods considered hot in Tokyo. All consumption trends, such as the slight shift toward a liberal (modern, Western) lifestyle, have started in this city. This is most apparent in consumption, fashion, and pop culture among Japanese under 35 years old.

Third, the new Japanese consumer wants to be similar to all other Japanese consumers. Virtually all Japanese think of themselves as middle class. They pay careful attention to dressing alike, but look for small differences in products to express individuality. The Japanese are amused by youthful indiscretions (e.g., wearing jeans instead of business suits), but they know juniors eventually marry, form families, and become middle class.

Fourth, the new Japanese consumer wants products that have "established reputation." Sometimes this means famous brands. More often this means famous brands bought at an honored store. Most often this means famous brands bought at an honored store that come with a reputation of success from Europe or the United States. Image instead of content is the most important criterion that determines whether the famous brand gift bought at an honored store meets the obligation required on White Day.

Fifth, the new Japanese consumer cannot afford to own houses. So the treat is to buy luxury overseas travel, richly appointed watches and jewelry, expensive cars, highly prized opera tickets, and a sumptuous night on the Queen Elizabeth II. Liquid assets rather than fixed assets make the affluent consumer in Japan.

Sixth, the new Japanese consumer wants the highest quality possible in goods and services. And the

packaging of these products must reflect the care one takes in selling these goods and services to the consumer in Japan. Every detail is dwelt upon as essential. The task of wrapping individual items, packaging all items in a box, wrapping the box, and putting ribbons around the total package supercedes all other tasks. The Japanese practice the art form of concentrated quality in which the wrapped package succeeds or fails entirely insofar as it achieves concentration. Beauty is not so much in the product itself, but in the concentration of preparing the package for the customer.

Seventh, the new Japanese consumer receives so much more information from *manga*, magazines, books, newspapers, radio, TV, and on-line computer services than do European and American consumers. All Japanese get the same information from Tokyo 24 hours each day, 7 days per week, 365 days per year. They use this information to determine which goods and services are of the highest quality, and which of these are the trends of emerging new lifestyles appearing from the interaction of western ides and Japanese values.

To avoid "humbling" feedback, U.S. marketers must pay attention to the real national differences between Americans and Japanese. Also marketers must recognize that Japanese consumers are changing along with other groups in the world, but Japanese consumers are changing at a much slower pace than are the Americans and the Europeans. Caution and care in collecting good consumer information give us better products, higher sales, and more satisfied customers in one of the toughest markets in the world, Japan.

Summary: Scanning Consumer Information

Marketers make Japanese sales by paying close attention to humor, fantasy, harmony, *nihonjin*, and other cultural insights. Marketing executives also make sales to Japanese juniors and other younger age-period peer groups by building assertiveness, green chic, value, and casual fashion into their products. Moreover, marketers make sales to Japanese younger and older age-period cohort groups by promoting collectivism and material success. This Japan is more different from than similar to Europe and America.

Source: Douglas Lamont (1996), *Global Marketing*, (Cambridge, MA: Blackwell), pp. 162–163.

keted Britain as a destination focusing on the country's reputation for old-fashioned hospitality and featuring shots of some of the country's famous sites. In Britain, the positioning was patriotic and emphasized the importance of flying the national carrier. In many other countries, much of the positioning was oriented toward price and vacation packages.

The inaugural global positioning chosen by Saatchi & Saatchi for British Airways (BA) was "The world's favorite airline." The basis for the theme was that, according to

1983 statistics, BA led the world's airlines in the number of passengers carried, the number of flights, and the number of passenger miles. The main concept was executed in a 90-second TV commercial called "Manhattan Landing" showing the island of Manhattan rotating slowly through the sky across the Atlantic to London, accompanied by the statement "Every year, we fly more people across the Atlantic than the entire population of Manhattan."

Although the commercial was an artistic and creative success, the difficulty of positioning the airline globally became clear when research showed the following reactions:

- How many people in the world know the population of Manhattan?
- Why only the execution flying over the Atlantic? People flying from New Delhi to London do not fly over the Atlantic Ocean.
- The word *favorite* can mean many things. One definition is related to the volume of people flying. However, another is more attitudinal in nature. BA did not have the best reputation at the time for customer service. Many managers around the world felt that the term could be misinterpreted in their local market or lack credibility where the local flag carrier had the dominant market position.
- In some countries, only the national flag airline could be advertised on TV. How would the theme translate into print media?
- Other BA country managers felt that their customers were more interested in a positioning related to vacationing. For example, in Japan, 70% of BA's passengers were vacationers heading to Britain on holiday. In these markets, the positioning was viewed as being better for business travelers, who valued the implied benefits of a large airline.

Thus, it is easy to see the limits of using a global positioning strategy, even a simple one such as that used by BA.

Global Branding

The arguments for or against global branding are consistent with the international versus global marketing orientation discussed earlier in this chapter, as well as the prior discussion on product positioning. A necessary condition for being interested in building a global name for a company, product, or service is a concomitant interest in having customers around the world view the equity in a name similarly. A key decision for F&P Gruppo is whether the Italian-sounding Gallo name will play well in Poland and other countries to which they are interested in expanding.

Recall that in Chapter 3 we defined brand equity as being composed of loyalty, awareness, perceived quality, favorable brand associations, and other assets (e.g., patents). If you are interested in building global brand equity, you must take steps in each country to focus on these components around a single brand name. In particular, most attempts to build a unified global image such as those described in this chapter (Orangina and British Airways, for example) focus on the awareness, associations, and perceived quality components and hope that greater purchasing and brand loyalty follow.

Proctor & Gamble's definition of a global brand is instructive: To obtain clear and consistent brand equity across geographic markets, a brand should be positioned the same, have the same formulation, provide the same benefits, and have a consistent advertising message. The company does this through the following principles:

- Understand the local consumer.
- Clearly define the brand's equity based on benefits that are common around the world.
- Expand what is successful in one market to other parts of the world.

An alternative approach to understanding global brand equity is to see how the international consulting group Interbrand develops quantitative estimates of brand equity, which are used to value companies and brands being bought or taken over by other companies. To judge a brand's strength, Interbrand examines the following:

- The industry in which the product competes (e.g., food is more highly valued than fashion because food industries are less susceptible to fads)
- The brand's stability
- Its market share or leadership
- The brand's internationality or global awareness
- The amount of marketing support behind it
- Its trademark protection
- The trend of the brand (whether its market share is increasing or decreasing)

The greatest weight is given to the third and fourth factors.[22]

◆ Illustration: Lucky-Goldstar

In 1995, Korean conglomerate Lucky-Goldstar changed its name to the LG Group.[23] The LG Group is a $70-billion company with interests in semiconductors, electronics, chemicals, and telecommunications. In 1995, the company invested in the U.S. company Zenith Electronics Corp. and now has more than 50% ownership of the company. The company has offices in more than 120 countries worldwide.

The company spent $30 million on a global campaign building the LG brand to compete against other global brands such as General Electric and Philips. It is the third-largest company in South Korea, behind Samsung and Hyundai, but is not nearly as well known worldwide. Therefore, part of the branding campaign was to build the awareness component of brand equity to offset the name change. In addition, the objective of the campaign was to create an image (association) that the company is a "gentle giant" through the tagline "We put people first." The objective is to show how technology fits into and improves everyday life around the world (i.e., how the company helps people).   ◆

Defending Local Markets

Thus far, this chapter has focused on companies that want to enter markets beyond their home markets. An alternative perspective is that of the home company that derives most of its sales in its local market: how do you defend your turf against large multinational and global marketers? Or, if yours is one of the latter two kinds of companies, how might you expect the local companies to defend themselves?

This is an important problem for local firms, which often face global companies with much more money. How does the local fast-food operator in India compete against the McDonald's that has opened down the street? How does a Russian personal computer company compete against Dell and Compaq?

The best approach for a local firm is to exploit the unique properties of their products in their culture or country. No matter how hard the global company attempts to "think local," the home company can do this better. The Kentucky Fried Chicken (KFC) restaurants in Shanghai compete against the regional chain Dicos Fried Chicken, which sells Chinese-style corn soup, green tea, and hot fruit juice. There is significant symbolism in emphasizing the local content of products. U.S. textile companies emphasize the American labor union labels in their clothing. As noted earlier in this chapter, every country's airline promotes itself based on a subtle (or sometimes, not so subtle) message of patriotism. The local company's value proposition should emphasize local content, color, and culture against which the large multinationals cannot compete. Such an approach will not eliminate the competitive threat from KFC and its counterparts, but to survive, home companies should exploit their natural competitive advantage as much as possible.

An additional strategy is to project a David versus Goliath image. Britvic soft drinks, a small British company, has been successful in fighting off Coke and Pepsi by showing TV commercials featuring a company executive in a boxing ring vowing to defend its Tango brand against any foreigner. The strategy has been extended to the Netherlands and Hungary.[24] A similar strategy was used by the Thai soap brand Parrot in response to the Asian currency problems in late 1997. An advertising campaign featuring a sadistic-looking foreigner (looking suspiciously like the U.S. Uncle Sam symbol) ordering a family to use a foreign brand of soap raised Parrot's market share to 50%, compared to just 13% before the campaign started.[25]

One way the global companies are fighting back is by marketing a combination of global and local brands. U.K.-based B.A.T. Industries markets 240 brands of cigarettes worldwide but only 10 of them are internationally marketed and distributed. Nestlé has 7,000 local brands. Table 16–7 shows the local brands owned by Coca-Cola and Proctor & Gamble. The local brands can be used to combat home-country brands or even expanded into a region. Some marketers view this local-global combination as beneficial because it induces locals to trade up to the global brands from their local brands as living standards around the world rise. However, from the customer's perspective, it is not clear that a strong local brand with significant cultural value is necessarily trading down from a global brand.

◆ Illustration: India

India is one of the most difficult markets in the world for consumer product manufacturers to crack.[26] Unlike China, where foreign brands such as Coke, Jeep, and Head & Shoulders are highly recognized and valued, Indians prefer Thums Up to Coke (interestingly, Coke owns Thums Up) and Titan watches to Timex. This is partly because of a long history of strict regulation of foreign investment and presence in the country, but it also results from the traditions and culture that Indians treasure, along with smart managers who have adapted modern marketing techniques to the home market. Particularly with respect to food, drink, and medicine, foreign countries can be difficult to penetrate.

One example is how the fast-food chain Nirula beat out McDonald's and other foreign competitors. The restaurant serves spicy chicken tikka burgers, mango lassis (a yogurt-flavored drink), vegetarian pizza with chili, and thalis (a sampler plate). Nirula emphasizes two differential advantages: low price and tradition. McDonald's sells its Maharaja Macs in New Delhi and Bombay, but is far outsold by Nirula. In addition, where competitors have innovated, Nirula has copied. When Pizza Hut introduced home delivery on scooters, Nirula did the same.

Dabur Ltd. is one of India's oldest and best-known ayurvedic medicine and cosmetic companies (using centuries-old mixtures of herbal and plant extracts). One of its best-known brands is Pudin Hara, a minty green digestive aid sold in brown bottles with 1950s packaging and labeling. Besides the dated look, the brand must be mixed with water and stirred before use. Because of the old packaging and the inconvenient product form, the brand was losing urban customers to foreign stomach ache remedies that came in tablet form. To help regain lost business, the company put the product in gel form for urban dwellers while continuing to sell the brown bottle in rural areas. In addition, the tradition of the brand was

Table 16–7 Local Brands Owned by Coca-Cola and Proctor & Gamble

Coca-Cola's national brands

Product	Description	Countries
Beverly	Herbal soft drink	Italy
Benaqua	Mineral water	Germany, Poland, Czech Republic, Hungary
Cappy	Juice drink	Turkey, Germany, Hungary, Slovak Republic, Poland, Romania
Cocke	Soft drink	Ireland
Kinley	Flavored tonic water	Germany, Czech Republic
Lilt	Citrus soft drink	United Kingdom, Ireland
Mezzo	Mineral water	Germany
Tab X-TRA	Sugar-free dark cola energy drink	Norway, Sweden, Iceland, Finland
Thumbs Up	Cola	India
Tiao Yi Di (Heaven & Earth)	Litchi, mango and pomegranate drink	China
Topper	Carbonated Icelandic water	Iceland
Splash	Fruit flavor juice drink for children	Germany, Spain
Urge/Surge	Low-carbonation citrus soft drink	Norway, United States

Proctor & Gamble's national brands

Product	Description	Countries
Az	Toothpaste	Italy
Blendax	Toothpaste	Germany, Austria, Eastern Europe
Bold	Laundry detergent	United Kingdom, United States
Daz	Laundry detergent	United Kingdom
Dreft	Dishwashing liquid	The Netherlands, Belgium
Fairy	Dishwashing liquid	United Kingdom
Kamille	Skincare product	Germany
Petrole Hahn	Haircare product	France

Source: Bill Britt (1997), "For multinationals, value lies in eyes of local consumers," *Advertising Age*, May, p. i18.

emphasized in advertising. For urban residents, the combination of the convenient form and the tradition has proven to be irresistible. ◆

MARKETING MIX IMPLICATIONS

Channels of Distribution

One of the issues raised in this chapter is the limit to true globalization, the concept that you can market a product or service around the world in the same manner.[27] The same question can be asked about distribution channels: Is it possible to have a global channel strategy? In Chapter 9, we discussed the fact that channel structures exist to serve the company's customers. In this chapter, we have noted that not only do customers' habits and tastes vary around the world, but so do economic, regulatory, and other conditions. Thus, cultural and other country differences affect strategic decisions such as positioning and branding but they also affect tactical decisions such as channels. No matter how you choose to enter a foreign market, whether through a joint venture, independent agents, or a wholly owned subsidiary, you have to consider global vagaries in retail and wholesale customs that restrict your ability to develop a truly global approach to channels. Some of these country and regional differences are the following.

Western Europe

The European retailing scene today looks very much like that of the United States. Increased price sensitivity has resulted in the proliferation of private label or "own" brands in the major chains such as Sainsbury, Safeway, Tesco, and Carrefours. Superstores such as Price/Costco have established footholds, as have well-known retailers such as Ikea, Toys "R" Us, and Staples.

However, local regulations still exist and must be considered. For example, Portugal has limited the establishment of new hypermarkets to protect small retailers. Germany has a large number of retail laws. The number of hours stores can remain open is significantly restricted, although the government is experimenting with relaxing those laws.

Russia and Other Former Soviet Bloc Countries

The lack of a high-quality distribution structure, not to mention a shortfall of disposable income, has hampered the development of retail activity in these countries. In addition, a significant amount of purchasing (up to 25% of grocery purchases by some estimates) is on the black market. Excise taxes can make the prices of consumer durables sold through conventional retailers such as cars prohibitively expensive (it is not surprising that the black market thrives). Brand loyalty is notoriously low. At the same time, foreign companies are entering major cities such as St. Petersburg, Moscow, and Warsaw. A first-time visitor to Prague or Budapest will be amazed at how Western the cities are (if you consider Pizza Hut and McDonald's representative of Western culture), sometimes to the detriment of their former charm.

Japan

It has been mentioned in this chapter that Japan is a difficult country for foreign companies to penetrate because of its maze of import and operational laws. For example, the Large-Scale Retail Store Law can delay a store's opening, reduce its size, force it to close early, and restrict the number of days it can be open. The retail market is extremely fragmented,

This electronics superstore is an exception to the rule in Japan, where mom-and-pop operations still dominate. Although import and operational laws make it a difficult country for foreign companies to penetrate, discounters and superstores such as this one have begun to penetrate Japan's market. (Kevin R. Morris/Corbis)

with mom-and-pop operations dominating; as a result, there is little price competition. However, these barriers are dropping as discounters in a number of categories, from men's clothing to toys, are springing up.

China and Other Asian Markets

In China, foreign firms are often forbidden to set up their own distribution networks; in fact, the Chinese Army (the People's Liberation Army) has a thriving subsidiary that distributes a variety of goods throughout the country. As in Japan, the retail market is extremely fragmented, with most Chinese living in rural areas. However, most global consumer and industrial companies are either in or looking at China simply because of its size and growing economic might.

Several examples already provided in this chapter indicate that southeast Asia is undergoing rapid economic development. Shopping malls have sprung up in Manila, Ho Chi Minh City, Singapore, and many other cities. However, the currency turmoil in late 1997 showed how vulnerable these economies can be to short-term economic problems.

◆ **Illustration: Proctor & Gamble** ────────────────────────────

Proctor & Gamble has been successful in entering both Japan and China, although it has been in the former country for a long time.[28] This illustration shows how the company used different approaches to distribution in each country by adapting to the local retail structure and consumer needs.

In 1995, P&G sold $450 million worth of shampoo and detergent, becoming the largest daily-use consumer products company in China. As we have noted, China has a poor infrastructure and is years away from having a national distribution system. How did P&G get its products into the millions of small and large stores throughout the country? The company targets the 228 Chinese cities with over 200,000 people and determines the location of every store in those cities. Then, they send in their "ground troops," thousands of trainees whose job is to get P&G products on the shelves of every store, into every kiosk, and even into street stalls. Thus, in a switch from traditional economics, the company is substituting labor for capital: The distribution system is based on human beings, not trucks or rail cars shipping vast amounts of products into warehouses. In addition, the company used an old Western distribution strategy of linking its Ariel and Tide brands with washing machine manufacturers, who pass out free products when a customer purchases a machine. Promotions such as free samples have been distributed generously.

Until 1995, P&G did not sell dish soap in Japan at all. By the end of 1997, the company had Japan's best-selling brand, Joy. Not only is the market for the product mature, but there are two giant Japanese competitors, Kao and Lion. The success was driven by introducing a new technologically advanced product (a more concentrated product requiring a smaller amount to be used) and popular TV commercials.

However, the product was also successful in winning over Japan's notoriously difficult retailers. Not surprisingly, retailers in Japan care about the same thing that retailers everywhere are concerned about: profitability of the category. Simply put, Joy is the most profitable product on the market. The Kao and Lion products were sold in long-necked bottles that wasted space. Joy is sold in a compact cylinder that takes less space in trucks, stores, warehouses, and, importantly, the shelves. This permits retailers to increase the number of units on the shelves, leading to lower restocking rates. That the product is sold for somewhat higher prices, giving higher margins per unit, does not hurt either.   ◆

Microsoft understands the huge potential in overseas markets.[29] More than half of the company's software sales come from its overseas operations, mainly in Europe and Japan. However, Latin America, Eastern Europe, Africa, and Asia account for about 10% of these overseas sales and are the company's fastest-growing markets.

How does Microsoft distribute its products in these emerging economies? The company hires local managers, who create partnerships with small companies that sell products such as Windows, Office, and NT. These companies then train other partners, creating a network somewhat like the multilevel marketing structures described in Chapter 9. This system allows Microsoft to keep its own staff small and highly productive; each overseas employee generates over $1 million of revenue, versus a company average of $500,000.   ◆

Gray Markets

The **gray market** is where trademarked goods are sold through channels of distribution that are not authorized by the holder of the trademark. It is common that gray markets develop across country lines; this phenomenon is often called **parallel importing.** Parallel importing is most often found when there are significant currency exchange rate or price differences between countries that make it profitable to purchase goods in one country and then import them into another for resale. Most readers are familiar with friends from foreign countries who find it cheaper to buy some products in the United States than in their home countries, and load up before returning. Parallel importing is exactly this behavior, except that institutions are involved in the purchasing and shipping and the products are resold in the home market. For example, an automobile dealer in Europe may find it prohibitively expensive to purchase and resell BMWs by going through normal channels. However, the dealer could purchase some in the United States and ship them back for resale at a lower price than legitimate BMW dealers can. Such gray markets are initiated by intermediaries known as **diverters.** These agents either purchase products or arrange for their purchase and divert the products away from normal channels.

It looks like a good deal for both the manufacturer and the customer; the former sells more products and the latter enjoys lower prices. However, legitimate channel members become agitated when a significant amount of gray market goods flood their markets. This leads to decreased goodwill in the channel. In addition, warranty support is not necessarily equivalent to that of goods bought through legitimate channels. Finally, brand image and equity can be diluted by gray marketers focusing on low prices.

Pricing

Because of the impact of gray market channels and other factors, price is very difficult to control in international markets. More precisely, a consistent global pricing policy is difficult to implement because of fluctuations in exchange rates, tariffs and other taxes that are added onto imported goods, and the price–quality effects of the country of origin.

Exchange rate fluctuations, unlike tariffs and taxes, are impossible to predict and play havoc with global pricing policies. In late 1997, over a 2-month period, the Korean currency, the won, decreased in value by nearly 50%, from $.0011 to $.00064. As a result, U.S. or other goods purchased in dollar terms doubled in terms of the local currency, assuming the exchange rate decline was passed along to customers. Retailers and other channel members usually raise their prices even though they purchased the inventory at a lower exchange rate because they will have to replace the inventory at the new, higher rates.

Thus, exchange rate changes in unfavorable directions and taxes and tariffs that are simply added to the imported costs result in wildly different prices around the world for the same products and a cost-plus pricing environment (see Chapter 11). In this environment, the final price is based only on costs. As a result, prices may be considerably higher than the value customers place on the product in the local market, resulting in significantly decreased sales. There is no reason that prices should not vary around the world; you would expect customer value to be different in different market segments and countries. However, arbitrarily adding costs, even those that are legitimately incurred, only creates a cost recovery rather than value recovery approach to pricing.

Interestingly, you do not have to be an exporter to be exposed to exchange rate fluctuations. Consider the situation in which a company that markets only in the United States faces foreign competitors, including some from Korea. All of a sudden, the Korean companies can significantly reduce their dollar prices in the U.S. market.

Table 16–8 shows different pricing and other policies under different currency conditions. When the domestic currency is weak, full-costing or cost-plus pricing does not hurt you so much because the exchange rate keeps the selling price down. However, when your currency is strong, cost-plus pricing would result in prices that are likely to be greater than customer value. As a result, marketing strategies focus on nonprice value propositions.

Some large price disparities exist even in regions of the world that are closely linked by geography and transportation. For example, in Europe, some of the extreme price differences are the following:[30]

- 115% for chocolate
- 65% for tomato ketchup
- 155% for beer
- 30% for natural yogurt

Table 16–8 Export Strategies Under Varying Currency Conditions

When Domestic Currency Is Weak	When Domestic Currency Is Strong
Stress price benefits	Engage in nonprice competition by improving quality, delivery, and after-sale service
Expand product line and add more costly features	Improve productivity and engage in vigorous cost reduction
Shift sourcing and manufacturing to domestic market	Shift sourcing and manufacturing overseas
Exploit export opportunities in all markets	Give priority to exports to strong-currency countries
Conduct conventional cash-for-goods trade	Deal in countertrade with weak-currency countries
Use full-costing approach, but use marginal-cost pricing to penetrate new or competitive markets.	Trim profit margins and use marginal-cost pricing
Speed repatriation of foreign-earned income and collections	Keep the foreign-earned income in host country, slow collections
Minimize expenditures in local, host country currency	Maximize expenditures in local, host country currency
Buy needed services (advertising, insurance, transportation, etc.) in domestic market	Buy needed services abroad and pay for them in local currencies
Minimize local borrowing	Borrow money needed for expansion in local market
Bill foreign customers in domestic currency	Bill foreign customers in their own currency

Source: S. Tamur Cavusgil (1988), "Unraveling the mystique of export pricing," *Business Horizons*, May–June, Figure 2, p. 58.

Despite geographic proximity, differences in regulations, competition, distribution structures, and consumer behavior create different levels of customer value and make it optimal to charge different prices. With the increasing size of the European Union resulting in fewer cross-country tariffs and regulations and the impending adoption of a common European currency, the Euro, on January 1, 2002 (when the Euro physically replaces national currencies), it is unclear whether these differences will be sustained.[31] It is still unlikely that a pan-European marketing strategy will and should be sustained, given the differences in customer tastes across country boundaries.

An additional factor to consider in global pricing is the effect that country of origin has on the price–perceived value relationship. In the United States, Japanese brands have high customer value, whereas Korean brands have lower value and are priced lower. German binoculars and cameras are premium-priced to take advantage of that country's reputation in optics. Similar situations hold for French wine, Swiss watches, and U.S. computers. These perceptual differences vary over product categories; although the French are known throughout the world for their wine, food, fashion, and movies, their reputation for making automobiles is concentrated mainly in Europe.

Advertising and Promotion

The discussions earlier in this chapter about global marketing and positioning noted the difficulty of using the same advertising campaign around the world. There are so many differences in language and culture that even a truly global advertising campaign requires some localization. For example, Taco Bell's wildly successful talking Chihuahua, Gidget, could not be used when the company expanded to Singapore as Muslims consider it taboo to touch a dog.[32] In addition, there are many differences around the world in regulation of advertising and promotion. Most countries regulate advertising content; for example, comparative advertising is widely frowned upon. Muslim countries have strict guidelines about how women can be portrayed in ads. Norway, Sweden, and Switzerland do not allow advertising on TV at all. Other countries have government-owned stations that limit advertising. However, with the global explosion of cable TV, many of these regulations are being relaxed. Many regulations also apply to sales promotion. For example, Austria, Germany, and Greece ban coupons. Sweepstakes and contests are strictly regulated in many countries.

 Despite local regulations, conventional advertising and sales promotional programs still work in many countries. At the end of 1995, research conducted by the Italian dairy products marketer Parmalat discovered that their products were found in only 19% of all Brazilian kitchens. By the end of 1996, the number was 96%. The reason? A wildly successful TV advertising campaign for milk based on equating milk with mammals and showing children aged 2–5 adorably dressed in big furry animal costumes. In November 1997, the company continued the campaign by launching a promotion allowing customers to obtain small stuffed animals based on the TV campaign. During the promotion, 60,000 Brazilians each day lined up to exchange the equivalent of $7 plus bar codes representing 20 purchases of Parmalat products for the toys. The campaign has been expanded to Venezuela and Argentina.[33]　◆

Table 16–9 Top 10 Global Advertisers, 1997

Advertiser	Global Ad Spending*	Asia	Europe	Latin America
Proctor & Gamble	$3,011.4	$ 63.2	$915.2	$354.2
Unilever	2,525.5	88.6	509.4	437.8
Nestlé	1,321.2	233.8	869.9	190.1
Toyota	1,254.4	871.6	300.4	22.4
Coca-Cola	1,026.4	246.7	437.6	307.2
General Motors	946.5	80.8	613.6	144.7
Volkswagen	898.2	41.4	740.3	98.4
PSA Peugeot Citroen	870.5	1.3	817.8	49.2
Nissan Motor Co.	866.9	561.6	259.8	19.6
Mars, Inc.	864.8	96.6	725.3	35.2

All figures in millions of dollars.

*Non-U.S. expenditures.

Source: Kevin Brown and Juliana Koranteng (1998), "Top global marketers," *Advertising Age*, November 9, p. 15.

Advertising expenditures around the world are substantial. Table 16–9 shows the top 10 global marketers ranked by their advertising spending outside the United States. It is interesting to note not only the totals but also the spending patterns in the major parts of the world.

THE IMPACT OF THE INTERNET

The Internet is having an important impact on global marketing. Companies in different countries can attract customers around the world by simply setting up a Web site and allowing customers to purchase, receive customer service, or collect product and company information. Thus, a Web-based business such as the book and CD seller Amazon.com is really a global company because anyone with access to the Web anywhere in the world can order books from their site. In this way, many of the difficult decisions about how to enter a new market are avoided. Web sites do not need foreign partners and they transcend country borders. They are essentially stateless.

Figure 16–5 shows the Web site for NZCrafts, a New Zealand–based company selling native crafts. No matter where they are, consumers with access to a PC and a modem can order mohair pullovers, wooden puzzles, shell jewelry, and other artifacts. A few clicks on the mouse while navigating Yahoo! gets you to such sites anywhere in the world, where you can purchase almost anything. Thus, many small companies like this one or large companies can sell their products and services to customers anywhere in the world without the complicated contracting and setting up a sales force.

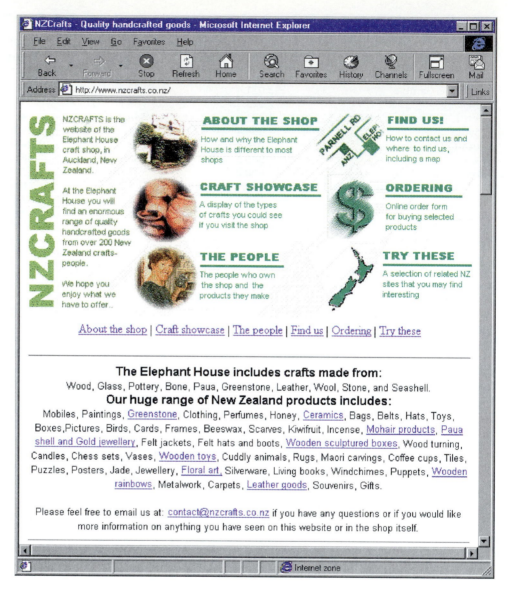

EXECUTIVE SUMMARY

The major points made in this chapter are the following:

- A distinction can be drawn between international marketing (tailoring a marketing program for each country or region) and global marketing (developing a uniform strategy for the product or service around the world).
- The concept of global marketing is grounded in the notion that because of enhanced communication and other technologies, the needs and tastes of customers around the world are becoming more similar.

- The case against global marketing is that this growing similarity of customers is overstated and that customers' tastes and needs should be examined on a market-by-market basis.
- Products that can be globally marketed most easily are those that are subject to economies of scale in manufacturing and those that are not culturally bound.
- A key decision in international marketing contexts is which markets to enter outside the home market. Three key subdecisions are which country or countries to enter, when to enter them, and how to operate in each one.
- Modes of operation in each country include exporting, contracting for production with a local firm, entering into a joint venture, or establishing a wholly owned subsidiary.
- The key to understanding customer behavior differences around the world is becoming familiar with the culture.
- Global positioning and branding decisions follow the problems and opportunities of international and global marketing. Depending on the product, it may or may not be possible to develop truly global brand positions and equity.
- If you are defending a local market, you should emphasize the unique properties and cultural aspects of your product.
- Marketing mix decisions (channels of distribution, price, and advertising and promotion) are bound by local regulations and customs.

CHAPTER QUESTIONS

1. What are the forces working in favor of global marketing? Against?
2. Many examples of successful global marketing strategies are for consumer products and services. Does the concept of global marketing apply as well to industrial products? What aspects of marketing outside your home market are most important to industrial products?
3. One important aspect of marketing a product in another country is the country-of-origin effect, or the effect that the home country has on the product's image. Develop a small survey measuring the perceived quality of TVs, soft drinks, and automobiles manufactured in the United States, Japan, Korea, and England and administer it to some of your colleagues. Can you explain the differences in perceived quality?
4. What factors would you consider in choosing which channels of distribution to use for marketing in a particular country?
5. Visit the Web site for a product or service from a foreign country. Does the company sponsoring the site exploit any characteristics or customs of its home country? How would you evaluate the site in terms of its ability to sell the product globally?

Application Exercises: Global Marketing and the PC Industry

Continuing the PC exercise, complete the following exercises:

1. Can PCs be marketed globally or is an international marketing approach more appropriate?
2. Pick two countries in different parts of the world and perform the following analyses:
   a. Analyze the country's culture or cultures.
   b. Research the institutions and regulations affecting distribution, pricing, and advertising and promotion in the two countries.
   c. Determine how most foreign companies enter these countries.

Integrated
Case

3. Choose a particular PC brand. Based on your analysis, develop a marketing strategy for the brand in both countries. Be clear on what parts of the strategy can be common (global) versus different (international).

4. Compare the answers to exercise 3 to the brand's strategy in the United States. What are the differences and similarities?

FURTHER READING

A good textbook on global marketing is Warren J. Keegan (1999), *Global Marketing Management,* 6th ed. (Englewood Cliffs, NJ: Prentice Hall). A paper describing a method for developing cross-country segments is by Frenkel ter Hofstede, Jan-Benedict E. M. Steenkamp, and Michel Wedel (1999), "International market segmentation based on consumer–product relations," *Journal of Marketing Research,* 36 (February), pp. 1–17. Readers interested in keeping up with research in the international marketing area should read the *International Journal of Research in Marketing,* which often features special articles about changing consumer behavior in different countries.

New Product Development

17

CHAPTER BRIEF

The purpose of this chapter is to highlight the importance of new products to firms and to describe alternative new product introduction processes. Key areas of learning include the following:

Why new products are important to organizations

Factors affecting new product success and failure

Three major approaches to developing new products: the linear process, the rugby approach, and the target costing method

The steps in bringing new products to market

Special topics in new product development, such as the importance of shorter development cycles and better integration of marketing and R&D

For nearly 10 years beginning in the mid-1980s, five multinational companies—Kodak, Fuji Photo Film, Minolta, Canon, and Nikon—worked together to develop a new photography system that Kodak called the advanced photo system or (APS).[1] The system is incompatible with existing 35-mm technology and is priced about 15% higher. However, the cameras are small and light, have easy film loading, and permit photographers to take three sizes of pictures on the same roll of film: classic (4 × 6 inches), group (4 × 7 inches), and panoramic (4 × 10 inches). In addition, some errors in picture taking when a flash is used can be corrected in the development process.

The cameras were introduced in early 1996. However, 4 months after the product introduction, most retailers did not have the cameras to sell because of production problems and demand forecasting mistakes. Poor packaging caused some consumers to buy the new film cartridges in the belief that they could be used in their existing 35-mm cameras (they cannot). The companies did not support the retailers well with in-store promotional materials. A multitude of brand names (Kodak called its APS camera the Advantix, Minolta used the brand name Vectis, and Nikon called it Nuvis) also created some confusion among consumers. Finally, when the cameras did arrive on the shelves, the negative publicity surrounding the new product kept consumers from purchasing them. Taking all the problems together, some observers called it the worst new product launch in the history of the photographic industry. In August 1996, the feeling was that the companies marketing the APS cameras had better recover within the next year or the camera would be history.

In April 1997, Kodak relaunched the Advantix camera with an estimated $60- to $100-million advertising campaign and extensive promotions, including a free camera to any woman who had a baby on Mother's Day. However, when a new photographic technology is introduced, film developers wait to see whether the camera will sell well (and, therefore, whether the film will sell) before investing in new processing equipment. This, in turn, affects whether consumers will buy the cameras—who will buy a camera with a new type of film if they cannot develop the pictures? Also, retailers, having been burned by Kodak and the other APS companies the previous year, were reluctant to carry the camera.

By 1999, however, the camera technology was well established. About 20% of all new camera sales used the APS system and advanced products were being launched by the major firms. A big boost to the market was Kodak's launch of one-time-use APS cameras, a very popular product form. Backed by a multi–million-dollar advertising campaign highlighted by a commercial in the popular *Seinfeld* TV series finale in 1998, Fuji's APS models have also sold very well.

The problems experienced by the companies manufacturing APS cameras are typical of those that occur when new products and services are launched. However, most companies rely on new products for their long-term health. Today, successful companies in a wide variety of industries generate a large percentage of their sales from new products. Figure 17–1 provides some evidence supporting the correlation between this percentage of sales from new products and industry position. As can be seen, the most successful companies generate nearly 50% (the "All Firms" line) of their sales from new products, as compared to around 10% for the least successful. For firms in high-tech industries, the gap is even larger. Hewlett-Packard, for example, obtains over 50% of its revenues from products introduced within the last 2 years.

In addition, companies spend a significant amount of money to develop new products. Table 17–1 shows the top 10 companies in the world in terms of their spending on research and development (R&D). Also, the number of patents issued by the U.S. Patent and Trademark Office is skyrocketing. A record 151,024 patents were issued in 1998, a 33% increase from 1997. The top five companies in this patent rush were IBM, Canon, NEC, Motorola, and Sony.[2] Most of these companies are enormous in terms of their revenues and can therefore afford to spend a significant amount of money on R&D. However, their large revenue streams are driven to a great extent by the success of their new product development efforts.

Figure 17–1

Percentage of Current Sales by New Products Developed in the Last 5 Years by the Company's Self-Reported Industry Rank

Source: Thomas P. Hustad (1996), "Reviewing current practices in innovation management and a summary of selected best practices," in M. D. Rosenau, Jr., A. Griffin, G. A. Castellion, and N. F. Anscheutz, eds., *The PDMA Handbook of New Product Development* (New York: Wiley), p. 490.

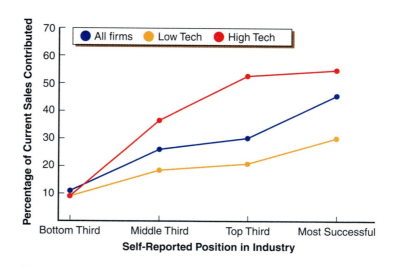

Table 17–1 Top 10 Global Spenders on Research and Development

Company	Country	1995 R&D Spending ($ millions)
General Motors	United States	$8,388
Ford Motor Co.	United States	6,509
Hitachi Ltd.	Japan	6,415
IBM	United States	5,227
Siemens A.G.	Germany	5,150
Matsushita Electric	Japan	4,857
Nippon Telephone	Japan	4,321
Fujitsu Ltd.	Japan	4,046
AT&T	United States	3,718
NEC Corp.	Japan	3,512

Source: *R&D Magazine*, October 1996.

Most companies recognize the importance of new products. In the high-tech marketing world described in Chapter 15, innovation is life. Even in slow-growth markets such as food industries, companies are constantly scrambling for ideas like Frito-Lay's flavored snack chips (e.g., Cool Ranch) or Nabisco's Snackwells that revitalize product categories and bring significant sales growth. Over 25,000 new products were introduced in 1997 in U.S. supermarkets and over 77,000 new universal product codes (UPCs) were generated.[3] The inevitability of the maturity and decline of the product life cycle means that there is constant pressure for companies to find their own "next big thing."[4] Thus, SmithKline Beecham generated $243 million in sales from its new smoking-cessation product Nicoderm CQ, introduced in 1997; revenues from this product replaces that of older products that are withdrawn or deemphasized.

New products can also form the foundation for a complete turnaround of a company's performance. For many years, Colgate-Palmolive had done a good job selling its toothpaste, deodorants, pet foods, and soaps in markets outside the United States. However, it had been consistently underperforming Proctor & Gamble and Unilever in the United States. In early

New products are critical to the long-term health of most companies. In the food industry, successful companies such as Frito-Lay are constantly introducing new snack ideas to revitalize the product category. Frito-Lay's new fat-free Ruffles and Lay's potato chips are part of a new snack line. (Felicia Martinez/Corbis)

1998, Colgate introduced a new toothpaste, Total, that is expected to help launch a corporate comeback in the U.S. market. Total contains triclosan, a germ-fighter found in many soaps and other personal care products. It has received approval from the Food and Drug Administration to claim that it helps to prevent gum disease, a claim no other toothpaste can match. Even in large, diversified companies like Colgate, such unique products can have a significant impact on the whole company's competitive performance.[5]

The new product development process is difficult and most new products fail.[6] The Kodak APS example illustrates only some of issues involved with launching new products. A larger list of such issues is the following:

- What are the sources of ideas for new products?
- How do you take the large list of possible ideas and winnow it down to a more feasible set?
- How do you go from product concept to prototype?
- How do you forecast the demand for a new product?
- What is the ideal organizational form for new product success?
- Once the new product is finalized, how do you introduce it into the marketplace?

Thus, the new product development and introduction process is complicated and fraught with difficulties. Some new product failures are famous:

- The Edsel
- The RCA Videodisk system and Polaroid's Polavision
- Microsoft Bob

For those interested in the legacy of new product failures in the supermarket, there is a museum in Ithaca, New York, dedicated to flops. The museum houses over 60,000 specialty food, personal care, and household cleaning products that were introduced and eventually withdrawn from the supermarket shelves.

A difficulty in the area of new products is defining exactly what constitutes a new product. New products are commonly divided into three categories:[7]

- Classically innovative products. These are also called new-to-the-world products because the firm has created a new product category. You might separate these into two subcategories: truly new products that are revolutionary (e.g., the disposable diaper, the personal computer) and other new products that create new categories but are based on existing products (e.g., the Kodak Advantix).
- New category entries. In this case, the product category already exists but the firm is just entering it. These are also commonly called new-to-the-company products. For example, Nike's entries into various sporting goods categories (e.g., in-line skates) fit into this classification.
- Additions to product lines or line extensions. These are new versions of existing products already marketed by the firm. Examples are new flavors, colors, or technical variations.

Other, more minor product changes could also result in what are thought of as new products:

- Product improvements. Most products on the market are eventually replaced by "new and improved" versions.

- Repositionings. Many products are repositioned for a new use or benefit. For example, Rolaids and Tums, antacids normally used as antidotes for heartburn, have been positioned as calcium supplements for women.
- Cost reductions. In some cases, the only change to the product is a cost reduction through manufacturing, operations, or product cost savings.

Obviously, although many new products are line extensions or the results of more minor changes, we will use the term *new product* to refer only to innovative products and new category entries. This is because considerably less time (sometimes none) is spent on the new product development process for line extensions, improvements, and repositionings.

FACTORS AFFECTING NEW PRODUCT SUCCESS OR FAILURE

There has been a considerable debate over the success rate of new products. The new product failure rate mentioned in the popular press and textbooks ranges from 67% to 80%. However, these numbers reflect variations in the definition of what constitutes a new product and how firms measure success, so you should interpret them cautiously. As we have already seen, a new product could be an invention such as the automobile or simply a new flavor of Jell-O. In addition, the notion of success is firm specific because most companies have their own internal criteria for determining whether a new product should be supported or withdrawn from the market.

Figure 17–2 presents survey data about the success rates of new products introduced in 1990 and 1995 by member firms of the Product Development and Management Association (PDMA). In 1990, for every 100 new product ideas, only about 10% were deemed successes by the companies that launched them. By 1995, improvements in the various stages of the new product development process had increased the success rate to over 20%. In general, the 20–33% success rule seems to hold, particularly for the first two categories of new products (inventions and new category entries).

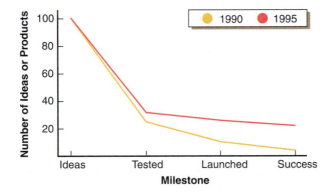

Figure 17–2

New Product Idea Mortality Curve for PDMA Member Firms, 1990 and 1995

Source: Thomas P. Hustad (1996), "Reviewing current practices in innovation management and a summary of selected best practices," in M. D. Rosenau, Jr., A. Griffin, G. A. Castellion, and N. F. Anscheutz, eds., *The PDMA Handbook of New Product Development* (New York: Wiley), p. 491.

What factors lead some products to be successes and others failures? Many studies have attempted to determine the factors that separate success from failure. One well-known list of the factors correlated with successful new product introductions is shown in Table 17–2:[8]

- A superior product with unique product benefits. This should not be a surprise. No product, whether new or old, can be successful with offering a value proposition that is unique in the marketplace. Note that this does not rule out clones or me-too products that imitate existing product offerings. In such cases, meaningful differentiation can be obtained through a lower price, better service, or some other non–product-based factor.
- A strong market orientation throughout the new product development process. This implies having a thorough understanding of the target customers, likely competitors, and the external environment. A market orientation helps to ensure that the product or service ultimately introduced has a unique value proposition.
- Sufficient time on up-front activities before the product is launched. Sometimes this is called the homework part of the new product development process. It includes casting the net broadly for obtaining ideas for new products and analyzing the opportunities thoroughly.
- Sharp product definition. This includes knowing the target market, specifying the benefits to be delivered to the target customers, having a basic idea of how the product will be positioned, and finalizing the features and attributes.
- High-quality execution of the steps of the process.
- The appropriate organizational structure. As we will see later in the chapter, successful product development involves people from across the organization in interfunctional

---

Table 17–2 New Product Success Factors

- Developing a superior, differentiated product, with unique benefits and superior value to the customer or user
- Having a strong market orientation throughout the process
- Undertaking the redevelopment homework upfront
- Getting sharp, early product definition before development begins
- High-quality execution-completeness, consistency, proficiency-of activities in the new product process
- Having the correct organization structure: multifunctional, empowered teams
- Providing for sharp project selection decisions, leading to focus
- Having a well-planned, well-resourced launch
- The correct role for top management: specifying new product strategy and providing the needed resources
- Achieving speed to market, but with quality of execution
- Having a multistage, disciplined new product game plan

Source: Robert G. Cooper (1996), "New products: what separates the winners from the losers," in M. D. Rosenau, Jr., A. Griffin, G. A. Castellion, and N. F. Anschuetz, *The PDMA Handbook of New Product Development* (New York: Wiley), p. 50.

teams. In addition, companies good at launching new products often have an entrepreneurial culture that encourages risk-taking and the open exchange of ideas.

- A good project prioritization process. Most companies can generate a significant number of ideas or concepts for new products. Because resources are always scarce, it is important to allocate those resources efficiently so that promising projects are not starved for cash. Often, difficult decisions must be made to discard concepts that will not be successful for the company.

- Careful launch planning. Earlier in this book, we stressed the importance of the marketing plan. This principle also applies to the launch of new products. The Kodak Advantix may be an excellent camera; however, that does not mean it will be a successful new product. The development and execution of the launch plan (i.e., the marketing) will ultimately determine whether the new product is successful.

- Strong support by top management. Goals must be set and articulated to employees, indicating that new products are an important component of the company's business. In addition, the product development process must be given adequate resources.

- Fast time-to-market. The hallmark of successful new product introductions in the 1990s is speed, reducing the time it takes from concept generation to launch. However, speed should not come at the expense of the other items in the list.

- A detailed new product development process. As we will see in the next section of this chapter, there are many ways to approach the development and launch of new products. Each company must determine for itself which approach best fits its culture and external environment. However, no matter which approach is chosen, the company should have a well-documented process for new products that employees can follow.

APPROACHES TO NEW PRODUCT DEVELOPMENT

The Classic Linear Approach

Figure 17–3 shows a typical linear design of a new product development process.[9] This process is described as linear because the firm using it goes through a series of processes that occur one after another; that is, after one set is complete, the next in sequence occurs. Although we describe these in more detail later in the chapter, a brief overview of each follows.

Opportunity Identification

In the first stage of the new product development process, the company determines which markets it wants to enter. This requires the integration of new product planning with more traditional marketing or strategic planning. For example, before Colgate developed Total, the germ-fighting toothpaste, the company had to decide that the therapeutic segment was valuable to enter, based on the existing competition, projections of growth, and other information. The company could have decided to enter the benefit customer segment more interested in whiter teeth, for example.

Once the market entry decision has been made, the company searches for new product ideas. As we will show later in the chapter, there are many possible sources for new product concepts. Some concepts are easy to develop; for example, a company wanting to enter an existing category with a product similar to a competitor's already has a reference point on which the new product can be based. However, for really new products or inventions, new product ideas are much sketchier and may not be feasible to produce.

Figure 17–3

New Product and
Service Development
Process

Source: John R. Hauser and
Glen L. Urban (1993), *Design
and Marketing of New Products,*
2nd ed. (Englewood Cliffs,
NJ: Prentice Hall), p. 38.

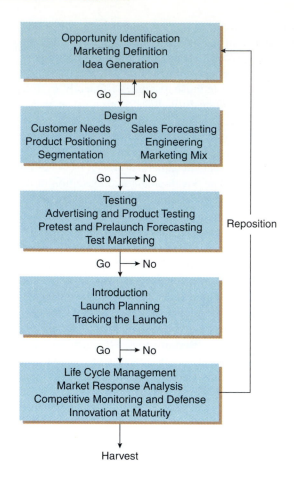

Design

Few new concepts ultimately make it to the marketplace. The design phase of the new product development process includes a step to screen the concepts developed in the first stage. Many of the concepts are not practical to make, require too much investment, or are not as good a fit to the strategic goals as others. Thus, the concepts are matched against customer needs and other requirements of the target segments and preliminary forecasts are developed. Those with lower estimates of potential sales are eliminated.

The concepts that survive are the focus of design efforts. Using information from customer research, prototypes are developed and subjected to further customer testing. These can be physical prototypes (in the case of manufactured products) or specific service concepts.

Testing

Once the prototype is developed, it is tested with customers from the target segment. Further refinements are made to make progress toward the final product. Advertising concepts are also tested. Based on the customer tests, more sales forecasts are developed and additional product concepts are eliminated. In some cases, the resulting products are test marketed in specific geographic regions. In test marketing, a company simulates the actual introduction of a product or service in a limited number of markets. Different pricing, advertising, packaging, and other features can be tried and evaluated. Unfortunately, test markets also provide an opportunity for competitors to learn about the new product, and some have been known to disrupt test markets using price promotions or other devices to confound the test.

Introduction

Following product testing (with or without test markets), the product or service is ready to be rolled out nationally or internationally. For all products, the rollout period is critical. For many kinds of products, the two key measures to monitor are trial and repeat. Clearly, for a product to be successful, you must get customers to try it. The greater the number of triers, the better; a product with a low trial rate will probably be withdrawn from the market. However, if customers do not repeat purchase, the product will also die. For consumer durables and other industrial products with long interpurchase cycles, trial or first-time purchasing is the key event.

Life Cycle Management

Although these are not specifically part of the new product development process, products and services require continuous updating and refinement. Pressure from customers and competitors force you to consider whether the price is appropriate, the advertising copy is working as well as it should, the distribution system is appropriate, and so on. In addition, particularly for durables and industrial products, whole product lines often have to be replaced (consider the frequent turnover in automobile models by most major global manufacturers).

The Rugby Approach

As we noted earlier, the classic new product development process is a linear process in which the new product concept goes through a number of stages before introduction. It is also a funnel: many new concepts start at the top but few make it out the bottom. In many companies, new product development is somewhat like a relay race in which different functional specialists carry the "baton" and hand it off to the next group. Often, marketing people develop product concepts, R&D engineers do the design work, production personnel make the product, and then it is given to the sales force to sell.

An alternative approach is more like a game of rugby: The product development process results from the constant interaction of a multidisciplinary team whose members work together from the beginning of the project to the product's introduction.[10] Thus, the team moves downfield in a pack from beginning to end. Companies using this method exhibit six characteristics in managing their new product development processes.

Built-In Instability

In this process, top management provides only a general strategic direction for the project team and establishes very challenging goals but provides a great deal of freedom. For example, Fuji Xerox gave a team a goal of producing a copier machine at half the cost of their most expensive line that performed just as well.

Self-Organizing Project Teams

Project teams are permitted to operate like startup companies within the larger organization by developing their own agendas and taking risks. They are normally given a great deal of autonomy. The result is that the project teams normally increase their goals throughout the new product development process, thus increasing the probability that they will develop breakthroughs rather than me-too products. The project teams usually consist of members with different functional specializations and personalities. This permits an extraordinary amount of learning within the group, which is translated to the project.

Canon's top management asked an interdisciplinary team to develop a high-quality automatic exposure camera that was small and easy to carry, easy to use, and priced 30% lower than the current prices of single-lens cameras. By the end of the project, the team had achieved several breakthroughs in camera design and manufacturing: an electronic brain made with chips from Texas Instruments, modularized production (which made automation and mass production possible), and 30–40% fewer parts. ◆

Overlapping Development Phases

The members of the project teams often start with different time horizons, which must be synchronized. At some point, the team begins to move forward together and they adapt to each other's styles and personalities. This movement forward is different from the linear process previously described. In that process, because there is a hand off of the baton after each phase, there is little integration between phases and a bottleneck at one phase stops the whole process. Under the rugby process, the phases overlap, enabling the team to continue to work on a later stage in the process even if there is a holdup in an earlier stage.

Multilearning

Members of these teams stay in close touch with external market conditions and continually learn from each other. This learning is transmitted across different levels (individual, group, and company) and functions (hence the term *multilearning*). Marketing people learn from engineers and vice versa.

Subtle Control

The project teams are not totally left alone. Senior management affects the process in a variety of ways, from choosing the people for the team to establishing an evaluation and reward system based on the performance of the group.

Canon has enjoyed long-term success with its line of traditional 35-mm cameras. Nonetheless, it has taken steps to ensure continued success by introducing new products, most recently this ultrasonic camera and its advanced photo system (APS) cameras. (Michael Newman/Photo Edit)

Transfer of Learning

An important byproduct of this process is the transfer of learning throughout the organization. Some of this is from project team to team. In some cases, the whole company learns from one project team's experiences. As a result of this transfer of learning, many of the companies using this approach have been successful in significantly reducing their cycle time for developing new products.

The Target Costing Approach

With the traditional linear new product development process, the retail price (or price to the customer) is set near the end of the process. Various price scenarios are used to perform the economic analyses necessary to screen product concepts and prototypes, but final manufacturing costs, a key input into many companies' pricing decisions, are not known until the design specifications are finalized and the size of the production run is known.

An alternative approach starts with the estimated price that the customers in the target segment are willing to pay. Before a company launches a new product, the ideal selling price must be determined, the feasibility of meeting that price assessed, and costs controlled in order to produce the product that can be sold at the target price. This process is called **target costing**.[11] Although a benefit of this approach is a decreased likelihood that low-margin products will be introduced, target costing ensures that market feedback is brought back into the development process right from the beginning.[12]

The steps of the approach are fairly straightforward. The company first researches its markets and segments and determines which it will target. It then calculates what price people are willing to pay in each segment it has chosen in order for the product to be successful. Subsequently, the company determines the levels of quality and functionality that are necessary to meet customer needs, given the target prices. Finally, the company arranges the sourcing of materials and the production and delivery processes that will enable it to achieve the target cost and profit margin at the desired price.

Figure 17–4 illustrates the target costing process. The leftmost circles designate the customer-based research that serves as the foundation for the target costing method. From this research, the quality and functionality targets emerge, as does the price target. Given the price, the organization must determine what its profit margin must be to reach corporate goals (the box labeled "Corporate Financial Requirements"). This then produces the target manufacturing cost. In other words, $C = P - \Pi$, where C (cost) is determined by subtracting the target profit margin per unit (Π) from the target price (P).[13] However, superimposed (top part of the figure) on these target costs are the expected costs from the current manufacturing process. The design challenge then becomes closing the gap between the target and expected costs.

 Illustration: Nissan

Nissan Motor Company uses the target costing system for developing its new car models.[14] The new product development system is divided into three different stages: the conceptual design stage, in which projects are initiated; the product development stage, in which the new car models are readied for production; and the production stage, in which they are manufactured. As of the early 1990s, the three stages lasted about 10 years, with the conceptual design stage lasting 2 years, the product development stage 4, and the production phase 4.

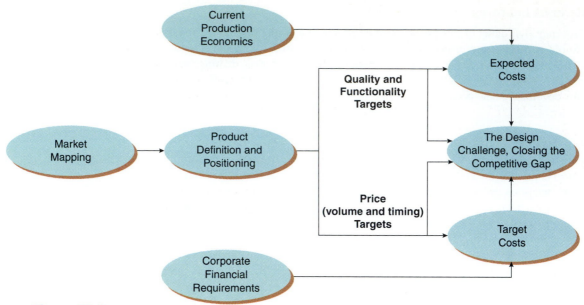

Figure 17–4

The Target Costing Process

Source: Robin Cooper and W. Bruce Chew (1996), "Control tomorrow's costs through today's designs," *Harvard Business Review,* January–February, p. 95.

Most target costing concepts are illustrated in the conceptual design stage. In this stage, the company starts with a matrix describing in general terms the numbers of each model the company wants to sell over the next 10 years. New entries in the matrix are obtained from detailed consumer studies. The company conceptualizes new models in terms of consumer mindsets, or how consumers view themselves in relation to their cars. Four mindsets used by Nissan are "value seeker," "confident and sophisticated," "aggressive enthusiast," and "budget/speed star." Where there is a significant cluster of potential consumers, the company attempts to introduce a model tailored to that segment. For example, the Sentra (a midpriced family sedan) was targeted to the confident/sophisticated and value seeker mindsets. The conceptual model is then categorized using three primary attributes: performance, aesthetics, and comfort.

The target price is the next factor estimated in the conceptual design stage. Both external and internal factors are considered in estimating the target price. In terms of external factors, besides consumer willingness-to-pay studies, Nissan also considers the company's image and the level of loyalty in the model's segment, the expected quality level and functionality of the model compared to competitive models, the model's expected market share, and the expected price of competing models. Internal factors include the position of the model in the matrix and the strategic and profit goals of senior management.

The allowable cost of the new model is determined by subtracting its target profit margin from the target price. The target margin is a function of the firm's long-term profit objectives, the anticipated future mix of products, and consumer information. Then, the size of the difference between the allowable cost and the current estimates of the manufacturing cost identifies how much costs must be reduced by a process called value engineering. To wring these costs out of the production process, all major functions, such as product design, engineering, purchasing, and parts, are brought into the discussion. If it is thought that the current and allowable costs can be brought into line, the process moves to the product development and production stages.

STEPS IN THE NEW PRODUCT DEVELOPMENT PROCESS

Although the three approaches to developing new products are quite different in concept, they all require the basic steps noted in Fig. 17–3. What varies is the sequencing of the activities. Even in the rugby and target costing approaches, new idea concepts must be generated, economic analyses and forecasts of the concepts must be made, products must move from concept to design and prototype stages, and the products launched. Therefore, in this section, we cover these major areas in more detail, focusing on the top three boxes of Fig. 17–3.[15]

New Product Concept Generation

A distinction can be made between two kinds of new product concepts: those that are provided by others, or ready-made, and those that are generated by some managed creative process.[16]

Sources of Ready-Made Concepts

Figure 17–5 shows the major internal and external sources of new product ideas in this category.

A variety of employees can be internal sources of new product ideas. Obviously, your own R&D department is an excellent source—that is what they are paid to do. In addition, many employees have customer contact: salespeople, customer service representatives, marketing managers conducting focus groups, and manufacturing personnel. Most companies today encourage suggestions from employees about new products; even if they are not in the categories not mentioned, for many products and services, employees are often customers as well and can therefore spot new product opportunities as well as external customers can.

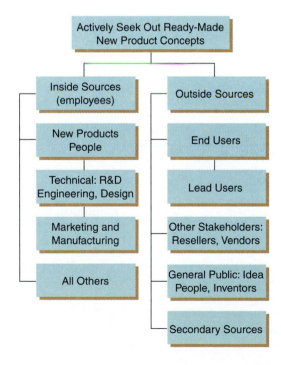

Figure 17–5

Sources of Ready-Made New Product Concepts

Source: C. Merle Crawford (1997), *New Products Management*, 5th ed. (Chicago: Irwin), p. 104.

Customers and other end users are logical external sources of new product ideas because they are seeking the benefits products and services seek to fulfill. Normally, new product ideas can emanate from focus and user group discussions. However, in some cases, customers will simply contact the company with suggestions. In Table 17–3, it can be seen that for several types of scientific instruments, customers accounted for over 80% of the innovations.

Other important external groups are channel members, vendors and suppliers, competitors, and independent inventors. Channel members have many customer contacts and are valuable for collecting information from the marketplace. As we noted in Chapter 7, many companies perform extensive analyses of competitors' products, looking for valuable information such as strengths and weaknesses. The invention industry is quite large, with many people developing new product ideas and then selling them to larger companies or obtaining venture capital and building their own companies.

Managing the Creative Process

Although there has been an increase in the number of courses offered in university business curricula on creativity, the creative process is still difficult to understand, predict, and manage. Companies may set up creative thinking groups or pay consultants to manage the process for them. Creative group methods generally involve a process in which group members are encouraged to think and speak freely outside the normal boundaries of their jobs.

One of the most common approaches to group creative thinking is brainstorming. In this approach, group members try to generate a large number of diverse ideas without criticism from other members. Variations on brainstorming exist, but all these methods have the following common elements:

- Openness and participation
- Encouraging many and diverse ideas
- Building on each other's ideas
- A problem orientation
- Using a leader to guide the discussion

These groups typically do not involve customers. Many experts believe that relying on customers for new products, particularly true innovations, is doomed to failure because of their limited ability to see into the future and conceptualize what could be.[17] Studies are being done to try to better understand what management processes can be applied to the problem of the development of radical rather than incremental innovations.[18]

Table 17–3 Sources of Innovation for Scientific Instruments

Major Improvement Innovations	% User Developed	Innovations Developed by			
		User	Manufacturer	NA	Total
Gas chromatograph	82%	9	2	0	11
Nuclear magnetic resonance spectrometer	79	11	3	0	14
Ultraviolet spectrophotometer	100	5	0	0	5
Transmission electron microscope	79	11	3	0	14
Total	81%	36	8	0	44

Source: Glen L. Urban and John R. Hauser (1993), *Design and Marketing of New Products*, 2nd ed. (Englewood Cliffs, NJ: Prentice Hall), p. 120.

Screening New Product Concepts

In order to reduce the number of concepts to a manageable number and to those that have good prospects for success, a variety of marketing research methods have been developed to enable you to screen the concepts by attempting to forecast ultimate demand.

Concept Testing

The initial test for most new products involves getting customer reactions to the product concept. The main purposes of a concept test are to choose the most promising from a set of alternatives, get an initial notion of the commercial prospects of a concept, find out who is most interested in the concept, and indicate what direction further development work should take. The subjects used in these tests should be taken from the target segments, if possible.

The most common approach is to present customers with a verbal or written statement of the product idea and then record their reactions. Recently, many researchers have chosen to include physical mockups and advertising statements in the concept test. (These are really prototype or prototype/concept tests.) The data gathered are both diagnostic ("Why do you like or dislike the product?") and predictive ("Would you buy it if it cost x?"). Including a concrete "Would you buy?" question is crucial if the results are to be useful from a predictive perspective. The data collection procedures fall into the following three major categories.

- Surveys. Surveys are useful for getting large samples for projection purposes. On the other hand, it is often difficult to effectively convey a concept in a survey, especially an impersonal one.
- Focus groups. The strength of focus groups is their diagnostic power in that they can be used to get detailed discussions of various aspects of the concept. As predictors of actual sales, they are fairly inaccurate because of their small sample sizes.
- Demonstrations. A popular way to present a concept is to gather a group of customers, present them with a description of the new product, and record their reactions. Questions typically asked are the following:
Do they understand the concept?
Do they believe the concept?
Is the concept different from other products in an important way?
If it is different, is the difference beneficial?
Do they like or dislike the concept? Why?
What could be done to make the product more acceptable?
How would they like to see the product (color, size, other features)?
Would they buy it?
What price would they expect to pay for it?
What would their usage be in terms of volume, purpose, channels for purchasing, and other factors?

The purpose of the concept tests can also vary. The most basic concept test is a screening test that describes several concepts briefly and asks subjects for an overall evaluation. Screening tests are used to reduce the concepts under consideration to a manageable number. Next, concept generation tests (often involving focus groups) are used to refine the concept statements. This is typically followed by concept evaluation tests. These tests are based on larger samples and attempt to quantitatively assess demand for the concept based on samples of 200–300. Such tests are typically done competitively in the sense that other new concepts or existing products are evaluated at the same time.[19]

Concept Testing Using Conjoint Analysis

Conjoint analysis is a very popular marketing research method that enables you to determine how customers value different levels of product attributes (e.g., a 350-megahertz microprocessor versus a 400-megahertz one) from theoretical profiles or concepts. The basic idea is that by rank ordering different product concepts (combinations of attributes), you can infer not only the most popular concept but also the utility customers derive from specific values of the attributes. This aids management in further refining the concept.

A classic example is from the carpet and upholstery spot remover product category.[20] The following attributes were analyzed as the main part of the concept test:

> Package design (A, B, C)
> Brand names (K2R, Glory, Bissell)
> Price ($1.19, $1.39, $1.59)
> Good Housekeeping seal of approval (yes or no)
> Money-back guarantee (yes or no)

A product concept is one combination of all five attributes (e.g., package design A, brand name K2R, $1.19 price, with a Good Housekeeping seal, and with a money-back guarantee). There are 108 such theoretical concepts if all combinations of attributes and their levels are combined ($3 \times 3 \times 3 \times 2 \times 2$). However, it is unlikely that any potential customer would be able to sensibly rank order all 108 different concepts. Thus, marketing researchers have developed methods for reducing the number of combinations while retaining as much of the original information from the 108 combinations as possible.

Table 17–4 shows the data obtained from one subject.[21] The first five columns of the table represent the different concepts (there are 18 in all). The last column is the respondent's rank ordering of the concepts. This respondent most preferred the combination C, Bissell, $1.19, Good Housekeeping seal, and money-back guarantee. This by itself is useful information in the new product development process. However, Table 17–5 is more informative because it shows the utilities for the different levels of the attributes and the overall importances of the attributes.[22] Assuming that this respondent is representative of the market, the concept can be further refined: Package design B, the Bissell brand name, a low price, and both the Good Housekeeping seal and money-back guarantee are more highly valued than the other levels of their respective attributes. In addition, by examining the size of the largest utility of a level, you can roughly infer the importance of the attributes. In this case, package design, price, and money-back guarantee appear to be the most important attributes.

Product Definition

Through concept testing and conjoint analysis, you now have an idea of what concepts appear to have the potential for success. The next stage in the new product development process is to translate the concepts into actual products for further testing, based on interactions with customers. This is usually called the **product definition** phase.

The key to successful new product design is building in quality from the beginning.[23] Historically, quality has meant quality control, that is, minimizing the number of defects in products coming off the production line. However, quality has come to mean incorporating customer feedback into the development process as early as possible in order to make products that meet their expectations. Good design then means not only high levels of functional quality but also not overengineering the product by having more features than the customers really want or need.

Table 17–4 Conjoint Analysis Illustration

Data Collected

Package Design	Brand Name	Price	Good Housekeeping Seal?	Money-Back Guarantee?	Respondent's Evaluation (rank number)
A	K2R	1.19	No	No	13
A	Glory	1.39	No	Yes	11
A	Bissell	1.59	Yes	No	17
B	K2R	1.39	Yes	Yes	2
B	Glory	1.59	No	No	14
B	Bissell	1.19	No	No	3
C	K2R	1.59	No	Yes	12
C	Glory	1.19	Yes	No	7
C	Bissell	1.39	No	No	9
A	K2R	1.59	Yes	No	18
A	Glory	1.19	No	Yes	8
A	Bissell	1.39	No	No	15
B	K2R	1.19	No	No	4
B	Glory	1.39	Yes	No	6
B	Bissell	1.59	No	Yes	5
C	K2R	1.39	No	No	10
C	Glory	1.59	No	No	16
C	Bissell	1.19	Yes	Yes	1

Source: Paul Green and Yoram Wind (1975), "New way to measure consumers' judgements," *Harvard Business Review*, 53 (July–August), p. 108, Copyright © 1975 by the President and Fellows of Harvard College; all rights reserved.

Customer needs are divided into three types. **Primary needs** are the main strategic benefits that the product or service attempts to satisfy. **Secondary needs** are more tactical needs associated with the primary perceptual benefit. **Tertiary needs** are the operational needs related to the engineering aspect of making the product. Table 17–6 is an example of this hierarchy of needs in the context of a car door. In this illustration, the primary need "good appearance" has three secondary needs and 6 tertiary needs. As you can see, the needs get more specific moving left to right.

Often, new product designers obtain several hundred tertiary needs from discussions with customers. This voice of the customer (VOC) approach is usually implemented by asking customers to develop short phrases in their own words about the benefits and needs of, for example, a car door. Table 17–6 lists only 21 of the more than 100 that were obtained for the car door.

Some attributes may conflict in terms of the ultimate design of the product. For example, in a personal digital assistant (PDA), customers may want the keys to be sufficiently large for typing but the PDA to be small enough to fit into a coat pocket. The VOC approach involves asking customers to rate the tertiary needs on some scale of importance to permit the design engineers to better understand the tradeoffs customers are willing to make. In addition, the customers are asked for their perceptions of the product they currently own and competitor's offerings on these tertiary needs. Figure 17–6 continues the car door example and shows a typical importance weighting and perception measurement. In this case, the customer places a much greater weight on the door being easy to close from the outside

Table 17–5 Conjoint Analysis Illustration Results

Feature	Utility
Package design	
A	.1
B	1.0
C	.6
Brand name	
K2R	.3
Glory	.2
Bissell	.5
Price	
1.19	1.0
1.39	.7
1.59	.1
Good Housekeeping seal	
Yes	.3
No	.2
Money-back guarantee	
Yes	.7
No	.2

Source: Paul Green and Yoram Wind (1975), "New way to measure consumers' judgements," *Harvard Business Review*, 53 (July–August), p. 110, Copyright © 1975 by the President and Fellows of Harvard College; all rights reserved.

than on the lack of road noise. In addition, the customer rated competitor's cars higher than his or her existing car in terms of the most important benefit.

In addition to the customer needs, it is necessary to build into the process the physical characteristics of the product necessary to meet those needs. This is the link between customer needs and engineering characteristics. Continuing the car door illustration, some of the engineering characteristics for the needs shown in Fig. 17–6 are given in Table 17–7.

How are the customer needs and engineering characteristics linked together? Figure 17–7 is an example of the **house of quality.** The horizontal customer needs are linked with the vertical engineering characteristics through the use of interfunctional teams, much like those specified in the rugby approach described earlier in the chapter. This use of interfunctional teams and VOC is called quality function deployment (QFD) and has been applied successfully in Japan.

The house of quality takes its name from the distinctive shape of the relationships between customer needs and engineering characteristics. In the center of the house, the matrix represents how each engineering characteristic affects each need. For example, decreasing the amount of energy necessary to close the door (the first column) increases the perception that the door is easier to close from the outside (the first row). These assessments are made by the interfunctional design team, possibly based on primary marketing research. The bottom rows are the physical or objective measurements on the engineering characteristics. The attic or roof of the house indicates the interrelationships between the characteristics. For example, the door seal resistance has a strong negative impact on the peak closing force.

Table 17–6 Hierarchy of Needs

Primary Needs	Secondary Needs	Tertiary Needs
Good operation and use	Easy to open and close door	Easy to close from outside Stays open on a hill Easy to open from the outside Doesn't kick back Easy to close from inside
	Isolation	Doesn't leak in rain No road noise Doesn't leak in car wash No wind noise Doesn't drop water when open Snow doesn't fall in car Doesn't rattle
	Arm rest	Soft, comfortable In right position
Good appearance	Interior trim	Material won't fade Attractive look
	Clean	Easy to clean No grease from door Stay clean
	Fit	Uniform gaps between panels

Source: John R. Hauser and Don Clausing (1988), "The house of quality," *Harvard Business Review*, May–June, p. 65.

To see how the house of quality affects the design, we can take the physical evidence that the doors of the current car are more difficult to close than those of the competitors (11 foot-pounds versus 9 and 9.5). The engineering characteristics affecting customer perceptions of this need are the energy to close the door, the peak closing force, and the door seal resistance (top row of the matrix). Because the first two characteristics are strongly positively related to customer perceptions, these are chosen by the engineers for improvement. However, by inspecting the attic, you can see that other characteristics are affected by changing

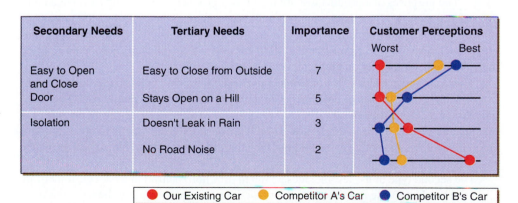

Figure 17–6

Consumers' Importance Weights and Evaluation of Competitive Products

Source: John R. Hauser and Glen L. Urban (1993), *Design and Marketing of New Products*, 2nd ed. (Englewood Cliffs, NJ: Prentice Hall), p. 38.

Table 17–7 List of Engineering Characteristics for a Car Door

Open-Close Effort	Sealing Insulation
Energy to close door	Door seal resistance
Check force on level ground	Acoustic transmission, window
Check force on 10-degree slope	Road noise reduction
Energy to open door	Water resistance
Peak closing force	

Source: Glen L. Urban and John R. Hauser (1993), *Design and Marketing of New Products*, 2nd ed. (Englewood Cliffs, NJ: Prentice Hall), p. 338.

the energy to close the door, such as the door opening energy and the peak closing force. This gives an indication of what other characteristics of the door will be affected by changing the energy to close the door. The team then sets a target of 7.5 foot-pounds (bottom row) for the new door.

Some writers have argued that in the case of high-technology products and services, it is important that the product definition not be locked in too soon.[24] This is because customer tastes, competition, or other factors characteristic of such markets could make the definition obsolete by the time the product is ready for launch. Deliberate product definition weighs the costs and benefits of delaying the final specifications closer to product launch. Unfortunately, in such markets, it is difficult to know exactly when the right time comes. Thus, it is not uncommon for new products in high-tech markets to have bugs and other defects, which early adopters of such products often must tolerate.

Forecasting Demand

Once the product has been designed with the customer in mind, a variety of approaches can be used to forecast demand.

Product Use Tests

This type of research consists of producing the product and getting potential customers to try it.[25] The purposes of a product test are to uncover product shortcomings, evaluate commercial prospects, evaluate alternative formulations, uncover the appeal of the product to various market segments, and, ideally, gain ideas for other elements of the marketing program. Such tests may be either branded (best for estimating sales) or unbranded or blind (best for focusing directly on physical formulation).

There are three major types of product use tests. Initially, such tests are usually conducted with small samples of customers, sometimes even only with employees. These initial tests are diagnostic and are directed toward eliminating serious problems with the product and getting a rough idea of how good it is compared to competitive products. This phase also allows the company to find out how the product is actually used and, possibly, to change the value proposition.

The second type of use test includes a limited time horizon trial in which customers are given the product to use and asked for their reactions to it. At the end of the trial, the company may simulate a purchase occasion. This may consist of a hypothetical "Would you

Figure 17–7

The House of Quality

Source: John R. Hauser and
Don Clausing (1988), "The
house of quality," *Harvard
Business Review*, 66, p. 72.

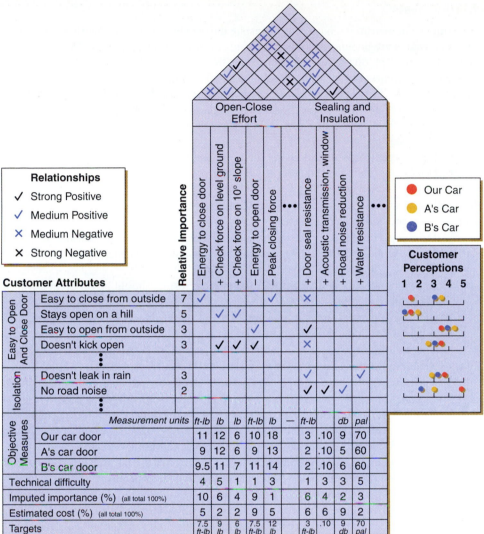

buy?" question or, better, an actual choice situation in which the customer either chooses one of a set of products, including the new product (usually at a reduced price), or simply chooses to buy or not buy the new product. To get a meaningful result, many researchers use a stratified sample. The strata are usually either product category usage rate (heavy, medium, light, none) or brand usually used. This stratification ensures adequate sample size in each segment to predict the popularity of the product.

The most elaborate form of product use test requires placement of the product in homes (or business settings for industrial products) for an extended period. For packaged goods, this period is usually about 2 months. The advantage of this extended period is that the results allow for both the wear-out of initial expectations and the development of problems that manifest themselves only over time (e.g., food that goes stale). Subjects complete before-and-after questionnaires and maintain a diary of actual use of the new and competitive products over the period of the test. The inclusion at the end of the test of an actual choice situation helps give the results a bottom-line orientation.

Market Tests

The ultimate in realism is a market test. Despite the problems mentioned earlier in the chapter, test markets are popular for testing all kinds of products and services. The purposes of such a test are to predict sales and profits from the prospective new product launch and to practice so that marketing, distribution, and production skills are developed before full-scale operations begin. Projections to national or international levels are typically made for both share and actual sales. The major measures to track are the following:

- Trial rate
- Repeat rate (for frequently purchased products)
- Usage rate or number bought per customer

In addition, awareness, attitudes, and distribution are usually monitored. Given these measures, a sales projection can be made.

In designing a market test, it is important to delineate clearly what information is to be gathered and why before proceeding. Several decisions must be made.

- Action standards. Standards for evaluating the results should be set up in advance. These standards should specify when the various possible decisions (e.g., stop the test, continue the test, revamp the product, go national) will be implemented.
- Where. The choice of where to test market is a serious problem. For consumer products, most market tests are done in two or three cities. (The test is not designed to try out numerous strategies; at most, two to three alternatives can be used.) Cities are chosen on the basis of representativeness of the population, the ability of the firm to gain distribution and media exposure in the area, and availability of good research suppliers in the area. Also, areas that are self-contained in terms of media (especially TV) are preferred. The result is that certain medium-sized cities are often chosen, such as Syracuse, New York; Fresno, California; and Fort Wayne, Indiana.
- What to do? The best test market designers are careful to make the effort in the geographic area proportional to what would reasonably be expected in a national launch. Note that what is meant by effort is not just budget; the goal is to make distribution, price, and so forth as representative as possible. However, typically the effort afforded the product is somewhat greater than the comparable national effort.
- How long? This question does not have an easy answer. Obviously, a longer run gives more information to the marketing manager, but it also costs more and gives competitors more time to formulate a counterattack. Consumer packaged goods may stay in test markets for 6–12 months in order to include several purchase cycles; this ensures that repeat usage as well as trial can be assessed accurately.
- How much? For a typical consumer packaged good, test marketing costs run over $1 million. Advertising and promotion typically account for 65–70% of the budget, with the rest of the budget divided between information gathering and analysis and miscellaneous administrative and other expenses.
- Information gathering. During a test market, a variety of information is gathered, most of it related to actual sales. In monitoring sales, it is important to recognize that a large percentage of first-year factory sales represent a one-time stocking up by the channels of distribution, not sales to final customers. The three major data sources are actual sales plus distribution and promotion; surveys that measure awareness, attitudes, and similar variables; and panels that report actual purchases and allow monitoring of trial and repeat rates.

Despite its limitations, test marketing new products often provides useful information to marketing managers. In 1997, Unilever, the giant British/Dutch consumer products company, developed a new ice cream snack called the Winner Taco, a taco-shaped wafer filled with ice cream and caramel, covered with chocolate and peanuts.[26] The product was developed at the company's innovation center in Rome and was intended to become a top-selling brand alongside its better-known Cornetto, Magnum, and Solero ice cream brands. As part of the new product development process, the product was first test marketed in April 1997 in Italy and Holland. After overshooting Unilever sales targets by 50%, the product was rolled out in Spain, Germany, and Austria in February 1998 and was launched in the rest of Europe in June. ◆

Sales Forecasting

Forecasting sales for a new product or service before it is launched and while you are going through the new product development process is always difficult. With no actual sales data at hand, marketing managers must rely on purchase intention surveys or other qualitative methods of forecasting (see Chapter 4).

Many approaches have been developed for frequently purchased products that rely on either test market data or very early data after the product is introduced. Most of these methods rely on some or all of the following factors to predict the ultimate success of the product:

- Brand awareness
- The eventual proportion of consumers who will try the product (trial)
- The proportion of triers who repeat purchase
- The usage rate of the product category by the eventual users

Notice that for durable goods, trial is basically first purchase; this may be the only purchase for several years. For frequently purchased products for which trial is easy to induce, repeat rates are the key to success.

- Awareness. The rationale for including awareness in a new product forecasting model is obvious: Customers cannot purchase a product or service unless they are aware of it. Most models attempting to predict success for new frequently purchased products either measure awareness directly through survey methods or attempt to predict it from other variables such as advertising spending and gross rating points.
- Trial. Like awareness, trial is tracked over time, with the objective of forecasting its ultimate level. Trial is simply the cumulative percentage of households (or companies) that have purchased the product or service at least once. Trial rates usually look like the graph in Fig. 17–8, with an increase in trial up to some asymptotic value (in this case, 45%). You can estimate the asymptote directly by plotting the points representing trial rates over time and then using some kind of curve-fitting method. The trial rates are obtained from a panel from the test market or early in the introductory phase.
- Repeat. The eventual repeat rate can be estimated using the same approach as that used for trial. Of course, unlike trial, which is nondecreasing, repeat rates tend to decrease (see Fig. 17–9). A product cannot be successful without a high repeat rate. A high trial rate with low repeat means poor product quality; eventually, you will run out of triers. High repeat rates, even among a few number of customers, can result in a profitable product. Figure 17–10 shows the relationship between product success and repeat rates.

Figure 17–8

Typical Penetration
for a New Brand
over Time

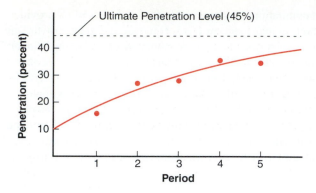

Figure 17–9

Typical Repeat Rate
for a New Brand
over Time

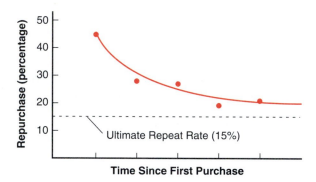

- Usage rate. This is simply an estimate of the average number of units purchased by customers. Like trial and repeat, it is derived from panels of customers measuring their actual purchasing of the product category.

An example of a simple market share forecasting model is the **Parfitt-Collins model.**[27] The three key elements of the model are an estimate of the eventual penetration rate (P), an estimate of the ultimate repeat rate (R), and an estimate of the relative prod-

Figure 17–10

Repeat Rates and
Product Performance

Source: NPD Research (1982),
*We Make the Answers to Your
Marketing Questions Perfectly
Clear* (New York: NPD
Research).

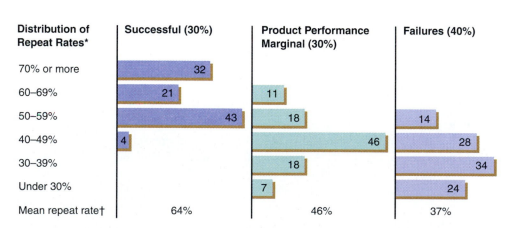

Distribution of Repeat Rates*	Successful (30%)	Product Performance Marginal (30%)	Failures (40%)
70% or more	32		
60–69%	21	11	
50–59%	43	18	14
40–49%	4	46	28
30–39%		18	34
Under 30%		7	24
Mean repeat rate†	64%	46%	37%

* Based upon 120 new products.
† Percentage of triers who will ever repeat.

uct category usage rate of buyers of the new brand (U). Eventual market share is predicted by simply multiplying the three variables together ($P \times R \times U$). Using the information from Figs. 17–8 and 17–9 and assuming that users of the new product consume it at a rate that is 80% of the market average, the predicted share is $45\% \times 15\% \times 80\% = 5.4\%$.

Other forecasting models use pretest market data from laboratory experiments to forecast sales. For example, ASSESSOR[28] uses a simulated shopping trip following advertising exposure and an in-home use period to predict how consumers will react to a new product. Evidence has shown that the market share estimates are within one share point of the share observed in the market.

Predicting the success of more radical innovations is much more difficult because customers may have difficulty understanding the product and how it will benefit them. One method, called information acceleration, attempts to place potential customers in a future world and familiarize them with a product (using multimedia technology) to improve the usefulness of their responses.[29]

◆ Illustration: Nestlé

In 1987, Nestlé Refrigerated Food Company (NFRC) contemplated entering the market for refrigerated pasta to be sold in supermarkets.[30] At that time, pasta was available in two forms in the United States. Fresh pasta was available in specialty food stores and restaurants, but was not generally sold in supermarkets. Dry pasta was a high-volume staple item for supermarkets. Fresh pasta was considered to be of higher quality and sold at a price premium.

NFRC did not have an entry in the refrigerated food category in the United States. In 1987, the company purchased Lambert's Pasta & Cheese, a small New York-based pasta company known for its fresh pasta and imported cheeses. Lambert had developed a process that extended the shelf life of its pastas from the usual 2–3 days to 40 days for sales in supermarket refrigerator cases. NFRC's goal was to introduce a national brand of refrigerated pasta under the Contadina brand name.

Nestlé's new product development process, established in the late 1980s, had seven steps:

1. Idea generation
2. Concept screening and idea refinement
3. Product development
4. Quantification of volume (forecasting)
5. Test marketing
6. Commercial evaluation
7. Introductory tracking   ◆

In 1987, NFRC was at the fourth stage in the development of the refrigerated pasta product. In order to estimate demand, NFRC used a concept testing and new product forecasting model sold by BASES, a marketing research firm. Among other things, NFRC wanted BASES to estimate first-year trial volume for pasta and sauces and simulate total year-1 sales volume.

In order to do this, BASES completed 300 concept tests (no real product was given to the consumers) in six different cities. All respondents were women, 18 years of age and older. Some of the key findings from the concept tests are shown in Table 17–8. The company forecasted demand based on the analysis shown in Fig. 17–11.

Of the 300 women shown the concept, 24% indicated they definitely would buy it and 51% said that they probably would. BASES then used industry shrinkage factors: 80% of the "definites" actually would buy and only 30% of the "probables" would buy. This reduced the interested total from 75% to 34.5%. They did not expect seasonality to be a factor. The 34.5% estimated to be interested was further reduced by the fact that the company planned

Table 17–8 Concept Test Results

Contadina Pasta and Sauce

Item	Total (301) %	Favorable (224) %	Unfavorable (77) %
Likes			
General variety	28	28	28
Filled variety	16	16	16
Natural/not artificial	28	30	23
Quick/fast/saves time	20	22	16
Easy to prepare/already prepared	17	20	11
Packed fresh/packed then refrigerated	6	8	1
Like small size	5	7	1
Clear package/can see what's inside	5	5	4
Like the shapes	5	5	5
Looks appetizing	4	5	1
Good/reasonable price	8	9	4
Fresh/made fresh & dated	26	27	21
Like/eat pasta	13	16	4
Like Contadina/ good name	9	11	4
Good meal/dinner	7	8	4
New/different	7	8	3
Dislikes			
Too expensive	8	3	23
Not like green/spinach color	6	5	11
Not like spinach taste	3	2	5
Not like pasta/rarely buy/eat	2	1	7
Not use this type of pasta	2	—	7
Nothing disliked	61	74	24
Concept Uniqueness			
Extremely new and different	15	17	8
Very new and different	38	41	32
Somewhat new and different	35	32	41
Slightly new and different	8	7	11
Not at all new and different	4	3	8
Mean uniqueness (5-point scale)	3.5	3.6	3.2

Source: V. Kasturi Rangan (1995), "Nestlé refrigerated foods: Contadina pasta & pizza (A)," Harvard Business School case #9-595-035, P. 20.

an advertising expenditure so that 48% of the potential consumers would be made aware of the new brand. In addition, they expected distribution in stores representing 70% of all commodity volume (ACV). This reduced the interested and able to buy number down to 11.6%. Multiplying this figure by the total number of U.S. households provided an estimated number of 9 million households trying and, assuming 1 unit per trial, 9 million trial units.

BASES then developed three different repeat purchase rates under alternative scenarios of product quality (see the bottom of Fig. 17–11). Assuming 2.5 repeat purchases in the first year and a claimed (by the women exposed to the concept) average repeat transaction amount of 1.4 units, the repeat purchase volume ranged from 8.5 million units (mediocre product) to 13.9 million units (excellent product). Given NFRC's hurdle rate of 20 million units for a product to be introduced, BASES recommended that the product be launched because the total units forecasted were greater than 20 million except for the mediocre qual-

Trial Volume

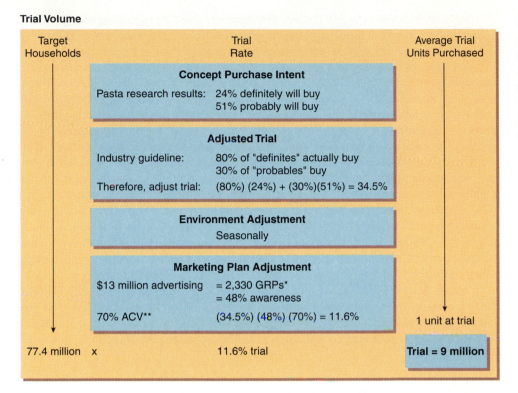

Figure 17–11

BASES Estimate of Contadina Year–1 Sales Volume

Source: V. Kasturi Rangan (1995), "Nestlé Refrigerated Foods: Contadina Pasta & Pizza (A)," Harvard Business School case #9-595-035, p. 32.

Repeat Volume

Trial Households	Repeat Rate	# Repeat purchase occasions:	Average repeat transaction amount:	
(77.4 million)(11.6%) = 9 million	Mediocre product - 27% Average product - 39% Excellent product - 44%	average 2.5	1.4 units	8.5 million units = 12.3 million units 13.9 million units

*GRPs: Gross Ratings Points (Reach x Frequency)

**ACV: All Commodity Volume

ity version (e.g., for excellent quality, the forecasted amount was 9 million units from trial plus the 13.9 million units from repeat). Contadina Fresh Pasta and Sauces were rolled out nationally in the second half of 1988 and sold 30 million units in only 6 months; the brand sold 60 million units in 1990.

TOPICS IN NEW PRODUCT DEVELOPMENT

The Importance of Shorter Product Development Cycles

Because of shorter product life cycles and faster technological obsolescence, companies are finding that quicker time-to-market with new products has become a competitive advantage. Although there is little empirical evidence that faster cycle times alone are positively correlated with a firm's overall financial performance,[31] speed clearly has become necessary in some industries just to keep pace. In addition, in industries such as semiconductors, where costs and prices fall rapidly over time, faster time-to-market can mean significantly higher prices over the lifetime of a specific product.

Table 17–9 shows some new product development cycle time reductions over the period 1988–1992. As can be seen, in many cases companies have reduced the new product introduction process by over 50% when moving from one generation of a product to the next.

A number of books have focused on speed to market and how to improve new product introduction processes.[32] One study has examined the relationship of some project and organizational characteristics to cycle time.[33] Not surprisingly, factors negatively correlated with shorter cycle times are the newness of the project (the amount of product redesign from the previous version) and the project's complexity (the number of functions performed by the product). Two important factors in shortening the new product development period are the institution of a formal new product planning process and the use of interfunctional teams.

The impact of new technologies is also helping to shorten cycle times. A significant improvement in new product design has occurred through the use of computer-aided design (CAD) software, which enables engineers to simulate very complex products that can then be given to manufacturing for production. However, except for some simple metal items, few of these designs can be instantly turned into three-dimensional objects by being fed into computer-controlled machine tools. This capability is necessary to create prototypes for customer testing and further refining. The construction of prototypes can take months. However, a new process called rapid prototyping (RP) enables companies to go directly from CAD prototypes on the computer monitor to physical products, using a machine that uses ink jets similar to those in a computer printer. Instead of ink, the machine deposits a liquid binder on layers of powdered ceramics to create different shapes. At Chrysler, RP machines

Table 17–9 Reported New Product Introduction Time Reductions

Product	Company	Cycle Times (months)	
		Previous	Now
Hybrid corn	Pioneer Hi-Bred	96	72
Construction equipment	Deere & Co.	84	50
Jet engine	General Electric	84	48
Helios (medical imaging)	Polaroid	72	36
Viper	Chrysler	60	36
Cars	Honda	60	36
9900 copier	Xerox	60	36
DeskJet printer	Hewlett-Packard	54	22
Personal computer	IBM	48	14
Thermostat	Honeywell	48	10
Checkout terminals	NCR	44	22
Air-powered grinder	Ingersol Rand	40	15
FX-3500 copier	Fuji-Xerox	38	29
Phone switchers	AT&T	36	<18
Electronic pager	Motorola	36	18
Electric clutch break	Warner	36	9
Communication gear	Codex	34	16
Machining center	Cincinnati Milacron	30	12
Pampers Phases	Proctor & Gamble	27	12
Leisure lantern	Coleman	24	12
Cordless phone	AT&T	24	12

Source: Abbie Griffin (1997), "The effect of project and process characteristics on product development cycle time," *Journal of Marketing Research*, February, p. 25.

turn out 3,000 objects each year, ranging from dashboards to transmission gears to intake manifolds. The latter can be made in transparent plastic in 4–8 days, whereas it used to take as long as 3 months to make the steel version.[34]

Improving the Integration of Marketing and R&D

Historically, marketing and R&D do not have a strong record of cooperation.[35] Various reasons have been given. One is that the personalities of the personnel are different (e.g., marketing people have shorter time frames than their R&D counterparts). Other reasons given are language (marketing emphasizes benefits and perceptions, R&D emphasizes specifications and performance), culture (business schools versus engineering departments), and physical barriers (different geographic locations).

Many studies have found that increased levels of cooperation between marketing and R&D results in higher levels of corporate success defined in a number of different ways. This success results from integration in the following areas:

- Analyzing customer needs
- Generating and screening new ideas
- Developing new products according to the market's needs
- Analyzing customer requirements
- Reviewing test market results

Some approaches for improving the cooperation between marketing and R&D are the following:

- Relocation and physical facility design. One obvious solution is to relocate one or both groups so they are geographically proximate. However, dramatic improvements in teleconferencing technology and document-sharing software make it easier for people with significant distance between them to communicate easily.
- Personnel movement. It is possible to give personnel in both departments temporary assignments to the other. However, barriers of the type mentioned previously make such transfers difficult. Education can help here; executive programs (e.g., "Marketing for Engineers," "Semiconductor Technology for Marketers") for cross-functional purposes are becoming more popular.
- Informal social systems. Developing a way for the two groups to interact informally would ultimately lead to better communication and coordination.
- Organizational structure. A rigid, departmentalized structure organized along functional groups is not likely to be successful for new product introductions. For example, as we have noted several times in this chapter, interfunctional teams tend to produce the most successful new products.
- Incentives and rewards. R&D and marketing personnel are often rewarded differently. In many companies, particularly consumer products, marketing managers are rewarded on the basis of their brands' market shares. R&D personnel are rewarded for patents, improvements in technology, and the number of new products developed. It has been suggested that more coordination would be achieved if both sets of personnel were rewarded on the basis of ultimate profits derived from new products introduced.

 Monsanto, one of the world's largest agricultural chemical and biotechnology companies, has developed a new approach to product development in order to transform itself from a chemical company into a life sciences company.[36] In 1996, the company decided to pair scientists and marketing specialists to lead new product development

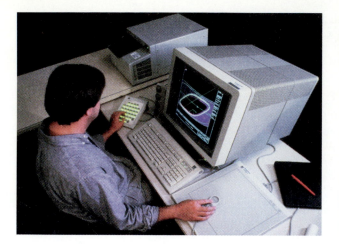

New Technologies are helping to shorten product development cycles significantly. The product engineer in the first photo is using computer-aided design to render automobile parts for Chrysler. In the second photo, a designer is using a desktop publishing program to create the layout for a book. In both cases, the use of technology means that less time is needed to make necessary modifications and refinements before reaching a final prototype. (Left: Bob Rowan; Progressive Image/Corbis; Right: Steve Weinrebe/Stock Boston/Picture Network International)

and other management functions within the company. The strategy is known internally as "two in the box" because the two managers normally work in adjoining cubicles, share a secretary, and keep each other posted about the product area of interest.

For example, in the company's huge agricultural sector, 30 pairs of box buddies lead most of the product teams. In the cotton division, a geneticist is paired with a manager with a background in marketing, business, and human resources. Box buddies earn the same pay and benefits, including bonuses. The goal is not only to develop new genetic technologies but to beat competitors to market with them.   ◆

EXECUTIVE SUMMARY

In this chapter, we have covered the following topics:

- New products are the lifeblood of companies and are therefore necessary for their long-term survival.
- Some key factors correlated with success in introducing new products are a superior product meeting customer needs, a customer orientation maintained throughout the new product development process, collection of the appropriate information, sharp product definition, interfunctional teams, and quick time-to-market.
- There are different approaches to new product development. The most common is the linear approach, which progresses from idea generation and initial screening to product design to testing to introduction, with fewer product concepts succeeding at each stage.
- New product concepts come either ready-made from sources such as employees, customers, and channels or from a managed creative process such as brainstorming.
- Product definition comes from combining customer input (voice of the customer) with engineering characteristics to create a house of quality chart.

- Forecasting the demand for new products is accomplished using procedures such as product use tests, test markets, and quantitative models based on market research data.

CHAPTER QUESTIONS

1. Consider the three major categories of new products: classically innovative products (ones that create new categories), new category entries, and line extensions. How does the job of the marketing manager differ for these three kinds of new products?
2. What are the pros and cons of the three approaches to new product development discussed in this chapter? Are there some circumstances (for example, different product categories) in which one approach might be better than another?
3. This chapter explores alternative methods for forecasting the demand for new products before they are launched. Compare these methods with those discussed in Chapter 4, which use existing sales data for products already on the market. How are the forecasting challenges facing marketing managers different in the two cases (beyond the fact that there are no sales data in the prelaunch phase for new products)?
4. For frequently purchased products, successful new products must have high trial and repeat rates. What tools can the marketing manager use to increase trial rates? Repeat rates?
5. How is launching industrial products or consumer products with infrequent purchasing rates (e.g., TVs) different from launching frequently purchased products? What key measures are used to assess trial and repeat rates for frequently purchased products?

Application Exercises: New Product Development and the PC Industry

Integrated Case

1. Identify several new computer products that have been successful and several that have been failures. What are the underlying reasons for success or failure?
2. Choose one of the major PC manufacturers and investigate its new product development process.
3. Convene a small group of your friends and colleagues. Discuss what they like and dislike about PCs. Based on the results of this focus group, develop a proposal for a new PC that integrates their comments (disregard engineering characteristics).
4. For this new concept developed in exercise 3, suggest ways to forecast demand. Be specific about the kind of information you would need to collect.

FURTHER READING

A book that integrates marketing, manufacturing, and a number of other business functions into new product development is Steven C. Wheelright and Kim B. Clark (1992), *Revolutionizing Product Development* (New York: Free Press). Other than the references in this chapter, a book with a number of examples of new product development processes is Jerry Patrick (1997), *How to Develop Successful New Products* (Lincolnwood, IL: NTC Business Books). An article focusing on a new creative approach for developing new product ideas is Jacob Goldenberg, David Mazursky, and Sorin Solomon (1999), "Toward identifying the inventive templates of new products: a channeled ideation approach," *Journal of Marketing Research,* 36 (May).

Notes

Chapter 1

1. This illustration is based on Fareena Sultan (1990), "Zenith: marketing research for high definition television (HDTV)," *Harvard Business School* case #9-591-025; Sylvia Rubin (1998), "In-your-face TV," *San Francisco Chronicle,* January 6, p. D1; and Kyle Pope and Evan Ramstad (1998), "HDTV sets: too pricey, too late?" *The Wall Street Journal,* January 7, p. B1.

2. For an explanation of the three different video standards, visit the Web site of Alken M.R.S.

3. See also Tobi Elkin (1998), "HDTV no longer a pipe dream, but still a marketing, branding challenge," *Brandweek,* January 19, p. 14.

4. For readers who would like a more formal definition of marketing, the American Marketing Association's definition is as follows: "Marketing is the process of planning and executing the conception, pricing, promotion, and distributing of ideas, goods, and services to create exchanges that satisfy individual and organizational objectives."

5. Although Apple has rebounded and staved off disaster with the success of the iMac, the company is still not as large and influential as many experts felt it could have been under different leadership.

6. See Franklin M. Houston (1986), "The marketing concept: what it is and what it is not," *Journal of Marketing,* 50 (April), pp. 81–87.

7. Peter F. Drucker (1954), *The Practice of Management* (New York: HarperCollins).

8. Theodore Levitt (1986), "Marketing and the corporate purpose," in *The Marketing Imagination* (New York: Free Press).

9. Of course, this must be done within local law. For example, public restaurants in the United States cannot deny service to any person on the basis of race.

10. This illustration is from Scott Woolley (1998), "Get lost, buster," *Forbes,* February 23, p. 90.

11. See John R. Hauser and Don P. Clausing (1988), "The House of Quality," *Harvard Business Review,* 66 (May–June), pp. 63–73.

12. Such as Frederick F. Reichheld (1996), *The Loyalty Effect* (Boston: Harvard Business School Press).

13. Some customers *are* interested in technology and gadgets. Unfortunately, there are not enough of them to make a product like the Newton a commercial success. This situation is discussed in more detail in Chapter 15.

14. Jerry Kaplan (1995), *Startup: A Silicon Valley Adventure* (Boston: Houghton Mifflin).

15. This illustration is drawn from Deborah E. Rosen, Jonathan E. Schroeder, and Elizabeth F. Purinton (1998), "Marketing high tech products: lessons in customer focus from the marketplace," *Journal of Consumer and Market Research,* published online at http://www.vancouver.wsu.edu/~jcmr/managerial/rosen06-98.html.

16. As you will see later in the chapter, Sony's product development approach is to lead customers (i.e., try to get them to adopt their new technologies) rather than developing products that fit existing needs.

17. Interestingly, in 1989 the National Highway Traffic Safety Administration concluded that there was no such phenomenon as "sudden acceleration." However, the damage had already been done.

18. Benson P. Shapiro (1988), "What the hell is 'market oriented'?" *Harvard Business Review*, 66 (November–December), pp. 119–125.

19. Gary Hamel and C. K. Prahalad (1994), *Competing for the Future* (Boston: Harvard Business School Press).

20. Hamel and Prahalad, *op. cit.*

21. Justin Martin (1995), "Ignore your customer," *Fortune,* May 1, pp. 121–126.

22. See Houston, *op. cit.*

23. Thomas A. Stewart (1995), "What information costs," *Fortune,* July 10, pp. 119–121.

24. See Rashi Glazer (1991), "Marketing in information-intensive environments: strategic implications of knowledge as an asset," *Journal of Marketing,* 55 (October), pp. 1–19.

25. Manufacturers working with the retailers on a category basis is called category management and is discussed in Chapter 12.

26. John Kavanagh (1998), "Internet is no substitute for EDI," *Financial Times,* June 3, pp. 5FT–IT.

27. See Regis McKenna (1997), *Real Time: Preparing for the Age of the Never Satisfied Customer* (Boston: Harvard Business School Press).

28. Allyson L. Stewart-Allen (1996), "Retail technology worth watching," *Marketing News,* January 29, p. 6.

29. Paul Taylor (1997), "Dawning of the information age," *Financial Times,* November 5, pp. 3FT–IT.

30. Evidence of the latter's success is the fact that as of late 1998, the market value of Microsoft (the value of the shares of the company's stock at a given price) was $270 billion, whereas that of industrial giant General Motors was only $57 billion.

31. To demonstrate the growth of the Web, in 1995 the Web search engine Lycos documented 8.5 million universal resource locators (URLs, or Web addresses). In April 1996, this figure was up to 22 million and in July 1996, 30 million.

32. Lucas Graves (1998), "Will the real online market please stand up?" *Marketing Computers,* January, p. 43; and Heather Green (1998), "The virtual mall gets real," *Business Week,* January 26, pp. 90–91.

33. Joel Kotkin (1998), "The mother of all malls," *Forbes ASAP,* April 6, p. 60.

34. *Business 2.0* (1999), January, p. 115.

35. An article by Donna L. Hoffman and Thomas P. Novak, "Marketing in hypermedia computer-mediated environments: conceptual foundations," *Journal of Marketing,* 60 (July), pp. 50–68, uses *hypermedia* to refer to networked links, largely the WWW. Our coverage is intended to be broader and includes CD-ROMs, kiosks, and other approaches to electronic marketing.

36. Much has been written on the topic of relationship marketing. One of the most popular references is Don Peppers and Martha Rogers (1993), *The One to One Future: Building Relationships One Customer at a Time* (New York: Doubleday).

37. B. Joseph Pine II (1993), *Mass Customization: The New Frontier in Business Competition* (Boston: Harvard Business School Press).

Chapter 2

1. This illustration is based on Frank V. Cespedes (1992), "Becton Dickinson Division: marketing organization," Harvard Business School case #9-593-070; Phillip L. Zweig and Wendy Zellner (1998), "Locked out of the hospital," *Business Week,* March 16, pp. 75–76; and Reynolds Holding and William Carlsen (1998), "Company markets unsafe needles despite reported risks," *San Francisco Chronicle,* April 14, p. A1.

2. See David Stipp (1998), "No more needles," *Fortune,* June 22, pp. 107–110.

3. For some history on the brand management system, see George S. Low and Ronald Fullerton (1994), "Brands, brand management, and the brand manager system: a critical-historical evaluation," *Journal of Marketing Research,* 31 (May), pp. 173–190.

4. For a more detailed discussion of the product manager's responsibilities and the pros and cons of different organizational forms, see Donald R. Lehmann and Russell S. Winer (1997), *Product Management,* 2nd ed. (Burr Ridge, IL: Irwin), Ch. 1.

5. OEM stands for original equipment manufacturer. OEMs are customers who incorporate a supplier's product into their own. For example, the laptop computer manufacturer Toshiba is an OEM for the hard disk drive manufacturer Quantum. This type of customer, often called a channel of distribution, is discussed in detail in Chapter 15.

6. This example is based on Beth Snyder (1998), "Digital revolution leaves Motorola playing catch-up," *Advertising Age,* October 19, pp. 32–33.

7. See Lehmann and Winer, *op. cit.,* and Donald R. Lehmann and Russell S. Winer (1997), *Analysis for Marketing Planning,* 4th ed. (Burr Ridge, IL: Irwin).

8. Sources for this case study are Charles G. Burck (1981), "A small surprise from Cadillac," *Fortune,* May 4, pp. 171–172; *Automobile Quarterly Magazine* (1983), "General Motors: the first 75 years" (New York: Crown); Charles R. Day, Jr. (1985), "Cadillac faces new foes and a stiffer fight," *Industry Week,* October 28, pp. 16–17; Alex Taylor III (1987), "Detroit vs. new upscale imports," *Fortune,* April 27, pp. 69–78; Christopher Power (1993), "Flops," *Business Week,* August 16, pp. 76–82; Alex Taylor III (1994), "Lincoln and Cadillac slip a gear," *Fortune,* August 22, p. 16; Parnelli Jones (1995), "5 automobiles that changed the world," *Forbes FYI,* October 23, pp. 178–179; Kathleen Kerwin (1995), "A Caddy that's not for Daddy," *Business Week,* December 18, p. 87; Mike Arnholt (1996), "Cars that made a difference," *Ward's Auto World,* May, p. 9; Brian S. Moskal (1996), "Cadillac's quest: find the fountain of youth," *Industry Week,* April 1, pp. 61–64; Kathleen Kerwin (1996), "GM warms up the branding iron," *Business Week,* September 23, pp. 153–154; Kathleen Kerwin and Keith Naughton (1997), "Can Detroit make cars that baby boomers like?" *Business Week,* December 1, pp. 134–148; and issues of *Autoweek.*

9. Sean Mehegan, "A picture of quality," *Brandweek,* April 8, 1996, pp. 38–40.

10. The case for the difficulty of automobile marketing is made in Steven P. Schnaars (1989), *Megamistakes* (New York: Free Press).

11. This industry overview is based on Das Narayandas and V. Kasturi Rangan (1995), "Dell Computer Corporation," Harvard Business School case #9-596-058.

12. Note that Apple is not on the list. Although it has made a comeback in 1999, one of the major business tragedies of the twentieth century is the decline of Apple, which once held nearly 30% of the U.S. market and, as of 1999, was down to about 5%.

13. See also Narayandas and Rangan, *op. cit.*

14. See Louise Kehoe and Paul Taylor (1998), "Long and winding download," *Financial Times,* March 12, p. 11.

15. The historical information on Compaq, IBM, and Hewlett-Packard is based on Adrian Ryans and Mark Vandenbosch (1995), "Compaq Computer Corporation in 1995," Richard Ivey School of Business case #95-A011.

16. Some of the IBM information is from Raju Narisetti (1997), "IBM to revamp struggling home-PC business," *The Wall Street Journal,* October 14, p. B1.

17. Raju Narisetti (1998), "How IBM turned around its ailing PC division," *The Wall Street Journal,* March 12, p. B1.

18. This is based on annual sales data; the data in Table 2–2 are from one quarter.

19. Lee Gomes (1997), "Hewlett-Packard sets its PC bar higher and higher," *The Wall Street Journal,* September 8, p. B4.

20. Sources for the Gateway case include Ira Sager and Peter Elstrom (1997), "Can Gateway round up the suits?" *Business Week,* May 26, pp. 132–136; and Jennifer Saba (1999), "Jeffrey Weitzen and Anil Arora," *Marketing Computers,* January, pp. 26–27.

Chapter 3

1. This illustration is based on Eric M. Olson and Stanley F. Slater (1996), "Smooth takeoff," *Marketing Management,* Fall, pp. 38–41.

2. Gretchen Morgenson (1991), "Is efficiency enough?" *Forbes,* March 18, pp. 108–109.

3. *Business Week* (1996), February 26, pp. 108–110.

4. Service businesses are discussed in more detail in Chapter 14.

5. Pepsi actually developed a new brand, Pepsi A.M., to compete with coffee and other beverages at breakfast. If the thought of drinking cola at breakfast does not excite you, you are not alone; the product was a failure.

6. This illustration is based on John Bowen (1998), "Pardon me. Grey Poupon is a niche brand," *Brandweek*, April 27, p. 14.

7. See Bernd Schmitt and Alex Simonson (1997), *Marketing Aesthetics* (New York: Free Press).

8. See Carl Shapiro and Hal R. Varian (1999), *Information Rules* (Boston: Harvard University Press), Ch. 6.

9. David A. Aaker (1995), *Strategic Market Management,* 4th ed. (New York: Wiley).

10. Derek F. Abell and John S. Hammond (1979), *Strategic Market Planning* (Englewood Cliffs, NJ: Prentice Hall).

11. See Robert D. Buzzell and Bradley T. Gale (1987), *The PIMS Principles* (New York: Free Press).

12. Many books have a detailed description of the experience curve. The best-known source is by the staff of the Boston Consulting Group (1972), *Perspectives on Experience* (Boston: Boston Consulting Group).

13. Normally, the horizontal axis is in cumulative units of production. However, because the relevant units for the two industries are different, time is used instead.

14. Michael Porter (1980), *Competitive Advantage* (New York: Free Press).

15. Porter, *op. cit.*

16. Porter, *op. cit.*

17. Two books that are important for this area of marketing are David A. Aaker (1991), *Brand Equity* (New York: Free Press); and David A. Aaker (1996), *Building Strong Brands* (New York: Free Press).

18. *The Economist* (1996), November 16, pp. 72–73.

19. See Aaker, *Brand Equity* or *Building Strong Brands.*

20. Interestingly, *position* is both a noun and a verb. A product's position is how customers perceive it relative to competition, as shown in the perceptual map in Fig. 3–7. Marketing managers position products by actively choosing the appropriate dimensions, differential advantage, and communications and other elements of the marketing mix that affect customer perceptions.

21. See Glen L. Urban and Steven H. Star (1991), *Advanced Marketing Strategy* (Englewood Cliffs, NJ: Prentice Hall).

22. Mark Fuller (1996), "Metaxa's new-found success is intoxicating," *Advertising Age International,* October, p. i6.

23. Metaxa does not have its own home page but is featured (perhaps *buried* is a better term) in the Stolichnya site. For an excellent example of how a Web page can reinforce a positioning strategy, see the Absolut vodka site.

24. Geoffrey A. Moore (1991), *Crossing the Chasm* (New York: HarperCollins), Ch. 6.

25. The source for this example is Don Clark (1996), "Informix revamps database technology," *The Wall Street Journal,* December 2, p. B3.

26. Sales histories of individual brands are called *brand life cycles.*

27. Alternative pricing approaches for the introductory phase of the PLC are discussed in more detail in Chapter 11.

28. See Glen L. Urban, Theresa Carter, Steven Gaskin, and Zofia Mucha (1986), "Market share rewards to pioneering brands: an empirical analysis and strategic implications," *Management Science,* June, pp. 645–659.

29. See Peter N. Golder and Gerard J. Tellis (1993), "Pioneer advantage: marketing logic or marketing legend?" *Journal of Marketing Research,* 30 (May), pp. 158–170. This possible lack of a true pioneering advantage results from the fact that the performance of nonsurviving pioneers several years after the product category develops cannot be measured, leaving only the presumably more successful survivors, who look like the pioneers. This measurement problem therefore creates an upward bias in the apparent performance of the presumed pioneers.

30. Linda Grant (1996), "Stirring it up at Campbell," *Fortune,* May 16, pp. 80–86.

31. Urban and Star, *op. cit.,* Ch. 16.

32. For more detail on the product portfolio, see Abell and Hammond, *op. cit.,* and David A. Aaker, *Strategic Market Management.*

Chapter 4

1. This example is based on Paula Kephart (1995), "The leader of the pack," *Marketing Tools,* September, pp. 16–19.

2. Del I. Hawkins and Donald S. Tull (1994), *Essentials of Marketing Research* (New York: Macmillan).

3. In this chapter *research* and *marketing research* are used synonymously.

4. A more detailed discussion of how to choose a marketing research supplier is beyond the scope of this book. However, in the United States a good place to start is the local chapter of the American Marketing Association.

5. Benchmarking can also be applied to processes such as new product development and organizational structure.

6. See Donald R. Lehmann, Sunil Gupta, and Joel H. Steckel (1998), *Marketing Research* (Reading, MA: Addison-Wesley).

7. The United States, Canada, and Mexico have developed the North American Industrial Classification System (NAICS) to replace SIC codes. More is said about this system in Chapter 6.

8. Special issue of *Marketing Management* on qualitative research, Summer 1996, p. 5.

9. Bobby J. Calder (1977), "Focus groups and the nature of qualitative marketing research," *Journal of Marketing Research*, August, pp. 353–364.

10. Calder, *op. cit.*

11. For some novel ways marketing researchers are attempting to understand buyer behavior, see Leslie Kaufman (1997), "Enough talk," *Business Week*, August 18, pp. 48–49.

12. Nancy K. Austin (1998), "The Buzz Factory," *Inc.*, May, pp. 54–64.

13. Kate Maddox (1998), "Virtual panels add real insight for marketers," *Advertising Age*, June 29, p. 34.

14. Raymond R. Burke (1996), "Virtual shopping: breakthrough in marketing research," *Harvard Business Review*, March–April, pp. 120–131.

15. The exception is when the universe is small. For example, if you are working for an aircraft manufacturer, the universe of airlines worldwide is sufficiently small that you could survey each potential customer.

16. In fact, to save money and make it easier to obtain the data, the U.S. government is strongly considering changing its 10-year census to a sampling approach.

17. Results from biased samples can be adjusted when the source and size of the bias are known, but this topic is beyond the scope of this book.

18. Gary S. Vazzana and Duane Bachman (1994), "Fax attracts," *Marketing Research*, 6 (Spring), pp. 19–25.

19. Martin Opperman (1995), "E-mail surveys: potentials and pitfalls," *Marketing Research*, 7 (Summer), pp. 29–33.

20. A panel is different from a tracking study. Both take measures from a set of respondents over time, but a panel uses the same set of respondents whereas a tracking study selects a new random sample at each measurement period.

21. Stephen J. Hoch, Xavier Drèze, and Mary E. Purk (1994), "EDLP, hi-lo, and margin arithmetic," *Journal of Marketing*, October, pp. 16–27.

22. Donald R. Lehmann and Russell S. Winer (1997), *Product Management*, 2nd ed. (Burr Ridge, IL: Irwin), Ch. 7.

23. Mediamark Research Inc. (1994), *Pet & Baby Products Report*.

24. For a good overview of different methods, see J. Scott Armstrong (1985), *Long-Range Forecasting: From Crystal Ball to Computer*, 2nd ed. (New York: Wiley).

25. Although our example is on market-level or product category data, the same techniques can be used to forecast individual product or brand sales.

26. Alternatively, one could fit the line using only data since 1992, where there is obviously a distinct change in slope.

27. If we use only data from 1992 on, the forecast is a more realistic 29,165,700 units. Thus, forecasts from this approach can be very sensitive to the time period of data used.

Chapter 5

1. This illustration is based on "Club Méditerranée," Harvard Business School case #9-579-061; Andrew Jack (1997), "Club Med turns its back on the idealism of the past," *Financial Times*, February 24, p. 19; and Andrew Jack (1998), "Redefining sun, sand, and sangria," *Financial Times*, January 29, p. 14.

2. Organizational or industrial buying behavior is examined in Chapter 6.

3. Diane Brady (1996), "Airlines in Asia offer personalized prices by age, race, gender," *The Wall Street Journal*, September 30, p. A13.

4. See Joseph Pine (1993), *Mass Customization: The New Frontier in Business Competition* (Boston: Harvard Business School Press); and Christopher W. Hart (1996), "Made to order," *Marketing Management*, Summer, pp. 11–23. We cover this topic more fully in Chapter 13.

5. This illustration is drawn from Patricia B. Seybold (1998), *Customers.Com* (New York: Times Books), Ch. CSF-7.

6. American Demographics (1991), *Going Global: International Psychographics* (Ithaca, NY: American Demographics Books).

7. A visitor to SRI's Web site can classify himself or herself into one of the groups.

8. Paul C. Judge (1998), "Are tech buyers different?" *Business Week,* January 26, pp. 64–68.

9. Greg Burns (1994), "It only Hertz when Enterprise laughs," *Business Week,* December 12, p. 44.

10. Karen Benezra (1998), "The fragging of the American mind," *Brandweek,* June 15, pp. S12–S19.

11. Another way to say this is that if the index numbers are similar across the levels of the variable, then that particular variable tells us nothing to help us discriminate between those who own the card and those who do not.

12. The material in this section is based on William R. Swinyard (1996), "The hard core and Zen riders of Harley Davidson: a market-driven segmentation analysis," *Journal of Targeting, Measurement and Analysis for Marketing,* June, pp. 337–362.

13. Many models of how consumers make decisions have been developed. A good overview of several classic models can be found in J. A. Lunn (1974), "Consumer decision-process models," in J. N. Sheth, ed., *Models of Buyer Behavior* (New York: HarperCollins), Ch. 3. An alternative approach is in James R. Bettman (1979), *An Information Processing Theory of Consumer Choice* (Reading, MA: Addison-Wesley).

14. One of the controversies of marketing is that many people believe that marketers can create customer needs. This is unlikely; although marketers certainly try and do influence how a customer satisfies those needs, the basic need must be established by the customer.

15. Abraham H. Maslow (1970), *Motivation and Personality,* 2nd ed. (New York: HarperCollins).

16. Susan Fournier (1996), "Land Rover North America, Inc.," Harvard Business School case #9-596-036.

17. The use of these weights in understanding customer decision-making is described later in this chapter.

18. It should be noted that the customer could choose not to choose, that is, conclude that none of the products in the evoked set satisfy the need and postpone the purchase decision.

19. There are several ways to ask this question besides the approach used in the text and different numbers of scale points can be used.

20. References to these methods are given at the end of the chapter in the Further Reading section.

21. Other data combination models or rules exist. For example, using a lexicographic rule, the customer selects one attribute as the most important and then chooses the brand that is rated the highest on that attribute. See William D. Wells and David Prensky (1996), *Consumer Behavior* (New York: Wiley), Ch. 12.

22. We will see this model of expectation formation and comparison to outcomes in Chapter 8 in the discussion about customer evaluation of service quality.

23. Michal Shapira and Sigahl Silvera (1999), "Cellular phone campaign brings hysterical demand," available at the Market Files Web site.

Chapter 6

1. This illustration is based on Edward O. Welles (1990), "Decisions, decisions," *Inc.,* August, pp. 80–89; and Leslie Brokaw (1991), "Anatomy of a start-up revisited," *Inc.,* November, p. 123.

2. Note that this is an example of leading the customer rather than being customer led, as we discussed in Chapter 1. This strategy is very common in technology-based companies.

3. The concept of a buying center applies to some consumer decisions. For example, the decision to purchase large-ticket durable goods such as autos may be done jointly between spouses, with input from children. Similarly, McDonald's realizes that children influence the purchases made by their parents. In these instances, some of the concepts of organizational buyer behavior can be applied.

4. Frederick E. Webster, Jr. (1979), *Industrial Marketing Strategy* (New York: Wiley).

5. Of course, this is not true for services, both consumer and business-to-business. In addition, as we will note in Chapter 13, many consumer businesses are looking for ways to develop ongoing relationships with customers.

6. V. Kasturi Rangan, Rowland Moriarty, and Gordon Swartz (1992), "Segmenting customers in mature industrial markets," *Journal of Marketing,* October, pp. 72–82.

7. Patrick J. Robinson, Charles W. Faris, and Yoram Wind (1967), *Industrial Buying and Creative Marketing* (Boston: Allyn & Bacon).

8. This illustration is based on Rowland T. Moriarty, Jr. (1985), "Signode Industries, Inc. (A)," Harvard Business School case #9-586-059.

9. Several comprehensive models of industrial buying behavior go into more detail about the steps of the decision-making process and the external and other factors that affect the process. Good reviews of these models can be found in Scott Ward and Frederick E. Webster, Jr. (1991), "Organizational buying behavior," in *Handbook of Consumer Behavior,* T. S. Robertson and H. H. Kassarjian, eds. (Englewood Cliffs, NJ: Prentice Hall), Ch. 12; and Wesley J. Johnston and Jeffrey E. Lewin (1996), "Organizational buying behavior: toward an integrative framework," *Journal of Business Research,* 35, pp. 1–15.

10. For more background on the market for copiers and how they are entering the digital age, see Raju Narisetti (1998), "Pounded by printers, Xerox copiers go digital," *The Wall Street Journal,* May 12, p. B1.

11. This illustration is from Patricia A. Seybold (1998), *Customers.Com* (New York: Times Books), Ch. CSF-1.

12. We devote more space to channels of distribution in Chapter 9.

13. Andy Reinhardt (1998), "Log on, link up, save big," *Business Week,* June 22, pp. 132–138.

Chapter 7

1. This illustration is based on Michael E. Porter (1991), "Coca-Cola versus Pepsi-Cola and the soft drink industry," Harvard Business School case #9-391-179; Mark Gleason (1996), "Coke, Pepsi repel thrust by alternative beverages," *Advertising Age,* September 30, p. S18; Patricia Sellers (1996), "How Coke is kicking Pepsi's can," *Fortune,* October 28, pp. 70–84; Richard Tomkins (1997), "Coca-Cola strives to rival tap water," *Financial Times,* October 27, p. 9; and Nikhil Deogun (1998), "For Pepsi, a battle to capture Coke's fountain sales," *The Wall Street Journal,* May 11, p. B1.

2. In 1997, Pepsi spun off its restaurants into a separate, publicly traded company, Tricon Global Restaurants, Inc.

3. Coca-Cola manufactures only the concentrate or syrup; its bottlers, some of which are company-owned, assume the costs of making the soft drink and distributing it.

4. Joe S. Bain (1968), *Industrial Organization* (New York: Wiley).

5. Tomkins, *op. cit.*

6. James P. Miller (1996), "Cereal makers fight bagels with price cuts," *The Wall Street Journal,* June 20, p. B1.

7. Tara Parker-Pope (1998), "P&G targets textiles Tide can't clean," *The Wall Street Journal,* April 29, p. B1.

8. A good source for these methods is Vithala R. Rao and Joel H. Steckel (1995), *The New Science of Marketing* (Chicago: Irwin), Ch. 4.

9. See Volney Stefflre (1972), "Some applications of multidimensional scaling to social science problems," in *Multidimensional Scaling: Theory and Applications in the Behavioral Sciences,* Vol. III, A. K. Romney, R. N. Shepard, and S. B. Nerlove, eds. (New York: Seminar Press); and S. Ratneshwar and Allan Shocker (1991), "Substitution in use and the role of usage context in product category structures," *Journal of Marketing Research,* August, pp. 281–295.

10. For more background information, see William Green (1998), "I spy," *Forbes,* April 20, pp. 90–100.

11. Ira Teinowitz (1995), "Marketing, ad woes choking RJR brands," *Advertising Age,* June 26, p. 3.

12. Priscilla C. Brown (1992), "Unisys' new marketing chief targets four key segments," *Business Marketing,* April, pp. 73–74.

13. See Pierre Wack (1985), "Scenarios: uncharted waters ahead," *Harvard Business Review,* 63 (September–October), pp. 73–89; and William R. Huss (1988), "A move toward scenario analysis," *International Journal of Forecasting,* 4, pp. 377–388.

14. For sources on competitor intelligence, see Leonard M. Fuld (1995), *The New Competitor Intelligence* (New York: Wiley).

15. For more inclusive lists, see Susan Greco (1996), "The on-line sleuth," *Inc.,* October, pp. 88–89; Rebecca Piirto Heath (1997), "Somewhere out there," *Marketing Tools,* January/February,

pp. 20–22; and B. G. Yovovich (1997), "Browsers get peek at rivals' secrets," *Marketing News,* November 10, p. 1.

16. For further information about how to maximize the information obtained from such tours, see David M. Upton and Stephen E. Macadam (1997), "Why (and how) to take a plant tour," *Harvard Business Review,* May–June, pp. 97–106.

17. This section draws on an article by K. Sridhar Moorthy (1985), "Using game theory to model competition," *Journal of Marketing Research,* 22 (August), pp. 262–282, as well as material from one of my colleagues, Debu Purohit.

18. Many formal definitions important to game theory are not discussed in detail here because they are beyond the scope of this book.

19. This simultaneous solution also assumes that both firms have complete information in that they both know the payoff matrix and know that it is the same for both of them. Of course, they still do not know with certainty what the other is going to do.

20. Game theory can be extended to include more than two participants and games over an extended period of time with multiple moves.

21. F. William Barnett (1995), "Making game theory work in practice," *The Wall Street Journal,* February 13, p. A14.

Chapter 8

1. The material for this example is from Susan Fournier (1996), "Land Rover North America, Inc.," Harvard Business School case #9-596-036.

2. For a classic reference in this area, see Wilbur Schram (1955), *The Process and Effects of Mass Communication* (Urbana: University of Illinois Press).

3. See E. Katz and P. F. Lazarsfeld (1955), *Personal Influence* (Glencoe, IL: Free Press).

4. This anecdote was provided by Thomas O'Guinn.

5. Electronic environments such as those discussed are called hypermedia computer-mediated environments. See Donna L. Hoffman and Thomas P. Novak (1996), "Marketing in hypermedia computer-mediated environments: conceptual foundations," *Journal of Marketing,* 60 (July), pp. 50–68.

6. Ralph S. Alexander, ed. (1965), *Marketing Definitions* (Chicago: American Marketing Association), p. 9.

7. This illustration is based on E. G. Martin (1997), "Losing its religion: Amdahl moves from IBM to platform agnosticism," *Marketing Computers,* February, pp. 46–49.

8. Mike Beirne (1998), "Feeding frenzy," *Brandweek,* October 5, p. 3.

9. *Advertising Age International* (1998), May 11, p. 15.

10. Several criticisms can be made of such hierarchical models, and alternative frameworks have been proposed. See George E. Belch and Michael A. Belch (1993), *Introduction to Advertising and Promotion* (Homewood, IL: Irwin), Ch. 6.

11. See Belch and Belch, *op. cit.*

12. A good reference on copy testing procedures is Rajeev Batra, John G. Myers, and David A. Aaker (1996), *Advertising Management,* 5th ed. (Upper Saddle River, NJ: Prentice Hall), Ch. 14.

13. Elizabeth Jensen (1996), "Networks blast Nielsen, blame faulty ratings for drop in viewership," *The Wall Street Journal,* November 22, p. A1.

14. H. Rao Unnava and Robert E. Burnkrant (1991), "Effects of repeating varied ad executions on brand name memory," *Journal of Marketing Research,* 28 (November), pp. 406–416.

15. Hubert A. Zielske (1959), "The remembering and forgetting of advertising," *Journal of Marketing,* 23 (January), pp. 239–243.

16. See David Kiley (1998), "Optimum target," *AdWeek,* May 18, pp. 39–42.

17. Michal Shapira and Sigahl Silvera (1999), "Cellular phone campaign brings hysterical demand," available on the Market Files Web site.

18. The Swatch wristwatch brand differentiates itself from competitors by being fashion oriented, with different watch face themes and colored bands.

19. See Adrian J. Slywotzky and Benson P. Shapiro (1993), "Leveraging to beat the odds: the new marketing mind-set," *Harvard Business Review,* September–October, pp. 97–107.

20. See John Philip Jones (1990), "Ad spending: maintaining market share," *Harvard Business Review,* January–February, pp. 38–48.

21. See Rita Koselka (1996), "The new mantra: MVT," *Forbes,* March 11, pp. 114–117.

22. These data are from Darral G. Clarke (1985), "G.D. Searle & Co.: Equal low-calorie sweetener (A)," Harvard Business School case #9-585-010.

23. John D. C. Little (1970), "Models and managers: the concept of a decision calculus," *Management Science,* 16, pp. B466–B485.

24. See J. Enrique Bigné (1995), "Advertising budget practices: a review," *Journal of Current Issues and Research in Advertising,* 2 (Fall), pp. 17–31.

25. Leonard M. Lodish, Magid Abraham, Stuart Kalmenson, Jeanne Livelsberger, Beth Lubetkin, Bruce Richardson, and Mary Ellen Stevens (1995), "How T.V. advertising works: a meta-analysis of 389 real world split cable T.V. advertising experiments," *Journal of Marketing Research,* 32 (May), pp. 125–139.

26. Naras Eechembadi (1994), "Does advertising work?" *The McKinsey Quarterly,* 3, pp. 117–129.

27. Gert Assmus, John U. Farley, and Donald R. Lehmann (1984), "How advertising affects sales: meta-analysis of econometric results," *Journal of Marketing Research,* 21 (February), pp. 65–74.

28. The vast majority of empirical research in this area has focused on consumer products and services. Thus, generalizing these findings to industrial products should be done with caution.

29. See Laura Rich (1997), "Count them in," *Brandweek,* February 3, pp. 24–29.

Chapter 9

1. This illustration is based on "How Kirin lost its sparkle," *The Economist,* September 14, 1996, pp. 66–67; and Norihiko Shirouzu (1997), "Asahi investors get giddy," *The Asian Wall Street Journal,* May 19, p. 22.

2. The potential components of this value are described later in the chapter.

3. Many would argue that even company-owned or captive channels should be a focus of marketing. This is often called internal marketing.

4. Evan Ramstad (1996), "Dell takes another shot at selling to home-PC users," *The Wall Street Journal,* December 16, p. B4; Silvia Ascarelli (1997), "Dell finds U.S. strategy works in Europe," *The Wall Street Journal,* February 3, p. A8; Andy Serwer (1998), "Michael Dell rocks," *Fortune,* May 11, pp. 59–70.

5. The companies also innovated in how the sales force is compensated. Their method, called multilevel selling, is covered later in this chapter.

6. John R. Hayes (1997), "Watch out, Dell," *Forbes,* March 24, p. 84.

7. Direct and indirect channels could be company owned (captive) or independent. For the purposes of simplification, we assume that the indirect channels are independent. Clearly, the company has more control over captive than independent indirect channels.

8. V. Kasturi Rangan, Melvyn A. J. Menezes, and E. P. Maier (1992), "Channel selection for new industrial products: a framework, method, and applications," *Journal of Marketing,* 56 (July), pp. 69–82.

9. A good discussion of the problems involved with multiple channels can be found in V. Kasturi Rangan (1994), "Reorienting channels of distribution," Harvard Business School case #9-594-118.

10. This example is based on V. Kasturi Rangan and E. Raymond Corey (1989), "Ingersoll-Rand (A): managing multiple channels," Harvard Business School case #9-589-121.

11. Rowland T. Moriarty and Ursula Moran (1990), "Managing hybrid systems," *Harvard Business Review,* November–December, pp. 146–155.

12. This illustration is based on Anne Bilodeau (1997), "Digital is weaned from direct sales, and finds it likes the freedom," *Marketing Computers,* April, pp. 60–63.

13. Louis W. Stern, Adel I. El-Ansary, and Anne T. Coughlan (1996), *Marketing Channels,* 5th ed. (Upper Saddle River, NJ: Prentice Hall), p. 286.

14. See Zachary Schiller (1994), "Making the middleman an endangered species," *Business Week,* June 6, pp. 114–115.

15. Joseph Pereira (1997), "Toys 'R' Us Inc. warned manufacturers on sales to warehouse club discounters," *The Wall Street Journal,* March 6, p. C22.

16. Stern, El-Ansary, and Coughlan, *op. cit.,* Ch. 7.

17. Daniel Roth (1996), "Card sharks," *Forbes,* October 7, p. 14.

18. Arthur Buckler (1988), "Holly Farms' marketing error: the chicken that laid an egg," *The Wall Street Journal,* February 9, p. 36.

19. Gary L. Frazier and John O. Summers (1986), "Perceptions of interfirm power and its use within a franchise channel of distribution," *Journal of Marketing Research,* 23 (May), p. 172.

20. Patricia Sellers (1999), "Inside the first e-Christmas," *Fortune,* February 1, pp. 70–73.

21. *Business 2.0,* March 1999, p. 8.

22. Eryn Brown (1997), "Could the very best PC maker be Dell Computer?" *Fortune,* April 14, p. 26.

23. For a good overview, see Laurie Freeman (1995), "CRP sticks as product movement mantra," *Advertising Age,* May 8, pp. S1–S9.

24. Suzanne Oliver (1997), "Million-man sales force," *Forbes,* March 24, p. 63.

25. These statistics are from Laura Loro (1996), "'96 B-to-B direct marketing sales hit $543 billion," *Business Marketing,* October, p. 35; and Laura Hansen (1997), "Dialing for dollars," *Marketing Tools,* January/February, pp. 47–53.

26. *Iconocast,* January 22, 1999.

27. The use of databases for building customer relationships is discussed in Chapter 10.

28. Hansen, *op. cit.*

29. Joan Throckmorton (1996), "Discovering DM," *Marketing Tools,* November/December, pp. 51–57.

30. This example is based on Joshua Levine (1996), "Give me one of those," *Forbes,* June 3, p. 134.

31. This example is based on John Spooner (1996), "Inside ON Technology's direct marketing machine," *Marketing Computers,* November, pp. 54–57.

Chapter 10

1. This illustration is based on Erika Rasmusson (1998), "GE Capital: dual obsessions with growth and quality drive Jack Welch's fast-growing division to the top," *Sales & Marketing Management,* July, pp. 34–37.

2. Frank V. Cespedes (1994), "Hewlett-Packard imaging systems division: Sonos 100 C/F introduction," Harvard Business School case #9-593-080.

3. MCI Communications Corporation: National Accounts Program, Harvard Business School case #9-587-116.

4. William A. O'Connell and William Keenan, Jr. (1990), "The shape of things to come," *Sales & Marketing Management,* January, pp. 36–41.

5. This illustration is from Sanjit Sengupta, Robert E. Krapfel, and Michael A. Pusateri (1997), "The strategic sales force," *Marketing Management,* Summer, pp. 29–34.

6. Increasingly, salespeople are also being rewarded on customer satisfaction measures. See Chapter 13 for further discussion.

7. Theodore Levitt (1986), "Relationship management," in *The Marketing Imagination* (New York: Free Press), Ch. 6.

8. In addition to the model used in this book, the interested reader can also consult Gilbert A. Churchill, Jr., Neil M. Ford, and Orville C. Walker, Jr. (1993), *Sales Force Management,* 4th ed. (Homewood, IL: Irwin), Ch. 9.

9. Of course, the firm may have better investment opportunities than to generate only $1 in contribution margin. The method can be adjusted to set a hurdle rate for the return of a salesperson beyond a given opportunity cost of capital.

10. This illustration is based on Darral G. Clarke (1983), "Syntex Laboratories (A)," Harvard Business School case #9-584-033.

11. In recent years, it has become more common for pharmaceutical companies to use advertising to target the end users directly and attempt to get the patients to request certain drug brands.

12. See Leonard J. Lodish (1971), "CALLPLAN: an interactive salesman's call planning system," *Management Science,* 18 (December), pp. 25–40; and Leonard M. Lodish (1974), "'Vaguely right' approach to sales force allocations," *Harvard Business Review,* 52 (January/February), pp. 119–124.

13. This method is becoming more common and is discussed in more detail in Chapter 13.

14. *Sales and Marketing Management* (1998), December, p. 42.

15. See Churchill, Ford, and Walker, *op. cit.,* Chs. 16–18.

16. Rowland T. Moriarty and Gordon S. Swartz (1989), "Automation to boost sales and marketing," *Harvard Business Review,* 89 (January–February), p. 100.

17. Thomas M. Siebel and Michael S. Malone (1996), *Virtual Selling* (New York: Free Press).

18. Edmund O. Lawler (1995), "A tour de sales force," *Business Marketing,* January, p. 21.

19. This topic is discussed further in Chapter 9.

20. Ken Dulaney (1996), "The automated sales force," *Marketing Tools,* October, pp. 57–63.

21. Michel Marchetti (1998), "Helping reps count every penny," *Sales & Marketing Management,* July, p. 77.

22. This illustration is based on Peter Leach and Wendy Close (1999), "Card games: how Lanier Worldwide automated its sales force," *Executive Edge,* February–March, pp. 50–54.

23. David W. Cravens (1995), "The changing role of the sales force," *Marketing Management,* Fall, pp. 49–57.

Chapter 11

1. This illustration is based on Carleen Hawn (1998), "General Mills tests the limits," *Forbes,* April 6, p. 48.

2. In fact, Peter Drucker calls cost-driven pricing a "deadly sin," in Drucker (1993), "The five deadly business sins," *The Wall Street Journal,* October 21, p. A–16.

3. This notion was first introduced to me by pricing consultant Daniel A. Nimer.

4. Elliot B. Ross (1984), "Making money with proactive pricing," *Harvard Business Review,* November–December, pp. 145–155.

5. We are intentionally vague about what constitutes cost; this is explained later in the chapter.

6. Brandon Mitchener (1996), "Audi shifts gears with a luxury car targeted at young European drivers," *The Wall Street Journal,* July 29, pp. 1A–5A.

7. See Eric M. Olson and Jeffrey M. Ferguson (1998), "Crash landing," *Marketing Management,* Summer, pp. 54–58.

8. Connie Ling and Wayne Arnold (1998), "Prospective customers compete to buy Nokia's new mobile phone," *The Asian Wall Street Journal,* September 21, p. 12.

9. A *retailer* may set the price of a product, usually called a loss leader, below cost. The intent of loss-leader pricing is to lure customers into the store by offering a deep discount on a popular item. For example, cranberry sauce is often used as a loss leader at Thanksgiving. We assume that a manufacturer would not do this intentionally.

10. The vertical bars indicate absolute value.

11. Gerard J. Tellis (1988), "The price elasticity of selective demand: a meta-analysis of econometric models of sales," *Journal of Marketing Research,* 25 (November), pp. 331–341.

12. John L. Forbis and Nitin T. Mehta (1981), "Value-based strategies for industrial products," *Business Horizons,* May–June, pp. 32–42.

13. "What buyers will pay for PC brands," *The Wall Street Journal,* October 16, 1995.

14. An alternative way to phrase the question is to ask how much the consumer would have to be paid to be indifferent between the preferred brand and the other brand.

15. This example is drawn from Ted Kendall (1990), "And the survey says . . ." *The Marketer,* September, pp. 47–48.

16. This example is from Nicholas Negroponte (1997), "Pay whom per what when, part II," *Wired,* March, p. 220.

17. This illustration is based on Gerry Khermouch (1998), "Sticking their neck out," *Brandweek,* November 9, pp. 26–38.

18. Andrew E. Server (1994), "How to escape a price war," *Fortune,* June 13, pp. 82–90.

19. Joan O. Hamilton (1990), "Genentech: a textbook case of medical marketing," *Business Week,* August 13, pp. 96–97.

20. See Derek F. Abell and John S. Hammond (1979), *Strategic Market Planning* (Englewood Cliffs, NJ: Prentice Hall), Ch. 3.

21. Drucker, *op. cit.*

22. For some examples showing the difficulty of raising prices, especially in periods of low inflation, see Christopher Farrell and Zachary Schiller (1993), "Stuck! How companies cope when they can't raise prices," *Business Week,* November 15, pp. 146–155.

23. For a literature review in this area, see Gurumurthy Kalyanaram and Russell S. Winer (1995), "Empirical generalizations from reference price research," *Marketing Science* 14, no. 3, pp. G161–G169.

24. Steve Ditlea (1997), "Grand illusions," *Marketing Computers,* May, pp. 27–34.

25. For some background on why odd prices seem to affect consumer decision-making, see Mark Stiving and Russell S. Winer (1997), "An empirical analysis of price endings with scanner data," *Journal of Consumer Research,* 24 (June), pp. 57–67.

26. See Ross, *op. cit.*

27. Paul B. Brown (1990), "You get what you pay for," *Inc.,* October, p. 155.

28. For an excellent description of this value pricing environment, see Stratford Sherman (1992), "How to prosper in the value decade," *Fortune,* November 30, pp. 90–103.

29. For a good discussion of the legal aspects of pricing, see Thomas T. Nagle and Reed K. Holden (1995), *The Strategy and Tactics of Pricing* (Englewood Cliffs, NJ: Prentice Hall), Ch. 14.

30. This is not always the case. Canadian retailer Loblaw has a private-label brand, President's Choice, that is fully competitive with national brands in quality and sells at about the same price level.

31. John A. Quelch and David Harding (1996), "Brands versus private labels: fighting to win," *Harvard Business Review,* January–February, pp. 99–109.

32. Larry Armstrong and Kathleen Kerwin (1998), "Downloading their dream cars," *Business Week,* March 9, pp. 93–94.

33. See Amy E. Cortese and Marcia Stepanek (1998), "Good-bye to fixed pricing?" *Business Week,* May 4, pp. 71–84.

34. Claire Tristram (1999), "Takin' it to the street," *Marketing Computers,* February, pp. 22–28.

35. See Scott Woolley (1998), "I got it cheaper than you," *Forbes,* November 2, pp. 82–84.

36. Ira Sager and Heather Green (1998), "So where are all the bargains?" *Business Week,* June 22, pp. 162–164.

Chapter 12

1. This illustration is based on Sean Mehegan (1998), "True blue," *Brandweek,* March 2, p. R7, as well as information collected from a variety of Web sites.

2. For tips on cleaning up the mess, see the Crayola Web site.

3. Robert C. Blattberg and Scott A. Neslin (1990), *Sales Promotion* (Englewood Cliffs, NJ: Prentice Hall).

4. Julie Pitta (1999), "Squeeze play: databases get ugly," *Forbes,* February 22, pp. 50–51.

5. Raju Narisetti (1997), "Move to drop coupons puts Proctor & Gamble in sticky PR situation," *The Wall Street Journal,* April 17, p. A1.

6. Carl F. Mela, Sunil Gupta, and Donald R. Lehmann (1997), "The long-term impact of promotion and advertising on consumer brand choice," *Journal of Marketing Research,* 34 (May), pp. 248–261.

7. See also John C. Totten and Martin P. Block (1994), *Analyzing Sales Promotion,* 2nd ed. (Chicago: Dartnell Corporation).

8. Cox Direct (1997), *Navigate the Promotional Universe* (Largo, FL: Cox Direct).

9. The amount of coupon misredemption decreases dramatically where electronic scanners are used because most coupons are bar coded and can be matched to brands that have actually been purchased.

10. Information Resources, Inc. (1994), *The Marketing Fact Book* (Chicago: Information Resources, Inc.).

11. Kathleen Kerwin (1998), "Carmakers may be flooding the engine," *Business Week,* May 18, p. 43.

12. Gerry Khermouch (1997), "Read this. It's free," *Brandweek,* June 16, p. 42.

13. This illustration is based on "Nivea Vital" (1996), *Ad Age International,* December, p. i8.

14. Matthew G. Nagler (1997), "An empirical analysis of cooperative advertising across product groups," unpublished working paper, Federal Communication Commission.

15. The marketing manager may want to reward loyal customers and aid retention, particularly in the face of competitor promotions, by giving them a discount. However, if they would normally pay the regular price, this is a cost of the promotion.

16. Scott A. Neslin and Robert W. Shoemaker (1983), "A model for evaluating the profitability of coupon promotions," *Marketing Science,* 2, pp. 361–388.

17. Certainly, companies in different industries advertise in appropriate trade journals that target channel members. However, this is usually a small amount of the advertising budget compared to the amount spent targeting end customers.

18. This illustration is based on John A. Quelch (1983), "Proctor & Gamble (B)," Harvard Business School case #9-584-048. Note that retail promotions are omitted because those decisions are made by the retailers.

19. A partial liquidator is a premium program in which the money the customer pays does not fully cover the costs of the promotion.

20. Hillary Rosner (1995), "Most buys are impulse," *Brandweek,* October 2, p. 5. For further information on in-store decision-making, see J. Jeffrey Inman and Russell S. Winer (1998), "Where the rubber meets the road: a model of in-store consumer decision-making," working paper, University of California at Berkeley.

21. Readers should not expect to get these kinds of results for every brand or kind of product.

22. Paul W. Farris and Robert D. Buzzell (1979), "Why advertising and promotional costs vary: some cross-sectional analyses," *Journal of Marketing,* 43 (Fall), pp. 112–122.

23. Robert M. Prentice (1977), "How to split your marketing funds between advertising and promotion," *Advertising Age,* January 10, p. 41.

24. A company providing such a Web-based coupon service to other companies is Coupons Online.

Chapter 13

1. This illustration is based on Richard Cross (1997), "High-octane loyalty," *Marketing Tools,* April, pp. 4–7.

2. Jim Carlton (1997), "Don't hang up," *The Wall Street Journal,* September 11, p. R11.

3. Theodore Levitt (1986), "Relationship management," in *The Marketing Imagination* (New York: Free Press), Ch. 6.

4. Barbara Bund Jackson (1985), "Build customer relationships that last," *Harvard Business Review,* November–December, pp. 120–128.

5. Chuck Pettis (1997), "A customer's loyalty for $200," *Marketing Computers,* September, pp. 67–70.

6. For a more detailed look at this acquisition/retention decision, see Robert C. Blattberg and John Deighton (1996), "Manage marketing by the customer equity test," *Harvard Business Review,* July–August, pp. 136–144.

7. This illustration is from Martha Rogers (1998), "Fingerhut forever: the advantages of modeling lifetime value," *Inside 1to1,* November 18.

8. See the references in Eugene W. Anderson, Claes Fornell, and Donald R. Lehmann (1993), "Economic consequences of providing quality and customer satisfaction," Marketing Science Institute Report #93-112, Cambridge, MA.

9. Thomas O. Jones and W. Earl Sasser, Jr. (1995), "Why satisfied customers defect," *Harvard Business Review,* November–December, pp. 88–99.

10. Jones and Sasser, *op. cit.*

11. In addition, there are many different measures of loyalty, from survey-based measures such as purchase intentions to behavioral measures such as share-of-requirements, the percentage of all purchases of a product that are of a particular brand.

12. Bradley T. Gale (1994), *Managing Customer Value* (New York: Free Press). For another approach to understanding and managing customer value, see Robert B. Woodruff and Sarah F. Gardial (1996), *Know Your Customer: New Approaches to Understanding Customer Value and Satisfaction* (Cambridge, MA: Blackwell).

13. Robert D. Buzzell and Bradley T. Gale (1987), *The PIMS Principles* (New York: Free Press).

14. This point about the Lexus 400 was made in Chapter 9 in the context of value pricing.

15. Jan Carlzon (1987), *Moments of Truth* (Cambridge, MA: Ballinger).

16. Kathy Chen (1997), "Would America buy a refrigerator labeled 'Made in Qingdao'"? *The Wall Street Journal,* September 17, p. A1.

17. Bob Tasca (1996), *You Will Be Satisfied* (New York: HarperCollins).

18. James L. Heskett, W. Earl Sasser, and Christopher W. L. Hart (1990), *Service Breakthroughs: Changing the Rules of the Game* (New York: Free Press).

19. Chad Kaydo (1998), "Riding high," *Sales & Marketing Management,* July, pp. 64–69.

20. "International Business Machines (B): Applitronics Account Strategy," Harvard Business School case #9-581-052.

21. Gina Imperato (1999), "MindSpring does a mind-flip," *Business 2.0,* March, pp. 40–42.

22. Geoffrey Naim (1997), "Retailers get smarter," *Financial Times,* September 3, FT–IT 7.

23. Rebecca Piirto Heath (1997), "Loyalty for sale," *Marketing Tools,* July, pp. 40–46; see also Grahame R. Dowling and Mark Uncles (1997), "Do customer loyalty programs really work?" *Sloan Management Review,* Summer, pp. 71–82; Louise O'Brien and Charles Jones (1995), "Do rewards really create loyalty?" *Harvard Business Review,* May–June, pp. 75–82.

24. Laura Loro (1998), "Loyalty programs paying off for B-to-B," *Business Marketing,* September, p. 49.

25. Pat Long (1997), "Customer loyalty, one customer at a time," *Marketing News,* February 3, p. 8.

26. Frederick F. Reichheld (1996), "Learning from customer defections," *Harvard Business Review,* March–April, pp. 56–69.

27. See B. Joseph Pine II (1993), *Mass Customization: The New Frontier in Business Competition* (Boston: Harvard Business School Press); and Don Peppers and Martha Rogers (1993), *The One to One Future: Building Relationships One Customer at a Time* (New York: Currency/Doubleday).

28. James H. Gilmore and B. Joseph Pine II (1997), "The four faces of customization," *Harvard Business Review,* January–February, pp. 91–101.

29. Christina Binkley (1997), "Harrah's builds database about patrons," *The Wall Street Journal,* September 2, p. B1.

Chapter 14

1. This illustration is based on Richard Teitelbaum (1997), "The Wal-Mart of Wall Street," *Fortune,* October 13, pp. 128–130.

2. *Wired* (1998), May, p. 54.

3. See Philip Nelson (1970), "Advertising as information," *Journal of Political Economy,* July–August, pp. 729–754; and Michael R. Darby and E. Karni (1973), "Free competition and the optimal amount of fraud," *Journal of Law and Economics,* April, pp. 67–86.

4. See David Garvin (1987), "Competing on the eight dimensions of quality," *Harvard Business Review,* November–December, pp. 101–109; and Christian Grönroos (1990), *Service Management and Marketing* (Lexington, MA: Lexington Books).

5. Daniel Kahneman and Amos Tversky (1979), "Prospect theory: an analysis of decision under risk," *Econometrica,* 47, pp. 263–291.

6. Valarie A. Zeithaml, A. Parasuraman, and Leonard L. Berry (1990), *Delivering Quality Service: Balancing Customer Perceptions and Expectations* (New York: Free Press).

7. Zeithaml, Parasuraman, and Berry, *op. cit.,* Appendix A.

8. Shelly Reese (1996), "Happiness isn't everything," *Marketing Tools,* May, pp. 52–58.

9. Philip B. Crosby (1979), *Quality Is Free: The Art of Making Quality Certain* (New York: McGraw-Hill).

10. Roland T. Rust, Anthony J. Zahorik, and Timothy L. Keiningham (1994), *Return on Quality: Measuring the Financial Impact of Your Company's Quest for Quality* (Chicago: Probus).

11. Malcolm Fleschner and Gerhard Gschwandtner (1994), "The Marriott miracle," *Personal Selling Power,* September, pp. 17–26.

12. See Theodore Levitt (1986), *The Marketing Imagination* (New York: Free Press), Ch. 5.

13. Valarie A. Zeithaml and Mary Jo Bitner (1996), *Services Marketing* (New York: McGraw-Hill), Ch. 10.

14. This illustration is based on Sandra Vandermerwe and Christopher H. Lovelock (1991), "Singapore Airlines: using technology for service excellence," IMD case #592-014-1.

15. Zeithaml and Bitner, *op. cit.,* Ch. 12.

16. This section is based on Donna Legg and Julie Baker (1987), "Advertising strategies for service firms," in C. Suprenant, ed., *Add Value to Your Service* (Chicago: American Marketing Association), pp. 163–168.

17. The material for this section is drawn from Seth Lubove (1996), "Cyberbanking," *Forbes,* October 21, pp. 108–116; *The Economist* (1996), "Turning digits into dollars," October 26, special survey of technology in finance; Matthew Schifrin (1997), "Cyber-Schwab," *Forbes,* May 5, pp. 42–43; Matthew Schifrin (1997), "The new enablers: chief information officers," *Forbes,* June 2, pp. 138–143; Erick Schonfeld (1998), "The customized, digitized, have-it-your-way economy," *Fortune,* September 28, pp. 115–124; *The Wall Street Journal* (1998), special report on on-line trading, September 8; Jeffrey M. Laderman (1998), "Remaking Schwab," *Business Week,* May 25, pp. 122–128.

18. In 1998, Wells Fargo merged with Norwest Bank.

Chapter 15

1. This illustration is based on John Deighton (1996), "Rogers Communications, Inc.: The Wave," Harvard Business School case #9-597-050. In 1997, Rogers took an equity position in @Home, a company developing networks for cable TV providers to hook to the Internet. In 1998, The Wave was rebranded as Rogers@Home.

2. For a moderately technical description of how cable modems work, see Les Freed (1998), "Faster connections," *PC Magazine,* February 10, pp. 229–230.

3. Rowland Moriarty and Thomas J. Kosnik (1987), "High-tech vs. low-tech marketing: where's the beef?" Harvard Business School case #9-588-012.

4. The life cycles of previous generations of chips are not completely extinguished because they continue to be used in lower-tech products such as toys.

5. A good example is the impact of the drop in Asian currencies in late 1997 on purchases of high-tech equipment such as PCs and their components.

6. Everett M. Rogers (1995), *Diffusion of Innovations,* 4th ed. (New York: Free Press).

7. In the high-tech literature, network externalities are often discussed in the context of increasing returns, in which the value of an additional unit of production produces more profits than the last one. See John Hagel III and Arthur G. Armstrong (1997), *net.gain: Expanding Markets Through Virtual Communities* (Boston: Harvard Business School Press). For an extensive discussion of network externalities in the context of information goods, see Carl Shapiro and Hal R. Varian (1999), *Information Rules* (Boston: Harvard Business School Press), Ch. 7.

8. This illustration is based on Michael J. Enright (1993), "The Japanese facsimile industry," Harvard Business School case #9-391-209.

9. Actually, Federal Express was prescient in seeing that fax machines would ultimately be a major competitor to its document delivery service. Because fast plain-paper fax machines are very inexpensive today, fax transmissions do indeed substitute for many former FedEx shipments.

10. Wayne D. Hoyer and Deborah J. MacInnis (1997), *Consumer Behavior* (Boston: Houghton Mifflin), Ch. 2.

11. This idea was originally popularized by John Naisbitt (1982) in *Megatrends: Ten New Directions for Transforming Our Lives* (New York: Warner Books).

12. See Rogers, *op. cit.* However, this framework was actually developed in the first edition of the book, published in 1962.

13. This section is based on Geoffrey A. Moore (1991), *Crossing the Chasm* (New York: HarperBusiness); and Geoffrey A. Moore (1995), *Inside the Tornado* (New York: HarperBusiness).

14. Interestingly, in some ways network PCs are a full-circle return to an old technology. Some readers might remember the old dumb terminals, which connected users to a mainframe computer. The difference is that a network PC is connected to a much more powerful and global network than a stand-alone mainframe.

15. This illustration is based on Nikhil Hutheesing (1997), "Auto-Baan," *Forbes,* October 6, pp. 109–113.

16. This illustration is based on Bill Taylor (1997), "Homer's Odyssey," *Marketing Computers,* November, pp. 41–52. Netscape is now owned by America Online.

17. This section is based on Shapiro and Varian, *op. cit.,* Ch. 5.

18. It is not necessarily true that high switching costs are bad for buyers if the sellers do a sufficiently good job of maintaining the value of their products and services so that there is little incentive for buyers to consider switching.

19. Hubert Gatignon and Thomas S. Robertson (1985), "A propositional inventory for new diffusion research," *Journal of Consumer Research,* 11 (March), pp. 849–867.

20. Eric Von Hippel (1986), "Lead users: a source of novel product concepts," *Management Science,* 32 (July), pp. 791–805.

21. For an illustration of how marketing research can help to uncover lead users, see Glen L. Urban and Eric Von Hippel (1988), "Lead user analysis for the development of new industrial products," *Management Science,* 34 (May), pp. 569–582.

22. This illustration is based on Ray A. Goldberg (1994), "DNA Plant Technology Corporation (DNAP)," Harvard Business School case #9-595-044.

23. This illustration is based on David Weinstein (1994), "Intel Inside," INSEAD case #594-038-1; and Steve Ditlea (1997), "Running scared," *Marketing Computers,* October, pp. 30–39.

24. Devavrat Purohit (1994), "What should you do when your competitors send in the clones?" *Marketing Science,* 13 (Fall), pp. 392–411.

25. This is not always the case. An OEM channel may want a long-term relationship with a supplier because it gives the latter an incentive to invest in improving its own technology and bringing down its costs, which ultimately benefits the OEM. An OEM may also require an investment on

the part of the supplier to tailor the product in some way, such as making a special adapter to fit into the product.

26. This illustration is based on David Einstein (1997), "Building a better mouse," *San Francisco Chronicle,* August 12, p. C1; Adrian B. Ryans (1992), "Logitech," Richard Ivey School of Business, University of Western Ontario, case #92-A012; and various information collected from the Web.

27. This illustration is based on John Spooner (1997), "The LANtastic voyage: Artisoft sets off in search of new markets," *Marketing Computers,* January, pp. 44–47.

Chapter 16

1. This illustration is based on John Quelch (1993), "Gallo Rice," Harvard Business School case #9-593-018.

2. Philip R. Cateora (1993), *International Marketing,* 8th ed. (Homewood, IL: Irwin), Ch. 1.

3. This approach is discussed more fully in the next section of this chapter.

4. Dexter Roberts (1997), "Where's that pot of gold? Drugs: plenty of bitter pills," *Business Week,* February 3, pp. 58–60.

5 Matt Moffett (1996), "Bruised in Brazil: Ford slips as the market booms," *The Wall Street Journal,* December 13, p. A10.

6. Theodore Levitt (1983), "The globalization of markets," *Harvard Business Review,* May–June, pp. 92–102.

7. For more background, see John A. Quelch (1984), "British Airways," Harvard Business School case #9-585-014.

8. See Susan P. Douglas and Yoram Wind (1987), "The myth of globalization," *The Columbia Journal of World Business,* 22 (Winter), pp. 19–29.

9. Bernard Wysocki, Jr. (1997), "In developing nations, many youths splurge, mainly on U.S. goods," *The Wall Street Journal,* June 26, p. 1.

10. Yumiko Ono (1997), "McCann finds global a tough sell in Japan," *The Wall Street Journal,* June 19, p. B2.

11. John A. Quelch and Edward J. Hoff (1986), "Customize global marketing," *Harvard Business Review,* May–June, pp. 59–68.

12. Bruce Crumley (1997), "Juicing up a strategy," *Advertising Age International,* March, p. i22.

13. In 1998, Coca-Cola attempted to purchase Orangina, but the French government prohibited it. An interesting question is what (if anything) would have happened to its uniquely French positioning.

14. Yumiko Ono (1997), "Tampax ads address cultural obstacles," *The Wall Street Journal,* March 17, p. B6.

15. A good reference on country selection is Franklin R. Root (1994), *Entry Strategies for International Markets* (New York: Lexington).

16. See Susan P. Douglas and C. Samuel Craig (1995), *Global Marketing Strategy* (New York: McGraw-Hill), Ch. 7.

17. For a detailed explanation of how to enter China via joint venture, see Wilfried Vanhonacker (1997), "Entering China: an unconventional approach," *Harvard Business Review,* March–April, pp. 2–7.

18. This illustration is based on Benjamin Gomes-Casseres (1991), "Xerox and Fuji Xerox," Harvard Business School case #9-391-156; and David P. Hamilton (1996), "United it stands," *The Wall Street Journal,* September 26, p. R19.

19. Frank Bradley (1991), *International Marketing Strategy* (New York: Prentice Hall), Ch. 5.

20. See Cateora *op. cit.*, Ch. 5.

21. Fara Warner (1997), "Nike laces up to improve the spirits of gloomy Thais—and sell sneakers," *The Asian Wall Street Journal,* December 8, p. 6.

22. Fara Warner (1997), "Names take on new value," *The Asian Wall Street Journal,* July 28, p. 7.

23. This illustration is based on Laura Petrecca (1997), "Korea's LG Group breaking $30 million branding campaign," *Advertising Age,* July 28, p. 10.

24. Bill Britt (1997), "For multinationals, value lies in the eyes of local consumers," *Ad Age International,* May, p. i18.

25. Fara Warner and Pichayaporn Utumporn (1997), "Ads in Southeast Asia capitalize on woes," *The Wall Street Journal,* December 10, p. B8.

26. This illustration is based on Fara Warner (1997), "Savvy Indian marketers hold their ground," *The Asian Wall Street Journal,* December 1, p. 1.

27. Some of the material in this section is based on Louis W. Stern, Adel I. El-Ansary, and Anne T. Coughlan (1996), *Marketing Channels,* 5th ed. (Upper Saddle River, NJ: Prentice Hall), Ch. 11.

28. This illustration is based on Joseph Kahn (1995), "P&G viewed China as a national market and is conquering it," *The Wall Street Journal,* September 12, p. A1; and Norihiko Shirouzu (1997), "P&G's Joy makes an unlikely splash in Japan," *The Wall Street Journal,* December 10, p. B1.

29. This illustration is based on Brent Schlender (1997), "Microsoft: first America, now the world," *Fortune,* August 18, pp. 214–217.

30. Hermann Simon and Eckhard Kucher (1995), "Pricing in the new Europe: a time bomb?" *Pricing Strategy & Practice,* 3, no. 1, pp. 4–13.

31. Since January 1, 1999, national currencies remain in circulation, but bank accounts, credit cards, and prices are measured in both local currency and Euros.

32. Normandy Madden and Andrew Hornery (1999), "As Taco Bell enters Singapore, Gidget avoids the ad limelight," *Ad Age International,* January 11, p. 13.

33. Laurel Wentz (1998), "DM9 nurtures Parmalat into a beloved brand," *Ad Age International,* October 5, p. 20.

Chapter 17

1. This illustration is based on Wendy Bounds (1996), "Camera system is developed but not delivered," *The Wall Street Journal,* August 7, p. B1; Emily Nelson (1997), "For Kodak's Advantix, double exposure as company relaunches camera system," *The Wall Street Journal,* April 23, p. B1; Laura Heller (1998), "APS sales nudge up to 20% market share," *Discount Store News,* June 22, pp. 43–44; and Tricia Campbell (1999), "Back in focus," *Sales & Marketing Management,* February, pp. 56–61.

2. Rodney Ho (1999), "Patents hit record in '98 as tech firms rushed to protect intellectual property," *The Wall Street Journal,* January 15, p. A2.

3. Judann Pollack (1998), "New products top ads in helping brands grow," *Advertising Age,* May 11, p. 28. A new UPC code is generated for new sizes, packages, flavors, and other variables, so there are many more UPCs than really different products.

4. See Michael J. McCarthy (1997), "Food companies hunt for a 'next big thing' but few can find one," *The Wall Street Journal,* May 6, p. A1.

5. See Tara Parker-Pope (1997), "Colgate places a huge bet on a germ-fighter," *The Wall Street Journal,* December 12, p. B1; and Linda Grant (1998), "Outmarketing P&G," *Fortune,* January 12, pp. 150–151.

6. See the next section of this chapter for a more detailed discussion about why new products fail.

7. See C. Merle Crawford (1997), *New Products Management,* 5th ed. (Chicago: Irwin), p. 9.

8. The person best known for studies in this area is Robert G. Cooper. Two articles he has written on this topic are R. G. Cooper and E. J. Kleinschmidt (1987), "New products: what separates winners from losers?" *Journal of Product Innovation Management,* 4, pp. 169–184; and Robert G. Cooper (1996), "New products: what separates the winners from the losers," in M. D. Rosenau, Jr., A. Griffin, G. A. Castellion, and N. F. Anscheutz, eds., *The PDMA Handbook of New Product Development* (New York: Wiley), Ch. 1.

9. This section is based on John R. Hauser and Glen L. Urban (1993), *Design and Marketing of New Products,* 2nd ed. (Englewood Cliffs, NJ: Prentice Hall), Ch. 2.

10. Hirotaka Takeuchi and Ikujiro Nonaka (1986), "The new product development game," *Harvard Business Review,* January–February, pp. 137–146.

11. Robin Cooper and W. Bruce Chew (1996), "Control tomorrow's costs through today's designs," *Harvard Business Review,* January–February, pp. 88–97; and Ogenyi Ejye Omar (1997), "Target pricing: a marketing management tool for pricing new cars," *Pricing Strategy & Practice,* 5, pp. 61–69.

12. New methods for incorporating the voice of the customer into a more traditional new product development process are described later in the chapter.

13. Note the difference from the traditional approach, whereby profit would be determined after a price is set that covers the manufacturing cost at a high enough level to satisfy corporate requirements ($\Pi = P - C$).

14. This illustration is based on Robin Cooper (1994), "Nissan Motor Company, Ltd.: target costing system," Harvard Business School case #9-194-040.

15. We do not cover new product launch issues, the fourth box of Fig. 17–3, because that is mainly the implementation of the product's marketing plan, the components of which have been covered in previous chapters.

16. See Crawford, *op. cit.,* Ch. 5.

17. Some researchers disagree. A new method called empathetic design obtains information from customers about potential new product ideas, not from focus groups or more traditional methods, but through observing their behavior in natural environments. See Dorothy Leonard and Jeffrey F. Rayport (1997), "Spark innovation through empathetic design," *Harvard Business Review,* November–December, pp. 102–113.

18. Otis Port and John Carey (1997), "Getting to 'Eureka,'" *Business Week,* November 10, pp. 72–74.

19. For more information about concept testing, see William L. Moore and Edgar A. Pessemier (1993), *Product Planning and Management* (New York: McGraw-Hill), Ch. 8.

20. Paul E. Green and Yoram Wind (1975), "New way to measure consumers' judgments," *Harvard Business Review,* July–August, pp. 107–117.

21. A conjoint analysis can be done on individual subjects. However, it is customary to ultimately determine the results at the segment level because that is more useful to marketing managers.

22. A detailed description of the methods used to estimate the utilities is beyond the scope of this book. A good reference is Moore and Pessemier, *op. cit.,* Ch. 5.

23. This section is based on John R. Hauser and Don Clausing (1988), "The house of quality," *Harvard Business Review,* 66, pp. 63–73.

24. G. Kalyanaram and V. Krishnan (1997), "Deliberate product definition: customizing the product definition process," *Journal of Marketing Research,* 34 (May), pp. 276–285.

25. The product used in this phase typically is specially produced and may not match the quality of the product after it reaches a large scale of production. For example, Knorr soup product test samples were produced in Europe, whereas the actual mass-produced product was made in a new, computerized plant in Argo, Illinois, which produced a product of different quality. Therefore, the success or failure of the test product does not necessarily imply success or failure of the actual product.

26. This illustration is based on Suzanne Bidlake (1998), "Winner Taco wins over Europeans searching for snack," *Ad Age International,* April 13, p. 19.

27. J. H. Parfitt and B. J. K. Collins (1968), "Use of consumer panels for brand-share prediction," *Journal of Marketing Research,* May, pp. 131–145.

28. Alvin J. Silk and Glen L. Urban (1978), "Pre-test market evaluation of new packaged goods: a model and measurement methodology," *Journal of Marketing Research,* May, pp. 171–191.

29. Glen L. Urban, Bruce D. Weinberg, and John R. Hauser (1996), "Pre-market forecasting of really-new products," *Journal of Marketing,* January, pp. 47–60.

30. This illustration is based on V. Kasturi Rangan (1995), "Nestlé Refrigerated Foods: Contadina Pasta & Pizza (A)," Harvard Business School case #9-595-035.

31. Christopher D. Ittner and David F. Larcker (1997), "Product development cycle time and organizational performance," *Journal of Marketing Research,* February, pp. 13–23.

32. See Steven C. Wheelwright and Kim B. Clark (1992), *Revolutionizing Product Development: Quantum Leaps in Speed, Efficiency, and Quality* (New York: Free Press).

33. Abbie Griffin (1997), "The effect of project and process characteristics on product development cycle time," *Journal of Marketing Research,* February, pp. 24–35.

34. Gene Bylinsky (1998), "Industry's amazing instant prototypes," *Fortune,* January 12, pp. 120B–120D.

35. This section is based on Abbie Griffin and John R. Hauser (1994), "Integrating mechanisms for marketing and R&D," Marketing Science Institute research report #94-116.

36. This illustration is based on Timothy D. Schellhardt (1999), "Monsanto bets on 'box buddies,'" *The Wall Street Journal,* February 23, p. B9.

Glossary

acquisition costs   the incremental costs involved in obtaining any new customer (p. 361)

agent   a business unit that negotiates purchases, sales, or both but does not take title to the goods in which it deals (Table 9–1)

association/causal methods   a sales forecasting method that tries to develop statistical models relating market factors to sales (p. 99)

brand   a name, term, sign, symbol, or design (or a combination thereof) intended to identify the goods and services of a seller and differentiate them from the competition (p. 169)

brand equity   the value of a brand name in communicating quality or other aspects of a product (p. 60)

brand positions   customers' perceptions of one brand in relation to its competitors (p. 60)

breakdown method   a major method used to determine the size of the sales force that is based on the forecasted sales level divided by an assumed average sales per salesperson (p. 277)

broker   a middleman who serves as a go-between for the buyer or seller (Table 9–1)

budget competition   a level of competition that includes any product, related or unrelated, that could be viewed as substitutable in a budget (p. 171)

buy classes   a set of descriptor variables used in industrial marketing segmentation that is based on the newness of the purchasing situation (p. 148)

buying center   a group of individuals collectively involved in a purchase decision (p. 143)

cannibalization   the amount of sales for a new element of a product line that is taken away from an existing element of the line (p. 70)

category management   a process that considers product categories to be the business units that should be customized on a store-by-store basis in a way that satisfies customer needs (p. 258)

channel power   the ability of one channel member to get another channel member to do what it otherwise would not have done (p. 252)

channels of distribution   the system by which customers have access to a company's product or service (p. 234)

chasm   the large gap that can exist between the early adopters of an innovation and the early majority (p. 422)

cohort analysis   an analysis that develops age-related profiles of each generation to segment the market (p. 113)

commission   a form of compensation based directly on a sale or some other activity (p. 283)

compatibility   an attribute evaluated by customers of new technologically based innovations that refers to the compatibility of the innovation with existing systems, values, and beliefs or previously introduced ideas (p. 417)

compensatory model   any model in which a low score on one attribute can be compensated for by a higher score on another (p. 134)

competitive advantage   the strategic development of some basis on which customers will choose a firm's product or service over its competitor's (p. 52)

competitive pricing a pricing policy in which the objective is to maintain a competitive price by either pricing at the market average or copying a particular brand (p. 311)

competitor analysis an analysis in which the strengths and weaknesses of competitors and their current and likely future strategies are examined (p. 167)

complementary pricing an approach to product line pricing that applies to products that are used together when one of the products is a consumable that must be replenished continually (p. 316)

complexity one factor of an innovation that is negatively related to its success (p. 418)

conjoint analysis a popular marketing research method in new product development that uses theoretical profiles or concepts to determine how customers value different levels of product attributes (p. 490)

consumer franchise building (CFB) activities that build brand equity, including advertising, sampling, couponing, and product demonstrations (p. 351)

consumer-oriented promotions sales promotions oriented toward the consumer, often including devices such as coupons, point-of-purchase price deals, sweepstakes, rebates, and free samples (p. 202)

consumer promotion a marketing tool such as a coupon that targets consumers and is intended to generate a short-term change in a product's sales or market share (p. 333)

continuous replenishment program (CRP) a program wherein members of a supply chain partner with supermarkets, working together to attempt to accurately forecast demand, which is then used to generate inventory replenishment data electronically (p. 258)

contract manufacturing a contractual arrangement in international marketing in which the company provides the necessary technology for the local firm to manufacture the product but does the marketing itself (p. 456)

control group in an experiment, a set of respondents or experimental units who receive the normal level of the manipulation and against which the experimental group is compared (p. 95)

cooperative exporting an approach to entering international markets in which the company enters into a collaborative agreement with a host company to cooperate on marketing, distribution, or other necessary activities (p. 455)

core strategy designed by the marketing manager, a statement that communicates the reason to buy to a specific customer group (p. 46)

correlation method of forecasting an association/causal method of sales forecasting in which a correlation between two variables is used to indicate the strength of the association between them (p. 103)

counting methods sales forecasting methods that rely on customer data (p. 99)

count-recount trade promotions that provide an allowance based on sales, given after a promotion period (p. 341)

couponing a price-oriented promotion that offers a discount off the price of a product and is accompanied by a physical or electronic document indicating the amount of the discount (p. 333)

cross-elasticity of demand the percentage of change in one product's sales caused by a percentage change in a marketing variable for another product (p. 173)

customer service service that supplements or complements the main product or service purchased (p. 370)

customer value what a product or service is worth to the customer in monetary terms; also called perceived value (p. 294)

customer value management an approach to satisfying customers in which a key to achieving exceptional customer value is a high level of perceived quality (p. 367)

Delphi method of forecasting a judgment method of sales forecasting that relies on a jury of experts formed from a diverse population to provide individual estimates of forecasted sales, which then are collated and refined in order to produce a final number (p. 101)

descriptors variables that describe customers in terms of their inherent characteristics (p. 111)

differential advantage one of the three components of a core strategy, a statement of how a particular product or service is better than the competition (p. 52)

differentiation   an approach to creating a competitive advantage based on obtaining an observable point of difference that customers will value and for which they will be willing to pay (p. 56)

diffusion of innovations   a framework developed by Everett Rogers for conceptualizing the sizes of different cohorts of customers who typically buy new innovations at different stages in the innovation's life cycle (p. 420)

direct exporting   an approach to entering international markets in which the company establishes its own operations in the foreign country (p. 455)

direct mail marketing   a form of direct marketing that involves sending letters or catalogues to potential customers (p. 201)

direct marketing   any communication form that sends messages directly to a target market with the anticipation of an immediate or very-short-term response; also, any method of distribution that gives the customer access to the firm's products and services without any other intermediaries (p. 260)

direct price discrimination   a pricing strategy in which each market segment is charged the price that maximizes profit from that segment because of different price elasticities of demand (p. 318)

direct sales   in the context of direct marketing, an approach that involves the use of friends and neighbors as the sales force in reaching potential customers (p. 201)

distributor   any market institution between the seller and buyer in a channel of distribution system; usually refers to a channel member who takes physical possession of goods for distribution to other parties such as retailers (Table 9–1)

diverters   in international marketing, middlemen who purchase products or arrange for their purchase and thereby divert the products away from normal channels (p. 468)

dollarmetric method   in estimating customer value, a method used in conjunction with survey-based methods that creates a scale that puts survey responses in monetary terms (p. 304)

early adopters   one type of adopter in Everett Rogers's diffusion of innovations framework; buyers who are not the first to purchase an innovation but who follow innovators (p. 421)

early majority   one type of adopter in Everett Rogers's diffusion of innovations framework that follows early adopters; buyers who are interested in new technology and gadgets but who wait to see whether an innovative product is just a fad (p. 421)

econometric models   an association/causal method of sales forecasting that involves the use of large-scale, multiple-equation models most often used to predict the economic performance of a country or a particularly large business sector (p. 103)

economies of scale   also called economies of size, the rationale that larger sales mean that fixed costs of operations can be spread over more units, which lowers average unit costs (p. 54)

efficient consumer response (ECR)   a process seeking to reduce costs throughout the entire distribution system, resulting in lower prices and increased consumer demand (p. 258)

emotional appeals   an approach to developing advertising copy that strives to tap an underlying psychological aspect of the purchase decision (p. 211)

evoked or consideration set   in consumer behavior, the set of products from which the customer will choose to purchase (p. 132)

executive opinion method of forecasting   a judgment method of sales forecasting in which the marketing manager relies on his or her own opinion to predict sales, based on his or her experience and knowledge or consultations with internal or external experts (p. 101)

expectations confirmation/disconfirmation model   a basic customer satisfaction model that presumes that levels of customer satisfaction with a product or service are determined by how well the product performs compared to what the customer expects (p. 364)

experience curve   the notion that costs fall with cumulative production or delivery of a service and that, using the first few years of a product's life as a yardstick, the continued decline in costs is predictable (p. 55)

exponential smoothing method of forecasting   a time-series method of sales forecasting that relies on historical sales data, like the moving averages method, but also uses exponentially declining weights based on past sales values (p. 102)

external validity   the ability to generalize experimental results to the real world or, more generally, the target population (p. 95)

extranets   pipelines from an organization to other specific organizations such as channel members (p. 19)

facilitating agent   a business that assists in the performance of distribution tasks other than buying, selling, and transferring title (Table 9–1)

factor analysis   a multivariate statistical approach used to reduce a large number of survey questions to a few underlying factors based on the correlation of the responses to the questions (p. 125)

field experiment   an experiment that takes place in a realistic environment (p. 95)

flat-rate vs. variable-rate pricing   a pricing strategy often used in services that offers customers a choice between a fixed price and a variable usage fee (p. 319)

focus groups   small groups of people, typically recruited through their membership in various target groups of interest, who are brought together in a room to discuss a topic chosen by the marketing manager and led by a professional moderator (p. 89)

frequency marketing   also called loyalty programs, which encourage repeat purchasing through a formal program enrollment process and the distribution of benefits (p. 374)

game theory   a mathematical approach to competitive strategy formulation that takes into account the interdependence of economic factors and assumes that conflicts of interest exist in that the competitors differ in what they want to do and cannot collude actively (p. 189)

generic competition   a level of competition that includes all products or services that the customer views as fulfilling the need requiring satisfaction on a particular purchase or use occasion (p. 170)

global marketing   a generic term encompassing any marketing activities outside a company's home market; also, a standardization of the strategies used to market a product around the world (p. 20)

gray market   a market in which trademarked goods are sold through channels of distribution that are not authorized by the holder of the trademark (p. 468)

growth phase   in the product life cycle, the stage immediately following the introductory phase, in which product category sales are growing, competitors are increasing in number, and market segmentation begins to be a key issue (p. 67)

high-technology product market   a market in which both market and technology uncertainty are high, product life cycles are short, and market conditions are turbulent (p. 415)

house of quality   a matrix used in new product development that illustrates how customer needs and engineering characteristics influence one another (p. 492)

hybrid system   a modification of the multiple-channel system in which members of the channel system perform complementary functions, often for the same customer, thereby allowing for specialization and better levels of performance (p. 250)

inbound logistics   one way to differentiate a product and thereby gain competitive advantages over the competition; involves the selection of the highest-quality raw materials and other inputs, including technology (p. 58)

incentive payments   monetary awards for special performance (p. 283)

indirect exporting   an approach to entering international markets that involves the use of agents, trading companies, or other organizations to move the goods from the home market to the foreign country (p. 455)

industrial marketing   marketing of a product or service to another organization, also called organizational marketing (p. 143)

industry   a group of products that are close substitutes to buyers, are available to a common group of buyers, and are distant substitutes for all products not included in the industry (p. 168)

inert set   in consumer behavior, the set of products that the customer has no intention of buying or has no information about (p. 132)

informational appeals   an approach to developing advertising copy that focuses on the functional or practical aspects of the product (p. 211)

innovators   one type of adopter in Everett Rogers's diffusion of innovations framework; the first buyers of an innovation (p. 420)

integrated marketing communications (IMC)   the concept that the all elements of the marketing mix communicating messages that must be coordinated in order to reinforce what each is saying and to avoid customer confusion (p. 196)

internal validity   the degree to which experimental results are actually caused by the experimental manipulation (p. 95)

intranets   Web-based systems within a specific organization that cannot be penetrated from the outside without special access codes (p. 19)

introductory phase   in the product life cycle, the stage in which the product or service is new; sales volume increases slowly because of a lack of marketing effort and the reluctance of customers to buy the product (p. 65)

investment pricing   also called return on sales, a pricing policy that assumes you can set a price that will deliver the rate of return demanded by senior management; most often used when a product has a monopoly position (p. 311)

jobber   a middleman who buys from manufacturers and sells to retailers; another term for wholesaler (Table 9–1)

joint ventures   a form of contractual arrangement in international marketing in which the companies involved share ownership and control (p. 456)

judgment methods   sales forecasting methods that rely on pure opinion (p. 99)

laboratory experiment   an experiment run in an artificial environment (p. 95)

laggards   one type of adopter in Everett Rogers's diffusion of innovations framework that follows the late majority; buyers who are generally not interested in new technology and are the last customers to buy, if they ever do (p. 421)

late majority   one type of adopter in Everett Rogers's diffusion of innovations framework; buyers who are conservative in terms of how much of an industry infrastructure must be built before they will buy an innovative product (p. 421)

leading indicators   an association/causal method of sales forecasting in which certain macroeconomics variables are used to forecast changes in the economy, based on the fact that changes in these variables occur before changes in the economy (p. 103)

lead users   the first buyers of an innovation in industrial marketing situations; also called innovators (p. 421)

licensing agreement   a form of contractual arrangement in international marketing in which the company receives a royalty fee from the licenser in exchange for permission to use a patented technology, trademark, or brand name (p. 456)

lifetime customer value   the present value of a stream of revenue that can be produced by a customer (pp. 27, 361)

lock-in   a strategy for taking advantage of high customer switching costs (p. 426)

loss aversion   a psychological phenomenon characterized by customers reacting more strongly to unexpectedly poor service than to unexpectedly good service (p. 393)

loyalty programs   also called frequency marketing, programs that encourage repeat purchasing through a formal program enrollment process and the distribution of benefits (p. 374)

manipulation   in an experiment, the marketing variable that is of central interest and is experimentally controlled by the researcher (p. 94)

manufacturer's agent   an agent who generally operates on an extended contractual basis, often sells within an exclusive territory, handles noncompeting but related lines of goods, and has limited authority with regard to prices and terms of sale (Table 9–1)

marginal economic method   a major method used to determine the size of the sales force, based on the macroeconomic concept that a resource should be allocated up to the point at which the marginal revenue obtained from an additional unit of the resource equals the marginal cost (p. 278)

market development funds   any money a company spends to help channel members sell their products (p. 341)

market development strategy   one possible strategy in segmenting the market; the decision to target customers who have not yet purchased the product or service (p. 49)

marketing   the set of activities designed to influence choice whenever an individual or organization has a choice to make (p. 3)

marketing concept   the importance of having a customer focus (i.e., organizing the resources of the firm toward understanding customers' needs and wants and then offering products and services to meet those needs) (p. 6)

marketing plan   a written document containing the guidelines for a product's marketing programs and allocations over the planning period (p. 33)

marketing research   the function that links the consumer, customer, and public to the marketer through information used to identify marketing opportunities and problems, generate and evaluate marketing actions, monitor marketing performance, and improve understanding of marketing as a process (p. 76)

market penetration strategy   one possible strategy in segmenting the market; the decision to target current customers of a product or service (p. 49)

market potential   the maximum sales reasonably attainable under a given set of conditions within a specified period of time (p. 96)

market segmentation   breaking mass marketing into segments that have different buying habits; also refers to the decision about which customer groups a company will pursue for a particular brand or product line (p. 109)

market share pricing   also called penetration pricing, a pricing policy in which the objective is to gain as much market share as possible; often used as part of an entry strategy for a new product (p. 310)

market structure analysis   an analysis in which the marketing manager seeks to better understand who the competition is and thus define the market (p. 167)

market survey method of forecasting   a counting method of sales forecasting that relies on surveys to predict demand (p. 101)

market testing method of forecasting   a counting method of sales forecasting that uses primary data collection methods, such as focus groups and in-depth interviews, to predict sales (p. 101)

mass customization   also called one-to-one marketing, a new marketing process whereby a company takes a product or service that is widely marketed and develops a system for customizing it to each customer's specifications (pp. 21, 110, 378)

maturity phase   in the product life cycle, the stage in which the sales curve has flattened out and few new buyers are in the market (p. 68)

merchant middleman   a middleman who buys the goods outright and takes title to them (Table 9–1)

middleman   an independent business that operates as a link between producers and ultimate consumers or industrial buyers (Table 9–1)

mission statement   a general statement describing a company's major business thrusts, customer orientation, or business philosophy (p. 49)

modified rebuys   a kind of purchasing situation faced by an organization in which something has changed since the last purchase (e.g., a new potential supplier or a large change in price levels) (p. 148)

moving averages method of forecasting   a time-series method of sales forecasting that uses the averages of historical sales figures to make a forecast (p. 101)

multiattribute model   a popular model of decision making that requires information about how useful or important each attribute is to the customer making a brand choice (which involves assigning importance weights) and how customers perceive the brands in the evoked set in terms of their attributes (p. 133)

multiple-channel systems   a channel of distribution that uses a combination of direct and indirect channels and in which the multiple channel members serve different segments (p. 248)

naïve extrapolation   a judgment method of sales forecasting that takes the most current sales and adds a judgmentally determined x%, where x is the estimated percentage change in sales (p. 99)

Nash equilibrium   in game theory, the most common form of equilibrium, which involves a list of strategies, one for each player, with the property that no manager wants to change its strategy unilaterally (p. 189)

network externalities   the concept that, for many products and services, the value of owning them increases as the number of owners increases (p. 418)

new task purchase   a purchasing situation that is unusual or occurs infrequently in a given organization (p. 149)

nonpersonal channels of communication   mass-media communication channels, such as television, newspapers, radio, direct mail, and the Internet (p. 197)

observability   the degree to which an innovation or its results are visible to others (p. 418)

off-invoice allowances   trade promotions that give a channel member a discount on orders for a fixed period of time (p. 341)

organizational marketing   marketing a product or service to another organization, also called industrial marketing (p. 143)

original equipment manufacturers (OEMs)   a channel of distribution for technology-based products; companies that purchase ingredients or components (e.g., hard disk drives) from manufacturers (p. 431)

outsourcing   purchasing a service from an outside vendor to replace a company's own operation (p. 302)

panel   a set of customers enlisted to give responses to questions or to provide data repeatedly over a period of time (p. 93)

parallel importing   the development of gray markets across country lines, often as a result of significant currency exchange rate or price differences between countries that make it profitable to purchase goods in one country and import them into another for resale (p. 468)

Parfitt-Collins model   a simple market share forecasting model that uses an estimate of the eventual penetration rate, an estimate of the ultimate repeat rate, and an estimate of the relative product category usage rate of buyers of the new brand to determine eventual market share (p. 498)

payoff matrix   in game theory, a graphic depiction of the rewards or costs to each player for each possible combination of strategies (p. 189)

penetration pricing   also called market share pricing, a pricing policy intended to gain as much market share as possible; often used as part of an entry strategy for a new product (p. 310)

perceived risk   in regard to their adoption of new technologies, the extent to which customers are uncertain about the consequences of an action (p. 419)

perceived value   what a product or service is worth to the customer; also called customer value (p. 297)

perceptual map   a map, based on marketing research from customers, that measures perceptions of competing products on a variety of attributes (p. 59)

periodic discounting   a pricing strategy that varies price over time in order to take advantage of particular time periods during which some customers are willing to pay a higher price (p. 319)

personal channels of communication   communication channels that involve direct sales as well as face-to-face or word-of-mouth interactions between customers (p. 197)

personal selling   the use of face-to-face communications between seller and buyer (p. 202)

point-of-purchase (POP) advertising   a form of retailer promotion that includes information-related displays and other company-paid advertising inside the store (p. 342)

premiums   a product-oriented promotion in which free merchandise is provided with a purchase or some free or reduced-price item is made available (p. 339)

prestige pricing   also called skimming, a pricing policy used when there is a strong price-perceived quality relationship and the product is positioned at the high end of the market; often used when costs are not related to volume and gaining significant market share is not an objective (p. 310)

price bands or tiers   price variations within a product category (p. 295)

price bundling   an approach to product line pricing in which a set of products is offered to customers in a package, which is usually priced lower than the sum of the individual components (p. 316)

price discrimination   the practice of charging different prices to segments of the market according to their price elasticity or sensitivity (pp. 295, 318)

price elasticity of demand   the percentage change in a product's demand resulting from a 1% change in its price (p. 301)

price-oriented promotions   consumer promotions that focus on price, including coupons, bonus packs, refunds, and rebates (p. 333)

primary information sources   in market research, sources of information that are generated for the particular problem being studied by the marketing manager (p. 80)

primary needs   biological or physiological needs that a person must meet in order to stay alive (p. 491)

prisoner's dilemma game   a particular form of competitive game in which neither participant wants to change his or her current strategy because if one does and the competitor matches, both will be worse off (p. 190)

product category   also called a product class, one particular product segment of a particular industry (p. 168)

product class   also called a product category, one particular product segment of a particular industry (p. 168)

product class or product category competition   a level of competition in which products or services that have similar features and provide the same function are considered (p. 170)

product definition   a stage in the new product development process in which concepts are translated into actual products for further testing based on interactions with customers (p. 490)

product form competition   a level of competition in which only products or services of the same product type are considered (p. 169)

product life cycle (PLC)   a sketch of the sales history of a product category over time; used as a strategic tool because the importance of various marketing mix elements and strategic options available to the marketing manager vary over the life cycle (p. 65)

product line   a group of closely related products (p. 69)

product-line pricing   a pricing strategy covering a set of related products (p. 316)

product-line strategy   a marketing strategy covering a set of related products (p. 69)

product-oriented promotions   consumer promotions that give away the product itself or a closely related product (p. 339)

product positioning   considering the alternative differentiation possibilities and determining what differential advantages are to be emphasized and communicated to the target customers (p. 62)

product type   a group of products that are functional substitutes (p. 169)

product variants   also called product brands, different specific combinations of features within a specific product type (p. 169)

public relations   communications for which the sponsoring organization does not pay, often in some form of news distributed in a nonpersonal form (p. 202)

purchase set   in consumer behavior, the set of products that the customer has actually chosen within a specified period of time (p. 132)

qualitative research   market research that usually involves small samples of customers and produces information that by itself does not directly lead to decisions but is valuable as an input for further research (p. 88)

quantitative research   market research that typically involves statistical analysis of data, where the intent is to provide descriptive results or explicitly test a hypothesis (p. 88)

reference price   any standard of comparison against which an observed potential transaction or purchase price is compared (p. 311)

regression analysis   an association/causal method of sales forecasting in which the time-series extrapolation model is generalized to include independent variables other than simply time (p. 103)

relationship customers   customers who see the benefits of interdependency between the buyer and the seller (p. 359)

relative advantage   the concept that a customer will adopt an innovation only if he or she considers it to be an improvement over the current product being used to satisfy the same need (p. 417)

repositioning   seeking a new perceived advantage in order to improve on a product's current positioning (p. 62)

reputation   the key asset for service providers, based on customer perceptions of their overall quality (p. 401)

reservation price   the maximum price someone is willing to pay for a product or the price at which the product is eliminated from the customer's budget (p. 297)

retailer   a merchant middleman engaged primarily in selling to ultimate consumers (Table 9–1)

retailer promotions   trade promotions in which retailers provide a direct incentive to customers to buy (p. 342)

return on quality (ROQ) approach   attempts to quantify financial returns on investments in improved service quality (p. 396)

return on sales pricing   also called investment pricing, a pricing policy that assumes you can set a price that will deliver the rate of return demanded by senior management; most often used when a product has a monopoly position (p. 311)

rugby approach to new product development   approach that treats the process of new product development as a game of rugby; the product development process results from the constant interaction of a multidisciplinary team whose members work together from the beginning of the project to the product's introduction (p. 483)

salary   a form of compensation in which a basic amount of money is paid to a worker on a regular basis (p. 283)

sales contests   sales force competitions based on sales performance (p. 283)

sales force method of forecasting   a judgment method of sales forecasting in which salespeople form their own forecasts of the sales in their territories and the marketing manager sums them up to provide an overall forecast (p. 101)

sales forecast   the amount of sales expected to be achieved under a set of conditions within a specified period of time (p. 96)

sales promotion   communication activities that provide extra incentives to customers or the sales force to achieve a short-term objective (pp. 202, 328)

sales quotas   specific sales goals that salespeople are required to meet (p. 282)

sales territory   a group of present and potential customers assigned to a salesperson, often designed on a geographic basis (p. 276)

sampling   a product-oriented promotion in which a product is given away for free (p. 339)

scenario planning   planning that involves asking "what-if" questions to produce forecasts of alternative outcomes based on different assumptions about advertising spending, price levels, competitor actions, and other variables (pp. 99, 186)

secondary information sources   in market research, sources of information that already exist and were not developed for the particular problem at hand (p. 80)

secondary needs   social or psychological needs that can remain unsatisfied without any immediate danger to life or health (p. 491)

second market discounting   a pricing strategy, most useful when excess production exists, in which extra production is sold at a discount to a market separate from the main market (p. 318)

SERVQUAL   a popular survey instrument that measures service quality by grouping questions into five categories of service quality (p. 395)

skimming   also called prestige pricing, a pricing policy used when there is a strong price-perceived quality relationship and the product is positioned at the high end of the market; often used when costs are not related to volume and gaining significant market share is not an objective (p. 310)

slotting allowances   payments to store chains for placing a product on a shelf (p. 341)

straight rebuys   routine purchases made by an organization from the same supplier used in the past (p. 148)

supply chain   the organizations involved in the movement of raw materials and components that are part of a product's production process (p. 144)

switching costs   customer costs of switching brands (p. 358)

target costing   in new product development, an alternative approach to setting the price of a new product, in which the ideal selling price is determined, the feasibility of meeting that price is assessed, and costs are controlled in order to produce the product that can be sold at the target price (p. 485)

target market   a particular segment of the market that the marketing manager chooses to actively pursue in regard to a particular product (p. 110)

telemarketing   a form of direct marketing that uses the telephone as the mechanism for reaching potential customers (p. 201)

tertiary needs   a type of customer need considered in new product development; the operational needs related to the engineering aspect of actually making the product (p. 491)

time-series methods   sales forecasting methods that rely on historical sales data (p. 99)

trade promotions   sales promotions oriented toward the channels of distribution in an effort to get the channels to carry and promote the product, often including devices such as sales contests, quantity discounts, and training programs (pp. 202, 341)

transaction buyers   buyers who are interested only in the particular purchase at hand, rather than a long-term relationship (p. 359)

trialability   the ability of potential users of an innovative or new product to try it on a limited basis before adoption (p. 418)

umbrella branding   using the same brand name for a line of products (p. 69)

value-added resellers (VARs)   organizations that buy products from a variety of vendors, assemble them in packages, and resell the packages to specialized segments; part of the channel of distribution for technology-based products (p. 434)

value-in-use   a method of estimating customer value that puts the benefits of the product in monetary terms, such as time savings, less use of materials, and less downtime (p. 301)

value pricing   giving customers more value than they expect for the price paid (p. 317)

value proposition   a one-paragraph summary of a product or service's differentiation strategy and positioning to each target customer group; in short, a statement of why the customer should buy that product or service rather than the competitor's (p. 64)

virtual selling   the reengineering of sales in the 1990s, especially the impact of sales force automation and the salesperson's educated use of technological tools in working with prospective customers in a highly efficient way (p. 287)

virtual shopping   a new technology incorporating computer graphics and three-dimensional modeling that allows marketing managers to observe how consumers choose between different brands using a virtual reality setting (p. 91)

wholesaler   a merchant establishment operated by a concern that is engaged primarily in buying, taking title to, usually sorting and physically handling goods in large quantities, and reselling the goods to retail or industrial or business users (Table 9–1)

workload method   a major method used to determine the size of the sales force that is based on the ability to calculate the total amount of work necessary to serve the entire market (p. 277)

Index

Subject

A

Advantage program, American Airlines, 374
academic publications, 83–84
account planning matrix, 280
accounting departments, source for market research data, 81
achievers
    as psychographic segments, 115–17
    as VALS2 group, 116
acquisition cost, 361
action standards, in market tests, 496
activity-based quotas, 282
actualizers, as VALS2 group, 116
ACV. *See* All commodity volume (ACV).
adapters, as psychographic segments, 115–17
adaptive customizers, 379
advanced photo system (APS), 475, 484
Advertising Age (trade publication), 82
advertising and promotion strategies, 193–231
    agencies, 208, 210
    budgets, 349–40
    campaigns, 63
    channels, 233–64, 406–07
        See also Channels of distribution.
    copy, evaluating, 213–14
    effect measurements, 227–28
    free product promotions, 204
    on global basis, 470–72
    response process, 208–09
advertising goals. *See* Goal setting, as advertising decision-making stage.
advertising-to-sales ratios, 223–26
affordability method, 227
African American consumerism, 114–15
age cohorts in the U.S., 114
agent and broker sales channels, 236, 406
AIDS, 26, 108
aircraft designers, 148
airline industry, 45–46, 63
    See also British Airways; Southwest Airlines; United Airlines.

customer satisfaction, 366
    flight schedules online, 17
    price cutting, 312
all commodity volume (ACV), 500
alpha chip (DEC), 251
alternative channel systems, 237–38
American Marketing Association, 2, 76
animation 212
annual reports, 187
Appalachian region, 122
APS. *See* Advanced photo system (APS).
Argentina, 470
ARS persuasion copy-testing system, 215
Asian American consumerism, 114–15
association/causal methods, 99, 103
assurance, in service quality, 393
ATMs. *See* Automated teller machines (ATMs), 244
attribute perceptions, 134–35
attribute rating score, 135
auctions on the Web, 322
augmented product, 371
auto servicing, as credence goods, 312
automated teller machines (ATMs), 15, 244
automobile market, 36–39, 60, 132, 193–96, 198, 243–44, 261–62, 298, 302, 322, 335, 370, 445, 450
    See also Ford Motor Company; Mercedes Benz; SUVs.
    buying on the Web, 322
    dealers, 322
ayurvedic medicine, India, 464

B

baby boomers, 114, 124
baby-busters, 114
backstage customer contact points, 402
Baldrige competitions. *See* Malcolm Baldrige Award for Quality.
Barrons, 110
base profits, 361
basic communications model, 196–97

BCG porfolio, 70–71
Becton Dickinson Division Organization Chart, 27, 29–30
beer market, 58, 66, 227, 233–34
behavior model, 128
behavior shifts in consumers, 207–09, 211–13
Belgian Olympic team, 107
believers, as VALS2 group, 116
benchmarking, 81
Bernoulli boxes, 13
billboard advertising, 217, 220
blue-blood estates, as a PRIZM demographic cluster, 119, 122
booksellers industry, 64 *See also*, Amazon.com barnes & Noble
boomers I cohort, 114
boomers II cohort, 114
brand associations, 61–62
brand awareness, 60–62, 497
brand-based advantage, 53
brand-based differentiation, 59
brand communities, 199
branding
    as positioning, 60, 169, 177, 430–31
    versus OEM, 435–36
brand loyalty. *See* Loyalty to products and services.
Brazil, 470
breakdown method, for estimating sales force, 277
brick industry, 151
British beef, 62
brokers, 257
    as marketing intermediary, 236
budget/competition industry, 169, 171, 173, 176
budget/speed star customers, 486
budgets for promotion and advertising, 206, 221–22
built-in instability, 483
burgundy wine, as market segment, 70
Business Library and How to Use It, The, 84

People

Products and Companies